Artificial Intelligence: Innovation, Applications and Transformative Experiences

Artificial Intelligence: Innovation, Applications and Transformative Experiences

Guest Editors

Diego Vergara
Pablo Fernández-Arias

MDPI

Basel • Beijing • Wuhan • Barcelona • Belgrade • Novi Sad • Cluj • Manchester

Guest Editors
Diego Vergara
Technology, Instruction and Design in Engineering and Education Research Group (TiDEE.rg)
Universidad Católica de Ávila
Ávila
Spain

Pablo Fernández-Arias
Technology, Instruction and Design in Engineering and Education Research Group (TiDEE.rg)
Universidad Católica de Ávila
Ávila
Spain

Editorial Office
MDPI AG
Grosspeteranlage 5
4052 Basel, Switzerland

This is a reprint of the Special Issue, published open access by the journal *Future Internet* (ISSN 1999-5903), freely accessible at: https://www.mdpi.com/journal/futureinternet/special_issues/AI_IATE.

For citation purposes, cite each article independently as indicated on the article page online and as indicated below:

Lastname, A.A.; Lastname, B.B. Article Title. *Journal Name* **Year**, *Volume Number*, Page Range.

ISBN 978-3-7258-8127-7 (Hbk)
ISBN 978-3-7258-8128-4 (PDF)
https://doi.org/10.3390/books978-3-7258-8128-4

Contents

About the Editors

Diego Vergara

Diego Vergara is a distinguished academic and researcher with expertise in digital technologies applied to education and engineering, particularly within materials science and mechanical engineering. He currently holds the position of Dean of the Faculty of Sciences and Arts at Universidad Católica de Ávila, and leads the TiDEE.rg research group (Technology, Instruction, and Design in Engineering and Education). He actively engages in international conferences and contributes to high-impact publications in the fields of digital education and technological innovation. Dr. Vergara was recognized as one of the world's most influential researchers in both 2023 and 2024 by the Stanford Ranking, underscoring his significant contributions to enabling technologies and strategic materials. Furthermore, in 2024, he was awarded an honorary doctorate (Doctor Honoris Causa) by the Universidad Interamericana para el Desarrollo (UNID) in Peru, in acknowledgment of his outstanding academic accomplishments and international collaboration.

Pablo Fernández-Arias

Pablo Fernández-Arias in Science and Technology Studies. Industrial Engineer. Technical Industrial Mechanical Engineer. MSc in Social Studies of Science and Technology. MSc in Occupational Health and Safety. MSc in Business Administration and Management. Accredited Doctoral-level Lecturer. Senior Instructor for Nuclear Power Plant Operators. Head of Technological Development and Innovation, Operations and Training Department. Member of the Research Group: Technology, Instruction and Design in Engineering and Education (TiDEE.rg). Director of the Master's Degree in Industrial Engineering at Universidad Católica de Ávila. Vice-Dean of the Faculty of Sciences and Arts at the Catholic University of Ávila.

Preface

Artificial intelligence (AI) is playing a central role in the ongoing digital transformation of society, emerging as part of an increasingly interconnected environment where data-driven systems, intelligent algorithms, and adaptive technologies interact to support innovation, decision-making, and enhanced user experiences across sectors such as healthcare, education, industry, communication, and digital services. This Reprint brings together the contributions included in the Special Issue "Artificial Intelligence: Innovation, Applications and Transformative Experiences", with the purpose of providing a current overview of recent progress in the field, encompassing methodological advances, theoretical developments, and applied research in real-world contexts. Out of twenty-three submitted manuscripts, eleven were accepted following a rigorous peer-review process, including eight research articles and three review papers, reflecting the interdisciplinary scope of the topic. The selected contributions span a wide range of applications, including adaptive learning systems and generative AI in education, machine learning approaches for health insurance fraud detection, AI-based chatbots and intelligent healthcare solutions, deep learning methods for earthquake prediction, speech emotion recognition, intelligent e-commerce systems, software refactoring using large language models, AI-supported consensus-building mechanisms, and agentic AI systems. Taken together, these works illustrate the expanding influence of artificial intelligence in addressing complex challenges, improving human–machine interaction, and enabling more capable, adaptive, and impactful digital systems.

Diego Vergara and Pablo Fernández-Arias
Guest Editors

future internet

Editorial

Editorial for the Special Issue "Artificial Intelligence: Innovation, Applications and Transformative Experiences"

Diego Vergara * and Pablo Fernández-Arias

Technology, Instruction and Design in Engineering and Education Research Group (TiDEE.rg), Facultad de Ciencias y Artes, Universidad Católica de Ávila, C/Canteros s/n, 05005 Ávila, Spain; pablo.fernandezarias@ucavila.es
* Correspondence: diego.vergara@ucavila.es

Artificial intelligence (AI) is driving profound changes in the digital transformation of society. Rather than representing isolated technological developments, these approaches increasingly operate within a convergent ecosystem in which data-driven systems, immersive environments, and intelligent algorithms interact, generating new forms of innovation, interaction, and decision-making. Across sectors such as industry, healthcare, communication, education, and digital services, AI-based solutions are reshaping processes, enhancing efficiency, and creating novel user experiences [1,2]. Within this context, this Special Issue of *Future Internet*, "Artificial Intelligence: Innovation, Applications and Transformative Experiences (AI-IATE)", assembles recent advances, methodological contributions, and applied research regarding the development and deployment of artificial intelligence systems in real-world scenarios. This Special Issue is intended to provide a comprehensive overview of how AI is being used to address complex problems, improve processes, and support innovation across multiple domains, with a particular emphasis on its role in digital transformation and intelligent systems. A total of 23 manuscripts were submitted to this Special Issue. Following an initial editorial screening and a rigorous peer-review process, only 11 papers were ultimately accepted for publication, while 12 were rejected or did not progress through the review stages. Eight of the accepted manuscripts are research articles, while three are reviews.

Two of the studies included in this Special Issue pertain to education. The authors of [3] propose MACxRL, a lightweight multi-agent context-aware reinforcement learning framework designed to support intelligent decision-making in educational and smart learning environments. The system combines edge-based rule reasoning with a centralized learning module, enabling fast local responses and global coordination under dynamic conditions. The experimental results obtained reveal significant improvements over baseline methods, including a 45–60% reduction in energy consumption, faster convergence, and more stable system performance. Overall, MACxRL provides a scalable and efficient approach for adaptive, AI-driven environments that can be applied to the optimization of educational and learning contexts.

The second of these studies [4] analyses the adoption and educational impact of generative AI in high-school and university contexts in Sonora, Mexico, based on survey data from 1477 participants. It introduces a Learning Engagement Index (LEI) to measure students' interaction with ChatGPT, including with respect to reading, modifying, and integrating AI-generated content. The results obtained show widespread adoption, higher engagement among university students, and only weak alignment between perceived learning and actual engagement behaviors. A complementary experiment using GitHub Copilot Free (version GPT-4) indicates efficiency gains but also potential risks for deeper reasoning.

Overall, the study highlights a gap between perceived and actual learning, underscoring the need for more robust pedagogical and assessment strategies in AI-mediated education.

Two papers related to the use of artificial intelligence in healthcare are included in this Special Issue. One of them introduces PDHIF (Phases for Detecting Fraud in Health Insurance) [5], a novel six-phase methodological framework designed to overcome the limitations of ad hoc machine learning approaches in health insurance fraud detection. Its main contribution lies in integrating fraud theory, actor analysis, and fraud mechanisms with a full supervised machine learning lifecycle, thereby providing a systematic and reproducible pipeline for real-world deployment. The framework is validated using an extensive dataset of 8.5 million claims from Peru's public health system, addressing severe class imbalance through advanced techniques such as K-means SMOTE. The results show that while standard models perform poorly on highly imbalanced data, PDHIF enables a substantial improvement in performance, with the Random Forest model achieving near-perfect results (with an F1-score, sensitivity, and AUC of 0.994). Overall, PDHIF is a robust, scalable, and highly accurate approach to transforming large-scale health insurance data into actionable fraud detection systems.

This Special Issue also includes two reviews within the health domain. AI-based chatbots have emerged as key tools for managing public health emergencies, particularly during infectious disease outbreaks, as they enable rapid, scalable, and reliable communication between health authorities and the public, sparking the review on this topic [6] included in this Special Issue. The main contribution of this work is its comprehensive analysis of these chatbots' roles in crisis contexts, highlighting how they support the real-time dissemination of accurate information, reduce uncertainty and anxiety, and assist in triaging and guiding users toward appropriate health services. The review also systematizes the main challenges associated with their deployment, including information reliability, ethical accountability, data privacy (e.g., GDPR compliance), and accessibility for linguistically and culturally diverse populations. Overall, this work provides an integrative perspective on the opportunities and limitations of AI chatbots in public health, offering a clear framework with which to guide their effective and responsible implementation in emergency response systems.

The other review [7] focuses on patient-oriented smart applications supporting healthcare provision for individuals with Parkinson's disease. Based on an umbrella review of 85 prior reviews encompassing 1867 primary studies, this review systematically synthesizes evidence on smart technologies such as wearables, smartphones, serious games, and ambient intelligence systems for diagnosis, monitoring, rehabilitation, and disease management. Its main contribution is critically integrating and structuring the existing literature, revealing that although many solutions have been proposed, their clinical effectiveness, acceptability, and regulatory compliance remain insufficiently validated. The study highlights key gaps between technological development and clinical translation, emphasizing the need for standardized methodologies, improved interoperability with clinical systems, and stronger collaborative research efforts to avoid duplication and enhance real-world applicability. Overall, this review provides a comprehensive roadmap for future research aimed at bridging the gap between technological innovation and clinical practice regarding care for Parkinson's disease.

The remaining articles address applications across different domains. One of them focuses on earthquake detection and magnitude estimation [8], addressing one of the key challenges in seismology, namely, the reliable detection of earthquakes across different regions, wherein model generalization and the limited availability of high-quality datasets remain critical constraints. To overcome these issues, the authors propose a novel deep learning architecture, Earth–Transformer–LSTM (ETL), which combines Transformer encoders for feature extraction, LSTM networks for temporal modeling, and an MLP-based

https://doi.org/10.3390/fi18040219

feed-forward design to enhance predictive performance. Evaluated on the Turkey earthquake dataset (2000–2018), the model achieved superior accuracy relative to state-of-the-art approaches, with a notable reduction in error (RMSE = 0.7). Overall, this study provides a robust and innovative deep learning framework for earthquake magnitude estimation, with strong potential for real-time seismic monitoring and early-warning systems.

The authors of [9] focus on Speech Emotion Recognition (SER), a key task in human–computer interaction and emotion-aware systems. The main challenge addressed is the inconsistency between frame- and utterance-level emotional representations in conventional SER models, which typically rely on pooling strategies over utterance-level labels. To overcome this limitation, the authors introduce a novel framework based on a CLS token self-attention pooling mechanism, enhanced with two auxiliary loss functions: Emotional Attention Loss (EAL) and Frame-to-Utterance Alignment Loss (FUAL). These losses are designed to improve representation consistency by aligning emotional information across frames and stabilizing the training process. Evaluated on benchmark datasets such as IEMOCAP, CREMA-D, and RAVDESS, the proposed method demonstrates improved performance and robustness compared to baseline and state-of-the-art approaches. Overall, this study provides a simple yet effective and interpretable solution for SER, achieving strong performance using only utterance-level annotations and showing good generalization across datasets.

In [10], the focus is on applying artificial intelligence in the field of e-commerce and intelligent user experience design. The study addresses the limitations of traditional static user interfaces, which cannot adapt to dynamic user behavior and cultural preferences in digital environments. To overcome this issue, the authors introduce an AI-driven model-driven development (AI-MDD-UX) framework that integrates generative AI, multi-agent reinforcement learning, and behavioral analytics to enable real-time UI/UX adaptation. The system models user behavior, generates personalized interfaces, and continuously optimizes design through feedback-driven learning mechanisms. Evaluated across mobile, web, and VR shopping environments, the proposed approach demonstrated significant improvements in user engagement, conversion rates, and satisfaction compared to baseline methods. Overall, the study highlights the potential of combining generative AI and software engineering principles to deliver adaptive, personalized, and high-performing e-commerce experiences.

Finally, the remaining three articles focus more on the core aspects of artificial intelligence. One of them [11] investigates the use of generative AI, specifically ChatGPT, for automating software refactoring tasks, addressing the challenge of transforming imperative Java code, particularly for-loops introduced in legacy codebases, into more expressive functional-stream-based constructs enabled by Java 8. Unlike traditional rule-based refactoring approaches, which rely on strict preconditions and limited transformation templates, this work evaluates whether ChatGPT can generalize beyond such constraints. Based on an empirical analysis of 2132 loops extracted from open-source repositories, the authors assessed the correctness and quality of AI-generated refactorings. The results show that ChatGPT can successfully refactor many loops and, in some cases, outperform deterministic methods, although limitations remain in regard to handling complex control flows and semantic dependencies. Overall, the study highlights large language models' potential to serve as complementary tools for software transformation while also identifying important limitations that require human supervision and hybrid approaches.

In another case, [12] explores the use of large language models (LLMs) to support consensus-building in group decision-making processes. The authors propose a novel real-time facilitation framework in which LLMs act as automated moderators within a multi-user chat system, dynamically adapting their strategies based on the evolution of

https://doi.org/10.3390/fi18040219

the discussion. By incorporating techniques such as summarization, clarification, and compromise generation, the system iteratively refines consensus proposals using cosine similarity to measure alignment with participants' viewpoints. The approach was evaluated using state-of-the-art models, including ChatGPT 4.0, Mistral Large 2, and AI21 Jamba-Instruct, with the results showing that ChatGPT 4.0 achieved the highest alignment and required fewer iterations to reach agreement. Overall, this study demonstrates LLMs' potential to serve as effective facilitators in collaborative decision-making, opening new avenues for scalable, AI-driven consensus processes.

Finally, [13] (a review) addresses the emerging paradigm of agentic AI systems, which extend beyond traditional and generative AI by emphasizing autonomy, adaptability, and goal-driven reasoning. Based on an analysis of 143 studies, the study provides a comprehensive and structured overview of definitions, architectures, and frameworks, comparing agentic AI with related approaches such as multi-agent systems and autonomic computing. Its main contribution lies in systematizing key components—such as planning, memory, reflection, and orchestration—along with evaluation metrics, application domains, and real-world implementations. The review also identifies critical challenges, including technical complexity, coordination, ethical considerations, and security issues. Overall, this review establishes a solid foundation for understanding and advancing agentic AI, highlighting its potential to create more autonomous, adaptive, and intelligent systems across diverse domains.

Funding: This research received no external funding.

Conflicts of Interest: The author declares there are no conflicts of interest.

References

1. Vergara, D.; Lampropoulos, G.; Antón-Sancho, Á.; Fernández-Arias, P. Impact of Artificial Intelligence on Learning Management Systems: A Bibliometric Review. *Multimodal Technol. Interact.* **2024**, *8*, 75. [CrossRef]
2. Vergara, D.; del Bosque, A.; Lampropoulos, G.; Fernández-Arias, P. Trends and Applications of Artificial Intelligence in Project Management. *Electronics* **2025**, *14*, 800. [CrossRef]
3. Lakehal, A.; Annane, B.; Alti, A.; Roose, P.; Aljarboa, S. Adaptive and Sustainable Smart Environments Using Predictive Reasoning and Context-Aware Reinforcement Learning. *Future Internet* **2026**, *18*, 40. [CrossRef]
4. Torres-Peralta, R.; Cirett-Galán, F.; Heras-Sanchez, M.d.C.; Lerma-Molina, K.; Espinoza-Flores, I. Perceived Learning vs. Engagement in AI-Assisted Homework: A Comparative Study of ChatGPT Use Across High School, University, and Teachers in Sonora, Mexico (2024–2025). *Future Internet* **2026**, *18*, 122. [CrossRef]
5. Villegas-Ortega, J.; Quiroz Aviles, L.N.; Arancibia, J.N.; Montenegro, W.C.; Delgadillo, R.; Mauricio, D. Methodology for Detecting Suspicious Claims in Health Insurance Using Supervised Machine Learning. *Future Internet* **2025**, *17*, 584. [CrossRef]
6. Branda, F.; Stella, M.; Ceccarelli, C.; Cabitza, F.; Ceccarelli, G.; Maruotti, A.; Ciccozzi, M.; Scarpa, F. The Role of AI-Based Chatbots in Public Health Emergencies: A Narrative Review. *Future Internet* **2025**, *17*, 145. [CrossRef]
7. Bastardo, R.; Pavão, J.; Martins, A.I.; Silva, A.G.; Rocha, N.P. Patient-Oriented Smart Applications to Support the Diagnosis, Rehabilitation, and Care of Patients with Parkinson's: An Umbrella Review. *Future Internet* **2025**, *17*, 376. [CrossRef]
8. Ghavifekr, A.A.; Ghazaei, E.; Mirzajani, M.; Visconti, P. Earthquake Magnitude Detection Utilizing a Novel Hybrid Earth–Transformer–LSTM Architecture. *Future Internet* **2026**, *18*, 143. [CrossRef]
9. Byun, S.; Lee, S.-P. Frame and Utterance Emotional Alignment for Speech Emotion Recognition. *Future Internet* **2025**, *17*, 509. [CrossRef]
10. Alti, A.; Lakehal, A. AI-MDD-UX: Revolutionizing E-Commerce User Experience with Generative AI and Model-Driven Development. *Future Internet* **2025**, *17*, 180. [CrossRef]
11. Midolo, A.; Tramontana, E. Refactoring Loops in the Era of LLMs: A Comprehensive Study. *Future Internet* **2025**, *17*, 418. [CrossRef]

https://doi.org/10.3390/fi18040219

12. Triantafyllopoulos, L.; Kalles, D. From Divergence to Alignment: Evaluating the Role of Large Language Models in Facilitating Agreement Through Adaptive Strategies. *Future Internet* **2025**, *17*, 407. [CrossRef]
13. Bandi, A.; Kongari, B.; Naguru, R.; Pasnoor, S.; Vilipala, S.V. The Rise of Agentic AI: A Review of Definitions, Frameworks, Architectures, Applications, Evaluation Metrics, and Challenges. *Future Internet* **2025**, *17*, 404. [CrossRef]

https://doi.org/10.3390/fi18040219

future internet

MDPI

Review

The Role of AI-Based Chatbots in Public Health Emergencies: A Narrative Review

Francesco Branda [1,*], Massimo Stella [2], Cecilia Ceccarelli [3], Federico Cabitza [4,5], Giancarlo Ceccarelli [6], Antonello Maruotti [7], Massimo Ciccozzi [1] and Fabio Scarpa [8]

1 Unit of Medical Statistics and Molecular Epidemiology, Università Campus Bio-Medico di Roma, 00128 Rome, Italy; m.ciccozzi@unicampus.it
2 Department of Psychology and Cognitive Science, University of Trento, 38122 Trento, Italy; massimo.stella-1@unitn.it
3 Architectural Science School, Department of Architecture, Roma Tre University, 00100 Rome, Italy; cec.ceccarelli@stud.uniroma3.it
4 Department of Computer Science, Systems and Communication, University of Milano-Bicocca, 20126 Milan, Italy; federico.cabitza@unimib.it
5 IRCCS Ospedale Galeazzi-Sant'Ambrogio, 20157 Milan, Italy
6 Department of Public Health and Infectious Diseases, University of Rome Sapienza, 00161 Rome, Italy; giancarlo.ceccarelli@uniroma1.it
7 Department GEPLI, LUMSA University, 00192 Rome, Italy; a.maruotti@lumsa.it
8 Department of Biomedical Sciences, University of Sassari, 07100 Sassari, Italy; fscarpa@uniss.it
* Correspondence: f.branda@unicampus.it

Abstract: The rapid emergence of infectious disease outbreaks has underscored the urgent need for effective communication tools to manage public health crises. Artificial Intelligence (AI)-based chatbots have become increasingly important in these situations, serving as critical resources to provide immediate and reliable information. This review examines the role of AI-based chatbots in public health emergencies, particularly during infectious disease outbreaks. By providing real-time responses to public inquiries, these chatbots help disseminate accurate information, correct misinformation, and reduce public anxiety. Furthermore, AI chatbots play a vital role in supporting healthcare systems by triaging inquiries, offering guidance on symptoms and preventive measures, and directing users to appropriate health services. This not only enhances public access to critical information but also helps alleviate the workload of healthcare professionals, allowing them to focus on more complex tasks. However, the implementation of AI-based chatbots is not without challenges. Issues such as the accuracy of information, user trust, and ethical considerations regarding data privacy are critical factors that need to be addressed to optimize their effectiveness. Additionally, the adaptability of these chatbots to rapidly evolving health scenarios is essential for their sustained relevance. Despite these challenges, the potential of AI-driven chatbots to transform public health communication during emergencies is significant. This review highlights the importance of continuous development and the integration of AI chatbots into public health strategies to enhance preparedness and response efforts during infectious disease outbreaks. Their role in providing accessible, accurate, and timely information makes them indispensable tools in modern public health emergency management.

Keywords: artificial intelligence; disease surveillance; ChatGPT; misinformation; COVID-19; health communication; machine learning; statistical analysis; natural language processing

1. Introduction

The world is witnessing an increasing frequency of infectious disease outbreaks, such as the COVID-19, Ebola, and mpox pandemics, which exposed significant gaps in public health communication and crisis management [1]. In these scenarios, the dissemination of timely and accurate information is critical to control the spread of disease and manage public anxiety. Digital health solutions [2] have emerged as essential tools to address these challenges, offering scalable, immediate, and reliable communication solutions because, during these health emergencies, traditional communication channels are often saturated. In this context, artificial intelligence (AI)-based chatbots have emerged as powerful tools to address the growing need for immediate and reliable responses during public health crises. These AI-driven systems, capable of engaging in human-like conversations, offer a scalable solution to handle increased public inquiries and provide crucial information around the clock [3]. Despite their potential, the adoption of AI chatbots in public health remains an ongoing challenge. Initially, the technology faced considerable resistance due to concerns about the accuracy of the information provided, ethical implications, and the risk of misuse. Early research highlighted AI's limitations in comprehending complex human emotions and the dangers of misinformation, which could heighten public anxiety during health crises [4]. For example, Gao et al. [5] found that public trust in AI systems was initially low, driven by fears of biased or inaccurate responses. However, as the technology has advanced, so has its perceived utility. Innovations in natural language processing (NLP) and machine learning (ML) have greatly enhanced chatbots' ability to generate accurate, contextually relevant responses [6]. Moreover, the COVID-19 pandemic acted as a turning point, accelerating the widespread adoption of AI chatbots as healthcare systems worldwide struggled to cope with the overwhelming demand for reliable information and support [7]. The shift from skepticism to optimism can be attributed to several factors. First, the demonstrated ability of chatbots to handle large volumes of inquiries in real-time has alleviated some of the initial concerns about their reliability [8]. Second, the integration of AI chatbots into existing healthcare systems has shown tangible benefits, such as reducing the workload on healthcare professionals and improving patient outcomes through timely information dissemination [9]. Finally, the development of more sophisticated models, such as GPT-4, has enhanced the ability of chatbots to understand and respond to complex queries, further building trust among users [10].

The potential of AI chatbots in public health emergencies is manifold. First, they serve as frontline communicators, offering real-time answers to citizens' questions about symptoms, preventive measures, and local health guidelines [11]. This immediate access to information helps to alleviate public anxiety and promote adherence to health protocols, which is critical to curbing the spread of infectious diseases [12]. In addition, by providing accurate and consistent information, AI chatbots play a key role in countering the spread of misinformation, which has been identified as a significant challenge during health crises [13]. Beyond their role in public communication, AI chatbots also offer substantial support to healthcare systems. By sorting requests and providing initial guidance, these systems can help reduce the burden on healthcare providers, allowing them to focus on more complex cases and critical patient care [7]. This is especially valuable during the peak of epidemics, when healthcare resources are often limited. In addition, chatbots can help with data collection and analysis, providing health authorities with valuable information about public concerns and epidemic progression [8]. The implementation of artificial intelligence chatbots in healthcare emergencies, however, is not without its challenges. Ensuring the accuracy and reliability of the information provided by these systems is critical, as misinformation can have serious consequences in healthcare [9]. There are also privacy and data security concerns, particularly when dealing with sensitive health information [14]. In addition, the issue of public trust in AI systems remains a significant factor that can affect their effectiveness [5]. Despite these challenges, the potential benefits of AI chatbots in health emergency management are considerable. Their ability to provide immediate, scalable, and personalized responses makes them valuable tools in modern crisis communication strategies. As AI technology continues to advance, these systems are becoming more sophisticated, able to understand context, adapt to new information, and even detect emotional states to provide more empathetic responses [15].

In recent years, it has become clear that artificial intelligence chatbots are not just technological innovations, but essential tools in the fight against public health threats, bridging the gap between authorities and the public and ensuring that vital information reaches those who need it most, when they need it most. The ongoing development and integration of artificial intelligence chatbots into the public health infrastructure is a critical area of research and implementation. This review aims to explore the current state of the use of AI chatbots in public health emergencies, their benefits, challenges, and potential future developments, providing insights into how these technologies can be optimized to improve public health response efforts. By harnessing the power of AI in public health communication, we can potentially create more resilient and responsive health systems that can meet the complex demands of future public health emergencies.

In this paper, we systematically explore the role of artificial intelligence-based chatbots in public health emergencies, with a focus on infectious disease outbreaks. After a review of the psychological relevance of chatbots in health communication, we analyze their historical development, from early experiments such as ELIZA and PARRY to current advancements with generative artificial intelligence models (Section 2). Next, we examine the specific applications of these tools in genetics and genomics (Section 3), as well as their use for the dynamic management of healthcare spaces during epidemics (Section 4). The paper continues with an analysis of the potential of chatbots as statistical consultants in epidemiology (Section 5) and their reliability in clinical decision support (Section 6). Finally, we address the main challenges and limitations related to their use (Section 7), concluding with a discussion of future prospects and research needs to further improve the integration of these tools into public health strategies (Section 8).

2. Chatbots and Their Psychological Relevance for Public Health Communication

Chatbots have a long history within the domains of artificial intelligence and psychology, as summarized in Table 1. This section reviews historical (ELIZA, PARRY) and more recent (GPTs) contributions to the field. Focus is given to highlighting the psychological implications of chatbots for public health communication, in view of foundational and more recent scientific literature.

Table 1. A brief outline of the conversational systems tested in psychological fields and relevant for public health communication.

Aspect	Key Points
Historical Chatbots	- ELIZA (1960s): Mimicked a psychotherapist; demonstrated the "ELIZA effect" (users ascribed human qualities). - PARRY (1970s): Simulated paranoid schizophrenia; showcased personification of complex human traits.

Table 1. *Cont.*

Aspect	Key Points
Psychological Relevance	- Theory of Mind: Users project mental states onto chatbots, enabling trust and engagement. - Trust: Critical for effective public health communication and behavior change. - Personification: Human-like traits (empathy, understanding) enhance user engagement and retention.
Modern Chatbots (GPTs)	- Advancements: GPTs enable human-like text generation and context understanding. - Applications: Used in disease surveillance, health education, and behavior change. - Challenges: Inherit human biases and exhibit non-human biases (e.g., hallucinations, overconfidence).
Future Directions	- Address biases (human and non-human) in chatbot responses. - Foster interdisciplinary collaboration (psychology, computer science, public health) to optimize chatbot use in public health.

2.1. The ELIZA Effect and Its Implications in Public Health Communication

ELIZA was a protoypical chatbot developed in the 1960s by Joseph Weizenbaum [16]. ELIZA mimicked a psychotherapist, engaging users in text-based conversations based on if–else statements and simple pattern matching [16]. Despite its simplicity, ELIZA demonstrated that machines could interact with humans while providing simple recommendations or elements of psychotherapeutic knowledge adapting to human requests [17]. In the psychological literature, it is known that the patient–psychoterapist dialogue is founded not only on knowledge but also on trust, engagement, care and empathy, which all promote a soothing environment [18]. Weizenbaum observed an "ELIZA effect": Even when individuals were aware that ELIZA was a computer program, they still treated it as if it had genuine human qualities like intentions or emotions [16]. This phenomenon is linked with the theory of mind in developmental psychology [17,19]. A theory of mind is the cognitive ability to understand that others have thoughts, feelings, and perspectives, potentially different from one's own. This ability typically develops in early childhood and is fundamental to human social interactions, enabling empathy, communication, and prediction of others' behavior [19]. Despite knowing ELIZA's mechanistic nature, users projected mental states onto the machine, assuming that ELIZA could understand and respond to their emotional cues. This projection, a manifestation of the ELIZA effect, illustrates that the theory of mind can extend to chatbots: Humans talking to even simple chatbots have the tendency to ascribe mental states to the latter and make sense of their behavior.

The ELIZA effect and its theory-of-mind component have deep repercussions for public health communication. These psychological phenomena show that humans can engage psychologically with chatbots, ultimately building trustful rapports with them. In public health, trust is a critical emotion that underlies effective communication and the success of health interventions [20,21]. Public health communication can be considered as a service where users are gaining health knowledge from one or several sources. Extensive psychological research [22] has shown that trust in service relationships can rise from affective phenomena (trusting a person perceived as friendly) or cognitive phenomena (trusting someone after a logical reasoning). Furthermore, several scientific studies have emphasized the importance of building trust between public health communicators and the public to ensure the effective dissemination of health information, e.g., open data [23], and the adoption of recommended health behaviors, e.g., face masking [21]. The studies by Kasperson and colleagues [24] highlight the concept of the social amplification of risk: the public's perception of risk is significantly influenced by the trust they have in the source of information. When public health communicators are perceived as trustworthy, their messages are more likely to be accepted and acted upon by the public [24]. Trustworthiness, or its lack, can either amplify or attenuate the public's response to health risks, hampering engagement with safety health measures during a pandemic [25]. Hall and colleagues [26] emphasized that, beyond public health communication, higher trust was also found to be associated with higher satisfaction, better adherence to medical advice, and improved health outcomes. These elements underline how chatbots can be attributed trust by humans and could thus play a relevant role for building trustful, and hence more successful, communication campaigns about public health.

2.2. *PARRY, Personification in Chatbots and Its Relevance in Public Health*

PARRY [27] is a key example of personification in chatbots, i.e., the ability for chatbots to tune their responses according to a given set of human traits [18]. Developed in the 1970s, PARRY was designed to simulate a person with paranoid schizophrenia [27]. PARRY's ability to generate responses that closely mirrored some symptoms of paranoia, like suspiciousness or delusional thinking, demonstrated that a computer could be programmed to replicate some complex human thought patterns and thus impersonate some human traits in conversation. These achievements were obtained through significant advancement in NLP, at the time, incorporating decision-making models and weighted responses that simulated paranoid reasoning [27]. The dialogues produced by PARRY were convincing enough to induce even trained psychiatrists into believing that PARRY's quips came from human patients [28]. PARRY remains a historical example of how even simple chatbots can portray personifications of complex human features.

In public health communication, personification is crucial for chatbots' engagement and retention. Firstly, personification can make chatbots appear more relatable and approachable, fostering user engagement. According to Bickmore and Picard [29], users are more likely to engage in sustained interactions with chatbots perceived as having human-like characteristics, such as empathy and understanding. In public health contexts, where conveying information and promoting behavior change are key goals [23], increased engagement can enhance the effectiveness of health communication. For instance, a chatbot designed to encourage vaccination might be more persuasive if users feel it genuinely understands and cares about their concerns [30]. Secondly, chatbots with personified features may help improve user retention by making interactions more enjoyable and memorable. Studies suggest that when chatbots exhibit human-like behaviors, such as humor or even personalized conversations, users are more likely to return for subsequent interactions [31]. This is especially relevant in public health, where ongoing engagement can be critical for chronic disease management, health education, and behavior modification [20,30]. Personification in chatbots could be managed at the level of textual responses but also through other components, like avatars or animations. Importantly, the latter may also influence user engagement. For instance, Ciechanowski and colleagues [32] showed that simpler textual chatbots, without complex animations or avatars, induced in users less negative affect and less intense psychophysiological reactions than simpler, text-only, chatbots. These findings indicate that not only text but also additional visual elements might influence user engagement with public health chatbots.

2.3. From Early Chatbots to Generative Pre-Trained Transformers

After ALICE (Artificial Linguistic Internet Computer Entity) [33], the real breakthrough for chatbots began with the advent of generative pre-trained transformers (GPTs) in the mid-2010s [6]. GPTs enabled chatbots to generate more human-like text and understand context with greater accuracy. ELMo (Embedding from Language Model), BERT (Bidirectional Encoder Representations from Transformers) and the more recent Large Language Models (LLMs), like GPT-4, all represent advanced architectures of artificial neural networks, trained on vast amounts of human texts and able to produce human-like responses [34]. In public health, modern chatbots are now being deployed to assist in disease surveillance, health education, and behavior change interventions [35], as discussed in the remainder of this review.

From a psychological perspective, LLM-based chatbots can be powerful for public health communication since they (i) are capable of personification [18], like PERRY, fostering engagement; (ii) can be subject to the ELIZA effect [35], fostering trust; and (iii) can display basic elements of a theory of mind [36]. However, LLMs are also complex systems, trained via reinforcement learning to closely reproduce human data [35]. Consequently, LLM-based chatbots also end up inheriting human biases [37]. In cognitive psychology, biases are deformations from common ways of combining intuitive and logical reasoning when processing knowledge [18]. Biases can be considered cognitive shortcuts reducing the effort required for processing information. For instance, confirmation bias makes it easier to accommodate novel knowledge if it confirms one's own pre-existing information. In public health communication, LLMs displaying biases similar to human communicators' might be considered neutral addition to the system. However, LLMs also possess non-human biases, due to their artificial nature [37]: (i) myopic overconfidence, e.g., pushing through inaccurate reasoning while appearing overly self-confident, and (ii) hallucinations, i.e., attempting to satisfy users' requests while interpolating over missing data from training knowledge. In public health contexts, hallucinations represents a deeply concerning phenomenon. Hallucinations might range from subtle—like fake but vaguely familiar scientific papers mentioned as sources backing up health facts [38]—to outright disastrous—like recommending toxic levels of herbal remedies for clinical pathologies [39]. Hallucinations, like myopic overconfidence, stem from two key factors. On the one hand, the reinforcement learning used to train GPTs pushes LLMs to always provide an answer, even in the presence of faulty, missing, or inaccurate data [37]. On the other hand, LLMs and the chatbots based on them do not possess metacognitive skills for filtering out less reliable information. This is different from what humans can do, e.g., filtering out dubious info about vaccines coming from extremely unreliable sources [40]. This lack of metacognitive skills makes LLMs poor fact searchers and providers. Because of myopic overconfidence, LLM-based chatbots can produce recommendations sounding fair but ultimately completely false. For instance, Metze and colleagues [38] found that, while producing 50 small literature reviews on Chagas' disease, GPT 3.5 produced references with major hallucinations in 86.7% of the cases. Always when investigating GPT 3.5, recent studies [39,41] found that the LLM recommended to patients with the metabolic dysfunction-associated steatotic liver disease using herbal remedies that are considered by experts as harmful. These concrete examples underline the grave consequences that hallucinations can have over LLMs' performance as public health chatbots. The future developments of LLM-based chatbots for public health should keep capitalizing on the enormous potential for personification, trust-creation and cognitive reasoning that LLMs provide, while addressing key issues originating from human and non-human LLMs' biases. A synergy between psychology, computer science and public health communication would greatly push the scientific community towards such a promising future direction.

3. Artificial Intelligence in Genetics and Genomics

3.1. AI in Genetics and Computational Genomics

The convergence of artificial intelligence (AI) with genetic sciences has ushered in a new era of innovation in genomics, driven by the need to analyze vast quantities of biological data [42]. AI algorithms, especially those in the realms of ML and deep learning (DL), are pivotal in addressing the complex and multifaceted challenges posed by modern genomics [43]. With the advancement of high-throughput sequencing technologies, such as next-generation sequencing (NGS) and single-cell sequencing, the quantity of genomic data generated has exponentially increased. Interpreting this massive volume of data necessitates sophisticated computational tools that are capable of handling both the scale and complexity of the human genome, which is where AI systems have demonstrated transformative potential. A key application of AI in genomics is in variant calling. Genomic variation, such as single nucleotide polymorphisms (SNPs), insertions, deletions, and structural variants, are critical to understanding human disease, evolution, and genetic diversity [44]. Traditional approaches to variant calling, which heavily rely on statistical models, often struggle with distinguishing true variants from sequencing errors, particularly in the repetitive or poorly characterized regions of the genome [45]. AI, and more specifically deep learning models such as convolutional neural networks (CNNs), have been successfully employed to overcome these limitations by learning complex patterns directly from raw sequencing data [46]. For example, Google DeepVariant (available at https://github.com/google/deepvariant, accessed on 5 February 2025) is an AI-powered tool that uses deep learning techniques to improve the accuracy of variant calling, significantly reducing error rates compared to traditional bioinformatics pipelines. DeepVariant was trained on a diverse set of genomic data to predict genetic variants directly from sequencer reads, demonstrating how AI can surpass rule-based methods and enhance the fidelity of genomic data interpretation. Beyond variant calling, AI plays a crucial role in functional genomics, particularly in predicting the functional impact of genetic variants. Not all genetic variants are functionally significant; some may be benign, while others can have profound effects on gene regulation, protein structure, or cellular pathways [47]. AI models, such as those based on recurrent neural networks (RNNs) and attention mechanisms, have been used to predict the pathogenicity of variants [48]. These models are trained on annotated databases, like ClinVar (https://www.ncbi.nlm.nih.gov/clinvar/, accessed on 5 February 2025) and the Genome Aggregation Database (gnomAD) (https://gnomad.broadinstitute.org, accessed on 5 February 2025), which contain information on the clinical significance of known variants. By leveraging AI, it is possible to prioritize variants of unknown significance (VUSs) for further study, thus accelerating the identification of potential disease-causing mutations [42]. Additionally, AI-driven approaches like AlphaFold, developed by DeepMind, have revolutionized protein structure prediction, which is inherently linked to genomics [49]. AlphaFold's ability to accurately predict 3D protein structures from amino acid sequences has opened new avenues in understanding how genetic variants affect protein folding and function, which is crucial for identifying novel drug targets and understanding the molecular basis of diseases. In the context of genome-wide association studies (GWAS), which aim to identify associations between genetic variants and traits or diseases, AI techniques have been invaluable in managing the immense computational burden associated with these studies. GWAS typically involve scanning millions of genetic variants across large populations to identify those associated with specific phenotypes. Traditional GWAS methods rely on linear models and statistical thresholds to detect significant associations, but these approaches may fail to capture complex interactions between genetic variants (epistasis) or between genes and environmental factors. AI, particularly in the form of deep learning and neural networks, can model these nonlinear interactions and capture subtle genetic effects that might be missed by conventional methods [50]. For instance, AI algorithms can integrate genomic data with other layers of biological data, such as transcriptomics, epigenomics, and proteomics, to provide a more holistic view of the genetic architecture underlying complex diseases like cancer, diabetes, and neurodegenerative disorders [42,51]. One of the most promising areas of AI application in genomics is drug discovery and development [52]. Genomic data play a critical role in identifying drug targets and understanding the genetic basis of diseases, and AI can accelerate this process by analyzing large-scale genomic datasets to identify patterns that human researchers might miss [42]. For example, AI models can be trained on genomic data from patients with a particular disease to identify common genetic variants or gene expression profiles that could be targeted by new drugs, or can be utilized to predict the pathogenicity of variants, map an individual's sequence to genome references, and identify any clinically significant mutations (Figure 1). In addition to target identification, AI can also be used to predict how patients with different genetic backgrounds might respond to certain drugs, thus paving the way for more personalized treatments. This approach, often referred to as pharmacogenomics, is particularly important for diseases like cancer, where genetic mutations can influence drug efficacy and resistance. AI-driven insights from genomic data can help researchers develop targeted therapies that are more likely to be effective for specific patient populations, thereby reducing the time and cost associated with traditional drug discovery processes [51]. In addition to these specific applications, AI has become an integral part of data integration and interpretation in genomics. The wealth of genomic data generated by sequencing technologies is often accompanied by other types of omics data, such as transcriptomics (gene expression), proteomics (protein levels), and epigenomics (DNA methylation patterns) [53]. Integrating these diverse datasets is essential for gaining a comprehensive understanding of biological processes, but it is also extremely challenging due to the sheer volume and heterogeneity of the data. AI models, particularly those using unsupervised learning techniques, can help by identifying hidden patterns and relationships within the data that might not be apparent through traditional analytical methods. For example, AI-driven approaches can cluster similar samples based on multi-omic data, revealing subtypes of diseases that were previously unrecognized. This capability is especially valuable in cancer research, where tumors are often genetically heterogeneous, and identifying subtypes can lead to more effective, personalized treatment strategies [54].

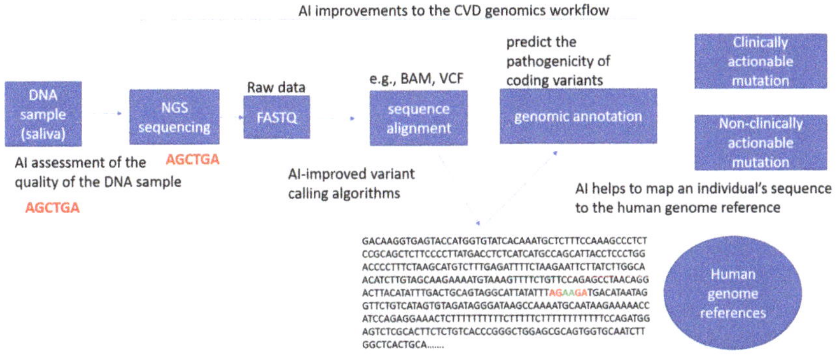

Figure 1. Example of the use of artificial intelligence to predict the pathogenicity of variants [55].

3.2. AI-Based Chatbots in Genomics

AI-based chatbots are emerging as valuable tools in genomics, offering new ways to provide instant access to complex genomic information for both professionals and the general public. In the genomic context, these chatbots have significant potential in streamlining data interpretation, facilitating patient engagement, and supporting personalized medicine [56]. One of the primary applications of chatbots in genomics is to assist researchers and clinicians in interpreting genetic data. Given the complexity and volume of data generated by genome sequencing technologies, AI-powered chatbots can serve as intermediaries, enabling users to query genomic databases, receive summaries of variant pathogenicity, or retrieve information on gene–disease associations in real time [48]. By integrating with genomic databases such as ClinVar, gnomAD, and Ensembl, these chatbots can provide quick, reliable responses to questions about specific genetic variants, their clinical relevance, or population frequency. Such tools can be especially useful in clinical settings, where genetic counselors or healthcare providers may need to rapidly access information to make informed decisions about patient care [57]. In addition to aiding professionals, AI chatbots can play a transformative role in genetic counseling by interacting directly with patients. The increasing availability of direct-to-consumer genetic testing services, such as 23andMe (https://www.23andme.com/en-int/, accessed on 5 February 2025) and AncestryDNA (https://www.ancestry.com, accessed on 5 February 2025), has led to a surge in individuals seeking to understand their genetic information. AI-driven chatbots can act as digital genetic counselors, answering common questions about genetic reports, explaining the implications of certain genetic variants, and even guiding users through the steps they should take after receiving potentially concerning results [58]. For example, a chatbot could explain whether a particular genetic variant is linked to an increased risk of cancer or other inherited conditions and advise the user on follow-up actions, such as consulting with a genetic counselor or undergoing further testing. This democratizes access to genetic insights, particularly for individuals who may not have easy access to professional genetic counseling services. By making genomic information more accessible and understandable, chatbots can help reduce the anxiety and confusion that often accompany the interpretation of personal genetic data. Another area where AI-based chatbots are gaining traction is in supporting personalized medicine by helping patients and healthcare providers interpret genomic data in the context of treatment options. Pharmacogenomics, the study of how genes affect an individual's response to drugs [59], is a key aspect of personalized medicine [60], and AI chatbots can play a crucial role in this field [61]. For example, a chatbot integrated with pharmacogenomic databases could help a physician determine whether a patient's genetic profile suggests a potential adverse reaction to a specific medication or whether they might benefit from a particular drug therapy based on their genetic makeup. This capability could significantly enhance the decision-making process in real-time, providing immediate, personalized recommendations for medication regimens that are tailored to an individual's genetic background. Furthermore, such chatbots could be designed to continually update and refine their knowledge base as new research and clinical trials provide more data, ensuring that patients and healthcare providers are working with the most current information available. Finally, AI-based chatbots also have the potential to address ethical concerns in genomics by promoting informed decision making and consent [62]. As genomic data become increasingly integrated into healthcare and research, ensuring that individuals understand the implications of sharing their genetic information is crucial. Chatbots can be programmed to explain the privacy risks, data-sharing policies, and potential consequences of genomic testing in simple, comprehensible language [63]. This empowers individuals to make informed choices about whether to participate in genomic studies or share their genetic data with healthcare providers. In research settings, chatbots could be used to facilitate the informed consent process, answering participant questions about genomic research protocols, data usage, and long-term storage, which can improve transparency and trust between researchers and participants. While the role of AI-driven chatbots in ensuring that patients understand the ethical and legal aspects of genomic data sharing is promising, particularly in the context of insurance and employment discrimination based on genetic information, further research is needed to explore the practical implementation of such functions. As the field of genomics evolves, chatbots may play a supportive role in helping individuals navigate the complex ethical landscape, but it remains to be seen how effectively they can address these concerns in real-world applications.

4. Leveraging AI-Driven Chatbots for Dynamically Adaptable Healthcare Spaces During Outbreaks

4.1. A Pragmatic Architectural Approach to the COVID-19 Response: The Lessons of the Pandemic

Early in the 2020 COVID-19 pandemic, the rapid construction of modular hospitals in Wuhan, China, using prefabricated components and negative-pressure ventilation, demonstrated the critical role of rapidly deployable quarantine facilities [64]. As the pandemic reached the United States, the American Institute of Architects (AIA) convened a task force to develop guidelines for converting existing structures into COVID-19 hospitals [65]. This effort resulted in a checklist, integrating expertise from diverse fields, to facilitate the rapid adaptation of buildings, prioritizing functionality over esthetics [66]. The initial phase of the pandemic response highlighted the challenge of determining optimal building typologies for quarantine hospitals. Open-plan structures (e.g., arenas) and closed-plan structures (e.g., hotels) each presented distinct advantages and disadvantages regarding patient isolation and infection control. By late spring 2020, following the first wave, it became clear that an ad hoc approach to such large-scale epidemiological and public health events was insufficient. Future pandemic preparedness necessitates a shift towards formalized pop-up testing infrastructure, prefabricated hospitals, and the integration of pandemic-resilient features into residential design, such as decontamination zones [67]. A growing consensus emerged that architects must address the challenge of designing built environments capable of maintaining essential societal functions, including work and education, during future pandemics, thereby mitigating the need for widespread societal shutdowns [67]. Shaping the future of architectural design to accommodate the possibility of recurring pandemic events requires a structured, predictive approach, integrating microbiological and epidemiological variables into the design process [66].

4.2. Post-Pandemic Architecture: Utilizing Digital Tools to Mitigate Airborne Transmission Risk

The COVID-19 pandemic has underscored the crucial role of architectural design in mitigating the spread of airborne infections. Digital simulation techniques, including CAD, CFD, and BIM, are increasingly employed to analyze the dynamics of viral particles within built environments [68,69]. These tools enable architects and engineers to model airflow patterns and assess the effectiveness of ventilation systems in reducing transmission risks. This interdisciplinary collaboration facilitates the development of predictive models that inform the design of more resilient architecture, addressing critical knowledge gaps regarding airborne viral transmission and ventilation efficacy.

4.3. Building the Future of Outbreak Response: AI Chatbots and Adaptive Hospital Design

The rapid emergence and spread of infectious diseases necessitate agile and adaptable healthcare infrastructure capable of responding effectively to diverse pathogens and evolving outbreak dynamics. Traditional healthcare facility design often proves inflexible and slow to adapt, hindering the effective management of rapidly unfolding public health crises [70]. This underscores the need for innovative approaches that leverage technology to create dynamically adaptable spaces capable of meeting the unique challenges posed by different outbreaks [71]. AI-driven chatbots, with their ability to process vast amounts of data and generate real-time insights, offer a promising avenue for achieving this goal (Table 2) [72,73].

Table 2. AI-driven chatbots for the rapid design of outbreak-specific context.

Strategy	Chatbots Role	Chatbots Functions
Data-Driven Design Parameters	Chatbots can be integrated with databases containing information on various pathogens, including their modes of transmission, incubation periods, and virulence. This data can inform the design parameters for outbreak-specific spaces.	• Transmission mode: The chatbot can determine the primary mode of transmission (airborne, droplet, contact) and recommend appropriate infection control measures, such as ventilation requirements, isolation protocols, and personal protective equipment guidelines [74]. • Incubation period: Knowing the incubation period helps determine the necessary duration of quarantine or isolation and informs the design of waiting areas and monitoring spaces [75]. • Virulence and severity: The severity of the disease influences the level of care required and the design of treatment areas, including the need for intensive care unit capabilities [76].
Rapid prototyping and space planning	Chatbots can assist with rapid prototyping and space planning by generating layout options based on the specific needs of the outbreak.	• Modular design: The chatbot can recommend modular designs that can be quickly assembled and reconfigured, allowing for flexibility and adaptability [77]. • Space allocation: Based on projected patient volumes and the required level of care, the chatbot can optimize space allocation for different functions, such as triage, testing, isolation, and treatment [78]. • 3D visualization: The chatbot can generate 3D visualizations of the proposed layouts, allowing stakeholders to review and approve the design before implementation [77].
Real-time adaptation and optimization	During an outbreak, the situation can change rapidly. Chatbots can continuously monitor data and adapt the design of the space accordingly.	• Patient flow management: The chatbot can analyze patient flow data and adjust the layout to optimize efficiency and minimize bottlenecks [79]. • Resource allocation: Based on real-time data on resource utilization, the chatbot can recommend adjustments to staffing levels, equipment allocation, and supply chain management [80]. • Infection control: The chatbot can update infection control measures based on the latest information about the pathogen and the evolving outbreak dynamics [81].

One of the potential benefits of using artificial intelligence-based chatbots in this context lies in their ability to integrate and analyze data from different sources. Linking chatbots to databases containing information on various pathogens—including modes of transmission, incubation periods, virulence, and susceptibility to different intervention measures—could support the definition of design parameters for spaces dedicated to managing epidemic outbreaks. Although chatbots cannot independently determine the transmissibility of a pathogen, they can be used to provide information from reliable sources, facilitating access to official guidelines on containment measures such as ventilation, isolation, and personal protective equipment. However, it is important to note that the reliability of such tools depends on the quality of the underlying data and their ability to interpret it. Because chatbots are probabilistic models of language, they may generate responses that appear plausible but are not necessarily correct. Therefore, their use should be considered a decision support rather than a definitive source, and any recommendations should be verified by experts in the field before being implemented.

Beyond informing initial design parameters, AI-driven chatbots can play a crucial role in rapid prototyping and space planning. By leveraging algorithms capable of generating multiple layout options based on specific outbreak characteristics and projected patient volumes, chatbots can significantly accelerate the design process. This can involve recommending modular designs that are easily assembled and reconfigured, optimizing the space allocation for different functions such as triage, testing, and isolation, and even generating the 3D visualizations of proposed layouts for stakeholder review. This rapid prototyping capability is essential for the timely deployment of adaptable healthcare spaces during outbreaks.

The dynamic nature of outbreaks demands continuous monitoring and adaptation. AI-driven chatbots can excel in this area by analyzing real-time data on patient flow, resource utilization, and emerging pathogen characteristics. This information can be used to adjust the layout of healthcare spaces, optimize staffing levels and equipment allocation, and update infection control protocols as needed. For example, a chatbot can analyze patient flow data to identify bottlenecks and recommend adjustments to the layout to improve efficiency and minimize wait times. Similarly, real-time data on resource utilization can inform decisions regarding the allocation of medical personnel, equipment, and supplies.

Furthermore, integrating chatbots with building management systems offers the potential for the automated control of environmental parameters. This can include adjusting ventilation rates and air filtration settings based on the specific needs of the outbreak, maintaining optimal temperature and humidity levels to inhibit pathogen growth, and optimizing energy consumption by adjusting lighting and climate control systems based on occupancy patterns. This level of integration can significantly enhance the efficiency and effectiveness of outbreak management.

4.4. Example Scenario

AI-driven chatbots can be valuable tools for rapidly designing and adapting spaces to manage different outbreaks, taking into account the specific characteristics of each pathogen (Figure 2).

The chatbot can access data on the virus's transmission characteristics and recommend a design that prioritizes airborne infection control measures, such as negative pressure rooms, HEPA filtration, and designated airflow patterns. As the outbreak progresses and more data become available, the chatbot can adapt the design to optimize patient flow, resource allocation, and infection control protocols (Figure 2). By leveraging AI-driven chatbots, we can create more responsive and adaptable healthcare spaces that are better equipped to manage the unique challenges of different outbreaks.

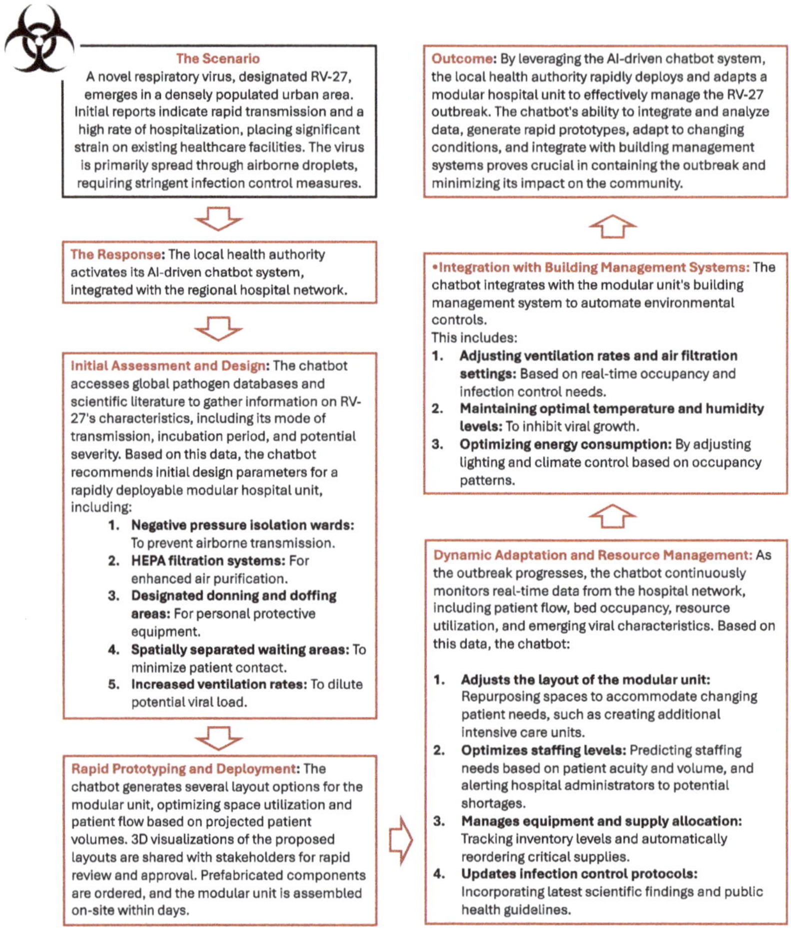

Figure 2. Example scenario of a novel hypothetic respiratory virus outbreak.

5. Chatbots as Statistical Consultants in Infectious Disease Settings: Potential and Reliability

In the field of infectious disease management, chatbots with advanced artificial intelligence, such as ChatGPT, are being studied not only as tools for disseminating information, but also to assist in data analysis and decision making. These artificial intelligence systems have the potential to guide public health officials, researchers, and even less experienced users through the complex process of selecting appropriate statistical techniques for epidemic data analysis. With the increasing use of large-scale data collection during epidemics, chatbots could provide accessible real-time advice on which statistical methods to employ based on the characteristics of the available data. However, the effectiveness and reliability of chatbots in this advisory role depend on several factors, including the accuracy of their recommendations, their interpretability, and their potential limitations.

5.1. Potential of Chatbots as Statistical Advisors

When faced with questions such as "I have this data set, what statistical method should I use?", chatbots such as ChatGPT can quickly generate plausible answers by leveraging their knowledge of general statistical principles. For example, if a user presents time series data on infection rates, the chatbot might suggest using techniques such as ARIMA (AutoRegressive Integrated Moving Average) models or exponential smoothing to predict future trends [82]. For spatial data involving epidemic outbreaks, the chatbot might recommend geospatial analysis tools such as kriging or spatial autocorrelation, which are useful for identifying disease clusters [83]. These recommendations can be useful, especially in situations where human expertise is not readily available, making chatbot-guided suggestions a scalable solution for public health workers during emergencies.

One of the strengths of the chatbot is its ability to handle different types of data. If asked a question about how to handle multivariable datasets, the chatbot might suggest principal component analysis (PCA) to reduce data dimensionality and identify key factors driving disease progression [84]. Where the user is dealing with survey data from affected populations, ChatGPT could recommend logistic regression or chi-square tests to explore relationships between variables, such as symptoms and risk factors. This wide range of functionality could support decision making at various stages of the epidemic response, from initial surveillance to resource allocation and intervention evaluation.

5.2. Evaluating the Reliability of Chatbots in Recommending Statistical Techniques

Although artificial intelligence chatbots such as ChatGPT have considerable potential to offer statistical guidance, their reliability in providing accurate and contextually appropriate recommendations is a critical issue. Language models are trained on vast datasets, often encompassing a wide range of disciplines, including statistics. However, they lack a deep understanding of the specific nuances of a given dataset or the subtleties of research questions in infectious disease contexts. This raises several reliability issues:

1. Accuracy of recommendations: AI chatbots are not immune from making mistakes or offering incorrect statistical advice. Although ChatGPT may suggest well-known statistical methods, it does not always recommend the techniques best suited to a specific dataset. For example, it might suggest the use of a linear regression when, given the distribution of the data, a nonlinear model would be more appropriate. Studies have shown that artificial intelligence models, despite their sophistication, are often unable to fully understand the domain-specific requirements of medical or epidemiological datasets [85]. This limitation could lead to erroneous recommendations, especially when users are unfamiliar with the subtleties of statistical techniques.
2. Assumptions and limitations: Every statistical technique has inherent assumptions, such as the normality of data distribution, independence of observations, or homoscedasticity. Chatbots do not always provide sufficient warning or detail about these assumptions, potentially leading to the misuse of statistical methods. For example, recommending ANOVA (analysis of variance) without clarifying the need for homogeneity of variances could lead to erroneous analysis results [86]. In this regard, human statisticians possess the nuances of judgment necessary to adapt methods based on data anomalies, something that current chatbots lack.
3. Interpretability and user understanding: Even when ChatGPT correctly identifies an appropriate statistical method, explaining why a particular technique should be used remains a challenge. Although the model can describe statistical concepts in general terms, it does not always provide clear guidance on why certain assumptions are important or how to interpret the results in a meaningful way. This limitation could be particularly problematic for users who do not have a strong background in statistics. A chatbot might recommend logistic regression for analyzing binary outcomes, but not guide the user through the necessary diagnostic tests, such as testing for multicollinearity or overfitting [87]. The absence of in-depth explanations could hinder the user's ability to effectively apply the recommended techniques.

4. Dependence on training data: ChatGPT and similar models are trained on large datasets that include vast amounts of information, but are not necessarily up-to-date with the latest advances in statistical theory or infectious disease epidemiology. This lag in knowledge could cause the chatbot to suggest outdated or less efficient methods. In addition, these models are based on probabilities derived from training data, which means they lack a true understanding of the problem at hand. They generate answers based on patterns and correlations in the data they have seen, but they do not reason about the statistical principles involved as a human expert would [88].
5. Risk of misinformation: One of the significant risks of using AI chatbots for statistical guidance is the potential for misinformation. ChatGPT, while very adept at generating human-like text, can sometimes produce "hallucinations", generating plausible but factually incorrect information [89]. In a statistical context, this could lead the chatbot to recommend inappropriate or even nonexistent methods. For example, it might suggest a test or statistical procedure that is not applicable to the user's dataset or, in extreme cases, does not exist in the statistical literature. In the world of public health, where data-driven decisions can impact millions of people, the consequences of such errors could be severe.

5.3. Enhancing the Reliability of Chatbots: A Hybrid Approach

To mitigate the risks associated with chatbot recommendations, a human-in-the-loop approach is advisable, especially in high-risk settings such as infectious disease management. In this context, chatbots provide preliminary recommendations that can be verified and refined by human experts. This hybrid approach ensures that the scalability and efficiency of AI is balanced with the critical judgment and domain-specific expertise provided by human statisticians. In addition, human experts can also review the chatbot's suggestions, providing additional insights or corrections that can improve the quality of the analysis. In addition, integrating real-time feedback systems that allow users to report inaccuracies or clarify uncertainties can help improve the chatbot's performance over time, increasing both accuracy and user confidence. Regular updates of the chatbot's training data can also ensure that it remains current with the latest developments in statistical methods and public health practices.

Future developments could focus on creating domain-specific chatbots trained on datasets directly relevant to public health and epidemiology. By incorporating knowledge about recent infectious disease outbreaks and advances in statistical methods adapted to these contexts, chatbots could become more reliable tools for public health professionals. This would also involve incorporating more sophisticated models for error detection, allowing the chatbot to flag potential risks in its recommendations and alert users to seek expert advice. Furthermore, collaboration with interdisciplinary teams that include statisticians, epidemiologists, and data scientists can help refine the chatbot's capabilities. This collaboration can improve the chatbot's ability to provide personalized recommendations that closely align with the specific needs of public health practitioners.

Artificial intelligence-based chatbots such as ChatGPT offer significant potential as statistical consultants in infectious disease settings, providing quick and accessible guidance on the use of appropriate analytical techniques. However, their recommendations should not be considered a substitute for expert judgment. Although these systems can suggest general methods, their limitations—such as lack of deep understanding, potential for error, and inability to explain complex statistical nuances—mean they should be used with caution. The future of chatbots in this role likely lies in hybrid models that combine the scalability of AI with the critical oversight of human experts, ensuring more reliable and contextually appropriate statistical advice. As public health continues to evolve in an increasingly data-driven world, the integration of these technologies can improve decision-making processes and, ultimately, health outcomes.

6. Clinical Insights from an Infectious Disease Specialist

6.1. *AI-Powered Chatbots for Clinical Management During Outbreaks*

Infectious disease outbreaks pose significant challenges to global health security, placing immense strain on healthcare systems. The rapid spread of infection, coupled with often-limited resources, necessitates efficient and timely patient management. Artificial intelligence-powered tools, particularly chatbots, offer a promising avenue for enhancing patient care and optimizing resource allocation during these critical periods. Chatbots can provide readily accessible information, facilitate preliminary triage, and enable remote monitoring, contributing to a more sustainable global healthcare paradigm [90].

Artificial intelligence is rapidly transforming healthcare delivery within hospitals and clinics. Its applications span various areas, from enhancing clinical decision making and streamlining operational efficiency to improving diagnostic accuracy and revolutionizing patient care. The evolution of AI has led to the development of increasingly sophisticated chatbots with diverse healthcare applications [91]. Historically, programs like MYCIN [92] aided physicians with differential diagnosis based on patient symptoms. Modern chatbots can play a crucial role during infectious disease outbreaks by providing up-to-date information about symptoms, prevention measures, and treatment options.

An example of such advanced AI technology is the BERT-based medical chatbot, which leverages Bidirectional Encoder Representations from Transformers (BERT) [93], a state-of-the-art deep learning model for natural language understanding (NLU). BERT, unlike traditional models that process text in a single direction (left-to-right or right-to-left), considers the context of a word by looking at both the words that come before and after it. This makes it highly effective in understanding the contextual meaning of sentences, especially in complex domains like medicine, where jargon and linguistic nuances are critical for accurate interpretation. Figure 3 illustrates the architecture of a BERT-based medical chatbot [94], where the BERT model processes user queries, extracts medical entities (such as symptoms or conditions), and generates relevant responses. Key components of the system include the user interface (frontend), which allows users to interact with the chatbot via text or voice input; the text processing module, which preprocesses queries by performing tokenization, stop word removal, stemming, lemmatization, and Part-of-Speech (PoS) tagging [95]; the BERT model, which parses text bidirectionally, recognizes medical entities and classifies user intent; context management, which maintains the history and context of the conversation to ensure consistent responses in complex interactions; the entity and intent recognition unit, which extracts medical entities and classifies intent using techniques such as Conditional Random Fields (CRFs) [96] and softmax [97]; dialogue management and response generation, which combines predefined templates, retrieval methods from a medical knowledge base, and generative templates to produce appropriate responses; the medical knowledge base, an up-to-date database with information on symptoms, conditions, treatments and guidelines, consulted by the chatbot to provide accurate advice; and finally, response delivery (backend), which sends the generated response to the user via the frontend interface, completing the interaction cycle.

They can also facilitate appointment scheduling and answer frequently asked questions, reducing the burden on healthcare workers. In particular, AI's evolution in healthcare has been driven by advancements in machine learning and neural networks, coupled with increased computational power and data availability. These technologies are empowering healthcare professionals with tools to analyze patient data more effectively, leading to more precise diagnoses and personalized treatment plans. AI is also optimizing hospital operations by automating administrative tasks, improving patient flow, and enhancing resource allocation. In medical diagnostics, AI is accelerating image analysis in radiology and pathology, enabling faster and more accurate results [98].

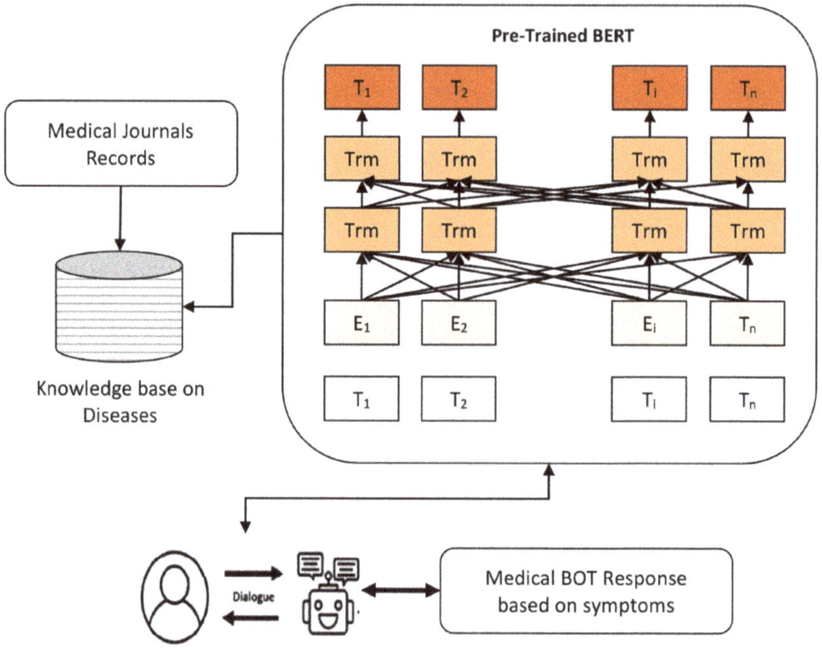

Figure 3. An example of BERT-based medical BOT [94].

Furthermore, chatbots contribute significantly to telehealth delivery, encompassing remote patient monitoring, medication reminders, and personalized health advice (https://www.irjmets.com/uploadedfiles/paper//issue_4_april_2024/53081/final/fin_irjmets1713334010.pdf, accessed on 9 March 2025) virtual assistance, creating new possibilities for patient–physician interaction. For example, recent advancements in voice-based AI technologies, as highlighted by Jadczyk et al. [99], demonstrate the potential of voice chatbots to streamline healthcare delivery during pandemics. These systems can automate patient triage, provide real-time health information, and support remote monitoring, reducing the burden on healthcare providers and improving patient outcomes. Figure 4 illustrates the workflow of an AI-driven voice chatbot in healthcare delivery, showcasing its integration with clinical decision support systems and electronic health records. The workflow begins with the user (patient or healthcare provider) interacting with the chatbot through a voice interface, such as a smartphone or smart speaker. The chatbot processes the user's input using NLP techniques and connects to a clinical decision support system (CDSS) to provide accurate, context-aware responses. The system then integrates the collected data with electronic health records (EHRs), enabling real-time updates and alerts for healthcare providers. This seamless integration allows for efficient patient triage, remote monitoring, and personalized care, reducing the workload on healthcare professionals and improving patient outcomes.

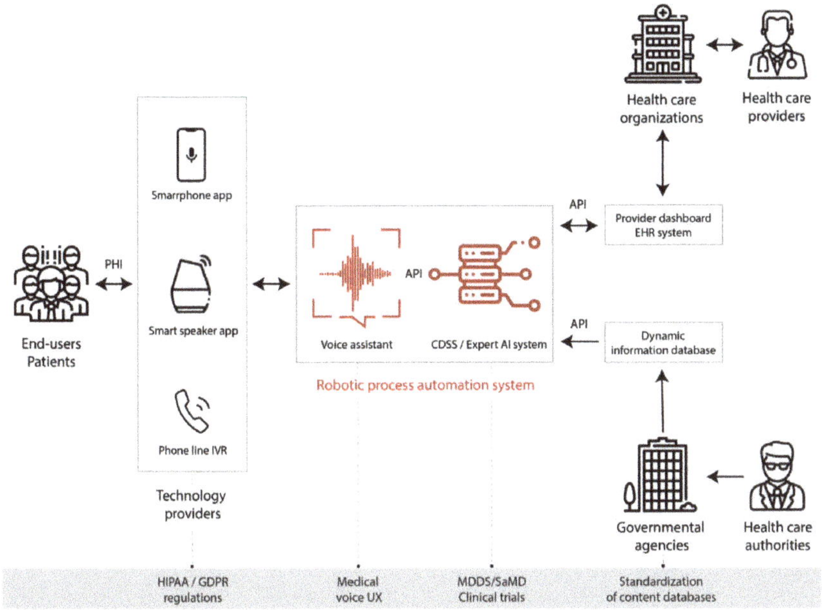

Figure 4. Workflow of the AI-driven voice chatbot in healthcare delivery [99].

6.2. Enhancing Outbreak Response with Chatbots: Benefits and Challenges in Clinical Management of Patients

AI-powered chatbots can play a significant role in improving clinical management during infectious disease outbreaks. These tools offer tangible benefits for both patients and healthcare professionals by optimizing workflows and enhancing operational efficiency.

For patients, chatbots serve as an immediate source of information and support. They can guide users through symptom assessment and triage, helping them determine the appropriate level of care and potentially reducing unnecessary hospital visits [3]. This is particularly crucial during outbreaks, as it minimizes exposure risk and alleviates the burden on healthcare facilities. Additionally, chatbots can disseminate accurate and up-to-date information about the outbreak, counteracting misinformation and enabling individuals to make informed decisions [3]. For patients managing their illness remotely, chatbots can facilitate remote monitoring by tracking symptoms and vital signs, allowing for the early detection of any health deterioration [100]. They can also provide medication reminders, support treatment adherence, and offer basic mental health assistance to help manage the stress and anxiety often associated with public health emergencies [101]. Furthermore, by analyzing individual patient data, chatbots can generate personalized health recommendations tailored to specific needs.

Healthcare professionals also stand to benefit from chatbot integration. By handling routine inquiries, distributing important updates, and reinforcing clinical guidelines, chatbots can reduce the workload of medical staff, enabling them to focus on more complex cases and direct patient care [101]. Additionally, chatbots can assist with contact tracing efforts and collect valuable epidemiological data for research purposes.

However, to ensure responsible and effective deployment, several challenges must be addressed. The accuracy and reliability of chatbot-provided information must be continuously monitored [102]. Safeguarding data privacy and security is paramount, and chatbot interfaces should be designed to support linguistic accessibility and cultural sensitivity. Furthermore, seamless integration with existing healthcare systems is crucial for successful implementation. Building trust and acceptance among both patients and healthcare providers is another key factor in widespread adoption.

It is important to emphasize that chatbots are not intended to replace healthcare professionals but rather to complement existing healthcare strategies. Their integration can enhance the quality and efficiency of healthcare delivery during outbreaks by providing timely and targeted support (Figure 5).

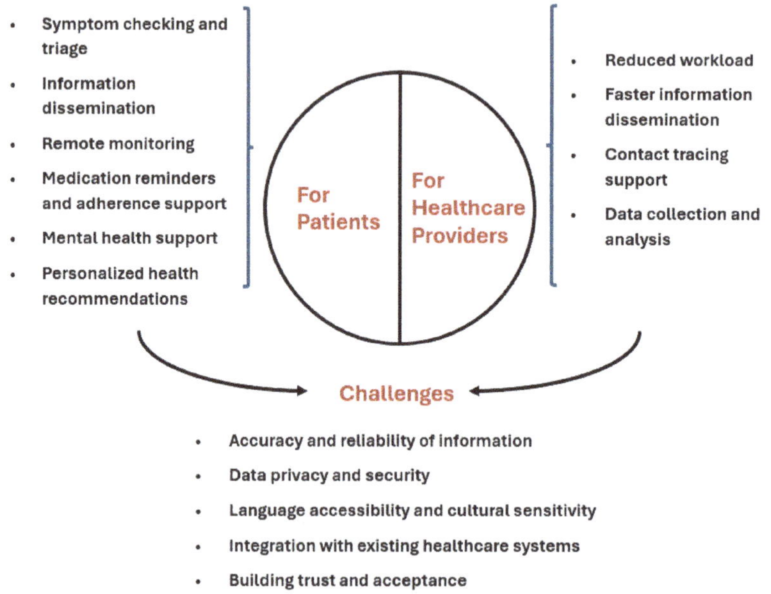

Figure 5. The role of chatbots in epidemic response.

6.3. Future Directions and Research Needs

Future research should focus on exploring the potential of AI-powered chatbots for handling more complex tasks, such as assisting with preliminary diagnosis and offering personalized treatment recommendations. A thorough evaluation of the effectiveness of chatbots in real-world outbreak scenarios is essential to assess their true impact on patient outcomes and the performance of healthcare systems. Ethical considerations regarding the use of chatbots, especially during public health emergencies, must be carefully addressed to ensure they are deployed responsibly and equitably. Despite these challenges, chatbots have considerable potential to transform patient management during infectious disease outbreaks. By providing timely and accurate information, facilitating remote monitoring, and alleviating the strain on healthcare systems, chatbots can contribute to more effective and equitable responses to public health crises. To fully realize their benefits, further research, careful implementation, and continuous evaluation are necessary. This will help maximize the advantages while minimizing the potential risks associated with the adoption of this emerging technology.

7. Challenges and Limitations of AI Chatbots in Infectious Disease Outbreaks

The integration of chatbots and large language models (LLMs) into healthcare communication during epidemics offers some notable advantages such as innovative ways to both collect and disseminate information and opportunities for resource optimization.

While these potential benefits can significantly support doctors, policymakers, and citizens by providing timely information and aiding in resource management, this class of software applications also present important limitations and risks in the context of infectious diseases, which must be known to allow for their cautious and responsible implementation.

The challenges and risks discussed below are similar to those associated with medical and health issues affecting individuals. However, they are intensified by the scale of those impacted, the uncertainty surrounding the nature of symptoms, the relationship between symptoms and disease severity, and the ambiguity regarding modes of disease transmission and mitigation. In other words, in what follows, we will survey problems that are known to be related to the use of conversational agents in the management of health issues, but exacerbated by the contexts in which epidemics and pandemic occur, that is, in contexts of heightened severity, spread, and uncertainty.

The main limitations and risks can be grouped in two broad ambits: capacity and alignment. Capacity refers to the intrinsic abilities of these systems in terms of their functions and skills. This domain encompasses quality dimensions such as accuracy, reliability, and effectiveness. Limitations in capacity involve technical shortcomings like misinformation propagation, the inability to interpret complex or ambiguous user inputs, and challenges in processing real-time updates. Essentially, capacity-related issues regard the tasks these AI systems are not capable of carrying out as expected and the kind of failure they can exhibit.

Alignment, on the other hand, pertains to the extent to which the capacities of these AI systems are coherent with the values, principles, and norms of the society and community they serve. This includes compliance with ethical standards, cultural sensitivities, and legal regulations such as data protection laws and medical practice guidelines. Limitations in alignment involve ethical dilemmas, privacy violations, lack of transparency, and potential misuse of technology. In essence, alignment-related issues regard shortcomings of these systems in adhering to societal expectations and legal requirements. For both ambit, we will discuss four main challenges, as they are reported in Table 3. The following sections will explore each of these challenges in detail, highlighting the critical issues that emerge in infectious disease contexts.

Table 3. Overview of issues related to AI-based chatbots in public health emergencies.

Capacity	**Information Accuracy and Reliability**
1.	Unpredictability and Reliability Issues
2.	Dissemination of Outdated Information
3.	Amplification of Misinformation
4.	Technical Limitations in Communication
Alignment	**Ethical and Legal Concerns**
1.	Ethical and Accountability Concerns
2.	Privacy and Data Security Risks
3.	Ineffectiveness with Diverse Populations
4.	Resource Allocation Concerns
5.	Unpredictability and Reliability Issues

7.1. Unpredictability and Reliability Issues

The unpredictability and potential unreliability of LLMs, such as GPT-3 and GPT-4, raise significant challenges when used in decision support tools during health crises like pandemics. These models generate responses based on patterns from extensive datasets without true understanding, which can lead to "hallucinations", that is, plausible yet factually incorrect information [89]. In critical situations, such misinformation can mislead individuals, potentially worsening disease spread. While LLMs offer scalable, immediate responses, their risks can undermine public trust and hinder effective health interventions [103].

Although improvements have been made to reduce inaccuracies [10], LLMs still struggle with maintaining factual consistency. Further research is needed to develop evaluation metrics and real-time verification systems to ensure reliability in high-stakes domains [104]. Enhancing training protocols by incorporating domain-specific data and real-time fact-checking algorithms are key technical measures to improve AI reliability [105]. Tools that promote AI explainability can also help identify and correct errors [106].

Beyond technical solutions, socio-technical measures are essential. Human-in-the-loop systems allow experts to validate AI outputs, reducing the risk of misinformation [107]. Educating users on AI's limitations and establishing clear regulatory frameworks are essential for responsible AI deployment in healthcare [108].

Research should focus on addressing AI hallucinations, enhancing real-time verification, and understanding how users interact with AI-generated health information [109,110]. Regulatory frameworks must evolve to ensure the safe, ethical deployment of AI in health crises [111].

7.2. Dissemination of Outdated Information

During health crises, AI chatbots that rely on outdated data risk providing incorrect guidance, leading to public confusion and non-compliance with current health measures [112]. AI models, especially LLMs, often require continuous updates to reflect the latest health guidelines, yet maintaining this real-time accuracy is technically challenging and resource-intensive. While dynamic knowledge graphs and incremental learning techniques show promise for keeping AI systems updated [113,114], gaps remain in ensuring the real-time integration of new data during fast-changing situations like pandemics.

Technical measures, such as integrating real-time data from authoritative sources via APIs, are necessary to ensure the accuracy of chatbot responses [115]. A modular AI design allows for more flexible updates by separating the knowledge base from the language model, which can significantly reduce the need for full retraining [116]. Incremental learning techniques can also enhance the system's adaptability, enabling it to learn from new information without large-scale retraining [117].

Socio-technical interventions, such as partnerships with health authorities like the WHO and CDC, ensure that AI systems receive timely updates [118]. User feedback systems allow individuals to report outdated information, helping improve chatbot accuracy and accountability [119]. Additionally, notifying users when significant updates occur fosters transparency and trust [120].

Key research areas include improving real-time update integration and maintaining data consistency in AI models [121]. Understanding how outdated information affects user behavior and trust is essential for developing design strategies that promote engagement with accurate, up-to-date data [122].

7.3. Amplification of Misinformation

Epidemics often trigger an "infodemic"—an overabundance of information, including rumors and misinformation [118]. AI chatbots, if not properly monitored, can unintentionally amplify false information due to their perceived authority, leading to harmful behaviors and undermining public health efforts [123]. Detecting misinformation is challenging because it evolves rapidly and is often context-dependent. While machine learning algorithms for misinformation detection exist, their integration into conversational AI systems remains underexplored [124].

To mitigate misinformation, it is necessary to integrate advanced NLP models capable of identifying false information in chatbot responses [125]. Chatbots should also cross-reference trusted databases from health organizations to ensure the reliability of the information provided [105]. Socio-technical measures, such as user reporting mechanisms and transparent disclaimers, foster a collaborative and trustworthy environment [126]. Partnering with fact-checking organizations can ensure that chatbots remain up-to-date with verified corrections [127].

Key research areas include developing real-time misinformation detection in AI chatbots, understanding the impact of misinformation on user behavior, and maintaining user trust through transparent content moderation policies [128]. Ethical considerations also require collaboration with policymakers to ensure responsible chatbot deployment, emphasizing transparency and accountability [111].

7.4. Ethical and Accountability Concerns

The deployment of AI chatbots in healthcare during crises raises ethical and accountability concerns, as users may over-rely on them for medical advice, potentially leading to self-diagnosis and the avoidance of professional consultation [129]. When chatbots provide incorrect or misleading information, determining liability is complex, as the advice comes from an AI system rather than a human. Current frameworks do not sufficiently address these issues, leaving gaps in legal and ethical responsibility [130].

While AI chatbots offer scalable solutions for disseminating health information, they also pose risks such as misdiagnosis and data privacy breaches. Users tend to trust these systems, which increases the likelihood of over-reliance on chatbot advice [131]. Balancing the benefits of widespread access to health information with the potential harms requires a comprehensive approach that includes technical and socio-technical measures.

On the technical side, ensuring transparency in chatbot decision making is fundamental for building trust. Chatbots should provide clear explanations for their recommendations, and safety protocols should be in place to alert users to seek professional help when necessary [132]. Protecting user privacy through compliance with regulations like GDPR is also essential to maintain confidentiality and secure sensitive data [133].

Socio-technical interventions are equally important. Ethical guidelines tailored to AI in healthcare must be integrated into chatbot design to ensure patient safety and fairness [134]. Educating users about the limitations of AI chatbots can prevent over-reliance and reinforce the importance of consulting healthcare professionals when needed [135]. Clear accountability frameworks should define the responsibilities of AI developers and healthcare providers to ensure ethical compliance and legal clarity [136].

Research is needed to develop frameworks for determining accountability when AI chatbots cause harm and to explore how users' over-reliance on AI affects their health outcomes [137]. Additionally, protecting user privacy while enabling personalized healthcare remains a critical challenge. Research into advanced encryption and anonymization techniques is essential for ensuring data security while providing personalized health solutions [138].

7.5. Privacy and Data Security Risks

The deployment of AI chatbots in healthcare often requires collecting personal health information (PHI) to provide tailored advice, raising significant privacy concerns [139]. Ensuring compliance with regulations such as HIPAA and GDPR is essential, but many chatbot platforms may lack the necessary infrastructure, posing risks to user data security [133]. The challenge is especially relevant during epidemics when individuals may share more sensitive data, increasing the potential for breaches that can lead to identity theft, discrimination, and a loss of trust in healthcare systems [63].

One of the key challenges is ensuring that chatbots collect only the minimum amount of data necessary to provide accurate responses. The principle of data minimization should be a cornerstone of chatbot design, ensuring that sensitive information is not unnecessarily stored or shared [140]. Additionally, end-to-end encryption and secure authentication protocols are critical to safeguarding PHI [141]. These technical measures must be complemented by user education, ensuring that individuals understand how their data are being used and what protections are in place [118]. Another important consideration is the transparency of data usage. Users should be informed about the types of data being collected, the purposes for which it will be used, and the entities with which it may be shared. This transparency is crucial for building trust, particularly in communities that may be skeptical of AI technologies [142]. Furthermore, real-time feedback mechanisms should be implemented to allow users to report privacy concerns or data breaches, enabling the continuous improvement of chatbot security measures [143]. The issue of data ownership also warrants attention. In many cases, the data collected by chatbots are stored and analyzed by third-party providers, raising questions about who ultimately controls this information. Clear guidelines and agreements must be established to ensure that data ownership remains with the individual or the healthcare provider, rather than the technology vendor [63]. Finally, the long-term storage of health data poses additional risks. While historical data can be valuable for research and improving chatbot performance, it also increases the potential for misuse. Policies must be put in place to ensure that data are anonymized and securely stored, with strict access controls to prevent unauthorized use [144].

To safeguard PHI, techniques like end-to-end encryption, anonymization, and secure authentication protocols are critical [141]. Anonymization reduces the risk of data breaches by ensuring that compromised data cannot be linked to individuals, while multi-factor authentication helps secure access to the chatbot system [143]. Regular security audits should be conducted to identify and mitigate vulnerabilities in the chatbot infrastructure [144]. Socio-technical strategies are also vital. Compliance with regulations like HIPAA and GDPR must be demonstrated, and users should be informed about data collection practices and asked for informed consent [142]. Adopting the principle of data minimization—collecting only what is necessary for the chatbot's function—can limit exposure to sensitive data [140]. Educating users on how their data are protected and their rights under privacy laws is key to fostering trust [118]. Research is needed to explore how AI chatbots can deliver personalized advice while maintaining compliance with privacy regulations. Incorporating privacy by design from the outset ensures that privacy considerations are integrated at every stage of chatbot development [142]. Additionally, advanced techniques like federated learning and real-time encryption should be investigated to balance data utility and privacy without compromising chatbot performance [63].

7.6. Ineffectiveness with Diverse Populations

AI chatbots often fail to meet the needs of diverse populations due to linguistic, cultural, and socioeconomic limitations. These systems struggle to interpret input from non-native speakers and lack cultural context, leading to miscommunication and misinformation, particularly among marginalized communities [145]. This shortfall exacerbates existing health disparities, as these groups face barriers in accessing reliable health information, increasing their risk during epidemics.

The biases in AI models, stemming from non-representative training data, limit their effectiveness in underrepresented languages and cultural contexts [146]. While multilingual models and culturally adaptive systems have been developed, significant gaps remain in scaling these solutions and ensuring they meet the needs of marginalized communities [147]. To address this, expanding training datasets to include more diverse languages and developing speech recognition systems that accommodate different dialects are critical steps [148]. In addition to technical innovations, socio-technical measures are essential. Community-centered design approaches, which involve local populations in chatbot development, ensure that the technology is culturally relevant and accessible [149]. Collaborations with health agencies and local organizations can help tailor information dissemination strategies to meet the specific needs of different communities [150]. Furthermore, digital literacy programs are vital for enabling marginalized populations to effectively engage with AI chatbots, improving access to critical health information. Key research areas include enhancing AI chatbots for low-resource languages, reducing bias, and assessing the public health impacts of communication barriers created by ineffective AI systems. Participatory design methods, which involve end-users in chatbot development, are essential for increasing engagement and trust among marginalized communities [151].

7.7. Technical Limitations in Communication

AI chatbots and LLMs face significant technical challenges in effectively communicating with users during health crises, often struggling with ambiguous queries, slang, and emotional cues. The misinterpretation of symptoms or concerns can result in inappropriate or unsafe advice, delaying necessary medical intervention [152]. This problem is exacerbated by limitations in NLP, as chatbots often fail to comprehend nuanced language or emotional states [153].

While transformer-based models like BERT and GPT-3 have improved language understanding, they still struggle with context-specific slang and emotion recognition [154]. Emotion recognition, a key area for improvement in healthcare chatbots, remains underexplored, and integrating it into real-world applications is challenging [155]. Expanding chatbot training datasets to include slang, colloquial language, and regional dialects is an important step for improving communication with diverse populations [156].

To address these challenges, adopting advanced NLP techniques and emotion recognition technologies is essential. Context-aware algorithms and multimodal systems that combine text analysis with speech and emotion recognition offer promising solutions for improving chatbot communication [157]. In addition, human–AI collaboration is also of paramount importance—systems should allow human experts to intervene when a chatbot detects ambiguity or emotional distress, ensuring appropriate responses [158,159].

User education is also important; informing users about chatbot limitations and encouraging clear communication can reduce misunderstandings [160]. Feedback mechanisms that enable users to report errors can lead to continuous improvements in chatbot performance [161].

Research is needed to explore how AI chatbots can better interpret ambiguous queries and context-specific language, especially in healthcare. Developing domain-specific language models and integrating emotion recognition technologies are critical steps toward improving chatbot effectiveness in high-stakes health scenarios [48]. Interdisciplinary approaches from linguistics, psychology, and human–computer interaction will be vital for enhancing chatbot communication [162].

7.8. Resource Allocation Concerns

The deployment of AI chatbots during health crises raises concerns about resource allocation, as investment in these technologies may divert funding and attention from essential public health interventions, such as vaccination campaigns and contact tracing [163]. While chatbots offer scalability and the ability to disseminate information quickly, their cost-effectiveness and impact on epidemic management remain uncertain [164]. Allocating resources to chatbots without clear evidence of their effectiveness may reduce the overall impact of traditional health measures [165].

To address these challenges, chatbots should be designed with cost-effective strategies in mind, such as using open source platforms and modular frameworks to enable scalability across different crises [166]. Integration with existing public health systems is a very relevant factor for ensuring that chatbots complement, rather than disrupt, traditional interventions [167]. Additionally, pilot programs and robust evaluation mechanisms can help assess chatbot effectiveness before wider deployment [168]. Socio-technical strategies are also important. Decision-making frameworks that evaluate the cost-effectiveness of chatbots should be implemented to ensure resources are allocated efficiently [169]. Engaging public health professionals, policymakers, and community representatives in the development process ensures that chatbots meet public health needs and do not undermine essential services [170].

Research is needed to compare the cost-effectiveness of chatbots with traditional public health interventions, explore integration frameworks that align chatbot deployment with existing health goals, and assess the long-term impact of chatbot investments on public health infrastructure [171].

8. Conclusions

AI-based chatbots have emerged as valuable tools in managing public health emergencies, particularly during infectious disease outbreaks. Their ability to provide immediate and reliable responses enhances communication between health authorities and the public, reducing anxiety and confusion while facilitating the timely dissemination of essential health information. However, the integration of these technologies into public health infrastructures presents several challenges that require careful consideration.

A primary concern is ensuring the accuracy and reliability of the information provided by chatbots. The rapid evolution of health crises demands real-time data integration, robust misinformation detection, and collaboration with health authorities to prevent the dissemination of outdated or false information. Ethical and accountability issues further complicate deployment, as misinformation during epidemics can have severe consequences. Addressing these challenges necessitates technical transparency, safety measures, and the establishment of ethical guidelines, user education, and clear accountability frameworks.

Privacy and data security risks also represent significant obstacles. AI chatbots handling sensitive health information must comply with stringent data protection laws, such as GDPR, and implement robust technical safeguards to maintain user trust. Transparency regarding data usage and user education on privacy measures are critical components in fostering public confidence in these systems.

Another key challenge is ensuring accessibility for linguistically and culturally diverse populations. Chatbots must be equipped with expanded language support, improved cultural competence, and enhanced NLP capabilities. Socio-technical strategies, such as community engagement and digital literacy programs, can help bridge communication gaps and mitigate health disparities. Incorporating emotion recognition, fostering human–AI collaboration, and promoting user education will contribute to making these tools more inclusive and effective.

The successful deployment of AI chatbots in public health settings requires a balanced approach that integrates both technical and socio-technical factors. Cost-effectiveness, scalability, and integration with existing healthcare systems are essential, alongside active stakeholder engagement and resource allocation. Evaluating long-term impact, effectiveness, and adaptability will shape the future role of AI in healthcare.

Looking forward, the potential of AI chatbots in public health remains significant. However, realizing this potential demands continuous research, human oversight, and a commitment to ethical and responsible AI deployment. By fostering collaboration between artificial intelligence experts, public health professionals, legislators, and local communities, we can develop AI systems that are not only effective and scalable but also equitable and trustworthy. The future of AI chatbots in healthcare will be determined by our ability to navigate these challenges, ensuring that these technologies contribute meaningfully to resilient and adaptive public health systems.

Author Contributions: Conceptualization, F.B.; supervision, M.C.; validation, M.C.; writing—original draft preparation, F.B., M.S., C.C., F.C., G.C., A.M., M.C. and F.S.; writing—review and editing, F.B., M.S., C.C., F.C., G.C., A.M., M.C. and F.S. All authors have read and agreed to the published version of the manuscript.

Funding: This work has been partially funded by The SMILE Project: "Statistical Modeling and Inference to Live the Environment", PRIN2023 grant number 2022XRHT8R.

Conflicts of Interest: The authors declare no conflicts of interest.

References

1. Managing Epidemics: Key Facts About Major Deadly Diseases, 2nd Edition. Available online: https://www.who.int/publications/i/item/9789240083196 (accessed on 28 August 2024).
2. Fagherazzi, G.; Goetzinger, C.; Rashid, M.A.; Aguayo, G.A.; Huiart, L. Digital health strategies to fight COVID-19 worldwide: Challenges, recommendations, and a call for papers. *J. Med. Internet Res.* **2020**, *22*, e19284.
3. Miner, A.S.; Laranjo, L.; Kocaballi, A.B. Chatbots in the fight against the COVID-19 pandemic. *NPJ Digit. Med.* **2020**, *3*, 65. [CrossRef] [PubMed]
4. Watters, C.; Lemanski, M.K. Universal skepticism of ChatGPT: A review of early literature on chat generative pre-trained transformer. *Front. Big Data* **2023**, *6*, 1224976. [CrossRef]
5. Gao, S.; He, L.; Chen, Y.; Li, D.; Lai, K. Public perception of artificial intelligence in medical care: Content analysis of social media. *J. Med. Internet Res.* **2020**, *22*, e16649.
6. Radford, A.; Narasimhan, K.; Salimans, T.; Sutskever, I. *Improving Language Understanding by Generative Pre-Training*; Technical report; OpenAI: San Francisco, CA, USA, 2018.
7. Judson, T.J.; Odisho, A.Y.; Neinstein, A.B.; Chao, J.; Williams, A.; Miller, C.; Moriarty, T.; Gleason, N.; Intinarelli, G.; Gonzales, R. Rapid design and implementation of an integrated patient self-triage and self-scheduling tool for COVID-19. *J. Am. Med. Inform. Assoc.* **2020**, *27*, 860–866.
8. Sezgin, E.; Huang, Y.; Ramtekkar, U.; Lin, S. Readiness for voice assistants to support healthcare delivery during a health crisis and pandemic. *npj Digit. Med.* **2020**, *3*, 122. [PubMed]
9. Kocaballi, A.B.; Berkovsky, S.; Quiroz, J.C.; Laranjo, L.; Tong, H.L.; Rezazadegan, D.; Briatore, A.; Coiera, E. The personalization of conversational agents in health care: Systematic review. *J. Med. Internet Res.* **2019**, *21*, e15360. [PubMed]
10. Brown, T.B. Language models are few-shot learners. *arXiv* **2020**, arXiv:2005.14165.
11. Nadarzynski, T.; Miles, O.; Cowie, A.; Ridge, D. Acceptability of artificial intelligence (AI)-led chatbot services in healthcare: A mixed-methods study. *Digit. Health* **2019**, *5*, 2055207619871808.
12. Jungmann, S.M.; Witthöft, M. Health anxiety, cyberchondria, and coping in the current COVID-19 pandemic: Which factors are related to coronavirus anxiety? *J. Anxiety Disord.* **2020**, *73*, 102239.
13. Cuan-Baltazar, J.Y.; Muñoz-Perez, M.J.; Robledo-Vega, C.; Pérez-Zepeda, M.F.; Soto-Vega, E. Misinformation of COVID-19 on the internet: Infodemiology study. *JMIR Public Health Surveill.* **2020**, *6*, e18444. [CrossRef] [PubMed]
14. Béranger, J. *Big Data and Ethics: The Medical Datasphere*; Elsevier: Amsterdam, The Netherlands, 2016.
15. Palanica, A.; Flaschner, P.; Thommandram, A.; Li, M.; Fossat, Y. Physicians' perceptions of chatbots in health care: Cross-sectional web-based survey. *J. Med. Internet Res.* **2019**, *21*, e12887.

16. Weizenbaum, J. ELIZA—A computer program for the study of natural language communication between man and machine. *Commun. ACM* **1966**, *9*, 36–45.
17. Dillon, S. The Eliza effect and its dangers: From demystification to gender critique. *J. Cult. Res.* **2020**, *24*, 1–15.
18. De Duro, E.S.; Improta, R.; Stella, M. Introducing CounseLLMe: A dataset of simulated mental health dialogues for comparing LLMs like Haiku, LLaMAntino and ChatGPT against humans. *Emerg. Trends Drugs Addict. Health* **2024**, *5, 100170.*
19. Frith, C.; Frith, U. Theory of mind. *Curr. Biol.* **2005**, *15*, R644–R645.
20. Cummings, L. The "trust" heuristic: Arguments from authority in public health. *Health Commun.* **2014**, *29*, 1043–1056. [PubMed]
21. Stella, M.; Vitevitch, M.S.; Botta, F. Cognitive Networks Extract Insights on COVID-19 Vaccines from English and Italian Popular Tweets: Anticipation, Logistics, Conspiracy and Loss of Trust. *Big Data Cogn. Comput.* **2022**, *6*, 52. [CrossRef]
22. Johnson, D.; Grayson, K. Cognitive and affective trust in service relationships. *J. Bus. Res.* **2005**, *58*, 500–507. [CrossRef]
23. Branda, F. Social impact: Trusting open science for future pandemic resilience. *Soc. Impacts* **2024**, *3*, 100058. [CrossRef]
24. Kasperson, J.X.; Kasperson, R.E.; Pidgeon, N.; Slovic, P. The social amplification of risk: Assessing fifteen years of research and theory. In *The Feeling of Risk*; Routledge: London, UK, 2013; pp. 317–344.
25. Devine, D.; Gaskell, J.; Jennings, W.; Stoker, G. Trust and the coronavirus pandemic: What are the consequences of and for trust? An early review of the literature. *Political Stud. Rev.* **2021**, *19*, 274–285. [CrossRef] [PubMed]
26. Hall, M.A.; Dugan, E.; Zheng, B.; Mishra, A.K. Trust in physicians and medical institutions: What is it, can it be measured, and does it matter? *Milbank Q.* **2001**, *79*, 613–639. [PubMed]
27. Colby, K.M.; Weber, S.; Hilf, F.D. Artificial paranoia. *Artif. Intell.* **1971**, *2*, 1–25. [CrossRef]
28. Heiser, J.F.; Colby, K.M.; Faught, W.S.; Parkison, R.C. Can psychiatrists distinguish a computer simulation of paranoia from the real thing?: The limitations of turing-like tests as measures of the adequacy of simulations. *J. Psychiatr. Res.* **1979**, *15*, 149–162. [CrossRef]
29. Bickmore, T.W.; Picard, R.W. Establishing and maintaining long-term human–computer relationships. *ACM Trans. Comput.-Hum. Interact. (TOCHI)* **2005**, *12*, 293–327.
30. Trzebiński, W.; Claessens, T.; Buhmann, J.; De Waele, A.; Hendrickx, G.; Van Damme, P.; Daelemans, W.; Poels, K. The effects of expressing empathy/autonomy support using a COVID-19 vaccination chatbot: Experimental study in a sample of Belgian adults. *JMIR Form. Res.* **2023**, *7*, e41148.
31. Fogg, B.J. Persuasive technology: Using computers to change what we think and do. *Ubiquity* **2002**, *2002*, 2. [CrossRef]
32. Ciechanowski, L.; Przegalinska, A.; Magnuski, M.; Gloor, P. In the shades of the uncanny valley: An experimental study of human–chatbot interaction. *Future Gener. Comput. Syst.* **2019**, *92*, 539–548.
33. Wallace, R.S. The anatomy of A.L.I.C.E. In *Parsing the Turing Test*; Springer: Berlin/Heidelberg, Germany, 2009; pp. 181–210.
34. Zhou, C.; Li, Q.; Li, C.; Yu, J.; Liu, Y.; Wang, G.; Zhang, K.; Ji, C.; Yan, Q.; He, L.; et al. A comprehensive survey on pretrained foundation models: A history from bert to chatgpt. *arXiv* **2023**, arXiv:2302.09419. [CrossRef]
35. Li, J.; Dada, A.; Puladi, B.; Kleesiek, J.; Egger, J. ChatGPT in healthcare: A taxonomy and systematic review. *Comput. Methods Programs Biomed.* **2024**, *245*, 108013.
36. Brunet-Gouet, E.; Vidal, N.; Roux, P. Can a Conversational Agent Pass Theory-of-Mind Tasks? A Case Study of ChatGPT with the Hinting, False Beliefs, and Strange Stories Paradigms. In Proceedings of the International Conference on Human and Artificial Rationalities, Paris, France, 19–22 September 2023; Springer: Cham, Switzerland, 2023; pp. 107–126.
37. Stella, M.; Hills, T.T.; Kenett, Y.N. Using cognitive psychology to understand GPT-like models needs to extend beyond human biases. *Proc. Natl. Acad. Sci. USA* **2023**, *120*, e2312911120. [PubMed]
38. Metze, K.; Morandin-Reis, R.C.; Lorand-Metze, I.; Florindo, J.B. Bibliographic research with ChatGPT may be misleading: The problem of hallucination. *J. Pediatr. Surg.* **2024**, *59*, 158. [CrossRef] [PubMed]
39. Giuffrè, M.; You, K.; Shung, D.L. Evaluating ChatGPT in medical contexts: The imperative to guard against hallucinations and partial accuracies. *Clin. Gastroenterol. Hepatol.* **2024**, *22*, 1145–1146.
40. Brashier, N.M. Do conspiracy theorists think too much or too little? *Curr. Opin. Psychol.* **2023**, *49*, 101504.
41. Pugliese, N.; Wong, V.W.S.; Schattenberg, J.M.; Romero-Gomez, M.; Sebastiani, G.; Castera, L.; Hassan, C.; Manousou, P.; Miele, L.; Peck, R.; et al. Accuracy, reliability, and comprehensibility of ChatGPT-generated medical responses for patients with nonalcoholic fatty liver disease. *Clin. Gastroenterol. Hepatol.* **2024**, *22*, 886–889. [PubMed]
42. Dixit, S.; Kumar, A.; Srinivasan, K.; Vincent, P.; Ramu Krishnan, N. Advancing genome editing with artificial intelligence: Opportunities, challenges, and future directions. *Front. Bioeng. Biotechnol.* **2024**, *1*, 1335901. [CrossRef]
43. Vilhekar, R.S.; Rawekar, A. Artificial intelligence in genetics. *Cureus* **2024**, *16*, e52035.
44. Abdelwahab, O.; Belzile, F.; Torkamaneh, D. Performance analysis of conventional and AI-based variant callers using short and long reads. *BMC Bioinform.* **2023**, *24*, 2956.
45. Krzysztof, K.; Magda, M.; Przemysław, B.; Bernt, G.; Joanna, S. Exploring the impact of sequence context on errors in SNP genotype calling with whole genome sequencing data using AI-based autoencoder approach. *NAR Genom. Bioinform.* **2024**, *6*, lqae131.

46. Vaz, J.; Balaji, S. Convolutional neural networks (CNNs): Concepts and applications in pharmacogenomics. *Mol. Divers.* **2021**, *6*, lqae131.
47. Sebiha, C.; Pei, Z.; Atiyye, Z.; Mustafa, S.P.; Wenyin, B.; Oktay, I.K. Matching variants for functional characterization of genetic variants. *G3 Genes Genomes Genet.* **2023**, *13*, jkad227.
48. Liu, Y.; Zhang, T.; You, N.; Wu, S.; Shen, N. MAGPIE: Accurate pathogenic prediction for multiple variant types using machine learning approach variants for functional characterization of genetic variants. *Genome Med.* **2024**, *16*, 3. [PubMed]
49. Jumper, J.; Evans, R.; Pritzel, A.; Green, T.; Figurnov, M.; Ronneberger, O.; Tunyasuvunakool, K.; Bates, R.; Žídek, A.; Potapenko, A.; et al. Highly accurate protein structure prediction with AlphaFold. *Nature* **2021**, *596*, 583–589.
50. Johnston, A.D.; Simões-Pires, C.A.; Thompson, T.V.; Suzuki, M.; Greally, J.M. Functional genetic variants can mediate their regulatory effects through alteration of transcription factor binding. *Nat. Commun.* **2019**, *10*, 3472. [PubMed]
51. Frasca, M.; La Torre, D.; Repetto, M.; De Nicolò, V.; Pravettoni, G.; Cutica, I. Artificial intelligence applications to genomic data in cancer research: A review of recent trends and emerging areas. *Discov. Anal.* **2024**, *2*, 10.
52. Qureshi, R.; Irfan, M.; Gondal, T.; Khan, S.; Wu, J.; Hadi, M.; Heymach, J.; Le, X.; Yan, H.; Alam, T. AI in drug discovery and its clinical relevance. *Heliyon* **2023**, *9*, e17575. [CrossRef]
53. Manzoni, C.; Kia, D.A.; Vandrovcova, J.; Hardy, J.; Wood, N.W.; Lewis, P.A.; Ferrari, R. Genome, transcriptome and proteome: The rise of omics data and their integration in biomedical sciences. *Brief. Bioinform.* **2018**, *19*, 286–3025.
54. Chen, F.; Zou, G.; Wu, Y.; Ou-Yang, L. Clustering single-cell multi-omics data via graph regularized multi-view ensemble learning. *Bioinformatics* **2024**, *40*, btae169.
55. Miner, A.S.; Milstein, A.; Hancock Jefferey, T.K.C.; Johnson, K.; Choi, E.; Kaplin, S.; Venner, E.; Murugan, M.; Wang, Z.; Glicksberg, B.; et al. Artificial Intelligence and Cardiovascular Genetics. *Life* **2022**, *12*, 279. [CrossRef]
56. Abe, S.; Tago, S.; Yokoyama, K.; Ogawa, M.; Takei, T.; Imoto, S.; Fuji, M. Explainable AI for Estimating Pathogenicity of Genetic Variants Using Large-Scale Knowledge Graphs. *Cancers* **2023**, *15*, 1118. [CrossRef]
57. Birney, E.; Andrews, T.; Bevan, P.; Caccamo, M.; Chen, Y.; Clarke, L.; Coates, G.; Cuff, J.; Curwen, V.; Cutts, T.; et al. An overview of Ensembl. *Genome Res.* **2004**, *14*, 925–928.
58. Al-Hilli, Z.; Noss, R.; Dickard, J.; Wei, W.; Chichura, A.; Wu, V.; Renicker, K.; Pederson, H.; Eng, C. A Randomized Trial Comparing the Effectiveness of Pre-test Genetic Counseling Using an Artificial Intelligence Automated Chatbot and Traditional In-person Genetic Counseling in Women Newly Diagnosed with Breast Cancer. *Ann. Surg. Oncol.* **2023**, *30*, 5990–5996. [PubMed]
59. Floris, M.; Moschella, A.; Alcalay, M.; Montella, A.; Tirelli, M.; Fontana, L.; Idda, M. Pharmacogenetics in Italy: Current landscape and future prospects. *Hum. Genom.* **2024**, *18*, 78.
60. Idda, M.; Zoledziewska, M.; Urru, S.; McInnes, G.; Bilotta, A.; Nuvoli, V.; Lodde, V.; Orrù, S.; Schlessinger, D.; Cucca, F.; et al. Genetic Variation among Pharmacogenes in the Sardinian Population. *J. Mol. Sci.* **2022**, *23*, 10058.
61. Chakraborty, C.; Pal, S.; Bhattacharya, M.; Dash, S.; Lee, S. Overview of Chatbots with special emphasis on artificial intelligence-enabled ChatGPT in medical science. *Front. Artif. Intell.* **2023**, *6*, 1237704.
62. Jeyaraman, M.; Balaji, S.; Jeyaraman, N.; Yadav, S. Unraveling the Ethical Enigma: Artificial Intelligence in Healthcare. *Cureus* **2023**, *15*, e43262.
63. Li, J. Security Implications of AI Chatbots in Health Care. *J. Med. Internet Res.* **2023**, *25*, e47551.
64. Mortice Z. 5 Insights as Architects Lead Hospital Conversion for COVID-19. Autodesk 2020. Available online: https://www.autodesk.com/design-make/articles/hospital-conversion (accessed on 1 October 2024).
65. AIA COVID-19 Task Force 1: Health Impact Briefing #2 COVID-19 Frontline Perspective Design Considerations to Reduce Risk and Support Patients and Providers in Facilities for COVID-19 Care. The American Institute of Architects 22 June 2020. Available online: https://content.aia.org/sites/default/files/2020-07/AIA_COVID_Frontline_Perspective.pdf (accessed on 1 October 2024).
66. Cogley B. AIA Task Force to Offer Advice on Converting Buildings into Healthcare Facilities-Dezeen 2020. Available online: https://www.dezeen.com/2020/03/27/aia-task-force-converting-buildings-into-healthcare-facilities/ (accessed on 1 October 2024).
67. De Yong, S.; Rachmawati, M.; Defiana, I. Theorizing security-pandemic aspects and variables for post-pandemic architecture. *Build. Environ.* **2024**, *258*, 111579.
68. Gan, V.J.; Luo, H.; Tan, Y.; Deng, M.; Kwok, H. BIM and data-driven predictive analysis of optimum thermal comfort for indoor environment. *Sensors* **2021**, *21*, 4401. [CrossRef]
69. Yang, T.; White, M.; Lipson-Smith, R.; Shannon, M.M.; Latifi, M. Design Decision Support for Healthcare Architecture: A VR-Integrated Approach for Measuring User Perception. *Buildings* **2024**, *14*, 797. [CrossRef]
70. Junaid, S.B.; Imam, A.A.; Balogun, A.O.; De Silva, L.C.; Surakat, Y.A.; Kumar, G.; Abdulkarim, M.; Shuaibu, A.N.; Garba, A.; Sahalu, Y.; et al. Recent advancements in emerging technologies for healthcare management systems: A survey. *Healthcare* **2022**, *10*, 1940. [CrossRef]
71. Chrysikou, E.; Papadonikolaki, E.; Savvopoulou, E.; Tsiantou, E.; Klinke, C.A. Digital technologies and healthcare architects' wellbeing in the National Health Service Estate of England during the pandemic. *Front. Med. Technol.* **2023**, *5*, 1212734.

72. Service, R.F. Could chatbots help devise the next pandemic virus? *Science* **2023**, *380*, 1211.
73. Cheng, K.; He, Y.; Li, C.; Xie, R.; Lu, Y.; Gu, S.; Wu, H. Talk with ChatGPT about the outbreak of Mpox in 2022: Reflections and suggestions from AI dimensions. *Ann. Biomed. Eng.* **2023**, *51*, 870–874. [PubMed]
74. Remuzzi, A.; Remuzzi, G. COVID-19 and Italy: What next? *Lancet* **2020**, *395*, 1225–1228.
75. Lauer, S.A.; Grantz, K.H.; Bi, Q.; Jones, F.K.; Zheng, Q.; Meredith, H.R.; Azman, A.S.; Reich, N.G.; Lessler, J. The Incubation Period of Coronavirus Disease 2019 (COVID-19) From Publicly Reported Confirmed Cases: Estimation and Application. *Ann. Intern. Med.* **2020**, *172*, 577–582. [CrossRef] [PubMed]
76. Branda, F.; Pierini, M.; Mazzoli, S. Monkeypox: Early estimation of basic reproduction number R0 in Europe. *J. Med. Virol.* **2023**, *95*, e28270. [PubMed]
77. Alavi, H.; Gordo-Gregorio, P.; Forcada, N.; Bayramova, A.; Edwards, D.J. AI-driven BIM integration for optimizing healthcare facility design. *Buildings* **2024**, *14*, 2354. [CrossRef]
78. Kaliappan, S.; Maranan, R.; Malladi, A.; Yamsani, N. Optimizing Resource Allocation in Healthcare Systems for Efficient Pandemic Management using Machine Learning and Artificial Neural Networks. In Proceedings of the 2024 International Conference on Advancements in Smart, Secure and Intelligent Computing (ASSIC), Bhubaneswar, India, 27–29 January 2024; pp. 1–7. [CrossRef]
79. Amiri, P.; Karahanna, E. Chatbot use cases in the COVID-19 public health response. *J. Am. Med. Inform. Assoc.* **2022**, *29*, 1000–1010. [CrossRef]
80. Wang, C.W.; Hsu, B.Y.; Chen, D.Y. Chatbot applications in government frontline services: Leveraging artificial intelligence and data governance to reduce problems and increase effectiveness. *Asia Pac. J. Public Adm.* **2024**, *46*, 488–511.
81. Chakraborty, S.; Paul, H.; Ghatak, S.; Pandey, S.K.; Kumar, A.; Singh, K.U.; Shah, M.A. An AI-based medical chatbot model for infectious disease prediction. *IEEE Access* **2022**, *10*, 128469–128483.
82. Shumway, R.H.; Stoffer, D.S.; Stoffer, D.S. *Time Series Analysis and Its Applications*; Springer: Berlin/Heidelberg, Germany, 2000; Volume 3.
83. Smith, C.M.; Le Comber, S.C.; Fry, H.; Bull, M.; Leach, S.; Hayward, A.C. Spatial methods for infectious disease outbreak investigations: Systematic literature review. *Eurosurveillance* **2015**, *20*, 30026.
84. Jolliffe, I.T.; Cadima, J. Principal component analysis: A review and recent developments. *Philos. Trans. R. Soc. A Math. Phys. Eng. Sci.* **2016**, *374*, 20150202.
85. Chen, S.; Yu, J.; Chamouni, S.; Wang, Y.; Li, Y. Integrating machine learning and artificial intelligence in life-course epidemiology: Pathways to innovative public health solutions. *BMC Med.* **2024**, *22*, 354.
86. Field, A. *Discovering Statistics Using IBM SPSS Statistics*; Sage Publications Limited: London, UK, 2024.
87. Harrell, F.E. *Regression Modeling Strategies*, 2nd ed.; Springer: New York, NY, USA, 2015. 10.10.1007/978-3-319-19425-7. [CrossRef]
88. Bender, E.M.; Koller, A. Climbing towards NLU: On meaning, form, and understanding in the age of data. In Proceedings of the 58th Annual Meeting of the Association for Computational Linguistics, Online, 5–10 July 2020; pp. 5185–5198.
89. Bender, E.M.; Gebru, T.; McMillan-Major, A.; Shmitchell, S. On the dangers of stochastic parrots: Can language models be too big? In Proceedings of the 2021 ACM Conference on Fairness, Accountability, and Transparency, Virtual Event, 3–10 March 2021; pp. 610–623.
90. Krishnan, G.; Singh, S.; Pathania, M.; Gosavi, S.; Abhishek, S.; Parchani, A.; Dhar, M. Artificial intelligence in clinical medicine: Catalyzing a sustainable global healthcare paradigm. *Front. Artif. Intell.* **2023**, *6*, 1227091.
91. Singh, J.; Sillerud, B.; Singh, A. Artificial intelligence, chatbots and ChatGPT in healthcare—Narrative review of historical evolution, current application, and change management approach to increase adoption. *J. Med. Artif. Intell.* **2023**, *6*, 30. 10.21037/jmai-23-92. [CrossRef]
92. Van Melle, W. MYCIN: A knowledge-based consultation program for infectious disease diagnosis. *Int. J. Man–Mach. Stud.* **1978**, *10*, 313–322.
93. Devlin, J.; Chang, M.W.; Lee, K.; Toutanova, K. Bert: Pre-training of deep bidirectional transformers for language understanding. In Proceedings of the 2019 Conference of the North American Chapter of the Association for Computational Linguistics: Human Language Technologies, Volume 1 (Long and Short Papers), Minneapolis, MN, USA, 2–7 June 2019; pp. 4171–4186.
94. Babu, A.; Boddu, S.B. Bert-based medical chatbot: Enhancing healthcare communication through natural language understanding. *Explor. Res. Clin. Soc. Pharm.* **2024**, *13*, 100419.
95. Chiche, A.; Yitagesu, B. Part of speech tagging: A systematic review of deep learning and machine learning approaches. *J. Big Data* **2022**, *9*, 10.
96. Yu, B.; Fan, Z. A comprehensive review of conditional random fields: Variants, hybrids and applications. *Artif. Intell. Rev.* **2020**, *53*, 4289–4333.
97. Franke, M.; Degen, J. The softmax function: Properties, motivation, and interpretation. *PsyArXiv* **2023**. [CrossRef]
98. Maleki Varnosfaderani, S.; Forouzanfar, M. The role of AI in hospitals and clinics: Transforming healthcare in the 21st century. *Bioengineering* **2024**, *11*, 337. [CrossRef]

99. Jadczyk, T.; Wojakowski, W.; Tendera, M.; Henry, T.D.; Egnaczyk, G.; Shreenivas, S. Artificial intelligence can improve patient management at the time of a pandemic: The role of voice technology. *J. Med. Internet Res.* **2021**, *23*, e22959. [CrossRef] [PubMed]
100. Haque, A.; Chowdhury, M.N.U.R.; Soliman, H. Transforming chronic disease management with chatbots: Key use cases for personalized and cost-effective care. In Proceedings of the 2023 Sixth International Symposium on Computer, Consumer and Control (IS3C), Taichung, Taiwan, 30 June–3 July 2023; IEEE: Piscataway, NJ, USA, 2023; pp. 367–370.
101. Sun, G.; Zhou, Y.H. AI in healthcare: Navigating opportunities and challenges in digital communication. *Front. Digit. Health* **2023**, *5*, 1291132. [CrossRef] [PubMed]
102. McKillop, M.; South, B.R.; Preininger, A.; Mason, M.; Jackson, G.P. Leveraging conversational technology to answer common COVID-19 questions. *J. Am. Med. Inform. Assoc.* **2021**, *28*, 850–855. [CrossRef]
103. Cinelli, M.; Quattrociocchi, W.; Galeazzi, A.; Valensise, C.M.; Brugnoli, E.; Schmidt, A.L.; Zola, P.; Zollo, F.; Scala, A. The COVID-19 social media infodemic. *Sci. Rep.* **2020**, *10*, 16598. [CrossRef]
104. Ji, Z.; Lee, N.; Frieske, R.; Yu, T.; Su, D.; Xu, Y.; Ishii, E.; Bang, Y.J.; Madotto, A.; Fung, P. Survey of hallucination in natural language generation. *ACM Comput. Surv.* **2023**, *55*, 1–38. [CrossRef]
105. Thorne, J.; Vlachos, A. Automated fact checking: Task formulations, methods and future directions. *arXiv* **2018**, arXiv:1806.07687.
106. Cabitza, F.; Campagner, A.; Malgieri, G.; Natali, C.; Schneeberger, D.; Stoeger, K.; Holzinger, A. Quod erat demonstrandum?—Towards a typology of the concept of explanation for the design of explainable AI. *Expert Syst. Appl.* **2023**, *213*, 118888. [CrossRef]
107. Amershi, S.; Weld, D.; Vorvoreanu, M.; Fourney, A.; Nushi, B.; Collisson, P.; Suh, J.; Iqbal, S.; Bennett, P.N.; Inkpen, K.; et al. Guidelines for human-AI interaction. In Proceedings of the 2019 CHI Conference on Human Factors in Computing Systems, Scotland, UK, 4–9 May 2019; pp. 1–13.
108. Lee, J.; Lee, E.H.; Chae, D. eHealth literacy instruments: Systematic review of measurement properties. *J. Med. Internet Res.* **2021**, *23*, e30644. [CrossRef]
109. Aljamaan, F.; Temsah, M.H.; Altamimi, I.; Al-Eyadhy, A.; Jamal, A.; Alhasan, K.; Mesallam, T.A.; Farahat, M.; Malki, K.H. Reference Hallucination Score for Medical Artificial Intelligence Chatbots: Development and Usability Study. *JMIR Med. Inform.* **2024**, *12*, e54345. [PubMed]
110. Vishwanath, P.R.; Tiwari, S.; Naik, T.G.; Gupta, S.; Thai, D.N.; Zhao, W.; Kwon, S.; Ardulov, V.; Tarabishy, K.; McCallum, A.; et al. Faithfulness Hallucination Detection in Healthcare AI. In Proceedings of the Artificial Intelligence and Data Science for Healthcare: Bridging Data-Centric AI and People-Centric Healthcare, Barcelona, Spain, 29 June 2024. Available online: https://openreview.net/forum?id=6eMIzKFOpJ (accessed on 25 March 2025).
111. Jobin, A.; Ienca, M.; Vayena, E. The global landscape of AI ethics guidelines. *Nat. Mach. Intell.* **2019**, *1*, 389–399.
112. Liu, Q.; Zheng, Z.; Zheng, J.; Chen, Q.; Liu, G.; Chen, S.; Chu, B.; Zhu, H.; Akinwunmi, B.; Huang, J.; et al. Health communication through news media during the early stage of the COVID-19 outbreak in China: Digital topic modeling approach. *J. Med. Internet Res.* **2020**, *22*, e19118. [CrossRef]
113. Peng, C.; Xia, F.; Naseriparsa, M.; Osborne, F. Knowledge graphs: Opportunities and challenges. *Artif. Intell. Rev.* **2023**, *56*, 13071–13102.
114. Wu, L.; Cui, P.; Pei, J.; Zhao, L.; Guo, X. Graph neural networks: Foundation, frontiers and applications. In Proceedings of the 28th ACM SIGKDD Conference on Knowledge Discovery and Data Mining, Washington, DC, USA, 14–18 August 2022; pp. 4840–4841.
115. Pap, I.A.; Oniga, S. eHealth Assistant AI Chatbot Using a Large Language Model to Provide Personalized Answers through Secure Decentralized Communication. *Sensors* **2024**, *24*, 6140. [CrossRef] [PubMed]
116. Lewis, P.; Perez, E.; Piktus, A.; Petroni, F.; Karpukhin, V.; Goyal, N.; Küttler, H.; Lewis, M.; Yih, W.t.; Rocktäschel, T.; et al. Retrieval-augmented generation for knowledge-intensive nlp tasks. *Adv. Neural Inf. Process. Syst.* **2020**, *33*, 9459–9474.
117. Fernández, I.; Aceta, C.; Fernandez, C.; Torres, M.I.; Etxalar, A.; Méndez, A.; Agirre, M.; Torralbo, M.; Del Pozo, A.; Agirre, J.; et al. Incremental Learning for Knowledge-Grounded Dialogue Systems in Industrial Scenarios. In Proceedings of the 25th Annual Meeting of the Special Interest Group on Discourse and Dialogue, Kyoto, Japan, 18–20 September 2024; pp. 92–102.
118. Eysenbach, G. How to fight an infodemic: The four pillars of infodemic management. *J. Med. Internet Res.* **2020**, *22*, e21820.
119. Ashktorab, Z.; Jain, M.; Liao, Q.V.; Weisz, J.D. Resilient chatbots: Repair strategy preferences for conversational breakdowns. In Proceedings of the 2019 CHI Conference on Human Factors in Computing Systems, Scotland, UK, 4–9 May 2019; pp. 1–12.
120. Khurana, A.; Alamzadeh, P.; Chilana, P.K. ChatrEx: Designing explainable chatbot interfaces for enhancing usefulness, transparency, and trust. In Proceedings of the 2021 IEEE Symposium on Visual Languages and Human-Centric Computing (VL/HCC), St. Louis, MO, USA, 10–13 October 2021; IEEE: Piscataway, NJ, USA, 2021; pp. 1–11.
121. Dhaliwal, N. Validating software upgrades with AI: Ensuring DevOps, data integrity and accuracy using CI/CD pipelines. *J. Basic Sci. Eng.* **2020**, *17*, 1–10. Available online: https://www.researchgate.net/publication/381002098 (accessed on 25 March 2025).

122. Wang, Y.; McKee, M.; Torbica, A.; Stuckler, D. Systematic literature review on the spread of health-related misinformation on social media. *Soc. Sci. Med.* **2019**, *240*, 112552.
123. Adebesin, F.; Smuts, H.; Mawela, T.; Maramba, G.; Hattingh, M. The role of social media in health misinformation and disinformation during the COVID-19 pandemic: Bibliometric analysis. *JMIR Infodemiology* **2023**, *3*, e48620. [CrossRef]
124. Tasnim, S.; Hossain, M.M.; Mazumder, H. Impact of rumors and misinformation on COVID-19 in social media. *J. Prev. Med. Public Health* **2020**, *53*, 171–174. [PubMed]
125. Zhou, X.; Zafarani, R. A survey of fake news: Fundamental theories, detection methods, and opportunities. *ACM Comput. Surv. (CSUR)* **2020**, *53*, 1–40.
126. Kim, K.; Shin, S.; Kim, S.; Lee, E. The relation between eHealth literacy and health-related behaviors: Systematic review and meta-analysis. *J. Med. Internet Res.* **2023**, *25*, e40778.
127. Graves, D. *Understanding the Promise and Limits of Automated Fact-Checking*; Reuters Institute for the Study of Journalism: Oxford, UK, 2018.
128. Bondielli, A.; Marcelloni, F. A survey on fake news and rumour detection techniques. *Inf. Sci.* **2019**, *497*, 38–55.
129. Longoni, C.; Bonezzi, A.; Morewedge, C.K. Resistance to medical artificial intelligence. *J. Consum. Res.* **2019**, *46*, 629–650.
130. Shen, J.; Zhang, C.J.; Jiang, B.; Chen, J.; Song, J.; Liu, Z.; He, Z.; Wong, S.Y.; Fang, P.H.; Ming, W.K.; et al. Artificial intelligence versus clinicians in disease diagnosis: Systematic review. *JMIR Med. Inform.* **2019**, *7*, e10010.
131. Dergaa, I.; Ben Saad, H.; Glenn, J.M.; Amamou, B.; Ben Aissa, M.; Guelmami, N.; Fekih-Romdhane, F.; Chamari, K. From tools to threats: A reflection on the impact of artificial-intelligence chatbots on cognitive health. *Front. Psychol.* **2024**, *15*, 1259845.
132. Guidotti, R.; Monreale, A.; Ruggieri, S.; Turini, F.; Giannotti, F.; Pedreschi, D. A survey of methods for explaining black box models. *ACM Comput. Surv. (CSUR)* **2018**, *51*, 1–42.
133. Voigt, P.; Von dem Bussche, A. *The EU General Data Protection Regulation (GDPR): A Practical Guide*, 1st ed.; Springer International Publishing: Cham, Switzerland, 2017. 10.1007/978-3-319-57959-7. [CrossRef]
134. World Health Organization. *Ethics and Governance of Artificial Intelligence for Health. WHO Guidance*; World Health Organization: Geneva, Switzerland, 2021.
135. Glikson, E.; Woolley, A.W. Human trust in artificial intelligence: Review of empirical research. *Acad. Manag. Ann.* **2020**, *14*, 627–660.
136. Bryson, J.; Winfield, A. Standardizing ethical design for artificial intelligence and autonomous systems. *Computer* **2017**, *50*, 116–119.
137. Goddard, K.; Roudsari, A.; Wyatt, J.C. Automation bias: A systematic review of frequency, effect mediators, and mitigators. *J. Am. Med. Inform. Assoc.* **2012**, *19*, 121–127.
138. Thapa, C.; Camtepe, S. Precision health data: Requirements, challenges and existing techniques for data security and privacy. *Comput. Biol. Med.* **2021**, *129*, 104130.
139. Abouelmehdi, K.; Beni-Hessane, A.; Khaloufi, H. Big healthcare data: Preserving security and privacy. *J. Big Data* **2018**, *5*, 1–18.
140. Hasal, M.; Nowaková, J.; Ahmed Saghair, K.; Abdulla, H.; Snášel, V.; Ogiela, L. Chatbots: Security, privacy, data protection, and social aspects. *Concurr. Comput. Pract. Exp.* **2021**, *33*, e6426.
141. Wangsa, K.; Karim, S.; Gide, E.; Elkhodr, M. A Systematic Review and Comprehensive Analysis of Pioneering AI Chatbot Models from Education to Healthcare: ChatGPT, Bard, Llama, Ernie and Grok. *Future Internet* **2024**, *16*, 219. [CrossRef]
142. Garcia Valencia, O.A.; Suppadungsuk, S.; Thongprayoon, C.; Miao, J.; Tangpanithandee, S.; Craici, I.M.; Cheungpasitporn, W. Ethical implications of chatbot utilization in nephrology. *J. Pers. Med.* **2023**, *13*, 1363. [CrossRef] [PubMed]
143. Yang, J.; Chen, Y.L.; Por, L.Y.; Ku, C.S. A systematic literature review of information security in chatbots. *Appl. Sci.* **2023**, *13*, 6355. [CrossRef]
144. Siponen, M.; Willison, R. Information security management standards: Problems and solutions. *Inf. Manag.* **2009**, *46*, 267–270.
145. Abd-Alrazaq, A.A.; Alajlani, M.; Alalwan, A.A.; Bewick, B.M.; Gardner, P.; Househ, M. An overview of the features of chatbots in mental health: A scoping review. *Int. J. Med. Inform.* **2019**, *132*, 103978.
146. Buolamwini, J.; Gebru, T. Gender shades: Intersectional accuracy disparities in commercial gender classification. In Proceedings of the Conference on Fairness, Accountability and Transparency, New York, NY, USA, 23–24 February 2018; PMLR: New York, NY, USA, 2018; pp. 77–91.
147. Anastasopoulos, A.; Neubig, G. Should all cross-lingual embeddings speak English? *arXiv* **2019**, arXiv:1911.03058.
148. Conneau, A. Unsupervised cross-lingual representation learning at scale. *arXiv* **2019**, arXiv:1911.02116.
149. Huang, K.; Altosaar, J.; Ranganath, R. Clinicalbert: Modeling clinical notes and predicting hospital readmission. *arXiv* **2019**, arXiv:1904.05342.
150. Mackert, M.; Mabry-Flynn, A.; Champlin, S.; Donovan, E.E.; Pounders, K. Health literacy and health information technology adoption: The potential for a new digital divide. *J. Med. Internet Res.* **2016**, *18*, e264. [PubMed]
151. Spinuzzi, C. The methodology of participatory design. *Tech. Commun.* **2005**, *52*, 163–174.
152. Miner, A.S.; Milstein, A.; Hancock, J.T. Talking to machines about personal mental health problems. *JAMA* **2017**, *318*, 1217–1218.

153. Hirschberg, J.; Manning, C.D. Advances in natural language processing. *Science* **2015**, *349*, 261–266.
154. Feine, J.; Morana, S.; Gnewuch, U. Measuring service encounter satisfaction with customer service chatbots using sentiment analysis. In Proceedings of the 14th International Conference on Wirtschaftsinformatik, Siegen, Germany, 24–27 February 2019.
155. Laymouna, M.; Ma, Y.; Lessard, D.; Schuster, T.; Engler, K.; Lebouché, B. Roles, Users, Benefits, and Limitations of Chatbots in Health Care: Rapid Review. *J. Med. Internet Res.* **2024**, *26*, e56930.
156. Han, B.; Baldwin, T. Lexical normalisation of short text messages: Makn sens a# twitter. In Proceedings of the 49th Annual Meeting of the Association for Computational Linguistics: Human Language Technologies, Portland, OR, USA, 19–24 June 2011; pp. 368–378.
157. Nikhil, G.; Yeligatla, D.R.; Chaparala, T.C.; Chalavadi, V.T.; Kaur, H.; Singh, V.K. An Analysis on Conversational AI: The Multimodal Frontier in Chatbot System Advancements. In Proceedings of the 2024 Second International Conference on Inventive Computing and Informatics (ICICI), Bangalore, India, 11–12 June 2024; IEEE: Piscataway, NJ, USA, 2024; pp. 383–389.
158. Jiang, J.; Karran, A.J.; Coursaris, C.K.; Léger, P.M.; Beringer, J. A situation awareness perspective on human-AI interaction: Tensions and opportunities. *Int. J. Hum.–Comput. Interact.* **2023**, *39*, 1789–1806.
159. Zhang, R.W.; Liang, X.; Wu, S.H. When chatbots fail: Exploring user coping following a chatbots-induced service failure. *Inf. Technol. People* **2024**, *37*, 175–195.
160. Følstad, A.; Brandtzæg, P.B. Chatbots and the new world of HCI. *Interactions* **2017**, *24*, 38–42.
161. Kocielnik, R.; Xiao, L.; Avrahami, D.; Hsieh, G. Reflection companion: A conversational system for engaging users in reflection on physical activity. *Proc. ACM Interact. Mob. Wearable Ubiquitous Technol.* **2018**, *2*, 1–26. [CrossRef]
162. Følstad, A.; Araujo, T.; Law, E.L.C.; Brandtzaeg, P.B.; Papadopoulos, S.; Reis, L.; Baez, M.; Laban, G.; McAllister, P.; Ischen, C.; et al. Future directions for chatbot research: An interdisciplinary research agenda. *Computing* **2021**, *103*, 2915–2942. [CrossRef]
163. Benatar, S.; Brock, G. *Global Health: Ethical Challenges*; Cambridge University Press: Cambridge, UK, 2021.
164. Vaidyam, A.N.; Wisniewski, H.; Halamka, J.D.; Kashavan, M.S.; Torous, J.B. Chatbots and conversational agents in mental health: A review of the psychiatric landscape. *Can. J. Psychiatry* **2019**, *64*, 456–464. [CrossRef] [PubMed]
165. Milne-Ives, M.; de Cock, C.; Lim, E.; Shehadeh, M.H.; de Pennington, N.; Mole, G.; Normando, E.; Meinert, E. The effectiveness of artificial intelligence conversational agents in health care: Systematic review. *J. Med. Internet Res.* **2020**, *22*, e20346. [CrossRef]
166. Martins, A.; Nunes, I.; Lapão, L.; Londral, A. Unlocking human-like conversations: Scoping review of automation techniques for personalized healthcare interventions using conversational agents. *Int. J. Med. Inform.* **2024**, *185*, 105385. [CrossRef]
167. Kostkova, P. Grand challenges in digital health. *Grand Chall. Digit. Health* **2015**, *3*, 134. [CrossRef]
168. Ren, R.; Zapata, M.; Castro, J.W.; Dieste, O.; Acuña, S.T. Experimentation for chatbot usability evaluation: A secondary study. *IEEE Access* **2022**, *10*, 12430–12464. [CrossRef]
169. Drummond, M.F.; Sculpher, M.J.; Claxton, K.; Stoddart, G.L.; Torrance, G.W. *Methods for the Economic Evaluation of Health Care Programmes*; Oxford University Press: Oxford, UK, 2015.
170. Cameron, G.; Cameron, D.; Megaw, G.; Bond, R.R.; Mulvenna, M.; O'Neill, S.; Armour, C.; McTear, M. Best practices for designing chatbots in mental healthcare—A case study on iHelpr. In Proceedings of the British HCI Conference 2018, Belfast, UK, 2–6 July 2018; BCS Learning & Development Ltd.: Pimpri-Chinchwad, India, 2018.
171. Bermeo-Giraldo, M.C.; Toro, O.N.P.; Arias, A.V.; Correa, P.A.R. Factors influencing the adoption of chatbots by healthcare users. *J. Innov. Manag.* **2023**, *11*, 75–94. [CrossRef]

future internet

MDPI

Article

AI-MDD-UX: Revolutionizing E-Commerce User Experience with Generative AI and Model-Driven Development

Adel Alti [1,2,*] and Abderrahim Lakehal [1]

[1] LRSD Laboratory, Faculty of Sciences, Computer Science Department, University Ferhat Abbas Sétif-1, Sétif P.O. Box 19000, Algeria; abderrahim.lakehal@univ-setif.dz
[2] Department of Management Information Systems & Production Management, College of Business & Economics, Qassim University, P.O. Box 6633, Buraidah 51452, Saudi Arabia
* Correspondence: a.alti@qu.edu.sa

Abstract: E-commerce applications have emerged as key drivers of digital transformation, reshaping consumer behavior and driving demand for seamless online transactions. Despite the growth of smart mobile technologies, existing methods rely on fixed UI content that cannot adjust to local cultural preferences and fluctuating user behaviors. This paper explores the combination of generative Artificial Intelligence (AI) technologies with Model-Driven Development (MDD) to enhance personalization, engagement, and adaptability in e-commerce. Unlike static adaptation approaches, generative AI enables real-time, adaptive interactions tailored to individual needs, providing a more engaging and adaptable user experience. The proposed framework follows a three-tier architecture: first, it collects and analyzes user behavior data from UI interactions; second, it leverages MDD to model and personalize user personas and interactions and third, AI techniques, including generative AI and multi-agent reinforcement learning, are applied to refine and optimize UI/UX design. This automation-driven approach uses a multi-agent system to continuously enhance AI-generated layouts. Technical validation demonstrated strong user engagement across diverse platforms and superior performance in UI optimization, achieving an average user satisfaction improvement of 2.3% compared to GAN-based models, 18.6% compared to Bootstrap-based designs, and 11.8% compared to rule-based UI adaptation. These results highlight generative AI-driven MDD tools as a promising tool for e-commerce, enhancing engagement, personalization, and efficiency.

Keywords: generative AI; model-driven development (MDD); E-commerce UX/UI optimization; UI adaptation; AI-powered user interaction modeling

1. Introduction

Digital transformation in e-commerce has gained significant attention in recent years, driven by advancements in context-aware computing and Artificial Intelligence (AI) driven personalization [1]. E-commerce platforms serve as digital ecosystems that facilitate online transactions by providing businesses with essential tools to manage customer interactions, payments, and digital storefronts [2]. These platforms operate across multiple devices, enabling users to access services at home, in the office, or anywhere. They offer a wide range of services in domains such as healthcare, transportation, retail, and supply chain management, while leveraging cutting-edge technologies to optimize user engagement and decision-making.

The increasing role of technology in e-commerce demands rigorous enhancement of User Experience (UX) design, particularly as AI emerges as a transformative tool in e-commerce practices. Integrating AI in e-commerce opens new possibilities for dynamic personalization. It also improved customer experiences, making applications more interactive, adaptive, and data-driven.

Several studies highlight challenges related to automation, UI refinement, and the practical implementation of predictive models, which affect the accuracy of user behavior in specific scenarios [3–5]. Zhu et al. [3] introduced a context-aware heterogeneous graph attention network to predict user behavior, emphasizing the role of contextual information in user engagement. Sun et al. [4] explored Reinforcement Learning (RL) for continuous UI layout optimization based on user feedback. While these approaches present promising directions, they often lack predictive and priority guidance for user interactions, particularly through multi-agent RL-based adaptation, user clustering, and generative AI. Additionally, existing methods face challenges in scaling across different platforms and cannot quickly adapt to evolving user needs. Model-Driven Development (MDD) remains underutilized in AI-enhanced UX design, limiting the ability to formalize, reuse, and automate UI/UX adaptations. These limitations hinder the development of intelligent interfaces capable of learning from and responding to user behavior over time. The proposed framework addresses these limitations by combining generative AI with model-driven principles, enabling real-time UX optimization and enhanced adaptability.

Furthermore, studies indicate that nearly 90% of e-commerce platforms fail within the first three months of operation, due to suboptimal UX workflows and an inability to refine user interactions based on behavioral data. Many businesses outsource development, leading to a disconnection between UI design and market-specific user expectations, which exacerbates usability issues. This misalignment highlights the need for AI-driven, adaptive design methodologies that can bridge the gap between user expectations and digital storefront effectiveness.

This paper presents a novel approach to e-commerce by integrating generative AI with the Model-Driven Development approach (AI-MDD-UX) to enhance engagement, personalization, and user experiences. The methodology combines KMeans++ for user clustering, Generative Adversarial Networks (GANs) for UI generation, and RL agents for adaptive interface optimization. The structured multi-level MDD framework translates user behavior insights into dynamic UI interactions, enabling real-time personalization and continuous design improvements. The key contributions of this study are

1. We present a novel hybrid approach that combines generative AI and MDD to ensure real-time UI/UX optimization in e-commerce. AI leverages KMeans++ for behavior-driven user clustering, GANs for automated UI generation, and RL agents for continuous interface adaptation, while MDD provides the structural foundation for consistency and automated adaptation.
2. This study contributes to the growing body of research on AI-driven e-commerce by introducing a unified AI-MDD architecture that enables structured, scalable UX design and intelligent personalization. The framework integrates real-time user behavior analysis with multi-agent reinforcement learning and generative models to dynamically generate user interfaces. Meanwhile, AI continuously monitors user feedback to refine UI elements, ensuring an adaptive and user-centric experience.
3. We validate the system performance across diverse interaction scenarios in a Saudi Arabian e-commerce market through technical validation, evaluate system quality for different user behaviors and measure conversion rates, user engagement, and adaptive UI responsiveness for broader deployment.

The remainder of the document is structured as follows: Section 2 reviews existing works related to UI/UX adaptation in e-commerce. Section 3 defines the problem statement, presents the mathematical formulation, and explains key notations. Section 4 details the methodology, focusing on the integration of generative AI and MDD into an e-commerce platform and designing technical algorithms. Section 5 presents the used dataset, analyzes the evaluation metrics, and includes the numerical results to validate the proposed approach. Finally, Section 6 concludes the key findings and outlines directions for future research.

2. Literature Works

This study aims to address two key objectives: (1) analyzing the challenges associated with the dynamic adaptation of UI/UX, and (2) proposing a hybrid AI-MDD-UX framework capable of supporting both static UI adaptation through a rule-based approach and dynamic adaptation of UI/UX using multi-agent reinforcement learning. To provide a comprehensive overview, this section begins by highlighting contemporary methods for solving static UI adaptation, followed by a discussion of static UX optimization techniques. Additionally, it presents a concise review of AI-driven UX adaptation, highlighting challenges that parallel dynamic adaptation issues in AI-enhanced e-commerce platforms.

Although a significant body of literature exists on real-time monitoring and adaptive UX challenges covering topics such as conversation rate optimization, rule-based UI adaptation, behavioral engagement modeling, and AI-driven user interaction assistance, as discussed in [6–22]. This study particularly focuses on research directly relevant to the dynamic UI adaptation. Existing studies have explored various aspects of dynamic UI adaptation in domains such as transportation, supply chain management, market, and customer relationships management. However, this research considers a systematic approach to categorize existing studies, identifying key gaps in AI-driven UX adaptation for personalized e-commerce experiences.

2.1. The Static UI Adaptation Problem: SUIAP

Several studies have focused on adapting interfaces using static user profiles. For instance, the study presented in [7] addresses the static UI adaptation problem by modeling user profiles, emphasizing the role of preferences, behavior history, and demographic data in optimizing interface delivery for diverse users. They also highlight security and privacy challenges involved in identifying the most threatening issues in user profiling. To mitigate these concerns, the researchers proposed Adaptive User Interfaces (AUIs), which balance system-driven adaptation with user control. Their methodology integrates data-driven algorithms that dynamically adjust interface elements for enhanced user experiences. The accuracy of this approach is rigorously tested against realistic benchmark instances, with quantitative analyses demonstrating its effectiveness in reducing solution times as system complexity increases.

In the context of Adaptive UI Personalization (AUP), Zhang et al. [8] introduced a population-based hybrid method combining adaptive (system-initiated) and adaptable (user-initiated) user interfaces to enhance usability and user performance in complex systems. Their findings suggest that such a combination can simplify complex UI structures, enhancing both usability and efficiency.

Abrahão et al. [9] conducted an in-depth analysis on UI adaptation across different contexts using model-based approaches. They introduced a conceptual framework for intelligent UI adaptation, explored the integration of machine learning techniques, and identified key challenges that must be addressed to optimize user experiences.

These works rely heavily on static data and lack scalability across platforms with real-time and dynamic interaction needs. Moreover, UI layouts are typically fixed at deployment, preventing adaptation to behavioral changes during runtime.

2.2. *The Dynamic UI/UX Adaptation Problem: DUIAP*

Dynamic adaptation introduces real-time responsiveness based on evolving user interactions. To tackle the Dynamic UI/UX Adaptation Problem (DUIAP), Jean [10] applied Reinforcement Learning (RL) to optimize UI/UX in real-time based on continuous user interactions. Their study dynamically adjusts UI elements, refining layout and content presentation according to evolving user preferences and behavioral patterns.

Zosimov et al. [11] developed a robust adaptable framework that addresses DUIAP by implementing pseudo-identification techniques to construct anonymous user profiles and rule-based adaptation mechanisms. By analyzing user activity in web applications, their system autonomously personalizes UI elements, ensuring seamless adaptation to individual user needs and improving overall usability.

Mezhoudi and Vanderdonckt [12] introduced TADAP, machine learning-driven UI adaptation framework that integrates user feedback to enable real-time UI adaptation. This mixed-initiative approach enables a dynamic collaboration between users and the system, allowing continuous UI refinement. By personalizing interface elements based on real-time interactions, TADAP enhances usability.

Heinrich et al. [13] proposed a model-driven approach for developing self-adaptive user interfaces. Their approach utilizes Domain-Specific Languages (DSLs) for context modeling and adaptation rules, facilitating automatic UI adaptations based on changing user context. This ensures that interface elements remain responsive and tailored to evolving user needs, reinforcing adaptability and usability in diverse interaction scenarios.

Nandoskar et al. [14] presented an AI-driven system that automates UI generation using Generative Adversarial Networks (GANs) to personalize web design based on user preferences. The system incorporates an interactive questionnaire, response analysis, and a recommendation engine to generate custom UI mock-ups tailored to individual needs. While this approach significantly enhances UI diversity and personalization, it requires additional manual refinement to meet UX standards, highlighting the need for more precise usability optimization and enhancement of user engagement.

2.3. *Comparative Summary and Innovation of This Study*

Table 1 summarizes key studies and their contributions. As shown, existing approaches lack full integration of four critical components: (1) real-time UI adaptation via multi-agent reinforcement learning, (2) behavioral clustering through unsupervised methods like KMeans++, (3) automated UI generation using GANs, and (4) model-driven development (MDD) for scalable and maintainable implementation.

Table 1. Comparative summary among existing works.

Related Works	Adaptation Type	Technique Used	Key Limitation
[7]	Static	Rule-based AUI	Limited runtime flexibility
[8]	Static	Hybrid Adaptive/Adaptable UI	Lacks deep personalization
[9]	Static	Model-based UI	Limited AI integration
[10]	Dynamic	Reinforcement Learning (RL)	No MDD integration
[11]	Dynamic	Rule-based and Pseudo-ID	Limited to activity logs
[12]	Dynamic	TADAP (ML and Feedback)	UX not fully automated
[13]	Dynamic	DSLs for MDD	No AI or learning ability
[14]	Dynamic	GANs	Manual refinement required
Proposed	Static and Dynamic	GANs + RL + KMeans++ + MDD	Addresses limitations of exiting studies

The proposed AI-MDD-UX framework is the first to unify behavioral clustering, generative AI, reinforcement learning and MDD to enable real-time, context-aware adaptive UI/UX. Unlike traditional GAN-based models that focus mainly on visual generation through reused design components, our approach integrates 4-level MDD pipeline (CIM, PIM, PSM, Code) to ensure scalability and maintainability. AI-MDD-UX enhances the user experience by integrating both direct and indirect feedback mechanisms for personalization. It combines static rule-based logic with dynamic adaptation using KMeans++ for unsupervised user clustering, GANs for generating diverse UI variations without manual effort, and multi-agent reinforcement learning for continuous interface optimization.

3. Problem Statement and Mathematical Formalization

3.1. Problem Statement

Dynamic UI adaptation differs fundamentally from static approaches by leveraging AI-driven strategies for real-time interface optimization. Traditional methods rely on predefined rules and fixed user segments, making them ineffective at adapting to shifts in user behavior. This approach often leads to suboptimal user experiences. In contrast, dynamic adaptation continuously monitors user interactions and context, enabling interfaces to evolve in real time.

We identify three key aspects that define this challenge:

- **Real-time UI adaptation:** Unlike static UI adaptation, which relies on predefined rules and remains unchanged during runtime, dynamic UI adaptation continuously updates UI components based on real-time user interactions and personalized needs. These updates capture the evolving nature of user behavior, enabling more adaptive and responsive decision-making process.
- **Personalized and Evolving User Needs:** Dynamic UI adaptation tailors experiences at an individual level, whereas static UI adaptation applies a uniform interface for all users. Since user needs evolve over time, dynamic adaptation requires sophisticated optimization mechanisms to ensure continuous relevance, engagement, and user satisfaction.
- **User experiences Optimization:** Effective dynamic UI adaptation must prioritize user satisfaction and interaction quality. Traditional static approaches fail to consider real-time user feedback and adaptive refinements. By dynamically personalizing UI layouts, optimizing responsiveness, and reducing dropout rates, dynamic adaptation enhances fosters higher engagement and an enhanced user experience.

The proposed AI-MDD-UX framework addresses these challenges by integrating reinforcement learning and generative models into a model-driven development pipeline. This enables scalable, real-time, and context-aware UI adaptation that responds effectively to the diverse and evolving needs of users.

3.2. Mathematical Formalization

We formulate the problem of this study as follows:

- Let U be the set of users, $I_u(t)$ represent the set of interactions for a given user u at time t.
- Each interaction $i \in I_u(t)$ consists of multiple behavioral features:
    - Click frequency c_u
    - Page views p_u
    - Session duration s_u
    - Search queries q_u
    - Checkout behavior ch_u
    - Device type d_u

These features are aggregated into a user-specific feature vector X_u as follows:

$$X_u = [c_u, p_u, s_u, q_u, ch_u, d_u]. \quad (1)$$

- The UI adaptation function, which determines the UI for a given user u at time t, is defined as

$$UI(u,t) = f(P_u, I_u(t), H_u), \quad (2)$$

where P_u represents the user's preferences, $I_u(t)$ captures real-time user intercation and H_u denotes the user's intercation history.

- To improve personalization, users are grouped based on interaction patterns using K-Means++ clustering.
    - Let $G = \{G_1, G_2, \ldots G_L\}$ denote the set of user clusters.
    - Each user u belongs to a cluster G_i, where:

$$G_i = argmin\ d(X_u, C_k), \quad (3)$$

where $d(X_u, C_k)$ is the distance metric between the user's features and cluster centroid C_k. This clustering mechanism enables the creation of adaptive UI groups, allowing for more targeted and personalized UI adaptations.

- The effectiveness of a dynamic UI adapation strategy is evalauted using optimization function:

$$max \in \sum\nolimits_{u\ \epsilon U} \alpha \cdot E_u + \beta \cdot UX_u + \gamma \cdot S_u - \delta \cdot D_u, \quad (4)$$

where

- E_u measures the level of user interaction with the system. It quantifies user actions (click frequency, page views, session duration, search queries, checkout behavior) that indicate engagement.

$$E_u = w_1 \cdot c_u + w_2 \cdot p_u + w_3 \cdot s_u + w_4 \cdot q_u + w_5 \cdot ch_u. \quad (5)$$

The coefficients w_i represent the weights assigned to various user engagement actions. Theses weights reflect the relative importance of each action in contributing to business objectives. Actions with a higher impact on outcomes such as "purchase" or "checkout" are assigned greater weights (e.g., w_1 = 10, w_2 = 8) than actions like "view" or "scroll" (e.g., w_3 = 6, w_4 = 4). This prioritization aligns with key business metrics such as revenue generation and purchase intent.

To ensure adaptability, the weights are dynamically updated over time based on user behavior and real-time feedback. The adjustment follows the update formula:

$$w_i(t) = w_i(t-1) + \alpha \cdot \sigma_i, \quad (6)$$

where

- $w_i(t)$ is the updated weight for the ith action at time t.
- $w_i(t-1)$ is the previous weight at time $t-1$.
- α is a learning rate controlling the adjustment speed.
- σ_i represent the influence of new data or feedback on the ith action.

- UX_u represent the user experience score which evaluates UI fluidity, responsiveness, and ease of use. It is defined by sum of retention rate R_u, response time R_u and error rate R_u at time t that computed as:

$$UX_u = \frac{1}{T}\sum_{t=1}^{T} \lambda_1 \cdot R_u(t) + \lambda_2 \cdot RT_u(t) + \lambda_1 \cdot ER_u(t), \quad (7)$$

λ_i are the weighting factors to i^{th} aspect.

The coefficients λ_i represent the weighting factors for the ith aspect of user experience, such as ease of use, visual design, and content satisfaction. These weights are derived by combining user survey responses with interaction log data. Users are asked to rate each UX aspect on a Likert scale (e.g., 1 to 5), and these ratings are aggregated across the user base. To determine which aspects, contribute most significantly to the overall UX score, we apply Principal Component Analysis (PCA). PCA helps identify the most influential dimensions by analyzing variance across the collected ratings and interactions. This approach ensures that aspects most strongly correlated with user satisfaction receive higher weight, making the UX evaluation both data-driven and user-centric.

- S_u represent user satisfaction and capture subjective user feedback through surveys, ratings, or implicit behavior analysis. It is defined by sum of net promoter score NPS_u, customer satisfaction score $CSAT_u$ and click-through rate CTR_u that computed as:

$$S_u = \varnothing_1 \cdot NPS_u + \varnothing_1 \cdot CSAT_u + \varnothing_1 \cdot CTR_u, \quad (8)$$

$\varnothing_i$ are the weighting factors.

- D_u represent dropout rate (e.g., users abandoning session).
- $\alpha, \beta, \gamma, \delta$ are weighting factors for engagement, retention, satisfaction and dropout.

This optimization ensures that UI updates maximize engagement and retention while minimizing dropouts, dynamically refining UI components based on user behavior.

4. Methodology

The integration of generative AI with MDD for the e-commerce platform requires a robust technical framework to ensure seamless, real-time interactions and adaptability across diverse user behaviors. This section outlines the architectural and technological advancements that enable dynamic UI adaptation, cross-platform code generation, and AI-driven UI customization tailored to user's needs. These innovations aim to enhance engagement, improve user experience outcomes

To guarantee adaptive user experiences, the framework integrates generative AI with Multi-Agent Reinforcement Learning (RL) that allow users to profit from intelligent decision-making in UI/UX design. This achieved through generative AI, feedback loops, and structured designs principals that decompose behavioral interactions into optimized UI components. Table 2 summarizes the complementary roles of generative AI and MDD in dynamic UI adaption for e-commerce platform.

Table 2. Roles of generative AI and MDD in dynamic UI adaption.

Aspect	Generative AI's Role	MDD Role
UI Personalization	Learns user behavior and preferences	Defines adaptable UI structures through models.
UI Generation	Generates dynamic UI designs	Transforms models into functional UI components
UI Optimization	Uses RL to refine UI layouts	Automates adaptation through transformation rules
UI Adaptation	Adjusts UI in response to user actions	Ensures structured evolution of UI models

4.1. Architectural Framework for Real-Time UX Adaptation

The system architecture is illustrated in Figure 1 and was designed to process real-time interactions while ensuring modularity, UI generation, and contextual adaptation. The real-time multi-agent reinforcement learning was the core approach for enabling dynamic UI refinements, enhancing user engagement, and delivering customized UI experiences.

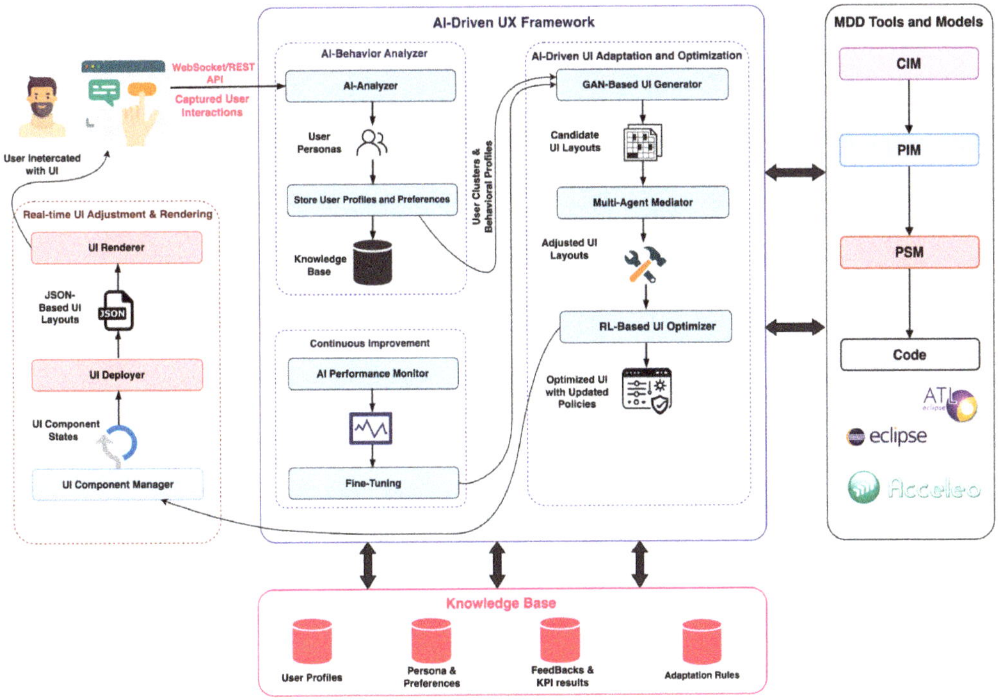

Figure 1. The general architecture of AI-MDD-UX. (1) Magenta color for CIM, (2) Blue color for PIM, (3) Red color for PSM, and (4) Gray color for Code.

Figure 1 also presents a four-layer architecture, including: Front-End, Back-End, and Knowledge Base MDD tool. Front-End layer communicates with the Back-End layer via Web-Sockets and RESTful APIs to enable seamless real-time interactions and dynamic UI adjustments.

1. **Front-End Layer:** This layer is responsible for displaying adaptive UI layouts, collecting user interactions and rendering optimized UI components. This layer consists of two main modules:
   - User Interaction Tracker Module: captures scrolls, clicks, hovers, dwell time, and gestures. It sends real-time events to the Multi-Agent System (MAS) layer for processing.
   - Real-time UI Adjustment and Rendering Module: This module dynamically updates and renders UI elements based on AI-driven recommendations. It consists of:
     - UI Component Manager: Handles UI components and maintains UI states.
     - UI Deployer: Converts JSON-based UI models into deployable interfaces for platforms, such as React.js, Flutter, and WebVR, using MDD tools.
     - UI Render: Displays the final UI layout after adaptation and optimization.

2. **Back-End Layer:** This layer processes user interactions, clusters user behavior, and adapts UI layouts through three main modules:
   - AI-Behavior Analyzer Module: This module receives user interaction logs and applies unsupervised clustering (KMeans++) to group users into different personas. It also stores personas and preferences in the Knowledge Base (KB) and shares insights with the AI-Driven UI Adaptation and Optimization Module.
   - AI-Driven UI Adaptation and Optimization Module: This module enables AI driven personalization and optimization. It consists of:
     - GAN-Based UI Generator: Generates adaptive UI layouts based on user preferences and behavioral clusters. It also uses a discriminator network to validate usability and coherence.
     - Multi-Agent Mediator: Acts as an intermediary between GAN and RL components, ensuring smooth decision-making based on adaptive rules and performance metrics. Multiple agents may share policies while executing dedicated adaptation tasks.
     - RL-Based Optimizer: Implements Q-learning-based UI refinement engine that optimizes layouts and applies logical adaptation rules for early, priority, and predictive guidance.
   - Continuous Improvement Module: This module monitors user engagement and interaction data to fine-tune models dynamically. It consists of
     - AI Performance Monitor: Monitors new user interactions and system performance while computing CTR (Click-Through Rate), engagement scores, and load time performance.
     - Fine-tuning Module: generate UI updates and adjust learning parameters based on user interaction metrics, and system performance.
3. **Knowledge Base Layer:** Serves as the central repository for storing historical user interactions, UI performance data, and contextual information. It includes
   - User Profiles: stores individual user behaviors and preferences.
   - Historical UI Performance: Logs past UI adaptations and their success rates, including state–action–reward experiences to improve RL learning.
   - Adaptation Rules: stores logical rules for priority and predictive guidance.
   - Persona Repository maintains essential information on user personas and preferences for personalized UI adaptation.
4. **MDD Tools Layer** consists of various tools (e.g., eclipse IDE, ATL transformation language and Acceleo) and models organized into four abstraction levels: (1)—Computational Independent Model (CIM) that captures business logic without system details, (2)—Platform Independent Model (PIM) that defines functional behavior independent of implementation technologies, (3)—Platform Specific Model (PSM) that adapts UI models for different target platforms and (4)—Code Generation and Deployment: Converts UI models into executable code for web and mobile platforms.

To enable intelligent and personalized UI adaptation, we combine KMeans++, GANs, and Multi-Agent Reinforcement Learning (MARL) to build an adaptive, user-centered UI system. KMeans++ clusters users based on raw interaction data, providing stable groupings that simplify learning, while GANs generate synthetic data to enrich training, avoid overfitting and improve generalization by exposing it to a wider range of behaviors. MARL leverages both real and synthetic data to train agents that dynamically adjust UI elements based on user feedback, enhancing personalization and overall performance. This hybrid approach addresses current limitations in adaptability, personalization, and engineering integration, offering a comprehensive, next-generation solution for dynamic e-commerce platforms.

4.2. Metamodels in AI-MDD-UX Vision

The AI-MDD-UX framework leverages layered metamodels to support automated UI generation, adaptive personalization, and real-time optimization based on user behavior and context. These metamodels guide the transformation from abstract user interactions to platform-specific implementations, integrating AI techniques throughout. The core metamodels, as illustrated in Figure 2, include:

- **CIM Metamodel—User Interaction Modeling:** Captures user behavior without technical constraints. Key classes include: (1) User, (2) Interaction, (3) Persona, and (4) UI Elements classes. The User is defined by User ID, interaction history, and preferences (e.g., shopping habits, browsing interactions). User Persona represents structured behavior types and shopping patterns. Interaction includes attributes such as click rate, session duration, and device type. The UI Elements class denotes adaptive components with engagement metrics.
- **PIM Metamodel—Cluster Modeling and Feature Vectors:** The PIM metamodel abstracts behavioral clustering and feature representation. It includes: (1) User-Cluster class that defines a set of similar user behaviors, (2) Feature-Vector class that captures metrics like click rate and purchase history, and (3) Persona Embeddings class encodes behavior into AI-compatible vectors.
- **PSM Metamodel—AI-Driven UI Generation and Optimization**: The PSM metamodel focuses on UI generation through GANs and RL.
    - **GAN-Driven UI Generation Metamodel:** This metamodel defines generative processes for adaptive UI design.
    - **Multi-Agent RL-Driven UI Adaptation and Optimization Metamodel:** This meta-model integrates RL to fine-tune UI in response to user interactions. It consists of several key classes: UI State class that represents the current UI layout and personalization option, RL-Agent class that learns optimal UI adjustments with attributes such as state, action, reward, policy, Adaptation Rule class that encapsulates rule-based UI adjustments, and Reward Function class that computes feedback for RL optimization.
- **UI Code Generation and Deployment Metamodel**: This metamodel defines platform-specific models for web, mobile, and VR interfaces. The Web Platform includes React components, dynamic layouts, and responsive designs. The Mobile Platform focuses on Flutter widgets, touch interactions, and mobile-optimized UIs. The VR Platform covers WebVR-specific components such as 3D models, VR UI elements, and immersive interactions. The core elements include (1) **Code Generator,** which is defined by language, framework, and target platform (e.g., React.js for Web, Flutter for Mobile, WebVR for VR), and (2) **Deployment Manager** that manages deployment configurations across platforms.

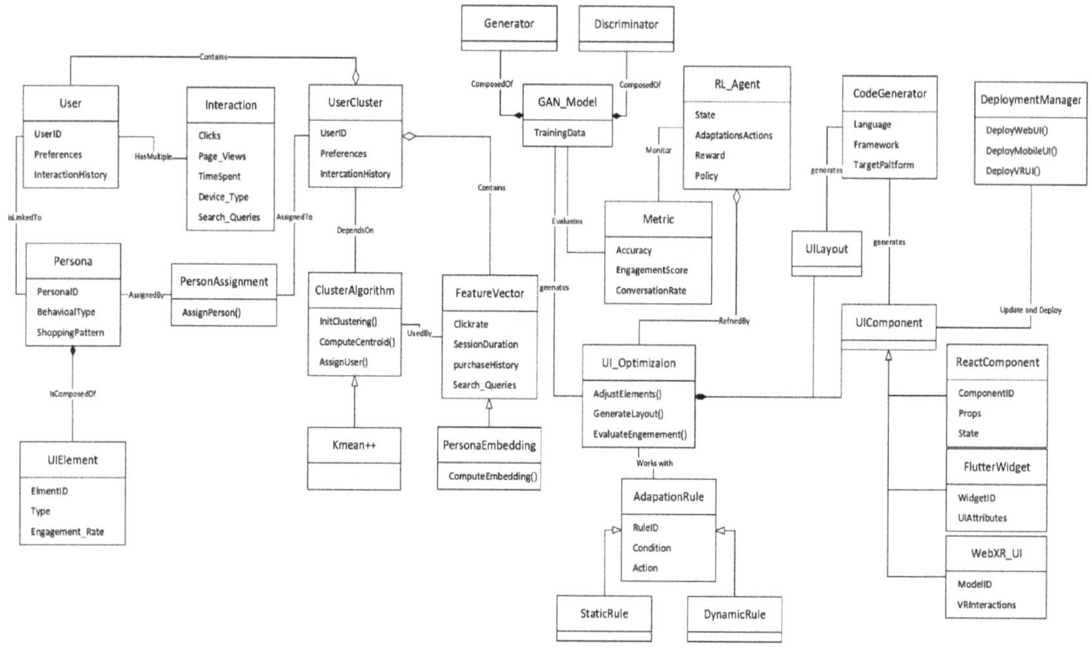

Figure 2. Metamodel of AI-MDD-UX approach.

4.3. The Workflow for Real-Time UI/UX Adaptation in AI-MDD-UX

The real-time UI/UX adaptation workflow is designed to enhance user engagement and ensure high-quality UI personalization. The workflow consists of six key steps: (1)—capturing user interaction, (2) clustering user behavior using KMeans++, (3)—generating persona embeddings, (4) GAN-based UI generation, (5)—multi-agent R-driven UI optimization, and (6)—(re-) deployment with real-time monitoring.

As illustrated in Figure 3, the process of the AI-MDD-UX approach begins by collecting user interaction data, such as clicks, session duration, and navigation patterns. This data is clustered using KMeans++, which generates stable user group labels based on behavioral patterns. GANs then use these labels to produce realistic synthetic interactions, enriching the dataset and improving model generalization. Both real and synthetic interactions are fed into the Multi-Agent Reinforcement Learning (MARL) module, where each agent is responsible for a specific UI element and earns adaptive policies based on user behavior and feedback. This architecture enables dynamic, personalized UI decisions through continuous learning. Finally, the optimized UI layouts are deployed across platforms to enhance user experience in real time. These steps are detailed as follows:

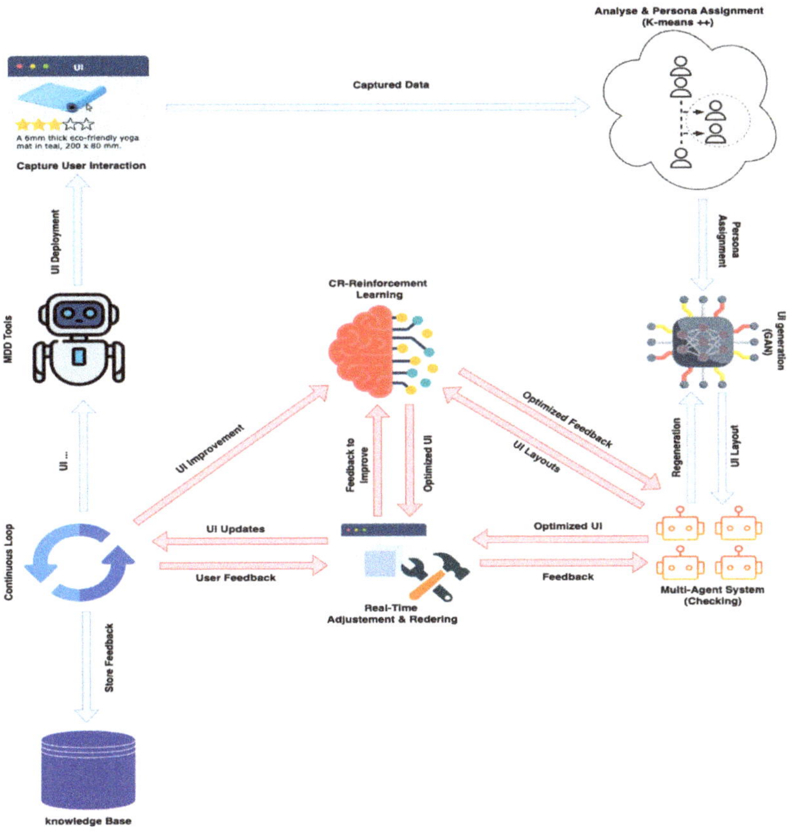

Figure 3. The workflow of AI-MDD-UX.

4.3.1. User Interaction Capture

User activity logs, clicks, page views, time spent, search queries, checkout, and other interactions are captured in the front-end layer from UI components. This raw interaction data is then structured into feature vectors and sent to the real-time AI-analyzer via WebSocket.

4.3.2. KMeans++ Based User Behavior Clustering

Users' behavioral feature vectors are clustered to ensure personalized UI adaptations, improved engagement, and optimized user experience based on their interaction patterns through the unsupervised K-means++ technique.

- K-means++ technique [15]: Grouping users into clusters based on their similar interaction patterns, such as using checkout behavior. It allows the system to generate tailored UI designs dynamically.
- Improve convergence and accuracy: Enhancing the traditional K-Means algorithm by optimizing centroid initialization, leading to faster convergence and more accurate clustering.
- Persona-based Adaptation: Allowing the generative AI models to handle UI experiences according to user persona.

The K-Means++ algorithm iteratively refines clusters, ensuring that users within the same cluster exhibit highly similar behaviors while maintaining distinct group separations.

Each user is dynamically assigned to the most relevant cluster based on their behavioral features, and persona profiles are continuously updated until optimal grouping is achieved.

Despite its improved efficiency, K-Means++ relies on Euclidean distance, which may limit its ability to capture complex spatial patterns, particularly in irregular or non-linear temporal distributions of user interactions. Nonetheless, it remains a computationally efficient and scalable approach for user segmentation. Future research could explore alternative clustering techniques, such as Density-Based Spatial Clustering of Applications with Noise (DBSCAN) [16] or hierarchical clustering, to better accommodate non-linear behavioral patterns.

The steps of K-means++ algorithm are detailed in Algorithm 1.

Algorithm 1 Enhanced K-Means++ Clustering for User Behavior Algorithm

Inputs: U_I: *Collected User Interaction Data;*
U_f: *Extracted features* (e.g., *clicks, page views, product preferences*), *n: number of users*

Outputs: *Groups* $G = \{G_1, G_2, \ldots, G_L\}$ *// Groups of similar user behaviors*
Centroids $C = \{C_1, C_2, \ldots, C_L\}$ *// Representative points of each group*

Begin

(1) : Initialize k cluster centers using K-Means++.
(2) : **Repeat**
(3) : Assign each user (U) to the nearest cluster based on Euclidean distance.
(4) : Update each center by averaging the feature values of assigned users.
(5) : **Until** no significant change in cluster assignments.
(6) : **Foreach** user (U) in a cluster **Do**
(7) : **IF** (moving U to a different cluster improves grouping quality) **Then**
(8) : Reassign U and update cluster centers.
(9) : **End IF**
(10) : **Until***Stability of centroids*
(11) : **Return** final clusters (G) and centroids (C).

End

4.3.3. Persona Embeddings Generation

The system computes persona embeddings by extracting key features of each user group, including preferred product categories, purchase frequency, and interaction style. Once user cluster are established, the system applies a neural network-based embedding layer to map cluster assignments into a lower-dimensional space as follows:

$$P_u = \varphi(G_i), \tag{9}$$

where P_u represents the persona embedding for user u, and $\varphi(G_i)$ is an encoding function that transforms clusters to embeddings. These embeddings provide a compact meaningful representation of different user personas, enabling the system to distinguish between profiles such as frequent buyers, casual browsers, and high-engagement users.

4.3.4. GAN-Based UI Generation

The GAN-based UI generation model enhances user experience by generating personalized and context-aware design. It dynamically adjusts the layout structure, component positioning and visual features to align with user preferences and behavior. To automate UI generation, the model processes persona embeddings and user interactions, generating UI layouts that make interactions more intuitive and engaging. Beyond the GAN model, the system **includes a generator that uses** embedded persona and user interaction to generate UI layouts. Additionally, a discriminator evaluates the authenticity of the generated UI against a training set of real UI components, ensuing UI remains personalized and aligned with the user's engagement level. The primary objectives of GANs in UI adaption are to:

- Automate UI creation and generate diverse variations from historical user data, enabling faster prototyping, and adaptation to user needs.
- Adjust UI layouts, colors, and element placements based on real-time interaction data, ensuring and optimized user experience without human intervention.
- Generate personalized UI designs by training on engagement metrics such as clicks, time spent, and conversion rates.
- Ensure visual appealing and functional UI layouts that enhance engagement.

Figure 4 shows the architecture of GAN for UI generation. It consists in two-network architecture: (1) Generator (G), which takes user interaction data as input and generates a new UI layout by proposing adjustments to UI components that aligns with user preferences, (2) Discriminator (D), which evaluates the usability of the generated UI, determines whether the layout matches high-performing UI examples and provides feedback to refine the generator's output.

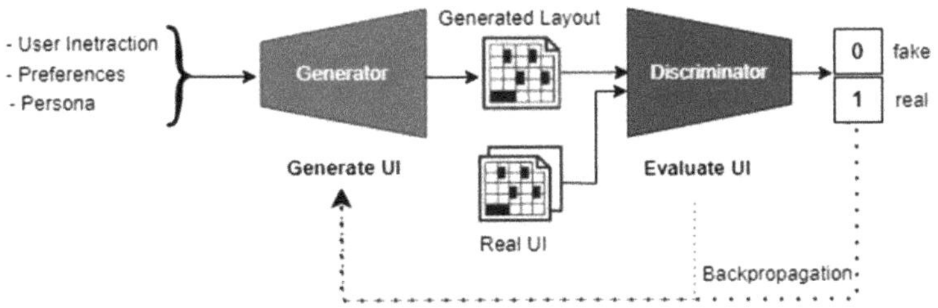

Figure 4. GAN-based UI generation architecture.

The UI generation process begins by initializing generator (G) and discriminator (D) networks with random weights. The generator synthesizes UI layouts by processing three key inputs: (1) persona embeddings P_u, (2) interaction feature vectors X_u, and (3) a random noise vector $z \sim \mathcal{N}(0,1)$ to ensuring diversity. The generation process is formally expressed as:

$$\widehat{UI} = G(P_u, X_u, z). \tag{10}$$

The discriminator then evaluates both generated and real historical UIs, assigning authenticity probabilities:

$$D(UI) \to [0,1] \ D\left(\widehat{UI}\right) \to [0,1], \tag{11}$$

where

- $D(UI)$: Probability a real UI is correctly identified.
- $D\left(\widehat{UI}\right)$: Probability a generated $\widehat{UI}$ is misclassified as real.

A higher value of $D(UI)$ close to 1 indicates successful real UI recognition. A lower value of $D\left(\widehat{UI}\right)$ close to 0 shows effective fake UI detection.

As depicted in Algorithm 2, the training process involves an adversarial competition between the generator and discriminator networks, using both real historical UI layouts and artificially generated ones. The discriminator's goal is its ability to distinguish between real and generated layouts by widening the gap in their probability scores, while the generator progressively enhances its output quality to produce more convincing UI designs that can deceive the discriminator. This adversarial dynamic is captured by the min-max objective function:

$$L \min_{G} \max_{D} \mathbb{E}_{UI \sim \widehat{UI}}[\log D(UI)] + \mathbb{E}_{\varkappa \sim P_{\varkappa}}[\log D(1 - D(G(P_u, X_u, \varkappa)))], \quad (12)$$

where

- $\mathbb{E}_{UI \sim \widehat{UI}}[\log D(UI)]$ drives the discriminator to accurately identify genuine UI layouts.
- $\mathbb{E}_{\varkappa \sim P_{\varkappa}}[\log D(1 - D(G(P_u, X_u, \varkappa)))]$ pushes the generator to create outputs that the discriminator will incorrectly classify as authentic.

During training, the discriminator continuously refines its classification ability through weight updates, while the generator simultaneously adjusts its parameters via gradient descent to produce more convincing layouts according to the update rule:

$$G = G - \eta \nabla_G \mathbb{E}_{\varkappa \sim P_{\varkappa}}[\log D(1 - D(G(P_u, X_u, \varkappa)))]. \quad (13)$$

Through iterative adversarial training, the generator's outputs gradually become indistinguishable from real UI designs, eventually reaching an equilibrium where the discriminator can no longer reliably differentiate between them. Once the training process converges, the system adapts dynamically UI elements in response to user behavior patterns, resulting to improved usability, user engagement levels, and retention rates. The generated UI components are intelligently composed into a personalized interface design based on user clusters while maintaining full responsiveness across diverse devices. Additionally, the system incorporates cultural adaptation features such as automatic adjustments for right-to-left language support, regionally preferred color schemes, and localized shopping behavior patterns to create truly customized user experiences.

4.3.5. Multi-Agents Reinforcement Learning Based UI Optimization

Once the GAN generates candidate UI layouts which include diverse configurations of interface elements like buttons, menus, and content blocks. These layouts serve as starting points for a multi-agent reinforcement learning system that dynamically adapts interfaces in real-time. As users interact with the generated UI, a coordination of specialized agents evaluates and refines the interface through continuous adaptation. Six core agents collaborate and operate in cooperative manner to optimize the user experience:

- **User Behavior Agent (UBA)**: Tracks interactions such as button clicks, form inputs, and hover actions.
- **Contextual Information Agent (CxIA)**: Collects environmental data, including device type (mobile or tablet), screen size, and network conditions.
- **Urgency Agent (UA)**: Monitors high-priority alerts, such as flash sales, security notifications, or order status updates.
- **Layout Optimization Agent (LOA)**: Dynamically adjust the position and size of UI elements to improve readability and accessibility based on user behavior and screen size.
- **Personalization Agent**: Adapts content and recommendations in real-time based on browsing history and user preferences to enhance engagement and sales.
- **Conflict Resolution Agent (CRA):** Resolves conflicts when multiple layout changes need to be made simultaneously.

Algorithm 2 GAN-Based UI Generation Algorithm

Inputs:
X_u: *User feature vectors*
P_u: *Personna embedding*
z: random noise.
UI: *Historical UI dataset*

Outputs: $\widehat{UI}$// *Optimized UI layouts*

Begin

(1) : Initialize GAN with random weights for generator G and discriminator D.
(2) : Extract feature vectors X_u
(3) : Compute persona embeddings from clustered user interactions P_u.
(4) : **While** convergence criteria not met **Do**
(5) : Sample real UI layouts UI from historical data.
(6) : Generate fake UI layouts using Equation (5).
(7) : Train the discriminator by maximizing discriminative distance using Equation (6)
(8) : Train the generator by updating parameters to detect fake UI using Equation (8)
(9) : Update weights of G and D using gradient descent.
(10) : Monitor training loss and adjust hyperparameters if needed.
(11) : **End While.**
(12) : **Select the best UI layouts** based on engagement and retention metrics.
(13) : **Return** $\widehat{UI}$.

End

The system's decision-making follows formalized adaptation rules (see Table 3) that translate user interactions into interface improvements:

Table 3. Adaptation rules for enhancing user experiences.

User Behavior Agent	
R1	$user\_interacted(t) \Rightarrow State2$
R2	$user\_scroll(s,t) \wedge dwell\_time(s,t) < threshold \Rightarrow adjust\_layout(s,t+1)$
Personalization Agent	
R3	$purchase\_history(u) \wedge browsing\_history(u) \wedge high\_engagement(u) \Rightarrow recommend\_items(u,t+1)$
CTA Monitoring Agent	
R4	$user\_hover(button,t) \wedge \neg user\_click(button,t) \Rightarrow modify\_CTA(button,t+1)$
UI Visibility Agent	
R5	$ambient\_light(low,t) \wedge visibility\_score(element,t) < threshold \Rightarrow enhance\_contrast(element,t+1)$
Feedback Processing Agent	
R6	$user\_action(a,s,t) \wedge positive\_feedback(s',t+1) \Rightarrow update\_reward(s,a,t+1)$
User Behavior Agent	
R7	$inactivity(t) > threshold \Rightarrow display\_timeout\_warning(t+1)$
Contextual Information Agent	
R7	$page\_load\_time(t) > threshold \Rightarrow optimize\_assets(t+1)$

The dynamic UI adaptation problem is formally modeled as a Markov Decision Process (MDP) within the reinforcement learning framework, defined by the tuple:

$$M = (Ag, S, \Omega, V, A_{act}, T, Ra),$$

where

- Ag represents a set of UI adaptation agents.
- S denotes all possible UI states.
- Ω describes UI elements and layout configurations.
- V maps UI element states to interaction metrics.
- A_{act} contains possible adaptation actions.
- T defines the transition probability between UI states.
- Ra represents the engagement-based reward function.

The system learning process follows a continuous cycle of state transitions and policy updates:

$$s \rightarrow a \rightarrow P(s' \mid s,\ a) \rightarrow s' \rightarrow R(s,\ a,\ s') \rightarrow PolicyUpdate \rightarrow \pi', \tag{14}$$

where $P(s' \mid s,\ a)$ determines the probability of transiting to state s' after taking action a in a state s, and $R(s,\ a,\ s')$ quantifies the engagement improvement from each adaptation. Three distinct guidance strategies are used based on interaction patterns: predictive adjustments for routine optimizations, priority-based adaptations for urgent situations and proactive refinements anticipating user needs.

(1) **Early Guidance Strategy (Algorithm 3)**

When multiple actions are equally important, the system prioritizes agent actions using Early Guidance Strategy. The *User Behavior Agent* tracks user interactions and guides the *UI Layout Agent* to apply immediate changes. However, the system implements mobile-first adaptations when detecting smaller screens, automatically enlarging form fields and highlighting interactive elements. For desktop interfaces, it enhances visual feedback through dynamic color changes, creating a responsive experience tailored to each device's interaction paradigms.

Algorithm 3 Early Guidance for UI Layout Adaptation

Inputs: *s: UI State, UAgt: Urgency Agent, CRA: Conflict Resolution Agent*
Outputs: *UIL: UI Layout.*
Begin
(1) : **Foreach** *UI state (s) monitored by UBA* **Do**
(2) : **If** device type = mobile **Then**
(3) : **If** form interaction detected **Then**
(4) : Guide (π(s), UI Layout Agent) //UBA suggests increasing form field size.
(5) : UIL ← Enlarge Form Fields
(6) : **If** button hover detected **Then**
(7) : Guide (π(s), UI Layout Agent) // UBA advises UI Agent to highlight buttons.
(8) : UIL ← Highlight Button
(9) : **Else if** the device type = Desktop **Then**
(10) : **If** button click detected **Then**
(11) : Guide (π(s), UI Layout Agent) // UBA recommends changing button color
(12) : UIL ← Change Button Color
(13) : **End For**
(14) : **Return** UIL
End

(2) **Priority Guidance Strategy (Algorithm 4)**

When critical notifications emerge, the system immediately suspends routine optimizations to prioritize urgent alerts through prominent visual treatments, ensuring users never miss time-sensitive information regardless of other interface modifications in progress. This strategy uses predefined urgency thresholds and context-awareness rules to determine when to trigger priority guidance.

Additionally, fallback mechanisms are employed to re-engage users with suspended tasks once the alert has been acknowledged.

Algorithm 4 Priority Guidance for UI Layout Adaptation

Inputs: *s: UI State, Augst: Urgency Agent, CRA: Conflict Resolution Agent*
Outputs: *UIL: UI Layout.*
Begin
(1) : **Foreach** *UI state (s) monitored by UBA* **Do**
(2) : **If** urgent alert detected **Then**
(3) : Guide (π(s), UI Layout Agent) //Ensures the user responds to the alert immediately.
(4) : UIL ← Prioritize Alert (e.g., pop-up, emphasis)
(5) : **End If**
(6) : **End For**
(7) : **Return** UIL
End

(3) **Predictive Guidance Strategy to UI Layout Adaptation:**

By analyzing engagement levels, device characteristics, and interaction history, the system anticipates user needs, preemptively adjusting layouts for mobile users or streamlining form interactions for frequent completers, often implementing improvements before explicit requests occur. For instance, if a mobile device is detected, the layout is reshaped before interaction, ensuring elements are stacked vertically for better accessibility. Based on past interactions, if the user frequently fills out forms, the UI automatically expands form fields to improve input efficiency (Algorithm 5).

Algorithm 5 Predictive Guidance for UI Layout Adaptation

Inputs: *UEngLvl: User Engagement Level, ScrSize: Screen Size*
PastInt: Past Interaction History, CtxAw: external factors (e.g., *location, time of day).*
UI: UI application. // Manage Dynamic UI refinements
Outputs: *UIAdapt: UI Layout adaptation before user requests.*
(1) : **Foreach** *UI state (s) in the system* **Do**
(2) : **If** UEngLvl is high **OR** ScrSize indicates mobile **OR** PastInt **Then**
(3) : Apply UIAdapt (Predictive UI adjustments)
(4) : **End If**
(5) : **End For**
(6) : **Return** *UIAdapt*
End

Through this integrated approach—combining generative design with multi-agent reinforcement learning—the system delivers interfaces that adapt continuously to user preferences, device capabilities, and business goals, while ensuring cross-platform consistency. Figure 5 visualizes agent interactions, highlighting state transitions and reward mechanisms that drive optimization.

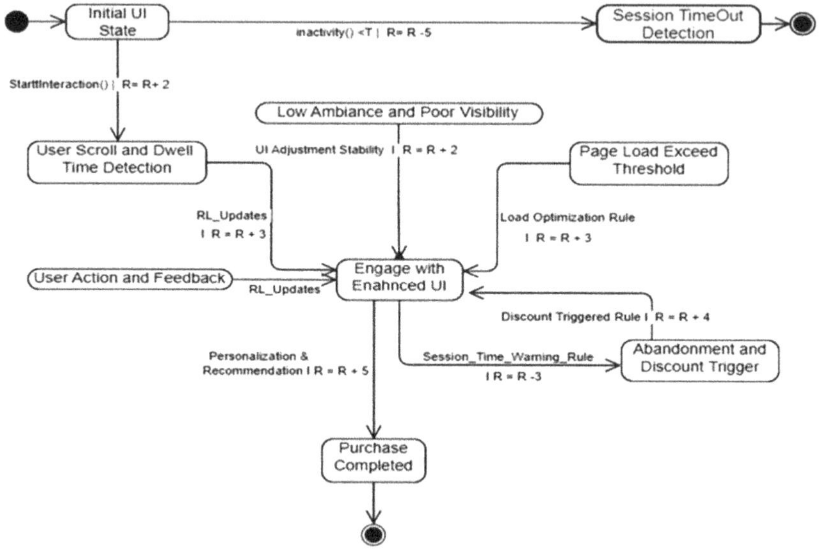

Figure 5. State transition diagram and reward actions.

4.3.6. (Re) Deployment and Real-Time Monitoring

Following the generation and refinement of UI layouts through the proposed multi-agent reinforcement learning system, the optimized interfaces undergo deployment across various platforms. For web applications, the final UI is packaged as modular HTML, CSS, and JavaScript bundles, leveraging modern frameworks like React, Angular, or Vue.js to ensure dynamic rendering capabilities. For mobile applications, the UI components are converted into platform-specific native code, utilizing Java/Kotlin for Android implementations, while maintaining design consistency across devices through responsive layout techniques. The deployed UI establishes connections with backend services through RESTful APIs, enabling real-time data fetching for dynamic content such as product catalogs, personalized recommendations, and user profile information. This API-driven architecture supports seamless content updates while preserving the adaptive layout structures generated by our system.

Critical to the continuous improvement cycle is our comprehensive real-time monitoring infrastructure, which captures and analyzes user interactions at granular levels. Sophisticated analytics tools track key engagement metrics including conversion funnel progression (e.g., add-to-cart click-through rates), content engagement duration (e.g., product browsing time), interface element interaction frequency, and task completion success rates.

Through continuous multi-agent RL, the system dynamically identifies performance patterns. For instance, discovering that minimalist UI designs yield 20% higher conversion rates among millennial users during evening browsing sessions. These insights trigger automatic refinement of UI adaptation rules, progressively optimizing interface elements for different user groups. The learning loop operates in real-time, with the system deploying updated UI configurations through our pipeline while maintaining version control for rollback capabilities when needed.

5. Implementation and User Scenario

5.1. Implementation

We opt Eclipse ATL (Atlas Transformation Language) model for its graphical modeling and transformation capabilities to ensure model-to-code transformations across different platforms. Furthermore, Python (Version 3.10), Google Colab is used to simulate user behavior, providing a convenient method to test different scenarios and verify user engagement. The e-commerce application is modeled in the editor zone, and user behavior processes are simulated using Python. In Table 3, we have developed a set of rules to model a reasoning-based predictive decision support system. To improve the user experience, we integrate the AI-MDD-UX framework to enhance the system's ability to dynamically update UIs based on evolving user preferences and behaviors. It continuously collects data on user interactions, analyzes behavior patterns, and monitor past purchases to personalize and refine UIs with relevant products. The system then adjusts UI elements dynamically based on browsing history, search queries, and real-time user actions to ensure a personalized and engaging experience.

5.2. Functional Details

AI-MDD-UX provides a dynamic and adaptive shopping experience for e-commerce platforms by facilitating real-time UI updates. Users interact with the e-commerce platform via a web page, mobile app, or VR interface. The front-end captures real-time interaction data (e.g., clicks, scrolls, session time) to analyze user engagement. This data is continuously monitored, allowing the system to adjust the UI dynamically based on pre-defined rules. The system applies K-Means++ clustering to segment users based on their interaction patterns. Once clusters are established, GANs generate adaptive UI layouts tailored to each group. The generated UI models undergo validation through multi-agent reinforcement learning, ensuring that the layouts align with user preferences and optimize engagement. Once validated, the layouts are passed to the code generation layer, where they are transformed into platform-specific specific. For instance, Figure 6a illustrates an example of automatic code generation for web (React.js), while Figure 6b shows code generation for mobile (Flutter).

```
const App = () => {
    return (
            <div className="app">
              <Button />
              <TextInput />
              <Image />
            </div>
        );
};
export default App;
```

(**a**)

```
class MyApp extends StatelessWidget {
  @override
  Widget build(BuildContext context) {
    return Scaffold(
      body: Stack(
        children: [
          ButtonWidget(),
          TextInputWidget(),
          ImageWidget(),
        ],
      ), );   }
}
void main() {   runApp(MyApp());}
```

(**b**)

Figure 6. Code generation for (**a**) Web (React.js) and (**b**) Mobile (Flutter).

5.3. Diverse User Scenarios: Saudi Arabian E-Commerce

The AI-MDD-UX is demonstrated through its dynamic UI adaptation in the context of Saudi Arabian E-Commerce. The first interaction for users with an e-commerce platform is the Main GUI Interface. In this scenario, Adam, a business manager, seeks to personalize the shopping experience for users of his e-commerce platform, Smartshop. The UI should adapt based on user profiles, such as fast shopper, detail-oriented shopper, or discount seeker. Instead of designing multiple UI variations manually, Adam integrates AI-MDD-UX to automate the UI generation, adaptation, and optimization process.

To illustrate the principle of AI-MDD-UX, let's follow Mohamed, who is a detail-oriented shopper with a history of purchasing home electronics. Currently, he is browsing Smartshop, having previously bought a smart speaker and shown interest in smart home devices. Below are key scenarios that demonstrate the AI-driven UI adaptation process:

Scenario 1# Initial Interaction and UI Adjustment

When Mohamed logs into Smartshop, the GAN model generates a personalized main UI layout, displaying recommended electronic products. Based on his browsing history, the system prioritizes smart home devices such as smart lights and thermostats (Figure 7). As Mohamed scrolls through the product list, the MAS system continuously tracks his interactions in real time by monitoring time spent on specific products, clicks, checkout behaviors and hover interactions over CTA buttons like "Add to Cart" and "Similar Products".

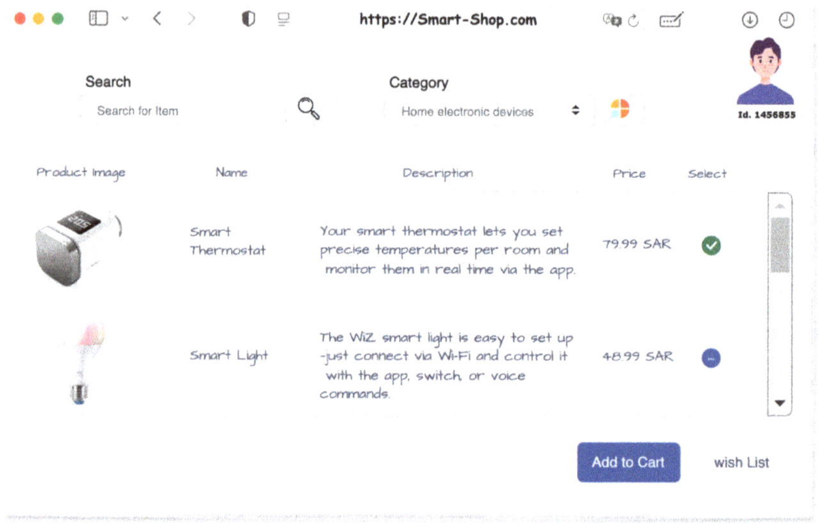

Figure 7. Main GUI of the e-commerce platform.

Scenario 2# Adaptative CTA

The system detects that Mohamed hovers over a smart thermostat but does not click on it. Recognizing interest without immediate action, the early guidance strategy is activated. The MAS layer applies the adaptive CTA rule, enlarging the smart thermostat's CTA button and changing its color to a more attention-grabbing shade of blue. These UI adjustments are sent to the RL layer, which learns that early engagement with UI elements increases click-through rates. The rendering layer immediately updates Mohamed's UI with the newly adjusted CTA buttons (see Figure 8).

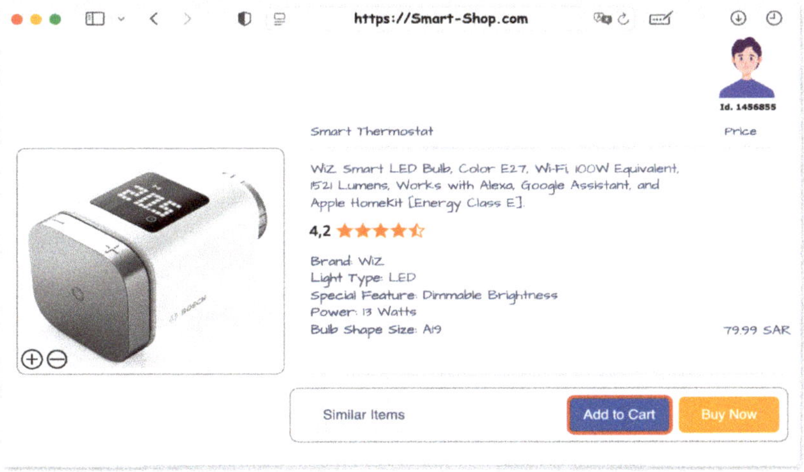

Figure 8. Adjustment of CTA buttons.

Scenario 3# Predictive Product Placement

After adding the smart thermostat to his cart, the MAS layer applies the predictive guidance and triggers a predictive product placement rule. The RL layer anticipates that users who add smart thermostats to their cart are also likely to purchase home automation hubs. By analyzing Mohamed's purchase history, the RL layer refines its prediction. The rendering layer updates the UI to prominently display a recommended smart home hub, increasing the likelihood of an additional purchase (Figure 9).

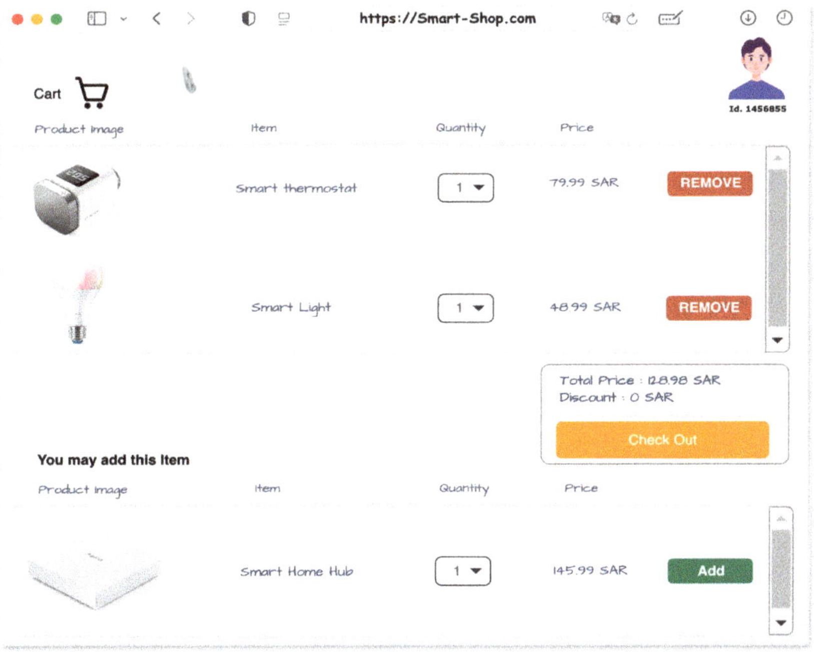

Figure 9. Predicted products with similar profiles.

Scenario 4# Purchase Completion and Continuous Learning

Mohamed completes his purchase. The MAS layer analyzes his engagements, detecting positive feedback. The RL layer updates its reward function to reinforce this positive outcome Additionally, the MAS layer evaluates Mohamed's overall experience, particularly his engagement with UI adjustments and product recommendations. The Continuous Improvement Layer detects that Mohamed responded well to the early visualization cue of enlarged CTA buttons. Based on this learning, the RL system refines its UI Adjustment Rule, ensuring more effective adaptations for future users with similar interaction patterns (Figure 10).

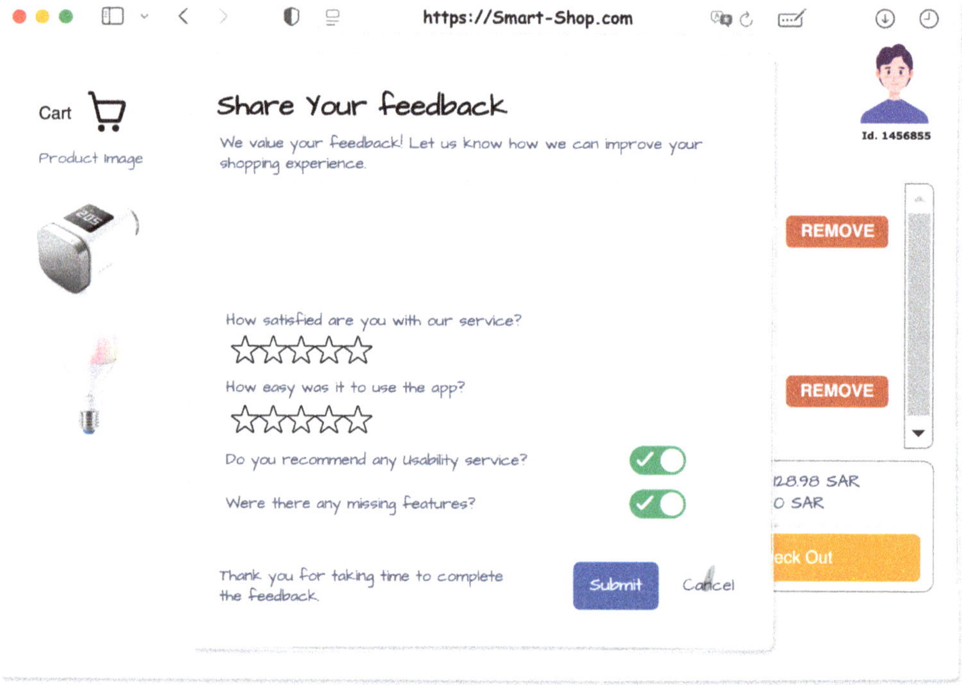

Figure 10. User engagement and feedback analysis.

5.4. Technical Validation and Experimental Results

The technical validation process was designed to assess the system's adaptability, accuracy, and execution speed under diverse conditions to ensure a thorough and rigorous evaluation. Building upon initial input accuracy and response efficiency, additional measures were implemented to address usability and user engagement. The system was validated on different platforms to ensure seamless interaction across multiple modalities.

User feedback was collected to evaluate the system's practicality and effectiveness in a real-world context by measuring key aspects such as conversational quality, accessibility, engagement, and overall user satisfaction. Additionally, feedback on the system's ability to maintain user interest was gathered to identify areas for further enhancement.

The experimental validation consists of two main evaluations:

1. **User Behavior Clustering and Persona Modeling**

   The first focuses on the clustering of user behaviors and personas. We conducted tests using an e-commerce user behavior dataset to assess the effectiveness of the proposed KMeans++ based approach in terms of cluster quality and execution speed. We compared our method against state-of-the-art techniques, KMeans [16], Density-Based

Spatial Clustering of Applications with Noise (DBSCAN) [17], and Agglomerative Algorithm [18]. The objective was to highlight the superior performance of our approach in solving the dynamic UI adaptation problem by improving clustering accuracy and execution efficiency. The selection of KMeans++ and DBSCAN was motivated by their complementary strengths in handling different aspects of user behavior analysis, which we elaborate on below:

- **KMeans++ for Efficiency and Scalability:** KMeans++ is prioritized due to its computational efficiency in centroid initialization, which ensures faster convergence while maintaining clustering accuracy, which is a critical requirement for real-time adaptive systems. The algorithm's scalability makes it well-suited for processing large-scale user interaction data, and its widespread adoption in behavior analysis provides a robust baseline for evaluation.
- **DBSCAN for Robustness to Irregular Patterns**: To address potential limitations of centroid-based methods, we incorporated DBSCAN as a comparative density-based approach. Its ability to: (1) identify arbitrarily shaped clusters, (2) detect and isolate noisy or atypical user behaviors, and (3) operate without predefining the number of clusters makes it invaluable for capturing nuanced or irregular behavior patterns that KMeans++ might overlook.

2. **Dynamic UI Adaptation and Performance Comparison**

   The second evaluation focuses on the dynamic UI adaptation problem, conducting a comparative analysis involving AI-MDD-UX, rule-based adaptation, heuristic-driven UI optimization, and traditional machine learning-based adaptation methods. This comparative analysis aims to demonstrate the effectiveness of AI-MDD-UX in enhancing user experiences and addressing dynamic UI adaptation challenges. Performance was evaluated using key metrics, including cluster quality, execution speed, user engagement, and layout adaptability. We provide strong evidence of AI-MDD-UX's efficiency and suitability for optimizing UI adaptations across various user behaviors and real-world scenarios.

5.4.1. Datasets

The system was tested using two different simulated datasets developed in Python via Google Colab. Both datasets were designed to simulate realistic user interactions in an e-commerce environment with dynamic UI requirements. The first dataset contains diverse user sessions to assess the dynamicity, quality, and adaptability of the system. The second focused on cross-platform performance, ensuring the system's functionality across multiple platforms. It consists of 100,000 simulated user sessions, each representing a sequence of interactions. These sessions are categorized into three key attributes: behavioral (18 features), demographic (14 features), and engagement (14 features). Table 4 shows an overview of the dataset, detailing the number of features and users across different instances.

Table 4. User behavior testing dataset.

Instance Name	Behavioral Features (Count)	Demographic Features (Count)	Engagement Features (Count)	Number of Users
Inst-1	10	6	8	10.000
Inst-2	12	7	10	25.000
Inst-3	15	8	12	50.000
Inst-4	18	10	14	100.000

The data was generated using modeling behavior patterns based on real-world interaction heuristics. The simulation was conducted using Python libraries, ensuring a balanced distribution across interaction types (e.g., clicks, page views, purchases) and user contexts (e.g., time of day, location, and engagement state). Our approach systematically collects and analyzes user behavior, clustering users into personas using the KMeans++ algorithm. Based on these clusters, the system dynamically generates UI updates using a multi-agent reinforcement learning algorithm, ensuring personalized UX adaptation.

The system was also validated across different platforms to ensure seamless interactions and UI adaptation across multiple modalities. The dataset captures various user scenarios and platform types (see Table 5). Tests ensured that performance metrics, such as CTR, conversion rate, session duration, user experience, and user satisfaction, remained stable even during transitions between different platform environments.

Table 5. UI Dynamic Adaptation Testing dataset.

Platform Name	Description	Platform	User Type	Interaction Complexity
E-commerce Web	Online shopping platform	React.js	Consumers	High
Mobile App	Mobile Shopping app	Flutter	App Users	Medium
VR Store	VR shopping experience	WebVR	VR Users	Very High
Smartwatch UI	Minimal shopping interface	Watch-OS	Go Users	Low
Automotive UI	In-car shopping dashboard	In-car OS	Drivers	Medium

5.4.2. User Feedback Collection

To strengthen the subjectivity and personalization of the UX model, we adopt a dual-feedback strategy that combines both direct (e.g., surveys and user ratings) and indirect feedback derived from user interaction patterns and behavioral data. This ensures comprehensive coverage of both perceived and behavioral aspects of the user experience.

- **Direct Feedback via Surveys:** A structured survey is designed to capture users' subjective evaluations across key interface dimensions, including ease of navigation, visual appeal, responsiveness, content relevance, and overall satisfaction. Each dimension is rated using a 5-point Likert scale ranging from "Strongly Disagree" to "Strongly Agree". These surveys are contextually triggered, typically following the completion of key actions, such as purchase and product comparison. The responses are stored in a feedback matrix $R_{u,i}$, where u represents the user and i represents the corresponding UX dimension.
- **Indirect Feedback via Interaction Logs:** Behavioral signals such as time spent on the UI, click-through rates, drop-off points, scroll depth, and hesitation metrics are captured anonymously through embedded tracking scripts. These signals are then associated with specific UX dimensions using heuristic mapping rules. For instance, prolonged hesitation during the checkout process may be interpreted as reduced ease of navigation.

All feedback was collected automatically during simulation runs using Python scripts. Each user session was logged in detail, including state transitions, user actions, and system-driven UI adaptations. These logs are stored in a structured format using *pandas* DataFrames, enabling structured analysis and comparative evaluation between static and dynamically adapted UI models.

5.4.3. Evaluation Criteria and Metrics

To assess the performance and effectiveness of the proposed system, we used a diverse set of metrics that capture both behavioral and perceptual aspects of user experience across static and dynamically adapted UI models. All metrics were computed using structured logs generated during simulation runs, and performance comparisons were conducted based on relative percentage changes.

1. **Conversion Rate (*CR*):** Conversion rate measures the percentage of users who successfully complete a target task (e.g., purchase, sign-up):

$$CR = \frac{N_c}{N_u}, \tag{15}$$

where

- N_c: Number of successful conversions (e.g., purchases)
- N_u: Number of unique users

A relative improvement of over **20%** in CR was used as a threshold to evaluate the effectiveness of UI adaptations.

2. **Click-Through Rate (*CTR*):** CTR reflects user interest and engagement by quantifying how often users click on actionable elements:

$$CTR = \frac{N_{clicks}}{N_{impression}} \times 100, \tag{16}$$

where

- N_{clicks}: Number of user's clicks on actionable elements.
- $N_{impression}$: Number of times elements were shown.

CTR serves both as a standalone indicator and a component of the overall engagement score (defined in Section 5.4.2).

3. **Session Duration (*SD*):** Session duration measures the average length of time users remain actively engaged with the interface:

$$SD = \frac{\sum_{i=1}^{S} t_i}{S} \times 100, \tag{17}$$

where

- t_i: Duration of session i.
- S: Number of sessions.

Longer session durations may indicate higher content relevance or user interest but are balanced against task completion time to avoid usability concerns.

4. **Task Completion Time (*TCT*):** This metric captures the average time users take to complete predefined tasks. Faster completion is considered indicative of a more efficient and user-friendly interface:

$$TCT = \frac{T_{static} - T_{adaptive}}{T_{static}} \times 100. \tag{18}$$

- T_{static}, $T_{adaptive}$: Average task completion times under static and adaptive conditions.

A reduction of **15% or more** was set as a performance improvement threshold.

5. **User Satisfaction (*US*):** User satisfaction is derived from direct feedback collected via Likert-scale surveys (see Section 5.4.2). Users rate their experience across key aspects such as ease of navigation, content relevance, and visual appeal. Satisfaction is calculated as an average rating per user across dimensions:

$$US_u = \frac{1}{N} \times \sum_{i=1}^{N} R_{u,i}, \tag{19}$$

where

- $R_{u,i}$: rating of user u for UX aspect i.
- N: number of UX aspects evaluated.

6. **Navigation Efficiency (*NU*):** As described earlier, navigation efficiency evaluates the directness of user paths during task execution:

$$NU = \frac{L_{optimal}}{L_{actual}}, \tag{20}$$

where

- $L_{optimal}$: Optimal number of steps to complete the task.
- L_{actual}: Observed number of steps.

Higher values indicate smoother and more intuitive user engagement.

5.4.4. Results of Simulated User Behavior

The technical validation conducted thorough assessment of AI-MDD-UX's performance across diverse user sessions. The key findings are summarized as follows:

- **Evaluation and Comparison of Cluster Quality**

To assess the clustering quality of AI-MDD-UX using KMeans++, we compared its performance against three other state-of-the-art algorithms: DBSCAN [16], KMeans [17], and Agglomerative [18]. Figure 11 illustrates the evolution of cluster quality achieved by different algorithms over multiple sessions. Our analysis reveals that KMeans++ provides superior cluster quality with achieving higher silhouette scores. This means that users are effectively segmented into meaningful personas based on their behavioral, demographic, and engagement attributes, enabling more accurate and personalized UI adaptation. In contrast, Agglomerative provides stable and well-formed clusters but lacks scalability to large datasets. DBSCAN offer some robust noise handling but is limited by its sensitivity to parameter tuning and encounters obstacles with dynamic adaptation when user behaviors shift over time.

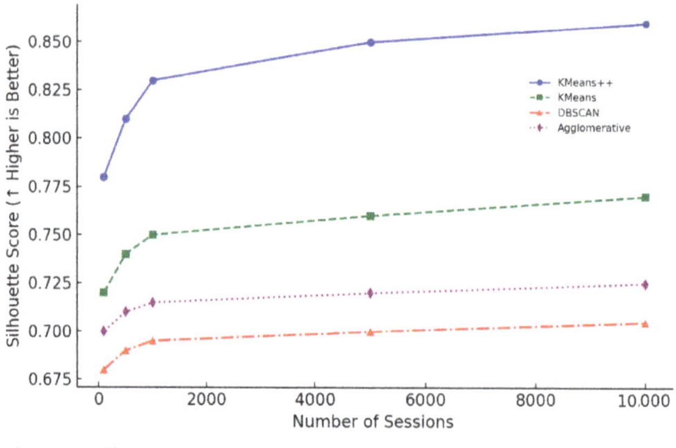

Figure 11. Cluster quality over sessions.

- **Evaluation and Comparison of Execution Speed**

Execution speed was evaluated across multiple test sessions, with up to 2000 sessions analyzed. As shown in Figure 12, the system demonstrated good execution speed, increasing linearly until reaching approximately 20 s for 10,000 sessions. This indicates a strong linear relationship between the number of sessions and execution time. However, DBSCAN struggles with execution speed due to its density-based clustering approach, making it impractical for highly dynamic e-commerce platforms that require real-time adaptability. In contrast, KMeans++ strikes a balance by delivering high clustering quality while maintaining efficient execution times, making it a more suitable choice for such environments.

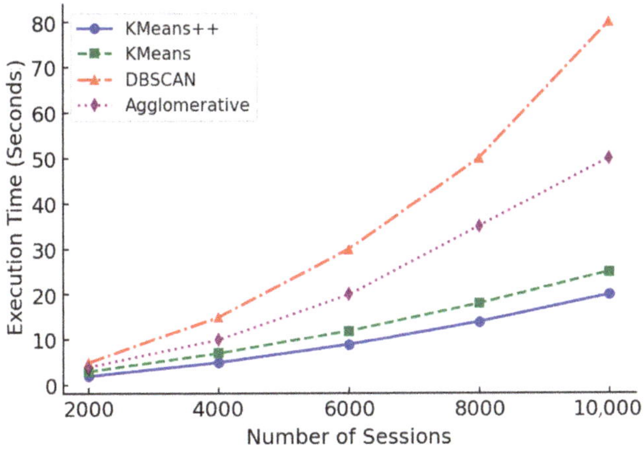

Figure 12. Execution speed over sessions.

5.4.5. Results of UI/UX Performance

- **Cross-Platform Performance Evaluation**

The system's performance was evaluated across five different UI platforms (web, mobile, VR, Smartwatch UI, and Automotive Interface) to ensure consistency in interaction and experiences. Table 6 presents the performance evaluation results of AI-MDD-UX across these platforms. AI-MDD-UX achieved a user experience score of 9.4 with an average user satisfaction of 94.7% in the VR platform, highlighting its strong engagement in immersive environments. Compared to the web platform (user satisfaction 91.2%, user experience of 9.0), AI-MDD-UX showed a slightly reduced user experience, with an unchanged UI layout. Smartwatch UI results show relatively lower click-through rate (CTR: 8.9%) and conversion rate (32.1%), which can be attributed to the limited screen real estate and interaction time. Despite this, a user experience score of 8.1 and user satisfaction of 85.5% indicate that AI-MDD-UX successfully maintained functionality and clarity in a compact interface. The system prioritized glanceable content, adaptive button resizing, and gesture-aware navigation to enhance interactions. In the Automotive Interface, the system achieved a user satisfaction rate of 90.3% and a user experience score of 8.8, reflecting the effectiveness of context-aware UI adaptations. The system dynamically minimized distraction by prioritizing essential content, adjusting contrast and layout based on lighting conditions, and suppressing non-critical elements during driving. Despite safety constraints, it maintained a solid CTR (11.1%) and conversion rate (37.8%) through voice-activated menus and driver-profile-based personalization.

Table 6. Performance evaluation of AI-MDD-UX for different UI instances.

Platform Name	CTR (%)	Conversation Rate (%)	Session Duration(m)	User Experience	User Satisfaction
E-commerce Web	12.5	42.3	5.8	9.0	91.2%
Mobile App	10.3	39.2	4.9	8.5	88.4%
VR Store	14.7	48.6	7.4	9.4	94.7%
Smartwatch UI	8.9	32.1	2.7	8.1	85.5%
Automotive UI	11.1	37.8	6.1	8.8	90.3%

Overall, the results indicate that AI-MDD-UX significantly improved conversation rates and session duration. The improvements stem from behavior-driven UI refinement, adaptive rules, and reinforcement learning (RL)-based optimizations that dynamically adjusted the interface in response to user interactions. Smartwatch and automotive results reinforce the system's potential in minimalist and safety-critical interfaces, although further tuning is required to maximize interactivity without overwhelming the user.

- **Evaluation with Simulated User Personas**

To comprehensively evaluate the system's adaptability, we conducted testing using simulated user personas representing distinct interaction behavior: (1) Power User, characterized by frequent engagement, preference for shortcuts and rapid navigation, (2) Cautious Browser, exhibiting thorough exploration before taking action, (3) First-Time User, lacking interaction history and requiring additional guidance and (4) Accessibility-Focused User which relies on larger text. As shown in Table 7, our performance evaluation demonstrated AI-MDD-UX's robust personalization capabilities. The system showed particular effectiveness for power users, who benefited from efficiency-optimized layouts and interaction shortcuts. While first-time and accessibility-focused users exhibited slightly longer task completion times due to their need for adaptive guidance and specialized interface elements, satisfaction levels remained consistently high across all groups. Notably, all personas rated the adaptive UI above 8.7, confirming the system's capacity to accommodate diverse needs and usage habits.

Table 7. Performance evaluation of AI-MDD-UX for different user personas.

Platform Name	CTR (%)	Conversation Rate (%)	Session Duration(m)	User Experience	User Satisfaction
Power User	15.2	50.1	3.5	9.6	93.8%
Cautious Browser	10.4	41.5	6.8	9.1	90.1%
First-Time User	9.6	34.2	7.2	8.6	86.7%
Accessibility User	8.8	30.5	8.3	8.9	88.4%

- **Evaluation with Various Business Domains**

To further demonstrate the broad applicability of the AI-MDD-UX framework, we tested it in various business domains (healthcare, education, finance, and retail), focusing on user satisfaction and user experience. As shown in Figure 13, in the healthcare domain, physics had a higher user experience score (9.3) compared to patients (8.4), due to the system's greater utility for healthcare professionals. In education, advanced learners scored higher (9.5) than new learners (8.7), reflecting greater familiarity and effective use of the system. In finance, investors had a higher score (9.4) than casual users (8.2), suggesting the system is more beneficial for those with deeper engagement. For retail stores, repeat customers scored higher (9.0) than first-time users (8.3), indicating that familiarity with the system leads to better experiences. As illustrated in Figure 14, user satisfaction mirrored the user experience scores. Healthcare professionals and investors were more satisfied, while new users in education and retail had lower satisfaction levels.

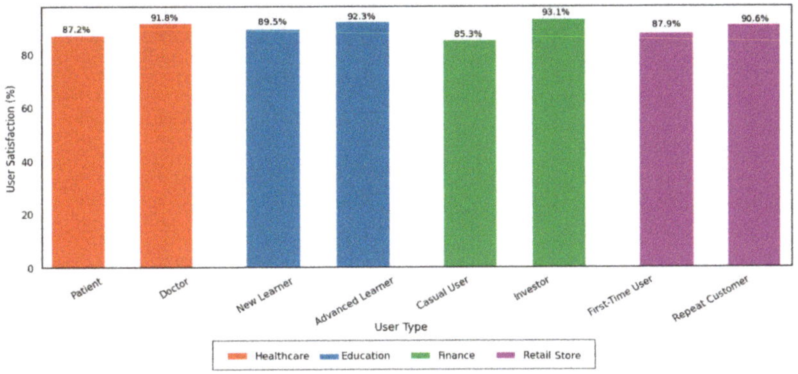

Figure 13. Evaluation of user satisfaction by user type and domain.

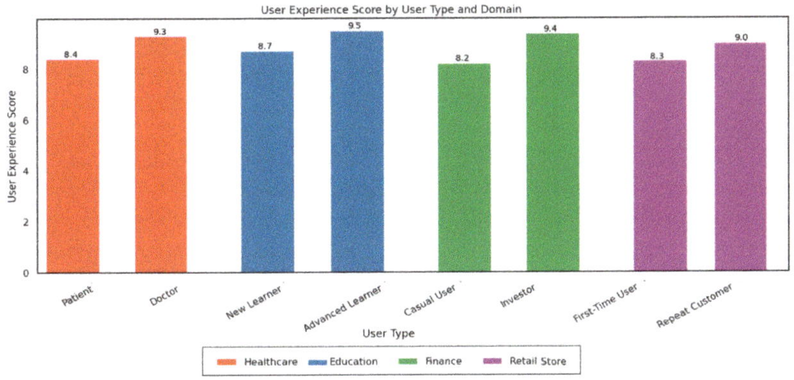

Figure 14. Evaluation of user experience by user type and domain.

- **Comparative Analysis with Other Approaches**

A comparative evaluation was conducted across 100 sessions, assessing the performance of AI-MDD-UX against a rule-based UI adaptation approach [20], a static UI design approach (Bootstrap) [6], and a GAN-based UI adaptation approach [14]. The comparison is focused on click-through rate (CTR), conversion rates, session duration, user experience, and user satisfaction, with results presented in Table 8. AI-MDD-UX achieved the highest user satisfaction rate at 91% (user experience score = 9.0/10), compared to 88% (user experience score = 8.8/10) for GAN-based UI adaptation, 79% (user experience score = 7.8/10) for rule-based UI adaptation and 72.5% (user experience score = 7.0/10) for Bootstrap. Engagement scores further demonstrated the AI-MDD-UX's effectiveness, with an average session duration of 5.8 m, outperforming GAN-based UI adaptation (5.5 m) and rule-based UI adaptation (4.6 m). The superior performance of AI-MDD-UX is attributed to its real-time, multi-agent reinforcement learning-driven refinements, which dynamically optimize UI elements based on user interactions, leading to a more personalized and engaging experience.

Table 8. Performance Comparisons of different approaches against various UI instances.

Instance Name	Evaluation Metric	Rule-Based UI Adaptation	Static UI Design (Bootstrap)	GAN Model	Proposed Approach
E-commerce Web	CTR (%)	9.8	8.2	11.7	**12.5**
	Conversation Rate (%)	35.2	29.1	40.5	**42.3**
	Session Duration (m)	4.6	3.9	5.5	**5.8**
	User Experience	7.8	7.0	8.8	**9.0**
	User Satisfaction (%)	79.4	72.5	88.9	**91.2**
Mobile App	CTR (%)	8.7	7.6	10.1	**10.3**
	Conversation Rate (%)	32.6	26.4	37.1	**39.2**
	Session Duration (m)	3.8	3.5	4.7	**4.9**
	User Experience	7.4	6.8	7.9	**8.5**
	User Satisfaction (%)	75.6	69.3	79.8	**88.4**

5.4.6. Discussion

The validation results highlight the AI-MDD-UX's strong performance and adaptability across diverse user groups and platforms. Testing with simulated users of different behaviors confirmed the system's effectiveness in delivering personalized experiences, achieving high engagement across mobile, web, and VR platforms. Performance remained consistent across modalities, demonstrating the system's ability to dynamically adjust UI elements based on user interactions. However, minor usability challenges were observed in scenarios involving less technical users, suggesting potential refinements to further streamline UI complexity and enhance accessibility for all user demographics.

Platform testing confirmed AI-MDD-UX's high accuracy and consistent interaction quality across different environments. Execution speed is compared to desktop systems (1.5 s vs. 1.2 s). This disparity reflects the additional computational hardware integration demands within AI-MDD-UX. While the proposed AI-MDD-UX approach shows promising results in optimizing the dynamic UI Adaptation, there are several limitations that should be acknowledged:

(1) **Scalability for Emerging Platforms:** The current implementation supports UI adaptation across Web (React.js), Mobile (Flutter), and VR interfaces, but extending adaptation to voice-based UIs, wearables, and automotive systems requires platform-specific customization and broader training datasets. Future works will focus on developing platform-agnostic interaction models that unify multimodal inputs (e.g., gesture, voice, and haptic feedback) for AI processing while exploring cross-modal transfer learning to adapt existing interface knowledge across different platforms, such as translating VR interface patterns to voice-controlled environments.

(2) **Computational Efficiency**: The combination of GAN-based UI generation, Multi-Agent Systems (MAS), and Reinforcement Learning (RL) imposes significant computational costs. While these components enhance UI adaptability, achieving real-time performance on large-scale platforms may necessitate high-performance computing resources or cloud-based solutions to efficiently handle the workload. Future enhancements will prioritize architectural optimization, including lightweight GAN variants and distilled RL policies to reduce inference time, combined with a hybrid

cloud-edge processing that strategically distributes computational workloads, maintaining resource-intensive UI generation on cloud servers while preserving real-time adaptation capabilities on end-user devices. Additionally, we will leverage parallel computation, particularly within RL components, to improve throughput and reduce latency, as discussed in [23].

(3) **Latency in Real-Time Adaptation:** Despite AI-MDD-UX's ability to dynamically track and respond to user interactions, latency issues may arise in high-traffic scenarios. The computational demands of KMeans++ clustering, RL-based policy learning, and UI rendering updates contribute to potential delays. Future improvements will integrate intelligent caching mechanisms and edge computing infrastructure to optimize processing time while reducing latency. This will be combined with an asynchronous RL architecture that separates policy updates from real-time interaction handling, enabling continuous model improvement without compromising system responsiveness.

(4) **Interpretability and Explainability Issues**: The black-box nature of GANs and RL-based UI adaptation presents challenges in explainability, making it difficult for UX designers and business stakeholders to fully understand how UI changes are generated. Enhancing transparency through Explainable AI (XAI) techniques could improve trust and provide actionable insights into UI decision-making. Future development will integrate Explainable AI (XAI) tools, particularly SHAP-based visualization tools, to make UI adaptation decisions transparent. We will concurrently assess how these system explanations impact user trust, evaluating statements such as "this interface adjusted based on your frequent interactions with a given feature".

Future enhancements to AI-MDD-UX would benefit from meta-learning techniques to improve UI adaptation for new users and adaptive reinforcement learning strategies to improve decision-making speed.

5.4.7. Practical Implementation Challenges and Ethical Considerations

Although the AI-MDD-UX framework shows potential for improving user engagement, satisfaction, and personalization, its real-world deployment presents practical and ethical hurdles. Overcoming these challenges is critical to maintaining the system's trustworthiness, scalability, and user-centricity.

(1) **Data Privacy and Security**

The framework AI-MDD-UX depends on continuous collection and analysis of user data such as browsing history, behavioral interactions, device context, and feedback, raising concerns about data misuse, unauthorized access, or regulatory violations. To mitigate these risks, future implementations will incorporate privacy-preserving measures, including: (1) end-to-end data-encryption using advanced, lightweight techniques to prevent unauthorized access or leakage during transmission (2) edge-based data processing, where feasible, to handle tasks like interaction tracking, basic UI adaptation, and feedback analysis directly on the user's device. This approach minimizes dependence on centralized servers, reducing risks tied to large-scale data aggregation.

(2) **Scalability and Platform Compatibility**

The farmwork aims to provide dynamic UI/UX personalization across diverse platforms such as web (React.js), mobile (Flutter), and VR. However, extending its functionality to emerging interfaces (e.g., wearables, voice assistants, and automotive systems) introduces challenges like: (1) adaptive UI design strategies, including modular components, reusable themes, and responsive layouts, to ensure consistency, (2) middleware standardization to unify interaction data (e.g., gestures, voice inputs) into a common format for AI processing, enabling seamless cross-platform compatibility.

6. Conclusions

This study explores multi-platform UI adaptation across mobile, e-commerce web, and VR shopping environments, focusing on the user experience enhancement by addressing the challenges of the dynamic UI adaptation problem, which considers the evolving nature of user interactions. To address this challenge, we developed an AI-driven software engineering model that integrates an AI approach with advanced UI generation. The proposed AI-MDD-UX approach is based on KMeans++ for clustering user behaviors, GANs for UI generation, and multi-agent RL for UI optimization. We evaluated the performance of AI-MDD-UX against other approaches, including rule-based UI adaptation, static UI design (Bootstrap), and GAN-based UI adaptation. Extensive testing based on performance metrics such as engagement, conversion, and navigation metrics has demonstrated the effectiveness of our approach in optimizing dynamic UI adaptation. The results show that the dynamically adapted UI using AI-MDD-UX outperformed static interfaces, with significant improvements in conversion rate (+24%) and user engagement (+21%). These enhancements are primarily attributed to real-time personalization driven by behavioral signals such as hesitation and dwell time. Moreover, the AI-MDD-UX framework achieved higher user satisfaction compared to other approaches, with a 2.3% improvement over GAN-based models, 18.6% over Bootstrap-based designs, and 11.8% over rule-based UI adaptation. These findings highlight the framework's effectiveness in context-aware UI adaptation, utilizing model-driven design, a dual feedback loop (both direct and indirect), and reinforcement learning to optimize user experience and performance outcomes.

Future work could improve the explanation of GANs and RL models by exploring the advantages of AI (XAI) techniques. This will provide transparent UI adaptation decisions, helping to justify UI changes while mitigating the black-box nature of deep learning-driven adaptation methods. So, AI-MDD-UX can further improve trust, usability, and interpretability, ensuring a more user-centric and adaptive digital experience.

Author Contributions: Conceptualization, A.A. and A.L.; methodology, A.A.; software, A.L. Writing—original draft preparation, A.L. and A.A.; writing—review and editing, A.A. and A.L.; visualization, A.L.; supervision, A.A. All authors have read and agreed to the published version of the manuscript.

Funding: This research received no external funding.

Data Availability Statement: Data is available on request due to restrictions.

Acknowledgments: This research was supported by the Center for Theoretical Colleges of Qassim University. We thank our colleagues from the marketing department who provided insight and expertise that greatly assisted the research.

Conflicts of Interest: No potential conflicts of interest were reported by the authors.

References

1. Sharma, R.; Srivastva, S.; Fatima, S. E-commerce and digital transformation: Trends, challenges, and implications. *Int. J. Multidiscip. Res. (IJFMR)* **2023**, *5*, 1–9.
2. Nationwide Group. Unveiling the Digital Storefront: How and Why You Should Leverage an E-Commerce-Enabled Website. 2024. Available online: https://www.nationwidegroup.org/unveiling-the-digital-storefront-how-and-why-you-should-leverage-an-e-commerce-enabled-website/ (accessed on 22 March 2025).
3. Zhu, P.; Wang, X.; Sang, Z.; Yuan, A.; Cao, G. Context-aware Heterogeneous Graph Attention Network for User Behavior Prediction in Local Consumer Service Platform. *arXiv* **2021**, arXiv:2106.14652.

4. Sun, Q.; Xue, Y.; Song, Z. Adaptive user interface generation through reinforcement learning: A data-driven approach to personalization and optimization. *arXiv* **2024**, arXiv:2412.16837.
5. Chunchu, A. Adaptive User Interfaces: Enhancing User Experience through Dynamic Interaction. *Int. J. Res. Appl. Sci. Eng. Technol.* **2024**, *12*, 949–956. [CrossRef]
6. Spurlock, J. *Bootstrap: Responsive Web Development*; O'Reilly Media, Inc.: Sebastopol, CA, USA, 2013.
7. Peissner, M.; Edlin-White, R. User control in adaptive user interfaces for accessibility. In Proceedings of the Conference on Human-Computer Interaction (IFIP), Cape Town, South Africa, 2–6 September 2013; pp. 623–640.
8. Zhang, L.; Qu, Q.X.; Chao, W.Y.; Duffy, V.G. Investigating the combination of adaptive UIs and adaptable UIs for improving usability and user performance of complex UIs. *Int. J. Hum.-Comput. Interact.* **2020**, *36*, 82–94. [CrossRef]
9. Abrahão, S.; Insfran, E.; Sluÿters, A.; Vanderdonckt, J. Model-based intelligent user interface adaptation: Challenges and future directions. *Softw. Syst. Model.* **2021**, *20*, 1335–1349. [CrossRef]
10. Jean, G. Dynamic UI/UX Adaptation in Mobile Apps Using Machine Learning for Individualized User Experiences. December 2024. Available online: https://www.researchgate.net/publication/386376034_Dynamic_UIUX_Adaptation_in_Mobile_Apps_Using_Machine_Learning_for_Individualized_User_Experiences (accessed on 22 March 2025).
11. Zosimov, V.V.; Khrystodorov, O.V.; Bulgakova, O.S. Dynamically changing user interfaces: Software solutions based on automatically collected user information. *Program. Comput. Softw.* **2018**, *44*, 492–498. [CrossRef]
12. Mezhoudi, N.; Vanderdonckt, J. Toward a task-driven intelligent GUI adaptation by mixed-initiative. *Int. J. Hum.-Comput. Interact.* **2021**, *37*, 445–458. [CrossRef]
13. Yigitbas, E.; Jovanovikj, I.; Biermeier, K.; Sauer, S.; Engels, G. Integrated model-driven development of self-adaptive user interfaces. *Softw. Syst. Model.* **2020**, *19*, 1057–1081. [CrossRef]
14. Nandoskar, V.; Pandya, R.; Bhangale, D.; Dhruv, A. Automated User Interface Generation using Generative Adversarial Networks. *Int. J. Comput. Appl.* **2021**, *174*, 4–9. [CrossRef]
15. Issam, Z.I.D.I.; Al-Omani, M.; Aldhafeeri, K. A new approach based on the hybridization of simulated annealing algorithm and tabu search to solve the static ambulance routing problem. *Procedia Comput. Sci.* **2019**, *159*, 1216–1228.
16. Ester, M.; Kriegel, H.P.; Sander, J.; Xu, X. A density-based algorithm for discovering clusters in large spatial databases with noise. In Proceedings of the 2nd International Conference on Knowledge Discovery and Data Mining (KDD-96), Portland, Oregon, 2–4 August 1996; pp. 226–231.
17. Lei, Y.; Yu, D.; Bin, Z.; Yang, Y. Interactive K-Means Clustering Method Based on User Behavior for Different Analysis Target in Medicine. *Comput. Math. Methods Med.* **2017**, *1*, 4915828.
18. Müllner, D. Modern hierarchical, agglomerative clustering algorithms. *arXiv* **2011**, arXiv:1109.2378.
19. Liu, Y.; Zhao, M.; Yang, M.; Eswaran, D.; Dhillon, I. Behavior Sequence Transformer for E-commerce Recommendation in Alibaba. In Proceedings of the 27th ACM SIGKDD Conference on Knowledge Discovery and Data Mining (KDD '21), Virtual Event, Singapore, 14–18 August 2021; pp. 2724–2732.
20. Paskalev, P.; Serafimova, I. Rule based framework for intelligent GUI adaptation. In Proceedings of the 12th International Conference on Computer Systems and Technologies (CompSysTech '11), Vienna, Austria, 16–17 June 2011; pp. 101–108.
21. Karchoud, R.; Roose, P.; Dalmau, M.; Illarramendi, A.; Ilarri, S. One app to rule them all: Collaborative injection of situations in an adaptable context-aware application. *J. Ambient. Intell. Humaniz. Comput.* **2019**, *10*, 4679–4692. [CrossRef]
22. Zhou, S.; Zheng, W.; Xu, Y.; Liu, Y. Enhancing user experience in VR environments through AI-driven adaptive UI design. *J. Artif. Intell. Gen. Sci.* **2024**, *6*, 59–82. [CrossRef]
23. Anokhin, I.; Rishav, R.; Riemer, M.; Chung, S.; Rish, I.; Kahou, S.E. Handling Delay in Real-Time Reinforcement Learning. *arXiv* **2025**, arXiv:2503.23478.

future internet

MDPI

Systematic Review

Patient-Oriented Smart Applications to Support the Diagnosis, Rehabilitation, and Care of Patients with Parkinson's: An Umbrella Review

Rute Bastardo [1], João Pavão [2], Ana Isabel Martins [3], Anabela G. Silva [4] and Nelson Pacheco Rocha [3,*]

[1] Research Unit in Design and Communication—UNIDCOM, Science and Technology School, University of Trás-os-Montes and Alto Douro, 5000-801 Vila Real, Portugal
[2] Institute for Systems and Computer Engineering, Technology and Science—INESC-TEC, Science and Technology School, University of Trás-os-Montes and Alto Douro, 5000-801 Vila Real, Portugal
[3] Institute of Electronics and Informatics Engineering of Aveiro—IEETA, Department of Medical Sciences, University of Aveiro, 3810-193 Aveiro, Portugal
[4] Center for Health Technology and Services Research—CINTESIS@RISE, School of Health Sciences, University of Aveiro, 3810-193 Aveiro, Portugal
* Correspondence: npr@ua.pt

Abstract: This umbrella review aimed to identify, analyze, and synthesize the results of existing literature reviews related to patient-oriented smart applications to support healthcare provision for patients with Parkinson's. An electronic search was conducted on Scopus, Web of Science, and PubMed, and, after screening using predefined eligibility criteria, 85 reviews were included in the umbrella review. The included studies reported on smart applications integrating wearable devices, smartphones, serious computerized games, and other technologies (e.g., ambient intelligence, computer-based objective assessments, or online platforms) to support the diagnosis and monitoring of patients with Parkinson's, improve physical and cognitive rehabilitation, and support disease management. Numerous smart applications are potentially useful for patients with Parkinson's, although their full clinical potential has not yet been demonstrated. This is because the quality of their clinical assessments, as well as aspects related to their acceptability and compliance with requirements from regulatory bodies, have not yet been adequately studied. Future research requires more aligned methods and procedures for experimental assessments, as well as collaborative efforts to avoid replication and promote advances on the topic.

Keywords: umbrella review; Parkinson's disease; patient-oriented smart applications; Parkinson's symptoms; diagnosis; monitoring; rehabilitation; disease management

1. Introduction

Due to the increasing number and proportion of older adults, neurological disorders are a primary cause of disability globally, with Parkinson's disease emerging as the fastest growing among them [1,2]. Estimates indicate that, by 2040, the number of patients with Parkinson's (PwP) worldwide will range from 12 to 17 million [3]. This increasing prevalence of Parkinson's is associated with a rising burden for patients, families, and society, which demands the optimization of healthcare provision to improve health outcomes and reduce economic costs [2].

Currently, no pharmacological tools are available to modify the progression of Parkinson's disease, and dopamine replacement therapy and levodopa are the gold-standard treatments for alleviating the disease's symptoms [4,5]. Considering this pharmacological limitation, the scientific community is researching new drugs with potential disease-modifying properties to decelerate or halt the disease's progression [4]. Future disease-modifying therapies might emerge from these research efforts, but symptomatic treatment is likely to remain the foundation of Parkinson's disease management for many years to come [4].

Other lines of research seek to optimize the diagnosis of Parkinson's disease and care provision for PwP—specifically, by using digital technologies. In this respect, digital technologies can help clinicians to improve diagnosis (e.g., with support from medical imaging modalities [6]), particularly by employing machine learning and deep learning models [7–11] or to facilitate the screening of large populations to identify individuals requiring additional clinical evaluations. Moreover, there is an active research community developing patient-oriented smart applications to support the diagnosis, rehabilitation, and care of PwP in their home environments to increase their comfort and quality of life [4].

This umbrella review, carried out using systematic methods [12], aimed to identify, analyze, and synthesize existing literature reviews related to patient-oriented smart applications to support healthcare provision for PwP. To the best of the authors' knowledge, this is the first tertiary study on the topic and might guide researchers in developing future patient-oriented smart applications and give patients and practitioners a better understanding of the relevant clinical benefits of these applications.

2. Materials and Methods

This umbrella review was registered in the International Prospective Register of Systematic Reviews (PROSPERO) on 4 April 2025 (Registration CRD420251019601), and its planning and conduction were supported by the Joanna Briggs Institute (JBI) guidelines [13]. The report followed the Preferred Reporting Items for Systematic Reviews and Meta-analyses (PRISMA) guidelines [14].

2.1. Objective and Research Questions

This umbrella review aimed to analyze scientific literature reviews focused on the use of patient-oriented smart applications to support the diagnosis, rehabilitation, and care of PwP (as diagnosed using any recognized diagnostic criteria), and to identify patient-relevant clinical benefits. This objective was informed by the following research questions:

- RQ1: What measurement and interaction technologies are being used to develop patient-oriented smart applications to support healthcare provision for PwP?
- RQ2: What types of patient-oriented smart applications are being proposed?
- RQ3: What is the effectiveness of the proposed smart applications?
- RQ4: What limitations and open issues of current research were identified by the existing reviews?

RQ1 and RQ2 aimed to provide a comprehensive overview of current research interests as well as the types of smart technologies and applications being used, while RQ3 aimed to identify the clinical implications of the existing evidence. Finally, RQ4 aimed to synthesize the current limitations and future trends in the research on the topic.

2.2. Literature Search

The online databases chosen for the umbrella review were Scopus, Web of Science, and PubMed. These databases were selected due to (i) broad coverage, (ii) content update, (iii) the availability of the full text of the indexed references, (iv) the accuracy of the results obtained by automatic searches, and (v) the versatility of the mechanisms used to export the results of the automatic searches.

The search query comprised three major components: (i) Parkinson's disease, (ii) smart application, and (iii) review. For each component, relevant terms were identified:

- Parkinson's disease: Parkinson, neurodegenerative disorder, neurological disorder.

- Smart applications: smart, remote, computerized, ehealth, digital, mobile, sensor, biosensor, wearable, artificial intelligence, machine learning, deep learning, information technologies, and communication technologies.
- Review: review, secondary and systematic mapping.

The relevant terms of each component were merged using the Boolean connector OR and the expressions obtained were combined with the Boolean connector AND. Having defined the search query, it was instantiated to the syntax of each database together with the indication that the automatic search should be performed considering the title and abstract of the indexed references. The search query did not include time limits or restrictions in terms of the types of articles (e.g., review). Table 1 presents the instantiation of the general combination of keywords to the selected databases.

Table 1. Instantiation of the general combination of keywords to Scopus, Web of Science, and PubMed.

Database	Query
Scopus	TITLE-ABS ((Parkinson OR neurodegenerative OR neurological) AND (smart OR remote OR computerized OR ehealth OR digital OR mobile OR sensor OR biosensor OR wearable OR "artificial intelligence" OR "machine learning" OR "deep learning" OR ((technology OR technologies) AND (information OR communication))) AND (review OR secondary OR "systematic mapping"))
Web of Science	TS = (Parkinson OR neurodegenerative OR neurological) AND (smart OR remote OR computerized OR ehealth OR digital OR Mobile OR sensor OR biosensor OR wearable OR "artificial intelligence" OR "machine learning" OR "deep learning" OR ((technology OR technologies) AND (information OR communication))) AND TS = (review OR secondary OR "systematic mapping")
PubMed	(Parkinson [Title/Abstract] OR neurodegenerative [Title/Abstract] OR neurological [Title/Abstact]) AND (smart [Title/Abstract] OR remote [Title/Abstract] OR computerized [Title/Abstract] OR ehealth [Title/Abstract] OR digital [Title/Abstract] OR mobile [Title/Abstract] OR sensor [Title/Abstract] OR biosensor [Title/Abstract] OR wearable [Title/Abstract] OR "artificial intelligence" [Title/Abstract] OR "machine learning" [Title/Abstract] OR "deep learning" [Title/Abstract] OR ((technology [Title/Abstract] OR technologies [Title/Abstract]) AND (information [Title/Abstract] OR communication [Title/Abstract])) AND (review [Title/Abstract] OR secondary [Title/Abstract] OR "systematic mapping" [Title/Abstract]))

2.3. Inclusion and Exclusion Criteria

Studies were included in the umbrella review if they met the eligibility criteria presented in Table 2.

Although there are guidelines on the different forms of literature reviews (e.g., systematic reviews or scoping reviews) and how they should be conducted and reported, inconsistencies in concepts and methodological procedures are often identified. For instance, concepts such as reviews, systematic reviews, scoping reviews, comprehensive reviews, integrative reviews, or narrative reviews are sometimes used indiscriminately, and, in terms of reporting, several non-conformities may not allow results to be reproduced. Thus, based on questions 1 and 3 of the first version of the A MeaSurement Tool to Assess systematic Reviews (AMSTAR) checklist [15], the IC2 criterion was introduced. The remaining criteria were derived from the objective of this umbrella review.

Table 2. Eligibility criteria.

Inclusion Criteria	Exclusion Criteria
IC1: Reviews related to patient-oriented smart applications to support the diagnosis, rehabilitation, and care of PwP published in peer-reviewed journals. IC2: Reviews with a well-documented literature search strategy, allowing for its replication.	EC1: References without authors or abstract. EC2: Reviews focusing on smart applications oriented towards formal and informal caregivers. EC3: Reviews published in conference proceedings or as book chapters. EC4: Reviews that, although including studies targeting PwP, targeted other health conditions in 70% of their primary studies. EC5: Reviews that, although considered patient-oriented smart applications, were focused on smart applications oriented towards formal and informal caregivers in more than 70% of their primary studies. EC6: Reviews published in languages other than English. EC7: Articles whose full text was not available.

2.4. Identification Process

After the automatic search in the three online databases, all the references retrieved were imported into a Microsoft Excel spreadsheet. Then, the identification process included four steps. Duplicate articles and articles without authors or abstracts were excluded during the first step. In turn, during the second step, articles were excluded based on the analysis of their titles and abstracts. In the third step, the full texts of the articles not excluded in the first two steps were analyzed to verify their conformity with the eligibility criteria. Finally, the fourth step included a backward search (i.e., the references of the articles included were analyzed to identify additional potentially relevant studies).

In all four steps, all the articles were independently analyzed by at least two authors.

2.5. Quality Assessment

The AMSTAR 2 [16] was used to assess the methodological quality of the studies included in the umbrella review. Each study was randomly assigned to two authors who performed their assessment independently. Disagreements were resolved by consensus.

2.6. Data Extraction

Customized Microsoft Excel forms were used for data extraction, which were piloted using three studies. These forms were developed to extract all relevant information about the included reviews to assess their quality and answer the research questions of the umbrella review.

Considering the quality assessment, authors and publication dates were extracted together with data to answer the sixteen questions on the AMSTAR 2 checklist. Moreover, the following data were extracted to answer RQ1 to RQ3: (i) research objectives; (ii) primary studies included; (iii) experimental designs of the primary studies; (iv) measurement and interaction technologies; (v) types of patient-oriented smart applications; (vi) interventions and measured outcomes; (vii) gold-standard instruments used as comparators; (viii) body location of the wearable devices; and (ix) effectiveness of the proposed applications. Finally, to answer RQ4, key paragraphs from the discussion and conclusions of each review were extracted.

The data extraction of each article was manually completed by one author and checked by a second author.

2.7. Data Synthesis

The different measurement and interaction technologies described in the studies included were identified and classified according to four classes: (i) wearable devices; (ii) smartphones; (iii) serious computerized games; and (iv) other technologies. Within these categories, the subgroup of studies that applied machine learning and deep learning was also identified.

In terms of application areas, the smart applications analyzed by the studies were classified according to their purpose (i.e., patients' diagnosis and monitoring based on motor and non-motor clinical variables of Parkinson's disease), rehabilitation (i.e., physical and cognitive rehabilitation), and disease management.

For each area of application, the following information was synthesized: research objectives; experimental designs of the respective primary studies, including type of study, settings, number and characteristics of the participants, and clinical instruments used as comparators; technological characteristics of smart applications; and assessment results. Moreover, concerning diagnosis and monitoring based on motor and non-motor clinical variables, the clinical variables, respective measurement devices, and body locations of wearable devices were also synthetized.

Finally, a thematic analysis was made of important points of the discussions and conclusions presented by the reviews to identify current challenges and open issues on the topic. Therefore, after the extraction of key paragraphs from the discussion and conclusions of each review, two authors independently created a primary list of categories. This categorization was refined by further analyses, and the final list of categories was discussed as a group.

3. Results

3.1. Identification of Studies

The search on the selected databases was performed in February 2025, and 6856 references were retrieved. Figure 1 presents the PRISMAS flowchart [14] of the identification process.

During the title and abstract screening, 3729 references were excluded, according to the inclusion and exclusion criteria. The exclusion reasons include: (i) references not related to patient-oriented smart applications to support the diagnosis, rehabilitation and care of PwP (e.g., [17,18]); (ii) references targeting other pathologies than Parkinson's (e.g., [19,20]); (iii) references focusing on clinician-oriented smart applications (e.g., [21,22]); (iv) references not reporting reviews (e.g., [23,24]); and (v) references reporting reviews not supported by reproducible methods (e.g., [25,26]). During the full-text analysis, 71 references were excluded because they report on (i) reviews that, although including studies targeting PwP, targeted other health conditions in more than 70% of their primary studies, (e.g., [27–29]), (ii) clinician-oriented smart applications (e.g., [30–33]), and (iii) reviews that were not reproducible (e.g., [34–36]). Therefore, after the identification process, 85 studies [37–121] were included in the review.

3.2. Characteristics of Included Studies

According to Figure 2, the studies were published between 2014 (i.e., one study [37]) and the first months of 2025 (i.e., four studies [118–121]), and more than 75% of the studies were published since 2019.

Sixty-two reviews [38–44,46–56,58–60,62,64–70,73,74,76,77,81–83,87–92,94–97,99–105, 107,109,111,114–116,118–121] specifically targeted PwP. Another 14 reviews [37,45,61,71,72, 75,79,80,84,89,93,108,110,112] included primary studies targeting PwP and patients with other neurological disorders. Finally, nine reviews [57,63,78,85,86,98,106,113,117] included primary studies with patients with neurological disorders, including PwP, and other health conditions (e.g., musculoskeletal disorders [86,113] or healthy older adults [106]). By identifying all the references of the primary studies of the reviews and eliminating duplicates and studies that did not include PwP, a total of 1867 different primary studies were identified. From those studies, 14 [122–135] were analyzed in at least 10% of the reviews.

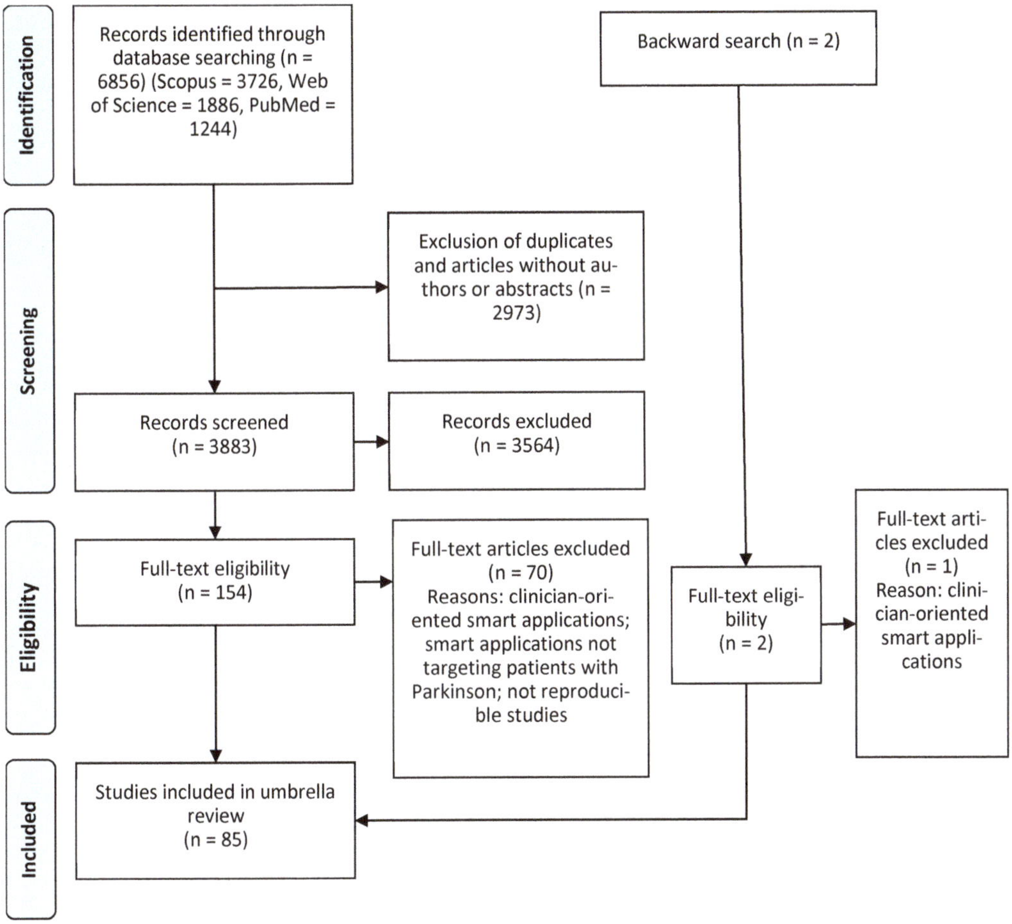

Figure 1. PRISMA flowchart.

Overall, only eight included studies [65,71,77,78,80,99,106,115] performed meta-analyses. All the other studies only conducted a qualitative synthesis, either because this was their objective or because they were forced to exclude meta-analyses due to the small number or heterogeneity of the primary studies available.

3.3. Quality Assessment

Figure 3 presents the results of the quality assessment of the reviews included according to AMSTAR 2. The AMSTAR items with the highest scores were Q1 (i.e., research questions and inclusion criteria) and Q16 (i.e., report of potential sources of conflict of interest, including funding sources), while the items with the lowest scores were related to the report on the sources of funding for the studies included in the review (Q10), the list of excluded studies and exclusion justifications (Q7), satisfactory technique for assessing the risk of bias (Q9), duplicate data extraction (Q6), and duplicate study selection (Q5). Moreover, items Q2 (review methods established a priori), Q3 (explanation of the selection of the studies' designs) and Q4 (comprehensive literature search strategy) have a high percentage of partial yes when compared with yes, due to the absence of an explicit statement that the respective review protocol was registered (Q2), an explanation of the type of primary studies' design included in the review (Q3), and complementary search strategies such as backward search in addition to the databases' queries (Q4).

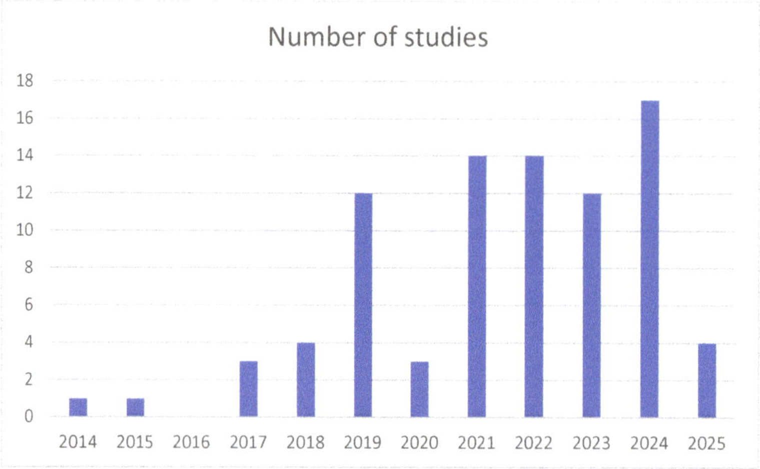

Figure 2. Number of studies published by year.

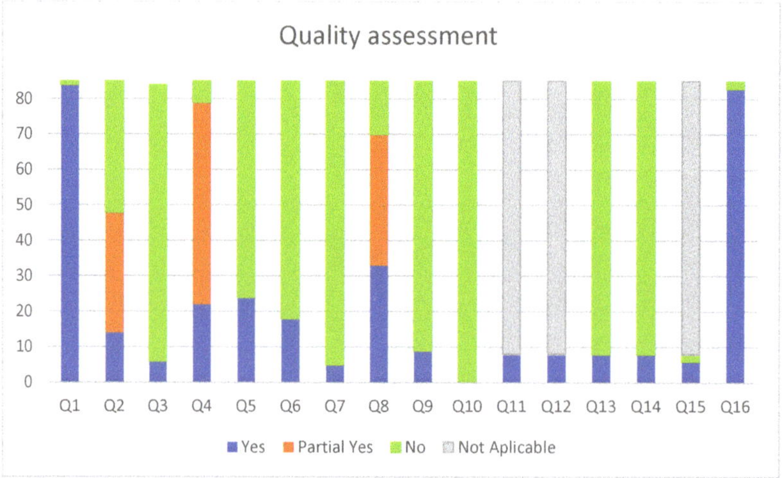

Figure 3. The quality of the reviews included according to the appraisal items of AMSTAR 2 [16]: Q1—research questions and inclusion criteria; Q2—review methods established a priori; Q3—explanation of the selection of the studies' designs; Q4—comprehensive literature search strategy; Q5—study selection performed in duplicate; Q6—data selection performed in duplicate; Q7—list of excluded studies and exclusions justified; Q8—description of the included studies in adequate detail; Q9—satisfactory technique for assessing the risk of bias; Q10—report on the sources of funding for the studies included in the review; Q11—use of appropriate methods for statistical combination of results when a meta-analysis was performed; Q12—assessment of the potential impact of risk of bias when a meta-analysis was performed; Q13—risk of bias accounted for when interpreting or discussing the results of the review; Q14—a satisfactory explanation for any heterogeneity observed in the results of the review; Q15—quantitative synthesis performed and publication bias discussed when a meta-analysis was conducted; Q16—report of potential sources of conflict of interest, including funding sources.

3.4. Measurement and Interaction Technologies

Figure 4 presents the types of measurement and interaction technologies reported in the reviews included. A significant number of them (i.e., 65 reviews) analyzed the application of wearable technologies, including biomechanical wearable devices (e.g., inertial measurement units, accelerometers, gyroscopes, magnetometers, force-sensitive insoles, or custom-made gloves) and physiological wearable devices (e.g., electromyography, electroencephalography, electrocardiography, actigraphy and polysomnography devices, or devices to measure galvanic skin response). In turn, 26 reviews analyzed the use of smartphones, and 12 others analyzed the use of serious computerized games. Finally, other technologies, such as ambient intelligence (e.g., force platforms or motion capture systems), computer-based objective assessments, or online platforms, were identified in 16 studies. Moreover, 18 studies reported the simultaneous use of different types of measurement and interaction technologies. For instance, Bansal et al. [97], Taniguchi et al. [101], Jeyasingh-Jacob et al. [110], and Silva-Batista et al. [114] reported the use of wearable devices and other technologies, while Tuena et al. [98] reported the integration of serious computerized games and wearable devices.

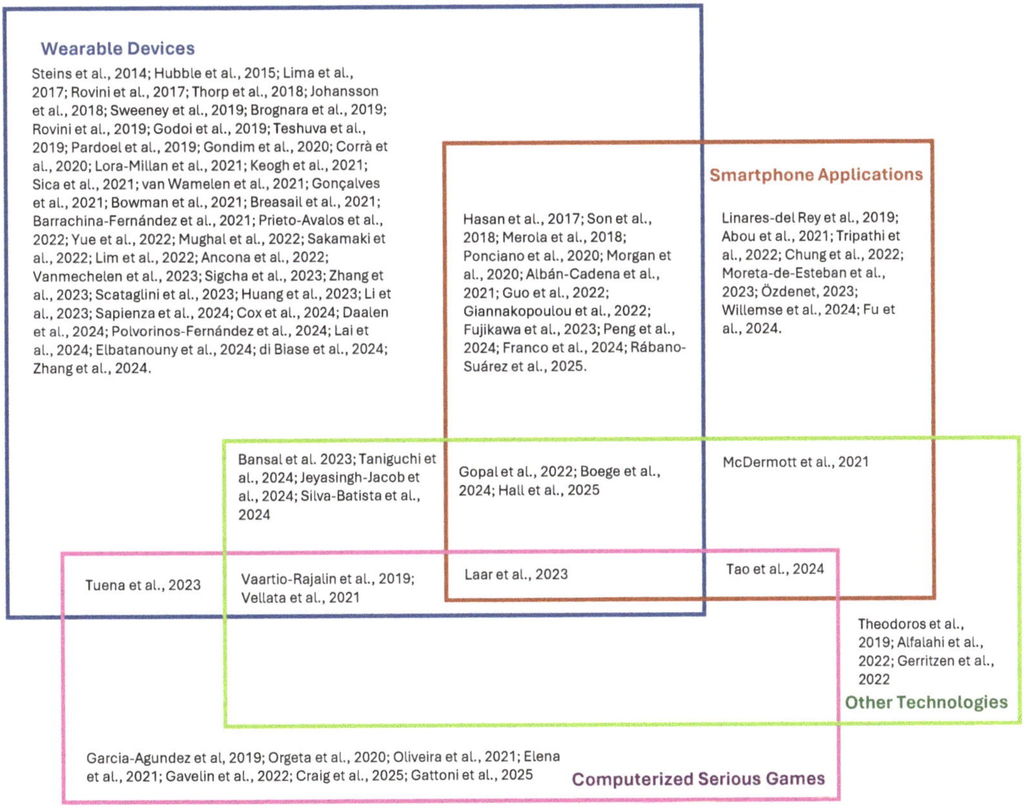

Figure 4. Measurement and interaction technologies reported by the reviews included: Steins et al., 2014 [37]; Hubble et al., 2015 [38]; Silva de Lima et al., 2017 [39]; Rovini et al., 2017 [40]; Hasan et al., 2017 [41]; Son et al., 2018 [42]; Thorp et al., 2018 [43]; Merola et al., 2018 [44]; Johansson et al., 2018 [45]; Sweeney et al., 2019 [46]; Brognara et al., 2019 [47]; Rovini et al., 2019 [48]; Linares-Del Rey et al., 2019 [49]; Godoi et al., 2019 [50]; Vaartio-Rajalin et al., 2019 [51]; Garcia-Agundez et al., 2019 [52];

Theodoros et al., 2019 [53]; Teshuva et al., 2019 [54]; Pardoel et al., 2019 [55]; Orgeta et al., 2020 [56]; Ponciano et al., 2020 [57]; de Oliveira Gondim et al., 2020 [58]; Morgan et al., 2020 [59]; Corrà et al., 2020 [60]; Lora-Millan et al., 2021 [61]; de Oliveira et al., 2021 [62]; Keogh et al., 2021 [63]; Sica et al., 2021 [64]; Elena et al., 2021 [65]; van Wamelen et al., 2021 [66]; Vellata et al., 2021 [67]; Abou et al., 2021 [68]; McDermott et al., 2021 [69]; Gonçalves et al., 2021 [70]; Bowman et al., 2021 [71]; Ó Breasail et al., 2021 [72]; Albán-Cadena et al., 2021 [73]; Barrachina-Fernández et al., 2021 [74]; Prieto-Avalos et al., 2022 [75]; Tripathi et al., 2022 [76]; Gavelin et al., 2022 [77]; Alfalahi et al., 2022 [78]; Guo et al., 2022 [79]; Yue et al., 2022 [80]; Giannakopoulou et al., 2022 [81]; Gerritzen et al., 2022 [82]; Mughal et al., 2022 [83]; Gopal et al., 2022 [84]; Sakamaki et al., 2022 [85]; Lim et al., 2022 [86]; Chung et al., 2022 [87]; Ancona et al., 2022 [88]; Vanmechelen et al., 2023 [89]; Sigcha et al., 2023 [90]; Zhang et al., 2023 [91]; Fujikawa et al., 2023 [92]; Scataglini et al., 2023 [93]; Moreta-de-Esteban et al., 2023 [94]; Huang et al., 2023 [95]; Laar et al., 2023 [96]; Bansal et al., 2023 [97]; Tuena et al., 2023 [98]; Özdenet, 2023 [99]; Li et al., 2023 [100]; Taniguchi et al., 2024 [101]; Sapienza et al., 2024 [102]; Cox et al., 2024 [103]; Janssen Daalen et al., 2024 [104]; Polvorinos-Fernández et al., 2024 [105]; Lai et al., 2024 [106]; Elbatanouny et al., 2024 [107]; Peng et al., 2024 [108]; di Biase et al., 2024 [109]; Jeyasingh-Jacob et al., 2024 [110]; Boege et al., 2024 [111]; Willemse et al., 2024 [112]; Fu et al., 2024 [113]; Silva-Batista et al., 2024 [114]; Zhang et al., 2024 [115]; Franco et al., 2024 [116]; Tao et al., 2024 [117]; Craig et al., 2025 [118]; Hall et al., 2025 [119]; Rábano-Suárez et al., 2025 [120]; and Gattoni et al., 2025 [121].

Among all the studies included, five [81,86,90,109,116] specifically expressed in their titles the application of machine learning or deep learning techniques, and other reviews (i.e., [37,40,43,55,64,74,78,91,92]) reported the use of machine and deep learning techniques. Several techniques were identified, including adaptative boosting, decision tree, extra gradient booster, gradient booster, hidden Markov model, linear discriminant analysis, linear regression, logistic regression, naïve Bayes, random forest, support vector machines, artificial neural networks, convolutional neural networks, deep autoencoder, multilayer perceptron, neural networks, recurrent neural networks, and temporal convolutional networks. However, in general, according to the reviews, the primary studies did not provide sufficient details on implementation of the machine learning and deep learning models and their validation.

These machine learning and deep learning models were mainly developed to process spatiotemporal gait parameters to assess movement impairments (e.g., [55,74,81,86,116]), analyze diverse kinematic data collected by a broad range of wearable devices to assess functional activities such as sitting and standing (e.g., [37]), or process kinematic and keystroke timing data to discriminate voluntary and involuntary movements such as the movements resulting from tremors (e.g., [40,43,64,78,92]). Specifically, Pardoel et al. [55] performed a comparative analysis of the performance of different techniques when applied for the freezing of gait detection using wearable devices.

3.5. Application Areas

Most reviews reported smart applications to support the diagnosis and monitoring of PwP, considering both motor and non-motor clinical variables. Moreover, the studies reported smart applications to improve the rehabilitation of PwP, in terms of physical and cognitive rehabilitation, as well as smart applications to help patients improve their disease management.

Therefore, five major application areas were identified (Figure 5): (i) motor, 57 studies, and (ii) non-motor diagnosis and monitoring, 15 studies; (iii) physical rehabilitation, 18 studies; (iv) cognitive rehabilitation, 8 studies; and (v) disease management, 9 studies. By comparing the application areas with measurement and interaction technologies, it is possible to conclude that wearable devices and smart applications are prominent in patients' diagnosis and monitoring based on motor and non-motor clinical variables, physical rehabilitation, and disease management; meanwhile, for cognitive rehabilitation, most studies applied computerized serious games. In turn, computerized serious games are not relevant to the other application areas, and technologies such as online platforms and videoconferencing assume relevance in terms of disease management.

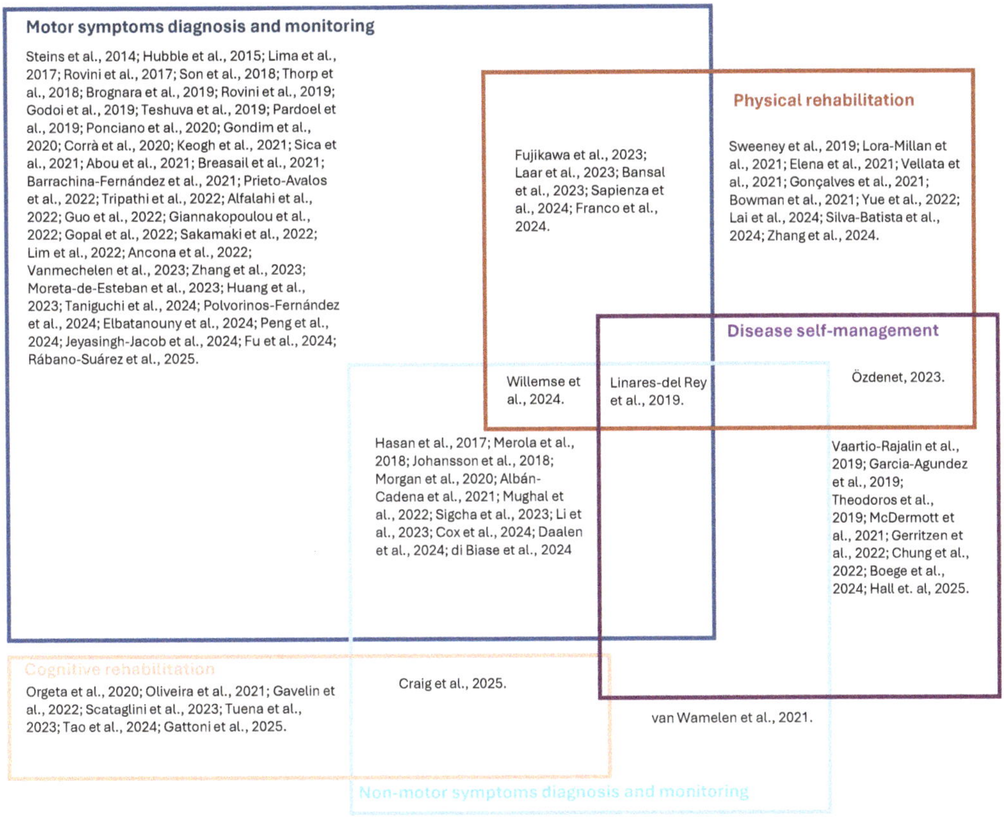

Figure 5. Application areas. Steins et al., 2014 [37]; Hubble et al., 2015 [38]; Silva de Lima et al., 2017 [39]; Rovini et al., 2017 [40]; Hasan et al., 2017 [41]; Son et al., 2018 [42]; Thorp et al., 2018 [43]; Merola et al., 2018 [44]; Johansson et al., 2018 [45]; Sweeney et al., 2019 [46]; Brognara et al., 2019 [47]; Rovini et al., 2019 [48]; Linares-Del Rey et al., 2019 [49]; Godoi et al., 2019 [50]; Vaartio-Rajalin et al., 2019 [51]; Garcia-Agundez et al., 2019 [52]; Theodoros et al., 2019 [53]; Teshuva et al., 2019 [54]; Pardoel et al., 2019 [55]; Orgeta et al., 2020 [56]; Ponciano et al., 2020 [57]; de Oliveira Gondim et al., 2020 [58]; Morgan et al., 2020 [59]; Corrà et al., 2020 [60]; Lora-Millan et al., 2021 [61]; de Oliveira et al., 2021 [62]; Keogh et al., 2021 [63]; Sica et al., 2021 [64]; Elena et al., 2021 [65]; van Wamelen et al., 2021 [66]; Vellata et al., 2021 [67]; Abou et al., 2021 [68]; McDermott et al., 2021 [69]; Gonçalves et al., 2021 [70]; Bowman et al., 2021 [71]; Ó Breasail et al., 2021 [72]; Albán-Cadena et al., 2021 [73]; Barrachina-Fernández et al., 2021 [74]; Prieto-Avalos et al., 2022 [75]; Tripathi et al., 2022 [76]; Gavelin et al., 2022 [77]; Alfalahi et al., 2022 [78]; Guo et al., 2022 [79]; Yue et al., 2022 [80]; Giannakopoulou et al., 2022 [81]; Gerritzen et al., 2022 [82]; Mughal et al., 2022 [83]; Gopal et al., 2022 [84]; Sakamaki et al., 2022 [85]; Lim et al., 2022 [86]; Chung et al., 2022 [87]; Ancona et al., 2022 [88]; Vanmechelen et al., 2023 [89]; Sigcha et al., 2023 [90]; Zhang et al., 2023 [91]; Fujikawa et al., 2023 [92]; Scataglini et al., 2023 [93]; Moreta-de-Esteban et al., 2023 [94]; Huang et al., 2023 [95]; Laar et al., 2023 [96]; Bansal et al., 2023 [97]; Tuena et al., 2023 [98]; Özdenet, 2023 [99]; Li et al., 2023 [100]; Taniguchi et al.,

2024 [101]; Sapienza et al., 2024 [102]; Cox et al., 2024 [103]; Janssen Daalen et al., 2024 [104]; Polvorinos-Fernández et al., 2024 [105]; Lai et al., 2024 [106]; Elbatanouny et al., 2024 [107]; Peng et al., 2024 [108]; di Biase et al., 2024 [109]; Jeyasingh-Jacob et al., 2024 [110]; Boege et al., 2024 [111]; Willemse et al., 2024 [112]; Fu et al., 2024 [113]; Silva-Batista et al., 2024 [114]; Zhang et al., 2024 [115]; Franco et al., 2024 [116]; Tao et al., 2024 [117]; Craig et al., 2025 [118]; Hall et al., 2025 [119]; Rábano-Suárez et al., 2025 [120]; and Gattoni et al., 2025 [121].

3.5.1. Patients' Diagnosis and Monitoring Based on Motor Clinical Variables

The reviews addressing Parkinson's motor clinical variables reported the use of the following types of measurement devices (Figure 6): (i) wearable devices that collect biomechanical data, 44 studies; (ii) wearable devices that collect physiological data, 18 studies; (iii) smartphones, 16 studies; and (iv) other technologies such as computer-based objective measures or online platforms, 12 studies.

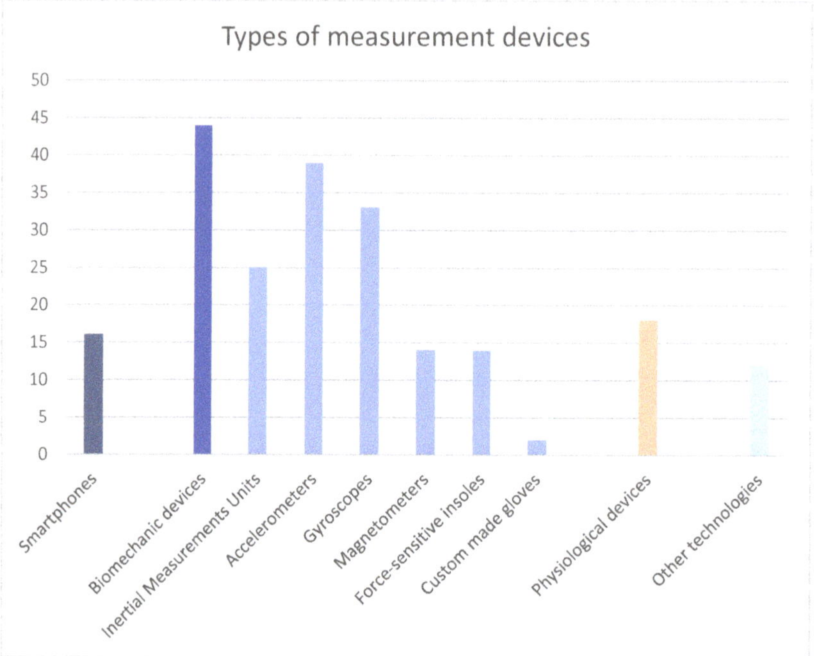

Figure 6. Distribution of the types of measurement devices related to motor clinical variables reported in the studies.

Although some primary studies used single wearable devices, in most cases the strategy was to use a combination of multiple devices. In this respect, the number of wearable devices used by the proposed smart applications to measure motor clinical variables varied considerably. For instance, Brognara et al. [47] reported that the number of wearable devices combined varied from two to eight, Giannakopoulou et al. [81] found that the same number varied from two to fourteen, and Polvorinos-Fernández et al. [105] concluded that 23% of the studies they analyzed used more than ten wearable devices.

Some of the reviews did not report on the body location of the wearable devices. Considering the available information, Figure 7 presents the distribution of studies according to the body location of the wearable devices being reported.

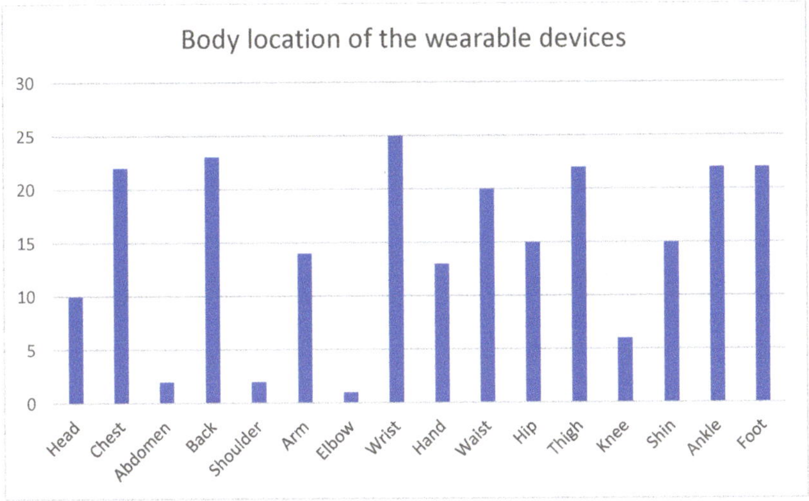

Figure 7. Distribution of the number of studies according to the body location of the wearable devices being reported.

Table 3 identifies the Parkinson's motor clinical variables considered as well as the measurement devices used and respective studies, while Figure 8 presents the frequency of these variables among the reviews included.

Table 3. Motor clinical variables and measurement devices considered in the reviews included.

Motor Clinical Variables	Wearable Devices	Smartphones	Other Technologies
Freezing of gait	[39,40,43–45,48,55,58,59,64,73,79,81,83,85,90,91,95–97,103,107,116,120]	[44,59,68,73,79,81,112,116,120]	[97,110] [(a)]
Other gait disturbances	[37,38,40–42,44,45,47,50,57–59,63,64,73–75,79,81,83,85,86,88,90,96,100,102,105,109,110,116,120]	[41,42,44,49,57,59,68,73,79,81,112,116,120]	[110] [(a)]
Tremor	[40–45,73,75,79,81,83,85,89,90,92,100,103,105,108,109]	[41,42,44,49,73,76,79,81,92,94,108,112]	
Balance	[38,40,42,44,45,58,73,75,79,81,85,88,105,109,120]	[42,44,68,73,76,79,81,112,120]	
Bradykinesia	[41–44,49,54,64,73,75,79,83,88–90,100,103]	[41,42,44]	
Dyskinesia	[40–43,45,48,73,75,79,85,88,89,100,103,109]	[41,42,73,79]	
Functional activities	[37,40,42,59,60,72,73]	[42,73,112,120]	
Physical activity	[42,45,59,63,64,72,73,96,100]	[42,73,112]	
Falls	[39,45,48,59,64,73,75,85,95]	[42,68,73]	
Fine motor impairments	[73,79,81,84,105,109]	[73,79,81,112,113]	[78,84] [(b,c)]
Rigidity	[40,41,44,54,83,109]	[41,44]	
Swallowing disorders	[104,109]	[104]	
Hypokinesia	[43,73]	[73]	
Impaired bed mobility	[101]		[101] [(d)]

[(a)] Motion capture systems; [(b)] computer-based objective assessments based on special-purpose keyboards; [(c)] online platforms; [(d)] ambient intelligence.

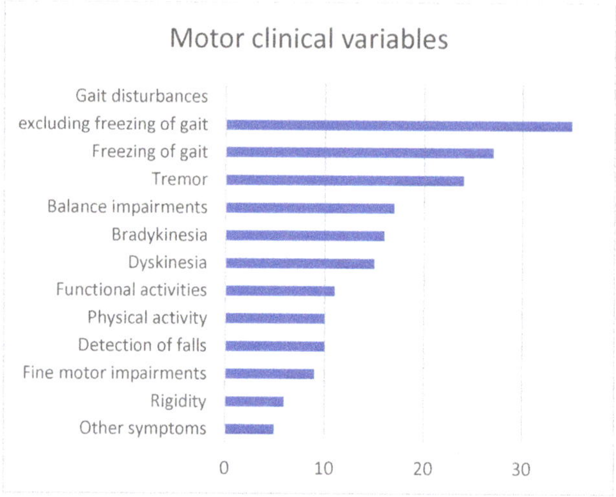

Figure 8. Frequency of the motor clinical variables addressed in the reviews.

The proposed smart applications related to the measurement of motor clinical variables had two main purposes: (i) to discriminate PwP; or (ii) to track the disease progression for those patients already diagnosed with Parkinson's disease. In terms of the assessment of the smart applications, for the first purpose, the objective was to verify the smart applications' capacity to discriminate PwP from healthy controls or patients with other chronic conditions (i.e., accuracy studies), while, for the second purpose, the objective was to verify the smart applications' clinical validity by comparing their outcomes to the outcomes of gold-standard clinical instruments, such as objective clinical assessments or standardized clinical assessment scales. Among the reviews, the Unified Parkinson's disease rating scale (UPDRS) and the Modified Unified Parkinson's Disease Rating Scale (MDS-UPDRS) emerged as the most frequently used standardized clinical assessment scales for comparators: the first scale was reported by 30 reviews [37,38,40–45,47–50,54,59,60,64,73,76,81,84,88–90,92,94,97,101,105,116,120], and the second scale was reported by 18 reviews [38,40–42,54,59,68,76,81,84,88–90,94,105,113,116,120]. The Hoehn and Yahr scale was the third most used clinical assessment scale and was reported by five reviews [38,42,47,89,101].

The experimental designs of the primary studies were quite heterogeneous in terms of methods (e.g., case studies, cross-sectional, case–control, or randomized and non-randomized studies) and in terms of the number and characteristics of the participants (e.g., disease severity or duration). Specifically, the number of participants seems to be a methodological drawback of most primary studies, since it was relatively small in most studies. For instance, Hubble et al. [38] reported that, among the primary studies they reviewed, a significant percentage included fewer than 15 participants in the intervention or control groups.

Eight studies [59,84,85,88,90,100,102,103] only reviewed primary studies that assessed smart applications in home settings, simulated home environments, or free-living environments. Considering the remaining reviews targeting Parkinson's motor clinical variables, all of them included a small percentage of studies performing long-term data collection in home settings or free-living environments. Therefore, most of the primary studies only collected data in research labs or clinical settings over short periods.

When collecting data in clinical settings, the patients perform constrained tasks, such as standardized tests (e.g., Timed UP and Go Test for assessing gait, the Romberg test for assessing balance, or tasks from the MDS-UPDRS for assessing other motor clinical variables), but, in general, the tasks patients performed were poorly specified by the primary studies. Measurement of motor clinical variables in home settings or free-living settings requires that the devices can measure motor parameters during unconstrained daily activities, which introduces added levels of complexity that need further research.

Most of the studies reviewed gave a narrative synthesis of the primary studies, and a few of them presented quantitative results. Table 4 presents the assessment results of smart applications considering the information provided by the reviews.

Table 4. Assessment results of the proposed smart applications based on the quantitative results presented by the reviews.

Motor Clinical Variables	Assessment Results
Freezing of gait	Johansson et al. [45] showed good agreement between wearable and video-based ratings regarding the number of freezing episodes and the percentage of time with freezing of gait, while other studies [39,68,79,90,103] concluded that wearables and smartphone devices might be used to detect freezing of gait. However, inconsistencies in the assessment processes still hinder the use of these applications in clinical practice [91].
Gait disturbances excluding freezing of gait	Some gait outcomes, such as jerk, harmonic stability or oscillation range, were able to differentiate PwP and healthy controls [38,40,90]. Additionally, good correlations were found between gait outcomes measured by wearable devices and clinical scales such as UPDRS, MDP-UPDRS or Hoehn and Yahr [81]. However, significant differences in gait spatiotemporal parameters were found between the primary studies, with high variability in terms of parameters and placement of the wearable devices [47]. This led to contradictory findings, which seem to indicate that some parameters are more consistent than others [38].
Tremor	Some reviews [40,43,89,94] found good results for correlation with gold-standard clinical tremor measurements (e.g., UPDRS or MDS-UPDRS), while other studies [49,73,76,81,90,94,103,109] demonstrated good accuracy in identifying tremor presence and severity and in differentiating PwP with tremor from healthy individuals.
Balance	Considering diverse parameters (e.g., mean acceleration, jerk, or sway distance), Abou et al. [68] found significant correlations between smartphone balance assessments and balance clinical tests, Barrachina-Fernández et al. [73] demonstrated that wearable devices can detect fluctuations of the center of gravity, and Johansson et al. [38] and di Biase et al. [109] found smart applications with good accuracy when discriminating PwP from healthy controls. However, it seems that the measured parameters have different consistency levels [38].
Bradykinesia	Some applications can accurately measure bradykinesia [41,54,73,88–90,103] since their outcomes present good correlations with clinical assessment scales [41,54,73,88,89,103] or the severity of bradykinesia assessed by experienced clinicians [90]. Moreover, Son et al. [42] and Thorp et al. [43] reported smart applications with good accuracy in detecting bradykinesia versus no bradykinesia.
Dyskinesia	Some measurements provided by the proposed smart applications might support discrimination between dyskinetic and non-dyskinetic events [43,45,89,103] compared to clinical ratings [43,45,89,103] such as UPDRS or an experienced observer [43]. However, considering the significant differences in accuracy between the proposed smart applications, Thorp et al. [43] suggested that the location of the wearable devices influences the precision of the measurements, making the detection of dyskinesia more accurate when the wearable devices are not attached to body parts involved in the tasks performed by patients. Moreover, Rovini et al. [40] and Thorp et al. [43] concluded that detecting dyskinesia during daily activities is particularly complex due to the difficulty in distinguishing voluntary movements from dyskinetic movements.

Table 4. *Cont.*

Motor Clinical Variables	Assessment Results
Functional activities	According to two studies [37,42], the proposed applications are not only capable of assessing the type, quantity and quality measures, but also of differentiating the Parkinson's disease-specific mobility patterns of healthy controls and classifying disease severity and progression within PwP.
Physical activity	There is some evidence of good correlations between physical activity measurements and clinical instruments [42,59] and capacity to discriminate sedentary or upright and walking behavior [45].
Detection of falls	Johansson et al. [45] reported that the quantification of missteps and risk of falls was shown to discriminate non-fallers and fallers, Abou et al. [68] suggested the discriminative ability of smartphone applications to predict future falls, and Sica et al. [64] reported the ability to predict future falls, even in patients without a prior history of falling.
Fine motor impairments	Keystroke dynamics presents good accuracy, sensitivity and specificity to discriminate and classify PwP [78]. Moreover, Tripathi et al. [76] and Gopal et al. [84] concluded that statistically significant correlations with traditional clinic metrics were most frequently reported, and Polvorinos-Fernández et al. [105] highlighted finger tapping as a particularly strong indicator for diagnosing and monitoring disease progression.
Rigidity	Teshuva et al. [54] suggested that some of the proposed applications have the capacity to discriminate between patients with rigidity and healthy controls but concluded that the accuracy of the applications measuring rigidity was not very high.
Other motor clinical variables (i.e., swallowing disorders, hypokinesia, and impaired bed mobility)	Due to the reduced number of primary studies addressing swallowing disorders, hypokinesia, and impaired bed mobility, it was not possible to systematize evidence about the effectiveness of the respective applications.

In terms of measurement of fine motor impairments, the meta-analysis performed by Alfalahi et al. [78] analyzed 29 independent models supported by machine learning or deep learning techniques to process keystroke timing data, concluding that keystroke dynamics presents good accuracy, sensitivity, and specificity to discriminate and classify PwP. The classification methods based on keystroke presented a pooled AUC of 0.85 (95% confidence interval (CI) 0.83–0.88; I2 = 94.04%) and a pooled accuracy of 0.82 (95% CI 0.78–0.86; I2 = 71.55%). These referred methods presented a pooled sensitivity of 0.86 (95% CI 0.82–0.90, I2 = 79.49%) and a pooled specificity of 0.83 (95% CI 0.79–0.87, I2 = 83.45%). These results were corroborated by other studies [76,84,105] that reported statistically significant correlations between finger tapping and traditional clinical metrics used to diagnose and monitor disease progression.

Moreover, good correlations between gold-standard clinical evaluations were found for the use of smart applications to assess the freezing of gait [45], other gait outcomes [81], tremor [40,43,89,94], balance [68], bradykinesia [41,54,73,88,89,103], dyskinesia [43,45,89,103], functional activities [37,42], and physical activity [42,59]. Some smart applications present good accuracy at detecting the freezing of gait [39,68,79,90,103], differentiating PwP and healthy controls based on other gait disturbances [38,40,90], identifying tremor presence and severity and differentiating PwP with tremor from healthy individuals [49,73,76,81,90,94,103,109], discriminating PwP from healthy controls based on balance measurements [38,109], detecting bradykinesia versus no bradykinesia [42,43], differentiating Parkinson's disease-specific patterns from those of healthy controls and classifying disease severity and progression within PwP patients based on the measurement of functional activities [37,42], discriminating between sedentary or upright and walking behavior [45], discriminating between non-fallers and fallers [68] or predicting future falls [64], and successfully distinguishing patients from healthy controls based on the measurement of rigidity [54].

However, inconsistencies in the assessment processes [91], significant differences in gait spatiotemporal parameters due to high heterogeneity in terms of measures and placement of the wearable devices [43,47], contradictory findings (since some of the outcomes may be more robust than others [38]), or difficulties in discriminating between voluntary and non-voluntary movements still hinder the use of smart applications to measure motor clinical variables of Parkinson's disease [40,43].

3.5.2. Patients' Diagnosis and Monitoring Based on Non-Motor Clinical Variables

Considering non-motor clinical variables, this umbrella review identified wearable devices [41,44,45,59,66,73,83,90,100,103,104,109], smartphones [41,44,49,73,104,112], and serious computerized games [118] as being used to measure diverse non-motor clinical variables (Table 5). Only the assessments of sleep disturbances, cognition, constipation, depression, voice and speech quality, and urinary dysfunction were reported by more than one review. In terms of sensing devices, diverse types were identified, including blood pressure, electromyography, electroencephalography, polysomnography, and abdominal electrodermal activity devices, smart vests, or ingestible smart pills.

Table 5. Non-motor clinical variables.

Non-Motor Clinical Variables	Wearable Devices	Smartphones	Serious Computerized Games
Affective state		[49]	
Anxiety	[104]		
Autonomic function	[44]	[44]	
Brain dysfunction	[90]		
Cognition	[41,66,90,104]	[41,104,112]	[118]
Constipation	[66,83,104]		
Depression	[66,83,104]		
Emotional dysfunction	[90]		
Fatigue	[104]		
Hallucinations and delusions	[104]		
Heart rate variability	[104]		
Impulse control disorder	[66]		
Skin impedance	[104]		
Orthostatic hypotension	[104]		
Pain	[104]		
Sleep disturbances	[44,45,59,66,73,83,103,104]	[44,73]	
Voice and speech quality	[41,90,109]	[41]	
Urinary dysfunction	[66,104]		

The studies related to non-motor clinical variables reported assessments both in clinical settings and home environments and highly heterogeneous validation methods, which limit generalization of the results. Moreover, some of the non-motor clinical variables (i.e., affective state, anxiety, brain dysfunction, constipation, depression, emotional dysfunction, fatigue, hallucinations and delusions, impulse control disorders, pain, voice and speech quality, and urinary dysfunction) were addressed in a limited number of primary studies, mainly proof-of-concept studies; therefore, there is not sufficient evidence to draw conclusions.

Regarding the remaining non-motor measurements, analyzing correlations against gold-standard clinical instruments, wide differences between devices were found for heart variability [104], significant modest correlations were found for sleep disturbance [59], and considerable correspondence was found for orthostatic hypotension [104]. In turn, significant differences were observed between PwP and healthy controls for autonomic function [44]. Finally, concerning cognition, contradictory findings were reported: (i) Daalen et al. [104] found sensitivity to progression towards mild cognitive impairment and dementia; (ii) van Wamelen et al. [66] suggested that gait parameters measured by wearable inertial devices could be useful as an indirect indicator of cognitive decline; and (iii) Craig et al. [118] concluded there are mixed results on how digitalized tests compare with paper/pencil versions.

3.5.3. Physical Rehabilitation

Eighteen studies [46,49,61,65,67,70,71,80,92,96,97,99,102,106,112,114–116], including six meta-analyses [65,71,80,99,106,115], addressed the physical rehabilitation of PwP.

One study, a meta-analysis [65], compared exergaming rehabilitation and conventional physiotherapy in relation to the quality of life of PwP and concluded that the analyzed randomized control trials, most of them performed in clinical settings or research labs, showed statistically significant improvements in quality of life and function when performing daily activities in the exergame rehabilitation experimental groups compared to conventional physiotherapy control groups.

The other studies addressed the rehabilitation of gait disorders (i.e., 11 studies [46,49, 70,71,97,99,102,106,112,115,116]), balance (i.e., 6 studies [67,70,71,80,96,114]), and tremor disorders (i.e., 2 studies [61,92]).

Wearable devices [46,71,97,102,106,115,116], smartphones [49,99,112], and online platforms [67] were used for the rehabilitation of gait disorders, some of them at home. Turning to the results of the meta-analyses of randomized control trials, Lai et al. [106] concluded that the intervention group showed a significant improvement in gait speed, and stride length was also shown to improve, but heterogeneity across studies was moderate. Zhang et al. [115] concluded that wearable cueing devices did not demonstrate efficacy on gait functions, Özdenet found smart application-based rehabilitation not superior to standard rehabilitation [99], and Bowman et al. [71] concluded that it was not possible to reach firm conclusions about the effectiveness of wearable devices' biofeedback rehabilitation due to the current quality of the literature.

In terms of balance rehabilitation, the reviews reported on wearable devices [70,71,80], exergames [96], and online platforms [67,114] in clinical settings, research labs, or at home. The meta-analysis performed by [71] included a small number of randomized control trials to draw significant conclusions, while the meta-analysis by Yue et al. [80], with the data of 14 primary studies, indicated that wearable-based exercise had a significant short-term effect on balance, although improvements did not reach statistical significance in other outcomes such as functional gait capacity or risk of falls.

Finally, two studies [61,92] reported the use of wearable devices to support the rehabilitation of tremor disorders. However, the primary studies related to tremor rehabilitation were limited and mainly cross-sectional and proof-of-concept studies.

3.5.4. Cognitive Rehabilitation

Cognitive rehabilitation was addressed by eight studies [56,62,77,93,98,117,118,121]: (i) five studies [56,62,77,118,121], including a meta-analysis [77], analyzed cognitive training applications based on serious computerized games applied to different settings, including home, community, long-term care, and rehabilitation settings; (ii) one study [98] analyzed smart applications integrating virtual-reality-based computerized cognitive training and wearable devices; (iii) and two studies [93,117] analyzed music interventions in institutional settings [93] supported by wearable devices (e.g., headphones) and mobile applications, and dance interventions [117], including home interventions, supported by mobile and online smart applications.

Due to the reduced number of primary studies and the heterogeneity of the respective designs, it was not possible to draw conclusions about the effectiveness of virtual-reality-based computerized cognitive training, music, and dance interventions. In terms of the impact of computerized cognitive training on cognitive functions (e.g., global cognition, attention, memory, or processing speed), Orgeta et al. [56] found no clear evidence that cognitive training improves global cognition at the end of treatment, although the cognitive training groups present improvements in attention and verbal memory compared to control groups, and Gavelin et al. [77] concluded that the overall cognitive effect of serious computerized games was small and statistically significant with moderate heterogeneity.

3.5.5. Disease Management

In total, ten studies [49,51–53,69,82,87,99,111,119], including a meta-analysis [99], addressed disease management smart applications: (i) two studies [53,111] reported the use of wearable devices, smartphones, and online platforms (e.g., synchronous technologies in the form of videoconference) to support the management of communication and swallowing disorders; (ii) four studies [51,52,69,99] addressed smart applications based on the use of wearable devices [51,69,99] or exergames [52] to promote physical activity; (iii) one study [82] addressed peer support based on social networks; (iv) and three studies [49,87,119] addressed smart mobile applications to empower PwP in terms of disease management (e.g., applications providing information on the disease and assistance in treatment).

Theodoros et al. [53] and Boege et al. [111] concluded that using smart applications to support the management of communication and swallowing disorders showed generally high user acceptance but were not able to determine the effectiveness of the applications due to the respective study designs. Similarly, the number of primary studies and their quality do not support conclusions about peer support and disease management applications. Finally, in terms of physical activity, due to the heterogeneity of the primary studies, the meta-analysis reported by Özdenet [99] only included two primary studies.

3.6. Challenges and Open Issues

The challenges and open issues were identified using a thematic analysis of the discussions and conclusions presented by the reviews. As shown in Figure 9, four major categories cut across all areas of application identified by this umbrella review: (i) experimental design, (ii) clinical viability, (iii) acceptability, and (iv) regulatory conformity. The subcategories of these major categories are presented in Table 6.

One important aspect emerging from the thematic analysis is that, in terms of primary studies, extensive engineering-oriented research has been undertaken, but clinical research significantly lags behind its engineering counterpart. This is evident in the experimental design of the primary studies, since 61 reviews reported several inconsistencies in terms of experimental designs of the primary studies.

As a result, it is not possible to confirm the clinical viability of the proposed smart applications due to a broad range of issues pointed out by the 81 reviews.

Moreover, 36 reviews reported challenges related to the acceptability of smart applications in terms of adherence, user experience, and comfort; improving this requires the proposed smart applications, to be minimally invasive, as well as training and technical assistance, and 15 reviews pointed out unsolved regulatory aspects regarding conformity requirements, security and data protection, risk analysis, and standardized assessment criteria.

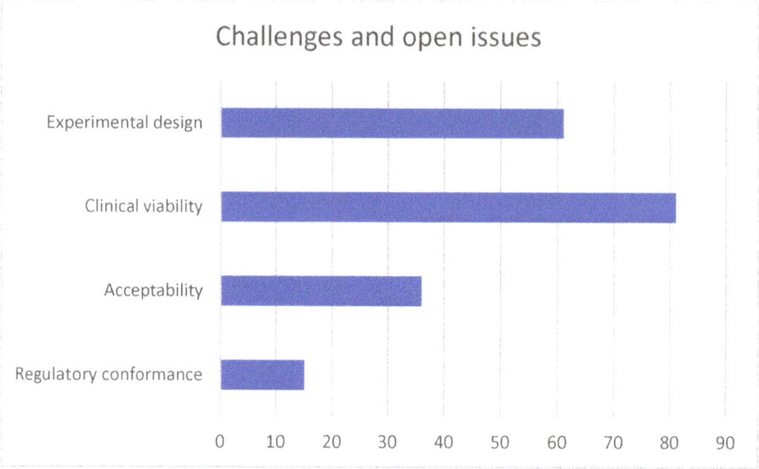

Figure 9. Challenges and open issues.

Table 6. Challenges and open issues: categories and sub-categories.

Category	Sub-Category
Experimental design	Heterogeneity of methods. Heterogeneity of outcomes. Heterogeneity of participants. Representativeness of the participants. Number of participants. Variability and specification of scripted tasks. Specification of the placement of the wearable devices. Correlations with clinical assessment instruments. Learning effects. Confounding variables.
	Reproducibility.
Clinical viability	Clinical utility. Limited research evidence on the efficiency and efficacy of smart applications with contradictory findings, namely when used in home environments. Translation to clinical practice. Long-term impact on health outcomes. Sociocultural factors affecting adherence to new clinical models. Cost effectiveness. Integration within clinical workflows. Efficient clinical management tools. Unscripted and unconstrained daily tasks and activities. Variability of metrics. Usefulness of some metrics. Non-motor clinical variables. Variability of the number and placement of the wearable devices. Transparency of the outcomes. Passive monitoring versus active monitoring. Closed-loop applications. Interoperability.

Table 6. *Cont.*

Category	Sub-Category
Acceptability	Adherence. User experience. Comfort. Invasiveness. Stakeholders' perspectives. Technical and training assistance.
Regulatory conformaty	Conformance requirements. Security and data protection. Risk analysis. Standardized assessment criteria.

4. Discussion

4.1. Measurement and Interaction Technologies

Concerning the measurement and interaction technologies being used (i.e., the first research question), most studies reported the use of biomechanical wearable devices (e.g., inertial measurement units, accelerometers, gyroscopes, magnetometers, force-sensitive insoles, or custom-made gloves), or inertial sensors embedded in the current smartphones. The studies also reported the use of other wearable devices to measure physiological parameters (e.g., electrical activity of brain, heart, or muscles; reactivity cycles; sleep parameters; or galvanic skin response). In addition, serious computerized games, including virtual-reality-based serious games, were used for rehabilitation, and other technologies, such as ambient intelligence (e.g., force platforms or motion capture systems), computer-based objective assessments, or online platforms, were also identified. Notably, ambient intelligence devices assume little importance, although they can be useful in passively monitoring the patients [136].

Additionally, some studies used a broad range of machine and deep learning techniques, either alone or in combination, to process monitoring data for improving diagnostic accuracy.

4.2. Types of Smart Applications

Considering the types of patient-oriented smart applications being proposed for improving healthcare provision for PwP (i.e., the second research question), about 70% of studies investigated the use of smart applications to support continuous patient monitoring, mainly using wearable devices and smartphones. This is an important aspect, considering that continuous monitoring of patients allows for the tracking of disease progression and treatment optimization.

Since wearable devices and smartphones can measure movement parameters, most studies focus on the measurement of motor clinical variables (e.g., gait disturbances, including the freezing of gait, balance, tremor, bradykinesia, dyskinesia, hypokinesia, fine motor impairments, rigidity, impaired bed mobility, functional activities, physical activity, falls, and swallowing disorders). In turn, although non-motor clinical variables (e.g., cognitive impairment or pain) also impact the quality of life of the patients, only a small number of studies targeted non-motor clinical variables.

Symptom changes must be accompanied by responses to changes, including rehabilitation (i.e., physical and cognitive rehabilitation) and disease management (e.g., healthy behaviors) to maintain a healthy life for as long as possible. In this respect, 21% of studies analyzed smart applications to support physical rehabilitation, 7% analyzed smart applications focused on cognitive rehabilitation, and 9% reviewed the use of smart applications to support disease management, including the empowerment of the patients, peer support, and the adoption of healthy behaviors (e.g., physical activity).

4.3. Effectiveness of the Proposed Smart Applications

In terms of the effectiveness of the proposed smart applications (i.e., the third research question), one of the drawbacks of current research on the topic is the heterogeneity of primary studies in terms of objectives, methods, procedures, outcomes, placement of the wearable devices, or characteristics and number of participants, which limits quantitative comparisons. This justifies the small number of meta-analyses included in this umbrella review and the fact that most studies give qualitative synthesis of primary studies instead of quantitative synthesis, which prevents drawing robust conclusions about the effectiveness of the proposed smart applications. Therefore, the analysis of the effectiveness of the proposed smart applications was based on the results expressed by the reviews, and no standardized qualitative assessments were performed.

Starting by analyzing the meta-analyses, in terms of the measurement of motor clinical variables, Alfalahi et al. [78] concluded that the analysis of keystroke dynamics presents good accuracy, sensitivity and specificity to discriminate PwP from healthy controls, although the quality of evidence was moderate based on the application of the Quality Assessment of Diagnostic Test Accuracy [137] to the included primary studies. Concerning physical rehabilitation, the meta-analyses concluded: (i) when compared to conventional physiotherapy, exergaming rehabilitation has a positive, statistically significant impact on patients' quality of life and their daily activities [65]; (ii) wearable devices are associated with a significant improvement in gait speed and stride length, although heterogeneity across studies was moderate [106]; (iii) physical rehabilitation monitored using wearable devices had a significant impact on balance, but there is no evidence of improved postural control during daily activities [80]; (iv) smart application-based rehabilitation was not superior to standard rehabilitation [99]; and (v) firm conclusions about the effectiveness of biofeedback rehabilitation based on wearable devices could not be drawn due to the current quality of the literature [71]. Regarding cognitive rehabilitation, Orgeta et al. [56] concluded that there was no clear evidence of the impact of cognitive training on global cognition, and Gavelin et al. [77] concluded that the overall cognitive effect of serious computerized games was small and statistically significant with moderate heterogeneity. Finally, considering disease management, Özdenet [99] could not analyze the effectiveness of physical activities due to the heterogeneity of the primary studies, which meant that the meta-analysis only included two primary studies.

Considering the reviews that present quantitative results, for gait disturbances, significant differences in gait spatiotemporal parameters were found between the primary studies, which present high variability in terms of the measurement and placement of the wearables [47]. However, according to several studies [39,45,68,79,90,103], wearable devices and smartphones might be used to detect the freezing of gait or to differentiate between PwP and healthy controls [38,40,90], while gait outcomes measured using wearable devices present good correlations with clinical scales such as UPDRS, MDP-UPDRS, and Hoehn and Yahr [81].

In terms of other motor clinical variables, good results for correlation with gold-standard clinical instruments were found for tremor [40,43,89,94], balance [68], bradykinesia [41,54,73,88–90,103], and dyskinesia [43,45,89,103], while other studies found good accuracy in the identification of tremor disorders and their severity [49,73,76,81,90,94,103,109], balance impairment [38,109], bradykinesia [42,43], or dyskinesia [43,45,89,103]. Additionally, Steins et al. [37] and Sou et al. [42] reported applications that are able to discriminate the Parkinson's disease-specific mobility patterns of healthy controls based on the measurement of functional activity, Johansson et al. [45] reported the capacity to discriminate between sedentary or upright and walking behavior, and the quantification of missteps and risk of falls was shown to discriminate between non-fallers and fallers, Abou et al. [68] suggested the discriminative ability of smartphone applications to predict future falls, and Sica et al. [64] reported that the processing of measures from wearable devices was able to predict future falls even in patients with no previous fall history.

Concerning non-motor clinical variables, considerable correspondence with gold-standard instruments was found for orthostatic hypotension [104], and significant modest correlations were identified for sleep disturbance [59], but wide differences between devices were identified for heart variability [104].

Furthermore, concerning cognition, smart applications are sensitive to progression towards mild cognitive impairment and dementia [104], and gait parameters measured by wearable inertial devices could be useful as an indirect indicator of cognitive decline [68]. However, there are mixed results for how digitalized tests compare with paper/pencil versions [118].

Finally, for disease management, Theodoros et al. [53] and Boege et al. [111] concluded that smart applications used to support the management of communication and swallowing disorders showed generally high user acceptance, despite not being able to determine the effectiveness of the applications, due to the study designs. Similarly, the number of primary studies and their quality did not allow for conclusions to be drawn about the peer support and disease management applications.

4.4. Limitations and Open Issues in Current Research

Concerning the fourth research question (what limitations and open issues of current research were identified by existing reviews?), the studies identified several limitations and open issues that make it difficult to translate the proposed smart applications into clinical practice. Most of these limitations and open issues are not related to the limitations of existing technologies, since they primarily result from the lack of adequate study designs tailored to provide robust evidence about the improvement of smart applications in health outcomes, which was also pointed out by other tertiary studies related to remote monitoring [138,139]. In fact, the full clinical potential of the proposed applications is not yet demonstrated; this is due to different reasons, including the quality of the clinical assessments of those applications, and aspects related to their acceptability and compliance with regulatory bodies that have not yet been adequately studied.

4.4.1. Experimental Design

Different methods, including case studies, cross-sectional, case–control or randomized and non-randomized longitudinal studies, were employed to assess the proposed smart applications. Moreover, the primary studies had specific objectives or constraints [116], which resulted in significant variability in the outcomes measured and results reported.

As for the number of participants, most primary studies were performed with relatively small sample sizes, so they are not representative of the entire population of PwP, although they involve patients in different stages of the disease. To obtain accurate results, the applications must be validated by involving a large number of PwP [40]. Moreover, for studies on diagnostic accuracy, experimental studies should include patients in the early stage of the disease [40].

Usually, during tests to diagnose Parkinson's disease, the patient performs specific tasks while clinicians assign scores as defined by clinical instruments such as UPDRS or MDS-UPDRS. Similarly, measurements of motor clinical variables based on the reported smart applications follow this paradigm, and the patients should perform predefined tasks such as resting tasks, postural tasks, or a 10 m walkway [40]. However, in the studies, tasks vary greatly, and, in some cases, they are not detailed. Additionally, some studies explicitly specify the placement of the wearable devices, while others merely refer to general anatomical regions [105].

Unfortunately, poorly detailed specifications are not exclusive to applications targeting motor clinical variables, as the same occurs in other types of applications, such as non-specification of the level of cognitive training intensity performed by participants during the validation of the smart applications to support cognitive rehabilitation [102].

All these inconsistencies hinder comparison between studies.

Although a significant number of studies identified correlations between experimental measurements and clinical scales, such as UPDRS or MDS-UPDRS, it is possible that these scales do not accurately reflect patients' free-living state [54]. Therefore, if we consider the hypothesis that new measurement instruments may be more sensitive than traditional clinical scales, their correlation with these clinical measures may not be desirable [54,120]. In turn, outcomes presenting weak or no correlations with clinical measures are unlikely to be adopted [120]. Consequently, their ability to measure changes that are meaningful to PwP should be analyzed as complementary rather than equivalent to existing gold-standard scales [120].

Other methodological issues identified were the inadequate assessment of learning effects [84] and inappropriate detail regarding the influence of confounding variables (e.g., psychological state, fatigue severity, discomfort, medication adherence, and timing) [38]. The paucity of studies conducting repeated trials of the assessment limits identification of any learning effects with the use of a new device [84]. In turn, if confounding variables are not properly considered, manifestations of uncontrolled variables might be reported as significant changes [38].

Therefore, research on the topic would benefit from more focused efforts with aligned methods, namely longitudinal randomized controlled trials to assess long-term outcomes, protocols, data collection instruments, and their specific positioning on the body, collected parameters, tasks performed by the patients, data analysis procedures, and reports of the results [43].

These more focused efforts should be supported in existing guidelines (e.g., determining the sample size for research [140], diagnostic accuracy studies [137], or intervention studies [141]) and are fundamental to allowing the reproducibility of experiments and fostering confirmation and comparison of the results and, consequently, their generalization, which is fundamental to guaranteeing the clinical viability of the proposed smart applications [39].

4.4.2. Clinical Viability

The results of this umbrella review show that numerous smart applications specifically designed for PwP are potentially useful. However, independently of the type of applications (i.e., measurement of motor and non-motor clinical variables, physical and cognitive rehabilitation, and disease management), scientific evidence of their effectiveness is scarce and of poor quality and presents contradictory findings, calling for high-quality experimental assessments with rigorous methods and procedures and an adequate number of participants and disease profiles. Moreover, evidence of the clinical utility of smart applications, defined as improved health outcomes or clinical decisions following their use [102], is scarce. Therefore, to facilitate the translation of research into clinical practice, future research should include longitudinal randomized studies to evaluate the long-term impact on health outcomes such as quality of life, self-efficacy, or treatment adherence, and to allow for comprehensive assessments of sociocultural factors that influence the adherence of patients, relatives, and clinicians to new clinical models and how these clinical models might be effectively translated to clinical practice [48]. Additionally, cost-effectiveness studies evaluating smart applications to support PwP are required [41,53,103,107].

This means that the real-world benefits of these smart applications in terms of improving clinical outcomes are not yet known. However, this knowledge is essential to translating the research findings into improved healthcare provision [109].

To guarantee the usefulness of smart applications, clinicians should be able to interact with them. Therefore, efficient clinical management platforms are required to provide efficient user-friendly interfaces for clinicians [40] and to guarantee the integration of patients' clinical information—specifically, in terms of existing electronic health record systems used to support clinical workflows [109].

The effective use of smart applications favors the participation of the patients and respective informal caregivers and their cooperation with clinicians [48]. Although the validity and usefulness of many smart applications were assessed in controlled settings (e.g., clinic or laboratory settings), models of their remote use in real free-living environments such as home settings need to be established to advance patient care [42,54,81,86,90,95].

Real-life validation of the practical effectiveness of smart applications is essential to guaranteeing their translation into clinical practice. However, real-life validation requires longer data collection periods and may require more complex outcome measures [109].

The basis of most research related to measuring motor clinical variables assumes that the patients perform predefined scripted tasks. In this respect, passive monitoring based on wearable devices or ambient intelligence devices may provide similar metrics with a reduced participant time burden [84,105]. This is particularly important for patients suffering from apathy or depression, who might not have the motivation to complete the scripted tasks [41]. However, both passive monitoring and the use of ambient intelligence devices (encountered extremely rarely in the literature [81]) need further research [105].

Moreover, in terms of the measurement of motor clinical variables, additional research should validate their application during unscripted and unconstrained daily tasks and activities rather than in scripted tasks (i.e., to support home-based measurements). This requires high-quality algorithms to discriminate between voluntary and involuntary movements [88].

Another critical limitation is the high variability in the metrics used to quantify motor symptoms [61]. Considering the broad range of parameters being measured, their clinical utility should be assessed in future studies. Moreover, considering the low importance ascribed to the measurement of non-motor clinical variables when compared with motor clinical variables, additional research is required on this topic [50,59].

Some of the studies analyzed the use of machine learning and deep learning techniques. However, they found that most of the primary studies did not provide sufficient details on the implementation of machine learning and deep learning models, training settings, and the validation procedure, which limits the validity of the results and reduces transparency and reproducibility [90]. Consequently, the application of these techniques is difficult to interpret, and, therefore, they are not easily adopted by clinicians [90].

Moreover, the translation to clinical practice in the home environment requires the optimization of the number and optimal body placement of the monitoring devices.

The selection of an ideal device system for the quantification of motor clinical variables is complex. Different individual devices or combinations of devices were proposed for measuring motor clinical variables. Their selection was mainly based on the type of symptoms being considered, and no single device was able to capture all the motor clinical variables related to PwP [43]. Similarly, multiple body parts were identified for the placement of the wearable devices, since different symptoms are detected by different device placements. Therefore, currently, there are no consensual guidelines regarding the number of monitoring devices and where they should be placed in the body [47]. Thus, accuracy, redundancy of different wearable devices, and body placement deserve further investigation [47].

A possible future direction is the integration of data collected by continuous monitoring of smart applications that can deliver treatments [41]. However, this possibility was not reported by the studies included.

Finally, the interoperability of smart applications and respective devices is a key problem requiring high-quality standards to aggregate data from different non-compatible devices [83] and integrate these data in healthcare workflows. According to the reviews included in this umbrella review, the interoperability of smart applications has not been sufficiently studied, despite having a significant impact on their clinical viability.

4.4.3. Acceptability

Acceptability needs particular attention, as the effective use of patient-oriented smart applications depends on a set of characteristics, such as usability, wearability, comfort of use, aesthetics, instructions for use, and support. These aspects might affect patients physically or psychologically but are frequently ignored by researchers [64], despite the existing literature on how to assess them (e.g., [142,143]).

Smart applications to be used by patients should not affect their daily activities negatively, which means the development of obtrusive bulky devices should be avoided since they can be invasive when used in the community [48]. In fact, uncomfortable solutions with negative user experience, together with their costs and skepticism about their effectiveness, are substantial barriers to their adoption [61,107].

Although wearable devices facilitate the capture of relevant motor parameters, to increase their acceptability and reduce their invasiveness, it is important to minimize the number of wearable devices required and place them in a way that does not interfere with daily activities [40].

To increase the acceptability of smart applications, it is imperative to consider the perspectives of PwP and their relatives. Despite these perspectives being critical for operative and effective clinical smart application, in general, they were not considered by the primary studies [48]. Moreover, the perspectives of clinicians and service providers are not duly considered by researchers [53]. Therefore, future studies should consider the involvement of all stakeholders [53,79] and implement user-centered design methods, namely co-design approaches.

Additionally, users should first become familiar with smart applications before using them in daily practice, and clear descriptions of their use should be available [96]. This means preparing structured training packages with adequate documentation. Moreover, to overcome difficulties in daily use, technical support teams should be available to tackle technical issues such as individual calibrations [97] or battery loss [96]. Despite its seemingly simple nature, patients' lack of trust in technological solutions, their geographical dispersion, their living conditions, and the heterogeneity of communication infrastructures can make technical support a highly complex process, which is why it is one of the constraints placed on the use of smart applications.

Although some experimental studies were conducted over several weeks or months, further research is required to determine long-term adherence to smart applications.

4.4.4. Regulatory Conformity

An important issue is approval of the smart application by regulatory authorities (e.g., the European Medicines Agency or the Federal Drugs Agency) [59], which might be supported by existing literature (e.g., [144–147]).

Certification by regulatory bodies not only guarantees the medical-grade accuracy, reliability, and safety of the smart applications [49,75], but it is also important to allow for reimbursement of the costs.

However, this certification is associated with several open issues. First, the developers of smart applications, in general, do not properly consider the conformity requirements needed for certification (e.g., certifiability, safety, security, stability, or trustworthiness). Second, even when smart applications are noninvasive and pose a relatively low safety risk, data protection should be guaranteed [84] (e.g., as defined, for instance, by the Health Insurance Portability Accountability Act [144]), but this was not generally addressed in the primary studies. Third, additional research is required to develop computationally efficient risk assessment models able to provide continuous risk assessments of the smart applications [78]. Finally, the heterogeneity of parameters, measurement protocols, types of devices, and body locations can hinder standardization, although it is expected that obligatory certification by recognized regulatory authorities will require standard criteria for the assessment of clinical applications [100].

4.5. Limitations of the Umbrella Review

When analyzing the results of this review, some limitations inherent to its scope and methodology must be considered. Given the vastness of the topic, it was challenging to define the search strategies, which means that the chosen keywords and the databases that were used, as well as the judgment of the authors when screening the articles, might potentially exclude relevant studies.

The results of this umbrella review should be analyzed with caution considering the methodological issues of the primary studies reported by the reviews included. Moreover, by analyzing the quality assessment performed on the reviews, it is possible to conclude that they present some limitations, specifically in terms of the explicit statement that the respective review protocol was registered before the study was carried out, the explanation of the selection of the designs of the primary studies, comprehensive literature search strategies, duplicated study selection and data extraction, and satisfactory techniques for assessing the risk of bias. Additionally, most of the reviews included in the umbrella review only performed qualitative synthesis, either because this was their objective or because the small number or heterogeneity of the primary studies they reviewed did not allow meta-analyses. Therefore, an important limitation of this umbrella review was the impossibility of presenting more consolidated results on the effectiveness of smart applications to support healthcare provision for PwP.

5. Conclusions

Based on 85 reviews, analyzing a total of 1867 primary studies, this umbrella review systematized the efforts of a very active research community. Through extensive engineering-oriented research, a considerable number of smart applications have been developed. However, it is not possible to reach conclusions about the clinical viability of most of them due to limited research evidence, with contradictory findings about their clinical effectiveness, inconsistencies in their assessments, and unresolved issues related to their acceptability and regulatory conformity. Therefore, future research on the topic requires more focused efforts with aligned methods, protocols, data collection, data analysis, and reporting of the results, allowing for reproducibility of the experiments and the confirmation and comparison of the results.

An important research gap is the translation of patient-oriented applications to clinical practice to support the diagnosis, rehabilitation, and care of PwP. This translation requires the integration of interoperable smart applications with existing electronic health record systems supporting clinical workflows, as well as their real-life validation, which requires longer data collection periods and more complex outcome measures. For their application to home environments, smart applications should be optimized in terms of algorithms able to analyze unscripted and unconstrained daily tasks and activities, rather than scripted tasks, measurements of non-motor clinical variables, metrics to quantify motor symptoms, and number and body placement of the monitoring devices.

Finally, since there are so many separate groups working across the world on similar smart applications to support healthcare provision for PwP, collaborative efforts are needed to avoid the replication of developments already achieved and instead promote advances on the topic.

Author Contributions: Conceptualization, N.P.R.; methodology, A.I.M., A.G.S. and N.P.R.; investigation, R.B., J.P., A.I.M., A.G.S. and N.P.R.; writing—original draft preparation, R.B., J.P. and N.P.R.; writing—review and editing, R.B., J.P., A.I.M., A.G.S. and N.P.R. All authors have read and agreed to the published version of the manuscript.

Funding: This research received no external funding.

Data Availability Statement: Data sharing is not applicable.

Conflicts of Interest: The authors declare no conflicts of interest.

References

1. Dorsey, E.R.; Sherer, T.; Okun, M.S.; Bloem, B.R. The emerging evidence of the Parkinson pandemic. *J. Park. Dis.* **2018**, *8*, S3–S8. [CrossRef]
2. Chaudhuri, K.R.; Azulay, J.P.; Odin, P.; Lindvall, S.; Domingos, J.; Alobaidi, A.; Kandukuri, P.L.; Chaudhari, V.S.; Parra, J.C.; Yamazaki, T.; et al. Economic burden of Parkinson's disease: A multinational, real-world, cost-of-illness study. *Drugs Real World Outcomes* **2024**, *11*, 1–11. [CrossRef]
3. Dorsey, E.; Bloem, B.R. The Parkinson pandemic—A call to action. *JAMA Neurol.* **2018**, *75*, 9–10. [CrossRef]
4. Stocchi, F.; Bravi, D.; Emmi, A.; Antonini, A. Parkinson disease therapy: Current strategies and future research priorities. *Nat. Rev. Neurol.* **2024**, *20*, 695–707. [CrossRef]
5. Antonini, A.; Moro, E.; Godeiro, C.; Reichmann, H. Medical and surgical management of advanced Parkinson's disease. *Mov. Disord.* **2018**, *33*, 900–908. [CrossRef] [PubMed]
6. Samson, E.; Noseworthy, M.D. A review of diagnostic imaging approaches to assessing Parkinson's disease. *Brain Disord.* **2022**, *6*, 100037. [CrossRef]
7. Wang, J.; Xue, L.; Jiang, J.; Liu, F.; Wu, P.; Lu, J.; Zhang, H.; Bao, W.; Xu, Q.; Ju, Z.; et al. Diagnostic performance of artificial intelligence-assisted PET imaging for Parkinson's disease: A systematic review and meta-analysis. *NPJ Digit. Med.* **2024**, *7*, 17. [CrossRef]
8. Grigas, O.; Maskeliunas, R.; Damaševičius, R. Early detection of dementia using artificial intelligence and multimodal features with a focus on neuroimaging: A systematic literature review. *Health Technol.* **2024**, *14*, 201–237. [CrossRef]
9. Ghaderi, S.; Mohammadi, M.; Sayehmiri, F.; Mohammadi, S.; Tavasol, A.; Rezaei, M.; Ghalyanchi-Langeroudi, A. Machine learning approaches to identify affected brain regions in movement disorders using MRI data: A systematic review and diagnostic meta-analysis. *J. Magn. Reson. Imaging* **2024**, *60*, 2518–2546. [CrossRef]
10. Bacon, E.J.; He, D.; Achi, N.; Wang, L.; Li, H.; Yao-Digba, P.D.; Monkam, P.; Qi, S. Neuroimage analysis using artificial intelligence approaches: A systematic review. *Med. Biol. Eng. Comput.* **2024**, *62*, 2599–2627. [CrossRef]
11. Aggarwal, N.; Saini, B.S.; Gupta, S. Role of artificial intelligence techniques and neuroimaging modalities in detection of Parkinson's disease: A systematic review. *Cogn. Comput.* **2024**, *16*, 2078–2115. [CrossRef]
12. Chandler, J.; Cumpston, M.; Li, T.; Page, M.J.; Welch, V.J.H.W. *Cochrane Handbook for Systematic Reviews of Interventions*, 2nd ed.; Wiley: Hoboken, NJ, USA, 2019.

13. Aromataris, E.; Fernandez, R.; Godfrey, C.M.; Holly, C.; Khalil, H.; Tungpunkom, P. Summarizing systematic reviews: Methodological development, conduct and reporting of an umbrella review approach. *JBI Evid. Implement.* **2015**, *13*, 132–140. [CrossRef] [PubMed]
14. Moher, D.; Liberati, A.; Tetzlaff, J.; Altman, D.G.; Prisma Group. Preferred reporting items for systematic reviews and meta-analyses: The PRISMA statement. *Int. J. Surg.* **2010**, *8*, 336–341. [CrossRef]
15. Shea, B.J.; Bouter, L.M.; Peterson, J.; Boers, M.; Andersson, N.; Ortiz, Z.; Ramsay, T.; Bai, A.; Shukla, V.K.; Grimshaw, J.M. External validation of a measurement tool to assess systematic reviews (AMSTAR). *PLoS ONE* **2007**, *2*, e1350. [CrossRef]
16. Shea, B.J.; Reeves, B.C.; Wells, G.; Thuku, M.; Hamel, C.; Moran, J.; Moher, D.; Tugwell, P.; Welch, V.; Kristjansson, E.; et al. AMSTAR 2: A critical appraisal tool for systematic reviews that include randomised or non-randomised studies of healthcare interventions, or both. *BMJ* **2017**, *358*, j4008. [CrossRef]
17. Aljarallah, N.A.; Dutta, A.K.; Sait, A.R.W. A systematic review of genetics-and molecular-pathway-based machine learning models for neurological disorder diagnosis. *Int. J. Mol. Sci.* **2024**, *25*, 6422. [CrossRef]
18. Kaushal, A. A central role of stimulator of interferon genes' adaptor protein in defensive immune response. *Immunol. Res.* **2025**, *73*, 39. [CrossRef]
19. Kaur, A.; Mittal, M.; Bhatti, J.S.; Thareja, S.; Singh, S. A systematic literature review on the significance of deep learning and machine learning in predicting Alzheimer's disease. *Artif. Intell. Med.* **2024**, *154*, 102928. [CrossRef]
20. Mahavar, A.; Patel, A.; Patel, A. A Comprehensive Review on Deep Learning Techniques in Alzheimer's Disease Diagnosis. *Curr. Top. Med. Chem.* **2025**, *25*, 335–349. [CrossRef]
21. Dennis, A.G.P.; Strafella, A.P. The identification of cognitive impairment in Parkinson's disease using biofluids, neuroimaging, and artificial intelligence. *Front. Neurosci.* **2024**, *18*, 1446878. [CrossRef]
22. Dzialas, V.; Doering, E.; Eich, H.; Strafella, A.P.; Vaillancourt, D.E.; Simonyan, K.; van Eimeren, T.; International Parkinson Movement Disorders Society-Neuroimaging Study Group. Houston, we have AI problem! quality issues with neuroimaging-based artificial intelligence in Parkinson's disease: A systematic review. *Mov. Disord.* **2024**, *39*, 2130–2143. [CrossRef]
23. Lamba, R.; Gulati, T.; Alharbi, H.F.; Jain, A. A hybrid system for Parkinson's disease diagnosis using machine learning techniques. *Int. J. Speech Technol.* **2022**, *25*, 583–593. [CrossRef]
24. Bruno, M.K.; Dhall, R.; Duquette, A.; Haq, I.U.; Honig, L.S.; Lamotte, G.; Mari, Z.; McFarland, N.R.; Montaser-Kouhsari, L.; Rodriguez-Porcel, F.; et al. A general neurologist's practical diagnostic algorithm for atypical parkinsonian disorders: A consensus statement. *Neurol. Clin. Pract.* **2024**, *14*, e200345. [CrossRef]
25. Pratihar, R.; Sankar, R. Advancements in Parkinson's Disease Diagnosis: A Comprehensive Survey on Biomarker Integration and Machine Learning. *Computers* **2024**, *13*, 293. [CrossRef]
26. Sankineni, S.; Saraswat, A.; Suchetha, M.; Aakur, S.N.; Sehastrajit, S.; Dhas, D.E. An insight on recent advancements and future perspectives in detection techniques of Parkinson's disease. *Evol. Intell.* **2024**, *17*, 1715–1731. [CrossRef]
27. Bawa, A.; Banitsas, K.; Abbod, M. A review on the use of Microsoft Kinect for gait abnormality and postural disorder assessment. *J. Healthc. Eng.* **2021**, *2021*, 4360122. [CrossRef] [PubMed]
28. Anikwe, C.V.; Nweke, H.F.; Ikegwu, A.C.; Egwuonwu, C.A.; Onu, F.U.; Alo, U.R.; Teh, Y.W. Mobile and wearable sensors for data-driven health monitoring system: State-of-the-art and future prospect. *Expert Syst. Appl.* **2022**, *202*, 117362. [CrossRef]
29. Yen, J.M.; Lim, J.H. A clinical perspective on bespoke sensing mechanisms for remote monitoring and rehabilitation of neurological diseases: Scoping review. *Sensors* **2023**, *23*, 536. [CrossRef]
30. Ngo, Q.C.; Motin, M.A.; Pah, N.D.; Drotár, P.; Kempster, P.; Kumar, D. Computerized analysis of speech and voice for Parkinson's disease: A systematic review. *Computer Methods Programs Biomed.* **2022**, *226*, 107133. [CrossRef]
31. Lam, W.W.; Tang, Y.M.; Fong, K.N. A systematic review of the applications of markerless motion capture (MMC) technology for clinical measurement in rehabilitation. *J. Neuroeng. Rehabil.* **2023**, *20*, 57. [CrossRef]
32. Islam, M.A.; Majumder, M.Z.H.; Hussein, M.A.; Hossain, K.M.; Miah, M.S. A review of machine learning and deep learning algorithms for Parkinson's disease detection using handwriting and voice datasets. *Heliyon* **2024**, *10*, e25469. [CrossRef]
33. Park, K.W.; Mirian, M.S.; McKeown, M.J. Artificial intelligence-based video monitoring of movement disorders in the elderly: A review on current and future landscapes. *Singap. Med. J.* **2024**, *65*, 141–149. [CrossRef] [PubMed]
34. Pereira, C.R.; Pereira, D.R.; Weber, S.A.; Hook, C.; De Albuquerque, V.H.C.; Papa, J.P. A survey on computer-assisted Parkinson's disease diagnosis. *Artif. Intell. Med.* **2019**, *95*, 48–63. [CrossRef] [PubMed]
35. Chudzik, A.; Śledzianowski, A.; Przybyszewski, A.W. Machine learning and digital biomarkers can detect early stages of neurodegenerative diseases. *Sensors* **2024**, *24*, 1572. [CrossRef] [PubMed]
36. Sánchez-Fernández, L.P. Biomechanics of Parkinson's Disease with Systems Based on Expert Knowledge and Machine Learning: A Scoping Review. *Computation* **2024**, *12*, 230. [CrossRef]
37. Steins, D.; Dawes, H.; Esser, P.; Collett, J. Wearable accelerometry-based technology capable of assessing functional activities in neurological populations in community settings: A systematic review. *J. Neuroeng. Rehabil.* **2014**, *11*, 36. [CrossRef]

38. Hubble, R.P.; Naughton, G.A.; Silburn, P.A.; Cole, M.H. Wearable sensor use for assessing standing balance and walking stability in people with Parkinson's disease: A systematic review. *PLoS ONE* **2015**, *10*, e0123705. [CrossRef]
39. Silva de Lima, A.L.; Evers, L.J.; Hahn, T.; Bataille, L.; Hamilton, J.L.; Little, M.A.; Okuma, Y.; Bloem, B.; Faber, M.J. Freezing of gait and fall detection in Parkinson's disease using wearable sensors: A systematic review. *J. Neurol.* **2017**, *264*, 1642–1654. [CrossRef]
40. Rovini, E.; Maremmani, C.; Cavallo, F. How wearable sensors can support Parkinson's disease diagnosis and treatment: A systematic review. *Front. Neurosci.* **2017**, *11*, 555. [CrossRef]
41. Hasan, H.; Athauda, D.S.; Foltynie, T.; Noyce, A.J. Technologies assessing limb bradykinesia in Parkinson's disease. *J. Park. Dis.* **2017**, *7*, 65–77. [CrossRef]
42. Son, H.; Park, W.S.; Kim, H. Mobility monitoring using smart technologies for Parkinson's disease in free-living environment. *Collegian* **2018**, *25*, 549–560. [CrossRef]
43. Thorp, J.E.; Adamczyk, P.G.; Ploeg, H.L.; Pickett, K.A. Monitoring motor symptoms during activities of daily living in individuals with Parkinson's disease. *Front. Neurol.* **2018**, *9*, 1036. [CrossRef] [PubMed]
44. Merola, A.; Sturchio, A.; Hacker, S.; Serna, S.; Vizcarra, J.A.; Marsili, L.; Fasano, A.; Espay, A.J. Technology-based assessment of motor and nonmotor phenomena in Parkinson disease. *Expert Rev. Neurother.* **2018**, *18*, 825–845. [CrossRef] [PubMed]
45. Johansson, D.; Malmgren, K.; Murphy, M.A. Wearable sensors for clinical applications in epilepsy, Parkinson's disease, and stroke: A mixed-methods systematic review. *J. Neurol.* **2018**, *265*, 1740–1752. [CrossRef]
46. Sweeney, D.; Quinlan, L.R.; Browne, P.; Richardson, M.; Meskell, P.; ÓLaighin, G. A technological review of wearable cueing devices addressing freezing of gait in Parkinson's disease. *Sensors* **2019**, *19*, 1277. [CrossRef]
47. Brognara, L.; Palumbo, P.; Grimm, B.; Palmerini, L. Assessing gait in Parkinson's disease using wearable motion sensors: A systematic review. *Diseases* **2019**, *7*, 18. [CrossRef]
48. Rovini, E.; Maremmani, C.; Cavallo, F. Automated systems based on wearable sensors for the management of Parkinson's disease at home: A systematic review. *Telemed. E-Health* **2019**, *25*, 167–183. [CrossRef]
49. Linares-Del Rey, M.; Vela-Desojo, L.; Cano-de La Cuerda, R. Mobile phone applications in Parkinson's disease: A systematic review. *Neurología* **2019**, *34*, 38–54. [CrossRef]
50. Godoi, B.B.; Amorim, G.D.; Quiroga, D.G.; Holanda, V.M.; Júlio, T.; Tournier, M.B. Parkinson's disease and wearable devices, new perspectives for a public health issue: An integrative literature review. *Rev. Da Assoc. Médica Bras.* **2019**, *65*, 1413–1420. [CrossRef]
51. Vaartio-Rajalin, H.; Rauhala, A.; Fagerström, L. Person-centered home-based rehabilitation for persons with Parkinson's disease: A scoping review. *Int. J. Nurs. Stud.* **2019**, *99*, 103395. [CrossRef]
52. Garcia-Agundez, A.; Folkerts, A.K.; Konrad, R.; Caserman, P.; Tregel, T.; Goosses, M.; Göbel, S.; Kalbe, E. Recent advances in rehabilitation for Parkinson's Disease with Exergames: A Systematic Review. *J. Neuroeng. Rehabil.* **2019**, *16*, 17. [CrossRef]
53. Theodoros, D.; Aldridge, D.; Hill, A.J.; Russell, T. Technology-enabled management of communication and swallowing disorders in Parkinson's disease: A systematic scoping review. *Int. J. Lang. Commun. Disord.* **2019**, *54*, 170–188. [CrossRef]
54. Teshuva, I.; Hillel, I.; Gazit, E.; Giladi, N.; Mirelman, A.; Hausdorff, J.M. Using wearables to assess bradykinesia and rigidity in patients with Parkinson's disease: A focused, narrative review of the literature. *J. Neural Transm.* **2019**, *126*, 699–710. [CrossRef]
55. Pardoel, S.; Kofman, J.; Nantel, J.; Lemaire, E.D. Wearable-sensor-based detection and prediction of freezing of gait in Parkinson's disease: A review. *Sensors* **2019**, *19*, 5141. [CrossRef]
56. Orgeta, V.; McDonald, K.R.; Poliakoff, E.; Hindle, J.V.; Clare, L.; Leroi, I. Cognitive training interventions for dementia and mild cognitive impairment in Parkinson's disease. *Cochrane Database Syst. Rev.* **2020**, *2*, CD011961. [CrossRef] [PubMed]
57. Ponciano, V.; Pires, I.M.; Ribeiro, F.R.; Marques, G.; Villasana, M.V.; Garcia, N.M.; Zdravevski, E.; Spinsante, S. Identification of diseases based on the use of inertial sensors: A systematic review. *Electronics* **2020**, *9*, 778. [CrossRef]
58. de Oliveira Gondim, I.T.G.; de Souza, C.D.C.B.; Rodrigues, M.A.B.; Azevedo, I.M.; de Sales, M.D.G.W.; Lins, O.G. Portable accelerometers for the evaluation of spatio-temporal gait parameters in people with Parkinson's disease: An integrative review. *Arch. Gerontol. Geriatr.* **2020**, *90*, 104097. [CrossRef]
59. Morgan, C.; Rolinski, M.; McNaney, R.; Jones, B.; Rochester, L.; Maetzler, W.; Craddock, I.; Whone, A.L. Systematic review looking at the use of technology to measure free-living symptom and activity outcomes in Parkinson's disease in the home or a home-like environment. *J. Park. Dis.* **2020**, *10*, 429–454. [CrossRef]
60. Corrà, M.F.; Warmerdam, E.; Vila-Chã, N.; Maetzler, W.; Maia, L. Wearable health technology to quantify the functional impact of peripheral neuropathy on mobility in Parkinson's disease: A systematic review. *Sensors* **2020**, *20*, 6627. [CrossRef]
61. Lora-Millan, J.S.; Delgado-Oleas, G.; Benito-León, J.; Rocon, E. A review on wearable technologies for tremor suppression. *Front. Neurol.* **2021**, *12*, 700600. [CrossRef]
62. de Oliveira, L.C.; Mendes, L.C.; de Lopes, R.A.; Carneiro, J.A.; Cardoso, A.; Júnior, E.A.; de Oliveira Andrade, A. A systematic review of serious games used for rehabilitation of individuals with Parkinson's disease. *Res. Biomed. Eng.* **2021**, *37*, 849–865. [CrossRef]
63. Keogh, A.; Argent, R.; Anderson, A.; Caulfield, B.; Johnston, W. Assessing the usability of wearable devices to measure gait and physical activity in chronic conditions: A systematic review. *J. Neuroeng. Rehabil.* **2021**, *18*, 138. [CrossRef] [PubMed]

64. Sica, M.; Tedesco, S.; Crowe, C.; Kenny, L.; Moore, K.; Timmons, S.; Barton, J.; O'Flynn, B.; Komaris, D.S. Continuous home monitoring of Parkinson's disease using inertial sensors: A systematic review. *PLoS ONE* **2021**, *16*, e0246528. [CrossRef] [PubMed]
65. Elena, P.; Demetris, S.; Christina, M.; Marios, P. Differences between exergaming rehabilitation and conventional physiotherapy on quality of life in Parkinson's disease: A systematic review and meta-analysis. *Front. Neurol.* **2021**, *12*, 683385. [CrossRef]
66. van Wamelen, D.J.; Sringean, J.; Trivedi, D.; Carroll, C.B.; Schrag, A.E.; Odin, P.; Antonini, A.; Bloem, B.R.; Bhidayasiri, R.; Chaudhuri, K.R.; et al. Digital health technology for non-motor symptoms in people with Parkinson's disease: Futile or future? *Park. Relat. Disord.* **2021**, *89*, 186–194. [CrossRef] [PubMed]
67. Vellata, C.; Belli, S.; Balsamo, F.; Giordano, A.; Colombo, R.; Maggioni, G. Effectiveness of telerehabilitation on motor impairments, non-motor symptoms and compliance in patients with Parkinson's disease: A systematic review. *Front. Neurol.* **2021**, *12*, 627999. [CrossRef]
68. Abou, L.; Peters, J.; Wong, E.; Akers, R.; Dossou, M.S.; Sosnoff, J.J.; Rice, L.A. Gait and balance assessments using smartphone applications in Parkinson's disease: A systematic review. *J. Med. Syst.* **2021**, *45*, 87. [CrossRef]
69. McDermott, A.; Haberlin, C.; Moran, J. The use of ehealth to promote physical activity in people living with Parkinson's disease: A systematic review. *Physiother. Pract. Res.* **2021**, *42*, 79–92. [CrossRef]
70. Gonçalves, H.R.; Rodrigues, A.M.; Santos, C.P. Vibrotactile biofeedback devices in Parkinson's disease: A narrative review. *Med. Biol. Eng. Comput.* **2021**, *59*, 1185–1199. [CrossRef]
71. Bowman, T.; Gervasoni, E.; Arienti, C.; Lazzarini, S.G.; Negrini, S.; Crea, S.; Cattaneo, D.; Carrozza, M.C. Wearable devices for biofeedback rehabilitation: A systematic review and meta-analysis to design application rules and estimate the effectiveness on balance and gait outcomes in neurological diseases. *Sensors* **2021**, *21*, 3444. [CrossRef]
72. Ó Breasail, M.; Biswas, B.; Smith, M.D.; Mazhar, M.K.A.; Tenison, E.; Cullen, A.; Lithander, F.; Roudaut, A.; Henderson, E.J. Wearable GPS and accelerometer technologies for monitoring mobility and physical activity in neurodegenerative disorders: A systematic review. *Sensors* **2021**, *21*, 8261. [CrossRef]
73. Albán-Cadena, A.C.; Villalba-Meneses, F.; Pila-Varela, K.O.; Moreno-Calvo, A.; Villalba-Meneses, C.P.; Almeida-Galárraga, D.A. Wearable sensors in the diagnosis and study of Parkinson's disease symptoms: A systematic review. *J. Med. Eng. Technol.* **2021**, *45*, 532–545. [CrossRef] [PubMed]
74. Barrachina-Fernández, M.; Maitín, A.M.; Sánchez-Ávila, C.; Romero, J.P. Wearable technology to detect motor fluctuations in Parkinson's disease patients: Current state and challenges. *Sensors* **2021**, *21*, 4188. [CrossRef] [PubMed]
75. Prieto-Avalos, G.; Sánchez-Morales, L.N.; Alor-Hernández, G.; Sánchez-Cervantes, J.L. A review of commercial and non-commercial wearables devices for monitoring motor impairments caused by neurodegenerative diseases. *Biosensors* **2022**, *13*, 72. [CrossRef]
76. Tripathi, S.; Malhotra, A.; Qazi, M.; Chou, J.; Wang, F.; Barkan, S.; Hellmers, N.; Henchcliffe, C.; Sarva, H. Clinical review of smartphone applications in Parkinson's disease. *Neurologist* **2022**, *27*, 183–193. [CrossRef]
77. Gavelin, H.M.; Domellöf, M.E.; Leung, I.; Neely, A.S.; Launder, N.H.; Nategh, L.; Finke, C.; Lampit, A. Computerized cognitive training in Parkinson's disease: A systematic review and meta-analysis. *Ageing Res. Rev.* **2022**, *80*, 101671. [CrossRef]
78. Alfalahi, H.; Khandoker, A.H.; Chowdhury, N.; Iakovakis, D.; Dias, S.B.; Chaudhuri, K.R.; Hadjileontiadis, L.J. Diagnostic accuracy of keystroke dynamics as digital biomarkers for fine motor decline in neuropsychiatric disorders: A systematic review and meta-analysis. *Sci. Rep.* **2022**, *12*, 7690. [CrossRef]
79. Guo, C.C.; Chiesa, P.A.; de Moor, C.; Fazeli, M.S.; Schofield, T.; Hofer, K.; Belachew, S.; Scotland, A. Digital devices for assessing motor functions in mobility-impaired and healthy populations: Systematic literature review. *J. Med. Internet Res.* **2022**, *24*, e37683. [CrossRef]
80. Li, X.; Chen, Z.; Yue, Y.; Zhou, X.; Gu, S.; Tao, J.; Guo, H.; Zhu, M.; Du, Q. Effect of wearable sensor-based exercise on musculoskeletal disorders in individuals with neurodegenerative diseases: A systematic review and meta-analysis. *Front. Aging Neurosci.* **2022**, *14*, 934844. [CrossRef]
81. Giannakopoulou, K.M.; Roussaki, I.; Demestichas, K. Internet of things technologies and machine learning methods for Parkinson's disease diagnosis, monitoring and management: A systematic review. *Sensors* **2022**, *22*, 1799. [CrossRef]
82. Gerritzen, E.V.; Lee, A.R.; McDermott, O.; Coulson, N.; Orrell, M. Online peer support for people with Parkinson disease: Narrative synthesis systematic review. *JMIR Aging* **2022**, *5*, e35425. [CrossRef]
83. Mughal, H.; Javed, A.R.; Rizwan, M.; Almadhor, A.S.; Kryvinska, N. Parkinson's disease management via wearable sensors: A systematic review. *IEEE Access* **2022**, *10*, 35219–35237. [CrossRef]
84. Gopal, A.; Hsu, W.Y.; Allen, D.D.; Bove, R. Remote assessments of hand function in neurological disorders: Systematic review. *JMIR Rehabil. Assist. Technol.* **2022**, *9*, e33157. [CrossRef]
85. Sakamaki, T.; Furusawa, Y.; Hayashi, A.; Otsuka, M.; Fernandez, J. Remote patient monitoring for neuropsychiatric disorders: A scoping review of current trends and future perspectives from recent publications and upcoming clinical trials. *Telemed. E-Health* **2022**, *28*, 1235–1250. [CrossRef]

86. Lim, A.C.Y.; Natarajan, P.; Fonseka, R.D.; Maharaj, M.; Mobbs, R.J. The application of artificial intelligence and custom algorithms with inertial wearable devices for gait analysis and detection of gait-altering pathologies in adults: A scoping review of literature. *Digit. Health* **2022**, *8*, 20552076221074128. [CrossRef]
87. Lee, J.; Yeom, I.; Chung, M.L.; Kim, Y.; Yoo, S.; Kim, E. Use of mobile apps for self-care in people with Parkinson disease: Systematic review. *JMIR Mhealth Uhealth* **2022**, *10*, e33944. [CrossRef] [PubMed]
88. Ancona, S.; Faraci, F.D.; Khatab, E.; Fiorillo, L.; Gnarra, O.; Nef, T.; Bassetti, C.L.A.; Bargiotas, P. Wearables in the home-based assessment of abnormal movements in Parkinson's disease: A systematic review of the literature. *J. Neurol.* **2022**, *269*, 100–110. [CrossRef] [PubMed]
89. Vanmechelen, I.; Haberfehlner, H.; De Vleeschhauwer, J.; Van Wonterghem, E.; Feys, H.; Desloovere, K.; Aerts, J.M.; Monbaliu, E. Assessment of movement disorders using wearable sensors during upper limb tasks: A scoping review. *Front. Robot. AI* **2023**, *9*, 1068413. [CrossRef] [PubMed]
90. Sigcha, L.; Borzì, L.; Amato, F.; Rechichi, I.; Ramos-Romero, C.; Cárdenas, A.; Gascó, L.; Olmo, G. Deep learning and wearable sensors for the diagnosis and monitoring of Parkinson's disease: A systematic review. *Expert Syst. Appl.* **2023**, *229*, 120541. [CrossRef]
91. Zhang, W.; Sun, H.; Huang, D.; Zhang, Z.; Li, J.; Wu, C.; Sun, Y.; Gong, M.; Wang, Z.; Sun, C.; et al. Detection and prediction of freezing of gait with wearable sensors in Parkinson's disease. *Neurol. Sci.* **2023**, *45*, 431–453. [CrossRef]
92. Fujikawa, J.; Morigaki, R.; Yamamoto, N.; Nakanishi, H.; Oda, T.; Izumi, Y.; Takagi, Y. Diagnosis and treatment of tremor in Parkinson's disease using mechanical devices. *Life* **2023**, *13*, 78. [CrossRef] [PubMed]
93. Scataglini, S.; Van Dyck, Z.; Declercq, V.; Van Cleemput, G.; Struyf, N.; Truijen, S. Effect of music based therapy rhythmic auditory stimulation (ras) using wearable device in rehabilitation of neurological patients: A systematic review. *Sensors* **2023**, *23*, 5933. [CrossRef] [PubMed]
94. Moreta-de-Esteban, P.; Martin-Casas, P.; Ortiz-Gutierrez, R.M.; Straudi, S.; Cano-de-la-Cuerda, R. Mobile applications for resting tremor assessment in parkinson's disease: A systematic review. *J. Clin. Med.* **2023**, *12*, 2334. [CrossRef] [PubMed]
95. Huang, T.; Li, M.; Huang, J. Recent trends in wearable device used to detect freezing of gait and falls in people with Parkinson's disease: A systematic review. *Front. Aging Neurosci.* **2023**, *15*, 1119956. [CrossRef]
96. Laar, A.; de Lima, A.L.S.; Maas, B.R.; Bloem, B.R.; de Vries, N.M. Successful implementation of technology in the management of Parkinson's disease: Barriers and facilitators. *Clin. Park. Relat. Disord.* **2023**, *8*, 100188. [CrossRef]
97. Bansal, S.K.; Basumatary, B.; Bansal, R.; Sahani, A.K. Techniques for the detection and management of freezing of gait in Parkinson's disease–A systematic review and future perspectives. *MethodsX* **2023**, *10*, 102106. [CrossRef]
98. Tuena, C.; Borghesi, F.; Bruni, F.; Cavedoni, S.; Maestri, S.; Riva, G.; Tettamanti, M.; Liperoti, R.; Rossi, L.; Ferrarin, M.; et al. Technology-assisted cognitive motor dual-task rehabilitation in chronic age-related conditions: Systematic review. *J. Med. Internet Res.* **2023**, *25*, e44484. [CrossRef]
99. Özden, F. The effect of mobile application-based rehabilitation in patients with Parkinson's disease: A systematic review and meta-analysis. *Clin. Neurol. Neurosurg.* **2023**, *225*, 107579. [CrossRef]
100. Li, P.; van Wezel, R.; He, F.; Zhao, Y.; Wang, Y. The role of wrist-worn technology in the management of Parkinson's disease in daily life: A narrative review. *Front. Neuroinformatics* **2023**, *17*, 1135300. [CrossRef]
101. Taniguchi, S.; Yamamoto, A.; D'cruz, N. Assessing impaired bed mobility in patients with Parkinson's disease: A scoping review. *Physiotherapy* **2024**, *124*, 29–39. [CrossRef]
102. Sapienza, S.; Tsurkalenko, O.; Giraitis, M.; Mejia, A.C.; Zelimkhanov, G.; Schwaninger, I.; Klucken, J. Assessing the clinical utility of inertial sensors for home monitoring in Parkinson's disease: A comprehensive review. *NPJ Park. Dis.* **2024**, *10*, 161. [CrossRef]
103. Cox, E.; Wade, R.; Hodgson, R.; Fulbright, H.; Phung, T.H.; Meader, N.; Walker, S.; Rothery, C.; Simmonds, M. Devices for remote continuous monitoring of people with Parkinson's disease: A systematic review and cost-effectiveness analysis. *Health Technol. Assess.* **2024**, *28*, 1. [CrossRef]
104. Janssen Daalen, J.M.; van den Bergh, R.; Prins, E.M.; Moghadam, M.S.C.; van den Heuvel, R.; Veen, J.; Mathur, S.; Meijerink, H.; Mirelman, A.; Darweesh, S.K.L.; et al. Digital biomarkers for non-motor symptoms in Parkinson's disease: The state of the art. *NPJ Digit. Med.* **2024**, *7*, 186. [CrossRef] [PubMed]
105. Polvorinos-Fernández, C.; Sigcha, L.; Borzì, L.; Olmo, G.; Asensio, C.; López, J.M.; Arcas, G.; Pavón, I. Evaluating Motor Symptoms in Parkinson's Disease Through Wearable Sensors: A Systematic Review of Digital Biomarkers. *Appl. Sci.* **2024**, *14*, 10189. [CrossRef]
106. Lai, P.; Zhang, J.; Lai, Q.; Li, J.; Liang, Z. Impact of Wearable Device-Based Walking Programs on Gait Speed in Older Adults: A Systematic Review and Meta-Analysis. *Geriatr. Orthop. Surg. Rehabil.* **2024**, *15*, 21514593241284473. [CrossRef] [PubMed]
107. Elbatanouny, H.; Kleanthous, N.; Dahrouj, H.; Alusi, S.; Almajali, E.; Mahmoud, S.; Hussain, A. Insights into Parkinson's Disease-Related Freezing of Gait Detection and Prediction Approaches: A Meta Analysis. *Sensors* **2024**, *24*, 3959. [CrossRef]
108. Peng, Y.; Ma, C.; Li, M.; Liu, Y.; Yu, J.; Pan, L.; Zhang, Z. Intelligent devices for assessing essential tremor: A comprehensive review. *J. Neurol.* **2024**, *271*, 4733–4750. [CrossRef]

109. di Biase, L.; Pecoraro, P.M.; Pecoraro, G.; Shah, S.A.; Di Lazzaro, V. Machine learning and wearable sensors for automated Parkinson's disease diagnosis aid: A systematic review. *J. Neurol.* **2024**, *271*, 6452–6470. [CrossRef]
110. Jeyasingh-Jacob, J.; Crook-Rumsey, M.; Shah, H.; Joseph, T.; Abulikemu, S.; Daniels, S.; Sharp, D.; Haar, S. Markerless motion capture to quantify functional performance in neurodegeneration: Systematic review. *JMIR Aging* **2024**, *7*, e52582. [CrossRef]
111. Boege, S.; Milne-Ives, M.; Ananthakrishnan, A.; Carroll, C.; Meinert, E. Self-Management Systems for Patients and Clinicians in Parkinson's Disease Care: A Scoping Review. *J. Park. Dis.* **2024**, *14*, 1387–1404. [CrossRef]
112. Willemse, I.H.; Schootemeijer, S.; van den Bergh, R.; Dawes, H.; Nonnekes, J.H.; van de Warrenburg, B.P. Smartphone applications for Movement Disorders: Towards collaboration and re-use. *Park. Relat. Disord.* **2024**, *120*, 105988. [CrossRef]
113. Fu, Y.; Zhang, Y.; Ye, B.; Babineau, J.; Zhao, Y.; Gao, Z.; Mihailidis, A. Smartphone-Based Hand Function Assessment: Systematic Review. *J. Med. Internet Res.* **2024**, *26*, e51564. [CrossRef] [PubMed]
114. Silva-Batista, C.; de Almeida, F.O.; Wilhelm, J.L.; Horak, F.B.; Mancini, M.; King, L.A. Telerehabilitation by Videoconferencing for Balance and Gait in People with Parkinson's Disease: A Scoping Review. *Geriatrics* **2024**, *9*, 66. [CrossRef] [PubMed]
115. Zhang, T.; Meng, D.T.; Lyu, D.Y.; Fang, B.Y. The Efficacy of Wearable Cueing Devices on Gait and Motor Function in Parkinson Disease: A Systematic Review and Meta-analysis of Randomized Controlled Trials. *Arch. Phys. Med. Rehabil.* **2024**, *105*, 369–380. [CrossRef] [PubMed]
116. Franco, A.; Russo, M.; Amboni, M.; Ponsiglione, A.M.; Di Filippo, F.; Romano, M.; Amato, F.; Ricciardi, C. The Role of Deep Learning and Gait Analysis in Parkinson's Disease: A Systematic Review. *Sensors* **2024**, *24*, 5957. [CrossRef]
117. Tao, D.; Awan-Scully, R.; Ash, G.I.; Cole, A.; Zhong, P.; Gao, Y.; Sun, Y.; Shao, S.; Wiltshire, H.; Baker, J.S. The Role of Technology-based Dance Intervention for Enhancing Wellness-A Systematic Scoping Review and Meta-synthesis. *Ageing Res. Rev.* **2024**, *100*, 102462. [CrossRef]
118. Craig, S.N.; Dempster, M.; Curran, D.; Cuddihy, A.M.; Lyttle, N. A systematic review of the effectiveness of digital cognitive assessments of cognitive impairment in Parkinson's disease. *Appl. Neuropsychol. Adult* **2025**, 1–13. [CrossRef]
119. Hall, A.M.; Allgar, V.; Carroll, C.B.; Meinert, E. Digital health technologies and self-efficacy in Parkinson's: A scoping review. *BMJ Open* **2025**, *15*, e088616. [CrossRef]
120. Rábano-Suárez, P.; Del Campo, N.; Benatru, I.; Moreau, C.; Desjardins, C.; Sánchez-Ferro, Á.; Fabbri, M. Digital Outcomes as Biomarkers of Disease Progression in Early Parkinson's Disease: A Systematic Review. *Mov. Disord.* **2025**, *40*, 184–203. [CrossRef]
121. Gattoni, M.F.; Gobbo, S.; Feroldi, S.; Salvatore, A.; Navarro, J.; Sorbi, S.; Saibene, F.L. Identification of Cognitive Training for Individuals with Parkinson's Disease: A Systematic Review. *Brain Sci.* **2025**, *15*, 61. [CrossRef]
122. Tripoliti, E.E.; Tzallas, A.T.; Tsipouras, M.G.; Rigas, G.; Bougia, P.; Leontiou, M.; Konitsiotis, S.; Chondrogiorgi, M.; Tsouli, S.; Fotiadis, D.I. Automatic detection of freezing of gait events in patients with Parkinson's disease. *Comput. Methods Programs Biomed.* **2013**, *110*, 12–26. [CrossRef]
123. Tzallas, A.T.; Tsipouras, M.G.; Rigas, G.; Tsalikakis, D.G.; Karvounis, E.C.; Chondrogiorgi, M.; Psomadellis, F.; Cancela, J.; Pastorino, M.; Arredondo, M.T.; et al. PERFORM: A system for monitoring, assessment and management of patients with Parkinson's disease. *Sensors* **2014**, *14*, 21329–21357. [CrossRef]
124. Arora, S.; Venkataraman, V.; Zhan, A.; Donohue, S.; Biglan, K.M.; Dorsey, E.R.; Little, M.A. Detecting and monitoring the symptoms of Parkinson's disease using smartphones: A pilot study. *Park. Relat. Disord.* **2015**, *21*, 650–653. [CrossRef] [PubMed]
125. Ferreira, J.J.; Godinho, C.; Santos, A.T.; Domingos, J.; Abreu, D.; Lobo, R.; Gonçalves, N.; Barra, M.; Larsen, F.; Fagerbakke, Ø.; et al. Quantitative home-based assessment of Parkinson's symptoms: The SENSE-PARK feasibility and usability study. *BMC Neurol.* **2015**, *15*, 89. [CrossRef] [PubMed]
126. Kim, H.; Lee, H.J.; Lee, W.; Kwon, S.; Kim, S.K.; Jeon, H.S.; Park, H.; Shin, C.W.; Yi, W.J.; Jeon, B.S.; et al. Unconstrained detection of freezing of Gait in Parkinson's disease patients using smartphone. In Proceedings of the 37th Annual International Conference of the IEEE Engineering in Medicine and Biology Society (EMBC), Milano, Italy, 25–29 August 2015. [CrossRef]
127. Pan, D.; Dhall, R.; Lieberman, A.; Petitti, D.B. A mobile cloud-based Parkinson's disease assessment system for home-based monitoring. *JMIR Mhealth Uhealth* **2015**, *3*, e3956. [CrossRef]
128. Rezvanian, S.; Lockhart, T.E. Towards real-time detection of freezing of gait using wavelet transform on wireless accelerometer data. *Sensors* **2016**, *16*, 475. [CrossRef]
129. Capecci, M.; Pepa, L.; Verdini, F.; Ceravolo, M.G. A smartphone-based architecture to detect and quantify freezing of gait in Parkinson's disease. *Gait Posture* **2016**, *50*, 28–33. [CrossRef]
130. Ginis, P.; Nieuwboer, A.; Dorfman, M.; Ferrari, A.; Gazit, E.; Canning, C.G.; Rocchi, L.; Chiari, L.; Hausdorff, J.M.; Mirelman, A. Feasibility and effects of home-based smartphone-delivered automated feedback training for gait in people with Parkinson's disease: A pilot randomized controlled trial. *Park. Relat. Disord.* **2016**, *22*, 28–34. [CrossRef]
131. Kassavetis, P.; Saifee, T.A.; Roussos, G.; Drougkas, L.; Kojovic, M.; Rothwell, J.C.; Edwards, M.; Bhatia, K.P. Developing a tool for remote digital assessment of Parkinson's disease. *Mov. Disord. Clin. Pract.* **2016**, *3*, 59–64. [CrossRef]
132. Lee, C.Y.; Kang, S.J.; Kim, Y.E.; Lee, U.; Ma, H.I.; Kim, Y.J. A validation study of a smartphone-based finger tapping application for quantitative assessment of bradykinesia in Parkinson's disease: 553. *Mov. Disord.* **2016**, *31*, S180. [CrossRef]

133. Camps, J.; Samà, A.; Martín, M.; Rodríguez-Martín, D.; Pérez-López, C.; Alcaine, S.; Mestre, B.; Prats, A.; Crespo, M.C.; Cabestany, J.; et al. Deep learning for detecting freezing of gait episodes in Parkinson's disease based on accelerometers. In Proceedings of the 14th International Work-Conference on Artificial Neural Networks, IWANN 2017, Cadiz, Spain, 14–16 June 2017. [CrossRef]
134. Rodríguez-Martín, D.; Samà, A.; Pérez-López, C.; Català, A.; Moreno Arostegui, J.M.; Cabestany, J.; Bayés, À.; Alcaine, S.; Mestre, B.; Prats, A.; et al. Home detection of freezing of gait using support vector machines through a single waist-worn triaxial accelerometer. *PLoS ONE* **2017**, *12*, e0171764. [CrossRef]
135. Lipsmeier, F.; Taylor, K.I.; Kilchenmann, T.; Wolf, D.; Scotland, A.; Schjodt-Eriksen, J.; Cheng, W.Y.; Fernandez-Garcia, I.; Siebourg-Polster, J.; Jin, L.; et al. Evaluation of smartphone-based testing to generate exploratory outcome measures in a phase 1 Parkinson's disease clinical trial. *Mov. Disord.* **2018**, *33*, 1287–1297. [CrossRef] [PubMed]
136. Queirós, A.; Dias, A.; Silva, A.G.; Rocha, N.P. Ambient assisted living and health-related outcomes—A systematic literature review. *Informatics* **2017**, *4*, 19. [CrossRef]
137. Whiting, P.F.; Rutjes, A.W.; Westwood, M.E.; Mallett, S.; Deeks, J.J.; Reitsma, J.B.; Leeflang, M.M.; Sterne, J.A.; Bossuyt, P.M.; QUADAS-2 Group. QUADAS-2: A revised tool for the quality assessment of diagnostic accuracy studies. *Ann. Intern. Med.* **2011**, *155*, 529–536. [CrossRef]
138. Boyle, L.D.; Giriteka, L.; Marty, B.; Sandgathe, L.; Haugarvoll, K.; Steihaug, O.M.; Husebo, B.; Patrascu, M. Activity and Behavioral Recognition Using Sensing Technology in Persons with Parkinson's Disease or Dementia: An Umbrella Review of the Literature. *Sensors* **2025**, *25*, 668. [CrossRef]
139. Wartenberg, C.; Elden, H.; Frerichs, M.; Jivegård, L.L.; Magnusson, K.; Mourtzinis, G.; Nyström, O.; Quitz, K.; Sjöland, H.; Svanberg, T.; et al. Clinical benefits and risks of remote patient monitoring: An overview and assessment of methodological rigour of systematic reviews for selected patient groups. *BMC Health Serv. Res.* **2025**, *25*, 133. [CrossRef]
140. Ahmed, S.K. How to choose a sampling technique and determine sample size for research: A simplified guide for researchers. *Oral Oncol. Rep.* **2024**, *12*, 100662. [CrossRef]
141. Hopewell, S.; Chan, A.W.; Collins, G.S.; Hróbjartsson, A.; Moher, D.; Schulz, K.F.; Tunn, R.; Aggarwal, R.; Berkwits, M.; Boutron, I. CONSORT 2025 statement: Updated guideline for reporting randomised trials. *Lancet* **2025**, *405*, 1633–1640. [CrossRef]
142. Martins, A.I.; Queirós, A.; Silva, A.G.; Rocha, N.P. Usability evaluation methods: A systematic review. In *Human Factors in Software Development and Design*; Daeed, I., Bajwa, I.S., Mahmood, Z., Eds.; IGI Global: Hershey, PA, USA, 2014; pp. 250–273. [CrossRef]
143. Silva, A.G.; Caravau, H.; Martins, A.; Almeida, A.M.P.; Silva, T.; Ribeiro, Ó.; Santinha, G.; Rocha, N.P. Procedures of user-centered usability assessment for digital solutions: Scoping review of reviews reporting on digital solutions relevant for older adults. *JMIR Hum. Factors* **2021**, *8*, e22774. [CrossRef]
144. O'herrin, J.K.; Fost, N.; Kudsk, K.A. Health Insurance Portability Accountability Act (HIPAA) regulations: Effect on medical record research. *Ann. Surg.* **2004**, *239*, 772–778. [CrossRef]
145. Shuren, J.; Patel, B.; Gottlieb, S. FDA regulation of mobile medical apps. *JAMA* **2018**, *320*, 337–338. [CrossRef]
146. Keutzer, L.; Simonsson, U.S. Medical device apps: An introduction to regulatory affairs for developers. *JMIR Mhealth Uhealth* **2020**, *8*, e17567. [CrossRef]
147. van Vroonhoven, J. *Risk Management for Medical Devices and the New BS EN ISO 14971*; BSI Standards Ltd.: London, UK, 2020.

future internet MDPI

Review

The Rise of Agentic AI: A Review of Definitions, Frameworks, Architectures, Applications, Evaluation Metrics, and Challenges

Ajay Bandi [1,*], Bhavani Kongari [1,†], Roshini Naguru [1,†], Sahitya Pasnoor [2,†] and Sri Vidya Vilipala [1,†]

1 School of Computer Science and Information Systems, Northwest Missouri State University, Maryville, MO 64468, USA; s575201@nwmissouri.edu (B.K.); s574380@nwmissouri.edu (R.N.); s576118@nwmissouri.edu (S.V.V.)
2 Independent Researcher, Omaha, NE 68022, USA; sahitya.ce@gmail.com
* Correspondence: ajay@nwmissouri.edu
† These authors contributed equally to this work. The authors are listed alphabetically by last name.

Abstract: Agentic AI systems are a recently emerged and important approach that goes beyond traditional AI, generative AI, and autonomous systems by focusing on autonomy, adaptability, and goal-driven reasoning. This study provides a clear review of agentic AI systems by bringing together their definitions, frameworks, and architectures, and by comparing them with related areas like generative AI, autonomic computing, and multi-agent systems. To do this, we reviewed 143 primary studies on current LLM-based and non-LLM-driven agentic systems and examined how they support planning, memory, reflection, and goal pursuit. Furthermore, we classified architectural models, input–output mechanisms, and applications based on their task domains where agentic AI is applied, supported using tabular summaries that highlight real-world case studies. Evaluation metrics were classified as qualitative and quantitative measures, along with available testing methods of agentic AI systems to check the system's performance and reliability. This study also highlights the main challenges and limitations of agentic AI, covering technical, architectural, coordination, ethical, and security issues. We organized the conceptual foundations, available tools, architectures, and evaluation metrics in this research, which defines a structured foundation for understanding and advancing agentic AI. These findings aim to help researchers and developers build better, clearer, and more adaptable systems that support responsible deployment in different domains.

Keywords: agentic ai; ai agents; ai systems; adaptive ai; goal-directed ai; ai frameworks and architectures; langchain; metaGPT; chatGPT; multi-agents; ethical ai

1. Introduction

Agentic AI refers to AI systems that do not just answer prompts; they set sub-goals, choose tools, and take multi-step actions to achieve a user's objective with limited supervision. In practice, these systems coordinate multiple agents, each handling part of the job, and an orchestration layer that keeps them aligned with the goal [1]. An agent is a system that senses its environment, decides what to do, and takes action to achieve a goal. A simple example is a travel planner agent: Given 'plan a 3-day trip to Chicago under USD 1500', it breaks the task into subtasks such as flights, hotel, itinerary, queries real-time sources, compares options, book reservations, then produces a shareable plan that asks for confirmation only at key steps. This goes beyond traditional chatbots by planning, acting, and verifying outcomes in a loop [2]. The term AI agent refers to an autonomous software entity that perceives, reasons, and acts to complete specific adaptively directed tasks. The term agentic AI refers to a multi-agent system where specialized agents collaborate, coordinate, and plan to achieve complex, high-level objectives. The difference in these terms for the flight booking example is shown in Figure 1.

Figure 1. Agentic AI vs. AI agents.

Interest in agentic AI is rising quickly as organizations look for automation that impacts real work, not just content generation. Industry analysts now track "AI agents" as a distinct market, estimating ~USD 5.3–5.4B in 2024 and projecting ~USD 50–52 B by 2030 (≈41–46% CAGR), reflecting strong enterprise demand for agents that can reason, use tools, and execute workflows [3,4]. Scholarly research suggests the same movement. One work from Stanford HAI [5] shows human agent that did exhibit human behavior and sustained personas. Additionally, industry advice such as by AWS [2] describes increasing levels of autonomy of which the agent iteratively planned, acted, checked experience, and adjusted each step of the way autonomously rather than expecting prompts step by step from a human. Together, these advances move AI from reactive assistants to proactive collaborators in various fields [6–8].

According to Google Trends, interest in "agentic AI" remained minimal for years, then spiked beginning in April 2024, reaching its peak in July 2025. A value of 100 represents the term's highest recorded popularity, as shown in Figure 2. This sharp rise reflects a global shift toward building AI that can plan, act, and adapt with minimal human guidance.

Traditional systems enabled the automation of individual steps that complied with limited rules; agentic AI connect these steps, track progress, recover from errors, and they are able to automate any end-to-end process, month-end close, claims adjudication, outreach in sales, and even research workflows, previously limited to human effort. Early enterprise reporting highlights this architectural turn from smarter models to agentic, process-embedded systems [9]. This review synthesizes how the field defines agentic AI, the architectures that enable it, where it is being applied, how it is measured, and the open challenges, such as reliability, coordination, safety, and governance, that must be addressed for widespread deployment.

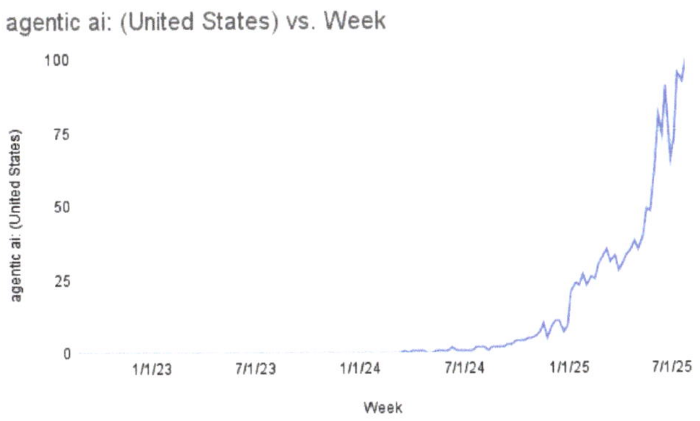

Figure 2. Google Trends shows the popularity of agentic AI.

1.1. Research Purpose

The purpose of this research is to provide a comprehensive review of agentic AI by synthesizing its definitions, frameworks, and architectures, while comparing agentic AI from related paradigms. This study aims to find current tools and frameworks that support agentic capabilities, describe available architectural models of such systems, and explore their applications across domains. Furthermore, it concentrates on the input–output mechanism of agentic AI, existing testing methods, and metrics used to assess agentic performance, and addresses the key challenges and limitations. By doing so, the paper establishes a structured foundation for understanding, assessing, and advancing the field of agentic AI.

1.2. Research Questions

The motivation for this research resulted from the growing importance of agentic AI and the need to better understand what it is and how it works. This study aims to provide researchers and developers with a clear overview of agentic AI by examining its definitions, how it differs from related technologies, the tools and frameworks that support it, its system design, the types of tasks it can perform, how it interacts with inputs and outputs, methods for evaluating it, and the challenges it faces. The objective is to support responsible development and deployment while also assisting in the improvement of agentic system design, use, and evaluation across various domains.

RQ1 How is agentic AI conceptually defined, and how does it differ from related paradigms?

Ans: We define agentic AI's core characteristics, distinguishing it from generative AI, autonomic computing, and multi-agent systems. A Venn diagram-based taxonomy illustrates overlaps and distinctions, clarifying terminology and providing a structured foundation.

RQ2 To what extent do current LLM-based and non-LLM-driven agentic AI, tools, and frameworks enable agentic capabilities?

Ans: We analyze frameworks like LangChain, AutoGPT, BabyAGI, OpenAgents, Autogen, CAMEL, MetaGPT, SuperAGI, TB-CSPN, and non-LLM-driven agentic systems. Their features planning, memory, reflection, and goal pursuit are compared to evaluate how effectively current LLM-based tools enable agentic capabilities and approach true autonomy.

RQ3 What are the core components or architectural models used to build agentic AI systems?

Ans: We define the core architectural components of agentic AI, emphasizing planning modules, memory system, and reasoning engines.

RQ4 What types of goals and tasks are currently being solved using agentic AI across domains?

Ans: We provide a comprehensive classification of goals and tasks being addressed by agentic AI across multiple domains, along with their application contexts and corresponding systems used in the literature, presented in a tabular format.

RQ5 What kinds of input and output formats do agentic AI systems handle in comparison to traditional AI systems?

Ans: We provide a detailed overview of the input and output formats handled by agentic AI systems, along with the specific tasks and corresponding applications, summarized in a tabular format, and compare this with the input–output mechanisms of traditional AI systems.

RQ6 What evaluation methods and metrics are used to assess the performance of agentic AI systems?

Ans: We presented a classification for both the testing methods and the evaluation metrics to evaluate agentic AI systems. The evaluation metrics are further classified into qualitative and quantitative.

RQ7 What are the key challenges and limitations in designing and deploying agentic AI systems?

Ans: We presented different challenges of agentic AI, including architecture and technical challenges, performance and tool integration issues, coordination between multi-agents, and user experience issues, along with ethical and security challenges.

1.3. *Contributions and Research Significance*

This survey provides detailed answers for research questions that show the importance and impacts of agentic AI systems in the real world. Exploring these definitions, frameworks, and architectural models of agentic AI provides important guidance and information to researchers and developers. Understanding these foundational elements is useful for designing agentic AI systems capable of autonomous planning, decision-making, and adaptive behavior. Also, this study reviews current tools and frameworks of agentic AI systems, their input and output mechanisms, and describes how agentic capabilities are implemented in real-time applications. Organizing architectures, applications, and evaluation methods in a clear overview helps people understand and choose the right approaches and tools easily for different tasks and areas.

Additionally, this research examines the key challenges and limitations in developing and deploying agentic AI, including reliability, safety, interpretability, and governance concerns. By highlighting these challenges and discussing robust evaluation methods, it contributes to establishing reliable assessment frameworks that improve the credibility and practical application of agentic AI systems. These insights facilitate informed decision-making in both academic and industrial contexts and support the development of more advanced, dependable, and context-aware agentic AI solutions. Overall, this study offers critical knowledge on conceptual, architectural, and practical aspects of agentic AI, advancing understanding and guiding future research and implementation efforts.

1.4. *Organization of the Paper*

The remainder of this paper is organized as follows. Section 1 introduces the motivation and background for studying agentic AI, the research purpose, proposed research questions, and outlines the overall organization of the paper. Section 2 describes the methodology used to conduct the review and analysis. Section 3 presents the results, beginning with the conceptual definition of agentic AI and its differences from related paradigms. It then examines the extent to which current LLM-based frameworks enable agentic capabilities, followed by a discussion of core components and architectural models, including a comparison between architectures and components. The section further explores the types of goals and tasks addressed by agentic AI across domains, the input–output mechanisms in comparison to generative AI systems, and the evaluation methods and metrics used to assess performance. Challenges and limitations in designing and deploying agentic AI systems are also highlighted. Section 4 concludes the paper by summarizing the findings and offering directions for future research. Appendix A presents tables summarizing the bibliographic search results of primary studies, including publication venues, years, and paper types, while Appendix B lists the abbreviations used throughout the paper.

2. Methodology

To carry out this study, we searched several academic databases, including Library Search, ACM Digital Library, ScienceDirect, Google Scholar, and Semantic Scholar. We created a precise search query ("agentic AI" OR "agent" OR "autonomous AI" OR "multi-agent systems" OR "autonomic computing" OR "generative AI" OR "AI planning" OR "AI memory systems" OR "AI feedback loops") AND ("survey" OR "overview" OR "review" OR "summary" OR "literature review") to find studies relevant to our research. After collecting the results, we removed duplicates and examined abstracts and conclusions to determine relevance. We included papers that discussed agentic AI concepts, systems, or challenges, using case studies, surveys, and other research methods. We also looked at the references of these papers to find additional useful studies. Finally, we extracted key information from all selected studies to summarize current knowledge on agentic AI.

As a result of the search process, we used these 143 primary studies to extract the data, which were published from the year 2005 to the present. More than 90% of these papers were published in 2024 and 2025; from this, it is clear that most of the agentic-AI-system-related papers are being published in recent times. More statistics related to year-wise agentic AI papers publications are shown in Table A1. Out of these papers 17% are conference proceedings, 46% are peer-reviewed journals, and 28% are preprints. Others are dissertations, articles, workshops, etc. Table A2 is a clear distribution format of the type of publication corresponding to the number of papers.

Turning to the publication platform, 32 of these selected papers are published on the arXiv platform, followed by 27 papers from conference proceedings, including ACM International Conferences such as on Autonomous Agents and Multi-agent Systems, Interactive Media Experiences, Information and Knowledge Management, Human Factors in Computing Systems, etc. Additionally, we found 43 papers that are published in journal-based venues such as IEEE Access, Engineering Applications of Artificial Intelligence. One of the selected papers is a PhD dissertation, and the other papers are from Procedia CIRP, MethodsX, etc. Table A3 provides the complete list of venues. We observed that most of the publications are multidisciplinary, which makes sense in the context of agentic AI, as these disciplines are focusing on solving their problems using agentic AI.

Along with the main research papers, we also studied 21 survey and review articles that provide useful perspectives on agentic AI. Each of these surveys was examined based on our chosen dimensions, and their contributions were marked as L, M, H, or NA to represent low, medium, high, and not applicable. As shown in Table 1, many of the surveys emphasize specific aspects such as taxonomy, system architecture, or domain-focused applications of LLM-based agents, while giving little attention to evaluation methods or input–output classifications. Some papers discuss specialized areas like planning, reasoning, integration with 6G networks, or retail systems, while others examine broader themes including trust, risk, operational practices, and public attitudes toward AI.

From this analysis, it is clear that most existing surveys cover only selected dimensions, leaving important areas such as standardized benchmarks, performance evaluation, and input–output modeling less developed. In contrast, our paper provides complete coverage of all six dimensions' definitions and concepts, taxonomy, architecture, applications, input–output classifications, evaluation metrics, and challenges. By taking this wider and unified approach, our research deals with the issues faced in prior research and provides a better understanding of agentic AI that will help address the questions or challenges of any future research and real practice.

Table 1. Summary of important surveys on agentic AI (L—Low, M—Medium, H—High, NA—Not Applicable).

Reference	Year Published	Definition and Concept Taxonomy	Architecture	Applications Classification	Input/Output formats Classification	Evaluation Metrics Metric Classification	Challenges and Limitations	Remarks
[10]	2021	H	M	H	L	M	H	Review of agent-based programming languages and frameworks for multi-agent systems, bridging theory and practice while identifying future research directions.
[11]	2024	M	L	H	NA	L	L	Focuses on use of LLMs and LLM-based agents, highlighting their applications, limitations, and future research directions across key SE tasks.
[12]	2024	L	M	NA	L	NA	NA	Focus on unified taxonomy and decision model to enhance the architectural design, operational understanding of foundation-model-based AI agents.
[13]	2024	H	M	H	NA	NA	H	Survey on unified framework detailing the architecture, applications, and challenges of LLM-based multi-agent systems.
[14]	2024	H	H	M	M	NA	M	Focuses on unified framework for LLM-based autonomous agents, covering their construction, evaluation methods, and future challenges.
[15]	2024	M	M	H	M	M	H	Survey on LLMs enhancing agent-based simulations across physical, cyber, social, and hybrid domains, highlighting challenges and future directions.
[16]	2024	L	NA	L	NA	L	L	The study investigates U.S. public comfort with AI across occupations, showing attitudes vary by automation likelihood and individual traits.
[17]	2024	L	L	L	NA	L	L	Focus multi-AI agent model using LLMs to fully automate and streamline the systematic literature review process.
[18]	2025	M	H	L	M	NA	L	This paper explores 6G network integration with agentic AI, emphasizing automation and support intelligent, energy-efficient, low-latency operations.
[19]	2024	M	H	L	L	M	M	This survey systematically reviews LLM-based agent planning, providing a taxonomy and analyzing recent approaches to improve planning abilities.
[20]	2025	NA	NA	NA	NA	M	M	Focuses on reasoning methods in LLMs, offering a systematic framework to understand evolving LLM reasoning capabilities and trends.

Table 1. *Cont.*

Reference	Year Published	Definition and Concept Taxonomy	Architecture	Applications Classification	Input/Output formats Classification	Evaluation Metrics Metric Classification	Challenges and Limitations	Remarks
[21]	2025	M	M	L	L	M	H	Focus on LLMs and autonomous AI agents, covering benchmarks, frameworks, applications, and future research directions.
[22]	2025	M	NA	L	NA	NA	L	This survey explores the evolution from generative AI to agentic AI, highlighting enhanced reasoning, autonomy, and key challenges for future research.
[23]	2025	M	H	M	L	M	M	The paper proposes an agentic AI framework using LLMs and TDD to enhance reliability, scalability, and decision-making in retail systems.
[24]	2025	M	M	L	L	M	H	Reviews trust, risk, and security management in LLM-based agentic multi-agent systems and proposes a roadmap for responsible deployment.
[25]	2025	M	H	L	L	H	M	Survey on LLM-based planning, categorizing methods and discussing evaluation frameworks and future directions.
[26]	2025	H	M	L	L	M	H	Reviews on LLMOps, AgentOps, and MLOps, outlining best practices and challenges for operationalizing generative AI systems.
[27]	2025	L	H	H	L	M	M	Review of AGI and agentic AI, emphasizing their definitions, architectures, applications, and associated challenges.
[28]	2024	L	M	NA	L	L	M	Review of AI-enhanced tools for SLRs, focusing on screening, extraction, and the integration of LLMs.
[29]	2025	H	H	M	L	M	M	Focuses on taxonomy and comparative analysis of AI agents and agentic AI, highlighting their divergent architectures, applications, and challenges.
[30]	2025	H	M	H	L	L	M	Reviews agentic AI applications in SMMEs, highlighting about enhancing efficiency, adaptability, and innovation through interconnected autonomous agents.
This Paper	2025	H	H	H	H	H	H	Our paper focuses on all six areas and contributes significant results such as definition and concept taxonomy, architecture, applications classification, input/output format classification, evaluation metrics, challenges, and limitations.

3. Results

3.1. How Is Agentic AI Conceptually Defined, and How Does It Differ from Related Paradigms?

Agentic artificial intelligence (agentic AI) marks a major change in how AI systems are designed. Moving beyond passive and reactive tools, agentic AI refers to autonomous, goal-driven systems that can operate on their own for long periods, requiring minimal human supervision [27,31–33]. Unlike traditional AI or standard large language models (LLMs) that respond only to single prompts [34], these systems can understand broad objectives, break them down into smaller tasks, and carry out multi-step plans while adapting to feedback from changing environments [35–37]. Their "agentic" nature also highlights their ability to take on responsibilities from humans [32], act purposefully, and be accountable for the results they produce.

What makes agentic AI stand out is its combination of key abilities in one system. These include strategic planning, memory that preserves context over time, using external tools to extend capabilities, and collaborating with other agents [38–40]. By combining foundation models with planners, knowledge bases, sensors, actuators, and feedback mechanisms, these systems can understand complex environments, adjust strategies in real time, and achieve their goals independently [37,41,42]. However, in the real world, autonomy can be defined as a system's capacity to establish sub-goals, finish tasks without human involvement, and adjust to unexpected events [22]. Even though existing frameworks show some autonomy, they are frequently still constrained by problems like reliance on human-defined goals, vulnerability to mistakes in long-term planning, and difficulties with accountability. This makes them highly valuable in areas like scientific research, industrial automation, and compliance management [43–45], where precision, continuous learning, and smart decision-making are essential.

At the heart of agentic AI is self-directed, goal-focused intelligence. These systems operate with a "degree of agenticness," meaning they can work proactively, plan ahead, and shape outcomes over time [14,46]. As research and industry continue to adopt these systems, agentic AI has the potential to become a reliable partner for humans extending our abilities while raising new questions about trust, oversight, and collaboration [36].

Agentic AI goes beyond simple automation by enabling systems to understand high-level intent, create actionable plans, and carry them out with minimal human input [27,31,38,47]. These systems combine goal-driven behavior, flexible decision-making, and adaptive reasoning to work effectively in dynamic and evolving situations [48–50]. They can pursue multiple goals at once, plan for the long term, and collaborate across several agents or components [37,38,51]. Architecturally, they often integrate large AI models with knowledge bases, planners, access to external tools, and persistent memory to improve understanding and independence [21,42,52]. By continuously learning from experience and adjusting to complex, unpredictable environments [53], agentic AI shifts from simple automation toward reflective, autonomous systems capable of achieving complex objectives.

The purpose of the comparative overview is to present the similarities and differences between multi-agent systems, generative AI, and agentic AI in a structured format, as shown in Table 2. By organizing the paradigms across key aspects such as decision-making, adaptability, learning approach, and workflow management, it highlights their distinctive features. The side-by-side format illustrates the progression from distributed coordination in MAS and pattern-based generation in GenAI toward the autonomy and goal-driven reasoning of agentic AI. This approach ensures complex concepts are communicated clearly.

The purpose of the below Venn diagram in Figure 3 is to provide a visual representation of how multiple fields of artificial intelligence overlap and intersect while emphasizing the importance of agentic AI. It shows how agentic AI overlaps with reinforcement learning and multi-agent systems and places it within the broader universe of AI. This format allows us to better understand and visualize the dependencies and shared characteristics between agentic AI and related fields. In general, the diagram serves as complement to the written discussion in providing a concise and more accessible picture of how agentic AI is situated and interacts within the greater ecosystem of AI technologies.

Table 2. Comparative analysis of AI paradigms: multi-agent systems, generative AI, and agentic AI.

Aspects	Multi-Agent Systems (MAS)	Generative AI (GenAI)	Agentic AI	Ref.
Primary Function	Task division among multiple autonomous agents for collaboration/competition	Task division among multiple autonomous agents for collaboration/competition	Goal-oriented autonomous decision-making with multi-step workflow execution	[27,35,37,39,41,43,45,47,49,54–56]
Decision-Making	Distributed across multiple agents with coordination mechanisms	Pattern-based responses from training data	Independent analysis, reasoning, and contextual decisions	[11–15,19,20,25–27,31,41,44,47,57,58]

Table 2. *Cont.*

Aspects	Multi-Agent Systems (MAS)	Generative AI (GenAI)	Agentic AI	Ref.
Task Scope	Complex goals broken into smaller tasks for individual agents	Single-turn interactions focused on content creation	Multi-step, multi-layered tasks over extended time frames	[10,27,37,47,59–63]
Learning Approch	Individual agent learning with inter-agent communication	Static dataset learning during training phase	Interactive learning with continuous feedback loops and adaptation	[41,57,64,65]
Architecture	Multiple coordinated agents with communication protocols	Primarily transformer-based neural networks	Planning modules, memory systems, tool integration, reasoning components	[27,35,47]
Adaptability	Coordination challenges; varies by system design	Limited to training data patterns; requires retraining for adaptation	Dynamic adaptation to changing environments and goals	[27,41,47,57]
Human Intervention	Varies by implementation; often requires coordination oversight	Moderate intervention for prompt engineering and guidance	Low intervention; operates autonomously with minimal supervision	[47,57,66–68]
Goal Orientation	Distributed goal achievement through agent collaboration	Content generation goals defined by prompts	Self-defined and executed goal-oriented behavior	[18,22–24,27,33,34,37,38,41,47,47,48]
Workflow Management	Distributed workflow across multiple agents	Cannot manage end-to-end workflows independently	Comprehensive end-to-end workflow orchestration	[37,69–73]
Memory Systems	Individual agent memory with shared knowledge bases	No persistent memory between interactions	Sophisticated memory systems with reflection and experience storage	[35,37,39,41,74]
Real-time Adaptation	Complex goals broken into smaller tasks for individual agents	Single-turn interactions focused on content creation	Multi-step, multi-layered tasks over extended time frames	[27,37,47]
Use Cases	Complex distributed problem-solving, simulation systems	Content creation, text generation, image synthesis	Virtual assistants, autonomous systems, adaptive planning, scientific discovery	[37,47,56,75,76]

Figure 3 shows the relationships between different areas of artificial intelligence. At the broadest level, everything falls under AI, with Machine Learning (ML) as a major subset. Inside ML, deep learning (DL), generative AI (Gen AI), and LLMs are shown as nested areas, reflecting their strong connection. Reinforcement learning (RL) also sits within ML but separately. Agentic AI overlaps with these technologies, as it draws from both LLMs and RL, while also sharing ideas with MAS [77,78]. Autonomic computing is placed outside, showing that it is related but not fully inside the AI family; it focuses on self-managing systems that can configure, heal, optimize, and protect themselves, which overlaps with AI but also extends into broader fields like distributed systems and IT infrastructure.

Agentic AI is built strongly on top of LLMs and RL. LLMs give agents the ability to understand and generate natural language, enabling them to reason, plan, and interact in ways that feel human-like. RL, meanwhile, allows agents to learn from their actions and continually improve their decisions, making them adaptive and focused on achieving goals [31,79]. Together, LLMs provide intelligence in communication and knowledge, while RL contributes the ability to learn from experience. This combination is at the heart of how agentic AI systems can plan tasks, solve problems, and act independently.

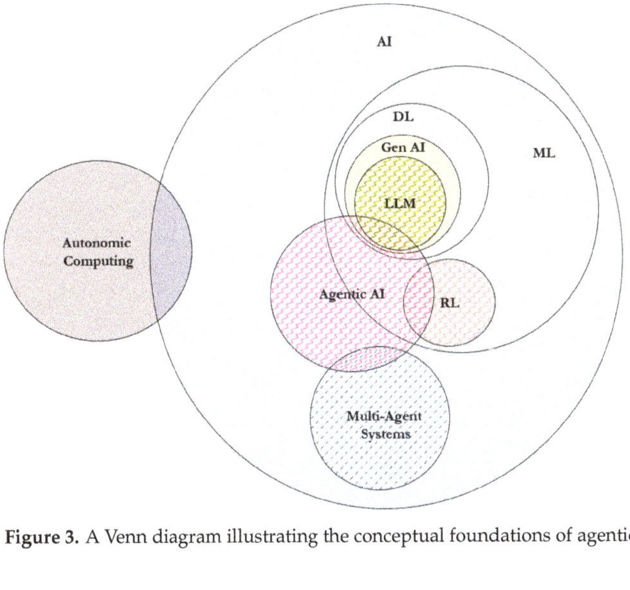

Figure 3. A Venn diagram illustrating the conceptual foundations of agentic AI.

The overlap between MAS and agentic AI is also important. MAS focus on how multiple autonomous agents interact, cooperate, or compete within a shared environment. These skills are essential for agentic AI, where several agents often need to coordinate to achieve complex objectives. Beyond using LLMs and RL, agentic AI depends on planning algorithms and memory systems, which help agents remember past experiences and develop long-term strategies. Altogether, these components form the foundation of agentic AI, allowing it to act not just as a tool but as an intelligent, goal-driven partner.

3.2. To What Extent Do Current LLM-Based and Non-LLM-Driven Agentic Systems, Tools, and Frameworks Enable Agentic Capabilities?

3.2.1. LLM-Based Agentic Systems

The development of LLM-based frameworks like LangChain [26,31,78,80], AutoGPT [26,31,78], BabyAGI [31], AutoGen [80], and OpenAgents [26] shows a clear trend toward building smarter, more independent AI systems. These frameworks give AI agents the ability to plan, remember past actions, reflect on their performance, pursue goals, and use external tools. By equipping agents with these cognitive skills, they become more adaptable and capable of handling complex tasks with minimal human guidance.

Table 3 presents an organized overview of major LLM-based frameworks. It highlights each framework's, primary purpose, key agentic capabilities, and the underlying LLM used. Structuring this information in tabular form makes complex details easier to navigate. The format also facilitates side-by-side comparison, enabling the identification of unique features as well as areas of overlap in agentic capabilities.

Table 3. Agentic capabilities across current LLM-based frameworks.

Framework	Primary Purpose	Key Agentic Capabilities	Primary LLM Used	Ref.
LangChain	Building structured workflows with LLMs	Planning, memory, tool use	OpenAI, Cohere, Anthropic	[26,31,78,79]
AutoGPT	Fully autonomous multi-step task execution	Goal pursuit, planning, reflection, tool use	GPT-4	[43,45,47]
BabyAGI	Accessible autonomous task management	Task decomposition, memory, adaptive execution	OpenAI	[49,81,82]
OpenAgents	Multi-agent collaboration and coordination	Multi-agent reasoning, goal pursuit, iterative planning	GPT-4	[26,78,79]
Autogen	Coordinating multiple AI agents via dialogue	Multi-agent collaboration, planning, reflection	GPT-4	[41]
CAMEL	Simulating multi-agent dialogues with defined roles	Role-based interaction, dialogue simulation, collaborative exploration	GPT-4, LLaMA	[83]
MetaGPT	Multi-agent collaborative problem solving	Automated problem decomposition, role assignment, coordination of agent societies	GPT-4	[84]
SuperAGI	Open-source framework for developing and deploying autonomous agents	Task orchestration, multi-agent workflows, deployment at scale	LLM-agnostic (commonly GPT-4, OpenAI, Anthropic, LLaMA)	[85]
TB-CSPN	Context-aware agentic reasoning beyond prompt chaining	Task decomposition, constraint satisfaction, context-driven decision-making	No specific LLM	[86]

LangChain is a popularly used open source framework that connects LLM to external tools, data sources and APIs, which simplifies the work of constructing complex workflows with multiple steps [26,31,78,79]. It allows developers to construct sequences of reasoning steps (i.e., chains) to help the model reach an objective. LangChain has basic memory that allows you to store and recall information and integrate external knowledge using Retrieval-Augmented Generation (RAG), which gives agents access to documents and databases or search results while they reason [77,80]. While it facilitates task planning and chaining, it does not natively include self-reflection or optimization, so its intelligence is largely guided by the developer. LangChain is ideal for creating structured, goal-oriented workflows where models can interact with external systems and perform contextual reasoning.

AutoGPT is built as a fully autonomous agent capable of completing complex tasks without needing constant human guidance [43,45,47]. It can take high-level goals, break them down into smaller actionable steps, and adjust its plan dynamically as circumstances change. With both short-term and long-term memory, AutoGPT keeps track of context and can handle tasks that go beyond a single interaction. It also leverages tools like web search, code execution, and file management to operate effectively in real-world settings [29,44]. Through its iterative process, AutoGPT can analyze outcomes and refine its actions, combining planning, memory, reflection, and goal-oriented execution to manage tasks autonomously.

BabyAGI approaches the idea of autonomous agents with a slightly different approach, emphasizing simplicity and general accessibility for task generation [49,81]. It can decompose high-level goals into smaller, actionable steps for task outputs and has memory to keep track of progress made on a particular multi-step task. BabyAGI has extensions for working with external tools, such as those for code generation and robotics, so it can effectively act in both digital and physical environments. Although it does not have a fully explicit reflection ability like AutoGPT, and it is still all iterative, meaning that it can execute a task, receive feedback, and refine or adopt new actions over time, to give it a practical level of self-correction for goal achievement [82]. BabyAGI should provide developers the ability to implement autonomous problem-solving agents of moderate complexity.

AutoGen is designed for multi-agent systems, allowing several AI agents to communicate, collaborate, and work together to solve tasks [41]. Each agent can create its own plan while coordinating with others, using memory to track past actions and shared context. The framework supports reflection and optimization, so agents can evaluate their plans and improve them over time. By combining tool use with teamwork, AutoGen reduces errors, boosts performance, and can tackle complex, distributed goals more effectively. This makes it especially useful for research or applications that rely on multi-agent reasoning and collaborative workflows.

OpenAgents focuses on developing LLM-based agents that can work together in a shared ecosystem to accomplish complex goals [26,78,79]. The framework uses contextual memory to keep interactions coherent over multiple steps, and it supports iterative planning and reasoning so agents can refine their decisions over time. By integrating external tools, agents can carry out tasks effectively while combining internal reasoning with knowledge from outside sources [31,77,80]. OpenAgents also lets agents improve themselves through repeated reasoning cycles and supports collaboration among multiple agents on tasks that require continuous decision-making, dynamic problem-solving, or integrating diverse sources of knowledge .

Communicative Agents for "Mind" Exploration of Large-Scale Language Model Society (CAMEL) is a framework for multiple agents that enables role-playing: LLM agents discuss with each other to see what new behaviors they come up with. In order to solve tasks, it assigns complementary roles (such as "User" and "Assistant") and promotes dialogue-based collaboration [83,87]. CAMEL facilitates autonomous reasoning, negotiation, and iterative solution refinement by breaking down objectives into conversational exchanges. In contrast to conventional single-agent systems, CAMEL makes use of multiple agents' interactions to produce more complex results. The majority of implementations use GPT-4 and Large Language Model Meta AI (LLaMA) as the underlying models, though it can operate on other LLMs. In constrained or open-ended environments, CAMEL is especially helpful for studying agent coordination, cooperation, and emergent problem-solving. MetaGPT is an advanced framework for multi-agent collaborative problem-solving that leverages GPT-4 as a central intelligent agent. It automates tasks that can be represented as a series of smaller sub-problems by breaking each problem into sub-problems, automatically assigning sub-problems to agents based on their specialization, and coordinating agents' interactions to solve the overlying problem [84,87]. By managing an organized "society" of agents, MetaGPT can achieve efficiency and scalability in solving challenging problems. MetaGPT can be used to automate workflows or research or to support decision-making and reasoning tasks that draw upon diverse expertise and collaborative reasoning. It is best designed with seamless communication and task management of dynamic complexity among multiple agents, showcasing a highly advanced evolution of AI-enabled collaboration.

SuperAGI is an open-source framework for autonomous agents. Developers can quickly define, deploy, and manage LLM-powered agents, with great flexibility. The software is mostly model-agnostic and supports LLMs from many providers (LLaMA, Anthropic, and OpenAI). SuperAGI agents have the capability for goal-directed execution; memory management; multi-step planning; and tool use, among others [85]. In addition, SuperAGI includes resource controls and monitoring to constrain autonomous behavior. Unlike lighter-weight orchestration tools, SuperAGI is oriented toward production readiness, allowing agents to be scaled and monitored within real-world workflows. Its modularity and extensibility make it a strong contender for enterprise-level autonomous agent applications.

A hybrid framework called Task-Based Cognitive Sequential Planning Network (TB-CSPN) blends selective LLM use with formal rule-based coordination [86]. Its architecture limits LLM involvement to semantic topic extraction and uses Colored Petri Nets for deterministic task planning and execution. This eliminates the possibility of LLM visions or non-determinism by guaranteeing that reasoning and sequencing are logically consistent and verifiable. Instead of using unrestricted LLM reasoning, TB-CSPN agents use structured tokens to communicate, and their interactions are guided by formal cognitive models. TB-CSPN demonstrates a more cautious integration of AI balancing LLM flexibility with symbolic rigor, in contrast to frameworks that mainly rely on language models for planning. It works particularly well in fields that need topic-driven task coordination, auditability, and dependability.

3.2.2. Non-LLM-Driven Agentic Systems

Intelligent agents can act and make decisions outside of large language models. Non-LLM-dependent agentic systems achieve autonomy through either rules, learning, planning, or reactive behaviors; they have been used extensively in robotics, simulations, and automated decision-making. These systems show that AI can be effective and adaptive without natural language understanding.

One important type is rule-based multi-agent systems. In these systems, agents follow predefined rules or logic to interact and achieve coordinated outcomes. Examples include CLIPS, Drools, and JADE [88], which are used for simulations, workflow automation, and decision-support tasks. Another key category is RL [89,90] agents, which learn from trial and error. Using algorithms like Q-learning, Deep Q-Networks (DQN), [91] and Policy Gradient methods, RL agents improve their performance over time by interacting with their environment. These agents are commonly used in robotics, autonomous vehicles, and dynamic systems.

Other non-LLM agentic systems include planning agents, which use algorithms such as STRIPS or PDDL [92] to achieve goals; agent-based simulation frameworks like NetLogo [93] and MASON [94], which model complex social, ecological, or economic behaviors; and behavior-based robotic agents, such as those using subsumption architectures, which respond to environmental stimuli through simple sensorimotor rules. Together, these systems demonstrate that intelligence, adaptability, and autonomous behavior can emerge through rules, learning, and planning, highlighting the broad potential of agentic AI beyond language-based models.

3.3. Core Components and Architectural Models for Agentic AI

This section defines a set of agent components and uses them to compare architectures by control flow and module wiring rather than terminology: perception, world/state, memory, planning, execution/tooling, reflection/evaluation, orchestration, and interaction. We then outline five orchestration models, ReAct (Reasoning + Acting) single-agent, supervisor/hierarchical, Hybrid reactive–deliberative, BDI, and layered neuro-symbolic, highlighting when to use each.

3.3.1. Core Functional Components of Agentic AI Systems

Core components are the reusable building blocks of agentic AI, wired together by architectural choices. A common set includes the following:

- Perception and world modeling—Ingests and structures external inputs (e.g., text, sensors, APIs) into internal representations [41,95].
- Memory (Short-Term, Long-Term, Episodic)—Stores short- and long-term knowledge; retrieval/promotion rules connect past to present reasoning [39,95].
- Planning, Reasoning, and Goal Decomposition—Transforms goals into actionable steps, evaluates alternatives, and selects next actions [95].
- Execution and Actuation—Carries out actions via APIs or actuators, with monitoring and dynamic replanning [41].
- Reflection and Evaluation—Enables self-critique, verification, and refinement of actions and plans [50].
- Communication, Orchestration, and Autonomy—Coordinates task flow, retries, and timeouts, either centrally (e.g., LLM-based supervisor) or via decentralized protocols [50,96].
  This component stack recurs across both academic and industry implementations, including high-stakes domains like finance [39].

The model, typically an LLM, large agent model (LAM), or foundation model (FM), provides the system's core intelligence. It often serves as the reasoning engine, perceptual front-end, and, in many cases, the orchestrator. In Multi-Agent Artificial Intelligence (MAAI) frameworks, the model forms a base layer for perception, action, orchestration, workflows, and user interaction [96]. Tutorials increasingly integrate LLMs/LAMs with planners, memory, tools, and knowledge bases [42].

Agentic AI behavior arises from a coordinated set of reusable components rather than from a single model, as shown in Figure 4. In the following, we synthesize the modules and how they interact.

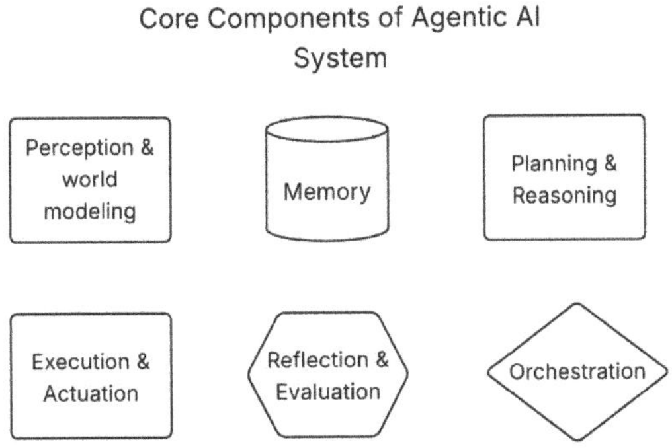

Figure 4. Core components of agentic AI system.

Perception and World Modeling: Perception ingests external inputs (text, events, sensors/APIs) and normalizes them into structured observations. World/state modeling maintains an internal representation used for prediction, consistency checks, and counterfactual simulation. In embodied or data-rich settings, perception is multimodal and frequently layered with probabilistic inference to manage uncertainty before symbolic planning or execution [41,42,95].

Memory (Short-Term, Long-Term, Episodic): Memory provides temporal continuity. Short-term memory (STM) maintains episode context (e.g., current plan, recent exchanges); long-term memory (LTM) stores episodic/semantic knowledge (e.g., preferences, histories, artifacts). Retrieval and promotion rules connect STM and LTM so that prior outcomes inform future decisions, reflection, and personalization [47,50,95].

Planning, Reasoning, and Goal Decomposition: The planning/reasoning module transforms goals into actionable steps, evaluates alternatives, and selects next actions across short and long horizons. Granularity varies by paradigm: BDI filters desires into intentions; HRL decomposes abstract goals into sub-tasks; single-agent ReAct interleaves reasoning with action (often with tool calls) [41,47,95].

Execution and Actuation: Execution bridges cognition to impact. It invokes tools/APIs, actuators, or workflow steps; validates outcomes against expectations; and triggers retries or replanning on deviation. Production-oriented variants emphasize schema checks, budget/latency limits, and robust error handling to support closed-loop operation in dynamic environments [41,42,95].

Reflection and Evaluation: Reflection/evaluation modules verify intermediate or final outputs, critique candidate plans, and trigger selective replanning. Practical patterns include self-critique, external tool-assisted verification, and nested "critic" roles that reduce hallucination and improve reliability while adding computational overhead [50,95].

Communication, Orchestration, and Autonomy: Interaction modules support human–agent and agent–agent dialogue (clarification, negotiation, oversight) and surface trace information (e.g., actions, tools, sources) for transparency. Autonomy emerges when perception, planning, execution, memory, and reflection are orchestrated over time; in many systems, an LLM-based supervisor coordinates sub-agents, invokes memory or tools, and maintains coherence across steps [41,50,97].

3.3.2. Architectural Models in Agentic AI

Agentic AI systems are not monolithic; their capabilities emerge from architectures that coordinate planning, execution, memory, reasoning, and interaction. Below, we outline five commonly used models and their control flows.

ReAct Single-Agent:

Figure 5 represents the architecture flow of ReAct single agent. ReAct instantiates a single agent that interleaves stepwise reasoning and acting, optionally inserting a lightweight evaluator before committing an output [98]. The core components are perception/world-state, planning/reasoning, execution and actuation, memory (STM/LTM), and reflection/evaluation; the architecture wires these into a minimal, locally orchestrated pipeline with no external supervisor. The agent observes via perception, reasons in plan/reason to select the next step, acts in execute/tools to affect the world or produce a user reply, may evaluate the result, and then updates memory before repeating. The goal is fast iteration on well-bounded tasks, where a compact loop outperforms heavier orchestration.

Components and flow: Data and control proceed left to right: the agent observes (perception), optionally retrieves salient context from memory, reasons in plan/reason to select the next step with success criteria, acts in act/execute via a tool/API, and may evaluate the outcome before logging/promoting state and repeating. In the diagram, rounded rectangles denote processing modules (perception → reason/plan → act/execute) connected by solid arrows (primary progression); memory is shown as a cylinder with an upward arrow to reason/plan (retrieval) and dashed downward arrows from act/execute (and, if present, the evaluator) for logging/promotions; evaluation appears as a hexagon branching by a solid arrow from act/execute and returning dashed feedback to reason/plan and/or memory. User-visible responses are produced in act/execute; the loop closes at the environment boundary when the updated world or next user turn re-enters perception as a new observation.

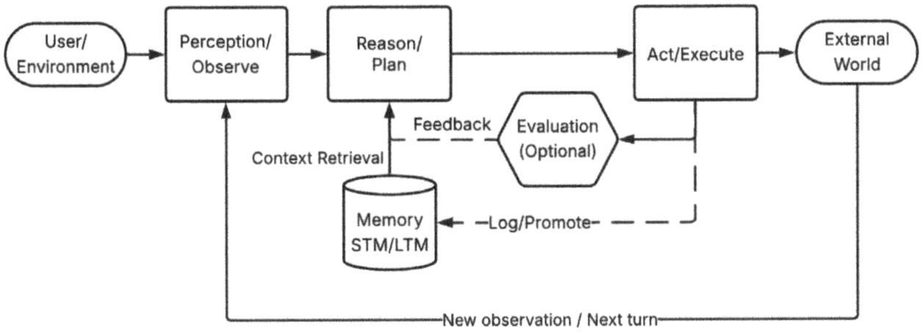

Figure 5. ReAct single-agent loop.

Use and trade-offs: Interleaving reasoning with action tends to improve multi-step task success, and brief critique/verification further suppresses hallucinations; both, however, introduce extra inference steps and wall-clock latency. ReAct is therefore a strong baseline for bounded, single-persona workloads and rapid prototyping. Its simplicity does not scale gracefully: the loop affords little parallelism, weak long-horizon coordination, and increasing tool-selection brittleness as the tool surface and dependency depth grow. For tasks requiring persistent goals, specialization, or oversight, escalation to supervisor/hierarchical (delegation and parallel execution) or Hybrid reactive–deliberative (real-time reflexes with planning) is appropriate despite added coordination overhead [98].

Supervisor/Hierarchical:

A supervisor/orchestrator as shown in Figure 6 decomposes high-level goals into subtasks and delegates them to role-specialized sub-agents, each of which executes locally using a compact ReAct-style loop, perception → reason/plan → act/execute, with optional evaluation and memory, while an optional shared/federated state maintains coherence across agents [47,50,95].

Components and flow: Operationally, control proceeds as planning → delegation → execution → reporting → possible re-planning. The supervisor (diamond) issues assignments (solid progression) and receives reports (dashed) that trigger retries or re-planning when outcomes deviate. Within each sub-agent, memory supports retrieval (solid) into planning and accepts logging/promotions (dashed) from execution/evaluation; evaluation appears as a hexagon branching from act/execute, feeding feedback into planning/memory.

Use and trade-offs: This architecture is well-suited to decomposable, multi-stage tasks that benefit from parallel specialization and clear ownership; it improves scalability via hierarchical delegation but incurs coordination overhead and risks a supervisor bottleneck/single point of failure if the controller is not engineered for throughput, fault-tolerance, and observability [47,50,95].

Hybrid reactive–deliberative:

A hybrid architecture runs two coordinated loops in parallel, as shown in Figure 7. A fast reactive loop that handles time-critical events and a slower deliberative loop that maintains goals and plans. The loops share a common memory and are overseen by an Arbitrator (diamond) that resolves conflicts when immediate reactions and long-horizon plans disagree [38,47,95].

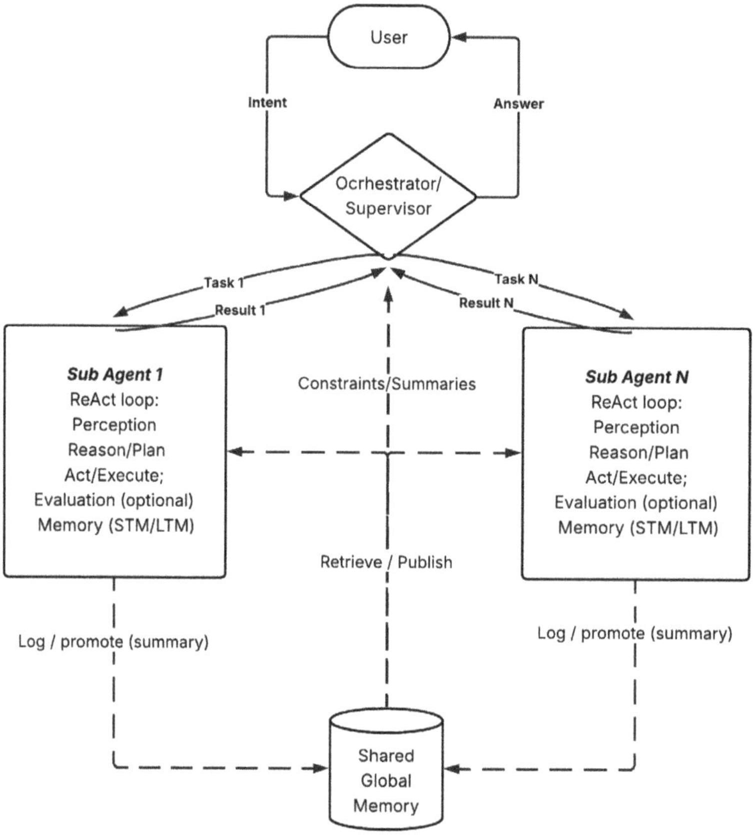

Figure 6. Supervisor/hierarchical architecture.

Components and flow: The reactive path couples perception of events to actions/actuation with minimal latency; safety/guard checks are typically embedded here. The deliberative path performs planning/reasoning over longer horizons, updating goals and selecting action sequences; it reads from and writes to memory (cylinder) to maintain temporal coherence. A shared memory module synchronizes state between the loops. The Arbitrator (diamond) mediates which loop has control when their recommendations diverge, using task/goal priorities and policy constraints. Flow proceeds: perceive (reactive and abstract inputs) → (branch) fast react vs. slower plan → arbitrate (diamond) → execute → evaluate (hexagon) → update memory → possibly re-plan.

Use and trade-offs: The hybrid model balances speed with strategic reasoning, but this comes with arbitration complexity and a requirement for reliable state synchronization across loops to avoid instability or "thrash." Empirically and in surveyed practice, it is preferred for real-time operations with long-horizon objectives; risks concentrate in arbitration design and consistency across loops [38,47,95].

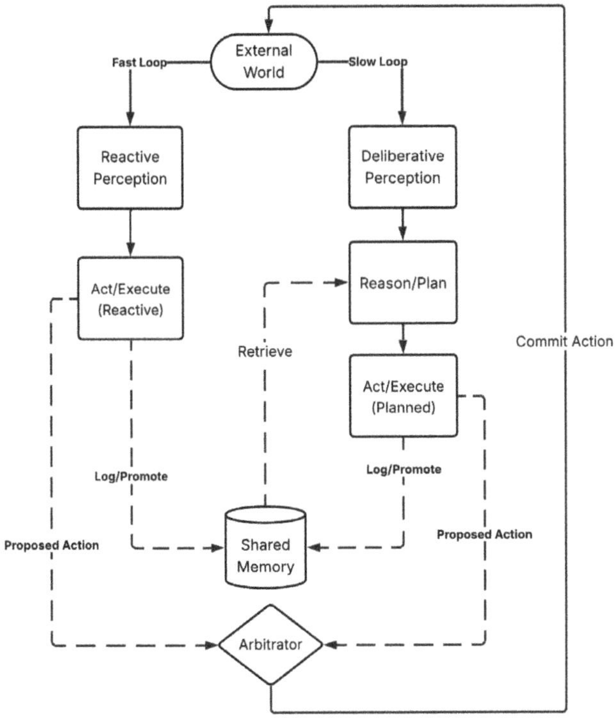

Figure 7. Hybrid reactive–deliberative.

Belief–Desire–Intention (BDI):

The BDI architecture models, as shown in Figure 8, deliberation with explicit mental states: beliefs (world information/state), desires (candidate goals), and intentions (the subset of goals the agent commits to pursue). A canonical cycle is observe → update beliefs → generate desires → filter to intentions → act → repeat; commitment rules maintain intentions until a goal is achieved, becomes impossible, or is superseded [38,95].

Components and flow: External world inputs are observed and update beliefs/world state. The agent derives desires and filters them into intentions according to domain rules and commitment policies. Act/execute realizes the current intention via tools/APIs/actuators, producing effects on the external world. An optional evaluation gate verifies outcomes or constraints and can feed revisions back to the desire set or commitment filter. Memory supplies retrieval to the desire/intention stage (schemas, facts, episodic traces) and receives logs/promotions from act/execute and evaluation (summaries, artifacts, outcomes). Control proceeds top→down, world → beliefs → desires → intentions → act/execute, followed by evaluation and memory update; the loop closes when the changed world yields the next observation back into beliefs [38,95].

Use and trade-offs: BDI is a strong fit for tasks where explainability, goal discipline, and traceability matter (e.g., auditability or safety cases). It trades some adaptability for clarity: commitment rules and symbolic state make reasoning legible but can become brittle in open-world settings without robust belief-revision and exception policies [47,50,95].

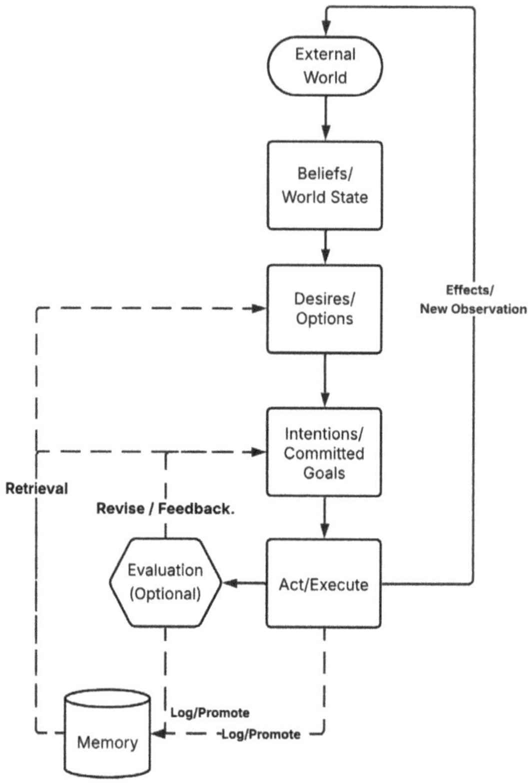

Figure 8. Belief–desire–intention (BDI) architecture.

Layered Decision (Neuro-Symbolic):

Layered decision architecture is shown in Figure 9. Layered decision architectures integrate neural perception and probabilistic inference with a symbolic planner and an execution layer, typically followed by evaluation and memory update. The aim is to handle uncertainty via statistical inference while preserving interpretability and traceable decisions through symbolic planning [38,39,41,95].

Components and flow: Perception ingests signals (text, images, telemetry) and encodes features. Probabilistic inference converts these into calibrated state estimates and event hypotheses, exposing uncertainty to discrete reasoning. The symbolic planner operates on this structured state with explicit rules, goals, and constraints; it retrieves schemas, facts, and episodic traces from memory. Act/execute materializes the chosen step via tools/APIs/actuators, producing effects on the external world. An optional evaluation stage performs verification (e.g., constraint checks, cross-model critics), returning feedback to the planner and logging/promoting artifacts to memory; act/execute likewise logs/promotes to memory. Control is top→down, external world → perception → probabilistic inference → symbolic planner → act/execute, followed by evaluation and memory updates; the loop closes as the updated world re-enters perception [38,95].

Use and trade-offs: Layered neuro-symbolic designs are well-suited to open-world decision-making under uncertainty and to domains needing transparent, auditable reasoning (e.g., public-sector workflows). The principal cost is integration and representation alignment, bridging neural encodings with symbolic state/rules and evaluation/feedback, which increases design and maintenance overhead. These strengths and costs are summarized in your comparative table and discussion.

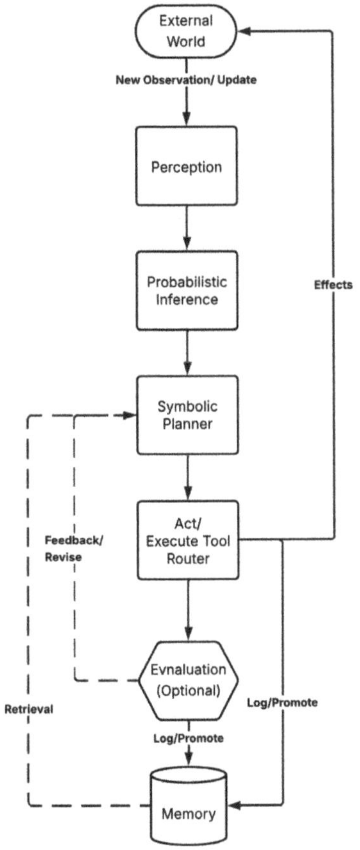

Figure 9. Layered decision (neuro-symbolic) architecture.

3.3.3. Coordination and Modularity in Agentic Architectures

Agentic AIs succeed or fail not only by which components they contain but by how those components are modularized and coordinated at runtime. This section summarizes dominant coordination mechanisms and their trade-offs.

Modular Composition:

Architectures commonly encapsulate perception, planning/reasoning, memory, execution/tooling, and reflection into independently deployable subsystems with clear interfaces. This promotes scalability (scale out specific modules), fault isolation (contain failures), and parallelism (concurrent role execution). Modularity also enables "plug-and-play" evolution, e.g., swapping a planner or adding a compliance checker, without redesigning the full system. Design guidance emphasizes tight control of interfaces and state contracts between modules to support predictable orchestration and observability [42,47,50,96].

Orchestration and Supervisory Control:

Centralized orchestration: Many systems employ a supervisor (often LLM-based) to route tasks, maintain shared context, trigger reflection or replanning, and arbitrate conflicts between competing goals. The supervisor coordinates specialist agents (planner, retriever, executor, critic), aggregates results, and enforces guardrails and approval gates where required [50,95].

Decentralized orchestration: In multi-agent settings, decision-making is distributed via message-passing and shared-state protocols; roles negotiate or vote to coordinate actions. This improves fault tolerance and throughput but increases testing and observability complexity and requires robust protocols for consensus and backoff [42,47,96].

When to prefer which: Centralized control suits tightly regulated or safety-critical workflows with clear accountability; distributed control fits large, decomposable workloads with dynamic specialization and resilience needs.

Communication Protocols and Workflow Graphs:

Production systems typically (i) exchange structured messages (e.g., JSON) including task intents, state snapshots, and tool results, enabling replay and lineage; (ii) use workflow graphs to represent control flow (branching, retries, compensations); and (iii) attach evaluation hooks (critics, policy checks) at key transitions to gate risky actions and trigger replanning or escalation. Graph-based orchestration frameworks and multi-agent planning protocols are frequently reported to improve robustness under non-determinism while preserving transparency for operators [41,42,50,96].

3.3.4. Integration of Components into Architecture

Agentic AI differ from conventional pipelines in that components are integrated into continuous decision loops that sense, plan, act, evaluate, and learn.

Layered and Modular Pipelines:

A common integration pattern is a layered flow that couples components into an end-to-end decision loop: perception $\rightarrow$ world/state modeling $\rightarrow$ planning/reasoning $\rightarrow$ execution/tooling $\rightarrow$ evaluation/feedback $\rightarrow$ memory $\rightarrow$ (back to) planning. Although often depicted linearly, these flows are event-driven and cyclic: evaluation and feedback can branch to retries or replanning; memory promotion/demotion changes subsequent retrieval; and perception can interrupt with high-priority events. Effective designs define explicit interfaces (inputs/outputs, schemas, confidence) at each boundary and attach gates (e.g., policy checks, critics) before risky actions [41,42,95]. This organization supports persistent goal pursuit (long horizon), real-time adaptation (short horizon), and safe recovery from deviations [41,95].

Orchestration Mechanisms:

Centralized orchestration: Many systems elevate an LLM to a supervisor role that maintains shared context, routes tasks to specialist modules/agents (planner, retriever, executor, critic), triggers reflection or replanning, and arbitrates conflicts among goals. The supervisor executes a graph (DAG/state machine) with branching, retries, compensations, and evaluator hooks at critical transitions to keep lineage auditable and side effects idempotent [42,50,97].

Graph-based execution:

Regardless of centralization, integrating components with an explicit workflow graph improves robustness under non-determinism. Nodes encapsulate component calls (with contracts for inputs/outputs and budgets), and edges encode control logic (success/failure, timeouts, escalation). Evaluators or policy guards can be placed at ingress/egress of high-risk nodes (e.g., external tools) [42,50].

Trade-offs: Centralized supervisors simplify accountability and debugging but may bottleneck or introduce single-point-of-failure risk; decentralized flows increase resilience and throughput but require stronger state contracts, message protocols, and observability [42,47,50].

Multi-Agent Integration and Decentralization:

In decentralized designs, agents each own a subset of components (e.g., local planner + executor + memory) and coordinate via shared context and message passing. Common patterns include role-based teams (planner/solver/critic), peer networks with negotiation/voting, and hybrid hierarchies that mix supervisor(s) with collaborating peers. Integration hinges on (i) shared state (what is global vs. local), (ii) protocols for task handoff and conflict resolution, and (iii) placement of evaluators/approvals for safety or compliance. This model yields fault tolerance and parallel specialization but increases testing/monitoring complexity and demands clear traceability of who decided what and why [39,47,97].

3.3.5. Architectural Models vs. Core Components

Table 4 synthesizes how common architectural families connect the components introduced earlier and compares the core agent components between the major architectural families, highlighting their typical uses and associated risks. It shows how different designs emphasize particular strengths: BDI architectures rely on explicit beliefs, desires, and intentions to support explainable decision systems, but require extensive symbolic modeling and can be brittle under uncertainty [38,41]; hierarchical/HRL models scale well for decomposable tasks through multi-level goal delegation, though they risk supervisor bottlenecks [50,96]; ReAct single agents offer lightweight reasoning–action loops for rapid iteration, but struggle with parallelism and reliable tool selection [47]; Hybrid reactive–deliberative systems balance fast reflexes with long-horizon planning, yet require careful arbitration design [38]; and layered neuro-symbolic approaches integrate neural inference with symbolic reasoning to manage uncertainty and provide traceability, though at the cost of added integration complexity [39,41,95]. Together, the table underscores how architectural choices map to trade-offs in scalability, transparency, and robustness, guiding when each model is most appropriate.

Table 4. Components and risks across architecture families

Architecture	Perception/State	Planning and Reasoning	Memory	Execution and Action	Reflection/ Feedback	Orchestration/ Autonomy	Typical Uses	Salient Risks
BDI (Belief–Desire–Intention)	✓ explicit beliefs	✓ desire filtering, intention commitment	○ belief updates persistent	✓ goal-driven loop	○ intention revision	✓ central loop, commitment	Explainable decision systems; simulations	Symbolic modeling effort; brittle under high uncertainty [38,41]
Hierarchical (HRL/ modular)	✓ local/implicit state	✓ multi-level goal decomposition	○ episodic (reward/trace)	✓ layered policies, sub-task execution	○ performance driven replans	✓ supervisor(s) (top-down)	Decomposable, large programs; parallel teams	Supervisor bottlenecks; debugging across tiers [50,96]
ReAct single-agent (LLM)	✓ LLM-driven interpretation	✓ stepwise CoT / ReAct	○ STM/LTM as needed	✓ tool/API invocation	○ language based self-critique	✓ local orchestration	Fast baselines; scoped assistants	Limited parallelism; tool-selection errors at scale [47]
Hybrid (reactive-deliberative)	✓ sensor + abstract model	✓ deliberative planner	○ localized recall	✓ reactive+ planned actions	○ arbitration triggered	✓ Supervisor arbitration	Real-time ops with long horizon	Consistency across loops; arbitration design [38]
Layered Neuro-Symbolic	✓ neural perception+ inference	✓ symbolic planner	✓ memory for rules/episodes	✓ planner to actuator tools	✓ verification/ reflection	✓ structured orchestration	Open-world planning under uncertainty; public sector	Integration overhead; representation alignment [39,41,95]

✓ = typically required; ○ = optional.

3.4. *What Types of Goals and Tasks Are Currently Being Solved Using Agentic AI Across Domains?*

Agentic AI is used in a large number of areas and applications in order to accomplish a large variety of goals and tasks. Agentic AI systems can determine a high-level objective, breaking that objective down into smaller tasks, and efficiently accomplishing those tasks, even in environments that are evolving and that are inherently unpredictable and/or complex processes. Agentic AI can reason, build plans, and act autonomously to adapt to a new scenario, work as part of a team, and produce results that may be difficult or impractical to produce with other types of AI.

Agentic AI systems are used to complete routine activities, support in real-time decision-making, handle complex tasks or problems, and provide personalized assistance by adapting to the context. The system's strength is in combining data from many sources, making ethical and informed decisions, and coordinating multiple agents to work together in real time.

The rationale for creating a domain-based categorization of agentic AIs is to clarify how these systems are molded and shaped by the specific needs, boundaries, and objectives of each of the fields deployed. The domain-based framework not only provides the clarity in displaying agentic capabilities across multiple domains highlighting similarities in abilities that were common but others that would be unique to a specific agent. The overview of the application categories is shown in Figure 10. Moreover, it allowed the reader to identify active patterns within a specific domain, while allowing for tabular comparison of other domains.

There are three components of Table 5: the domain, the application, and the tasks and/or considerations associated with the agents' work. This allows for quick access to important information without reading full paragraphs. The diagram serves as a companion piece, but includes an additional layer to represent a domain with relationships to their applications, as well as where domains share characteristics. Viewing where the table and diagram intersect means the reader has both meaningful representation, and sufficient detail to challenge if agentic AIs are acting as agents in real and experimental contexts.

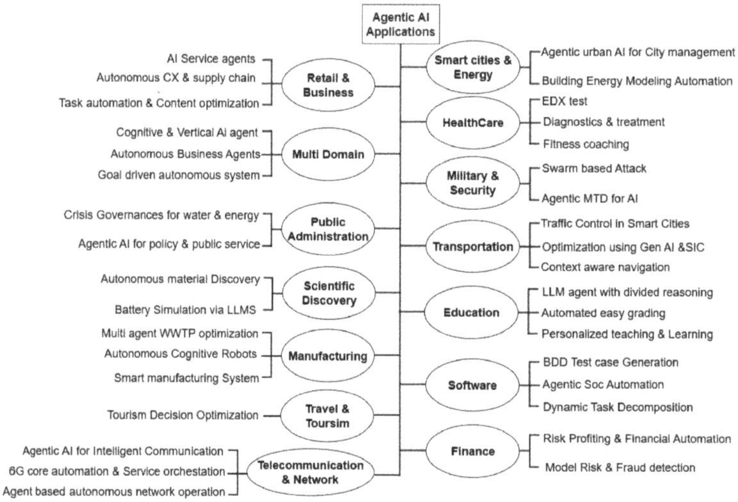

Figure 10. Overview of agentic AI applications across multiple domains.

Table 5. Agentic AI applications and tasks across multiple domains.

Domain	Application	Goal/Task Attempted by Agentic AI	Ref.
Healthcare	Diagnostics and treatment planning	Enhancing healthcare decision support, diagnosis, and personalization.	[59]
	Fitness Coaching	Personalized, adaptive fitness coaching using multimodal multi-agent digital twin systems.	[60]
	Neuromuscular Electrodiagnostic	Standardized, AI-assisted interpretation and reporting of neuromuscular EDX tests for electrophysiologists.	[99]
	Genomic analysis and dynamic health management	Personalized, real-time healthcare management using agentic AI for prediction, intervention, monitoring, and workflow optimization.	[35]

Table 5. *Cont.*

Domain	Application	Goal/Task Attempted by Agentic AI	Ref.
	Ethical oversight in generative AI	Ethical, compliant, and trustworthy deployment of GenAI in healthcare via agentic oversight.	[44]
	Computer vision (medical CV)	Autonomous construction and execution of medical image segmentation pipelines via agentic AI.	[100]
	Bioethical clinical decision support	Advisory system for ethical clinical decision support in complex healthcare scenarios.	[101]
	Clinical Decision and Drug Discovery	Transforming healthcare to enable accurate diagnostics, personalized treatment planning, real-time patient monitoring, workflow automation, and drug discovery.	[56]
	Clinical Risk Assessment	Real-time identification and assessment of DILI risks using LLM on clinical notes.	[102]
Transportation	Traffic control in Smart Cities	Enhancing traffic control, safety, and sustainability in urban transportation systems.	[103]
	Industrial Systems –Transportation, and Biomanufacturing	Real-time optimization, control, and personalization in industrial and biomanufacturing systems.	[43]
	Autonomous Vehicle Control and Safety	Multimodal model predictive control for safe, context-aware autonomous vehicle navigation.	[74]
	Multi-Agent Routing and Scheduling	Multi-agent routing and scheduling optimization in logistics and guidepath networks.	[61]
	Human-Machine Transportation Systems	Multi-agent management of transportation systems across lifecycle phases to improve travel outcomes, safety, and system adaptability.	[104]
Software	Automated query and task processing	Autonomously decompose complex queries, select relevant tools, and execute tasks efficiently with real-time feedback.	[105]
	BDD Test Case Generation	Automate BDD test case generation from natural language while supporting code mapping and user collaboration.	[106]
	Computer vision in healthcare, robotics	Enable autonomous, real-time decision-making and adaptive behavior from visual data for complex perception and interaction tasks.	[107]
	Software and task automation in SMMEs	Automate software engineering and business tasks through autonomous, goal-driven multi-agent systems.	[30]
	Fraud and sensor drift management.	Automate and optimize data pipelines with adaptive, interpretable, and balanced agent-driven learning.	[54]
	Personalized search and recommendations	Develop AI agents for personalized, relevant, and fair information retrieval across complex and multimodal queries.	[108]
	CV task automation for non-expert users.	Automate CV tasks via natural language commands for non-experts.	[109]
	Fault-Tolerant Multi-agent Software Systems	Design fault-tolerant software systems with autonomous multi-agent control and recovery.	[62]
	Automatic Programming for End-Users	Enable end-user software development from natural requirements to deployment using LLMs.	[110]
	SLM-based software and IT task automation	Automate software and IT tasks and coordinate multi-agent workflows using SLMs.	[111]
	Personalized and autonomous IR systems.	Improve relevance, accuracy, and personalization in IR systems with autonomous task handling.	[112]
Software	Autonomous software development	Automate multi-step software development and optimize workflows, code quality, and maintenance autonomously.	[50,51]
	Web and file automation	Execute complex digital tasks with minimal oversight using modular multi-agent systems.	[113]
	Human-algorithmic agency modeling	Clarify and theorize agency in human-algorithmic ensembles to inform organizational governance and socio-technical system design.	[114]
	Conversational software testing agent	Develop SOCRATEST, an autonomous LLM-based conversational agent for software testing.	[115]
	Conversational MLOps	Facilitate human–AI collaborative MLOps using conversational interfaces.	[116]
	Agentic SOC automation	Automate SOC operations for proactive detection, mitigation, and response to cyber threats.	[117]
	Autonomous IT operations and automation	Autonomous IT operations for real-time incident detection, prediction, and resolution. LLM-driven autonomous IT operations enabling adaptive, collaborative incident detection, prediction, and resolution.	[49,118]
Military and Security	Multi-Agent Attack-Defense Coordination	Autonomous swarm decision-making for coordinated attack-defense in military confrontations.	[119]
	AI Workloads and Infrastructure Defense	Automated moving-target defense for AI workloads through ephemeral infrastructure rotation in Kubernetes.	[120]
Manufacturing and Industrial	WWTP optimization	Optimize full-scale wastewater treatment plant operation to cut costs and improve water quality under varying conditions.	[63]
	Smart Manufacturing and robotic assembly	Develop autonomous, multi-agent systems to optimize manufacturing workflows, task sequencing, and adaptive production processes.	[33,121]
	Automated Supply Chain Decisions	Enable autonomous decision-making in food supply chains to improve efficiency, safety, and reduce waste.	[55]
	Cognitive robots for collaboration	Develop autonomous, cognitive robotic agents that can safely cooperate with humans, learn continuously, and plan for future scenarios.	[122]
	Autonomic quality management	Achieve self-managing, autonomic manufacturing systems that reduce human effort, ensure compliance, and optimize execution for total quality achievement.	[123]
	Human–Robot Collaboration	Predict 3D human motion to enable safe and efficient human–robot collaboration in construction tasks.	[124]
	Multi-Agent Pickup and Delivery	Enable multi-agent pickup and delivery systems to complete tasks efficiently and without deadlocks in complex environments.	[69]
Smart Cities and Energy	Optimize city services and coordination	Autonomously manage, optimize, and adapt urban systems for resilient, equitable, and sustainable cities.	[125]
	Energy management and fault detection	Optimize building energy use, operations, and maintenance for efficiency, cost reduction, and reliability.	[58,70,126]
Public Administration	Resource and service management	Optimize governance, public services, and policy-making for efficiency, equity, and sustainability.	[37,41]
Tourism and Traveling	Decision optimization in tourism	Optimize tourism management decisions using agentic AI for pricing and personalized services.	[127]
Finance, Banking, and Insurance	Autonomous banking operations	Enhance financial decision-making, risk profiling, and automated banking operations using AI.	[80]
	Financial modeling and risk management	Automate financial modeling and model risk management workflows using LLMs to ensure compliance, robustness, and accurate decision-making.	[39]
	AI for BFSI customer support	Assist consumers in BFSI by providing information, recommendations, decision aid, and delegated actions.	[128]
	Risk and fraud detector	Enhance banking risk management and fraud using LLMs, ML, XAI.	[129]
Finance, Banking, and Insurance	Personalized banking	Provide trustworthy, personalized banking experiences and financial guidance through autonomous agentic AI.	[130]
	AI-driven automated customer service	Enable AI-driven, autonomous customer service and decision-making to improve efficiency, personalization, and workflow automation in business and insurance contexts.	[96,131]
Multi-Domain	Personalized recommendations and task management	Develop foundation model-powered agents for autonomous, multi-domain task execution, combining personalized recommendations and general task automation with planning, reasoning, and collaboration.	[32,75,76,132–134]
	Multi-agent system	Enable autonomous, goal-driven AI agents and multi-agent systems to plan, act, reason, and adapt across multiple domains, completing complex, long-horizon tasks with minimal human intervention.	[31,34,36,47,53,77,135, 136]
	Coding and problem solving	Enable autonomous agents to reason, plan, and solve complex tasks across diverse domains.	[46,137]
	Cost-efficient plan caching	Enable autonomous LLM agents to perform multi-step reasoning and planning efficiently across domains while reducing computational costs.	[66,138]
	Radiology and predictive crime analytics	Enable autonomous, agentic AI systems to support decision-making, diagnostics, and automated scheduling in professional and medical domains.	[67]
	Memory-Augmented Agent Systems	Enable LLM agents to perform multi-domain tasks with memory for reflection, recall, and long-term planning.	[139]

Table 5. *Cont.*

Domain	Application	Goal/Task Attempted by Agentic AI	Ref.
Retail, Business and E-commerce	Retail and supply chain automation	Automate and personalize retail customer interactions and supply chain operations.	[27,78,140]
	Digital task automation	Autonomously optimize digital tasks, schedules, and workflows across platforms using agentic AI.	[141,142]
	Enterprise automation	Automate enterprise decision-making and workflows to enhance productivity and reduce errors.	[68,143,144]
	Cognitive robots for collaboration	Develop autonomous, cognitive robotic agents that can safely cooperate with humans, learn continuously, and plan for future scenarios.	[122]
	Customer service and retail support	Optimize AI chatbots for customer service, decision support, and human-agent collaboration in retail.	[145,146]
	Interactive Recommender Systems	Deliver interactive, personalized, multi-turn recommendations using LLM-enhanced chatbots.	[79]
	Automate tasks and coordinate AI agents	Enable AI agents to autonomously reason, plan, and act across enterprise systems while securely automating tasks.	[40]
Education	Personalized educational assistance	Enhance learning, teaching, and educational administration through personalized and adaptive support	[57,97,147]
	Evolution of AI in Education	Improve consistency, reliability, and fairness in automated essay grading using multi-agent systems.	[148]
	Research and task management	Enhance research, decision-making, and cognitive support through intelligent task execution.	[149]
Scientific Discovery Research	Automated Scientific Research	Automate and accelerate scientific discovery across chemistry, materials science, bioinformatics, and molecular biology.	[45,150,151]
	LLM model battery simulation	Integrate LLMs with physical models to autonomously simulate, analyze, and guide advanced battery research.	[64]
	LLM-driven materials discovery	Accelerate materials discovery using knowledge-guided LLMs with autonomous labs.	[65]
	Science Exocortex for Research Automation	Augment human cognition and automate scientific research using a "science exocortex" of AI agents.	[152]
	Automated interview and data coding	Automate and streamline qualitative interviews and analysis in social and health sciences.	[153]

3.4.1. Healthcare

For agentic AI in healthcare, it will include diagnostics, treatment plans, and personalized care. Agentic AI enables pinpoint risk stratification, rapid segmentation of medical images, personalized diets from scratch, real-time seizure prediction, and robust human–robot interaction [59]. Fitness and wellness agents have enabled adaptive coaching, strengthened posture analysis paradigms, and offered multimodal feedback, tracked progress, and coordinated recommendations [60]. The EDX test standardized factor could have organized EMG/NCS data, smartly enabled incorporation of known diagnostic contexts through RAG, and offered accurate level physician reports [99]. Genomic assessment could predict risk for disease, specify treatments, indicate progression, and personalize care for costs, in accordance with safeguards of security [35]. Agents could indicate the ethical framework for generative AI [44], clean and automate medical computer vision pipelines [100], develop bioethical decision support [101], greatly enhance clinical decision-making of some use cases for workflows in surgery and drug discovery workflows [56], and would streamline real-time differential diagnosis of DILI derived from clinical notes [102].

3.4.2. Military

In military and cybersecurity efforts, agentic AI makes it possible to have groups of autonomous agents to carry out both offensive actions and defensive actions based on collective coordinated decisions. Every agent can independently act based on its own preferences. They can defend their positions, attack enemy positions, move around as needed, adapt their movements based on performance metrics, and choose to deploy a variety of effective formations [119]. For example, in cloud-based AI platforms, these forms of agentic AI systems can facilitate a kind of continual protective action to foster security by allowing the rotation of particular active services in order to minimize some risk, preemptively defend against known threats, limit vulnerabilities associated with repeated attacks, apply strict security rules, report unusual activity, and automatically respond with system changes [120].

3.4.3. Transportation

Intelligent agentic traffic control systems simulate traffic situations, control dynamic routing and implement on-demand signal operations, coordinate agents over distributed transport networks, and work toward improving safety, efficiency, and sustainability [103]. Real-time process optimization using generative models and soft inputs with SIC architectures predicts quality variables, performs closed-loop control, allows for closed-loop control with soft sensors to scale biomanufacturing, personalize product design, and minimize energy use and emissions [43]. Context-aware navigation reduces risk of collision in dynamic environments and complex place types through multimodal perception to inform actions and behavior used with semantic understanding for informing decision-making [74]. Multi-agent routing and scheduling coordinate agents traveling multiple traffic channels to eliminate delays, avoid deadlock, and provide opportunity for agents to reach locations given occupancy constraints [61]. Multi-phase transportation lifecycle management is human-centered and adaptable and strive to address barriers toward inclusion while engaging with persistent issues of congestion, collisions, environmental impact, and equity while optimizing travel outcomes for individuals and collectives [104].

3.4.4. Software

Agents independently decompose complex queries, determine which tools are relevant, and execute subtasks, while providing adjustable feedback in real time [105]. Behavior-based development agents use a natural language query as an input and generate structured test cases to collaborate across teams [106], whereas autonomous visual intelligence agents fuse spatial context into multimodal sensory data to perceive the environment, adapt, and collaborate in real-time for tasks such as robotic surgery, disaster response, and augmented/mixed reality applications [107]. Software engineering and business automation agents take a goal and decompose it to oversee who is assigned to each role and to automate workflows, including inventory management, customer relationship management, invoicing, and demand forecasting [30]. Self-directed AI pipelines autonomously select models, make use of data featuring imbalanced learning classes, and manage knowledge-aware, interpretable decision-making [54]. Agentic search, reviews, and personalization systems are capable of multi-step reasoning, retrieval in cross-lingual forms, and bias mitigation [108]. Multi-agent orchestration systems can facilitate computer vision task automation and manage complex, fault-tolerant, high-risk systems [62,109].

End-user programming agents are giving rise to democratized software development [110]. Near real-time multi-agent frameworks simultaneously can be used for software development, controlling operational IT workflows, and strategic decision-making [111]. Autonomous software development and multi-domain digital task agents will plan, assign, execute, and self-correct the software development, browsing, coding, and file operations associated with a release [50,113]. Human-algorithmic agency modeling also theorizes an evolving model for collective human–AI agency [114]. Conversational agents will become increasingly integrated into software development to improve software test case development, ML workflow improvement, and SOC automation through natural language interpretation, test case generation, pipeline and incident monitoring and detection, rule zero-trust enforcement and multi-agent interaction coordination [115–117]. Fully autonomous software development, predictive incident detection, IT automation, and other tasks do not require a fully autonomous agent to decompose prompts, write and test code, integrate third-party APIs, optimize resource use and performance, manage Git workflows, or manage incidents using coordinated multi-agent planning [49,51,118].

3.4.5. Finance, Banking and Insurance

Agents operating in finance, banking, and insurance have improved customers' risk profiling, automated forecasting for loans, treasury management, and fraud detection by examining real-time data and behavioral patterns [80]. Agents also increase model risk management by using automated ML workflows, compliance checks, and by cooperating agent to agent [39]. Further, customer services receive outstanding support 24/7, recommendations on investments and insurance, and automated transactions, due diligence, and KYC [128]. Risk and fraud detection agents can spot risky actions, break down complicated processes, and use AI that clearly explains how it works [129]. Personalized banking agents automate budgeting, product recommendations, and can provide instant behavioral interventions which also support inclusion through quasi-real-time feedback mechanisms [130]. Agents for insurance claims evaluation utilize multimodal inputs, decompose tasks into assigned subtasks, and respond in a policy-compliant way [96]. Finally, customer-centric chatbots improve sales, diagnostic ability, predictive analytics, and can automate IoT-driven processes for better interactive engagement across organizational partners [131].

3.4.6. Manufacturing and Industrial

Agents are useful within the manufacturing and industrial contexts in terms of increasing efficiency, safety, and decision-making across production and supply chains. Multi-agent systems play a role in the optimization of a number of tasks spanning wastewater treatment, factory operations, predictive maintenance, and energy-aware task scheduling, among others [33,63]. Supply chain agents may also forecast demand and monitor for contamination and then recommend actions with respect to quality and pricing [55]. Cognitive robots and collaborative human–robot agent systems can also be used to predict the possible states of a scenario, learn from social interactions with humans, adapt movements based on learning, and collaborate in shared tasks with humans safely [122,124]. Workflow agents and autonomic computing agents can also increase efficiency in robotic assembly, and automate the tasks of compliance, scheduling, and resource planning [121,123]. Multi-agent pickup and delivery systems address the coordination task, collision avoidance tasks, and other delay reduction tasks [69].

3.4.7. Tourism and Traveling

They optimize pricing, planning, and customer service using human–AI teams. They provide real-time decision support ethically and transparently, through RAG, Interactive Cognitive Agents (ICAs), and other management support systems [127].

3.4.8. Multi-Domain

Agents model user behavior, provide recommendations and context, coordinate processes across domains, automate business processes, break down goals, utilize external knowledge, and coordinate safely and ethically [53,132,133]. Agents also engage in real-time decision-making, minimize costs, make better use of resources, produce intelligible outputs, and plan and execute tasks under uncertainty [36,135]. Multi-domain agents engage with tools and/or APIs, manage workflows that will inevitably be very complex, such as coding, healthcare, finance, crime analysis, etc., and provide memory-based learning that allows them to continue a task by absorbing adaptive information from external cues [31,67,75–77,136,139]. Agents also enhance personal assistants, cybersecurity, and autonomous knowledge management, while realizing reduced computation cost and smarter cross-domain problem solving [32,46,66,134,137,138].

3.4.9. Scientific Discovery and Research

Autonomous systems are aiding scientific inquiry by making hypotheses, automating the literature review and analysis, and designing experiments. They can physically perform majority of robotic chemical and biological experiments, analyze data across all domains, and iteratively refine experiments to facilitate efficient experimentation for drug discovery, material science, and energy applications [64,65,150,151]. Multi-agent systems of LLMs can incorporate physical models with domain knowledge to plan simulations, make predictions for material properties, and develop multimodal outputs (numerical data, charts, text reports) for engineers [64,65]. Agents can facilitate automatic writing of research papers, analyze textual or hypertext content, organize qualitative interviews or conversations, and create knowledge graphs while embedding factors such as interpretability, bias detection, and collaborative reasoning throughout scientific workflows [45,152,153].

3.4.10. Retail, Business, and E-Commerce

Autonomous systems create customized customer interactions and coordinated management of supply chains by offering personalized shopping experiences, situation-aware support in the form of chatbots and virtual assistants, navigation support inside buildings or stores, and through coordinated autonomous operation by multi-agent systems like inventory management, logistics, and fulfillment [78]. Autonomous systems also manage automating task scheduling, digital management of content, and automating multi-step workflows like travel booking or e-commerce tasks [141,144]. Autonomous systems depend on using natural language processing (NLP) and situational reasoning algorithms to adapt to changing situationals [144]. There are also autonomous decision-making agents that are intended to quickly assist an organization or team by helping with aspects of strategic and tactical planning, or rapid data analytics along with error detection or forecasting to improve productivity and customer satisfaction [143]. The increasingly sophisticated capabilities of AI service agents and chatbots allow for continued personalized interactions, as well as the use of financial advice, reservations, smart device activation, and decreased human workload [140,145]. Workflow automation is at play in areas such as law and retail along with automating Kubernetes tasks with minimal supervision, and e-commerce process optimization provides opportunities for reduced costs and increased customer satisfaction [27,142]. Human–machine collaboration is added by using humanoid robotics and agentic LLMs for claims handling, smart marketing, HR, and trust establishment in customer service [68,146]. Interactive recommender systems will provide conversational personalized recommendations across movies/entertainment and retail domains [79]. GenAI agents showcase multi-domain reasoning, planning, and task execution capabilities, including finance and banking, cybersecurity, healthcare/remote healthcare, and software operation/administrative tasks [40].

3.4.11. Smart Cities and Energy

Autonomous systems support a city's services, like transport, health, and emergency management, and can proactively provide solutions to problems like pollution and traffic in real time [125]. Agents can take on responsibility for building energy work that now involves data processing, coding, and simulations [58]. Multi-agent systems use less energy in smart buildings while maintaining comfort, reducing cost, and preventing energy spikes [70]. Digital twin agents support monitoring buildings, fault detection, maintenance to avoid faults, and energy efficiency for use [126].

3.4.12. Public Administration

Autonomous systems assist public administration with efficiently managing resources (water and energy), correctly anticipating demand, simulating policies with digital twins, and making adjustments in real-time. Autonomous systems also enhance services to citizens, automate administrative workflows, aid with fraud detection, and help with smart cities and population health decision-making [37,41].

3.4.13. Education

The personalized learning capabilities of autonomous systems in education derive from tracking student performance, adjusting content, giving timely feedback, taking on administrative responsibilities, identifying signs of disengagement, and promoting collaborative learning [57]. They can also help automate objective essay questions, thus offering a consistent, fair, and explainable way of marking via collaborative engagement of multiple agents [148]. Adaptive AI agents would be described as metacognitive support, facilitating the diagnosis of gaps in learning, providing scaffolding for complex content, relieving learner burden and acknowledgement from remote participation, and automation in marking [147]. Multi-agent LLM systems help deliver personalized and consistent results for both subjective and objective purposes, merging agent coordinate reasoning, validation, and quality coding of data generation [97]. In addition to helping learners, agents help the cognitive workflows related to research, decision-making, report writing, organizing travel, and many other complex academic workloads [149].

3.5. What Kinds of Input and Output Formats Do Agentic AI Systems Handle in Comparison to Traditional AI Systems?

Agentic AI systems designed for operation in complex environments are developed with flexible input–output structures for independent decision-making. Various agentic AI models use input–output schemes suited to the nature of the task, which will differ in terms of structural design and user styles of interaction. This section presents the various interaction methods with agentic AI systems, including how they process different input forms and produce appropriate outputs. Table 6 is categorized according to the input types given to the system, along with the task performed and the technologies used to produce that output.

The rationale for the agentic AI models for input–output formats is to demonstrate how agentic AI systems are designed by directly mapping input modalities to their outputs, the tasks performed, and the technologies used. This comprehensive table is organized for easy comparison of how a single input can produce multiple types of output and perform different types of tasks. This provides important information about system flow in the real world applications of agentic AI systems. The table also highlights the diversity and specialization of agentic AI systems to help researchers and practitioners identify models or technologies appropriate for particular applications.

Table 6. Agentic AI models for various input–output transformations.

Input	Output	Task Performed	Technology	Ref.
Text	Actions	Process user prompts to run tasks and coordinates the agents	LLMs, MCP servers	[120]
		Processes and handles the user query to handling multi-step workflows	RAG systems, Vectara-agentic	[27]
		Manages live network operations and delivers network services	Autonomous Agents, Orchestration APIs	[82]
		Automatically generate efficient robotic assembly workflows	MAPE-K, ML, knowledgebase	[121]
		Design and implement fault-tolerant software	Multi-agent AI and concurrent SE techniques	[62]
		Enables direct network control as per Telecom control	Decision-making module	[71]
		Coordinate multiple home appliances for energy saving	MAS, enhanced by LLMs	[38]
		Decide next action by self-reflection or knowledge use and generate signals	LLMs, KnowSelf, DeepSpeed, vLLM	[144]
		Executes arbitrary computer tasks	LLMs, Adept ACT-1, AutoGPT, OpenAI's tools	[34]
		Critical self-analysis and refinement of its previous outputs	LLMs, SELF-REFINE	[50]
		Learn from feedback, self-improve dynamically	BrainBody-LLM, RASC, REVECA, AIFP	[75]
		Resolve ambiguity and adapts to user preferences	LAM, Neuro-symbolic program, LLM	[154]
	Text	Parse user intent, maps, retrieve and combine data to respond back	Router Agent (LLM), domain APIs	[77]
		Understanding/responding to inquiries quickly	AI agents, LLM workflows	[41]
		AI agent learns and shares this expertise with other agents	LLM, AI Agent with locally privacy-preserving learning	[143]
		Understand, search, compute, combine results	LLaMA-3-70B, Bee agent (ReAct)	[52]
		Complex problem-solving through iterative reasoning	GPT-4, GPT-3.5, Claude, Self-refinement, CoT	[137]
		Plans and handles multi-step support for customer interactions	GPT-3.5, service robots	[140]
		Assist software development by completing codes	LLM	[155]
		Generating and refining novel research ideas and hypotheses	LLMs, reinforcement learning, RAG	[150]
		Understanding, planning, and error correction in codes	GPT-4, fine-tuned LlaMA 2, ItemCF, SASRec	[110]
		Planning and generating executable synthesis plans	GPT-4, 18 tools, RoboRXN	[65]
		Splits big goals, step-by-step plans and achieve multiple targets	Autonomous HVAC agents	[37]

Table 6. *Cont.*

Input	Output	Task Performed	Technology	Ref.
Audio	Text/JSON scripts	Break down, assign, execute, and monitor tasks	LLM orchestrators, FAISS	[105]
	JSON scripts	Automate research by assigning tasks to AI agents	RAG, LLM, citation traversal	[151]
	Text/Charts	Battery material analysis, SEI growth prediction	AgentGPT, DFT, VASP, APIs, Cloud, SEI Models	[64]
	YAML config file/image	Plan steps, generate YAML, verify, self-correct, execute	LLM, SimpleMind	[100]
	Numerical data	Extract, plan, and refine financial data	GPT-4o-mini, LLaMa-3.2-8B	[138]
	Text/numerical results	Clinical decision support for epilepsy detection	MAS, agent abstraction, ML	[59]
	Logs/audit events	Workflow execution and data retrieval	LLM, RAG, LangChain, LangFlow, AutoGen, CrewAI	[40]
	Text	Data review, ethical decision-making and gives advice	Agentic AI, LLMs, fairness tools	[101]
	Text/Audio	Goal parsing, context-aware feedback generation	ASR, STM, LTM, GPT-4	[60]
	Audio	Conduct structured, empathetic interviews	GPT-4o mini, Whisper3-turbo, Llama3.2	[153]
Real-time data	Action	Analyze sensor data to detect issues and optimize operations	IIoT, ML, DT, Cloud	[131]
		Buildings adjust energy use to support the power grid	MADRL, AC, AM, DNN, CityLearn	[70]
		Multi-agent navigation and collision avoidance	PIBT+, Priority Decentralized Ctrl	[72]
		Monitor, analyze, plan, optimize to enhance system performance	MAPE-K loop, sensors, Machine Learning	[123]
		Smart nano-grid energy management	Fuzzy Logic Control, VSI, SAF	[73]
		Automated threat detection, response, and system optimization	Agentic AI, OOAD, CIF, DA	[156]
		Adjust plans in response to disruptions	Agentic AI with RL + MAS	[30]
		Learn through trial and error to improve strategies	RL, Q-learning, DQN, PPO	[36]
		Goal setting and strategic adaptation, decision-making	Urban sensing, LLMs	[125]
	Text/Dataset	Suggests better routes to prevent traffic and manage flow	ACP, ABT, AI/ML, DS, AI, VA, CB	[103]
Real-time coordinates	Actions	Autonomous task completion, movement decision-making	Swarm algorithms, Stepwise decisions	[119]
Datasets	Text	Monitoring and providing feedback for employee performance	AI, NLP, SML, DL, MA	[146]
		Generate E-commerce product descriptions, updates and manages catalogs	Transformer model, PyTorch	[142]
		Learn and adjust prices to increase profits	Reinforcement Learning (RL), Q-learning	[157]
		Provide coaching and insights for team members	CoachBot, BRiN, Amanda	[145]
	Actions	Real-time feedback-based adaptation	MPA, A-Core integration	[66]
		Analyze datasets, detect threats, autonomously mitigate threats	LLMs, agentic AI, AI agents, networks of specialized models	[117]
		Adapted task performance	LLMs, RLHF, RAG	[152]
		Automated trading and investment	Agentic AI, Neural Nets, Trading algs	[80]
		Optimize processes, identify opportunities	Agentic AI, Agentic platform, Pred. analytics, adaptive reasoning	[158]
		Make quick decisions to adjust plant controls, improves results	MARL and G2ANet	[63]
	Dataset	Predictive policing and analysis	CAS, ML algorithms	[67]
		Extracts datasets split into training/testing sets and subsamples	Code execution tool + GPT-3.5 Turbo	[39]
		Data analysis and pricing strategy formulation	Explainable AI (XAI), Rule-based logic	[127]
	Alerts	Monitor data, detect risks, notify	Autonomous AI system with LLMs	[102]
		Fraud detection and risk management	AI, ML, LLMs, NLP, GNN	[129]
	Images/Visuals	Communicate complex info visually	Kubernetes bots, OSSD bots, Gatekeeper	[32]
	Dataset/Text	Analyze and predict health outcomes	Agentic AI, LLM	[35]
Text/Images	Text	Review policy, verify claims, craft response, coordinate agents	Multi-agent AI, Pretrained LMs, RAG	[96]
		Diagnosis issue, generates treatment plan, and healthcare process	LLMs, DL, ML, multimodal AI	[56]
Text/Dataset	Text	Create, modify, and guide BDD test steps with user feedback	LLMs, NLP, RAG, ReAct agent, BDD frameworks, Streamlit UI	[106]
	Text/Test code	Autonomous software testing, Planning and executing tests	MW, LLMs, MA, LC, ACM, NN	[115]
	Text, JSONL data	Generates personalized, contextual data and synthetic data	LLaMA 3.2 3B, LoR, JSONL	[97]
	Text/Actions	User intent retrieval and action mapping	LLMs, RAG, RL, Knowledge Graphs	[159]
Text	Text/Code/Logs	Problem-solving, adaptive execution, information gathering	Agentic AI/LLM-based assistant	[46]
Images Dataset	Text/Audio/Actions	Personalized service, actions monitoring, fault detection	Agentic AI, NLP, ML, DL, RL	[160]
Images/Video/Text	Actions	Predict and align with human intent to adapt robot behavior	LSTM-based deep learning	[124]
Images/Video	Coordinates/Image	Object detection, classification, result refinement	YOLO, ResNet, LLMs, RAG, VCG16	[109]
Video/Audio	Actions	Perception, reasoning about complex situations	MM pipelines, adaptive mechanisms; spatial and temporal reasoning	[95]
Text/Images/Audio	Actions	Adaptive decision-making and optimized task execution	LLMs, VLMs, RL, Embodied AI	[135]
Text/Images/Audio /Video	Actions	Strategy refinement and optimization	Self-supervised and RL	[33]
Image/Real-time data	Actions	Real-time prediction and adjustment of navigation	Agentic AI, DRL, computer vision	[107]
Text/Audio	Actions	Plan and execute complex tasks like booking hotel rooms	GPT-4, APIs, web automation	[141]
Text/Audio/Image	Actions	Understand and fulfill user needs by NPL interaction	CLIP, Multimodal Foundation Models	[132]
Text/Images/Audio /Graphs/Charts	Graphs/charts	Recommend products, provide feedback, and manage tasks	Agentic knowledge graphs, ML	[134]
Text/Image/Audio	Text/Image/Audio	Customer query and feedback handling	Transf. models, PT, CUDA	[42]
Text/Video/Audio	Text/Visual analytics	Real-time adaptation, intelligent decision-making	RL, NLU, contextual reasoning	[57]
Graph/Code/Text	Numeric data	Predicts and ranks workflow performance without execution	GNNs, MLPs, T5/BERT (MiniLM)	[81]
Numeric + Text	Word document	Compile FDD results and analyses to comprehensive report	AI Agent, Code Interpreter, LangSmith	[126]
Spatial coordinates	Actions	Agents plan collision-free moves to complete tasks	Decentralized control algorithms, PI, BT, PIBTTP, PIBTTP-TA	[69]
Numeric	Actions	Adjusting crystallization residence time and optimizes emission	Data denoising, SCADA integration	[43]
Alert	Actions/Alerts	Analyze alerts, mitigate risks, manage Tier 1/2 responses	Agentic AI with generative AI	[161]
Code files like .cs	Code files	Modifies code, generates git diffs, logs, summaries	Codex (OpenAI), git diff, sandbox	[51]
CSV file	ML model(.pt,.pkl)	Generate and debug energy modeling code	gpt-4o on LangGraph (ReAct), PythonREPL	[58]
PDFs	Dataset	Extract and organize clinical data	AANEM references, LLM Gemini 1.5 API	[99]

3.5.1. Text to Actions

Text as input is a free-form language from user to system; mostly, it is a natural language that can be structured or unstructured. In agentic AI models, actions as output means executing something in the system to complete the tasks [120]. More advanced models, like Vectara-agentic [27] and AutoGPT [34], can take text input, read the user's prompt to create outputs or undertake actions, and coordinate with other agents without human assistance.

Beyond task executions, agentic AI systems also contribute to robotic process automation. It is possible for an agentic AI model to analyze manufacturing data and automatically execute optimized robotic assembly sequences, based on a structured framework like MAPE-K [121]. Similarly, in network operations [71], an agentic AI can interpret controlling commands and independently react to failure by interpreting and implementing possible actions in real-time [82] to make a decision to execute an action. In doing so, these models improve the fault tolerance of systems and enhance resilience [62]. Moreover, in the case of smart environments, agentic AI can drive energy savings by connecting power supply across home appliances [38] using multiple AI agents collaborating in a coordination process enhanced with LLMs.

Agentic AI models can improve themselves. BrainBody-LLM and RASC [75] utilize feedback in self-reinforcement to continue learning and optimizing over time. In scenarios where the past outputs have been wrong, self-reflective models like SELF-REFINE [50] can improve their behaviors by reviewing their own actions to create their improvement without relying on outside parties. Agency AI Systems can remove ambiguity, enact user preferences [154], and derive next actions through self-reflection to generate signals [144].

3.5.2. Text to Text

Text as output is human-readable language, which is a combination of formatted and structured text that is read and understood by people. Recent LLM models can share their knowledge amongst other agents, resulting in a multi-agent ecosystem capable of collective learning [143]. LLaMA-3 models [40] can help users in information retrieval by parsing users' prompts [77], looking for responses to the prompts, and aggregating information from other sources [52]. LLM models support problem-solving [137] and programming [155] by completing or correcting code, and describing runtime errors [110]. The GPT models can also help automate customer interaction process workflows [140], logic-based processing in automated support [137], and responding to inquiries [41].

3.5.3. Text to Multimodel Data

Agentic AI systems can produce structured outputs, such as JSON or YAML scripts, after completing complex tasks [105], orchestration [100], or documenting research in research documents [151]. AgentGPT models can also produce multimodal data as output, which can be data visualizations such as projecting future growth using an interactive timeline [138] or charting their current and historical data and actions [64]. LLM models can fill logs and audits when they process textual input and produce structured records of activity [40].

3.5.4. Audio Files to Text/Audio

Audio as input in agentic AI systems can be speech, music, or signals, which are processed by the system to understand the goal, supporting human experience by allowing for more natural, context-rich interactions. Audio as output is a sound-based content as a response, which is human-perceivable sound for listening. Agentic AI systems utilize technologies including Automatic Speech Recognition (ASR), short-term and long-term memory, and advanced language models such as GPT-4 or Llama 3.2 to process spoken language and operationalize it into actionable insights. It is possible to use audio input for ethical advisory scenarios where agentic AIs can generate fairness-aware decisions through parsing spoken queries [101]. Similarly, feedback-generating interactive systems can use audio to goal parse and make context-aware outputs [60]. In cases such as empathetic interviewing, multimodal agentic AI are a more advanced use of audio input as both parse input and response are captured and subsequently provided in a structured, emotionally intelligent discussion [153]. Audio input allows agentic AI to extend their capabilities of real-time communications that exhibit human-like attributes.

3.5.5. Real-Time Data to Actions

Agentic AI can receive continuous real-time data from a sensor or camera, allowing it to obtain live information. Sensor data can detect a building's power grid [73], analyze how it is being used, and instruct the building to save energy [70]. Agentic AI also suggests the optimal routes in traffic [103]. ML-based agentic systems can detect the issue [131] to optimise the operations [123]. When the AI is engaged in operational tasks, it is also measuring and detecting threats, assessing the environment and deciding on an immediate action [156], response to disruptions [30]. Using a trial RT learning approach, the system recognizes and stabilizes performances in the system's strategizing over time [36]. Real-time data can also involve coordinates or the accurate location of a person, car, or agent in a game, allowing the system to respond immediately and perform actions timely manner [72,119].

3.5.6. Datasets to Text

Dataset as input for agentic AI systems is a pre-collected, structured set of data, and helps systems to analyze, learn from, or make decisions. When datasets are used as inputs in agentic AI systems, they can implement a whole hierarchy of autonomous and semi-autonomous actions in employee management and coaching, product management, risk identification, and pricing. These datasets can be textual, tabular, or multimodal. Datasets with employee feedback and behaviors are provided to employee management [146] and coaching applications [145] to be processed using agentic AI, NLP, SML, and deep learning models, to create performance assessments and feedback loops. In e-commerce applications, datasets with product metadata and customer interaction data are provided to transformer models using PyTorch, an open-source deep learning framework [142] to automatically generate and update product descriptions. Pricing applications typically employ Q-learning-based reinforcement learning algorithms [157] in order to learn from sales datasets and modify pricing for maximum profitability.

3.5.7. Datasets to Actions

In applications where action or intelligence is needed, such as for safety or efficiency management through automation with utilities, robotics or autonomous vehicles or processes and systems (such as supply chains), agentic AI systems use action-based datasets, which contain information about conducted actions, so they can learn how to recognize anomalies [117], mitigate threats, or identify the best actions to optimize processes [63,158]. Based on how the system adapted, feedback is generated autonomously in real time [66]. Based on given datasets, an agentic AI system can autonomously participate in trading, investments [80], and adapt to tasks [152].

3.5.8. Dataset to Dataset

The purpose of datasets extends to predictive applications, such as health, policing, and financial services, where agentic AI apply structured datasets to predict where possible threats or issues might arise, using XAI [127], ML algorithms [67], and LLMs [35] for forecasting, risk assessment, or strategy formulation, etc. Agentic AI also helps in software applications by providing the training and testing datasets, used for ML models, if a raw dataset is given. This supports that agentic AI uses streaming data, providing both static and dynamic datasets.

3.5.9. Dataset to Alerts

Alerts as output are notifications or warnings to inform users about specific events; these events, most of the time, will be detecting risks [102] or fraud detections [129] in agentic AI systems. Here, the dataset acts as an input knowledge source for the system, which is analysed to detect risks or fraud.

3.5.10. Multimodel Data to Multimodel Data

Agentic AI can utilize multimodal data from various types, including text, video, images, audio, graphs, and datasets to generate personalized outputs to act more intelligently, flexibly, and responsively. Agentic AI uses a number of sensory channels to help the machine perceive complex environments, actuate behavior to align with human intentions, and make decisions based on the real-world context. Reviewing work using LSTM-based deep learning and reinforcement learning effectively aligned behaviors of robots with human goals using simultaneous visual and textual trainable inputs [124]. Additionally, multimodal pipelines based on audio and video can build a spatial–temporal reasoning capability, enabling perception and context decision-making amidst complex situations [95]. Models like LLMs and VLMs enable adaptive decision-making in agentic decision-making when processes use combinations of text, images, and audio, thus enabling an agentic system to demonstrate embodied reasoning and task execution towards articulated goals [33,135].

Structured representations of user goals, and multimodal input like speech signals, visual cues, and brief actions are the main methods of prompting agents to behave in particular ways [132]. The agents act upon abstract, high-level user goals instead of explicit commands, which allows the agent to figure out how and when to respond. Many of the processes used intermediate representations of states and often had feedback loops to make decisions in dynamic environments, as we depicted in the annotation [71,105].

3.5.11. Beyond Conventional Input–Output Methods

In addition to standard input–output models, which usually use structured text inputs or standard datasets and files, agentic AI systems are increasingly utilizing other kinds of input data that are spatial, document, or alert-based. These different media for inputs give AI agents very high degrees of freedom, control, and adaptability for a number of actions they typically perform in a domain-oriented task. Exact coordinates of the agent help to plan a path that is entirely collision-free with respect to any agents involved [69]. This enables robotics and multi-agent systems to function without any centralized controller. Numeric data supporting SCADA connections allow AI agents [43] to optimize key process parameters, such as emission output, generally used in chemical factories. Alert-based inputs represent real-time set triggers where agentic AI can respond autonomously to reduce risk associated with incidence and Tier 1 and Tier 2 Incident response actions [161].

Code files, including .cs files, represent an input to AI agents like Codex that modify codebases or create Git diffs and logs to be able to allow for agentic to autonomous software maintenance and version tracking [51]. CSV files can provide AI with inputs and can be used in combination with pretrained ML models to cue AI to produce and debug the energy modeling code with tools like LangGraph with ReAct and PythonREPL [58]. PDFs are mostly considered unstructured input types. LLM APIs like Gemini 1.5 [99] can be used to parse and extract, and then structure clinical datasets, so AI has passed the milestone of being able to handle semi-structured documents. These examples represent agentic systems which push beyond the inputs of traditional models toward AI systems that accommodate varied formats of data in order to operationalize in specialized and high-stakes contexts.

3.5.12. Core Input–Output Mechanisms in Agentic vs. Traditional Systems

Traditional AI systems generally work on structured, static inputs and produce fixed [71] or predefined outputs [135]. The systems evaluate input against rule-based logic or supervised learning models that have been trained by available labels on training sets, all within an institutional context that necessitates human action or intervention to make decisions and take action [47]. Inputs typically comprise historical data [78], clearly defined user commands or queries, and are mapped to singular outputs such as classifications or recommendations [132]. Based on narrow sets of inputs and outputs, these systems work well in a constrained environment with predictable data structure and have less success in contexts with complex and evolving problems [95,106]. Research papers [57,80] emphasize that traditional AI with structured inputs provides shallow outputs, and becomes exhausting to use with frequent human intervention.

In comparison, agentic AI systems operate with multimodal [33], dynamic [106], and contextual inputs like real-time sensor data [116], natural language [126], intent-based actions [148], and feedback and results in autonomous outputs and/or actions that are goal-directed multi-step plans, executable actions, and adaptive decisions [157]. Agentic AI reasoning is temporally continuous, socially collaborative, and learns from its environments [38,136]. Paper [77] supports the argument that agentic AI outputs are indicative of rich, contextual information and proactive responses, while [143] describes the agentic AI system's adaptability to user-defined workflows through its contextually adapted inputs and predictions-oriented predictions. Unlike non-agentic systems, agentic AI operates continuously, proactively, and is not dependent on an input to act; rather, it anticipates requirements, operates autonomously, provides strategic options, remembers and learns, and frequently works collaboratively with other agents to produce an output, as compared to making a prediction based on data input with a simple action [55,161].

Researchers of papers [37,132] discuss real-time adaptability of agentic AI and long-term modeling of preferences, while [31,125] start to explore deeper meanings of situational awareness and internal goals. Papers [38,71] make explicit comparisons, comparing the ordering of decision-making chains and the moments when systems are orchestrated. In evaluating quality and how useful those offering applied system analyses or definitive architectural comparisons, [31,41,95] closely align with research pointing toward modeling agentic input–output pathways. Learning about these input–output functions is important for designing future AI systems that are both intelligent and autonomously able to demonstrate self-direction and situational awareness, and also be able to operate in an unattended state.

3.6. What Evaluation Methods and Metrics Are Used to Assess the Performance of Agentic AI Systems?

Evaluation metrics used to assess the performance of agentic AI systems are increasingly critical as these systems are expanding in every domain. With the increasing applications of agentic AI in areas ranging from autonomous robotics to intelligent decision-making, it is very important to validate and test the system's performance to ensure reliability, efficiency, and safety. This evaluation helps to identify the strengths and limitations of the system, which supports their improvement and responsible use. This section discusses more about various evaluation metrics and testing methods.

Figure 11 represents the categorization of performance measures of agentic AI, which diverges with two categories. They are evaluation metrics and testing methods. In practice, testing and evaluation metrics are closely related but not the same. Testing is where the system will be given experiments or scenarios on its performance. Evaluation metrics are the specific measures used to quantify how well the agentic AI system performs. They are used to interpret the results from testing.

The rationale for our performance analysis of agentic AI classification is to present the different types of testing methods and evaluation metrics of agentic AI systems. It organizes methods and metrics based on the aspects that are being tested in the system. It presents different testing methods from the literature in one place, and the results from those tests are interpreted to obtain evaluation metrics. Using these metrics, the system's performance is evaluated. Figure 11 divides methods and metrics separately because many methods in agentic AI have different metrics that overlap, such as accuracy. Each metric is further specified as qualitative or quantitative to independently identify what is being measured and how it is measured.

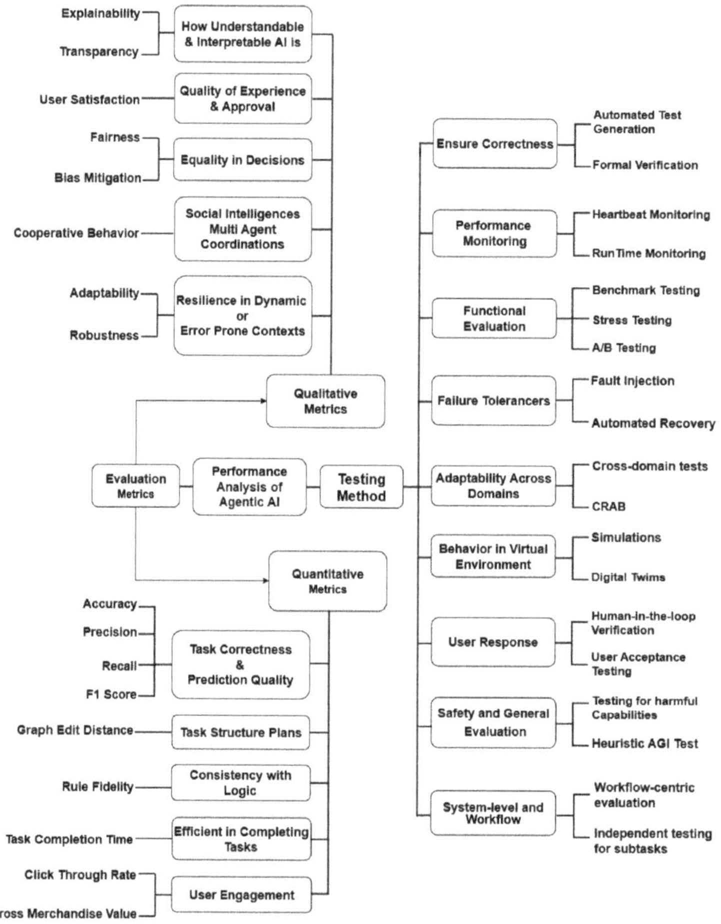

Figure 11. Classification diagram for testing methods and evaluation metrics that are used to assess the performance of agentic AI systems.

3.6.1. Testing Methods

Automated Test Generation [110] is a method in which tools like CodeT, Reflexion, and ClarifyGPT are used to refine code and detect ambiguous requirements. Formal

Verification [95] is used to test whether the system is exactly as specified, without errors or unexpected behavior.

Runtime monitoring [51] is a live, ongoing test to find how well the system is running in real time. This allows for the identification of errors and abnormal behavior, allowing agents to quickly respond, like making a rollback or remediate before a system crash. Heartbeat monitoring [123] simply checks if the system is alive by sending requests periodically. It helps in detecting failures and alerting IT without interrupting users.

Fault injection [123] is the act of injecting errors or faults into a model so that one may observe the model's behavior and use this methodology to ensure that the model can still perform its job correctly in a faulty state. Automated recovery [150] is deployed to test the system's capabilities to reflect and recover from failures while returning to normal operation without human intervention.

Benchmark testing [61,113] is a process that includes evaluation of an agentic AI system's performance on standardized tasks and metrics that validate its operational and reliable capabilities in real-world applications. Stress testing [39] is to test the model with unusual or extreme inputs to see if it stays reliable and functionally adaptable to change. A/B testing [132] is a process of running live experiments with users to see which version works better in real life.

Cross-domain tests [76] allow us to evaluate whether an agentic AI is performing well across different models or tasks with registers outside its original training. It involves tests in different domains like MineDojo, ALFRED, and ScienceWorld. Cross-platform Agent Benchmark (CRAB) [75] evaluates multimodal embodied language model agents with graphic-based tests and a unified Python interface.

Simulations [162] are used to model ethical dilemmas, especially in areas like autonomous vehicles and healthcare, allowing people to evaluate AI decisions in realistic and interactive scenarios. Digital twins [163] are real-time virtual models used for fault prediction and performance optimization, combined with LLMs, enabling smart, safe, and automated management of the system.

Human-in-the-loop verification [45] includes human involvement to improve the reliability, interpretability, and trustworthiness of AI-driven scientific discoveries. It highlights the need for human oversight to address AI limitations and support validation and accountability. User Acceptance Testing (UAT) [104] examines the system with real users to validate that the system satisfies their needs, wants, and user expectations to ensure user satisfaction and accountability.

Testing for Harmful Capabilities [46] is testing whether agents generate harmful outputs or enable malicious actions so they can be mitigated, to ensure safety. Heuristic AGI [134] testing is a simple way to evaluate models based on certain achievements, like passing a Turing test or solving important problems. This is quick as it does not involve fully measuring their true abilities.

Workflow-centric evaluation [50] considers evaluating the full decision-making process from perception to reasoning to acting rather than just evaluating the end product. Here, the agentic AI's behavior is validated and verified across workflows when using AI-driven testing workflows, advanced monitoring, and metrics. Independent Testing of Subtasks [46] is a process of isolating each of the subtasks of complex tasks and testing each subtask by itself for reliability; high-risk actions will always take precedence.

3.6.2. Evaluation Metrics

The evaluation metrics are divided into qualitative metrics and quantitative metrics to be able to assess the system's overall performance, behavior, and machine and human interaction. Quantitative metrics measure numerical performance, while qualitative metrics measure the quality and adaptation of the system, along with the user experience of interaction with the system.

Explainability: The degree to which the system produces clear and understandable reasons or explanations for its actual decisions or outputs. Explainability is tested using self-reflection and cross-agent reflection for foundation models like GPT-4 [133,150], LLaMA [133], and Compliance Agentic Model (CAM) [44] through reasoning traceability and in Artificial Cognitive Agents [122] by evaluating how well they mimicked human reasoning and explained decisions clearly.

Transparency: A measure of how openly the AI system's inner workings and decision processes are made visible or available for inspection. Transparency for models like AMBY and Drawcto [135] is tested through user-facing clarity, Constitutional AI models [44] using predefined ethical principles and Hybrid Transparency Models [37] are tested through open-source governance components and external audits.

User Satisfaction: It is a measure of how well the agentic AI system meets the needs, expectations, and preferences of users [163]. Models like Bi-level are Learnable LLM Planner (BiLLP) [132], and user satisfaction is evaluated by measuring how well the agent balances short-term and long-term user preferences in recommended tasks. For user satisfaction in agentic chatbots for achieved and ideal customer service [47], satisfaction can be measured by the system accommodating for user mood and personalizing decision-making responses.

Fairness: It can be used to identify biases system in agentic AI, for example, responding in different ways, or differing response quality in different demographic groups [56]. Fairness can also use methods such as SHAP [101], or counter-factual analysis [101] to measure fairness and bias in the agentic AI experience.

Bias Mitigation: It can be used to reduce or eliminate bias from agentic AI systems. If agentic AI systems that amplify societal biases can lead to unfair outcomes, [49], particularly oscillating more aggregated biases in regards to vulnerable groups. It is important for LLMs to implement bias mitigation in contexts, such as citing GPT-4 [56], ensuring commitment for both equitable and ethical deployment.

Co-operative Behavior: It can be used to measure how well AI agents collaborate and coordinate with one another to achieve mutual goals. Agentic AI systems can collaborate via social contract rules, for example, using shared rules [157] or cooperating and learning agentic AI behavior via reinforcement learning rules. Cooperation behavior is actively promoted using the MAAC model [70] to improve resource management across multiple agents.

Adaptability: It encompasses ongoing interpersonal learning and agile feedback and tuned goals and measures via conceptual multi-agent models, formal policy operationalizations such as Petri Nets [154], and applied second burst benchmark measures that simulate unpredictable, complex, and dynamic environments [75]. Adaptability is tested by how AI agents and humanoid robots adjust tasks and processes dynamically in real time [68].

Robustness: It is a measure of the ability of an agentic AI system to maintain goal-directed performance [48] despite internal failures and external adversities. For agentic coding systems like Codex (OpenAI) [51] and Google Jules [51], robustness is tested via sandboxed execution, traceability, and rollback. AgentHarm Benchmark [136] is used to test robustness against adversarial LLM agent behavior.

Accuracy: It is a measure of how correct and precise an agentic AI system's outputs are compared to the expected or true results. Agentic frameworks like LangGraph [53] and CrewAI [53] show around 94% accuracy in complex task execution. Models like Claude 3.5 [138] and LLaMa-3.2 [138] can show 96% accuracy with efficient plan caching and keyword-based retrieval. Platforms like IBM Watson Health [66] and tools like E-rater [57] and IntelliMetric [57] maintain high scoring accuracy in predicting and evaluating.

Precision: It is a measure of how many were actually correct out of all positive predictions made by a model, to find the accuracy of positive predictions. Most models like YOLO [109] and Mask R-CNN [109] have nearly perfect precision (almost equal to 1) for automated injury detection tasks. Models like GPT-3 [65] and LLaMA-2 [102] achieved higher precision than BERT [81], and the Swarm Agent [119] framework is better in precision than the Decision Tree [116] for classifications.

Recall: It measures how many the model gets right out of all actual positives, to obtain all positive instances. Agentic AI models have maintained high recall across different applications like EcoptiAI [142] in e-commerce retrieval, LLaMA 3.1 [102] in clinical text extraction, InteRecAgent potentially using RecLLaMA [79] in recommendation systems, and GPT-4o [126] in digital twins in fault detection.

F1 score: It is a measure that combines precision and recall into a single number by calculating their harmonic mean. The F1 score is calculated by multiplying precision and recall, and its double is dividing by the sum of precision and recall [126,142]. So, it is clear that the F1 score will depend on precision and recall.

Graph Edit Distance (GED): An important structural metric in agentic AI, using the level of structural similarity between an AI-generated task graph and a ground-truth graph as a measurement. When using the frameworks within a GPT-4-based algorithms [52,105] (gpt-4-0613), GED was estimated based on the minimum number of edits to the nodes and edges of a graph. This ultimately allows you to quantify the accuracy of the multi-hop reasoning and tool-use planning measured by the metrics; the lower the score, the closer to expert behavior we are.

Rule Fidelity: A measure of how accurately the symbolic, human-readable rules generated by the system reflect the actual decision-making process. The frameworks building the Neuro-Symbolic Agent [161], AutoML Agent [54], and the Agentic Planner [54] achieve roughly 94% rule fidelity based on their ability to concisely convert the decision-made learned model to human-readable rules.

Task Completion Time (TCT): It measures the time taken by the agent to plan, execute, and complete a particular task. This is a measure of how well the system performs operationally, along with the speed at which the AI completes complex workflows without human involvement. Model implementations LangGraph [58], Autogen [151], and GoEX [53] averaged 12 ± 2 min TCT, which is a 34.2% improvement against traditional AI in general.

Click-Through Rate (CTR): It assesses how good of a job the agentic AI system interacts with the user to click a recommendation or content we list to them, e.g, associating CTR with the system's relevance, impact, etc. Models like the GPT-4 (ColdLLM)6, the CG4CTR6 and the LLM-InS6 simulators were used to test if it was possible to associate different scenarios of CTR to the recommendation list through simulations of common interest content personalization, visual design impact, Inter environmental dialog personality, or deferred dialog.

Gross Merchandise Value (GMV): It measures the total dollar amount of the items sold or the total dollar amount of completed transactions due to the actions of, or recommendations made by, the AI. The ColdLLM [132] simulations used user interaction to gain improvements in making recommendations for new items, which positively impacted the returned GMV in actual A/B testing.

Agentic AI accuracy is context-dependent and evaluated in different ways. In many cases, we have seen systems that have numerical accuracy like ECG AI, that has an accuracy of 96–97% [164], and Organa, that can report >90% accuracy [150]. Otititi emphasized that these efficiencies do not mean the AI will have a fixed set of tasks or goals on which basis we evaluate it. Previously discussed systems have emphasized operational relevance rather than static scores [35,134]. Some ways accurate agentic AI improved were by issue structuring in modular team collaborations, simulations like Agent4Rec, that repeat user activity and modeling to run those activities in simulation [132], and self-improvement via reasoning through feedback loops and by using knowledge graphs [37,134]. Some papers say system success is based on accuracy only in domains like healthcare and fraud detection [41,47], while others say system success also depends on transparency, fairness, and misinformation suppression [156,161]. Our view suggests that accuracy in agentic AI is best understood not as a single metric but as a multi-faceted outcome shaped by goal alignment, domain context, and the AI's ability to plan, adapt, and reason.

Technologies like self-healing architectures can identify failures and correct problems on their own [71,121,123], while tools like retrieval-augmented generation, tree-of-thought backtracking, and iterative debugging can help rectify hallucinations and task-related mistakes [58,75,82,132]. Multi-agent cross-verification, confidence-based reruns, and actor–critic feedback loops improve reliability in dynamic scenarios [65,79,140]. These are all the mechanisms of error recovery in agentic AI systems. Metrics for error recovery remain underdeveloped, and systems often struggle with conceptual mistakes, cascading faults, or complex edge cases [105,136,165]. Human checks, backup systems, clear logs, and interpersonal support allow them to be more robust [39,95,135]. Future agentic AI systems will strive to automatically identify and recover from errors with reinforcement learning, dynamic replanning and fault-tolerant architectures [33,49,66,166].

Parallel processing, semantic filtering, and real-time planning reduce duplication and response delays, improving both speed and scalability of the system [36,81,105]. Task efficiency improves through modular multi-agent systems, lightweight models, and adaptive architectures [31,111,132]. While efficiency defines quick responses and low energy use, most studies agree that agentic AI performs better than traditional systems through goal-oriented, optimized task execution.

A further central key component for trust to operate in agentic AI systems is transparency, explainability, and ethical design. Papers [132,135] and [37] say that trust can be developed through reasonable explanations, fairness, and accountability. Papers [71] and [65] highlight the potential for trust to break down as large models remain subject to errors, attacks, and hallucinations. Some researchers suggest dynamic approaches like system refresh [120] or incremental querying and reflection [133] to manage these risks.

Some papers talk about conceptual models based around trust, for example, cognitive, affective and social trust cited as [128], and other papers talk about metrics, for example, Explainability Scores [105], and reliability [99]. It illustrates how agentic AI trust research is still emerging. Some studies say that user satisfaction depends on how easy and trustworthy using an agentic AI system [130,141], while others say it depends more on how well the AI adapts and matches the user's values [31,37]. But the actual user satisfaction depends on many factors like meeting user's expectations, usefulness, ease of use, speed, task completion, and accuracy.

3.7. What Are the Key Challenges and Limitations in Designing and Deploying Agentic AI Systems?

Agentic AI systems bring a number of technical and social challenges. The impact of these systems depends largely on the need to constantly sense, plan, and act in dynamic environments, which requires well-designed architectural and layered systems. At the same time, the implementation of agentic AI systems raises challenges with trust, safety, ethics, and governance that require oversight and justifiable design frameworks.

Architectural/Technical Challenges: Architectural design is a key consideration for agentic AI systems. There are limitations surrounding dynamic task de-composition, hierarchical planning, and adaptive reasoning in changing environments [105]. Recent frameworks to support generalization to diverse tasks have limitations pertaining symbolic reasoning and structural rigidity [38]. Classical agent models do not support long-term strategic planning, leading to brittleness in dynamic settings [106]. Additionally, handling large and variable data including issues with volume, velocity, variety, and veracity places excessive strains on current system architecture [54]. The construction of opaque architecture limits interpretability and makes coupling with a real-world instantiation difficult [157]. Overall, we seek to develop modular, transparent scalable agent architectures that can operate under uncertainty [167].

Ethical/Societal/Governance Limitations: Agentic AI has many ethical, societal, and governance problems that need attention. There are privacy and security risks; almost 78% of organizations reported problems with data safety while using these, which shows they needed stronger rules to protect personal information [53]. Secondly, about accountability, as they are trained with reinforcement learning and, sometimes they act in unexpected ways. Even the developers cannot explain why the agentic AI made a certain choice, which makes it difficult to decide who is responsible [157]. Third, when several agentic AIs work together, there can be a communication failure. Due to these failures, it can create safety risks and increase unfair or biased decisions [105]. Finally, when the data are used by agentic AI, they may often be broken, incomplete, or poor in quality, so this also leads to biased and unfair outcomes, and that may affect trust and fairness [135].

Performance/Tool Integration Issues: Agentic AI systems continue to face ongoing problems regarding performance and tool integration. When executing multi-step and complicated tasks, there is often delay or issues pertaining to computational inefficiencies, especially during simultaneous interaction of the agents and the set of diverse external tools in real time [53]. The issues will not be improved as there is no standard interfaces offered in tool/software development to integrate with, especially with commercial or domain specific workflows [105]. Furthermore, limited design, test, and deployment support for agent design, testing and deploy environments limits the agents' scale and stable design and development [135]. This is especially true in critical areas such as healthcare, where the limits can threaten trust and effectiveness to operate. This highlights the need for effective agent architectures, and powerful toolchains to support reliable and scalable deployment.

Multi-Agent Coordination: Multi-agent coordination has recurrent difficulties in agentic AI systems, especially in terms of collaboration, synchronization, and scaling [105]. When multiple agents operate in shared environments, breakdowns in communication or strategy alignment between agents can lead to inefficiencies in establishing tasks, or complete system failure. Operational challenges that arise in the real-world are often the result of coordination failures like inconsistency in data access, communication latency, and misalignment stemming from a failure to share context [53]. Cooperative systems are also highly susceptible to correlated system failures resulting in collusion—even when there is no malicious intent—thereby diminishing issues of fairness, robustness, and transparency [135]. The problems demonstrate the necessity for scalable coordination protocols, methods for context awareness, and safety guarantees in multi-agent systems.

Human–AI Interaction: Human–AI interaction presents ongoing difficulties for the effective deployment of agentic AI systems. Many agents have limited transparency and interpretability, discouraging trust for users, and limiting collaboration, particularly when the stakes are high [105]. Effective human–AI interaction often entails poor or insecure interface design, along with overly rigid communication protocols, which fail to address the differing user roles and contexts that may involve non-expert or at-risk user groups [53]. In addition, the lack of participatory aspects limits the opportunity for oversight and corrective feedback to occur in ethical or safety-critical contexts. Systems currently struggle to properly interpret and align with the subtlety of human intention, leading to misalignment of action, including on even simple tasks and moral misalignment on work meant to help others [162]. These problems suggest human-centered agent approaches that increase explainability, allow for adaptable interaction, while fostering broader value alignment in communities and environments characterized by diverse technical differences.

Security: Security is still a fundamental issue in the design and implementation of agentic AI systems. Agents often function autonomously, and will operate in dynamic and diverse real-world conditions that make them susceptible to a range of risks (e.g., adversarial attacks, data poisoning, or inappropriate use of external tools or APIs) [53]. Lack of verifiable pipelines to connect external knowledge sources or tools also presents a means for malicious misconduct to emerge and spread false information [105]. Lack of relevant oversight processes as a safeguard may also make it difficult for humans to detect or intervene in harmful behavior when it occurs [162]. To achieve resilience, agentic AI must establish secure-by-design principles, undertakes continuous audits, and establish guardrails that restrain misuse while continuing to perform their task [135].

4. Conclusions

Agentic AI refers to intelligent systems that act autonomously, plan and adjust steps, and operate in complex environments with minimal human oversight. Combining LLMs and reinforcement learning, these systems manage multi-step workflows, remember past interactions, and pursue multiple goals. Frameworks like LangChain, AutoGPT, BabyAGI, AutoGen, and OpenAgents illustrate this evolution, progressing from structured reasoning and iterative tasks to multi-agent collaboration and adaptive problem-solving. Agentic AI will share many of the following key components: perception, planning, execution, memory, reflection, orchestration, and interaction, but differ in terms of the orchestration style and control loop between agentic AI. LLMs are sometimes seen and used as reasoners, communicators, and orchestrators. The very best agentic systems build on the concept of explicit memory for behavior, and have built-in feedback and graph-based orchestration with their memory, to elicit adaptive, reliable behaviors. Agentic AI is capable of instilling efficiency, individualization, and decision-making in a wide variety of settings because of its offering of autonomous, coordinated, and responsive action. Agentic AI can complement humans, undertake more sophisticated processes, provide greater safety, as well as intelligent, real-time solutions covering all aspects of work. Agentic AI systems move well beyond simple input–output frameworks. They include a wide variety of data types like text, audio, multimodal inputs, datasets, real-time streams, and even specialized formats like code files and PDFs. They facilitate autonomous work across structured and unstructured environments while counteracting the unpredictable elements of the real world. Evaluating agentic AI systems is an important process, and it requires a multi-faceted approach that integrates technical accuracy with qualitative factors. The most successful agentic AI systems will balance performance through the operational aspect of the system with the explanation and fairness aspect of the system, ensuring its outputs best support users' needs, values, and expectations. Agentic AI systems must contend with deeply intertwined technical, social, and governance challenges. Necessary evolution to agentic AI must involve creating modular, transparent, scalable systems while balancing the problems of alignment with human values, accountability, and fairness. Secure-by-design practices, ongoing oversight, and physics guidelines for human interactions, will be vital for establishing trust in the use of agentic AI systems and ensure safety in the many types of real-world dynamic environments.

Funding: This research received no external funding.

Data Availability Statement: See Appendixes A and B.

Conflicts of Interest: The authors declare no conflict of interest.

Appendix A

Table A1. Numerical overview of papers published per year.

Year Published	Number of Papers
1999	1
2005	1
2007	1
2014	1
2017	1
2018	1
2019	1
2020	1
2021	3
2022	6
2023	12
2024	21
2025	93
Total	143

Table A2. Numerical overview of different publication types.

Paper Type	Number of Papers
Journals	70
Preprints	38
Conference Proceedings	26
Articles	2
Working papers	2
Book	2
Dissertation	1
Workshop	2
Total	143

Table A3. Numerical overview of different publication venues.

Publication Venue	Number of Papers	Reference Code
arXiv	32	[31,33,38–40,42,51,71,75,77,81,87,90,98,100,111,113,116,120,132,136–138,141,143,144,148,150,157,159,166,167]
SSRN	6	[27,37,41,55,129,160]
Preprints	3	[36,53,96]
IEEE Access	3	[47,89,142]

Table A3. *Cont.*

Publication Venue	Number of Papers	Reference Code
Companion Proceedings of the ACM on Web Conference	3	[45,112,139]
IFAC-PapersOnLine	3	[61,72,119]
AI	2	[30,88]
ACM Conference on Fairness, Accountability, and Transparency	2	[34,168]
Journal of Business Research	2	[131,146]
Engineering Applications of Artificial Intelligence	2	[62,76]
ACM International Conference on Intelligent User Interfaces	2	[52]
Neural Information Processing Systems	2	[83,92]
Metallurgical and Materials Engineering	2	[130,134]
American Advanced Journal for Emerging Disciplinaries	1	[78]
ACM Transactions on Software Engineering and Methodology	1	[110]
ACM International Conference on User Modeling, Adaptation and Personalization	1	[97]
Advanced Engineering Informatics	1	[124]
Rani Channamma University Belagavi	1	[57]
AIS Transactions on Human Computer Interaction	1	[114]
American Journal of Computing and Engineering	1	[103]
Annual review of psychology	1	[162]
Applied Energy	1	[70]
Architectural Intelligence	1	[169]
Array	1	[66]
Association for Computing Machinery	1	[79]
Automation in Construction	1	[58]
BioSystems	1	[158]
Cell Reports Physical Science	1	[64]
Chapman and Hall/CRC	1	[170]
Clinical Neurophysiology	1	[99]
Computer Methods and Programs in Biomedicine	1	[59]
Computers and Electrical Engineering	1	[73]
Computers in Human Behavior: Artificial Humans	1	[128]
Cureus	1	[101]
Current Opinion in Chemical Engineering	1	[43]
Digital Discovery	1	[152]
European journal of analytics and artificial intelligence	1	[35]
Engineering	1	[82]
European Management Journal	1	[68]
Expert Systems with Applications	1	[135]
Extreme Mechanics Letters	1	[165]
PhD Dissertation	1	[32]
Foreign Languages in Higher Education	1	[147]
Frontiers in Computational Neuroscience	1	[122]
Frontiers in Human Dynamics	1	[154]
Informatics and Health	1	[56]
Information and Organization	1	[67]
International Journal of Computational Mathematical Ideas	1	[54]
International Conference on the AI Revolution: Research, Ethics, and Society	1	[50]
International Journal of Human-Computer Studies	1	[164]
International Journal of Research Publication and Reviews	1	[107]
Journal of Retailing	1	[140]
Journal of Building Engineering	1	[126]
Journal of Clinical and Experimental Hepatology	1	[102]
Journal of Computer Information Systems	1	[161]
Journal of Computer Science and Technology Studies	1	[95]
Journal of Retailing and Consumer Services	1	[145]
Journal of Strategic Information Systems	1	[149]
Journal of Systems and Software	1	[133]
Journal of Water Process Engineering	1	[63]
MethodsX	1	[109]
Multidisciplinary, Scientific Work and Management Journal	1	[80]
NeurIPS 2024 Workshop on open-world Agents	1	[105]
Optical Switching and Networking	1	[163]
International Conference on Agents and Artificial Intelligence	1	[106]
Procedia CIRP	1	[121]
Conference on Human Factors in Computing Systems.	1	[155]
Australasian Computer Science Week	1	[44]

Table A3. *Cont.*

Publication Venue	Number of Papers	Reference Code
Special Interest Group on Management Information Systems—Computer Personnel Research.	1	[156]
ACM International Conference on Autonomous Agents and Multiagent Systems	1	[74]
ACM International Conference on Information and Knowledge Management	1	[108]
ACM International Conference on Interactive Media Experiences	1	[60]
ACM International Conference on Human Factors in Computing Systems	1	[153]
International Conference on Automated Assembly Systems	1	[123]
Pacific Asia Conference on Information Systems	1	[48]
IEEE/ACM International Conference on Automated Software Engineering	1	[115]
ACM on Software Testing and Analysis	1	[118]
OpenAI	1	[46]
Review of Materials Research	1	[65]
Telecommunications Policy	1	[117]
The Artificial Intelligence Business Review	1	[49]
Tourism Management	1	[127]
Transport Policy	1	[104]
UIUC Spring 2025 CS598 LLM Agent Workshop	1	[151]
Urban Informatics	1	[125]
International Conference on Learning Representations	1	[84]
Future Internet	1	[86]
Springer Science and Business Media LLC	1	[91]
Sage Publications, Thousand Oaks, CA	1	[94]
Wiley Online Library	1	[93]
SmythOS	1	[85]
Total	143	

Appendix B

Table A4. Commonly used abbreviations.

Acronym	Abbreviation
ABT	Agent-Based Traffic
ACP	Adaptive Control Planning
ASR	Automatic Speech Recognition
BDD	Behavior-Driven Development
BDI	Belief–Desire–Intention
BERT	Bidirectional Encoder Representations from Transformers
CAM	Compliance Agentic Model
CAMEL	Communicative Agents for "Mind" Exploration of Large Scale Language Model Society
CIF	Common Information Framework
CLIPS	C Language Integrated Production System
CRAB	Cross-Platform Agent Benchmark
CTR	Click-Through Rate
CUDA	Compute Unified Device Architecture
DILI	Drug-induced liver injury
DL	Deep Learning
DQN	Deep Q-Networks
EDX	Electrodiagnostic tests
FM	Foundation Model
GED	Graph Edit Distance
GMV	Gross Merchandise Value
ICA	Interactive Cognitive Agents
JADE	Java Agent DEvelopment Framework
LAM	Large Agent Model
LC	Logic-based Computing
LLMs	Large Language Models
LLaMA	Large Language Model Meta AI
LTM	Long-Term Memory
MADRL	Multi-Agent Deep Reinforcement Learning
MAAI	Multi-Agent Artificial Intelligence
MAS	Multi-Agent Systems
MASON	Multi-Agent Simulator Of Neighborhoods
MCTS	Monte Carlo Tree Search
ML	Machine Learning
NLP	Natural Language Processing
OOAD	Object-Oriented Analysis and Design
PDDL	Planning Domain Definition Language
PIBT	Priority Inheritance with Backtracking
PIBTTP	Priority Inheritance with Backtracking for Tree-shaped Paths
PPO	Proximal Policy Optimization
RAG	Retrieval-Augmented Generation
RL	Reinforcement Learning
RLHF	Reinforcement Learning with Human Feedback
SCADA	Supervisory Control and Data Acquisition
SOC	Security Operations Center
SOCRATEST	Self-Optimizing Contextual Reasoning and Adaptive Testing System
STM	Short-Term Memory
STRIPS	Stanford Research Institute Problem Solver
TCT	Task Completion Time
TB-CSPN	Task-Based Cognitive Sequential Planning Network
UAT	User Acceptance Testing
WWTP	Wastewater Treatment Plant Operation
XAI	Explainable Artificial Intelligence

References

1. IBM. Agentic AI. Available online: https://www.ibm.com/think/topics/agentic-ai (accessed on 14 August 2025).
2. Amazon Web Services. The Rise of Autonomous Agents: What Enterprise Leaders Need to Know About the Next Wave of AI. Available online: https://aws.amazon.com/blogs/aws-insights/the-rise-of-autonomous-agents-what-enterprise-leaders-need-to-know-about-the-next-wave-of-ai/ (accessed on 14 August 2025).

3. MarketsandMarkets. AI Agents Market. Available online: https://www.marketsandmarkets.com/Market-Reports/ai-agents-market-15761548.html (accessed on 14 August 2025).
4. Grand View Research. AI Agents Market Report. Available online: https://www.grandviewresearch.com/industry-analysis/ai-agents-market-report(accessed on 14 August 2025).
5. Stanford HAI. Simulating Human Behavior with AI Agents. Available online: https://hai.stanford.edu/policy/simulating-human-behavior-with-ai-agents (accessed on 14 August 2025).
6. Zou, J.; Topol, E.J. The rise of agentic AI teammates in medicine. *Lancet* **2025**, *405*, 457. [CrossRef]
7. Chawla, C.; Chatterjee, S.; Gadadinni, S.S.; Verma, P.; Banerjee, S. Agentic AI: The building blocks of sophisticated AI business applications. *J. AI Robot. Workplace Autom.* **2024**, *3*, 1–15. [CrossRef]
8. White, J. Building living software systems with generative & agentic AI. *arXiv* **2024**, arXiv:2408.01768. [CrossRef]
9. TechRadar Pro. The Enterprise AI Paradox: Why Smarter Models Alone Aren't the Answer. Available online: https://www.techradar.com/pro/the-enterprise-ai-paradox-why-smarter-models-alone-arent-the-answer (accessed on 14 August 2025).
10. Cardoso, R.C.; Ferrando, A. A review of agent-based programming for multi-agent systems. *Computers* **2021**, *10*, 16. [CrossRef]
11. Jin, H.; Huang, L.; Cai, H.; Yan, J.; Li, B.; Chen, H. From llms to llm-based agents for software engineering: A survey of current, challenges and future. *arXiv* **2024**, arXiv:2408.02479. [CrossRef]
12. Zhou, J.; Lu, Q.; Chen, J.; Zhu, L.; Xu, X.; Xing, Z.; Harrer, S. A taxonomy of architecture options for foundation model-based agents: Analysis and decision model. *arXiv* **2024**, arXiv:2408.02920. [CrossRef]
13. Li, X.; Wang, S.; Zeng, S.; Wu, Y.; Yang, Y. A survey on LLM-based multi-agent systems: Workflow, infrastructure, and challenges. *Vicinagearth* **2024**, *1*, 9. [CrossRef]
14. Wang, L.; Ma, C.; Feng, X.; Zhang, Z.; Yang, H.; Zhang, J.; Chen, Z.; Tang, J.; Chen, X.; Lin, Y.; et al. A survey on large language model based autonomous agents. *Front. Comput. Sci.* **2024**, *18*, 186345. [CrossRef]
15. Gao, C.; Lan, X.; Li, N.; Yuan, Y.; Ding, J.; Zhou, Z.; Xu, F.; Li, Y. Large language models empowered agent-based modeling and simulation: A survey and perspectives. *Humanit. Soc. Sci. Commun.* **2024**, *11*, 1259. [CrossRef]
16. Novozhilova, E.; Mays, K.; Katz, J.E. Looking towards an automated future: US attitudes towards future artificial intelligence instantiations and their effect. *Humanit. Soc. Sci. Commun.* **2024**, *11*, 132. [CrossRef]
17. Sami, A.M.; Rasheed, Z.; Kemell, K.K.; Waseem, M.; Kilamo, T.; Saari, M.; Duc, A.N.; Systä, K.; Abrahamsson, P. System for systematic literature review using multiple ai agents: Concept and an empirical evaluation. *arXiv* **2024**, arXiv:2403.08399. [CrossRef]
18. Dev, K.; Khowaja, S.A.; Singh, K.; Zeydan, E.; Debbah, M. Advanced architectures integrated with agentic ai for next-generation wireless networks. *arXiv* **2025**, arXiv:2502.01089. [CrossRef]
19. Huang, X.; Liu, W.; Chen, X.; Wang, X.; Wang, H.; Lian, D.; Wang, Y.; Tang, R.; Chen, E. Understanding the planning of LLM agents: A survey. *arXiv* **2024**, arXiv:2402.02716. [CrossRef]
20. Ke, Z.; Jiao, F.; Ming, Y.; Nguyen, X.P.; Xu, A.; Long, D.X.; Li, M.; Qin, C.; Wang, P.; Savarese, S.; et al. A survey of frontiers in llm reasoning: Inference scaling, learning to reason, and agentic systems. *arXiv* **2025**, arXiv:2504.09037. [CrossRef]
21. Ferrag, M.A.; Tihanyi, N.; Debbah, M. From llm reasoning to autonomous ai agents: A comprehensive review. *arXiv* **2025**, arXiv:2504.19678. [CrossRef]
22. Schneider, J. Generative to agentic ai: Survey, conceptualization, and challenges. *arXiv* **2025**, arXiv:2504.18875. [CrossRef]
23. Mishra, L.N.; Senapati, B. Retail Resilience Engine: An Agentic AI Framework for Building Reliable Retail Systems With Test-Driven Development Approach. *IEEE Access* **2025**, *13*, 50226–50243. [CrossRef]
24. Raza, S.; Sapkota, R.; Karkee, M.; Emmanouilidis, C. Trism for agentic ai: A review of trust, risk, and security management in llm-based agentic multi-agent systems. *arXiv* **2025**, arXiv:2506.04133.
25. Cao, P.; Men, T.; Liu, W.; Zhang, J.; Li, X.; Lin, X.; Sui, D.; Cao, Y.; Liu, K.; Zhao, J. Large language models for planning: A comprehensive and systematic survey. *arXiv* **2025**, arXiv:2505.19683. [CrossRef]
26. Joshi, S. LLMOps, AgentOps, and MLOps for Generative AI: A Comprehensive Review. *Int. J. Comput. Appl. Technol. Res.* **2025**, *14*, 1–11.
27. Joshi, S. Comprehensive Review of Artificial General Intelligence AGI and Agentic GenAI: Applications in Business and Finance. *Int. J. Multidiscip. Res. Growth Eval.* **2025**, *6*, 681–688. [CrossRef]
28. Bolanos, F.; Salatino, A.; Osborne, F.; Motta, E. Artificial intelligence for literature reviews: Opportunities and challenges. *Artif. Intell. Rev.* **2024**, *57*, 259. [CrossRef]
29. Sapkota, R.; Roumeliotis, K.I.; Karkee, M. Ai agents vs. agentic ai: A conceptual taxonomy, applications and challenge. *arXiv* **2025**, arXiv:2505.10468. [CrossRef]
30. Olujimi, P.A.; Owolawi, P.A.; Mogase, R.C.; Wyk, E.V. Agentic AI frameworks in SMMEs: A systematic literature review of ecosystemic interconnected agents. *AI* **2025**, *6*, 123. [CrossRef]
31. Shah, C.; White, R.W. Agents are not enough. *arXiv* **2024**, arXiv:2412.16241. [CrossRef]

32. Dharanikota, S. Psychological and Agentic Effects of Human-Bot Delegation in Open-Source Software Development (OSSD) Communities: An Empirical Investigation of Information Systems Delegation Framework. 2022.
33. Ren, Y.; Liu, Y.; Ji, T.; Xu, X. AI Agents and Agentic AI-Navigating a Plethora of Concepts for Future Manufacturing. *arXiv* **2025**, arXiv:2507.01376. [CrossRef]
34. Chan, A.; Salganik, R.; Markelius, A.; Pang, C.; Rajkumar, N.; Krasheninnikov, D.; Langosco, L.; He, Z.; Duan, Y.; Carroll, M.; et al. Harms from Increasingly Agentic Algorithmic Systems. In Proceedings of the 2023 ACM Conference on Fairness, Accountability, and Transparency, New York, NY, USA, 12–15 June 2023. [CrossRef]
35. Suura, S.R. Agentic artificial intelligence systems for dynamic health management and real-time genomic data analysis. *Eur. J. Anal. Artif. Intell. (EJAAI)* **2024**, *2*.
36. Pavani, S.; Shwetha, H. Agentic AI: Redefining Autonomy for Complex Goal-Driven Systems. 2025. Available online: https://scholar.google.com/scholar?hl=en&as_sdt=0%2C26&q=Agentic+AI%3A+Redefining+Autonomy+for+Complex+Goal-Driven+Systems.&btnG= (accessed on 14 August 2025)
37. Mohammed Salah, A.; Alnoor, A.; Abdelfattah, F.; Chew, D.X. Agentic Ai Forging Adaptive, Equity-Driven Governance Pathways for Sustainable Futures. In *XinYing, Agentic Ai Forging Adaptive, Equity-Driven Governance Pathways for Sustainable Futures*; 2025. Available online: http://dx.doi.org/10.2139/ssrn.5229744 (accessed on 14 August 2025).
38. Botti, V. Agentic AI and Multiagentic: Are We Reinventing the Wheel? *arXiv* **2025**, arXiv:2506.01463. [CrossRef]
39. Okpala, I.; Golgoon, A.; Kannan, A.R. Agentic AI Systems Applied to tasks in Financial Services: Modeling and model risk management crews. *arXiv* **2025**, arXiv:2502.05439.
40. Narajala, V.S.; Narayan, O. Securing agentic ai: A comprehensive threat model and mitigation framework for generative ai agents. *arXiv* **2025**, arXiv:2504.19956. [CrossRef]
41. Salah, M.; Alnoor, A.; Abdelfattah, F.; Al Halbusi, H. Agentic Artificial Intelligence in Public Administration: Foundations, Applications, and Governance. Applications, and Governance 2025. Available online: https://ssrn.com/abstract=5249100 (accessed on 10 May 2025).
42. Jiang, F.; Pan, C.; Dong, L.; Wang, K.; Dobre, O.A.; Debbah, M. From large ai models to agentic ai: A tutorial on future intelligent communications. *arXiv* **2025**, arXiv:2505.22311. [CrossRef]
43. Boskabadi, M.R.; Cao, Y.; Khadem, B.; Clements, W.; Nevin Gerek, Z.; Reuthe, E.; Sivaram, A.; Savoie, C.J.; Mansouri, S.S. Industrial Agentic AI and generative modeling in complex systems. *Curr. Opin. Chem. Eng.* **2025**, *48*, 101150. [CrossRef]
44. Menezes, V.P.; Chowdhury, M.J.M.; Mahmood, A. An Agentic Framework for Compliant, Ethical and Trustworthy GenAI Applications in Healthcare. In Proceedings of the 2025 Australasian Computer Science Week, New York, NY, USA, 10–13 February 2025. [CrossRef]
45. Huang, L.; Koutra, D.; Kulkarni, A.; Prioleau, T.; Wu, Q.; Yan, Y.; Yang, Y.; Zou, J.; Zhou, D. Towards Agentic AI for Science: Hypothesis Generation, Comprehension, Quantification, and Validation. In Proceedings of the Companion Proceedings of the ACM on Web Conference, Sydney, Australia, 28 April–2 May 2025; pp. 1639–1642.
46. Shavit, Y.; Agarwal, S.; Brundage, M.; Adler, S.; O'Keefe, C.; Campbell, R.; Lee, T.; Mishkin, P.; Eloundou, T.; Hickey, A.; et al. *Practices for Governing Agentic AI Systems*; Research Paper; OpenAI: San Francisco, CA, USA, 2023.
47. Acharya, D.B.; Kuppan, K.; Bhaskaracharya, D. Agentic AI: Autonomous Intelligence for Complex Goals—A Comprehensive Survey. *IEEE Access* **2025**, *13*, 18912–18936. [CrossRef]
48. Wissuchek, C.; Zschech, P. Exploring Agentic Artificial Intelligence Systems: Towards a Typological Framework. *arXiv* **2025**, arXiv:2508.00844.
49. Allam, H.; AlOmar, B.; Dempere, J.; et al. Agentic AI for IT and Beyond: A Qualitative Analysis of Capabilities, Challenges, and Governance. *Artif. Intell. Bus. Rev.* **2025**, *1*. Available online: https://theaibr.com/index.php/aibr/article/view/3 (accessed on 14 August 2025). [CrossRef]
50. Horne, D. *The Agentic AI Mindset–A Practitioner's Guide to Architectures, Patterns, and Future Directions for Autonomy and Automation*; 2025. Available online: https://www.researchgate.net/profile/Dwight-Horne/publication/390958865_The_Agentic_AI_Mindset_-_A_Practitioner's_Guide_to_Architectures_Patterns_and_Future_Directions_for_Autonomy_and_Automation/links/6805a1eadf0e3f544f432cad/The-Agentic-AI-Mindset-A-Practitioners-Guide-to-Architectures-Patterns-and-Future-Directions-for-Autonomy-and-Automation.pdf (accessed on 14 August 2025).
51. Sapkota, R.; Roumeliotis, K.I.; Karkee, M. Vibe coding vs. agentic coding: Fundamentals and practical implications of agentic ai. *arXiv* **2025**, arXiv:2505.19443. [CrossRef]
52. Brachman, M.; Kunde, S.; Miller, S.; Fucs, A.; Dempsey, S.; Jabbour, J.; Geyer, W. Building Appropriate Mental Models: What Users Know and Want to Know about an Agentic AI Chatbot. In Proceedings of the 30th International Conference on Intelligent User Interfaces, Cagliari, Italy, 24–27 March 2025; pp. 247–264.
53. Sawant, P. Agentic AI: A Quantitative Analysis of Performance and Applications 2025. Available online: https://www.preprints.org/frontend/manuscript/b540908df60641a985f056de30899adb/download_pub (accessed on 14 August 2025).

54. Peddisetti, S. Agentic AI Meets Data Engineering: Toward Self-Directed, Interpretable, and Balanced Pipelines. *Int. J. Comput. Math. Ideas (IJCMI)* **2025**, *17*, 17313–17325.
55. Pamisetty, A. Application of Agentic Artificial Intelligence in Autonomous Decision Making Across Food Supply Chains. 2024. Available online: https://ssrn.com/abstract=5231360 (accessed on 14 August 2025).
56. Karunanayake, N. Next-generation agentic AI for transforming healthcare. *Inform. Health* **2025**, *2*, 73–83. [CrossRef]
57. Raidas, M.A.; Bhandari, R. Agentic AI in Education: Redefining Learning for the Digital Era. In *Artificial Intelligence in EducationTransforming Learning for the Future*; Scholars' Press: London, UK, 2025; p. 89.
58. Zhang, L.; Fu, X.; Li, Y.; Chen, J. Large language model-based agent Schema and library for automated building energy analysis and modeling. *Autom. Constr.* **2025**, *176*, 106244. [CrossRef]
59. Montagna, S.; Mariani, S.; Schumacher, M.I.; Manzo, G. Agent-based systems in healthcare. *Comput. Methods Programs Biomed.* **2024**, *248*, 108140 . [CrossRef] [PubMed]
60. Vahdati, M.M.; Gholizadeh HamlAbadi, K.; Laamarti, F.; El Saddik, A. A Multi-Agent Digital Twin Framework for AI-Driven Fitness Coaching. In Proceedings of the 2025 ACM International Conference on Interactive Media Experiences, New York, NY, USA, 3–6 June 2025. [CrossRef]
61. Daugherty, G.; Reveliotis, S.; Mohler, G. Optimized Multi-Agent Routing in Guidepath Networks. *IFAC-PapersOnLine* **2017**, *50*, 9686–9693. [CrossRef]
62. Nourani, C. Multiagent AI implementations an emerging software engineering trend. *Eng. Appl. Artif. Intell.* **1999**, *12*, 37–42. [CrossRef]
63. Nam, K.; Heo, S.; Kim, S.; Yoo, C. A multi-agent AI reinforcement-based digital multi-solution for optimal operation of a full-scale wastewater treatment plant under various influent conditions. *J. Water Process Eng.* **2023**, *52*, 103533. [CrossRef]
64. hui Li, J.; Hu, Y.; Xia, G.; Mo, W.; Li, B.; Jia, Y.; Gao, Y.; Xuan, F.; Liu, H.; Lian, C. Coevolution of large language models with physical models boosts advanced battery research. *Cell Rep. Phys. Sci.* **2025**, *6*, 102553. [CrossRef]
65. Wang, G.; Hu, J.; Zhou, J.; Liu, S.; Li, Q.; Sun, Z. Knowledge-guided large language model for material science. *Rev. Mater. Res.* **2025**, *1*, 100007. [CrossRef]
66. Hosseini, S.; Seilani, H. The role of agentic ai in shaping a smart future: A systematic review. *Array* **2025**, *26*, 100399. [CrossRef]
67. Leonardi, P.M. Homo agenticus in the age of agentic AI: Agency loops, power displacement, and the circulation of responsibility. *Inf. Organ.* **2025**, *35*, 100582. [CrossRef]
68. Korzynski, P.; Edwards, A.; Gupta, M.C.; Mazurek, G.; Wirtz, J. Humanoid robotics and agentic AI: Reframing management theories and future research directions. *Eur. Manag. J.* **2025**, *43*, 548–560. [CrossRef]
69. Fujitani, Y.; Yamauchi, T.; Miyashita, Y.; Sugawara, T. Deadlock-Free Method for Multi-Agent Pickup and Delivery Problem Using Priority Inheritance with Temporary Priority. *Procedia Comput. Sci.* **2022**, *207*, 1552–1561. [CrossRef]
70. Xie, J.; Ajagekar, A.; You, F. Multi-Agent attention-based deep reinforcement learning for demand response in grid-responsive buildings. *Appl. Energy* **2023**, *342*, 121162. [CrossRef]
71. Sifakis, J.; Li, D.; Huang, H.; Zhang, Y.; Dang, W.; Huang, R.; Yu, Y. A Reference Architecture for Autonomous Networks: An Agent-Based Approach. *arXiv* **2025**, arXiv:2503.12871.
72. Deng, L.; Shu, Z.; Chen, T. Event-Triggered Robust Distributed MPC for Multi-Agent Systems with A Two-Step Event Verification. *IFAC-PapersOnLine* **2022**, *55*, 144–149. [CrossRef]
73. Coordination of modular nano grid energy management using multi-agent AI architecture. *Comput. Electr. Eng.* **2024**, *115*, 109112. [CrossRef]
74. Multimodal Agentic Model Predictive Control. In Proceedings of the 24th International Conference on Autonomous Agents and Multiagent Systems, Detroit, MI, USA, 19–23 May 2025.
75. Luo, J.; Zhang, W.; Yuan, Y.; Zhao, Y.; Yang, J.; Gu, Y.; Wu, B.; Chen, B.; Qiao, Z.; Long, Q.; et al. Large language model agent: A survey on methodology, applications and challenges. *arXiv* **2025**, arXiv:2503.21460. [CrossRef]
76. Liu, J.; Hao, W.; Cheng, K.; Jin, D. Large language model-based planning agent with generative memory strengthens performance in textualized world. *Eng. Appl. Artif. Intell.* **2025**, *148*, 110319. [CrossRef]
77. Bousetouane, F. Agentic Systems: A Guide to Transforming Industries with Vertical AI Agents. *arXiv* **2025**, arXiv:2501.00881. [CrossRef]
78. Kalisetty, S.; Singireddy, J. Agentic AI in Retail: A Paradigm Shift in Autonomous Customer Interaction and Supply Chain Automation. *Am. Adv. J. Emerg. Discip. (AAJED)* **2023**, *1*.
79. Huang, X.; Lian, J.; Lei, Y.; Yao, J.; Lian, D.; Xie, X. Recommender AI Agent: Integrating Large Language Models for Interactive Recommendations. *ACM Trans. Inf. Syst.* **2025**, *43*, 1–33. [CrossRef]
80. Paleti, S. Agentic AI in Financial Decision-Making: Enhancing Customer Risk Profiling, Predictive Loan Approvals, and Automated Treasury Management in Modern Banking. *Multidiscip. Sci. Work. Manag. J.* **2024**, *34*, 832–843.
81. Trirat, P.; Jeong, W.; Hwang, S.J. Agentic Predictor: Performance Prediction for Agentic Workflows via Multi-View Encoding. *arXiv* **2025**, arXiv:2505.19764. [CrossRef]

82. Li, X.; Shi, W.; Zhang, H.; Peng, C.; Wu, S.; Tong, W. The Agentic-AI Core: An AI-Empowered, Mission-Oriented Core Network for Next-Generation Mobile Telecommunications. *Engineering* 2025, *in press*. [CrossRef]
83. Li, G.; Hammoud, H.; Itani, H.; Khizbullin, D.; Ghanem, B. Camel: Communicative agents for" mind" exploration of large language model society. *Adv. Neural Inf. Process. Syst.* **2023**, *36*, 51991–52008.
84. Hong, S.; Zhuge, M.; Chen, J.; Zheng, X.; Cheng, Y.; Zhang, C.; Wang, J.; Wang, Z.; Yau, S.K.S.; Lin, Z.; et al. MetaGPT: Meta programming for a multi-agent collaborative framework. In Proceedings of the International Conference on Learning Representations, ICLR, Vienna, Austria, 7–11 May 2024.
85. De Ridder, A. SuperAGI vs LangChain: A Comprehensive Guide. Available online: https://smythos.com/developers/agent-comparisons/superagi-vs-langchain/ (accessed on 29 August 2025).
86. Borghoff, U.M.; Bottoni, P.; Pareschi, R. Beyond Prompt Chaining: The TB-CSPN Architecture for Agentic AI. *Future Internet* **2025**, *17*, 363. [CrossRef]
87. Liu, Z.; Yao, W.; Zhang, J.; Yang, L.; Liu, Z.; Tan, J.; Choubey, P.K.; Lan, T.; Wu, J.; Wang, H.; et al. AgentLite: A Lightweight Library for Building and Advancing Task-Oriented LLM Agent System. *arXiv* **2024**, arXiv:2402.15538. http://arXiv.org/abs/2402.15538
88. Thirumalainambi, R. Pitfalls of JESS for Dynamic Systems. In Proceedings of the Artificial Intelligence and Pattern Recognition, Citeseer, Orlando, FL, USA, 9–12 July 2007; pp. 491–494.
89. Nguyen, T.T.; Nguyen, N.D.; Nahavandi, S. Deep Reinforcement Learning for Multiagent Systems: A Review of Challenges, Solutions, and Applications. *IEEE Trans. Cybern.* **2020**, *50*, 3826–3839. [CrossRef]
90. Zhang, K.; Yang, Z.; Başar, T. Multi-Agent Reinforcement Learning: A Selective Overview of Theories and Algorithms. *arXiv* **2021**, arXiv:1911.10635. http://arXiv.org/abs/1911.10635. [CrossRef]
91. Hernandez-Leal, P.; Kartal, B.; Taylor, M.E. A survey and critique of multiagent deep reinforcement learning. *Auton. Agents Multi-Agent Syst.* **2019**, *33*, 750–797. [CrossRef]
92. Silver, T.; Hariprasad, V.; Shuttleworth, R.S.; Kumar, N.; Lozano-Pérez, T.; Kaelbling, L.P. PDDL planning with pretrained large language models. In Proceedings of the NeurIPS 2022 Foundation Models for Decision Making Workshop, 2022. Available online: https://drive.google.com/file/d/1PqCYzzfdUFitxG7NxFs0D6dn-TzI97q_/view (accessed on 14 August 2025).
93. Chiacchio, F.; Pennisi, M.; Russo, G.; Motta, S.; Pappalardo, F. Agent-based modeling of the immune system: NetLogo, a promising framework. *BioMed Res. Int.* **2014**, *2014*, 907171. [CrossRef] [PubMed]
94. Luke, S.; Cioffi-Revilla, C.; Panait, L.; Sullivan, K.; Balan, G. Mason: A multiagent simulation environment. *Simulation* **2005**, *81*, 517–527. [CrossRef]
95. Garg, V. Designing the Mind: How Agentic Frameworks Are Shaping the Future of AI Behavior. *J. Comput. Sci. Technol. Stud.* **2025**, *7*, 182–193. [CrossRef]
96. Allmendinger, S.; Bonenberger, L.; Endres, K.; Fetzer, D.; Gimpel, H.; Kühl, N. Multi-Agent AI. OSF Preprints. 2023. Available online: https://osf.io/hndm3 (accessed on 14 August 2025).
97. Nurturing Code Quality: Leveraging Static Analysis and Large Language Models for Software Quality in Education. In Proceedings of the Adjunct 33rd ACM Conference on User Modeling, Adaptation and Personalization, New York, NY, USA, 16–19 June 2025. [CrossRef]
98. Yao, S.; Zhao, J.; Yu, D.; Du, N.; Shafran, I.; Narasimhan, K.; Cao, Y. ReAct: Synergizing Reasoning and Acting in Language Models. In Proceedings of the International Conference on Learning Representations (ICLR), Kigali, Rwanda, 1–5 May 2023.
99. Gorenshtein, A.; Sorka, M.; Khateb, M.; Aran, D.; Shelly, S. Agent-guided AI-powered interpretation and reporting of nerve conduction studies and EMG (INSPIRE). *Clin. Neurophysiol.* **2025**, *177*, 2110792. [CrossRef]
100. Kim, J.; Wahi-Anwa, M.; Park, S.; Shin, S.; Hoffman, J.M.; Brown, M.S. Autonomous Computer Vision Development with Agentic AI. *arXiv* **2025**, arXiv:2506.11140. [CrossRef]
101. Roy, T.P.D. Bioethics Artificial Intelligence Advisory (BAIA): An Agentic Artificial Intelligence (AI) Framework for Bioethical Clinical Decision Support. *Cureus* **2025**, *17*, e80494. [CrossRef]
102. Suechkul, P.; Tribuddharat, N.; Kulthamrongsri, N. Toward Real-Time Detection of Drug-Induced Liver Injury Using Large Language Models: A Feasibility Study from Clinical Note. *J. Clin. Exp. Hepatol.* **2025**, *15*, 102627. [CrossRef]
103. Bharadiya, J.P. Artificial Intelligence in Transportation Systems A Critical Review. *Am. J. Comput. Eng.* **2023**, *6*, 35–45. [CrossRef]
104. Yu, J. Preparing for an agentic era of human-machine transportation systems: Opportunities, challenges, and policy recommendations. *Transp. Policy* **2025**, *171*, 78–97. [CrossRef]
105. Jeyakumar, S.K.; Ahmad, A.A.; Gabriel, A.G. Advancing Agentic Systems: Dynamic Task Decomposition, Tool Integration and Evaluation using Novel Metrics and Dataset. In Proceedings of the NeurIPS 2024 Workshop on Open-World Agents, Vancouver, BC, Canada, 16 December 2024.
106. Paduraru, C.; Zavelca, M.; Stefanescu, A. Agentic AI for Behavior-Driven Development Testing using Large Language Models. Available online: https://www.scitepress.org/Papers/2025/133744/133744.pdf (accessed on 14 August 2025).

107. Ogbu, D. Agentic AI in Computer Vision Domain-Recent Advances and Prospects. Available online: https://www.researchgate.net/profile/Daniel-Ogbu/publication/386292786_Agentic_AI_in_Computer_Vision_Domain_-Recent_Advances_and_Prospects/links/674c6ec6a7fbc259f1a33618/Agentic-AI-in-Computer-Vision-Domain-Recent-Advances-and-Prospects.pdf (accessed on 14 August 2025).
108. Zhang, Y.; Liu, Z.; Wen, Q.; Pang, L.; Liu, W.; Yu, P.S. AI Agent for Information Retrieval: Generating and Ranking. In Proceedings of the 33rd ACM International Conference on Information and Knowledge Management, Boise, ID, USA, 21–25 October 2024; pp. 5605–5607.
109. Saxena, A.; Chaudhari, A.Y.; Gupta, A. AgCV: An Agentic framework for automating computer vision application. *MethodsX* **2025**, *15*, 103424. [CrossRef]
110. Robinson, D.; Cabrera, C.; Gordon, A.D.; Lawrence, N.D.; Mennen, L. Requirements Are All You Need: The Final Frontier for End-User Software Engineering. *ACM Trans. Softw. Eng. Methodol.* **2025**, *34*, 141. [CrossRef]
111. Belcak, P.; Heinrich, G.; Diao, S.; Fu, Y.; Dong, X.; Muralidharan, S.; Lin, Y.C.; Molchanov, P. Small Language Models are the Future of Agentic AI. *arXiv* **2025**, arXiv:2506.02153. [CrossRef]
112. Wen, Q.; Zhang, Y.; Liu, Z.; McAuley, J.; Wei, H.; Pang, L.; Liu, W.; Yu, P.S. The 3rd Workshop on AI Agent for Information Retrieval: Generating and Ranking. In Proceedings of the Companion Proceedings of the ACM on Web Conference 2025, New York, NY, USA, 28 April–2 May 2025; WWW '25, pp. 1659–1662. [CrossRef]
113. Casper, S.; Bailey, L.; Hunter, R.; Ezell, C.; Cabalé, E.; Gerovitch, M.; Slocum, S.; Wei, K.; Jurkovic, N.; Khan, A.; et al. The AI Agent Index. *arXiv* **2025**, arXiv:2502.01635.
114. Meske, C.; Kuss, P.M. Theorizing the Concept of Agency in Human-Algorithmic Ensembles with a Socio-Technical Lens. 2022. Available online: https://core.ac.uk/download/pdf/542549024.pdf (accessed on 14 August 2025).
115. Feldt, R.; Kang, S.; Yoon, J.; Yoo, S. Towards Autonomous Testing Agents via Conversational Large Language Models. In Proceedings of the 38th IEEE/ACM International Conference on Automated Software Engineering, Luxembourg, 11–15 November 2024; IEEE Press: New York, NY, USA, 2024. [CrossRef]
116. Fatouros, G.; Makridis, G.; Kousiouris, G.; Soldatos, J.; Tsadimas, A.; Kyriazis, D. Towards Conversational AI for Human-Machine Collaborative MLOps. *arXiv* **2025**, arXiv:2504.12477. [CrossRef]
117. Transforming cybersecurity with agentic AI to combat emerging cyber threats. *Telecommun. Policy* **2025**, *49*, 102976. [CrossRef]
118. Bouzenia, I.; Pradel, M. You Name It, I Run It: An LLM Agent to Execute Tests of Arbitrary Projects. *Proc. Acm Softw. Eng.* **2025**. 2, 1054–1076. [CrossRef]
119. Wang, L.; Qiu, T.; Pu, Z.; Yi, J.; Zhu, J.; Zhao, Y. A Decision-making Method for Swarm Agents in Attack-defense Confrontation. *IFAC-PapersOnLine* **2023**, *56*, 7858–7864. [CrossRef]
120. Sheriff, A.; Huang, K.; Nemeth, Z.; Nakhjiri, M. ADA: Automated Moving Target Defense for AI Workloads via Ephemeral Infrastructure-Native Rotation in Kubernetes. *arXiv* **2025**, arXiv:2505.23805.
121. Ungen, M.; Kampert, D.; Feldotto, B.; Huber, E.; Riedel, O. Automated workflow generation supporting the value stream design of reconfigurable robot assembly cells. *Procedia CIRP* **2024**, *128*, 609–614. [CrossRef]
122. Sandini, G.; Sciutti, A.; Morasso, P. Artificial cognition vs. artificial intelligence for next-generation autonomous robotic agents. *Front. Comput. Neurosci.* **2024**, *18*, 1349408. [CrossRef]
123. Bennett, J.; Sterritt, R. Autonomic Computing in Total Achievement of Quality. In Proceedings of the The Twentieth International Conference on Autonomic and Autonomous Systems, Athens, Greece, 10–14 March 2024.
124. Contexts Matter: Robot-Aware 3D human motion prediction for Agentic AI-empowered Human-Robot collaboration. *Adv. Eng. Inform.* **2025**, *68*, 103591. [CrossRef]
125. Tiwari, A. Conceptualising the emergence of Agentic Urban AI: From automation to agency. *Urban Inform.* **2025**, *4*, 13. [CrossRef]
126. Yoon, S.; Song, J.; Li, J. Ontology-enabled AI agent-driven intelligent digital twins for building operations and maintenance. *J. Build. Eng.* **2025**, *108*, 112802. [CrossRef]
127. Stylos, N.; Okumus, F.; Onder, I. Beauty or the Borg: Agentic artificial intelligence organizational socialization in synergistic Hybrid Transformative Dynamic Flows. *Tour. Manag.* **2025**, *111*, 105205. [CrossRef]
128. Pathak, A.; Bansal, V. AI as decision aid or delegated agent: The effects of trust dimensions on the adoption of AI digital agents. *Comput. Hum. Behav. Artif. Humans* **2024**, *2*, 100094. [CrossRef]
129. Sriram, H.K.; Bharath M, B.M. Beyond Automation: Exploring the Potential of Agentic AI in Risk Management and Fraud Detection in Banks. *Eksplorium* **2025**, *46*, 192–220. [CrossRef]
130. Inala, R.; Somu, B. Building Trustworthy Agentic Ai Systems FOR Personalized Banking Experiences. *Metall. Mater. Eng.* **2025**, *31*, 1336–1360.
131. Wünderlich, N.V.; Blut, M.; Brock, C.; Heirati, N.; Jensen, M.; Paluch, S.; Rötzmeier-Keuper, J.; Tóth, Z. How to use emerging service technologies to enhance customer centricity in business-to-business contexts: A conceptual framework and research agenda. *J. Bus. Res.* **2025**, *192*, 115284. [CrossRef]
132. Huang, C.; Huang, H.; Yu, T.; Xie, K.; Wu, J.; Zhang, S.; Mcauley, J.; Jannach, D.; Yao, L. A Survey of Foundation Model-Powered Recommender Systems: From Feature-Based, Generative to Agentic Paradigms. *arXiv* **2025**, arXiv:2504.16420.

133. Liu, Y.; Lo, S.K.; Lu, Q.; Zhu, L.; Zhao, D.; Xu, X.; Harrer, S.; Whittle, J. Agent design pattern catalogue: A collection of architectural patterns for foundation model based agents. *J. Syst. Softw.* **2025**, *220*, 112278. [CrossRef]
134. Yellanki, S.K.; Kummari, D.N.; Sheelam, G.K.; Kannan, S.; Chakilam, C. Synthetic Cognition Meets Data Deluge: Architecting Agentic AI Models for Self-Regulating Knowledge Graphs in Heterogeneous Data Warehousing. *Metall. Mater. Eng.* **2025**, *31*, 569–586. [CrossRef]
135. Piccialli, F.; Chiaro, D.; Sarwar, S.; Cerciello, D.; Qi, P.; Mele, V. AgentAI: A comprehensive survey on autonomous agents in distributed AI for industry 4.0. *Expert Syst. Appl.* **2025**, *291*, 128404. [CrossRef]
136. Plaat, A.; van Duijn, M.; van Stein, N.; Preuss, M.; van der Putten, P.; Batenburg, K.J. Agentic large language models, a survey. *arXiv* **2025**, arXiv:2503.23037. [CrossRef]
137. Hu, S.; Lu, C.; Clune, J. Automated design of agentic systems. *arXiv* **2024**, arXiv:2408.08435. [CrossRef]
138. Zhang, Q.; Wornow, M.; Olukotun, K. Cost-Efficient Serving of LLM Agents via Test-Time Plan Caching. *arXiv* **2025**, arXiv:2506.14852.
139. Zhang, Z.; Dai, Q.; Chen, X.; Li, R.; Li, Z.; Dong, Z. MemEngine: A Unified and Modular Library for Developing Advanced Memory of LLM-based Agents. In Proceedings of the Companion ACM on Web Conference 2025, New York, NY, USA, 18 May 2025. [CrossRef]
140. Sohn, S.; Labrecque, L.; Siemon, D.; Morana, S. Artificial intelligence versus human service agents: How their presence shapes consumer information privacy concerns. *J. Retail.* **2025**, *101*, 263–278. [CrossRef]
141. Floridi, L.; Buttaboni, C.; Hine, E.; Morley, J.; Novelli, C.; Schroder, T. Agentic AI Optimisation (AAIO): What it is, how it works, why it matters, and how to deal with it. *arXiv* **2025**, arXiv:2504.12482. [CrossRef]
142. Alecsoiu, O.R.; Faruqui, N.; Panagoret, A.A.; Ceausescu, A.I.; Panagoret, D.M.; Nitu, R.V.; Mutu, M.A. EcoptiAI: E-Commerce Process Optimization and Operational Cost Minimization through Task Automation using Agentic AI. *IEEE Access* **2025**, *13*, 70254–70268. [CrossRef]
143. Narechania, A.; Endert, A.; Sinha, A.R. Agentic Enterprise: AI-Centric User to User-Centric AI. *arXiv* **2025**, arXiv:2506.22893.
144. Qiao, S.; Qiu, Z.; Ren, B.; Wang, X.; Ru, X.; Zhang, N.; Chen, X.; Jiang, Y.; Xie, P.; Huang, F.; et al. Agentic Knowledgeable Self-awareness. *arXiv* **2025**, arXiv:2504.03553. [CrossRef]
145. Chong, T.; Yu, T.; Keeling, D.I.; de Ruyter, K. AI-chatbots on the services frontline addressing the challenges and opportunities of agency. *J. Retail. Consum. Serv.* **2021**, *63*, 102735. [CrossRef]
146. Jeon, Y.A. Let me transfer you to our AI-based manager: Impact of manager-level job titles assigned to AI-based agents on marketing outcomes. *J. Bus. Res.* **2022**, *145*, 892–904. [CrossRef]
147. Sargsyan, L. Integrating Agentic AI in Higher Education: Balancing Opportunities, Challenges, and Ethical Imperatives. *Foreign Lang. High. Educ.* **2025**, *29*, 87–100. [CrossRef]
148. Kamalov, F.; Calonge, D.S.; Smail, L.; Azizov, D.; Thadani, D.R.; Kwong, T.; Atif, A. Evolution of ai in education: Agentic workflows. *arXiv* **2025**, arXiv:2504.20082. [CrossRef]
149. AI Agents: Potential implications for IS Research? Available online: https://www.sciencedirect.com/science/article/pii/S0963868725000216 (accessed on 14 August 2025) .
150. Gridach, M.; Nanavati, J.; Abidine, K.Z.E.; Mendes, L.; Mack, C. Agentic AI for scientific discovery: A survey of progress, challenges, and future directions. *arXiv* **2025**, arXiv:2503.08979.
151. Zhou, R.; Sikand, V.; Rao, S. AI Agents for Deep Scientific Research. In Proceedings of the UIUC Spring 2025 CS598 LLM Agent Workshop, Urbana, Illinois, United States, 27 Apr 2025, Submitted. Available online: https://openreview.net/forum?id=wODNrFtTT2 (accessed on 14 August 2025).
152. Yager, K.G. Towards a science exocortex. *Digit. Discov.* **2024**, *3*, 1933–1957. [CrossRef]
153. Budig, T.; Nißen, M.; Kowatsch, T. Towards the Embodied Conversational Interview Agentic Service ELIAS: Development and Evaluation of a First Prototype. In Proceedings of the Adjunct 33rd ACM Conference on User Modeling, Adaptation and Personalization, New York, NY, USA, 16–19 June 2025. [CrossRef]
154. Borghoff, U.M.; Bottoni, P.; Pareschi, R. Human-artificial interaction in the age of agentic ai: A system-theoretical approach. *Front. Hum. Dyn.* **2025**, *7*, 1579166. [CrossRef]
155. Weisz, J.D.; He, J.; Muller, M.; Hoefer, G.; Miles, R.; Geyer, W. Design Principles for Generative AI Applications. In Proceedings of the 2024 CHI Conference on Human Factors in Computing Systems, Honolulu, HI, USA, 11–16 May 2024. [CrossRef]
156. Vajpayee, P.; Hossain, G. Cyber Defense through Agentic AI Enabled Automation: An Approach to Reduce Cyber Risk. In Proceedings of the 2025 Computers and People Research Conference, Waco, TX, USA, 28–30 May 2025. [CrossRef]
157. Mukherjee, A.; Chang, H.H. Agentic AI: Expanding the Algorithmic Frontier of Creative Problem Solving. *arXiv* **2025**, arXiv:2502.00289.
158. Seifert, G.; Sealander, A.; Marzen, S.; Levin, M. From reinforcement learning to agency: Frameworks for understanding basal cognition. *BioSystems* **2024**, *235*, 105107. [CrossRef]

159. Zhang, R.; Tang, S.; Liu, Y.; Niyato, D.; Xiong, Z.; Sun, S.; Mao, S.; Han, Z. Toward agentic ai: Generative information retrieval inspired intelligent communications and networking. *arXiv* **2025**, arXiv:2502.16866. [CrossRef]
160. Motamary, S. Transforming Customer Experience in Telecom: Agentic AI-Driven BSS Solutions for Hyper-Personalized Service Delivery. 2024. Available online: https://ssrn.com/abstract=5240126 (accessed on 14 August 2025) .
161. Hughes, L.; Dwivedi, Y.K.; Malik, T.; Shawosh, M.; Albashrawi, M.A.; Jeon, I.; Dutot, V.; Appanderanda, M.; Crick, T.; De', R.; et al. AI agents and agentic systems: A multi-expert analysis. *J. Comput. Inf. Syst.* **2025**, *65*, 489–517. [CrossRef]
162. Bonnefon, J.; Rahwan, I.; Shariff, A.F. The Moral Psychology of Artificial Intelligence. *Annu. Rev. Psychol.* **2023**, *75*, 653–675. [CrossRef]
163. Cruzes, S. Revolutionizing optical networks: The integration and impact of large language models. *Opt. Switch. Netw.* **2025**, *57*, 100812. [CrossRef]
164. Cabitza, F.; Campagner, A.; Simone, C. The need to move away from agential-AI: Empirical investigations, useful concepts and open issues. *Int. J. Hum.-Comput. Stud.* **2021**, *155*, 102696. [CrossRef]
165. Ni, B.; Buehler, M.J. MechAgents: Large language model multi-agent collaborations can solve mechanics problems, generate new data, and integrate knowledge. *Extrem. Mech. Lett.* **2024**, *67*, 102131. [CrossRef]
166. Rathakrishnan, M.; Gayan, S.; Singh, R.; Kaur, A.; Inaltekin, H.; Edirisinghe, S.; Poor, H.V. Towards AI-Driven RANs for 6G and Beyond: Architectural Advancements and Future Horizons. *arXiv* **2025**, arXiv:2506.16070. [CrossRef]
167. Miehling, E.; Ramamurthy, K.N.; Varshney, K.R.; Riemer, M.; Bouneffouf, D.; Richards, J.T.; Dhurandhar, A.; Daly, E.M.; Hind, M.; Sattigeri, P.; et al. Agentic ai needs a systems theory. *arXiv* **2025**, arXiv:2503.00237.
168. Ajmani, L.H.; Abdelkadir, N.A.; Chancellor, S. Secondary Stakeholders in AI: Fighting for, Brokering, and Navigating Agency. In Proceedings of the 2025 ACM Conference on Fairness, Accountability, and Transparency, New York, NY, USA, 23–26 June 2025. [CrossRef]
169. Cheung, L.H.; Wang, L.; Lei, D. Conversational, agentic AI-enhanced architectural design process: three approaches to multimodal AI-enhanced early-stage performative design exploration. *Archit. Intell.* **2025**, *4*, 1–25. [CrossRef]
170. Jilk, D.J. Limits to verification and validation of agentic behavior. In *Artificial Intelligence Safety and Security*; Chapman and Hall/CRC: Boca Raton, FL, USA, 2018; pp. 225–234.

future internet

MDPI

Article

From Divergence to Alignment: Evaluating the Role of Large Language Models in Facilitating Agreement Through Adaptive Strategies

Loukas Triantafyllopoulos * and Dimitris Kalles

School of Science and Technology, Hellenic Open University, 263 31 Patras, Greece; kalles@eap.gr
* Correspondence: triantafillopoulos.loukas@ac.eap.gr

Abstract: Achieving consensus in group decision-making often involves overcoming significant challenges, particularly reconciling diverse perspectives and mitigating biases hindering agreement. Traditional methods relying on human facilitators are usually constrained by scalability and efficiency, especially in large-scale, fast-paced discussions. To address these challenges, this study proposes a novel real-time facilitation framework, employing large language models (LLMs) as automated facilitators within a custom-built multi-user chat system. This framework is distinguished by its real-time adaptive system architecture, which enables dynamic adjustments to facilitation strategies based on ongoing discussion dynamics. Leveraging cosine similarity as a core metric, this approach evaluates the ability of three state-of-the-art LLMs—ChatGPT 4.0, Mistral Large 2, and AI21 Jamba-Instruct—to synthesize consensus proposals that align with participants' viewpoints. Unlike conventional techniques, the system integrates adaptive facilitation strategies, including clarifying misunderstandings, summarizing discussions, and proposing compromises, enabling the LLMs to refine consensus proposals based on user feedback iteratively. Experimental results indicate that ChatGPT 4.0 achieved the highest alignment with participant opinions and required fewer iterations to reach consensus. A one-way ANOVA confirmed that differences in performance between models were statistically significant. Moreover, descriptive analyses revealed nuanced differences in model behavior across various sustainability-focused discussion topics, including climate action, quality education, good health and well-being, and access to clean water and sanitation. These findings highlight the promise of LLM-driven facilitation for improving collective decision-making processes and underscore the need for further research into robust evaluation metrics, ethical considerations, and cross-cultural adaptability.

Keywords: consensus-building; artificial intelligence; collaborative decision-support systems; large language models; cosine similarity

1. Introduction

The concept of "achieving consensus" is often misinterpreted as complete unanimity among group members [1]. In fact, consensus does not require absolute agreement but the acceptance of a proposal that is considered satisfactory by all interested parties, considering the existing constraints [2]. Nevertheless, achieving this kind of agreement is a complex challenge, especially when participants have conflicting views [3,4]. Differences in opinion often arise from personal beliefs and priorities [5], while biases like attachment to initial positions [6,7] and confirmation bias [8] can hinder consensus by limiting openness to alternative perspectives.

Given the importance of this issue in collective decision-making, particularly on matters of significant concern to humanity, various methods have been employed over time to facilitate the process. One common approach is including a facilitator, often an expert or knowledgeable individual on the topic under discussion [9,10]. The facilitator guides and structures the dialogue, helping participants navigate differing viewpoints, identify common ground, encourage critical thinking, and propose mutually acceptable ideas to reach consensus [11]. While this practice has proven effective in many cases, it has shown limitations when addressing particularly complex or contentious issues, especially in large-scale and fast-paced online discussions [12,13].

On this issue, the research community has increasingly focused on automating the role of the facilitator [14], with the use of artificial intelligence (AI) playing a pivotal role in advancing this effort in recent years [12]. Notably, a growing body of research highlights the increasing interest in the potential of AI-driven facilitators over their human counterparts [13,15]. This trend has further evolved with adopting large language models (LLMs), which are increasingly recognized as effective tools for facilitating complex discussions and consensus-building processes [16].

LLMs possess a unique ability to process and synthesize vast information [17]. Analyzing diverse perspectives, identifying common themes, and proposing neutral, balanced statements can serve as powerful tools for fostering consensus [18]. Additionally, as unbiased facilitators, these models can synthesize varied viewpoints, ensuring all group members have an equitable voice in the conversation [19].

Measures like cosine similarity are particularly useful for evaluating LLMs' success in achieving consensus [3,20,21]. Cosine similarity is effective in ranking alternatives and assessing how closely participants' views align during the consensus process [22], often providing more accurate results than Euclidean distance in such scenarios [23]. Additionally, cosine similarity allows for the assessment of alignment in high-dimensional spaces [24], which is common in LLM-based tasks where the complexity of the data often extends beyond simple scalar comparison.

In this framework, the current study aims to evaluate the effectiveness of three popular LLMs in facilitating consensus among individuals on critical issues. To accomplish this, a chat-based environment was developed from scratch, enabling synchronous communication between participating users and following a predefined discussion scenario where the LLM served as the facilitator. Its role was especially to synthesize consensus proposals based on user feedback, employing, in cases of disagreement, four well-known strategies from the literature for achieving consensus. After that, the study used cosine similarity to measure the alignment between users' initial positions and the final consensus, providing a precise metric to evaluate the effectiveness of these strategies and the overall ability of the LLMs to foster agreement.

The key contributions of this paper can be outlined as follows:

1. First, the development of a fully custom, synchronous multi-user chat platform that enables real-time LLM-facilitated discussions, going beyond existing static or asynchronous systems such as D-agree;
2. Second, the integration of an adaptive facilitation framework, allowing LLMs to dynamically select among five literature-based consensus strategies during live interactions—an innovation not previously tested with multiple LLMs in a controlled setting;
3. Third, the use of cosine similarity with sentence-level vectorization (via the Universal Sentence Encoder) to evaluate consensus quantitatively across iterative discussion rounds, offering a novel and replicable method to benchmark alignment between participants' opinions and LLM-generated consensus proposals;

4. Finally, the comparative empirical assessment of three cutting-edge LLMs across a diverse set of sustainability-related questions yielded new insights into their behavior, convergence speed, and performance variability across discussion topics.

Beyond its empirical findings, this study contributes conceptually by operationalizing a replicable framework for AI-facilitated consensus evaluation. It bridges real-time interaction design with measurable alignment metrics, offering a structured methodology for future research across models, domains, and facilitation styles. Nevertheless, these contributions should be interpreted in the context of discussions involving only two participants, which inherently limits the generalizability of the results obtained.

The organization of this paper is structured as follows: Section 2 reviews relevant literature and outlines the research questions that guide this study. Section 3 details the methodology employed, including the consensus-building framework and tools used, and explains the selection criteria for the sample in the pilot test. Section 4 presents the empirical findings. Section 5 discusses these results, explores their implications, and addresses the study's limitations. Finally, Section 6 offers concluding remarks and highlights the key insights derived from the research.

2. Background

Within the context of the relevant literature, we focus on two critical issues. The first concerns the role of artificial intelligence (AI) in facilitating consensus building; the second addresses the various approaches used to measure AI's effectiveness in this area. After reviewing the pertinent information, we present the current study's approach as an advancement over the existing literature, highlighting the gaps it aims to fill and its potential contributions to the scientific community.

2.1. The Role of Artificial Intelligence in Facilitating Consensus Building

A review of the recent literature reveals numerous research efforts aimed at evaluating AI as a reliable tool for mediating and facilitating consensus-building. For this purpose, scholars often compare the outcomes of two scenarios: one with AI assistance and one without it throughout the process.

One popular approach discussed in the literature involves regularly integrating conversational agents into discussion platforms such as D-agree [15,25–28]. This online text-based platform allows participants to exchange messages with each other and with conversational AI. The AI is based on the Issue-Based Information System (IBIS) framework [29], which helps guide participants toward consensus by deconstructing dialogues into issues, ideas, pros, and cons. Additionally, these agents can summarize data, visualize discussion structures, and enhance participation with adaptive messages. Utilizing this framework, Haqbeen et al. conducted studies on achieving consensus regarding sustainability issues in Kabul, Afghanistan, and addressing solidarity in the Ukraine conflict [25,26]. Similarly, Sahab et al. [28] noted the effectiveness of AI agents in facilitating consensus in diverse environments across five Afghan cities, while Ito et al. [15] assessed the social influence of this platform in Japan. Indeed, Sahab et al. [30] later compared the results between these two countries to evaluate the effectiveness of AI agents across different cultural settings. Finally, Hadifi et al. [27] explored how conversational agents could act as facilitators to bolster women's participation in online debates in culturally conservative settings.

Despite the popularity of the D-agree platform and the use of IBIS for guiding the behavior of AI agents, some researchers consider the use of IBIS problematic in facilitating consensus achievement. Dong [31] cites two critical issues. Regarding the discussion environment, he argues that it is not inclusive, as various characteristics of participants are ignored, leading to insufficient discussions. Additionally, he contends that the facilitation messages generated by IBIS-based AI agents are not sufficiently natural, resulting in reduced participant engagement and a lack of flow in topic discussions. As an ideal alternative, Dong et al. [13] propose using LLMs for guiding AI agents, presenting a series of additional functionalities that these models offer. They strengthen their position by comparing the results of the two approaches in their publication, distinguishing LLMs (tested using GPT-3.5) as more effective for assisting the consensus process. In a related development, Nomura et al. [32] have historically integrated LLMs with the IBIS framework to enhance brainstorming interactions. By employing GPT-3.5-turbo, they assigned AI agents roles that facilitated more dynamic and inclusive discussions, addressing potential concerns about engagement and the natural flow of dialogue. This approach leveraged the advanced capabilities of LLMs to improve the effectiveness of consensus-building processes, demonstrating the benefits of merging structured facilitation methods with the adaptability of modern AI technologies.

Other researchers recognize the superiority of LLMs as tools for facilitating consensus in various ways. For example, Ding and Ito [3] developed the Self-Agreement framework, utilizing GPT-3 to autonomously generate and evaluate diverse opinions, facilitating consensus without human input. Using a different approach, Song et al. [33] demonstrated how multi-agent AI systems powered by LLMs can significantly influence social dynamics and steer opinions towards consensus by increasing social pressure among participants. Additionally, Tessler et al. [34] introduced the "Habermas Machine," an AI designed to mediate discussions on divisive political topics. Their AI was trained to produce group statements that not only garnered broad agreement among UK groups discussing issues like Brexit and immigration but also did so more effectively than human mediators. The "Habermas Machine" helped create clearer, more logical, and informative statements, ensuring minority perspectives were not alienated, thus demonstrating another powerful application of LLMs in consensus-building within diverse groups.

Building on the capabilities of LLMs to facilitate consensus-building, Govers et al. [12] focused on the specific strategies that AI agents must use to mediate online debates effectively. Their research utilized the Thomas–Kilmann Conflict Mode Instrument (TKI) to implement conflict resolution strategies through LLMs. The study particularly emphasized high-cooperativeness strategies, which were most effective at depolarizing discussions and enhancing the perception of achievable consensus among participants. This approach demonstrated how tailored AI-driven strategies could significantly influence online interactions, guiding diverse groups toward agreement and more constructive dialogue.

2.2. Measuring the Effectiveness of AI in Consensus-Building

As noted in the previous section, various approaches illustrate how AI can be valuable and necessary for facilitating the consensus-building process. However, a subsequent step involves assessing the extent to which AI achieves this goal. In the literature, numerous metrics and methodologies have been proposed to measure AI's impact on consensus formation, ranging from semantic similarity scores to perceptual and qualitative assessments. This diversity reflects the complexity of consensus-building, shaped by objective factors, such as agreement metrics, and subjective elements, such as participant satisfaction and perceived fairness.

One prominent line of research focuses on using semantic models to compare participant views and gauge overall agreement. Specifically, Ding and Ito [3] introduce a scoring function that evaluates candidate agreements generated by improved language models, relying on semantic similarity scores—such as cosine similarity computed with BERT embeddings—to determine how well different viewpoints are unified. This logic is also applied by Pérez et al. [35], who draw on soft consensus measures and fuzzy logic to quantify partial agreements, using indices like Euclidean, Manhattan, and cosine distances, along with adaptive thresholds.

Another approach examines the broader social context influenced by AI. Song et al. [33] use a 6-point Likert scale to measure opinion shifts and polarization before and after AI-mediated discussions, shedding light on the social forces that foster or hinder consensus. Likewise, Hadfi and Ito [36] adopt "Augmented Democratic Deliberation," using feedback loops in knowledge graphs to assess the depth and quality of group deliberations.

Additionally, exploring participants' subjective experiences sheds further light on how AI can affect consensus outcomes. Govers et al. [12] introduce a Perceived Consensus Score that allows participants to indicate how realistic they believe potential agreements are, potentially revealing unspoken reservations or hidden divergences. This metric is complemented by qualitative insights from Pham et al. [5] and de Rooij et al. [37], who conduct interviews to capture richer details about participants' perceptions of AI's role in shaping group dynamics and decision-making.

Finally, integrating quantitative and qualitative data provides a comprehensive view of how AI can facilitate consensus. Kim et al. [38] and Sahab et al. [39] show that AI-facilitated platforms not only lead to measurable shifts in opinions but also improve perceptions of fairness and inclusivity. This dual impact underscores AI's potential to enhance the structural efficiency of consensus-building—via semantic modeling and feedback loops—and the human experience of collaboration. AI interventions increase the likelihood of durable and broadly accepted agreements by fostering more productive, transparent, and balanced discussions.

3. A Layered Path to Opinion Convergence

Building on the relevant literature on using AI to facilitate consensus-building, particularly the potential of LLMs for this purpose, we developed a systematic approach to the process and the measurement of its effectiveness. Specifically, we designed a web application from the ground up to enable structured communication and message exchange among participants, as well as interactions with the LLM models under examination, ChatGPT 4.0, Mistral Large 2, and AI21 Jamba. These models were integrated into an organized discussion framework incorporating specific consensus-facilitating strategies, allowing each model to select appropriate actions based on conversation history and user feedback. The discussions were analyzed to evaluate the extent to which participants reached a consensus proposal aligned with their initial positions. The following section outlines the employed approach and its key components.

3.1. System Architecture and Workflow

The system architecture of the web application was designed to facilitate efficient interaction between participants and the LLMs, supporting real-time consensus-building processes. Figure 1 illustrates the consensus formation workflow, which begins with participants responding to a question posed during the discussion and expressing their opinions on the topic. The LLM synthesizes these opinions to formulate a proposal to achieve consensus among the participants.

Participants then indicate their acceptance or rejection of the consensus proposal. In cases of rejection, the system collects feedback from the participant(s) who disagreed, while those who accepted the proposal await the next iteration. The LLM then evaluates the accumulated conversation history and the newly provided feedback to autonomously determine which of the five predefined facilitation strategies to apply. This choice was not governed by any fixed algorithm or manual intervention but emerged dynamically from the model's real-time interpretation of the dialogue. Each chosen strategy guides the LLM through tailored prompts to generate a revised proposal. This iterative process continues until a consensus is reached or the discussion ends, with the LLM adapting its strategy in real time to the evolving dynamics of the dialogue.

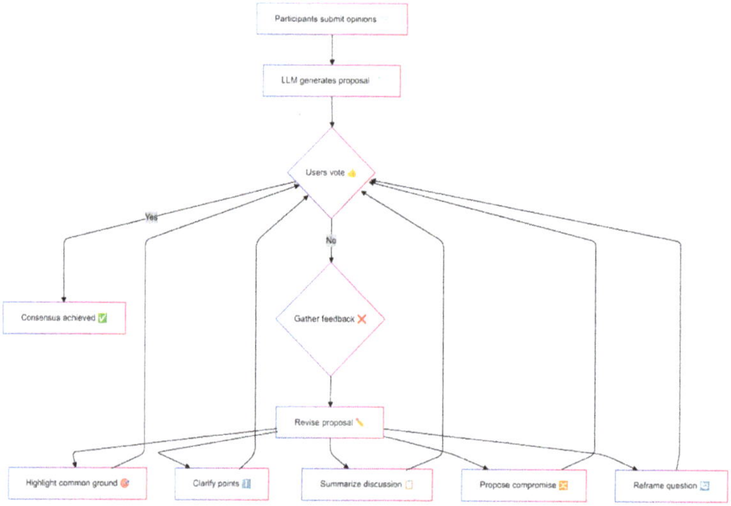

Figure 1. Consensus formation workflow.

The five strategies that the LLM could select from at each rejection point are summarized in Table 1. These strategies, derived from a literature review, aim to promote understanding, summarize key points, highlight agreements, propose compromises, and reframe questions when necessary. For instance, Bosch et al. [40] and Dworetzky et al. [41] emphasize the importance of the "ClarifyUnderstanding" strategy for eliminating ambiguities, while Chosokabe et al. [42] highlight the "SummarizeDiscussion" strategy for condensing complex conversations into their essential elements. Similarly, Nieto-Romero et al. [43] stress the value of the "HighlightCommonGround" approach, which effectively identifies shared agreements among diverse perspectives. Complementing these strategies is the "ProposeCompromise" method, emphasized by Opricovic [44] and Basuki [45], which seeks to offer balanced solutions that accommodate differing viewpoints. Additionally, Kettenburg et al. [46] advocate for the "ReframeQuestion" strategy, which involves skillfully rephrasing or redirecting research questions to foster new insights and facilitate consensus.

Table 1. Available strategies for selection by the LLM to achieve overall consensus.

Strategy	Prompt
ClarifyUnderstanding	Provide additional explanations, definitions, or examples to eliminate misunderstandings or ambiguities related to the research question or discussion points.
SummarizeDiscussion	Provide a concise summary of the discussion, highlighting key points of agreement and disagreement.
HighlightCommonGround	Identify and emphasize points of agreement among participants.
ProposeCompromise	Suggest potential compromises or middle-ground solutions.
ReframeQuestion	Rephrase or adjust the focus of the research question to make it more agreeable or clearer.

To support this architecture, we utilized several technologies, including HTML, JavaScript, PHP, CSS, and AJAX, to ensure the application's user-friendliness and compatibility across devices. An open-source server environment built using Node.js facilitated real-time interaction with the LLMs. Critical for sustained discussions, conversation history was stored in a specially configured MySQL database. Finally, API technology was employed to integrate the LLMs into the platform, with necessary code modifications to align with the previously described workflow in Figure 1.

3.2. *The Characteristics of the Evaluated LLMs*

The three LLMs selected in this research are distinguished by their popularity and promising results in addressing complex tasks. Developed by three companies, each model possesses unique features while sharing common attributes.

3.2.1. The ChatGPT Model

ChatGPT, developed by OpenAI, has rapidly gained popularity due to its powerful capabilities [47]. Version 4.0, released in March 2023, has been extensively tested by the research community across various tasks, including its effectiveness in facilitating consensus among participants [33].

This success is partly due to its architecture, which follows the Transformer model ([48]; see Figure 2), an approach that excels at processing input sequences and generating outputs by predicting the next word in a sentence based on context [49]; unlike previous recurrent neural network models, which process text sequentially from left to right, the Transformer can simultaneously consider all words in a sentence, even those at the ends of the input. It achieves this by employing multiple self-attention mechanisms, which calculate a weighted sum of the input sequence. These weights are determined based on the similarity between each input token and the rest of the sequence [50].

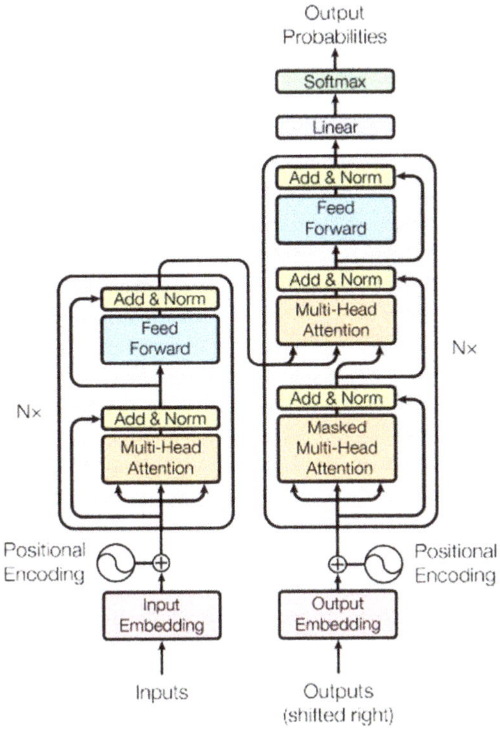

Figure 2. The Transformer—model architecture (Ashish [48]).

In addition, ChatGPT introduced some unprecedented advancements. Specifically, a unique training approach, based on unsupervised learning, was employed to process vast amounts of internet data autonomously. This approach involved incorporating approximately 1.76 trillion parameters [51] to capture intricate patterns and connections in textual information. Furthermore, reinforcement learning with human feedback was applied in a subsequent step to enhance the model's responses, refining its ability to generate contextually appropriate and accurate outputs [52].

3.2.2. The Mistral Large 2 Model

Mistral Large 2 is an LLM developed by Mistral AI and released in July 2024, significantly later than ChatGPT [53]. Unlike the previously mentioned LLM, this model was trained predominantly on French texts rather than English and utilizes a smaller number of parameters, approximately 123 billion [54]. Despite this difference, performance measurements indicate that it is an equally reliable choice, offering competitive results in general knowledge and reasoning tasks [55]. Furthermore, Mistral Large 2 supports dozens of foreign languages and more than 80 programing languages (e.g., Python, Java, C, C++, JavaScript, and Bash), making it highly capable in multilingual text processing and code generation [56,57].

Mistral Large 2 also builds upon the traditional Transformer architecture [55], introducing several improvements aimed at reducing computational complexity without significantly compromising the quality of its outputs. One notable enhancement is the Sliding Window Attention mechanism, which limits attention to a specific window of tokens. Additionally, the model incorporates mechanisms such as the Key-Value Cache with Rolling Buffer, enabling the storage and reuse of precomputed values during text generation. This reduces redundant calculations and improves the model's speed and efficiency [58]. Furthermore, as an open-source LLM, Mistral Large 2 allows the research community to make modifications, fostering further advancements and optimizations [53].

3.2.3. The AI21 Jamba-Instruct Model

The third and final model evaluated in this study is AI21's Jamba-Instruct, which was released in early May 2024 [59]. This particular LLM has been trained on a relatively minor number of parameters, approximately 52 billion [60]. Despite this, it achieves remarkable results across several performance indicators, making it a standout choice among open-source LLMs [61].

The architecture of the Jamba model series by AI21 Labs is particularly noteworthy. It employs an innovative hybrid approach that integrates Mamba layers beyond the traditional Transformer architecture. These layers enhance the processing of long-distance relationships in significant texts while reducing memory requirements. Additionally, the inclusion of Mixture of Experts (MoE) enables the use of multiple experts per layer, significantly increasing the model's capacity without a proportional increase in computational cost. It can handle content lengths of up to 256,000 tokens, with a KV cache memory footprint of only 4 GB—substantially lower than the 32 GB required by comparable LLMs. This efficiency enables Jamba to achieve top-tier performance in benchmarks such as HellaSwag and MMLU, all while being up to three times more efficient than other models of similar size [60,61].

3.3. *Calculating Text Similarity as a Surrogate for Consensus*

The cosine similarity index is a common and widely used method for comparing text similarity [62]. This index is efficient in computation [63] and its results are easy to interpret [64]. It quantifies the cosine of the angle between two non-zero vectors in a multidimensional space [65]. Specifically, its calculation formula is defined by the following equation [66]:

$$\text{Cosine Similarity}: \frac{A * B}{\|A\| \, \|B\|} \quad (1)$$

where

- A and B represent the user opinion and the consensus sentence provided by LLM, respectively, as the two vectors;
- A * B represents the dot product of the two vectors;
- ||A|| and ||B|| represent the magnitudes (or norms) of the vectors A and B.

The resolution of this relationship involves four distinct steps. First, the texts under consideration are converted into vector representations, followed by calculating the dot product between them. Next, the norms of these vectors are computed. Finally, the cosine similarity is determined by dividing the dot product by the product of the magnitudes of the two vectors.

In this study, this process was applied to analyze the cosine similarity between the initial opinions of the participants and the final proposal that was ultimately accepted in an effort to achieve consensus. It was also used to assess the differences between intermediate states, namely, participants' opinions regarding consensus proposals that were not accepted. The study required participants to provide feedback on the reasons for rejecting these proposals. This analysis helped to determine the extent to which participants maintained their original positions throughout the discussion or modified their stances by accepting proposals that did not align with their initial positions.

In the first step of this methodology, the examined texts were converted into vector representations using the Universal Sentence Encoder (USE) available from Tensor Flow Hub. This model was chosen over traditional approaches such as Term Frequency–Inverse Document Frequency (TF-IDF) and basic word embeddings, as it captures the semantic meaning of entire sentences and paragraphs more effectively [67]. Although more recent alternatives like Sentence-BERT (SBERT) offer state-of-the-art performance in semantic similarity tasks, USE was selected because it provided an optimal balance between accuracy, computational efficiency, and multilingual robustness. In particular, its proven performance across languages, including Greek, made it especially suitable for the present study, which required real-time processing of participant input during ongoing discussions. Furthermore, USE's lightweight integration with our development environment ensured consistent and fast embedding generation under the iterative consensus-building workflow. These features rendered USE not a matter of convenience but a methodologically appropriate and reliable choice for computing similarity scores across participant data. The entire vectorization process was implemented in Python using the Google Colab platform, which provided an accessible and efficient environment for embedding generation and data processing.

Next, we proceeded to calculate the dot product (numerator of Equation (1)), which concerns the sum of the vector products between each user's opinions and the consensus proposals from the LLMs. More specifically, we have Equation (2) as follows:

$$\mathrm{A} * \mathrm{B} = \sum_{i=0}^{n} A_i * B_i \quad (2)$$

where

- A_i and B_i are the elements of vectors A and B, respectively;
- n is the dimension of the vectors.

Then, we calculated the magnitudes (norms) of the vectors by taking the square root of the sum of the squares of their elements. These magnitudes represent the length of each vector in the multidimensional space. In this context, the following holds:

$$\|A\| = \sqrt{\sum_{i=1}^{n} A_i^2} \text{ and } \|B\| = \sqrt{\sum_{i=1}^{n} B_i^2} \quad (3)$$

Finally, we calculated the cosine similarity by dividing the dot product, as detailed in relation (2), by the product of the magnitudes of the two vectors from relation (3). This index ranges between -1 and 1, where:

- A cosine similarity of 1 indicates that the vectors are identical, meaning there is complete agreement between the user's proposal and the consensus proposal;
- A cosine similarity of 0 indicates that the vectors are orthogonal, suggesting no alignment between the user's proposal and the consensus proposal generated by the LLM;
- A cosine similarity of -1 indicates that the vectors are diametrically opposed, meaning the user's proposal and the consensus proposal from the LLM are completely opposite.

It should be noted that cosine similarity operationalizes consensus regarding semantic proximity to initial views. While this allows for a precise and reproducible comparison, it may underestimate cases where participants converge on a novel compromise distant from their original positions.

4. Experimental Setup

This study aimed to evaluate the AI-assisted application by focusing on a group with diverse views on sustainability, making students the ideal choice for participation [68,69]. In August 2024, the Hellenic Open University launched a call for volunteers, targeting Informatics students from all years through its official website. The announcement provided a straightforward application process with clear instructions, a consent form, and a video guide to ensure participants could easily navigate the application. To uphold ethical standards and protect privacy, the University's Ethics and Research Committee approved the study, requiring participants only to create a personal username and password, with anonymity fully safeguarded throughout.

Additionally, implementing the sessions between participants and using the three LLMs via API required resources, which were provided by both OpenAI and Amazon. Specifically, OpenAI offered free API access through the "OpenAI Researcher Access Program". At the same time, the other two models were made available through Amazon Bedrock at no cost as part of the Open Cloud for Research Environments (OCRE) initiative.

In total, 30 students expressed interest in participating in the research following the university's invitation. Using the specially designed management platform, these students organized sessions among themselves, sending invitations, selecting their questions, and scheduling the day and time for each session. As a result, between 24 August and 30 September 2024, a total of 75 sessions were conducted, with each student participating in at least one session. The sessions were evenly distributed across the three LLM models under study, with the platform occasionally adjusting the question availability to ensure a balanced evaluation of each model.

Six questions were selected for discussion, covering several SDGs, such as good health and well-being (Goal 3) and quality education (Goal 4). The set of questions used is listed in Table 2 below.

Table 2. Questions for discussion and consensus-building.

#	Question
1	Should patients with a healthy lifestyle be prioritized in healthcare provision compared to those who choose a lifestyle that increases the risk of serious conditions?
2	Should international collaborations be strengthened to address pandemics like COVID-19, or would it be better to focus on national strategies to protect public health?
3	Should priority be given to the integration of digital technologies in education to better prepare students for the modern age, or should we focus more on strengthening basic skills in literacy and numeracy?
4	Should educational policy place greater emphasis on personalized learning and support for students with different learning needs, or is it more important to maintain uniform standards and approaches for all students?
5	Should global cooperation be strengthened to improve access to clean drinking water and sanitation services, or is it better to tailor policies to the specific needs of each region?
6	Should economically disadvantaged countries adopt stricter policies to reduce carbon dioxide emissions, or should greater emphasis be placed on adaptation and the resilience of societies to climate change?

5. Results and Analysis

This section presents various analyses using cosine similarity calculations to compare the three LLMs in terms of their ability to facilitate users' consensus during a controversial discussion. This study was performed at two levels: first, by examining the distance between the participants' initial and final positions and, second, through a more detailed graphical evaluation of the intermediate stages that evolved, ultimately leading to an acceptable consensus proposal.

5.1. Evaluation of the Distance Between Users' Initial and Final Positions

Regarding the first part of the results, Tables 3 and 4 are presented. Table 3 initially analyzes the degree of similarity between the users' initial and final positions at the model level, using the average cosine similarity as a metric. As shown, ChatGPT-4 achieved the highest mean cosine similarity (M = 0.7015, SD = 0.1480, 95% CI [0.6605, 0.7425]), followed by A21-Lab (M = 0.6127, SD = 0.1485, 95% CI [0.5628, 0.6626]) and Mistral Large 2 (M = 0.5807, SD = 0.1807, 95% CI [0.5247, 0.6367]). For the total of 124 calculated values, the overall average cosine similarity index was 0.6381.

Table 3. Average cosine similarity per examined LLM.

LLM	No. of Occasions	Average Cosine Similarity	Std. Dev.	95% CI (Lower—Upper)
ChatGPT 4.0	50	0.701	0.1480	[0.6605, 0.7425]
Mistral Large 2	40	0.5807	0.1807	[0.5247, 0.6367]
AI21 Jamba	34	0.6126	0.1485	[0.5628, 0.6626]
Total	124	0.6381		

A one-way ANOVA revealed a statistically significant difference among the three models ($F(2, 121) = 6.98$, $p = 0.00136$), indicating that the type of LLM significantly affected the degree of semantic alignment between user positions and the generated consensus proposals.

Table 4. Average cosine similarity per sustainable task and LLM.

Sustainable Task	LLM	No. of Occasions	Avg. Cosine Similarity	Std. Dev.	95% CI (Lower—Upper)
Good Health and Well-Being	ChatGPT 4.0	22	0.70499	0.1558	[0.6399, 0.7701]
	Mistral Large 2	16	0.5962	0.0987	[0.5479, 0.6446]
	AI21 Jamba	14	0.6574	0.1531	[0.5773, 0.7376]
	Total	52	0.658	0.1449	[0.6194, 0.6981]
Climate action	ChatGPT 4.0	2	0.8488	0.0021	[0.8459, 0.8517]
	Mistral Large 2	2	0.5574	0.1365	[0.3682, 0.7466]
	AI21 Jamba	4	0.4966	0.0399	[0.4575, 0.5357]
	Total	8	0.599	0.1663	[0.4846, 0.7151]
Quality Education	ChatGPT 4.0	20	0.7069	0.1071	[0.66, 0.7539]
	Mistral Large 2	16	0.5922	0.2482	[0.4706, 0.7138]
	AI21 Jamba	12	0.6356	0.1457	[0.5532, 0.718]
	Total	48	0.650	0.1784	[0.6004, 0.7013]
Clean water and sanitation	ChatGPT 4.0	6	0.6212	0.2287	[0.4381, 0.8042]
	Mistral Large 2	6	0.5167	0.1751	[0.3766, 0.6568]
	AI21 Jamba	4	0.5033	0.1272	[0.3788, 0.628]
	Total	16	0.552	0.1842	[0.4623, 0.6428]

Next, Table 4 examines the extent to which the LLMs facilitated consensus, this time considering the discussion topics, which were drawn from four of the 17 SDGs. As shown, higher average cosine similarity indices were observed in discussions concerning good health and well-being and quality education, both of which were supported by a larger number of cases in this study. Specifically, for the two questions related to SDG 3 (good health and well-being)—"Should patients with a healthy lifestyle be prioritized in healthcare provision compared to those who choose a lifestyle that increases the risk of serious conditions?" and "Should international collaborations be strengthened to address pandemics like COVID-19, or would it be better to focus on national strategies to protect public health?"—the overall average cosine similarity was 0.658. Similarly, for the topics associated with SDG 4 and especially quality education—"Should priority be given to the integration of digital technologies in education to better prepare students for the modern age, or should we focus more on strengthening basic skills in literacy and numeracy?" and "Should educational policy place greater emphasis on personalized learning and support for students with different learning needs, or is it more important to maintain uniform standards and approaches for all students?"—the resulting average cosine similarity index reached 0.650. In contrast, a lower average cosine similarity score was observed for discussions on climate action (0.599), while the lowest average, 0.552, was recorded for the question addressing the global issue of clean water and sanitation. These descriptive results suggest that the alignment between participant views and consensus proposals may vary by topic. However, differences should be interpreted with caution due to differences in sample size across domains.

At the LLM level, ChatGPT-4 showed higher average cosine similarity scores across all four discussion topics included in this study (see Table 4). For example, ChatGPT-4 recorded a mean cosine similarity of 0.8487 in the context of climate action, compared to 0.5570 for Mistral Large 2 and 0.4966 for A21-Lab. In discussions related to good health and well-being, ChatGPT-4 achieved a similarity of 0.7050, while A21-Lab and Mistral Large 2 scored 0.6570 and 0.5962, respectively. The same pattern was observed in quality education, with ChatGPT-4 reaching 0.7069, compared to 0.6355 for A21-Lab and 0.5921 for Mistral Large 2. Even in the topic of clean water and sanitation, where scores were generally lower, ChatGPT-4 had a higher similarity (0.6211) than A21-Lab (0.5033) and Mistral Large 2 (0.5166).

While these results suggest a consistent trend in higher alignment scores for ChatGPT-4—meaning that its proposals remained more closely aligned with participants' initial positions—these observations should be interpreted descriptively rather than as evidence of broader facilitation success.

5.2. Assessment of the Intermediate State Until Users Reach Consensus

Figures 3–5 are presented below to help us better understand the consistency of the examined LLMs in generating proposals that align with the participants' feedback and the conversation history throughout the interaction until consensus is reached.

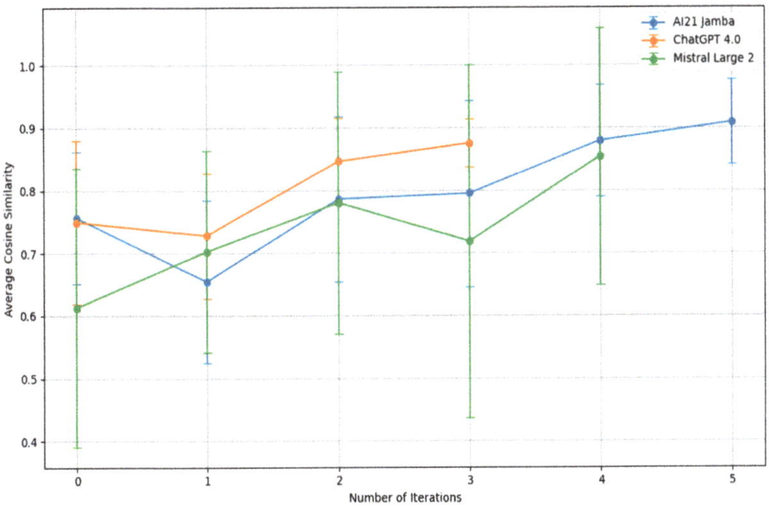

Figure 3. Average cosine similarity across iterations.

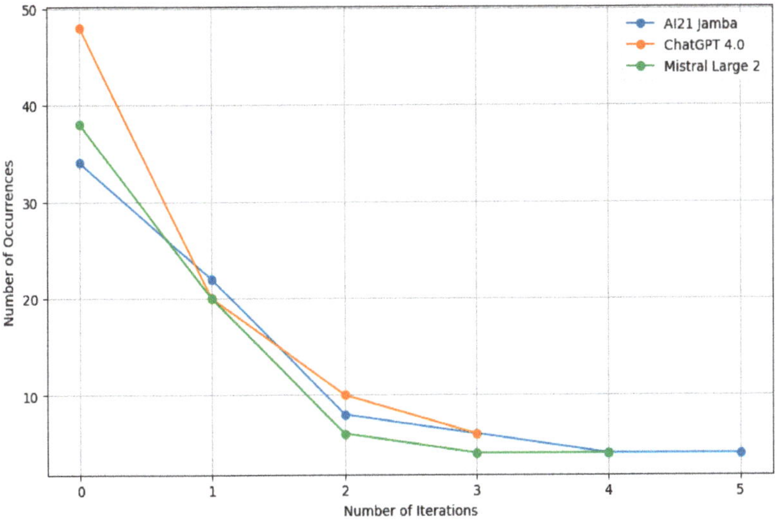

Figure 4. Number of cases per iteration for achieving consensus.

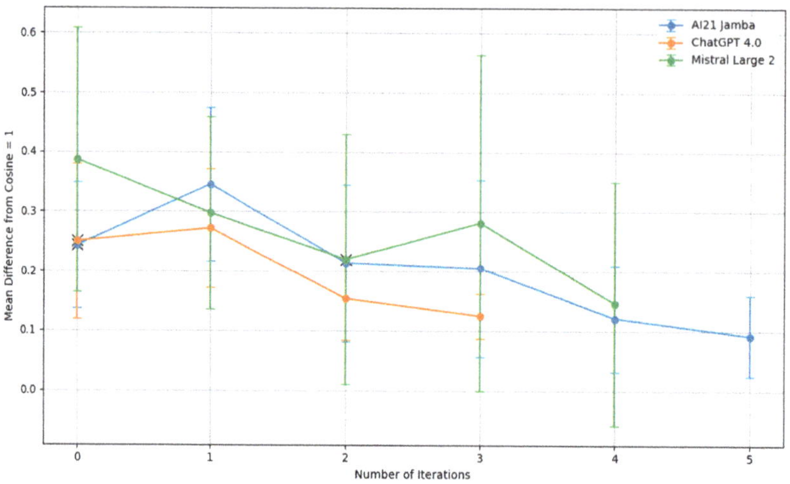

Figure 5. Mean difference in cosine similarity per iteration.

In Figure 3, the variation in the average cosine similarity per LLM is observed as the discussion progresses, particularly in cases where no acceptable consensus proposal exists among the participants. Even in the initial phase of interaction between the AI and users, ChatGPT 4.0 demonstrates a cosine similarity index close to 0.75. This value represents the similarity between the consensus proposal it generates and the initial opinions of the participants. The similarity increases significantly after the second and third iterations, as the model applies strategies to assist the discussion. Notably, in all discussions involving this LLM, no more than three iterations were required for the sample to reach a consensus. Similarly, AI21 Jamba achieves a high initial cosine similarity of 0.75. However, its behavior diverges as the process continues. According to Figure 3, its index drops significantly to 0.65 after the first round of user feedback but subsequently improves through better integration of user input. Finally, Mistral Large 2 starts with a lower initial cosine similarity index, slightly above 0.60, but shows improvement across iterations, ultimately reaching a peak of 0.85 after the fourth round. Standard deviation error bars have been included to illustrate the variability of similarity scores at each iteration step, offering a clearer view of performance consistency.

Next, Figure 4 illustrates the distribution of cases across different phases of the consensus-building process. ChatGPT 4.0 demonstrates faster convergence toward consensus compared to the other examined LLMs. Specifically, it achieves consensus more frequently within the first round of proposal generation, even without user feedback, reaching 50 cases. This surpasses the number of immediate unanimous cases observed with Mistral Large 2 and AI21 Jamba, which remain below 40. When user feedback is incorporated, the differences among the three LLMs diminish over the first three iterations. Mistral Large 2 and AI21 Jamba require additional iterations to reach consensus in some cases (up to the fourth and fifth rounds), whereas ChatGPT 4.0 achieves consensus earlier. As this figure displays frequency counts, error bars are not applicable.

Lastly, aiming to understand how the similarity between states evolved throughout the discussions, an additional analysis focused on identifying the elbow point [70] for each LLM by examining the average difference in cosine similarity from a value of 1 (entirely identical) across iterations.

Figure 5 shows no clear elbow point was detected for any model. ChatGPT 4.0 showed a steady decline in cosine difference over time, while Mistral Large 2 and AI21 Jamba exhibited fluctuations—indicating that more complex discussions may require additional iterations for convergence. To support interpretability, standard deviation error bars have also been included in this figure, providing insight into the variability of semantic drift across the interaction timeline.

6. Discussion

This study evaluated the potential of large language models (LLMs) to facilitate consensus during contentious discussions by developing a novel, real-time conversation platform. The platform employed cosine similarity as a reliable metric to assess the alignment between participants' views and proposed consensus solutions. Unlike previous studies that utilized AI tools with fixed facilitation functions, this research introduced a key innovation, dynamic and adaptive strategy selection by the AI itself, based on the discussion history. The performance of three popular LLMs—ChatGPT 4.0, Mistral Large 2, and AI21 Jamba—was compared in contemporary discussions on sustainability issues.

The analysis of all conducted conversations focused on two key areas: (1) the degree of differentiation between participants' initial positions and the consensus proposals ultimately accepted and (2) the effort required—measured by the number of iterative rounds—to reach agreement. Regarding the first axis, notable differences were observed in how each model formulated consensus proposals. ChatGPT 4.0 tended to generate proposals more closely aligned with participants' initial positions, as reflected in higher cosine similarity scores. In contrast, AI21 Jamba and Mistral Large 2 produced proposals that deviated more from participants' original views, which resulted in lower similarity scores under our operationalization. It should be emphasized that such deviations do not necessarily indicate weaker facilitation quality, as effective consensus-building may also involve movement away from initial views toward a shared compromise. This trend was consistent across all discussions in the pilot study. Specifically, ChatGPT 4.0 showed higher alignment in climate-change-related discussions, whereas AI21 Jamba adopted the most divergent approach in formulating consensus proposals on the same topic. As for the second research issue, ChatGPT 4.0 demonstrated a higher percentage of discussions that reached agreement more quickly, often requiring only one or two iterations of the scenario application process. In contrast, Mistral Large 2 and AI21 Jamba generally required more iterations—typically four to five—before producing proposals acceptable to all participants. This translated into increased time and effort under our study design.

Despite the promising results of this study, several limitations must be acknowledged, as they may have influenced the findings and affected the generalizability of the results. First, all participants were Computer Science students, a homogeneous group with high digital literacy and familiarity with structured reasoning and technological tools. While this choice reduced variability for pilot study, it may also have made participants unusually adept at interacting with LLMs, potentially inflating their apparent performance and limiting the generalizability of the findings. Second, the discussions took place in dyads, simplifying the consensus-building process by reducing the complexity of negotiation dynamics. In larger groups, where a wider range of perspectives and potential conflicts must be addressed, LLMs may require different facilitation strategies and more iterations to achieve consensus. Third, all conversations were conducted in Greek, which is not a primary training or instruction language for the evaluated LLMs. This linguistic mismatch may have impacted the models' ability to interpret nuance, produce syntactically correct responses, and engage effectively with participant input—particularly for models less optimized for multilingual tasks. Fourth, while cosine similarity is a widely used and effective metric for assessing textual alignment, it primarily measures the semantic proximity between the final consensus proposal and participants' initial views. This operationalization may underestimate successful facilitation in cases where participants reach consensus by moving away from their initial positions toward a novel compromise, as such outcomes would register lower similarity scores. In addition, cosine similarity mainly captures surface-level or lexical overlap and may overlook deeper aspects of consensus, such as shared reasoning, emotional alignment, perceived fairness, or mutual understanding. It also does not account for participants' satisfaction with the facilitation process or the perceived legitimacy of the outcome. Given that consensus involves both semantic and interpersonal dimensions, reliance on this metric alone may present an incomplete picture of facilitation effectiveness. Fifth, the study did not include a direct comparison with human facilitators, which could have offered valuable insights into the respective strengths and limitations of AI-mediated versus human-guided consensus building. However, it is essential to note that such a comparison was beyond the scope of this pilot study, as the platform was specifically designed for real-time facilitation using LLMs. Incorporating human mediators would have required a fundamentally different technical and procedural setup—including adjustments to interaction dynamics, facilitator training, and participant anonymity protocols—with any small-scale or isolated comparison under such divergent conditions potentially introducing biases that would undermine the interpretability and generalizability of the results. Finally, this study's thematic focus on sustainability—though timely and significant—may limit the transferability of findings to other domains or organizational contexts, where the nature and dynamics of discussion may differ substantially.

Given these limitations, future research could expand on the present study by involving larger groups of participants in the discussions. Engaging more individuals would introduce complex group dynamics and surface real-world challenges such as power imbalances, dominance of certain voices, or resistance to consensus. In such contexts, exploring additional facilitation strategies—such as voting mechanisms or structured debate formats—may become necessary to understand better how different interaction practices influence the consensus-building process. Moreover, incorporating participants with diverse demographic and cultural backgrounds could provide valuable insights into how these variables shape engagement with AI facilitators. Conducting discussions in the primary training languages of the LLMs would also help clarify the impact of language on facilitation quality, model comprehension, and overall user experience. Finally, expanding the thematic scope of the discussion scenarios beyond sustainability—into areas such as ethics, healthcare, or public policy—could shed light on the adaptability of LLMs in contexts marked by substantial social, moral, or ideological differences. Such extensions would be instrumental in assessing the broader applicability of AI-facilitated consensus-building in diverse real-world settings.

From a methodological perspective, an auspicious direction for future research involves conducting a comparative study between AI-driven and human-led facilitation, using a matched evaluation framework. Such a study would allow for direct assessment of differences in effectiveness, efficiency, and participant experience, offering a clearer understanding of each approach's unique contributions and limitations. Additionally, complementing cosine similarity with alternative computational metrics—such as Jaccard similarity—and incorporating qualitative indicators of agreement could offer a more nuanced understanding of conceptual convergence. This would help capture lexical overlap and the depth and substance of shared meaning among participants. To further enrich the analysis, participant-centered measures such as satisfaction ratings, perceptions of fairness, and post-discussion reflections could be integrated. These metrics would help assess whether the consensus reached was computationally valid and experienced as acceptable, equitable, and meaningful from the participants' perspectives.

Finally, an important avenue for future research involves the development of transparency and control mechanisms to safeguard ethical conduct among participants throughout the discussion process. Addressing this issue is essential for the design of AI facilitation systems that are not only effective but also inclusive, interpretable, and responsive to the ethical and social needs of diverse communities. Ensuring transparency in facilitation decisions and offering participants a degree of agency or oversight will be critical to fostering trust and legitimacy in AI-mediated deliberation.

7. Conclusions

The present study explored the use of LLMs in supporting consensus-building processes within structured online discussions. Among the three evaluated models, ChatGPT 4.0 achieved higher alignment with participants' initial views and required fewer iterations to reach agreement compared to Mistral Large 2 and AI21 Jamba based on cosine similarity measures. These findings suggest that LLMs can function as mediators in collaborative discussions and highlight important areas for further investigation, including the impact of language, cultural context, and participant diversity. Future research could build on these results by involving larger and more heterogeneous groups, testing additional facilitation strategies, and integrating qualitative assessments to capture the deeper dynamics of agreement formation. Such efforts may contribute to the continued refinement of AI-assisted decision-making frameworks in various domains.

Author Contributions: Conceptualization, L.T. and D.K.; methodology, L.T. and D.K.; software, L.T.; validation, L.T.; formal analysis, L.T.; investigation, L.T.; resources, L.T.; data curation, L.T.; original draft preparation, L.T.; writing—review and editing, D.K.; supervision, D.K.; project administration, D.K. All authors have read and agreed to the published version of the manuscript.

Funding: This research received no external funding.

Data Availability Statement: The data presented in this study is only contained in the article itself.

Acknowledgments: The authors would like to thank the students from the undergraduate IT department at the Hellenic Open University for their participation in the sessions conducted using the pilot version of the application.

Conflicts of Interest: The authors declare no conflicts of interest.

References

1. Hanson, M.P. *Clues to Achieving Consensus: A Leader's Guide to Navigating Collaborative Problem Solving*; Rowman & Littlefield Education: Lanham, MD, USA, 2005.
2. Neves, M.P. Consensus. In *Encyclopedia of Global Bioethics*; Springer: Cham, Switzerland, 2016; pp. 740–747.
3. Ding, S.; Ito, T. Self-agreement: A framework for fine-tuning language models to find agreement among diverse opinions. In *Pacific Rim International Conference on Artificial Intelligence*; Springer Nature Singapore: Singapore, 2023; pp. 298–309.
4. Foroughi, M.; de Andrade, B.; Roders, A.P.; Wang, T. Public participation and consensus-building in urban planning from the lens of heritage planning: A systematic literature review. *Cities* **2023**, *135*, 104235. [CrossRef]
5. Pham, T.V.; Weisswange, T.H.; Hassenzahl, M. Embodied Mediation in Group Ideation–A Gestural Robot Can Facilitate Consensus-Building. In Proceedings of the 2024 ACM Designing Interactive Systems Conference, Copenhagen, Denmark, 1–5 July 2024; pp. 2611–2632.
6. Kahneman, D.; Slovic, P.; Tversky, A. (Eds.) *Judgment Under Uncertainty: Heuristics and Biases*; Cambridge University Press: Cambridge, UK, 1982; pp. 3–20.
7. Liu, W.; Xiao, S.; Browne, J.T.; Yang, M.; Dow, S.P. ConsensUs: Supporting multi-criteria group decisions by visualizing points of disagreement. *ACM Trans. Soc. Comput.* **2018**, *1*, 1–26. [CrossRef]
8. Toma, C.; Butera, F. Hidden profiles and concealed information: Strategic information sharing and use in group decision making. *Personal. Soc. Psychol. Bull.* **2009**, *35*, 793–806. [CrossRef] [PubMed]
9. Straus, D. *How to Make Collaboration Work: Powerful Ways to Build Consensus, Solve Problems, and Make Decisions*; Berrett-Koehler Publishers: Oakland, CA, USA, 2002.

10. Pound, D. Designing and facilitating consensus-building–keys to success. In *Conflicts in Conservation: Navigating Towards Solutions*; Redpath, S.M., Gutierrez, R.J., Wood, K.A., Young, J.C., Eds.; Cambridge University Press: Cambridge, UK, 2015; pp. 240–256.
11. Cowell, S.; Begg, K.; Clift, R. Support for sustainable development policy decisions a case study from highway maintenance. *Int. J. Life Cycle Assess.* **2006**, *11*, 29–39. [CrossRef]
12. Govers, J.; Velloso, E.; Kostakos, V.; Goncalves, J. AI-Driven Mediation Strategies for Audience Depolarisation in Online Debates. In *Proceedings of the 2024 CHI Conference on Human Factors in Computing Systems*; ACM: New York, NY, USA, 2024; pp. 1–18.
13. Dong, Y.; Ding, S.; Ito, T. An Automated Multi-Phase Facilitation Agent Based on LLM. *IEICE Trans. Inf. Syst.* **2024**, *107*, 426–433. [CrossRef]
14. Filip, F.G.; Zamfirescu, C.B.; Ciurea, C. Collaborative activities and methods. In *Computer-Supported Collaborative Decision-Making*; Springer International Publishing: Cham, Switzerland, 2017; pp. 71–120.
15. Ito, T.; Hadfi, R.; Suzuki, S. An agent that facilitates crowd discussion: A crowd discussion support system based on an automated facilitation agent. *Group. Decis. Negot.* **2022**, *31*, 621–647. [CrossRef]
16. Zhou, L.; Farag, Y.; Vlachos, A. An LLM Feature-based Framework for Dialogue Constructiveness Assessment. *arXiv* **2024**, arXiv:2406.14760.
17. Burton, J.W.; Lopez-Lopez, E.; Hechtlinger, S.; Rahwan, Z.; Aeschbach, S.; Bakker, M.A.; Becker, J.A.; Berditchevskaia, A.; Berger, J.; Brinkmann, L.; et al. How large language models can reshape collective intelligence. *Nat. Hum. Behav.* **2024**, *8*, 1643–1655. [CrossRef]
18. Abdelnabi, S.; Gomaa, A.; Sivaprasad, S.; Schönherr, L.; Fritz, M. Cooperation, competition, and maliciousness: LLM-stakeholders interactive negotiation. *Adv. Neural Inf. Process. Syst.* **2024**, *37*, 83548–83599.
19. Westermann, H.; Savelka, J.; Benyekhlef, K. Llmediator: Gpt-4 assisted online dispute resolution. *arXiv* **2023**, arXiv:2307.16732. [CrossRef]
20. Xu, S.; Wu, Z.; Zhao, H.; Shu, P.; Liu, Z.; Liao, W.; Li, S.; Sikora, A.; Liu, T.; Li, X. Reasoning before comparison: LLM-enhanced semantic similarity metrics for domain specialized text analysis. *arXiv* **2024**, arXiv:2402.11398. [CrossRef]
21. Zhang, L.; Jijo, K.; Setty, S.; Chung, E.; Javid, F.; Vidra, N.; Clifford, T. Enhancing large language model performance to answer questions and extract information more accurately. *arXiv* **2024**, arXiv:2402.01722. [CrossRef]
22. Chiclana, F.; García, J.T.; del Moral, M.J.; Herrera-Viedma, E. Analyzing consensus measures in group decision making. *Procedia Comput. Sci.* **2015**, *55*, 1000–1008. [CrossRef]
23. Bakhshi, F.; Ashtiani, M. An approach for reaching consensus in large-scale group decision-making focusing on dimension reduction. *Complex. Intell. Syst.* **2024**, *10*, 4223–4251. [CrossRef]
24. Ingram, S.; Munzner, T. Dimensionality reduction for documents with nearest neighbor queries. *Neurocomputing* **2015**, *150*, 557–569. [CrossRef]
25. Haqbeen, J.; Takayuki, I.; Hadifi, R.; Nishida, T.; Sahab, Z.; Sahab, S.; Roghmal, S.; Amiryar, R. Promoting discussion with AI-based facilitation: Urban dialogue with Kabul city. In Proceedings of the 8th ACM Collective Intelligence, ACM Collective Intelligence Conference Series, Boston (Virtual Conference), South Padre Island, TX, USA, 18–19 June 2020.
26. Haqbeen, J.; Sahab, S.; Ito, T. A Case Study on the Comparison of AI-facilitated Threaded Conversation versus Threaded Conversation. *IIAI Lett. Inform. Interdiscip. Res.* **2023**, *4*. [CrossRef]
27. Hadfi, R.; Okuhara, S.; Haqbeen, J.; Sahab, S.; Ohnuma, S.; Ito, T. Conversational agents enhance women's contribution in online debates. *Sci. Rep.* **2023**, *13*, 14534. [CrossRef]
28. Sahab, S.; Haqbeen, J.; Ito, T. Conversational ai as a facilitator improves participant engagement and problem-solving in online discussion: Sharing evidence from five cities in afghanistan. *IEICE Trans. Inf. Syst.* **2024**, *107*, 434–442. [CrossRef]
29. Kunz, W.; Rittel, H.W.J. *Issues as Elements of Information Systems*; IURD Working Paper Series; Institute of Urban and Regional Development, University of California: Berkeley, CA, USA, 1 July 1970.
30. Sahab, S.; Haqbeen, J.A.; Ito, T. Comparative analysis of AI facilitator impact in online discussions: A cross-cultural study. In *INFORMATIK 2024*; Gesellschaft für Informatik eV: Berlin, Germany, 2024; pp. 715–725.
31. Dong, Y. The multi-agent system based on llm for online discussions. In Proceedings of the 23rd International Conference on Autonomous Agents and Multiagent Systems, Auckland, New Zealand, 6 May–10 May 2024; pp. 2731–2733.
32. Nomura, M.; Ito, T.; Ding, S. Towards Collaborative Brain-storming among Humans and AI Agents: An Implementation of the IBIS-based Brainstorming Support System with Multiple AI Agents. In *Proceedings of the ACM Collective Intelligence Conference*; Association for Computing Machinery: New York, NY, USA, 2024; pp. 1–9.
33. Song, T.; Tan, Y.; Zhu, Z.; Feng, Y.; Lee, Y.C. Multi-Agents are Social Groups: Investigating Social Influence of Multiple Agents in Human-Agent Interactions. *arXiv* **2024**, arXiv:2411.04578.
34. Tessler, M.H.; Bakker, M.A.; Jarrett, D.; Sheahan, H.; Chadwick, M.J.; Koster, R.; Evans, G.; Campbell-Gillingham, L.; Collins, T.; Parkes, D.C.; et al. AI can help humans find common ground in democratic deliberation. *Science* **2024**, *386*, eadq2852. [CrossRef] [PubMed]

35. Pérez, I.J.; Cabrerizo, F.J.; Alonso, S.; Dong, Y.C.; Chiclana, F.; Herrera-Viedma, E. On dynamic consensus processes in group decision making problems. *Inf. Sci.* **2018**, *459*, 20–35. [CrossRef]
36. Hadfi, R.; Ito, T. Augmented Democratic Deliberation: Can Conversational Agents Boost Deliberation in Social Media? In Proceedings of the 21st International Conference on Autonomous Agents and Multiagent Systems, Virtual Event, New Zealand, 9–13 May 2022; pp. 1794–1798.
37. de Rooij, A.; Broek, S.V.D.; Bouw, M.; de Wit, J. Co-Creating with a Robot Facilitator: Robot Expressions Cause Mood Contagion Enhancing Collaboration, Satisfaction, and Performance. *Int. J. Soc. Robot.* **2024**, *16*, 2133–2152. [CrossRef]
38. Kim, S.; Eun, J.; Seering, J.; Lee, J. Moderator chatbot for deliberative discussion: Effects of discussion structure and discussant facilitation. *Proc. ACM Hum. Comput. Interact.* **2021**, *5*, 1–26. [CrossRef]
39. Sahab, S.; Haqbeen, J.; Ito, T. Facilitating Collaborative Consensus Building in Web-based Discussion through Collective Task-Based Roles: A Case Study. *IIAI Lett. Inform. Interdiscip. Res.* **2023**, *4*. [CrossRef]
40. BOBosch, D.; Pease, J.; Wolfe, M.L.; Zobel, C.; Osorio, J.; Cobb, T.D.; Evanylo, G. Community DECISIONS: Stakeholder focused watershed planning. *J. Environ. Manag.* **2012**, *112*, 226–232. [CrossRef]
41. Dworetzky, B.; Paladino, M.J.; Cruze, E.; Fox, D.; Roy, S.; Bakewell, T.; Coleman, C. Family engagement in systems change: Use of a new assessment tool in quality improvement. *Pediatrics* **2024**, *153* (Suppl. 1), e2023063424D. [CrossRef]
42. Chosokabe, M.; Koie, S.; Oyamada, Y. Examining the Effect of ChatGPT on Small Group Ideation Discussions. In *International Conference on Group Decision and Negotiation*; Springer Nature: Cham, Switzerland, 2024; pp. 142–153.
43. Nieto-Romero, M.; Milcu, A.; Leventon, J.; Mikulcak, F.; Fischer, J. The role of scenarios in fostering collective action for sustainable development: Lessons from central Romania. *Land Use Policy* **2016**, *50*, 156–168. [CrossRef]
44. Opricovic, S. A compromise solution in water resources planning. *Water Resour. Manag.* **2009**, *23*, 1549–1561. [CrossRef]
45. Basuki, A. Sustainable strategies selection in SMEs using MCDM approach. In *MATEC Web of Conferences*; EDP Sciences: Les Ulis, France, 2016; p. 02007.
46. Kettenburg, A.J.; Hanspach, J.; Abson, D.J.; Fischer, J. From disagreements to dialogue: Unpacking the Golden Rice debate. *Sustain. Sci.* **2018**, *13*, 1469–1482. [CrossRef] [PubMed]
47. Easin, A.M.; Sourav, S.; Tamás, O. An intelligent llm-powered personalized assistant for digital banking using langgraph and chain of thoughts. In Proceedings of the 2024 IEEE 22nd Jubilee International Symposium on Intelligent Systems and Informatics (SISY), Pula, Croatia, 19–21 September 2024; pp. 625–630.
48. Ashish, V. Attention is all you need. In Proceedings of the 31st Conference on Neural Information Processing Systems (NeurIPS 2017), Long Beach, CA, USA, 4–9 December 2017; Volume 30.
49. Hariri, W. Unlocking the potential of ChatGPT: A comprehensive exploration of its applications, advantages, limitations, and future directions in natural language processing. *arXiv* **2023**, arXiv:2304.02017.
50. Dwivedi, Y.K.; Kshetri, N.; Hughes, L.; Slade, E.L.; Jeyaraj, A.; Kar, A.K.; Baabdullah, A.M.; Koohang, A.; Raghavan, V.; Ahuja, M.; et al. Opinion Paper: "So what if ChatGPT wrote it?" Multidisciplinary perspectives on opportunities, challenges and implications of generative conversational AI for research, practice and policy. *Int. J. Inf. Manag.* **2023**, *71*, 102642. [CrossRef]
51. Hao, X.; Demir, E.; Eyers, D. Exploring collaborative decision-making: A quasi-experimental study of human and Generative AI interaction. *Technol. Soc.* **2024**, *78*, 102662. [CrossRef]
52. Roumeliotis, K.I.; Tselikas, N.D. Chatgpt and open-ai models: A preliminary review. *Future Internet* **2023**, *15*, 192. [CrossRef]
53. Mistral AI. Mistral Large: Introducing Our Advanced Model. Available online: https://mistral.ai/news/mistral-large-2407 (accessed on 7 January 2025).
54. Da Silva, V.T.; Rademaker, A.; Lionti, K.; Giro, R.; Lima, G.; Fiorini, S.; Archanjo, M.; Carvalho, B.W.; Neumann, R.; Souza, A.; et al. Automated, LLM enabled extraction of synthesis details for reticular materials from scientific literature. *arXiv* **2024**, arXiv:2411.03484. [CrossRef]
55. Pawitan, Y.; Holmes, C. Confidence in the reasoning of large language models. *arXiv* **2024**, arXiv:2412.15296. [CrossRef]
56. Kanepajs, A.; Ivanov, V.; Moulange, R. Towards safe multilingual frontier ai. *arXiv* **2024**, arXiv:2409.13708.
57. Qiu, Z.; Liu, W.; Feng, H.; Liu, Z.; Xiao, T.Z.; Collins, K.M.; Tenenbaum, J.B.; Weller, A.; Black, M.J.; Schölkopf, B. Can Large Language Models Understand Symbolic Graphics Programs? *arXiv* **2024**, arXiv:2408.08313. [CrossRef]
58. Jiang, F. Identifying and Mitigating Vulnerabilities in LLM-Integrated Applications. Master's Thesis, University of Washington ProQuest Dissertations & Theses, Washington, DC, USA, 2024.
59. AI21 Labs. Announcing Jamba-Instruct. Available online: https://www.ai21.com/blog/announcing-jamba-instruct (accessed on 7 January 2025).
60. Team, J.; Lenz, B.; Arazi, A.; Bergman, A.; Manevich, A.; Peleg, B.; Aviram, B.; Almagor, C.; Fridman, C.; Padnos, D.; et al. Jamba-1.5: Hybrid transformer-mamba models at scale. *arXiv* **2024**, arXiv:2408.12570. [CrossRef]
61. Lieber, O.; Lenz, B.; Bata, H.; Cohen, G.; Osin, J.; Dalmedigos, I.; Safahi, E.; Meirom, S.; Belinkov, Y.; Shalev-Shwartz, S.; et al. Jamba: A hybrid transformer-mamba language model. *arXiv* **2024**, arXiv:2403.19887. [CrossRef]

62. Shahmirzadi, O.; Lugowski, A.; Younge, K. Text similarity in vector space models: A comparative study. In Proceedings of the 2019 18th IEEE International Conference on Machine Learning and Applications (ICMLA), Boca Raton, FL, USA, 16–19 December 2019; IEEE: New York, NY, USA, 2019; pp. 659–666.
63. Huang, A. Similarity measures for text document clustering. In Proceedings of the Sixth New Zealand Computer Science Research Student Conference (NZCSRSC2008), Christchurch, New Zealand, 14–18 April 2008; pp. 9–56.
64. Li, B.; Han, L. Distance weighted cosine similarity measure for text classification. In Proceedings of the 14th International Conference onIntelligent Data Engineering and Automated Learning (IDEAL 2013), Hefei, China, 20–23 October 2013; Springer: Berlin/Heidelberg, Germany, 2013; pp. 611–618.
65. Kalhori, H.; Alamdari, M.M.; Ye, L. Automated algorithm for impact force identification using cosine similarity searching. *Measurement* **2018**, *122*, 648–657. [CrossRef]
66. Mishra, H.; Soundarajan, S. Balancedqr: A framework for balanced query recommendation. In *Joint European Conference on Machine Learning and Knowledge Discovery in Databases*; Springer Nature: Cham, Switzerland, 2023; pp. 420–435.
67. TensorFlow. Semantic Similarity with TF Hub Universal Encoder. Available online: https://www.tensorflow.org/hub/tutorials/semantic_similarity_with_tf_hub_universal_encoder (accessed on 7 January 2025).
68. Sakamoto, M.; Yamaguchi, E.; Yamamoto, T.; Wakabayashi, K. An intervention study on students' decision-making towards consensus building on socio-scientific issues. *Int. J. Sci. Educ.* **2021**, *43*, 1965–1983. [CrossRef]
69. Levett-Jones, T.; Catling, C.; Cheer, S.; Fields, L.; Foster, A.; Maguire, J.; McIntyre, E.; Tracey Moroney, O.A.M.; Pich, J.; Pitt, V.; et al. Achieving consensus on the essential knowledge and skills needed by nursing students to promote planetary health and sustainable healthcare: A Delphi study. *J. Adv. Nurs.* **2024**, *00*, 1–19. [CrossRef] [PubMed]
70. Thorndike, R.L. Who belongs in the family? *Psychometrika* **1953**, *18*, 267–276. [CrossRef]

future internet

MDPI

Article

Refactoring Loops in the Era of LLMs: A Comprehensive Study

Alessandro Midolo and Emiliano Tramontana *

Dipartimento di Matematica e Informatica, University of Catania, 95125 Catania, Italy; alessandro.midolo@unict.it
* Correspondence: tramontana@dmi.unict.it; Tel.: +39-095-7383008

Abstract: Java 8 brought functional programming to the Java language and library, enabling more expressive and concise code to replace loops by using streams. Despite such advantages, for-loops remain prevalent in current codebases as the transition to the functional paradigm requires a significant shift in the developer mindset. Traditional approaches for assisting refactoring loops into streams check a set of strict preconditions to ensure correct transformation, hence limiting their applicability. Conversely, generative artificial intelligence (AI), particularly ChatGPT, is a promising tool for automating software engineering tasks, including refactoring. While prior studies examined ChatGPT's assistance in various development contexts, none have specifically investigated its ability to refactor for-loops into streams. This paper addresses such a gap by evaluating ChatGPT's effectiveness in transforming loops into streams. We analyzed 2132 loops extracted from four open-source GitHub repositories and classified them according to traditional refactoring templates and preconditions. We then tasked ChatGPT with the refactoring of such loops and evaluated the correctness and quality of the generated code. Our findings revealed that ChatGPT could successfully refactor many more loops than traditional approaches, although it struggled with complex control flows and implicit dependencies. This study provides new insights into the strengths and limitations of ChatGPT in loop-to-stream refactoring and outlines potential improvements for future AI-driven refactoring tools.

Keywords: AI-based code; code generation; software engineering

1. Introduction

The release of Java 8 introduced the functional programming paradigm in the Java language and library and enabled developers to implement more expressive and concise code. The functional paradigm reduces common programming errors, such as off-by-one mistakes, while promoting higher-level abstraction thanks to constructs like streams and lambda expressions [1,2], while the underlying libraries handle lower level details [3]. Despite the significant advantages offered by Java 8, traditional loops, particularly the for-loop, are still prevalent in available codebases [4]. The transition to a functional paradigm requires a change in mindset, which many developers have not yet fully adopted [5,6].

Generative AI technologies, such as ChatGPT, provide a very powerful coding assistant that can solve many software engineering problems, especially in the realm of code refactoring [7,8]. ChatGPT, a generative pre-trained transformer (GPT), allows users to input prompts and receive human-like responses across various media, including text and code [9]. Given the critical importance of refactoring [10,11], and the many automated tools proposed in the literature [12–16], the potential of ChatGPT to improve code quality and development efficiency deserves closer examination [17].

Researching ChatGPT's refactoring ability gives an opportunity to assess both the code quality and the efficiency of the development process in terms of time and cost.

Moreover, ChatGPT's ability to maintain context across multiple conversational exchanges and generate human-like dialogue offers unique advantages not found in other AI-based tools. Therefore, a thorough investigation of ChatGPT's capabilities in this domain could lead to significant advancements in software engineering.

Several studies have explored the role of ChatGPT in software engineering. Depalma et al. [8] examined ChatGPT's effectiveness in refactoring Java code, highlighting its strengths in improving code readability but suggesting the need for human oversight to maintain broader context and ensure correctness. White et al. [18] proposed a set of prompt patterns designed to leverage ChatGPT and other large language models (LLMs) for common software engineering tasks. Chavan et al. [19] analyzed the outcomes of ChatGPT on software development by studying the interactions on GitHub and Hacker News and focusing on its role in refactoring. Guo et al. [20] compared ChatGPT with the CodeReviewer tool, finding that ChatGPT performs better in specific code review tasks. Other studies [21–23] examined the effectiveness of ChatGPT in various development tasks and identified strengths and limitations in several contexts.

Although prior studies have examined various uses of ChatGPT in software engineering, none have specifically addressed the task of refactoring for-loops into stream pipelines. This gap presents a significant opportunity for further research. Investigating ChatGPT's suggestions for transitioning from an imperative to a functional programming style could provide valuable insights into ChatGPT's abilities. The literature describes two main deterministic approaches for refactoring loops into stream pipelines [12,24]. The more recent approach [12] introduced five templates for identifying and refactoring for-loops into streams, while the foundational work by Gyori et al. [24] explored multiple transformations. However, the applicability of both methods depends on the satisfaction of a strict set of preconditions that guarantees the correct transformation of each category of loops. More loops could be refactored if more categories or more sets of preconditions could be discovered.

To address such limitations, this paper proposes a comprehensive study that leverages ChatGPT's ability to refactor for-loops into stream pipelines. The study aims to (i) evaluate ChatGPT's effectiveness in preserving the semantics of code during refactoring, (ii) compare ChatGPT's performance to state-of-the-art (SOTA) approaches by analyzing whether it can overcome the limitations inherent in other approaches, and (iii) identify and analyze the scenarios in which ChatGPT fails to refactor code and explore the causes of failures.

For this study, we extracted five open source repositories on GitHub and isolated 2132 loops. Each loop was labeled according to the preconditions and templates defined by the SOTA approaches. The code fragments were then submitted to ChatGPT, which was tasked with generating a refactored version using stream pipelines. We provide a detailed discussion of the typical use cases for each label, highlight successful refactoring cases, and analyze the instances where ChatGPT's output was either flawed or counterproductive. The replication package of our experiments is publicly available [25].

The rest of the paper is structured as follows. In Section 2, we review the current state of the art on loop refactoring and the application of ChatGPT in software engineering. Section 3 details the methodology of our study, including its objectives and execution. Section 4 presents the results, discusses the implications, and outlines the limitations of ChatGPT's performance. Section 5 addresses potential threats to the validity of our study. Finally, Section 6 concludes with a summary of our contributions and suggestions for future research directions.

2. Related Works

This section reviews the main related works using LLMs and recommender systems for software development activities. Specifically, we focus on studies that (i) propose various approaches to refactoring for-loops and (ii) explore the use of ChatGPT in software-related tasks.

2.1. For-Loop Refactoring

The literature suggests two main approaches for refactoring for-loops into appropriate stream code. The first study introduces LambdaFicator [15], a tool designed to automate refactoring tasks in Java by leveraging functional features introduced in Java 8 [24]. LambdaFicator performs two key refactorings: converting anonymous inner classes to lambda expressions and transforming for-loops that iterate over collections into functional operations (like map or filter) using lambda expressions.

The second approach automatically refactors for-loops into stream-based code in Java, leveraging the functional programming features introduced in Java 8 [12]. The approach works by checking for-loop code against preconditions and matching it to predefined templates that represent equivalent stream-based operations. Once a match is found, the loop is replaced with the corresponding stream code, adapting and incorporating relevant statements from the original loop. Both approaches define a set of preconditions that guide the refactoring by discarding all for-loops that do not satisfy at least one of them. This paper focuses on the preconditions and investigates the ability of ChatGPT to overcome the limits imposed by preconditions and proposes innovative refactoring solutions.

Other approaches focused on refactoring for-loops, by optimizing their structure and execution or proposing parallel solutions to improve their efficiency. In [26], the authors introduced a technique for summarizing memoryless loops in C programs—loops that handle strings without maintaining memory across iterations—by replacing them with equivalent C standard library functions. This counterexample-guided synthesis approach aims to simplify string manipulation, which is often achieved through complex, error-prone loops in C.

One of the key advantages of the Java Stream API is the ability to easily parallelize streams using the parallel() method or by creating a stream using the parallelStream() method. However, before parallelizing stream operations, several factors must be considered as they may negatively impact performance. Khatchadourian et al. [27] analyzed stream operations to determine whether they are suitable for parallelization. They defined a set of conditions to ensure that converting sequential operations to parallel ones will enhance performance. Their approach is applicable to projects that include at least one stream declaration. Given the high-level abstractions provided by the Stream API, it can be challenging for developers to account for control and data flow relationships, particularly in the context of parallel operations [28]. To address this, Stein et al. [29] proposed an analysis of the user interface (UI) access in stream-based programs to ensure thread safety in parallelized environments.

Python (version 3.11.6) follows a set of conventions and best practices, known as Python Enhancement Proposals (PEPs) or Pythonic idioms [30], to enhance expressiveness and conciseness. Among these, some Pythonic idioms enable the refactoring of for-loops into a functional style. Zhang et al. [13,14] introduced a static analysis tool that automatically refactors anti-idiomatic code smells into Pythonic idioms. Similarly, Midolo et al. [31] evaluated the effectiveness of LLMs, specifically GPT-4o, in refactoring such code smells. Their comparison with the state-of-the-art tool [14] demonstrated that LLMs achieve comparable or superior performance.

2.2. AI for Software Engineering

In [8], the authors investigated ChatGPT's abilities and limitations in refactoring Java code, focusing on its capacity to improve code quality while preserving the behavior and providing accurate documentation. The study evaluates ChatGPT's performance on 40 Java code segments based on eight quality attributes. The analyzed for-loop refactoring focused solely on transforming traditional for-loops into enhanced for-loops and removing inefficient operations. Conversely, our approach investigates the ability of ChatGPT to refactor for-loop to stream pipelines, moving from an imperative style to a functional one.

A recent study investigated the effectiveness of general-purpose LLMs in automating software refactoring [32]. Through an empirical evaluation, the researchers assessed LLMs on a range of refactoring tasks, measuring both the correctness of the transformations and their impact on code quality metrics. The results showed that while LLMs can successfully suggest many refactored code snippets, challenges remain in preserving program semantics and handling complex or large codebases.

Another empirical analysis focused on StarCoder2's ability to perform code refactoring on 30 open-source Java projects [33]. The findings indicated that the model can reduce code smells by 20.1%, more than human developers on average, particularly excelling at systematic issues such as long statements, magic numbers, and empty catch clauses. However, developers still outperform the model in more complex design-level problems such as broken modularization and deficient encapsulation.

The EM-Assist tool has been proposed as an IntelliJ IDEA plugin that enhances the traditional Extract Method refactoring process by combining LLM-based reasoning with IDE-supported static analysis [34]. This approach addresses the challenge of identifying which statements in overly long methods should be extracted—a task where existing tools often fall short of matching developers' preferences.

An investigation into developer–ChatGPT interactions provided insights into how programmers use LLMs to support refactoring tasks [35]. By analyzing real refactoring conversations, the study highlights the prompts developers use, the types of refactoring suggested, and how developers respond—accepting, modifying, or rejecting the AI's recommendations. Common patterns emerge, alongside challenges such as potential behavioral changes in the code, incomplete understanding of developer intent, and trust issues.

White et al. [18] introduced prompt design techniques, structured as patterns, to address common challenges when using LLMs, e.g., ChatGPT, in software engineering tasks. These tasks include ensuring code decoupling from third-party libraries and generating API specifications from requirement lists.

In [19], an investigation of the impact of ChatGPT on software development was conducted to analyze developer conversations from GitHub and Hacker News. Through exploratory data analysis and data annotation, the study characterized interactions between developers and ChatGPT, with a specific focus on its role in code refactoring. By filtering relevant keywords, the researchers identified and analyzed refactoring facilitated by ChatGPT.

A study evaluating ChatGPT's performance in automated code review tasks was presented in [20]. The approach focused on the ability of ChatGPT to refine code based on the provided reviews. Using the existing CodeReview benchmark and a newly constructed dataset, the authors compared ChatGPT's performance against CodeReviewer, a state-of-the-art tool. The results show that ChatGPT significantly outperforms CodeReviewer.

The study in [21] examined the practical use of ChatGPT by developers through an analysis of the DevGPT dataset, which contains developer–ChatGPT conversations, including code snippets. The study addresses three key research questions: (1) whether ChatGPT generates Python and Java code with quality issues, (2) whether ChatGPT-generated code is merged into repositories and how much it is modified, and (3) the main use cases for ChatGPT beyond code generation. The findings reveal that ChatGPT-generated code often contains issues such as undefined variables, poor documentation, and security flaws.

The study in [22] explored software development practices by mining 1501 commits, pull requests (PRs), and issues from open-source projects to identify instances where ChatGPT was used. After filtering out false positives, the authors manually analyzed 467 true positive cases, resulting in a taxonomy of 45 tasks that developers automated by means of ChatGPT. These tasks, categorized and illustrated with representative examples, provided valuable insights for developers on how to integrate LLMs into their workflows and offer researchers a clear view of tasks that could benefit from further automation.

In [23], the authors systematically compared the unit test suites generated by ChatGPT and search-based software testing (SBST) tool EvoSuite [36]. The comparison focused on key aspects such as correctness, readability, code coverage, and bug detection capability. The study identified the strengths and weaknesses of ChatGPT in generating unit tests and its effectiveness against EvoSuite.

These studies explored various aspects of the usage of ChatGPT in software engineering tasks, highlighting both its strengths and weaknesses when assisting developers. However, the capability of ChatGPT to refactor for-loops into semantically equivalent stream pipelines has not been previously investigated. This gap indicates a need for further research into the model's ability to facilitate the transition from imperative programming styles to functional programming paradigms.

3. Investigation Approach

3.1. *Java Streams: A Functional Alternative to Looping*

Java streams, introduced in Java 8, offer a powerful and expressive alternative to traditional for-loops, enabling developers to process collections with a functional approach. While for-loops provide means to implement the iteration and the statements to execute over a set of elements, streams provide a way to implement a more concise and readable code, reducing boilerplate and improving maintainability. Streams support lazy evaluation, meaning that operations are executed only when a terminal operation is invoked, ensuring efficiency by avoiding unnecessary computations.

Listing 1 shows an example of a typical for-loop that iterates over a collection, requiring explicit control of the loop counter and conditions. This imperative style requires developers to manually specify the iteration, condition checking, and the actions to perform, which leads to verbose code, especially when having to perform complex transformations.

Listing 1. A traditional for-loop selecting from a list and printing some values.

```
List<String> names = Arrays.asList("Alice", "Bob", "Charlie");
for (String name : names) {
    if (name.startsWith("A")) {
        System.out.println(name.toUpperCase());
    }
}
```

Listing 2 shows the corresponding Java stream-based code. Here, the stream pipeline consists of a series of operations, including filtering and mapping, where each step clearly expresses its purpose. The filter() method allows an element of the stream to be checked according to the given condition and only provides as output the elements that match the condition; whereas the map() method transforms the elements according to the given operation. As a result, the code is more readable and maintainable.

Listing 2. A stream pipeline used to select values and print them.

```
List<String> names = Arrays.asList("Alice", "Bob", "Charlie");
names.stream()
     .filter(name -> name.startsWith("A"))
     .map(String::toUpperCase)
     .forEach(System.out::println);
```

The declarative nature of Java streams offers several significant benefits. First, streams improve conciseness. Where traditional loops require multiple lines of code to iterate, check conditions, and transform elements, streams reduce this to a single line per operation. The removal of boilerplate code allows developers to express complex logic in a much clearer and more compact way. Second, readability is greatly improved. By chaining operations, such as filter() and map(), the intent of the code is immediately apparent. This contrasts with traditional loops, where the mechanics of iteration can obscure the underlying logic. As a result, streams make it easier to understand what the code is doing at a glance.

Another advantage of streams is their inherent support for parallelism. Traditional loops require manual implementation of multithreading, often involving complex thread management. Streams, instead, offer built-in parallel processing capabilities by means of the parallelStream() method. This allows developers to efficiently distribute tasks across multiple processor cores, significantly improving performance in scenarios involving large datasets. Lastly, streams align with Java's broader move towards functional programming, introducing a more functional style through the use of lambdas and method references. This shift encourages developers to think in terms of operations on datasets rather than focusing on individual elements and control structures.

The current work aims to assess the power and reliability of ChatGPT to transform for-loops. This in turn provides developers with suggestions on whether complex for-loops could be transformed using ChatGPT, and whether refactoring is possible even though not documented in the literature. This knowledge is valuable for developers who wish to improve their code or implement new code.

3.2. Solutions and Limits of the State of the Art

We focus on the limits of SOTA approaches. In particular, we have analyzed the preconditions expressed in LambdaFicator [15,24] and in our previous work [12]. In both works, the preconditions serve to check the functional requisites of the for statements before the refactoring. If a for-loop does not satisfy any one precondition, it is not considered for the refactoring. Table 1 gives the main characteristics of the code that allow the loop to be labeled according to a category and the preconditions that have to be satisfied for such a category to be able to transform the loop. Table 2 shows each transformation template with the relevant label and description. These are the transformations proposed by both approaches above, which are apt to for-loops that satisfy the previous preconditions, and additionally a set of five templates presented in [12].

Table 1. Categories of loops and preconditions to allow refactoring defined by the approaches in [15,24].

Name	Label	Description	Precondition
Local Variables	LV	References to non-effectively final variables defined outside the loop	Only one reference allowed
Throw Clause	TC	Throwing checked exceptions	No throws allowed
Break	BR	Containing break statements	No break allowed

Table 1. *Cont.*

Name	Label	Description	Precondition
More Return	MR	Containing return statements	Only one return allowed
Continue	CO	Containing a continue statement	No continue allowed
Max Statements	MS	Number of statements	At most five statements (in if-then-else both branches are considered as one statement)
Nested Loop	NL	Containing nested loops	No nested loops allowed
Switch	SW	Containing switch statements	No switch statements allowed

Table 2. Categories of loops and templates suggested for the refactoring according to [12].

Name	Label	Description
One return	OR	The loop contains one return statement
Small size	SS	The loop has at most five statements
First template	1st	Loops that contain a conditional statement and one or more return statements giving back a primitive value or an object
Second template	2nd	Loops having a temp variable [10] declaration and assignment then a conditional statement whose expression uses the assigned variable and a return statement using the assigned variable
Third template	3rd	Loops having a temp variable and some other statements, such as a conditional statement using the current value of the iteration, and a method call
Forth template	4th	Loops where some operation is called on each element of the iteration to create a new value, then such a new value is inserted into a collection
Fifth template	5th	Loops having an if-then-else statement; hence, a secondary path of execution exists, followed when the condition evaluates false

3.3. Methodology for the Analysis of Suggested GPT Refactoring

To explore the capabilities of LLMs to refactor for-loops into Java streams, we used ChatGPT, as a representative of powerful LLMs, and more than two thousand inspected for-loops sampled from open source projects hosted on GitHub. Our study aims to provide answers to the following research questions.

- RQ_1 Can ChatGPT accurately refactor Java for-loops into stream pipelines while preserving the semantics of the generated code?
- RQ_2 Can ChatGPT overcome the limits of deterministic approaches based on preconditions to propose alternative for-loop refactoring?
- RQ_3 What limitations does ChatGPT encounter when proposing for-loop refactorings?

We answered such research questions by mining for-loops from several popular open-source Maven repositories. We mainly focused on repositories whose dependencies guaranteed ease of compiling the source code to make the validation of ChatGPT-generated solutions possible.

Figure 1 represents the three main steps of our methodology: the first one mines the for-loops candidates from the selected repositories; the second one asks ChatGPT to refactor the identified for-loops into stream-based pipelines; finally, the refactored code is injected in the source code and validated by compiling the application.

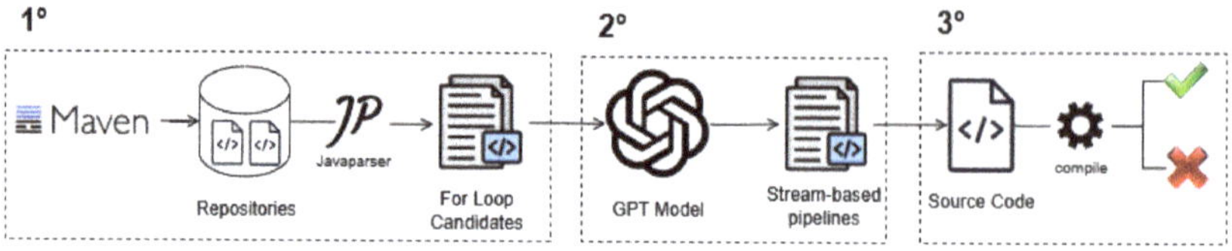

Figure 1. The methodology can be summarized in three main steps: mining for-loops, generating stream-based pipelines, and validation through compilation.

The objective of the first step was to systematically identify and extract for-loops by analyzing the source code of repositories [37]. By mining such repositories, we gathered valuable insights into how for-loops were implemented in real-world Java projects. We inspected the Maven repository [38] to identify the most popular projects suitable for our study. Starting from the highest-ranked projects, we applied two main selection criteria: (i) the presence of a substantial number of for-loops and (ii) the ability of the project to compile correctly without warnings or errors. We specifically focused on popular projects because their for-loops are likely written correctly and follow canonical coding practices, given the wide use and scrutiny of these codebases. Using these criteria, we selected five repositories that vary in size—both in terms of the number of files and lines of code—as well as in project scope. Our goal was to include a diverse set of projects representing different programming scenarios, ensuring that our analysis could be generalized across a range of real-world codebases.

To identify for-loops in the Java source files, the code was systematically parsed using the JavaParser library (https://javaparser.org, accessed on 23 May 2025), which allows source code analysis by means of an Abstract Syntax Tree (AST) [39], thereby providing a comprehensive representation of the source code's structure.

To perform code inspection, we employed the `VoidVisitorAdapter` class from JavaParser, which allows the definition of custom Visitor classes for traversing the abstract syntax tree (AST) of a Java source file and collecting specific nodes. Listing 3 shows the implementation of a `VoidVisitorAdapter` used to extract for-loops from the selected repositories. The custom visitor class, `CollectForEachStmt`, extends `VoidVisitorAdapter<HashSet <ForEachStmt>>`, specifying that enhanced for-loop nodes (`ForEachStmt`) will be collected in a `HashSet`. The `visit()` method is overridden to define the behavior when a `ForEachStmt` node is encountered: it calls `super.visit()` to continue traversing child nodes and adds the visited node to the collection, ensuring that all loops are captured without duplication.

Method `extractForEachStmt()` takes a `CompilationUnit` as input, instantiates the custom visitor and a `HashSet` to store the collected loops, invokes the visitor on the compilation unit, and returns the set of extracted loops. Traditional for-loops (`ForStmt`) are handled similarly using a separate visitor class. By employing this approach, we ensure that all loops are extracted accurately and efficiently. The extracted for-loops are then saved into separate files, which are subsequently provided to ChatGPT for the automated refactoring analysis. This strategy allows the study to focus specifically on loop refactoring, leveraging both canonical and enhanced loop structures from real-world, widely used Java projects.

The next step involved refactoring such extracted loops into stream-based code using the GPT. This step was automated by leveraging the OpenAI API, hence interacting programmatically with the model. We used the `GPT-3.5 turbo` model to generate the refactoring. Table 3 reports the parameters used for GPT-based for-loop refactoring. These settings were chosen to mimic the behavior of a developer requesting the model to refactor a specific code fragment into a stream-based implementation, rather than providing the entire file or enabling random sampling. Listing 4 shows a Python snippet that interacts with the OpenAI GPT API to automatically refactor Java for-loops into stream-based code. Function `ask_Gpt` constructs a system prompt, instructing the model to act as a skilled Java developer, and a user prompt containing the for-loop code to be refactored. It then sends these prompts to the GPT model via a chat completion request and returns the refactored code, ensuring that only the Java code is returned without explanations or additional formatting. Therefore, a prompt consists of two components: the system prompt and the user prompt. The system prompt defines the model's behavior through specific instructions, while the user prompt contains the input that describes the task. The formulation of these prompts significantly influences the LLM's code generation performance [40,41]. We designed our system and user prompts as shown in the following box.

Listing 3. A code fragment of the Visitors class used to identify and extract for-loop from the selected repositories.

```
public class Visitors {
....
    public static class CollectForEachStmt extends
        VoidVisitorAdapter<HashSet<ForEachStmt>>{
        @Override
        public void visit(ForEachStmt md, HashSet<ForEachStmt> methods) {
            super.visit(md, methods);
            methods.add(md);
        }
    }
    ....
    public static HashSet<ForEachStmt> extractForEachStmt(CompilationUnit
        cu){
        VoidVisitor<HashSet<ForEachStmt>> collectForEach = new
            CollectForEachStmt();
        HashSet<ForEachStmt> forEachstmts = new HashSet<>();
        collectForEach.visit(cu, forEachstmts);
        return forEachstmts;
    }
....
}
```

Listing 4. Example of the API call to the GPT model used to request the refactoring of a for-loop into a stream-based implementation.

```
from openai import OpenAI
from colorama import Fore, Style

client = OpenAI(api_key="")

def ask_Gpt(code):
    systemPrompt = "You are a software developer, skilled in writing Java
        source code and refactoring for loops into stream-based code"
    userPrompt = f"Please refactor this code to use streams, and provide
        only the Java code without any markdown, explanation, or comments:
        {code}"

    completion = client.chat.completions.create(
        model="gpt-3.5-turbo-0125",
        messages=[
            {"role": "system", "content":systemPrompt},
            {"role": "user", "content": userPrompt}
        ]
    )

    message = completion.choices[0].message.content
    print(f"{Fore.LIGHTBLUE_EX}{message}{Style.RESET_ALL}\n")
    return message
```

Table 3. Parameters used for GPT-based for-loop refactoring experiments.

Version	Temperature	Attempts	Context	Sampling
GPT-3.5 turbo	1.0	1	code fragment (not the entire file)	no

System and user prompts used for generation

System: 'You are a software developer, skilled in writing Java source code and refactoring for loops into stream-based code'
User: 'Please refactor this code to use streams, and provide only the Java code without any markdown, explanation, or comments: *code*'

Our prompt design follows the study proposed by Liu et al. [42] to ensure effective transformation of traditional for-loops into stream pipelines. To validate the clarity and correctness of the prompts, we manually executed them on representative code snippets, confirming that the model accurately understood the task and consistently generated the intended stream-based refactorings. By carefully structuring the prompts and verifying their effectiveness, we aimed to emulate the practical workflow of a developer using ChatGPT for targeted code refactoring.

To streamline the following refactoring process, we asked ChatGPT to omit any markdown, comment, or explanation, guaranteeing that the provided answer contained just the source code that will replace the original for-loop.

The last step aimed at injecting the stream-based code fragment into the proper method in the original source code. Each for-loop was replaced with the corresponding stream code. The injected code was then compiled using Maven. Each pair, for-loop, and corresponding stream-based code, was labeled according to the output of the compilation, which can be successful or not. If compilation was successful, refactoring was considered correct; otherwise, Maven output was collected to understand the issue.

4. Results of the Experiments

This section describes the results and addresses the three research questions expressed in Section 3.3. The study involved examining five GitHub projects, selected from the most recent Maven-based projects. Maven was chosen as the project manager due to its simplicity in compiling source code, ensuring semantic correctness. Since Java streams require Java 8 or higher, the focus was on recent repositories to avoid compatibility issues and ensure that the repositories are still actively maintained. The selected repositories are magpie [43], j2clmavenplugin [44], iridium [45], openrefine [46], and rapiddweller-benerator-ce [47]. Table 4 shows the number of stars, forks and contributors for each repository.

Table 4. GitHub characteristics of the selected repositories for the analysis

Repository	Stars	Forks	Contributors
iridium	123	17	11
magpie	191	33	15
j2clmavenplugin	8	3	3
rapiddweller-benerator-ce	151	26	10
openrefine	11,500	2100	395

4.1. RQ1: Semantic Preserving Transformation

The goal is to update the code to a more modern style while preserving the original semantics, ensuring that the new implementation does not encounter compilation problems, i.e., errors that were not present before.

Table 5 illustrates the results of the automated refactoring process carried out by ChatGPT on the five open-source repositories. The table columns display the repository name, the total number of for-loops identified, the number of successfully refactored loops, and the resulting status of the refactored code—specifically, whether it was compilable or uncompilable.

Table 5. Summary of for-loop refactoring outcomes across repositories.

Repository	For-Loops	Refactored	Compilable	Uncompilable
iridium	36	36	16	20
magpie	84	84	17	67
j2clmavenplugin	56	56	19	37
rapiddweller-benerator-ce	729	725	357	368
openrefine	1227	1200	196	1004
	2132	2101	605	1496

From the data, we see that in all cases, ChatGPT attempted to refactor the majority of for-loops in each repository. In the smallest repository, i.e., iridium, all 36 for-loops were refactored, and just 16 were compilable, leaving 20 uncompilable. Similar trends are seen in other repositories, such as magpie and j2clmavenplugin, where the majority of the for-loops were refactored; however, a significant portion of the resulting code was uncompilable. This points to the complexity involved in fully automating the refactoring process, especially when converting legacy for-loops to streams.

The larger repositories, rapiddweller-benerator-ce and openrefine, demonstrate the challenges of scaling the refactoring process. In rapiddweller-benerator-ce, 725 out of 729 loops were refactored by ChatGPT; however, only 357 were compilable, showing that larger codebases present more obstacles to successful refactoring. The largest repository, openrefine, had 1200 loops refactored, but only 196 were compilable, leaving over 1000 loops uncompilable.

In total, ChatGPT refactored 2101 out of 2132 identified for-loops, achieving a high success rate in terms of completing the refactoring itself. Only 605 of the refactored loops were compilable, while 1496 were uncompilable. This suggests that while ChatGPT is effective in automating loop refactoring, there are limitations to the process when it comes to ensuring that the resulting code is complete and readily compilable. The reasons for uncompilable code included contextual issues, syntax challenges, or differences in how stream-based code interacts with the rest of the codebase.

The inability of ChatGPT to refactor 31 for-loops is primarily influenced by the complex dependencies and potential side effects inherent to traditional loops. Streams, being designed with a functional and side-effect-free paradigm, contrast with the imperative style of for-loops. Additionally, streams are not always optimal for scenarios involving multi-level iteration, particularly when loops are interdependent or when there is intricate state sharing.

We manually evaluated a significant subset of the cases that successfully compiled. The manually inspected snippets were around 25% of the ones that compiled. We found that the refactored code preserved the original semantics; hence, the transformations were correct, most of the time, with only around 10% of code not being semantically correct. For the cases that failed to compile, we analyzed the code to identify the causes of compilation errors, categorizing them according to the type of issue encountered. The classification, along with examples and detailed discussion, is presented in Section 4.3. This process allowed us to rigorously assess both the correctness of successful refactoring and the limitations of the automatic approach in handling more complex or unconventional code patterns.

Gathered data underscore the potential of AI-driven code refactoring tools and highlight the need for human intervention to review and fine-tune the results, especially in complex or large-scale projects. ChatGPT is a helpful tool for programmers; however, it is not yet reliable enough to be used without human oversight [8].

> Answer to RQ1. Only 29% of the automatically refactored for-loops compiled successfully, and a manual evaluation suggested that these preserved the original semantics. The remaining 71% failed to compile due to (sometimes minor) flaws, underscoring the need for human review and refinement of the refactoring results produced by ChatGPT.

4.2. RQ2: Comparison with SOTA Approaches

State-of-the-art approaches for automated for-loop refactoring typically impose strict preconditions on the loops they can transform, limiting their applicability to only a subset of 'simple' or canonical loops. These preconditions often exclude loops with multiple return statements, break statements, local variables referenced from outside the loop, or throwing clauses, under the assumption that such constructs are too complex for reliable transformation. With this research question, we aim to challenge this perspective by showing that the GPT is capable of refactoring many loops that do not satisfy these traditional preconditions. Our results highlight that these 'old' limitations are overly conservative and that LLM-based approaches can handle a wider range of for-loop patterns, generating compilable stream-based code in scenarios that previous SOTA techniques would have deemed ineligible.

Tables 6–8 show the number of for-loops generated by ChatGPT and classified according to the categories discussed in Section 3.2. Each column is a category, and the two sub-columns 'c' and 'u' give the number of compilable and uncompilable for-loops generated, respectively.

Table 6. Number of for-loops that do not satisfy the first four preconditions listed in Table 1 and that were refactored by ChatGPT successfully (column c) or not (column u). Columns 'c' and 'u' indicate compilable and uncompilable, respectively.

Repository	LV		TC		BR		MR	
	c	u	c	u	c	u	c	u
iridium	0	1	4	0	1	6	0	0
magpie	0	0	2	5	0	1	0	0
j2clmavenplugin	0	0	2	4	0	0	0	0
rapiddweller-benerator-ce	11	22	12	45	11	8	0	5
openrefine	31	43	10	59	27	28	1	2

Table 7. Number of for-loops that do not satisfy the last four preconditions in Table 1, and were refactored successfully by ChatGPT (column c) or unsuccessfully (column u). Columns 'c' and 'u' indicate 'compilable' and 'uncompilable', respectively.

Repository	CO		MS		NL		SW	
	c	u	c	u	c	u	c	u
iridium	0	0	7	2	2	2	2	0
magpie	0	0	4	10	1	1	0	0
j2clmavenplugin	2	7	6	12	2	5	0	0
rapiddweller-benerator-ce	3	8	70	124	14	32	5	1
openrefine	32	48	91	351	59	68	2	2

Table 8. Number of for-loops refactored by ChatGPT for the templates presented in [12] (see Table 2). Columns 'c' and 'u' indicate compilable and uncompilable, respectively.

Repository	OR		SS		1st		2nd		3rd		4th		5th	
	c	u	c	u	c	u	c	u	c	u	c	u	c	u
iridium	0	1	9	18	0	1	0	0	0	0	0	4	0	0
magpie	1	3	13	57	0	0	0	0	0	0	4	36	0	0
j2clmavenplugin	1	0	13	25	0	0	0	0	0	0	0	0	0	0
rapiddweller-benerator-ce	9	37	287	244	4	18	2	6	3	4	34	10	3	0
openrefine	31	54	105	653	19	33	0	1	14	10	31	12	4	3

Table 6 shows the number of for-loops that were classified according to their characteristics, i.e., having local variables (LV), having throwing clauses (TC), having break statements (BR), and having more than one return (MR); however, they do not satisfy the respective preconditions presented in Table 1. Despite this, ChatGPT proposed a corresponding stream-based code fragment, whose successful compilation showed that its refactoring was possible. Although some transformations were successful, others posed significant challenges. A loop that does not satisfy the Throw Clause (TC) precondition is less likely to have a corresponding successful stream-based code. Specifically, in the rapiddweller and openrefine repositories, fewer than 22% of the generated fragments were compilable. Similarly, loops not satisfying the more return (MR) precondition resulted in very few compilable generated fragments for both repositories: 100% and 50%, respectively. These findings suggest that certain code blocks, i.e., those involving throwing exceptions and having many return statements, are more complex or less suitable for automated refactoring into stream pipelines since their paradigms are more relatable to an imperative style of programming rather than a functional one.

The largest number of refactoring attempts, as well as the highest rate of successful refactorings, occurred in the openrefine and rapiddweller-benerator-ce repositories. In openrefine, 31 loops not satisfying the precondition local variables (LV) were refactored successfully; however, 43 failed to compile. This indicates a substantial attempt to convert complex for-loops that involved more than one reference to non-effectively final variables defined outside the loop, albeit with a significant failure rate. Similarly, this repository saw notable success in refactoring loops not satisfying the BR precondition, with 27 successful compilations, although again accompanied by a comparable number of failures (28).

In contrast, smaller repositories, such as iridium, magpie, and j2clmavenplugin, saw relatively few refactoring attempts, with mixed results. In iridium, e.g., the Throw Clause (TC) precondition resulted in a full success rate with four compilable loops and no failures. This indicates that simpler loop structures, may be more amenable to automated refactoring despite containing exception-handling statements.

The refactoring of loops when the Break (BR) precondition was not satisfied consistently showed a higher success rate across the repositories, particularly in rapiddweller and openrefine, where the majority of transformed code snippets compiled successfully. This suggests that loops containing break statements can be effectively transformed into streams, even though state-of-the-art approaches have claimed that such cases are not feasible (we could more appropriately say not straightforward) for stream refactoring.

The overall success rates of compilable refactorings vary widely between repositories and preconditions, with certain combinations that prove more conducive to stream-based transformations. Notably, the openrefine repository shows both the highest volume of attempted refactorings and a reasonable number of successful compilations across multiple preconditions, indicating that it contains a broad variety of loops that are somewhat compatible with Java's Stream API. However, the relatively high number of failures in all preconditions indicates that while ChatGPT can handle simpler cases, more intricate loop structures involving complex control flow or variable manipulation remain challenging.

Listing 5 shows an example of a for-loop that does not satisfy the precondition local variables (LV); however, it was successfully refactored by ChatGPT to an equivalent stream pipeline. In the original loop, the local variable columnIndex is computed within the loop and used in the conditional check and to compute the local variable cellIndex, which is then assigned to an array. In the refactored version, these local variables are handled implicitly: the stream maps the loop index i to columnIndex, filters according to the same logic, maps to cellIndex, and finally performs the side-effect update on keyedGroup.cellIndices. This transformation demonstrates that ChatGPT can correctly manage multiple intermediate variables by embedding their computation within the stream pipeline stages.

Listing 5. Example of for-loop refactoring not satisfying the local variables (LV) precondition as it contains more than one local variable and successfully refactored by ChatGPT.

```
// original for loop
for (int i = 0; i < group.columnSpan; i++) {
    int columnIndex = group.startColumnIndex + i;
    if (columnIndex != group.keyColumnIndex && columnIndex <
        columnModel.columns.size()) {
        int cellIndex = columnModel.columns.get(columnIndex).getCellIndex();
        keyedGroup.cellIndices[c++] = cellIndex;
    }
}

// refactored stream pipeline
IntStream.range(0, group.columnSpan)
    .mapToObj(i -> group.startColumnIndex + i)
    .filter(columnIndex -> columnIndex != group.keyColumnIndex &&
        columnIndex < columnModel.columns.size())
    .map(columnIndex -> columnModel.columns.get(columnIndex).getCellIndex())
    .forEach(cellIndex -> keyedGroup.cellIndices[c++] = cellIndex);
```

Table 7 shows the results of the refactoring transformations attempted when considering the loops that exhibit the characteristics shown in Table 1 (max statements, MS; nested loops, NL; switch statements, SW; and continue statement, CO); however, such loops do not satisfy the respective preconditions given.

Transforming loops is less feasible when the loop body has more than five statements (hence they are classified as max statements (MS) loops). The results show that for repositories such as rapiddweller-benerator-ce and openrefine, ChatGPT struggles with this constraint, with 124 and 351 uncompilable cases, respectively. In contrast, iridium has a relatively balanced ratio of compilable (7) to uncompilable (2) cases. For repositories magpie and j2clmavenplugin, a higher number of uncompilable cases were given by ChatGPT, indicating that many loops exceed the complexity threshold for stream-based refactoring.

Nested loops are notoriously difficult to refactor using streams as they introduce more intricate control flows. This is reflected in the high number of uncompilable cases across the board. Repositories openrefine and rapiddweller-benerator-ce are particularly affected, with 68 and 32 uncompilable cases, respectively. Only iridium and magpie manage a more balanced ratio of compilable to uncompilable cases, but still, the presence of nested loops is a substantial barrier to stream refactoring.

Switch statements pose another challenge for stream refactoring. However, the number of switch statements in loops is relatively small compared to other constraints. Repositories rapiddweller-benerator-ce and openrefine have a few compilable and uncompilable cases, but the impact is less severe overall. This suggests that switch statements are less common within loops in the analyzed repositories, or developers might be avoiding their usage in situations conducive to refactoring.

In the repositories, the number of statements in the loop (MS) and the presence of nested loops (NL) are the most significant barriers to refactoring. Particularly, openrefine and rapiddweller-benerator-ce repositories show that a large portion of their loops exceed the complexity threshold, indicating that functional programming styles may not be suitable for these parts of the codebase. The results also show that control flow constructs such as switch statements (SW) are relatively rare in compilable stream refactoring.

Regarding for-loops including continue statements (CO), only j2clmavenplugin, rapiddweller-benerator-ce, and openrefine repositories have a few compilable cases, with openrefine standing out with 32 compilable cases. However, the large number of uncompilable cases in openrefine (48) and other repositories highlights that this remains a significant limitation.

While some repositories, such as iridium, have a more balanced number of compilable and uncompilable cases across multiple categories, repositories like openrefine and rapiddweller-benerator-ce present challenges in refactoring, primarily due to the complexity of loop bodies and control flow structures. These results suggest that while streams offer a more readable and functional style of programming, they are not always suitable for all types of loops, especially those with complex control flows or extensive nested structures.

Listing 6 shows an example of a for-loop that does not satisfy the precondition continue (CO); however, it was successfully refactored by ChatGPT to an equivalent stream pipeline. The original loop skips empty strings using a continue statement and applies a sequence of transformations to build a normalizedLocalName String. In the refactored version, the same logic was implemented using a stream pipeline: the filter step excludes empty strings, followed by two map operations to transform each path, and a reduce operation to concatenate the results. Despite the presence of the continue statement, which usually complicates refactoring, the transformation preserves the original behavior and produces an equivalent result using functional constructs.

Listing 6. An example of for-loop refactoring of the CO category where ChatGPT successfully refactors a for-loop containing a continue statement.

```
// original for loop
for (String p : paths) {
    if (p.equals("")) {
        continue;
    }
    p = currentFileSystem.toLegalFileName(p, '-');
    normalizedLocalName += String.format("%c%s", File.separatorChar, p);
}

// refactored stream pipeline
normalizedLocalName = paths.stream()
    .filter(p -> !p.equals(""))
    .map(p -> currentFileSystem.toLegalFileName(p, '-'))
    .map(p -> String.format("%c%s", File.separatorChar, p))
    .reduce("", (result, p) -> result + p);
```

Table 8 presents the evaluation of loops transformed into Java stream-based code for the cases of loops with one return statement (OR), loops having fewer than five statements, and the five templates presented in [12]. The results reveal variability in both the success and failure rates of stream-based refactoring depending on the repository and the type of for-loop template applied. Notably, the counts of compilable versus uncompilable transformations indicate that certain patterns of loops are more challenging to refactor into streams, particularly with template 1 (for-loops with a conditional statement and one or more return statements), in agreement with the results of Table 6 where statements with returns are more challenging.

Starting with loops having satisfied the one return (OR) precondition resulted in very few compilable generated fragments for both repositories: less than 20% and 37%, respectively. In contrast, column small size (SS) represents cases where the loop body size is less than five statements. Streams are generally suitable for such loops, and we observe a higher number of compilable cases in most repositories. For instance, openrefine has 105 compilable cases, but it is also noteworthy that there are 653 uncompilable cases, emphasizing that many loops are still too complex for straightforward refactoring. A deeper analysis of the compilation error is described in Section 4.3 to elucidate the main reasons behind the large number of uncompilable cases. Repository rapiddweller-benerator-ce shows a large number of cases (287 compilable vs. 244 uncompilable), suggesting a mixed suitability for streams in this repository.

The first template was found in two repositories: rapiddweller-benerator-ce and openrefine. Interestingly, openrefine achieved 19 compilable refactorings, but 33 instances failed to compile. This suggests that the first template, while somewhat effective, still poses significant challenges, particularly due to conditional structures that may not easily translate into a single stream operation. Similarly, rapiddweller-benerator-ce encountered several unsuccessful refactoring, with just 4 compilable for-loops and 18 uncompilable ones.

The second and fifth templates show few occurrences, showing that they are less common when writing for-loop structures. Nevertheless, the fifth template shows a higher success rate than the second, and this highlights that the temp variable's inclusion complicates the transformation, possibly due to scoping and reuse issues as streams are typically expected to be stateless and work more effectively with immutable data.

The results for the third template vary, and it appears to be another challenging pattern, particularly in openrefine (14 compilable and 10 uncompilable) and rapiddweller-benerator-ce (3 compilable and 4 uncompilable). The combination of a temp variable and method calls adds complexity that might interfere with stream semantics, particularly since method calls inside loops may cause side effects, which are difficult to express in functional streams.

The forth template is the most prevalent in the data, particularly in magpie (4 compilable and 36 uncompilable), rapiddweller-benerator-ce (34 compilable and 10 uncompilable), and openrefine (31 compilable and 12 uncompilable). Despite a high number of successful compilations in some repositories, the number of uncompilable transformations remains significant. This suggests that while this template fits well within the stream paradigm (as streams naturally support element-wise operations), edge cases, such as incorrect handling of the new value insertion logic, might still cause failure in the refactoring process.

The data suggest that stream-based refactoring is highly dependent on the specific structure of the loop and the repository's coding patterns. While some templates (like the fourth) are frequently encountered and refactored with relative success, others (such as the second and third) are more error-prone. This variability highlights the need for further improvements in automated refactoring tools to handle edge cases, particularly where temp variables and conditional branches are involved. Additionally, individual codebases vary significantly in how amenable they are to stream-based refactoring, suggesting that the nature of the existing code plays a crucial role in determining the success rate of such transformations.

According to the results previously shown, ChatGPT was able to correctly generate a refactored version of 414 for-loops that were originally discarded by the SOTA approaches because they violated their preconditions. This highlights that ChatGPT has overcome the limits of these approaches, suggesting innovative refactoring that was not previously proposed. This can be justified by the massive training process of the GPT model, which it applied to the billions of model code snippets that, unlike deterministic approaches, helped the model to properly combine stream APIs to obtain innovative stream pipelines. The remaining 903 uncompilable generated for-loops can be further analyzed to comprehend the reasons behind these failures.

Listing 7 displays an example of a for-loop corresponding to the fifth template presented in [12] that was successfully refactored by ChatGPT. The original code iterates over the list sg.getSnaks() using a classic enhanced for-loop. Inside the loop, it conditionally selects between two visitors—referenceSnakPrinter or mainSnakPrinter—depending on the value of the boolean variable reference and then writes the result of the accept method to the writer. The refactored version expresses the same logic using a stream pipeline. It transforms the collection into a stream, applies a map operation that performs the same conditional logic inline using the ternary operator, and finally consumes the result using forEach(writer::write).

Listing 7. An example of for-loop refactoring of the 5th template where ChatGPT successfully refactored a loop containing an if/else statement.

```
// original for loop
for (Snak s : sg.getSnaks()) {
    if (reference) {
        writer.write(s.accept(referenceSnakPrinter));
    } else {
        writer.write(s.accept(mainSnakPrinter));
    }
}

// refactored stream pipeline
sg.getSnaks().stream()
    .map(s -> reference ? s.accept(referenceSnakPrinter) :
        s.accept(mainSnakPrinter))
    .forEach(writer::write);
```

Answer to RQ2. ChatGPT successfully generated 414 innovative stream pipelines, surpassing the limitations of previous state-of-the-art (SOTA) approaches. The proposed refactoring effectively addresses the preconditions set by these approaches, offering interesting and novel solutions.

4.3. RQ3: Compilation Error Analysis

To address the third research question, we focus the study on the uncompilable refactorings generated by ChatGPT (see Section 4.2). Table 9 highlights the metrics extracted from the compilation errors. The columns are described according the tags introduced in Section 3.2, while rows represent the error name collected from the compilation report. A description of each error can be found in Table A1 in the Appendix A.

From Table 9, the 'cannot find symbol' error is the most prevalent across all categories. This suggests that these categories often involve references to variables or methods that are not defined within the scope. This could be due to misspelled variable or method names, variables or methods that are declared outside the loop but not accessible within it, and missing imports or incorrect package references.

The 'illegal character' error is relatively rare, appearing only in SS (seven occurrences) and the fifth template (six occurrences). Illegal characters can be caused by typographical error, copy-pasting code from different sources that include non-printable characters, and incorrect encoding settings in the development environment.

Table 9. Numbers of all compilation errors encountered for each analyzed category

Error	LV	TC	BR	OR	MR	CO	MS	SS	NL	SW	1st	2nd	3rd	4th	5th
illegal character	0	0	0	0	0	0	0	7	0	0	0	0	0	6	0
cannot find symbol	55	84	33	66	6	48	361	451	88	2	31	7	9	26	1
symbol expected	0	2	0	0	0	1	11	59	3	0	0	0	3	37	0
unreported exception	1	6	0	0	0	5	15	56	5	0	0	0	0	0	0
local variables referenced	11	7	7	1	0	10	34	18	5	1	0	0	0	0	0
variable is already defined	13	4	11	4	0	5	12	57	3	0	2	0	0	2	0
incompatible types	0	0	0	0	0	0	0	4	0	0	0	0	0	0	0
non-static variable	0	0	0	4	0	0	1	3	0	0	1	2	0	0	0
no suitable method	0	0	1	3	0	0	1	5	1	0	2	0	0	0	0
illegal start of type	0	0	0	0	0	0	1	1	1	0	0	0	0	0	0
try without	0	0	0	0	0	0	0	1	0	0	0	0	0	0	0
parse errors	4	2	2	2	0	4	14	21	11	0	1	0	2	0	1

The 'symbol expected' error is notable in SS (59 occurrences) and the fifth template (37 occurrences). It indicates syntax issues where the compiler expected a different token. Common causes include missing semicolons or braces, incorrect use of operators or delimiters, and incomplete statements or expressions.

Another common error is 'unreported exception', which occurs in SS (56 occurrences) and MS (15 occurrences). It suggests that these categories often involve operations that can throw exceptions not handled properly. This can happen when methods that throw checked exceptions are called without proper try–catch blocks and the throws clause is missing in the method signature.

'Local variables referenced' is often overlooked during refactoring. This error is relatively frequent in MS (34 occurrences) and SS (18 occurrences). It indicates issues with variable scope and usage, such as referencing variables outside their declared scope, modifying effectively final variables within lambda expressions, and conflicts between local and global variable names.

The 'variable is already defined' error is notable in SS (57 occurrences) and LV (13 occurrences). It suggests multiple declarations of the same variable within these categories. This can occur due to re-declaring variables within nested scopes, conflicts between parameter names and local variable names, and copy-pasting code without renaming variables.

The 'incompatible types' error is rare, with only four occurrences in SS. It indicates type mismatch issues, which can be caused by assigning values of incompatible types, incorrect method return types, and using raw types instead of parameterized types in generics.

The 'non-static variable' error appears in OR (four occurrences) and SS (three occurrences). It indicates issues with accessing non-static variables from static contexts. This can happen when trying to access instance variables from static methods, when the scope of static and non-static members is misunderstood, and when the static context is used incorrectly within lambda expressions.

The 'no suitable method' error is relatively rare, with the highest occurrence in SS (five occurrences). It indicates method signature mismatches, which can be caused by calling methods with incorrect parameters, overloading methods without proper parameter types, and using incorrect method references in lambda expressions.

The 'illegal start of type' error is very rare, with only one occurrence in SS. It indicates a syntax issue at the start of a type declaration, which can be caused by incorrectly placed annotations or modifiers, missing class or interface keywords, and typographical errors in type declarations.

The 'try without' error is extremely rare, with only one occurrence in SS. It indicates a missing try block, which can happen when forgetting to include the try keyword before a block of code that handles exceptions, incorrectly formatting the try–catch–finally structure, and overlooking exception handling during refactoring.

Finally, 'parse errors' is more common in SS (21 occurrences) and NL (11 occurrences). It indicates general syntax errors, which can be caused by incomplete or incorrect code statements, misplaced or missing punctuation, and errors in code structure or formatting.

The types of errors encountered can provide insights into both the severity of mistakes made by ChatGPT and potential underlying causes. Moreover, they offer an indication of the effort a developer may need to invest to resolve them.

Starting with the most common issue, the 'cannot find symbol' error often arises due to insufficient context provided to ChatGPT during code generation. Since the model was queried with a focus solely on refactoring a for-loop (see Section 3.3), it generated the corresponding stream-based code without including necessary imports and variable declarations, assuming that they are implicit. In these cases, the error can easily be rectified by adding the required imports or defining the missing variables. However, a more complex situation occurs when the missing symbol refers to a class or method that does not exist, having been 'hallucinated' by the model [48,49]. This could require more significant intervention by the developer.

Similarly, the 'variable is already defined' error is a result of inadequate context. In this case, the model unnecessarily redefines variables already declared outside the generated stream pipeline. The resolution here is straightforward: remove the redundant variable declaration and use the pre-existing one.

Errors such as 'illegal character', 'symbol expected', 'illegal start of type', and 'parse errors' fall under the category of syntactical mistakes. These errors result from the model improperly writing code, using incorrect symbols, or omitting required ones. These errors are typically simple to correct, requiring the developer to insert or replace the appropriate symbols.

Shifting to more complex errors, 'unreported exception' and 'try without' relate to exception handling in Java, specifically within the context of stream APIs. These errors occur when the model fails to properly handle exceptions, a task often better suited for traditional for-loops rather than stream pipelines. Fixing such errors may necessitate reverting to a more conventional approach or a detailed restructuring of the code to ensure proper exception handling, which diminishes the utility of stream-based refactoring.

Although rarer, the 'incompatible types' and 'non-static variable' errors demand a deeper contextual analysis. These errors typically occur when there is a mismatch between the expected and actual types or when non-static variables are used incorrectly within static contexts. Resolving these issues may not always be feasible due to the constraints imposed by the semantic structure of stream pipelines.

Finally, the 'local variable referenced from a lambda expression must be final or effectively final' error is tightly connected to one of the preconditions discussed in state-of-the-art approaches (see Section 4.2). By design, stream APIs do not allow the use of non-final local variables, meaning that certain for-loops cannot be easily refactored into streams. However, as indicated in Table 6, ChatGPT is often able to successfully refactor these loops despite this limitation, highlighting its potential to handle such complex refactorings.

Listing 8 highlights a typical compilation error that can arise when refactoring a for-loop into a Java stream. The generated code attempts to reassign the local variable `fileName` inside a lambda expression used within the `ifPresent` method. However, Java requires that variables captured by lambdas be final or effectively final, and reassignment violates this rule. As shown in the Maven output, the compiler fails with the error 'local variables referenced from a lambda expression must be final or effectively final', preventing successful compilation of the refactored code. Such variable scope and mutability dependencies are often subtle and non-trivial, making them particularly difficult for LLMs to detect and handle correctly during automated refactoring.

Listing 8. Example of a compilation error encountered during the analysis of a refactored for-loop. The code snippet shows the stream generated by the GPT, followed by the Maven compilation failure indicating an error of type `local variables referenced`.

```
Arrays.stream(new String[] { ".gz", ".bz2" })
    .filter(ext -> fileName.endsWith(ext))
    .findFirst()
    .ifPresent(ext -> fileName = fileName.substring(0,
        fileName.length() - ext.length()));

....
[ERROR] Failed to execute goal
    org.apache.maven.plugins:maven-compiler-plugin:3.13.0:compile
    (default-compile) on project main: Compilation failure: Compilation
    failure:
[ERROR]
    /C:/Users/Ale-m/Desktop/RepositoryMining/AnalyzedRepositories/openrefine
    /main/src/com/google/refine/importing/ImportingUtilities.java:
    [733,24] local variables referenced from a lambda expression must be
        final or effectively final
....
```

Answer to RQ3. ChatGPT successfully generated a range of stream pipelines but encountered errors primarily due to the lack of context during code generation. Common issues like 'cannot find symbol' were often easily resolved by adding imports or defining variables, while more complex errors such as handling exceptions in streams required deeper analysis.

5. Threats to Validity

This section discusses potential threats to the validity of our study, highlighting factors that may affect the reliability, interpretability, and generalizability of our findings. We categorize these threats into internal and external validity. Internal validity addresses the fidelity of the study's execution, including methodological choices, tool behavior, and dataset characteristics that could influence the observed outcomes. External validity concerns the extent to which our results can be generalized to other codebases, loop patterns, or large language models beyond the specific configurations and repositories considered in this work. By explicitly acknowledging these limitations, we aim to provide a transparent assessment of the study's strengths and constraints.

Internal validity pertains to the integrity of the study's execution. The non-deterministic nature of GPT-3.5, combined with the choice of hyperparameters and prompts, may influence the quality of the generated content without guaranteeing optimal solutions. Furthermore, since GPT-3.5's training data is not publicly available, there is a possibility that similar code patterns exist in its training set, potentially providing an advantage over benchmark solutions. We used the default parameters of GPT-3.5 (temperature = 1.0), which could maximize response diversity. This choice reflects typical developer usage as ChatGPT's UI does not provide options to adjust the temperature. Keeping the default parameters ensures that the experimental scenario closely resembles real-world usage. Finally, we selected five repositories from the Maven Central Repository. While this selection may not represent all publicly available projects, we aimed to choose the most popular ones, reflecting those most widely used by developers. Additionally, we ensured diversity in project type, scope, and size, in order to capture a range of realistic programming scenarios.

External validity concerns the generalizability of our findings. While our study focused on fifteen selected for-loop idioms, this set does not encompass all possible refactoring proposals, potentially limiting generalizability. However, prior studies emphasize these idioms as among the most widely used and impactful in Java development, supporting their relevance. Additionally, our analysis involves methods extracted from diverse GitHub repositories, highlighting the practical need to address missing refactorings. The number of extracted loops and the popularity of the chosen repositories should represent the majority of for-loop idioms. Moreover, the high number of compilation errors in some categories suggests that refactoring difficulties arise, especially when the code references or defines local variables or uses a context that is beyond the loop itself. Such recurrent difficulties should represent a common occurrence in for-loops. The study focuses exclusively on ChatGPT, without considering other LLMs. Nevertheless, ChatGPT is widely regarded as a state-of-the-art LLM, serving as a representative model. Future research could enhance generalizability by evaluating ChatGPT alongside other LLMs across a broader range of refactorings.

6. Conclusions

The adoption of the functional programming paradigm introduced in Java 8 offers significant advantages in terms of code conciseness, expressiveness, and abstraction. Despite these benefits, the transition from imperative constructs, such as for-loops, to stream pipelines remains underutilized in practice. This paper presented an empirical study evaluating ChatGPT's effectiveness in refactoring for-loops into stream pipelines compared to state-of-the-art (SOTA) approaches. Our findings indicate that ChatGPT can successfully refactor a substantial portion of loops while preserving code semantics, demonstrating its potential as a valuable tool for code transformation.

However, our analysis also revealed that ChatGPT's performance is inconsistent across different loop categories. Although it excels in cases that align closely with SOTA templates, it struggles with more complex loops that require nuanced contextual understanding or violate the preconditions of existing deterministic approaches. Notably, ChatGPT produced correct refactorings beyond the limitations of SOTA in specific cases, suggesting its capacity to generalize transformations where rigid rule-based methods fall short. Conversely, we identified failure patterns where ChatGPT either generated syntactically invalid code or produced semantically incorrect transformations, underscoring the need for human oversight.

These findings suggest a complementary role for ChatGPT alongside deterministic approaches. By leveraging ChatGPT's ability to generalize for diverse patterns and combining it with the precision of formal refactoring rules, future research could explore hybrid solutions that improve automation and reliability. Further investigations should also examine ways to mitigate failure cases and improve the interpretability of ChatGPT's outputs. This study provides a foundation for the advancement of automated refactoring techniques and underscores the potential of large language models to bridge the gaps left by traditional methodologies.

Author Contributions: Conceptualization, A.M. and E.T.; methodology, A.M.; software, A.M.; validation, A.M. and E.T.; data curation, A.M.; writing—original draft preparation, A.M.; writing—review and editing, E.T.; supervision, E.T. All authors have read and agreed to the published version of the manuscript.

Funding: This research received no external funding.

Data Availability Statement: Data derived from public domain resources.

Acknowledgments: We acknowledge the support of the University of Catania PIACERI project TEAMS.

Conflicts of Interest: The authors declare no conflicts of interest.

Appendix A

Table A1. Compilation error types with descriptions.

Error	Description
illegal character	The code contains a character not allowed in Java source code, often due to copy-paste or encoding issues.
cannot find symbol	A referenced variable, method, or class is undefined or out of scope.
symbol expected	Java expected a symbol (e.g., semicolon, bracket, or identifier) but found none or something invalid.
unreported exception	A checked exception may be thrown but is not caught or declared in the method signature.
local variables referenced	A local variable is used before it has been initialized.
variable is already defined	A variable is declared more than once in the same scope.
incompatible types	An assignment or operation involves mismatched data types that cannot be converted automatically.
non-static variable	A non-static variable is referenced from a static context.
no suitable method	A method call does not match any method signature available for the object.
illegal start of type	A statement or declaration is placed incorrectly in the class or method structure.
try without	A `try` block is missing a corresponding `catch` or `finally` block.
parse errors	Generic syntax errors preventing the compiler from parsing the code correctly.

Listing A1. Example of a compilation error encountered during the analysis of a refactored for-loop. The code snippet shows the stream generated by the GPT, followed by the Maven compilation failure indicating an error of type `cannot find symbol`.

```
XMLUtil.getChildElements(element)
    .stream()
    .filter(child -> !MEMBER_ELEMENTS.contains(child.getNodeName()))
    .map(child -> result.addSubStatement(context.parseChildElement(child,
        parentXmlPath, currentPath)))
    .collect(Collectors.toList());

....
[ERROR] Failed to execute goal
    org.apache.maven.plugins:maven-compiler-plugin:3.10.1:compile
    (default-compile) on project rapiddweller-benerator-ce: Compilation
    failure: Compilation failure:
[ERROR] ... CascadeParser.java:[70,5] cannot find symbol
[ERROR]   symbol:   method stream()
[ERROR]   location: class org.w3c.dom.Element[]
[ERROR] ... CascadeParser.java:[73,14] cannot find symbol
[ERROR]   symbol:   variable Collectors
[ERROR]   location: class
    com.rapiddweller.benerator.engine.parser.xml.CascadeParser
....
```

Listing A2. Example of a compilation error encountered during the analysis of a refactored for-loop. The code snippet shows the stream generated by the GPT, followed by the Maven compilation failure indicating an error of type `symbol expected`.

```
values.entrySet().stream()
    .forEach(entry -> MAP.put(entry.getKey(), new
        IncrementalIdGenerator(Long.parseLong(entry.getValue())));

....
[ERROR] Failed to execute goal
    org.apache.maven.plugins:maven-compiler-plugin:3.10.1:compile
    (default-compile) on project rapiddweller-benerator-ce: Compilation
    failure
[ERROR] ... LocalSequenceGenerator.java:[136,107] ')' expected
....
```

Listing A3. Example of a compilation error encountered during the analysis of a refactored for-loop. The code snippet shows the stream generated by the GPT, followed by the Maven compilation failure indicating an error of type `unreported exception`.

```
applicationTypes.stream()
    .filter(typeEntity ->
        typeEntity.getType().equals(ApplicationType.SINGLE_PAGE))
    .map(typeEntity ->
        ApplicationGenerator.generateIridiumApplication(entityManager,
        iridiumTenant, typeEntity))
    .forEach(application -> this.iridiumAppId = application.getClientId());

....
[ERROR] Failed to execute goal
    org.apache.maven.plugins:maven-compiler-plugin:3.11.0:compile
    (default-compile) on project iridium-cli: Compilation failure
[ERROR] ... InitCommand.java:[42,71] unreported exception
    java.security.NoSuchAlgorithmException; must be caught or declared to be
    thrown
....
```

Listing A4. Example of a compilation error encountered during the analysis of a refactored for-loop. The code snippet shows the stream generated by the GPT, followed by the Maven compilation failure indicating an error of type `variable already defined`.

```
String errorMessage = messages.stream()
    .collect(Collectors.joining("\n"));

....
[ERROR] Failed to execute goal
    org.apache.maven.plugins:maven-compiler-plugin:3.10.1:compile
    (default-compile) on project rapiddweller-benerator-ce: Compilation
    failure: Compilation failure:
[ERROR] ... CreateProjectPanel.java:[275,16] variable errorMessage is
    already defined in method showErrors(java.lang.Object...)
....
```

Listing A5. Example of a compilation error encountered during the analysis of a refactored for-loop. The code snippet shows the stream generated by the GPT, followed by the Maven compilation failure indicating an error of type `incompatible types`.

```
sources.stream()
        .filter(source -> !source.isThreadSafe())
        .findAny()
        .ifPresent(s -> { return false; });

....
[ERROR] Failed to execute goal
    org.apache.maven.plugins:maven-compiler-plugin:3.10.1:compile
    (default-compile) on project rapiddweller-benerator-ce: Compilation
    failure
[ERROR] ... MultiGeneratorWrapper.java:[149,19] incompatible types:
    unexpected return value
....
```

Listing A6. Example of a compilation error encountered during the analysis of a refactored for-loop. The code snippet shows the stream generated by the GPT, followed by the Maven compilation failure indicating an error of type `no suitable method`.

```
return Arrays.stream(unluckyNumbers)
    .anyMatch(test -> candidate.endsWith(test));

....
[ERROR] Failed to execute goal
    org.apache.maven.plugins:maven-compiler-plugin:3.10.1:compile
    (default-compile) on project rapiddweller-benerator-ce: Compilation
    failure
[ERROR] ... UnluckyNumberValidator.java:[189,22] no suitable method found
    for stream(java.util.Set<java.lang.String>)
....
```

Listing A7. Example of a compilation error encountered during the analysis of a refactored for-loop. The code snippet shows the stream generated by the GPT, followed by the Maven compilation failure indicating an error of type `illegal start of type`.

```
writeColumnInfos.stream()
        .map(info -> {
            Object jdbcValue = entity.getComponent(info.name);
            if (info.type != null) {
                jdbcValue = AnyConverter.convert(jdbcValue, info.type);
            }
            return new AbstractMap.SimpleEntry<>(info, jdbcValue);
        })
        .forEach(entry -> handleOracleType(tableName, statement,
            writeColumnInfos.indexOf(entry.getKey()), entry.getKey(),
            entry.getValue()););

....
[ERROR] Failed to execute goal
    org.apache.maven.plugins:maven-compiler-plugin:3.10.1:compile
    (default-compile) on project rapiddweller-benerator-ce: Compilation
    failure: Compilation failure:
[ERROR] ... AbstractDBSystem.java:[697,142] illegal start of expression
....
```

References

1. Urma, R.G.; Fusco, M.; Mycroft, A. *Modern Java in Action: Lambdas, Streams, Functional and Reactive Programming*, 2nd ed.; Manning Publications Co.: Shelter Island, NY, USA, 2018.
2. Mazinanian, D.; Ketkar, A.; Tsantalis, N.; Dig, D. Understanding the use of lambda expressions in Java. *Proc. ACM Program. Lang.* **2017**, *1*, 1–31. [CrossRef]
3. Møller, A.; Veileborg, O.H. Eliminating abstraction overhead of Java stream pipelines using ahead-of-time program optimization. *Proc. ACM Program. Lang.* **2020**, *4*, 1–29. [CrossRef]
4. Rosales, E.; Rosà, A.; Basso, M.; Villazón, A.; Orellana, A.; Zenteno, A.; Rivero, J.; Binder, W. Characterizing Java Streams in the Wild. In Proceedings of the 2022 26th International Conference on Engineering of Complex Computer Systems (ICECCS), Hiroshima, Japan, 26–30 March 2022; pp. 143–152. [CrossRef]
5. Khatchadourian, R.; Tang, Y.; Bagherzadeh, M.; Ray, B. An Empirical Study on the Use and Misuse of Java 8 Streams. In *Fundamental Approaches to Software Engineering*; Wehrheim, H., Cabot, J., Eds.; Springer: Cham, Switzerland, 2020; pp. 97–118.
6. Nostas, J.; Alcocer, J.P.S.; Costa, D.E.; Bergel, A. How Do Developers Use the Java Stream API? In Proceedings of the Computational Science and Its Applications—ICCSA 2021, Cagliari, Italy, 13–16 September 2021; Springer: Cham, Switzerland, 2021; pp. 323–335.
7. Champa, A.I.; Rabbi, M.F.; Nachuma, C.; Zibran, M.F. ChatGPT in Action: Analyzing Its Use in Software Development. In Proceedings of the MSR '24: 21st International Conference on Mining Software Repositories, Lisbon, Portugal, 15–16 April 2024; pp. 182–186. [CrossRef]
8. DePalma, K.; Miminoshvili, I.; Henselder, C.; Moss, K.; AlOmar, E.A. Exploring ChatGPT's code refactoring capabilities: An empirical study. *Expert Syst. Appl.* **2024**, *249*, 123602. [CrossRef]
9. Bulla, L.; Midolo, A.; Mongiovì, M.; Tramontana, E. EX-CODE: A Robust and Explainable Model to Detect AI-Generated Code. *Information* **2024**, *15*, 819. [CrossRef]
10. Fowler, M. *Refactoring: Improving the Design of Existing Code*; Addison-Wesley Professional: Reading, MA, USA, 2018.
11. Murphy-Hill, E.; Parnin, C.; Black, A.P. How We Refactor, and How We Know It. *IEEE Trans. Softw. Eng.* **2012**, *38*, 5–18. [CrossRef]
12. Midolo, A.; Tramontana, E. Refactoring Java Loops to Streams Automatically. In Proceedings of the CSSE '21: International Conference on Computer Science and Software Engineering, Singapore, 22–24 October 2021; pp. 135–139. [CrossRef]
13. Zhang, Z.; Xing, Z.; Xia, X.; Xu, X.; Zhu, L. Making Python code idiomatic by automatic refactoring non-idiomatic Python code with pythonic idioms. In Proceedings of the ESEC/FSE 2022: 30th ACM Joint European Software Engineering Conference and Symposium on the Foundations of Software Engineering, Singapore, 14–18 November 2022; pp. 696–708. [CrossRef]
14. Zhang, Z.; Xing, Z.; Zhao, D.; Xu, X.; Zhu, L.; Lu, Q. Automated Refactoring of Non-Idiomatic Python Code with Pythonic Idioms. *IEEE Trans. Softw. Eng.* **2024**, *50*, 2827–2848. [CrossRef]
15. Franklin, L.; Gyori, A.; Lahoda, J.; Dig, D. LambdaFicator: From imperative to functional programming through automated refactoring. In Proceedings of the 2013 35th International Conference on Software Engineering (ICSE), San Francisco, CA, USA, 18–26 May 2013; pp. 1287–1290. [CrossRef]
16. Purnima, N.; Salomi Nelaballi, V.S.P.; Kim, D.K. Deep Learning-Based Code Refactoring: A Review of Current Knowledge. *J. Comput. Inf. Syst.* **2024**, *64*, 314–328. [CrossRef]
17. Khojah, R.; Mohamad, M.; Leitner, P.; de Oliveira Neto, F.G. Beyond Code Generation: An Observational Study of ChatGPT Usage in Software Engineering Practice. *Proc. ACM Softw. Eng.* **2024**, *1*, 1819–1840. [CrossRef]
18. White, J.; Hays, S.; Fu, Q.; Spencer-Smith, J.; Schmidt, D.C. ChatGPT Prompt Patterns for Improving Code Quality, Refactoring, Requirements Elicitation, and Software Design. In *Generative AI for Effective Software Development*; Springer: Cham, Switzerland, 2024; pp. 71–108. [CrossRef]
19. Chavan, O.S.; Hinge, D.D.; Deo, S.S.; Wang, Y.O.; Mkaouer, M.W. Analyzing Developer-ChatGPT Conversations for Software Refactoring: An Exploratory Study. In Proceedings of the MSR '24: 21st International Conference on Mining Software Repositories, Lisbon, Portugal, 15–16 April 2024; pp. 207–211. [CrossRef]
20. Guo, Q.; Cao, J.; Xie, X.; Liu, S.; Li, X.; Chen, B.; Peng, X. Exploring the Potential of ChatGPT in Automated Code Refinement: An Empirical Study. In Proceedings of the ICSE '24: 46th IEEE/ACM International Conference on Software Engineering, Lisbon, Portugal, 14–20 April 2024. [CrossRef]
21. Siddiq, M.L.; Roney, L.; Zhang, J.; Santos, J.C.D.S. Quality Assessment of ChatGPT Generated Code and their Use by Developers. In Proceedings of the MSR '24: 21st International Conference on Mining Software Repositories, Lisbon, Portugal, 15–16 April 2024; pp. 152–156. [CrossRef]
22. Tufano, R.; Mastropaolo, A.; Pepe, F.; Dabic, O.; Di Penta, M.; Bavota, G. Unveiling ChatGPT's Usage in Open Source Projects: A Mining-based Study. In Proceedings of the MSR '24: 21st International Conference on Mining Software Repositories, Lisbon, Portugal, 15–16 April 2024; pp. 571–583. [CrossRef]
23. Tang, Y.; Liu, Z.; Zhou, Z.; Luo, X. ChatGPT vs SBST: A Comparative Assessment of Unit Test Suite Generation. *IEEE Trans. Softw. Eng.* **2024**, *50*, 1340–1359. [CrossRef]

24. Gyori, A.; Franklin, L.; Dig, D.; Lahoda, J. Crossing the gap from imperative to functional programming through refactoring. In Proceedings of the ESEC/FSE 2013: 9th Joint Meeting on Foundations of Software Engineering, Saint Petersburg, Russia, 18–26 August 2013; pp. 543–553. [CrossRef]
25. Midolo, A.; Tramontana, E. Replication Package. Available online: https://github.com/AleMidolo/Refactoring-Loops-in-the-Era-of-LLMs-A-Comprehensive-Study (accessed on 28 August 2025).
26. Kapus, T.; Ish-Shalom, O.; Itzhaky, S.; Rinetzky, N.; Cadar, C. Computing summaries of string loops in C for better testing and refactoring. In Proceedings of the PLDI 2019: 40th ACM SIGPLAN Conference on Programming Language Design and Implementation, Phoenix, AZ, USA, 22–26 June 2019; pp. 874–888. [CrossRef]
27. Khatchadourian, R.; Tang, Y.; Bagherzadeh, M. Safe automated refactoring for intelligent parallelization of Java 8 streams. *Sci. Comput. Programm.* **2020**, *195*, 102476. [CrossRef]
28. Midolo, A.; Tramontana, E. An API for Analysing and Classifying Data Dependence in View of Parallelism. In Proceedings of the ICCCM '22: 10th International Conference on Computer and Communications Management, Okayama, Japan, 29–31 July 2022; pp. 61–67. [CrossRef]
29. Stein, B.; Clapp, L.; Sridharan, M.; Chang, B.Y.E. Safe stream-based programming with refinement types. In Proceedings of the ASE '18: 33rd ACM/IEEE International Conference on Automated Software Engineering, Montpellier, France, 3–7 September 2018; pp. 565–576. [CrossRef]
30. The PEP Editors. Python Enhancement Proposals. 2000. Available online: https://peps.python.org (accessed on 28 August 2025).
31. Midolo, A.; Penta, M.D. Automated Refactoring of Non-Idiomatic Python Code: A Differentiated Replication with LLMs. In Proceedings of the 2025 IEEE/ACM 33rd International Conference on Program Comprehension (ICPC), Ottawa, ON, Canada, 27–28 April 2025; pp. 1–11. [CrossRef]
32. Liu, B.; Jiang, Y.; Zhang, Y.; Niu, N.; Li, G.; Liu, H. Exploring the potential of general purpose LLMs in automated software refactoring: An empirical study. *Autom. Softw. Eng.* **2025**, *32*, 26. [CrossRef]
33. Cordeiro, J.; Noei, S.; Zou, Y. An Empirical Study on the Code Refactoring Capability of Large Language Models. *arXiv* **2024**, arXiv:2411.02320. [CrossRef]
34. Pomian, D.; Bellur, A.; Dilhara, M.; Kurbatova, Z.; Bogomolov, E.; Bryksin, T.; Dig, D. Next-Generation Refactoring: Combining LLM Insights and IDE Capabilities for Extract Method. In Proceedings of the 2024 IEEE International Conference on Software Maintenance and Evolution (ICSME), Flagstaff, AZ, USA, 6–11 October 2024; pp. 275–287. [CrossRef]
35. AlOmar, E.A.; Venkatakrishnan, A.; Mkaouer, M.W.; Newman, C.; Ouni, A. How to refactor this code? An exploratory study on developer-ChatGPT refactoring conversations. In Proceedings of the MSR '24: 21st International Conference on Mining Software Repositories, Lisbon Portugal, 15–16 April 2024; pp. 202–206. [CrossRef]
36. Fraser, G.; Arcuri, A. EvoSuite: Automatic test suite generation for object-oriented software. In Proceedings of the ESEC/FSE '11: 19th ACM SIGSOFT Symposium and European Conference on Foundations of Software Engineering, Szeged, Hungary, 5–9 September 2011; pp. 416–419. [CrossRef]
37. Dabic, O.; Aghajani, E.; Bavota, G. Sampling Projects in GitHub for MSR Studies. In Proceedings of the 2021 IEEE/ACM 18th International Conference on Mining Software Repositories (MSR), Madrid, Spain, 17–19 May 2021; pp. 560–564.
38. maven. Mavenrepository. Available online: https://mvnrepository.com/popular (accessed on 2 September 2024).
39. Smith, N.; Van Bruggen, D.; Tomassetti, F. *Javaparser: Visited*; Leanpub: Victoria, BC, Canada, 2017; Volume 10.
40. Li, J.; Li, G.; Li, Y.; Jin, Z. Structured Chain-of-Thought Prompting for Code Generation. *ACM Trans. Softw. Eng. Methodol.* **2025**, *34*, 1–23. [CrossRef]
41. Li, J.; Zhao, Y.; Li, Y.; Li, G.; Jin, Z. AceCoder: An Effective Prompting Technique Specialized in Code Generation. *ACM Trans. Softw. Eng. Methodol.* **2024**, *33*, 1–26. [CrossRef]
42. Liu, C.; Bao, X.; Zhang, H.; Zhang, N.; Hu, H.; Zhang, X.; Yan, M. Improving ChatGPT Prompt for Code Generation. *arXiv* **2023**, arXiv:2305.08360. [CrossRef]
43. Raven, O. Magpie. Available online: https://github.com/openraven/magpie (accessed on 3 September 2024).
44. Vertispan. j2clmavenplugin. Available online: https://github.com/Vertispan/j2clmavenplugin (accessed on 3 September 2024).
45. IridiumIdentity. Iridium. Available online: https://github.com/IridiumIdentity/iridium (accessed on 3 September 2024).
46. OpenRefine. Openrefine. Available online: https://github.com/OpenRefine/OpenRefine (accessed on 3 September 2024).
47. Rapiddweller. Rapiddweller-Benerator-ce. Available online: https://github.com/rapiddweller/rapiddweller-benerator-ce (accessed on 3 September 2024).

48. Liu, F.; Liu, Y.; Shi, L.; Huang, H.; Wang, R.; Yang, Z.; Zhang, L. Exploring and evaluating hallucinations in llm-powered code generation. *arXiv* **2024**, arXiv:2404.00971. [CrossRef]
49. Alkaissi, H.; McFarlane, S.I. Artificial hallucinations in ChatGPT: Implications in scientific writing. *Cureus* **2023**, *15*, e35179. [CrossRef] [PubMed]

future internet

MDPI

Article

Frame and Utterance Emotional Alignment for Speech Emotion Recognition

Seounghoon Byun [1] and Seok-Pil Lee [2,*]

[1] Department of Computer Science, Graduate School, Sangmyung University, Seoul 03016, Republic of Korea; bshbsh72@gmail.com
[2] Department of Computer Science, Sangmyung University, Seoul 03016, Republic of Korea
* Correspondence: esprit@smu.ac.kr

Abstract: Speech Emotion Recognition (SER) is important for applications such as Human–Computer Interaction (HCI) and emotion-aware services. Traditional SER models rely on utterance-level labels, aggregating frame-level representations through pooling operations. However, emotional states can vary across frames within an utterance, making it difficult for models to learn consistent and robust representations. To address this issue, we propose two auxiliary loss functions, Emotional Attention Loss (EAL) and Frame-to-Utterance Alignment Loss (FUAL). The proposed approach uses a Classification token (CLS) self-attention pooling mechanism, where the CLS summarizes the entire utterance sequence. EAL encourages frames of the same emotion to align closely with the CLS while separating frames of different classes, and FUAL enforces consistency between frame-level and utterance-level predictions to stabilize training. Model training proceeds in two stages: Stage 1 fine-tunes the wav2vec 2.0 backbone with Cross-Entropy (CE) loss to obtain stable frame embeddings, and stage 2 jointly optimizes CE, EAL and FUAL within the CLS-based pooling framework. Experiments on the IEMOCAP four-class dataset demonstrate that our method consistently outperforms baseline models, showing that the proposed losses effectively address representation inconsistencies and improve SER performance. This work advances Artificial Intelligence by improving the ability of models to understand human emotions through speech.

Keywords: speech emotion recognition; self-supervised learning; frame-level emotion alignment; attention; artificial intelligence

1. Introduction

SER is the task of classifying emotional states from a speaker's audio signal. Recent advances in deep learning and Self-supervised Learning (SSL) frameworks have significantly improved SER performance [1,2]. SSL models leverage large-scale unlabeled audio data to learn generalized acoustic representations, enabling efficient adaptation to downstream tasks using only a limited amount of labeled data [3–5]. Among these, models such as wav2vec 2.0, HuBERT, and WavLM are widely adopted as backbone architectures in SER [6–8].

Traditional SER systems generate frame-level embeddings using an SSL backbone and then aggregate them into a single utterance-level representation through pooling operations. The resulting utterance-level representation is passed to a classifier for final emotion prediction [9,10]. However, this approach has two key limitations. First, emotional content is often non-uniformly distributed within an utterance, meaning that some frames may express different emotions than others. Since conventional SER models are trained using only utterance-level labels, they struggle to learn consistent intra-class frame representations, leading to a mismatch between frame-level and utterance-level features and causing training instability [11]. Second, traditional pooling methods such as mean or weighted sum cannot explicitly capture relationships between frames within the same emotion class. As a result, even utterances belonging to the same emotion category may produce inconsistent frame embeddings, obscuring decision boundaries and degrading overall performance.

To address these challenges, we propose two auxiliary loss functions: EAL and FUAL. Both loss functions are designed to improve representation learning by modeling the relationship between frames and the entire utterance, while requiring only labels at the utterance level. EAL encourages frames of the same emotion to cluster around a central representation while pushing frames of different classes apart, thereby sharpening class boundaries. FUAL enforces consistency between frame-level and utterance-level predictions, ensuring that each frame reflects the overall emotional structure of the utterance.

To effectively implement these objectives, we employ CLS-based self-attention pooling. from all frames into a single utterance-level representation through Multi-Head Attention (MHA), while simultaneously affecting the update of frame-level embeddings [12–14]. In this process, EAL and FUAL jointly influence the learning procedure, enabling the CLS to capture a concise and representative utterance-level context.

The training process proceeds in two stages. In Stage 1, the SSL backbone is fine-tuned with CE loss only, stabilizing frame-level embeddings for downstream tasks [15]. In stage 2, the model from Stage 1 is used as initialization, and EAL and FUAL are jointly optimized within the CLS-based self-attention pooling framework to refine emotional alignment and improve recognition performance.

Experiments on the IEMOCAP 4-class dataset demonstrate that the proposed method consistently outperforms baseline models in both Unweighted Accuracy (UA) and Weighted Accuracy (WA).

As Speech Emotion Recognition is a key component of affective computing and Human-Centered Artificial Intelligence, the proposed method directly contributes to advancing AI systems capable of understanding and responding to human emotions.

The remainder of this paper is organized as follows. Section 2 reviews related work on Speech Emotion Recognition and Self-Supervised Learning. Section 3 presents the proposed method and training strategy. Section 4 describes the experimental setup and results. Section 5 provides a discussion, and Section 6 concludes the paper.

2. Related Work

2.1. Traditional SER Approaches

Previous SER research involved manually extracting designed features such as MFCCs, pitch, energy, and mel spectrograms from audio signals, then classifying emotions using traditional machine learning algorithms like Support Vector Machine (SVM) or K-Nearest Neighbor (KNN). However, these features had limitations. They could not sufficiently capture complex, nonlinear patterns of emotion, and their generalization performance across datasets was not robust [16–18].

Subsequent advancements in deep learning enabled the application of Convolutional Neural Network (CNN) and RNN-based models to SER, significantly improving performance [19,20]. While Recurrent Neural Network (RNN)-based models demonstrated particular strength in learning time-series audio information, limitations persisted regarding data scarcity and the ability to learn diverse emotional expressions with precision [21].

To address this, SSL-based models, which leverage large-scale unlabeled audio data to learn powerful representations, have recently become widely used as the backbone for SER.

2.2. Wav2vec 2.0

The SSL model learns frame-level generalizable representations from unlabeled audio data, achieving remarkable performance on diverse downstream audio tasks using only a small amount of labeled data. The representative model, wav2vec 2.0, learns rich acoustic representations by masking parts of the raw waveform and predicting those masked segments [6].

It uses a convolutional feature encoder to capture local patterns and a Transformer network to model long-range temporal dependencies. Through contrastive learning, wav2vec 2.0 distinguishes true masked segments from negative samples, producing robust and discriminative features. Due to these characteristics, wav2vec 2.0 has become a widely used backbone for SER, offering superior performance to CNN and RNN-based models and reducing reliance on large labeled datasets.

2.3. Pooling Techniques for Utterance-Level Representations

SER models integrate frame-level audio representations to generate a single utterance-level vector, which is then used to classify emotion. Previous studies employed simple techniques like average pooling or max pooling, but these methods had limitations. They either processed all frames equally or extremely.

To improve this, attentive pooling was proposed, generating speech representations that assign higher weights to important frames through learned weights [22]. However, in this approach, weights are determined only indirectly during model training, making it difficult to guarantee that emotionally significant frames are directly reflected. Furthermore, since the relationships between frames are not explicitly captured, different frames can be mixed. This increases the likelihood of noise and unnecessary information being included, ultimately limiting the final prediction performance.

2.4. Frame Representation Alignment in SER

Existing SER research primarily relies on utterance-level labels, meaning that the roles and relationships of individual frames are not explicitly learned. Attention pooling methods assign higher weights to frames that are relatively more important for classification, based on the relationships between frames, to generate an utterance-level representation. Consequently, even among utterances belonging to the same emotion class, frame representations may fail to align consistently, and the representations of frames sharing the same emotion may be learned in a highly inconsistent manner.

Such inconsistencies blur the boundaries between emotion classes and introduce unnecessary variability into the training process, ultimately degrading the final prediction performance. Therefore, to enhance both the performance and generalization ability of SER models, a new approach is required that enables mutual learning between utterance-level and frame-level representations.

3. Proposed Method

This study utilizes SSL-based audio frame embedding to learn stable and emotionally consistent Utterance-level representations through a two-stage training procedure. The overall two-stage training framework is illustrated in Figure 1.

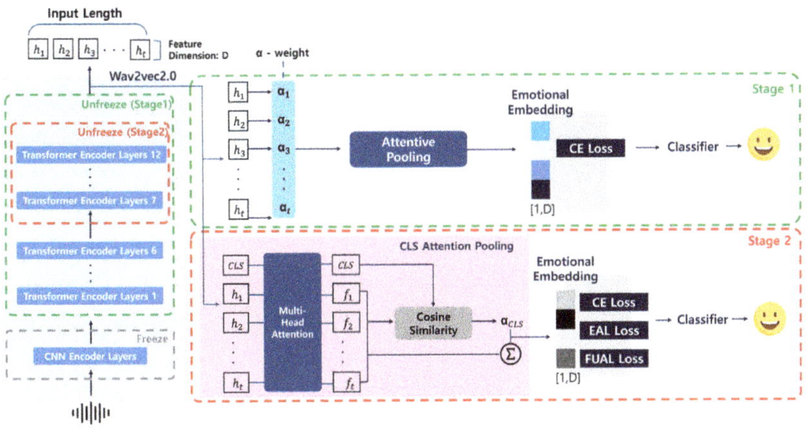

Figure 1. Architecture of the Frame-Align SER Model.

In stage 1, input audio is fed through the SSL model to extract frame-level embeddings. Subsequently, frame-specific weights are computed via attention pooling, which are then weighted to generate utterance-level representations. These generated utterance representations are learned through CE loss, enabling the SSL model to stably reflect frame-level embedded emotional information.

In stage 2, the SSL model trained in stage 1 is used as the initial value, and the frame representations that stably retain emotional information are utilized as input. At this stage, a CLS is added, and information from all frames is integrated via MHA, which is then learned as a global utterance vector. Subsequently, the utterance representation generated via CLS-based self-attention pooling is used for final emotion classification, simultaneously applying CE Loss, EAL, and FUAL throughout this process.

3.1. Stage 1: SSL Fine-Tuning with Attentive Pooling

We employ wav2vec 2.0 as the SSL backbone to extract frame-level embeddings $H = [h_1, h_2, \ldots, h_T]$ from the input waveform x. These frame embeddings are then integrated using an attentive pooling module to generate an utterance-level representation u, which is subsequently passed to the final classifier for emotion prediction.

The frame-wise attention weights α_t and the utterance-level representation u are computed as follows:

$$s_t = w^T h_t + b,\ \alpha_t = \frac{exp(s_t)}{\sum_{k=1}^{T} exp\ (s_k)},\ u = \sum_{t=1}^{T} \alpha_t h_t, \tag{1}$$

The utterance-level representation u obtained in (1) is trained using CE Loss, defined as:

$$L_{CE} = -\sum_{c=1}^{C} y_c log(\hat{y}_c), \tag{2}$$

C is the number of emotion classes, y_c is the ground truth as a one-hot vector, and $\hat{y}_c$ is the softmax probability for class c.

Through this process, the frame-level weights α_t are stabilized to accurately reflect emotional information. Thus, stage 1 focuses on learning a stable SSL-based initial model, providing a strong foundation for stage 2. This step ensures that the subsequent application of auxiliary losses in stage 2 is stable and effective, facilitating smooth training and improving overall performance.

3.2. *Stage 2: CLS-Based Self-Attention Pooling & Joint Objectives*

In stage 2, the SSL backbone from stage 1 is used for initialization. A CLS is prepended to the frame sequence and passed through a multi-head attention encoder to produce frame representations f_t and a global utterance-level representation c.

These outputs are aggregated to form the final utterance-level vector u. At this stage, CE Loss, EAL, and FUAL are jointly optimized to enhance both frame-level alignment and utterance-level consistency.

3.2.1. Self-Attention Pooling with CLS

The frame embedding sequence from the SSL backbone is given by $H = [h_1,\ h_2, \ldots,\ h_T]$. A CLS h_{CLS} is prepended to form the input sequence:

$$H' = [h_{CLS},\ h_1,\ h_2,\ \ldots,\ h_T], \tag{3}$$

The sequence H' is then processed by the multi-head attention encoder $Enc(\cdot)$:

$$[c, f_1,\ f_2, \ldots,\ f_T] = Enc(H'), \tag{4}$$

c represents the CLS output summarizing the entire utterance, and f_t represents the final frame-level representations. By concentrating the utterance information into c, this structure provides a foundation for EAL to guide emotion-specific alignment.

The similarity scores between the CLS and each frame are normalized using a softmax function to produce attention weights α_t. These weights determine the contribution of each frame to the final utterance-level representation, similar to the process described in stage 1.

3.2.2. Emotional Attention Loss (EAL)

EAL encourages frames within the same emotion class to align closely with the CLS while separating frames from different classes.

The cosine similarity between the CLS and each frame, s_t, is calculated as follows:

$$s_t = \frac{C \cdot f_t}{||C|| \cdot ||f_t||}, \tag{5}$$

To enforce alignment, a softplus-margin loss is applied so that emotionally salient frames maintain a similarity above margin m [23].

The frame-wise loss for each frame is defined as:

$$l_t = log\left(1 + {}^{(m - s_t)}\right), \tag{6}$$

The overall EAL is computed as the mean of these losses across all frames:

$$L_{EAL} = \frac{1}{T}\sum_{t=1}^{T} l_t, \tag{7}$$

While EAL improves class boundary clarity, the softmax function can still amplify small differences in similarity scores, causing attention weights to become overly concentrated on certain frames. The margin mitigates this effect by limiting updates for frames already close to the CLS, but it does not fully resolve the disproportionate allocation of attention.

As a result, EAL alone may not fully prevent this weight concentration, which can make training less stable and reduce the diversity of frame-level representations.

3.2.3. Frame-to-Utterance Alignment Loss (FUAL)

Using only EAL may cause the model to over-focus on a few specific frames, which can lead to unstable representations for other frames. To address this issue, FUAL is introduced to ensure that frame-level predictions are consistent with the utterance-level prediction distribution. Each frame output is passed through a softmax function to generate a probability distribution p_t, and the utterance representation is also passed through a softmax function to produce the utterance-level probability distribution q. The frame-level predictions are then aggregated using attention weights α_t to form a weighted average distribution $\overline{p}$.

Finally, FUAL minimizes the Kullback–Leibler (KL) divergence between these two distributions as follows [24]:

$$L_{FUAL} = KL\left(q_{\|}\overline{p}\right), \tag{8}$$

FUAL minimizes this divergence to encourage consistency between frame-level and utterance-level predictions, resulting in more stable and coherent emotional representations across both levels.

3.2.4. Total Loss

The final loss function combines CE, EAL, and FUAL:

$$L_{total} = L_{CE} + \lambda_{EAL} L_{EAL} + \lambda_{FUAL} L_{FUAL}, \tag{9}$$

λ_{EAL} and λ_{FUAL} are weighting factors controlling the influence of the auxiliary losses. By optimizing L_{total}, the model improves utterance-level classification accuracy while ensuring that frame-level representations remain aligned and consistent with the overall emotional structure.

4. Experiments

In this section, we present the dataset, training configurations, baseline models, and experimental results used to evaluate the performance of the proposed method.

4.1. Dataset

For performance evaluation, this study utilized the IEMOCAP corpus [25], a widely adopted benchmark dataset for SER. The corpus is multi-modal, containing audio, visual, and lexical modalities; however, only the audio modality was used in this work. It comprises five sessions, each consisting of dyadic conversations between one male and one female speaker.

To prevent speaker information leakage, we followed a leave-one-session-out five-fold cross-validation strategy. In this setup, four sessions were used for training, while the data from one speaker in the remaining session served as the validation set, and the data from the other speaker were used as the test set.

We focused on four emotion categories: Happy (including Excited), Sad, Neutral, and Angry. In total, 5531 audio utterances were selected for training and evaluation, and their distribution across the four classes is summarized in Table 1.

Table 1 summarizes the distribution of utterances across the 4 emotion classes.

Within the held-out session, the data were further divided by speaker gender: utterances from the male speaker were used for validation, and those from the female speaker were used for testing.

Table 1. Number of utterances per emotion and per session.

Session	Angry	Happy	Sad	Neutral	Total
1	229	278	194	384	1085
2	137	327	197	362	1023
3	240	286	305	320	1151
4	327	303	143	258	1031
5	170	442	245	384	1241
Total	1103	1636	1084	1708	5531

4.2. Evaluation Metrics

The model performance was evaluated using UA and WA. UA accounts for class imbalance by equally weighting all classes, providing a fair assessment of performance across different emotion categories. In contrast, WA measures the overall accuracy based on the total number of samples, reflecting the model's performance across the entire dataset.

$$UA = \frac{1}{C}\sum_{c=1}^{C} \frac{TP_c}{N_c}, WA = \frac{\sum_{c=1}^{C} TP_c}{\sum_{c=1} N_c}, \quad (10)$$

C denotes the number of classes, TP_c represents the number of correct predictions for class C, and N_c indicates the total number of samples in class C.

In addition, a Confusion Matrix was used to visually inspect class-wise prediction tendencies, allowing for an intuitive understanding of potential misclassification patterns.

4.3. Implementation Details

All experiments were conducted on a single NVIDIA RTX 5080 GPU using the PyTorch 2.8.0 framework with CUDA 12.8 and Python 3.10.8. The training process consisted of two sequential stages. In stage 1, the SSL backbone was fine-tuned to obtain stable frame-level representations using only CE loss. In stage 2, the model was jointly trained with CE and the proposed auxiliary losses to refine frame-to-utterance emotional alignment. The CNN-based feature extractor remained frozen in both stages to preserve general speech representations. AdamW was used as the optimizer with different learning rates (LR) for the backbone, attention module, and classification head. The pretrained model, facebook/wav2vec2-base, was obtained from the Hugging Face Transformers library.

Table 2 summarizes the core hyperparameter settings for both stages, allowing a direct comparison of key experimental configurations.

Table 2. Hyperparameter settings for stage 1 and stage 2.

Hyperparameters	Stage 1	Stage 2
Backbone	wav2vec 2.0 base	Stage-1 checkpoint
Epochs	40	30
Batch size	32	32
Backbone LR	1e-4	1e-5
Classifier LR	1e-4	3e-4
Attention LR	5e-4	3e-4
Weight decay	1e-2	1e-2
Pooling	attentive pooling	CLS + self-attention pooling
Trainable transformer layers	12	6

In stage 2, CLS-based self-attention pooling was configured with four attention heads, a depth of one, and no dropout. The hyperparameters of both EAL and FUAL were determined experimentally, and further analysis is provided in Section 4.4.2 (Ablation Study).

4.4. Results

4.4.1. Baselines

For comparison, two baseline models were established using the same dataset and the SSL backbone pre-trained in stage 1 to ensure a fair and consistent evaluation setting. The first baseline employed a conventional self-attention pooling mechanism, while the second utilized a CLS-based self-attention pooling approach, where the CLS serves as a global summary representation of the entire utterance. These baselines were designed to evaluate the effect of incorporating a global anchor token in emotion representation learning.

Building upon the CLS-based self-attention pooling baseline, we further examined the impact of the proposed auxiliary loss functions by gradually integrating the FUAL. Specifically, three CLS-based configurations were tested: one with EAL alone, another with FUAL alone, and a third with both EAL and FUAL applied together to form the proposed model. This progressive approach allowed us to systematically analyze the contribution of each individual loss function as well as their combined effect on overall performance.

All experiments were conducted using five-fold cross-validation, and performance was evaluated using UA and WA.

As shown in Table 3, the CLS-based self-attention pooling showed moderate performance improvements compared to conventional self-attention pooling, indicating that incorporating a global summary token can provide a more stable foundation for utterance-level representation. When either EAL or FUAL was added to the CLS-based framework, the model exhibited additional improvements over the CLS baseline, suggesting that each loss plays a supportive role in enhancing frame-level alignment and prediction consistency. When both losses were applied together, the proposed model achieved the best overall performance among all configurations, demonstrating clear performance gains compared to the baseline. These results confirm that the proposed auxiliary losses are effective within the CLS-based framework and provide consistent performance improvements under the given experimental setting.

Table 3. Performance of the proposed methods.

Methods	UA (%)	WA (%)
self-attention pooling	73.29	71.88
CLS-based self-attention pooling	73.50	72.33
+EAL	74.16	72.86
+FUAL	74.96	73.80
+EAL + FUAL	75.30	74.22

4.4.2. Ablation Study

To analyze the contribution of each component in the proposed framework, we conducted an ablation study focusing on the auxiliary losses, EAL and FUAL. The experiments were designed to investigate the effect of key hyperparameters that influence alignment learning.

EAL includes two key hyperparameters, the margin m and the loss weight λ_{EAL}. The margin m controls the degree of separation between frame-level representations, and we explored three different values, 0.4, 0.6, and 0.8. The loss weight λ_{EAL} determines how much influence the EAL term has on the overall loss function, and we tested three levels, 0.05, 0.10, and 0.15. Because these parameters can affect both the stability of training and the final recognition performance, we systematically investigated their impact through a structured hyperparameter search.

To conduct this study, we evaluated every possible combination of the margin and the loss weight, resulting in nine different experimental settings. All experiments were performed using five-fold cross-validation in order to provide reliable performance estimates. The results, reported in terms of UA and WA, are presented in Table 4.

Table 4. Ablation study of margin (m) and loss weight (λ_{EAL}) on UA and WA.

λ_{EAL} \ Margin	m = 0.4	m = 0.6	m = 0.8
0.05	74.80/73.54	74.54/73.39	75.30/74.22
0.10	75.15/74.07	75.10/73.84	74.60/73.65
0.15	74.62/73.39	74.59/73.39	75.11/74.10

As shown in Table 4, the performance of the model varied depending on the specific values of the margin and the loss weight. When the margin was either too low or too high, the improvement in accuracy was less consistent, which suggests that an appropriate balance is needed between encouraging frame clustering and maintaining sufficient separation. A similar trend was observed for the loss weight. When the loss weight was increased beyond a certain level, the performance did not continue to improve and slightly decreased in some cases, indicating that excessive weighting of EAL can interfere with the optimization of other objectives. Among all the tested combinations, the setting with a margin of 0.8 and a loss weight of 0.05 produced the most stable and consistent results.

To further validate the robustness of the proposed framework, an additional ablation study was conducted by varying λ_{FUAL} while fixing the best EAL parameters (m = 0.8, λ_{EAL} = 0.05). The results are summarized in Table 5.

Table 5. Ablation study of loss weight (λ_{FUAL}) on UA and WA.

λ_{FUAL}	UA (%)	WA (%)
0.05	75.3	74.22
0.10	74.81	73.8
0.15	74.7	73.42

As shown in Table 5, the model achieved the highest performance when λ_{FUAL} = 0.05. Increasing the loss weight beyond this value slightly degraded performance, indicating that an excessive emphasis on FUAL can dominate the optimization and reduce generalization. These findings suggest that moderate weighting of FUAL effectively complements EAL, maintaining stable alignment between frame- and utterance-level representations.

4.4.3. Visualization Analysis

To examine the effect of EAL and FUAL on aligning emotional representations across entire utterances, we visualized the learned embeddings using t-SNE [26].

As shown in Figure 2a,b, the comparison suggests that in Figure 2b, the utterance-level emotion distributions appear more clearly differentiated, showing a relatively clear boundary around the CLS token. This implies that the proposed loss functions help improve the separation and organization of emotion representations at the utterance level, indicating their potential in structuring the emotional feature space.

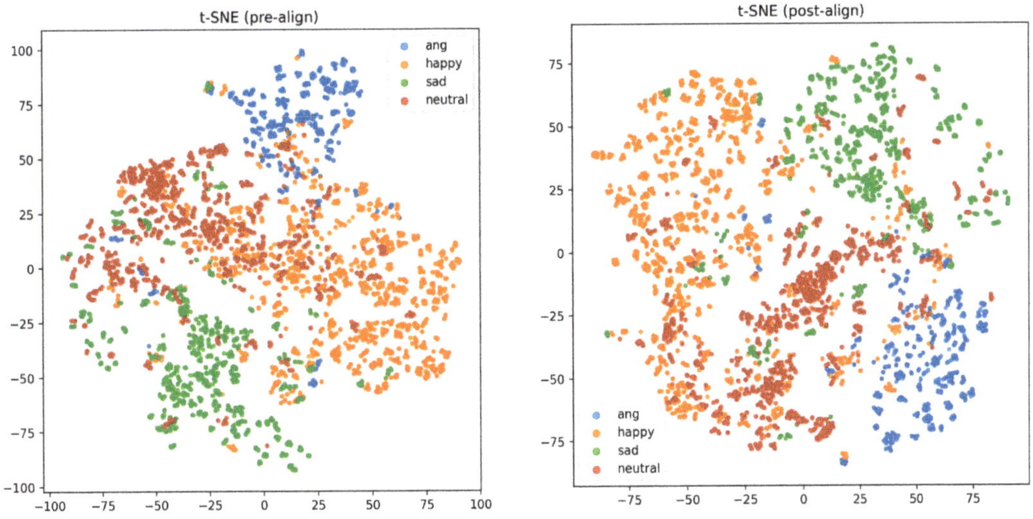

(**a**) (**b**)

Figure 2. t-SNE visualization of utterance-level embeddings. (**a**) Baseline; (**b**) Proposed.

4.4.4. Confusion Matrix

Figure 3 shows the confusion matrix of the final proposed model evaluated using 5-fold cross-validation. Each cell indicates the percentage of predicted classes for a specific true emotion class, clearly visualizing the model's tendency to misclassify particular emotions. The results indicate that while this model achieves high accuracy for the Anger and Sad classes, it exhibits relatively lower accuracy for the Happy and Neutral classes, showing notable confusion between these two emotion categories.

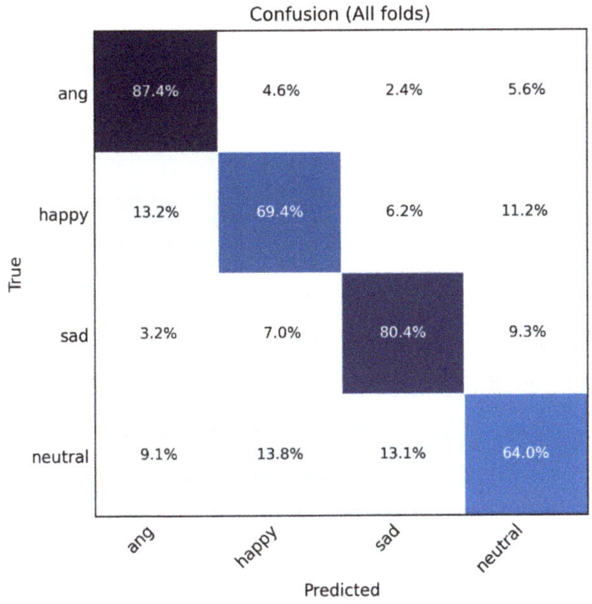

Figure 3. Confusion matrix of the proposed method.

As shown in Table 1, both Happy and Neutral classes contain significantly more utterances than other emotions, which may lead to class imbalance and bias the model toward these categories. In addition, the boundary between Happy and Neutral emotions is often ambiguous in conversational speech, making them difficult to distinguish clearly. These factors together likely contribute to the observed confusion between the two emotions.

4.4.5. Comparison with Other SER Systems

As shown in Table 6, the proposed model achieved a UA of 75.3% and a WA of 74.2%, demonstrating clear performance improvements over existing models such as SMW-CAT and ShiftCNN. Moreover, the proposed method achieved comparable performance to the state-of-the-art FLEA model, highlighting its effectiveness.

Table 6. Comparison with other SER systems.

Systems	UA (%)	WA (%)
P-TAPT [27]	74.3	-
SMW-CAT [28]	74.2	72.8
ShiftCNN [29]	74.8	72.8
Proposed	75.3	74.2
FLEA [30]	75.7	74.7

Importantly, our approach requires only utterance-level labels for training and does not rely on frame-level annotations. This demonstrates that the model can effectively achieve high SER performance without complex modules or additional labeling efforts, making it both efficient and scalable for practical applications.

4.4.6. Cross-Dataset Evaluation

To further assess the generalizability of the proposed method, additional experiments were conducted on two benchmark datasets, CREMA-D [31] and RAVDESS [32]. The CREMA-D dataset contains 7442 audiovisual clips of six emotions (happy, sad, neutral, anger, disgust, and fear) recorded by 91 actors [31]. The RAVDESS dataset includes 1440 utterances from 24 actors expressing eight emotions (calm, happy, sad, angry, fearful, surprise, disgust, and neutral) [32].

As shown in Table 7, the proposed CLS-based model achieved higher UA and WA scores than the baseline model on both datasets, confirming consistent performance improvements. These results demonstrate that the proposed method maintains stable recognition capability across different emotional corpora, validating its robustness beyond the IEMOCAP dataset.

Table 7. Cross-dataset comparison between the baseline and proposed model.

Dataset	Model	UA (%)	WA (%)
CREMA-D	Baseline	78.00	77.73
	Proposed	78.76	78.53
RAVDESS	Baseline	90.11	90.07
	Proposed	93.13	92.72

5. Discussion

This study aimed to address inconsistencies between frame-level and utterance-level representations in SER. To this end, we introduced two auxiliary loss functions: EAL and FUAL. EAL promotes clustering of frames belonging to the same emotion class around the CLS while separating frames of different classes, whereas FUAL encourages consistency between frame-level and utterance-level predictions, preventing the model from over-focusing on a few dominant frames. The CLS also plays a key role in integrating frame information into a coherent utterance-level representation, providing a stable reference point for subsequent alignment learning.

The results in Table 3 show that incorporating the CLS into the pooling mechanism provided modest improvements over conventional self-attention pooling. Adding EAL or FUAL individually led to further gains, while combining both losses achieved the best overall performance, demonstrating their complementary effects. t-SNE visualizations confirmed this by showing clearer and more distinct emotion clusters when both losses were applied, indicating that the proposed framework reshapes the representation space to better capture emotional structures.

The ablation analysis further highlighted the importance of carefully tuning alignment-related hyperparameters such as the margin and loss weights. These parameters influenced training stability and overall recognition performance, emphasizing the need for empirical balance to achieve stable and effective optimization.

The confusion analysis indicated that most emotions were accurately recognized, though minor overlap was observed between acoustically similar categories such as Happy and Neutral. In addition, comparison with previous methods demonstrated that our approach outperforms prior models such as SMW-CAT and ShiftCNN while reaching performance levels comparable to the state-of-the-art FLEA model. Importantly, this was achieved without requiring frame-level annotations, highlighting the practicality and scalability of our method.

To further validate its robustness, additional experiments were conducted on the CREMA-D and RAVDESS datasets. The proposed method maintained consistent performance across these benchmarks, confirming its generalizability across different emotional speech conditions.

Future studies will aim to further assess adaptability using more diverse and spontaneous speech data.

In summary, integrating EAL and FUAL within a CLS-based framework effectively improves both alignment and representation consistency in SER. This approach provides a simple yet effective way to enhance emotion recognition using only utterance-level labels, supporting its potential for broader practical applications.

6. Conclusions

This study proposed a CLS-based framework that integrates two auxiliary loss functions, EAL and FUAL, to address inconsistencies between frame-level and utterance-level representations in SER. The proposed method leverages a two-stage training strategy, where the wav2vec 2.0 backbone is first fine-tuned to obtain stable frame embeddings, and then EAL and FUAL are jointly optimized within a CLS-based self-attention pooling mechanism.

Through experiments on the IEMOCAP dataset, we demonstrated that the combination of EAL and FUAL effectively improves alignment and representation consistency, leading to stable training and higher recognition accuracy without requiring frame-level annotations. Additional experiments on the CREMA-D and RAVDESS datasets further confirmed that the proposed approach maintains consistent performance across different corpora, supporting its generalizability to varied emotional speech conditions. Furthermore, comparison with existing SER systems showed that the proposed method achieves performance comparable to recent state-of-the-art models while maintaining a simpler and more efficient architecture.

In conclusion, this framework provides a practical and interpretable solution for enhancing SER using only utterance-level labels, achieving a good balance between model simplicity, scalability, and recognition performance. Future work will extend this approach to multimodal emotion recognition by incorporating visual or textual modalities, and will explore its application to more diverse and spontaneous speech data to evaluate adaptability in real-world scenarios.

Author Contributions: Conceptualization, S.B. and S.-P.L.; methodology, S.B.; investigation, S.B.; writing—original draft preparation, S.B.; writing—review and editing, S.-P.L.; project administration, S.-P.L. All authors have read and agreed to the published version of the manuscript.

Funding: This research received no external funding.

Data Availability Statement: Experiments used publicly available datasets.

Conflicts of Interest: The authors declare no conflicts of interest.

References

1. Atmaja, B.T.; Sasou, A. Evaluating self-supervised speech representations for speech emotion recognition. *IEEE Access* **2022**, *10*, 124396–124407. [CrossRef]
2. Naini, A.R.; Kohler, M.A.; Richerson, E.; Robinson, D.; Busso, C. Generalization of self-supervised learning-based representations for cross-domain speech emotion recognition. In Proceedings of the ICASSP 2024—2024 IEEE International Conference on Acoustics, Speech and Signal Processing (ICASSP), Seoul, Republic of Korea, 14–19 April 2024; IEEE: New York, NY, USA, 2024; pp. 12031–12035. [CrossRef]
3. Morais, E.; Hoory, R.; Zhu, W.; Gat, I.; Damasceno, M.; Aronowitz, H. Speech emotion recognition using self-supervised features. In Proceedings of the ICASSP 2022—2022 IEEE International Conference on Acoustics, Speech and Signal Processing (ICASSP), Singapore, 22–27 May 2022; IEEE: New York, NY, USA, 2022; pp. 6922–6926. [CrossRef]
4. Schneider, S.; Baevski, A.; Collobert, R.; Auli, M. wav2vec: Unsupervised Pre-Training for Speech Recognition. *Proc. Interspeech* **2019**, *2019*, 3465–3469. [CrossRef]
5. Fang, Y.; Xing, X.; Xu, X.; Zhang, W. Exploring Downstream Transfer of Self-Supervised Features for Speech Emotion Recognition. *Proc. Interspeech* **2023**, *2023*, 3627–3631. [CrossRef]
6. Baevski, A.; Zhou, Y.; Mohamed, A.; Auli, M. wav2vec 2.0: A framework for self-supervised learning of speech representations. In *Advances in Neural Information Processing Systems*; NeurIPS: San Diego, CA, USA, 2020; Volume 33, pp. 12449–12460.
7. Hsu, W.N.; Bolte, B.; Tsai, Y.H.H.; Lakhotia, K.; Salakhutdinov, R.; Mohamed, A. Hubert: Self-supervised speech representation learning by masked prediction of hidden units. *IEEE/ACM Trans. Audio Speech Lang. Process.* **2021**, *29*, 3451–3460. [CrossRef]
8. Chen, S.; Wang, C.; Chen, Z.; Wu, Y.; Liu, S.; Chen, Z.; Li, J.; Kanda, N.; Yoshioka, T.; Xiao, X.; et al. Wavlm: Large-scale self-supervised pre-training for full stack speech processing. *IEEE J. Sel. Top. Signal Process.* **2022**, *16*, 1505–1518. [CrossRef]
9. Hyeon, J.; Oh, Y.H.; Lee, Y.J.; Choi, H.J. Improving speech emotion recognition by fusing self-supervised learning and spectral features via mixture of experts. *Data Knowl. Eng.* **2024**, *150*, 102262. [CrossRef]
10. Kakouros, S.; Stafylakis, T.; Mošner, L.; Burget, L. Speech-based emotion recognition with self-supervised models using attentive channel-wise correlations and label smoothing. In Proceedings of the ICASSP 2023—2023 IEEE International Conference on Acoustics, Speech and Signal Processing (ICASSP), Rhodes, Greece, 4–10 June 2023; IEEE: New York, NY, USA, 2023; pp. 1–5. [CrossRef]
11. Nagase, R.; Fukumori, T.; Yamashita, Y. Speech Emotion Recognition Using Sequences of Fine-grained Emotion Labels with Phoneme Class Attributes. *APSIPA Trans. Signal Inf. Process.* **2025**, *14*, e17. [CrossRef]
12. Chang, H.-S.; Sun, R.-Y.; Ricci, K.; McCallum, A. Multi-CLS BERT: An Efficient Alternative to Traditional Ensembling. In Proceedings of the 61st Annual Meeting of the Association for Computational Linguistics (ACL 2023), Toronto, ON, Canada, 9–14 July 2023; Association for Computational Linguistics: Stroudsburg, PA, USA; pp. 821–854. [CrossRef]
13. Chen, W.; Liang, Y.; Ma, Z.; Zheng, Z.; Chen, X. EAT: Self-supervised pre-training with efficient audio transformer. *arXiv* **2024**, arXiv:2401.03497.
14. Vaswani, A.; Shazeer, N.; Parmar, N.; Uszkoreit, J.; Jones, L.; Gomez, A.N.; Kaiser, Ł.; Polosukhin, I. Attention is all you need. In *Advances in Neural Information Processing Systems (NeurIPS 2017)*; NeurIPS: San Diego, CA, USA, 2017; Volume 30, pp. 5998–6008.
15. De Boer, P.T.; Kroese, D.P.; Mannor, S.; Rubinstein, R.Y. A tutorial on the cross-entropy method. *Ann. Oper. Res.* **2005**, *134*, 19–67. [CrossRef]
16. Mirsamadi, S.; Barsoum, E.; Zhang, C. Automatic speech emotion recognition using recurrent neural networks with local attention. In Proceedings of the 2017 IEEE International Conference on Acoustics, Speech and Signal Processing (ICASSP), New Orleans, LA, USA, 5–9 March 2017; IEEE: New York, NY, USA, 2017; pp. 2227–2231. [CrossRef]

17. Rajamani, S.T.; Rajamani, K.T.; Mallol-Ragolta, A.; Liu, S.; Schuller, B. A novel attention-based gated recurrent unit and its efficacy in speech emotion recognition. In Proceedings of the ICASSP 2021—2021 IEEE International Conference on Acoustics, Speech and Signal Processing (ICASSP), Toronto, ON, Canada, 6–11 June 2021; IEEE: New York, NY, USA, 2021; pp. 6294–6298. [CrossRef]
18. Li, R.; Wu, Z.; Jia, J.; Zhao, S.; Meng, H. Dilated residual network with multi-head self-attention for speech emotion recognition. In Proceedings of the ICASSP 2019—2019 IEEE International Conference on Acoustics, Speech and Signal Processing (ICASSP), Brighton, UK, 12–17 May 2019; IEEE: New York, NY, USA, 2019; pp. 6675–6679. [CrossRef]
19. Issa, D.; Demirci, M.F.; Yazici, A. Speech emotion recognition with deep convolutional neural networks. *Biomed. Signal Process. Control* **2020**, *59*, 101894. [CrossRef]
20. De Lope, J.; Grana, M. A hybrid time-distributed deep neural architecture for speech emotion recognition. *Int. J. Neural Syst.* **2022**, *32*, 2250024. [CrossRef] [PubMed]
21. Li, Y.; Wang, Y.; Yang, X.; Im, S.K. Speech emotion recognition based on Graph-LSTM neural network. *EURASIP J. Audio Speech Music. Process.* **2023**, *2023*, 40. [CrossRef]
22. Santos, C.D.; Tan, M.; Xiang, B.; Zhou, B. Attentive pooling networks. *arXiv* **2016**, arXiv:1602.03609. [CrossRef]
23. Glorot, X.; Bordes, A.; Bengio, Y. Deep sparse rectifier neural networks. In Proceedings of the Fourteenth International Conference on Artificial Intelligence and Statistics, Fort Lauderdale, FL, USA, 11–13 April 2011; JMLR Workshop and Conference Proceedings: New York, NY, USA, 2011; pp. 315–323.
24. Kullback, S.; Leibler, R.A. On information and sufficiency. *Ann. Math. Stat.* **1951**, *22*, 79–86. [CrossRef]
25. Busso, C.; Bulut, M.; Lee, C.-C.; Kazemzadeh, A.; Mower, E.; Kim, S.; Chang, J.N.; Lee, S.; Narayanan, S.S. IEMOCAP: Interactive emotional dyadic motion capture database. *Lang. Resour. Eval.* **2008**, *42*, 335–359. [CrossRef]
26. Maaten, L.V.D.; Hinton, G. Visualizing data using t-SNE. *J. Mach. Learn. Res.* **2008**, *9*, 2579–2605.
27. Chen, L.W.; Rudnicky, A. Exploring wav2vec 2.0 fine tuning for improved speech emotion recognition. In Proceedings of the ICASSP 2023—2023 IEEE International Conference on Acoustics, Speech and Signal Processing (ICASSP), Rhodes, Greece, 4–10 June 2023; IEEE: New York, NY, USA, 2023; pp. 1–5. [CrossRef]
28. He, Y.; Minematsu, N.; Saito, D. Multiple acoustic features speech emotion recognition using cross-attention transformer. In Proceedings of the ICASSP 2023—2023 IEEE International Conference on Acoustics, Speech and Signal Processing (ICASSP), Rhodes, Greece, 4–10 June 2023; IEEE: New York, NY, USA, 2023; pp. 1–5. [CrossRef]
29. Shen, S.; Liu, F.; Zhou, A. Mingling or misalignment? temporal shift for speech emotion recognition with pre-trained representations. In Proceedings of the ICASSP 2023—2023 IEEE International Conference on Acoustics, Speech and Signal Processing (ICASSP), Rhodes, Greece, 4–10 June 2023; IEEE: New York, NY, USA, 2023; pp. 1–5. [CrossRef]
30. Li, Q.; Gao, Y.; Wang, C.; Deng, Y.; Xue, J.; Han, Y.; Li, Y. Frame-level emotional state alignment method for speech emotion recognition. In Proceedings of the ICASSP 2024—2024 IEEE International Conference on Acoustics, Speech and Signal Processing (ICASSP), Seoul, Republic of Korea, 14–19 April 2024; IEEE: New York, NY, USA, 2024; pp. 11486–11490. [CrossRef]
31. Cao, H.; Cooper, D.G.; Keutmann, M.K.; Gur, R.C.; Nenkova, A.; Verma, R. Crema-d: Crowd-sourced emotional multimodal actors dataset. *IEEE Trans. Affect. Comput.* **2014**, *5*, 377–390.
32. Livingstone, S.R.; Russo, F.A. The Ryerson Audio-Visual Database of Emotional Speech and Song (RAVDESS): A dynamic, multimodal set of facial and vocal expressions in North American English. *PLoS ONE* **2018**, *13*, e0196391. [CrossRef] [PubMed]

future internet

MDPI

Article

Methodology for Detecting Suspicious Claims in Health Insurance Using Supervised Machine Learning

Jose Villegas-Ortega [1,2,*], Luis Napoleon Quiroz Aviles [3], Juan Nazario Arancibia [3], Wilder Carpio Montenegro [3], Rosa Delgadillo [1] and David Mauricio [1]

1 Faculty of System Engineering, Universidad Nacional Mayor de San Marcos, Lima 15081, Peru; rdelgadilloa@unmsm.edu.pe (R.D.); dmauricios@unmsm.edu.pe (D.M.)
2 Unidad de Postgrado, Universidad Peruana de Ciencias Aplicadas, Lima 15072, Peru
3 Ministerio de Salud, Seguro Integral de Salud, Lima 15018, Peru; lquiroza@minsa.gob.pe (L.N.Q.A.); consultor_grep_38@sisext.pe (J.N.A.); wcarpio@sis.gob.pe (W.C.M.)
* Correspondence: jose.villegas@unmsm.edu.pe

Abstract: Health insurance fraud (HIF) places a substantial economic burden on global health systems. While supervised machine learning (SML) offers a promising solution for its detection, most approaches are ad hoc and lack a systematic methodological framework that ensures replicability, adaptability, and effectiveness, especially in contexts with severe class imbalance. We developed PDHIF (Phases for Detecting Fraud in Health Insurance), a six-phase systematic methodology that introduces a holistic focus that integrates fraud theory, actors, manifestations, and factors with the complete SML lifecycle. We applied this methodology in a case study using a dataset of 8.5 million claims from a public health insurance system in Peru. We trained and evaluated three SML models (Random Forest, XGBoost, and multilayer perceptron) in two experimental scenarios: one with the original, highly unbalanced dataset and another with a training set balanced via the K-means SMOTE technique. When PDHIF was applied, the results revealed a stark contrast: in the unbalanced scenario, the models were ineffective at detecting fraud (F1 score < 0.521) despite high accuracy (>98%). In the balanced scenario, the performance improved dramatically. The best-performing model, RF, achieved an F1 score of 0.994, a sensitivity of 0.994, and an AUC of 0.994 on the test set, demonstrating a robust ability to distinguish suspicious claims.

Keywords: health insurance fraud; machine learning; fraud detection; class imbalance; systematic methodology; Peru

1. Introduction

Fraud, waste, and abuse in healthcare systems represent a global economic and social burden, consuming an estimated 3% to 10% of total annual healthcare spending [1] and costing hundreds of billions of dollars [2]. This diversion of resources not only compromises the financial sustainability of healthcare systems but also erodes patient trust and can negatively impact the quality of care.

Efforts to mitigate health insurance fraud (HIF) face significant challenges, including high initial detection costs and administrative complexities. While automated detection of health insurance fraud can result in substantial savings—estimated at 25% of total health-care spending in the United States [3]—identifying such practices in the healthcare sector is more complex than those in other insurance sectors, such as credit or auto insurance [4]. Furthermore, detecting health insurance fraud involves numerous challenges: information is often lacking or of poor quality, and reporting fraud can be arduous and cost-inefficient, resulting in high investigation costs and delays in legal action [5]. Fraudsters also evolve and adapt their strategies, making it difficult to analyze large volumes of overlapping data [6]. This is compounded by the lack of real-time detection [7] and the high costs of triage [8], which require human intervention to resolve doubtful claims [9]. Despite these efforts, it is estimated that $100 billion USD is lost annually to fraud, waste, and abuse in the U.S. healthcare system alone [2].

Methods for detecting health insurance fraud (HIF) require a deep understanding of the ecosystem in which it occurs. Five fundamental, interrelated elements are identified: (1) the conditions that define fraud as an intentional act that violates the law to obtain an illicit benefit [10]; (2) the actors who commit it (insurers, policyholders, and healthcare providers); (3) the specific manifestations of fraud for each actor; (4) the factors (macro, meso-, and microenvironmental) that influence fraudulent behavior; and (5) the key processes where fraud occurs (enrollment, service delivery, and billing/payment). The interaction of these elements is dynamic and adaptive. Figure 1 conceptualizes these relationships, providing an essential framework for designing robust detection strategies.

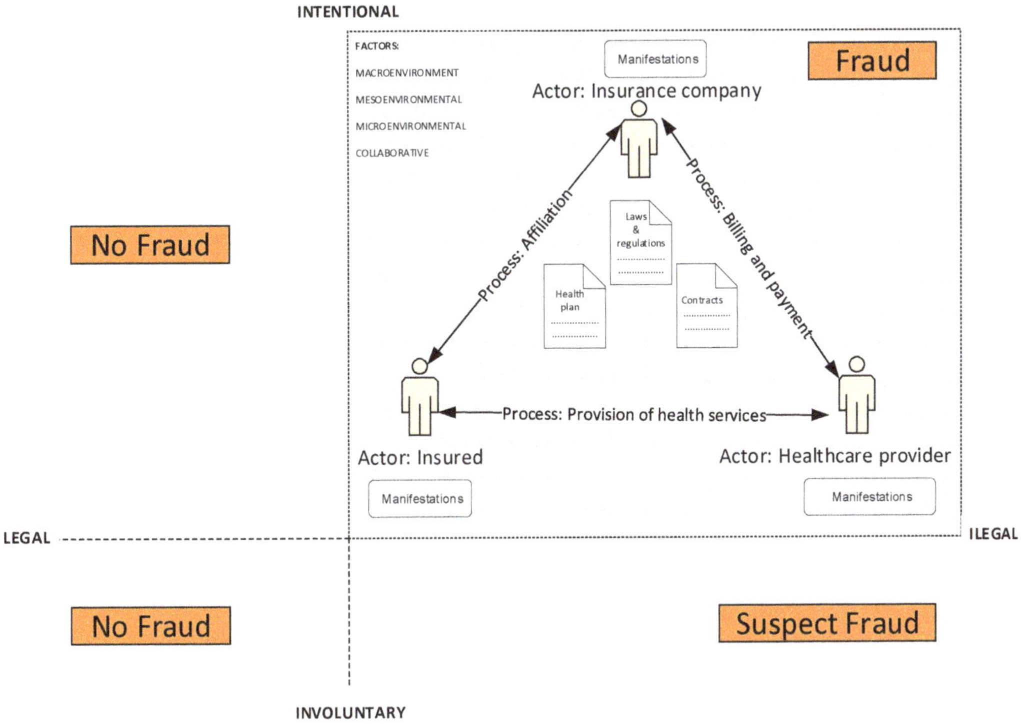

Figure 1. Diagram of the elements of health insurance fraud.

Furthermore, CRISP-DM exhibits low levels of adherence, which becomes evident when applied to highly complex domains such as health insurance fraud (HIF), given that its generalist and industry-independent nature lacks the necessary flexibility and operational focus [11,12]; this limitation is corroborated in the analysis of the 12 representative studies in Table 1, where although supervised machine learning (SML) techniques have become established as key tools for identifying suspicious patterns, significant methodological shortcomings persist, so the authors prefer to use ad hoc methodologies.

Table 1. Summary of previous studies on HIF detection based on SMLs.

Autor	Country | Database (Size)	Algorithm	Balancing Method	Accuracy	Precision	AUC	Recall	Specificity	F1 Score	DM Methodology
[13]	Chile | Banmédica SA, claims (500,000), abusive (169).	ANN–MLP	NR	NR	NR	82.0%	73.4%	NR	91.0%	Ad hoc
[14]	Taiwan | NHI (1,050,979 patients y 17,668 providers)	LR	NR	84.6%			NR			Ad hoc
		ANN		91.5%						
		DT		98.7%						
[15]	US | Medicaid US Wisconsin (Medication for 190 beneficiaries)	DT-CHAID	NR	95.3%	91.9%	NR	87.2%	96.5%	NR	Ad hoc
[16]	US | Medicare y Medicaid (182,809 invoices)	SVM	NR	99.0%	NR	NR	NR	NR	NR	Ad hoc
[6]	Republic of Korea | HIRA (3075 internal medicine providers)	DT-CDA Score				NR				Ad hoc
[17]	US | Medicare Part A, B, D (759,267 nonfraud, 473 fraud)	LR	SMOTE	NR		82.8%		NR		Ad hoc
		RF	RUS			82.8%				
		XGB	RUS			81.7%				
[18]	US | Nine datasets from Medicare part B, part D, DMEPOS.	XGB		NR		95.4%	84.9%	95.7%	NR	CRISP-DM
		RF				87.2%	NR			
		XGB				95.9%	86.2%	96.8%		
		RF				80.2%	NR			
		XGB				95.0%	85.5%	96.9%		
		RF				83.8%	NR			
[19]	US | Medicare Part D (5,344,106 instances, 0.07% fraud)	CATB		NR		95.7%		NR		Ad hoc
		XGB				95.6%				
		RF				86.4%				
		LGBM				84.8%				
		ET				84.1%				
		LR				83.5%				
	US | Medicare Part B (8,669,497 instances, 0.05% fraud)	CATB		NR		95.9%		NR		
		XGB				94.7%				
		RF				84.6%				
		LGBM				85.0%				
		ET				86.1%				
		LR				91.4%				
[20]	Saudi Arabia | Three providers from 2022	RF	SMOTE	98.2%	98.1%	90.0%	100.0%	80.0%	99.0%	Ad hoc
		LR	SMOTE	80.4%	97.6%	80.2%	80.4%	80.0%	88.2%	
		ANN	SMOTE	94.6%	98.0%	88.0%	96.1%	80.0%	97.0%	
[21]	US | Exclusive dataset (558,000).	RF	NR	92.4%	95.6%	90.7%	83.8%	NR	89.3%	Ad hoc
		XGB		91.7%	97.4%	96.2%	80.4%		88.1%	
		SVM		81.8%	81.6%	87.6%	67.1%		73.7%	
		IF		62.6%	51.5%	40.6%	21.9%		30.8%	
		DLM		91.7%	94.8%	90.9%	65.1%		77.2%	
		SEM		92.8%	93.6%	97.0%	86.9%		90.2%	
[22]	US | Medicare US Part B (9,449,361)	LR	SMOTE-ENN and cross-validation	65.0%	69.0%	73.0%	67.0%	NR	65.0%	Ad hoc
		DT		100.0%	99.0%	95.0%	100.0%		100.0%	
		RF		95.0%	95.0%	99.0%	95.0%		95.0%	
		XGB		96.0%	96.0%	99.0%	96.0%		96.0%	
		AdaGB		65.0%	70.0%	68.0%	67.0%		64.0%	
		LGBM		91.0%	90.0%	97.0%	91.0%		91.0%	

Table 1. *Cont.*

Autor	Country | Database (Size)	Algorithm	Balancing Method	Accuracy	Precision	AUC	Recall	Specificity	F1 Score	DM Methodology
[23]	China | Tianchi Precision Social Security Competition: Real Health Insurance Data (NR)	LR	D.Samp.	NR	95.6%	NR	73.0%	NR	82.8%	Ad hoc
		XGB	D.Samp.		81.1%		86.9%		83.9%	
		LR	SMOTE		95.8%		78.3%		86.2%	
		XGB	SMOTE		91.2%		90.3%		90.8%	
		LR	BSMOTE		95.6%		80.5%		87.4%	
		XGB	BSMOTE		92.6%		86.9%		89.6%	
		LR	GAN		93.8%		72.8%		81.9%	
		XGB	GAN		94.4%		96.4%		95.4%	

NR: Not reported. NHI: National Health Insurance. DM: Data mining. LR: Logistic regression. DT: decision tree. RF: random forest. IF: isolation forest. DLM: Deep learning Model. SVM: Support Vector Machine. SEM: stacking ensemble model. XGB: extreme gradient boosting. CATB: Categorical boosting. AdaGB: Adaptive boosting. LGBM: Light gradient boosting machine. ANN: artificial neural network. MLP: Multilayer perceptron. CHAID: Chi-square automatic interaction detection. HIRA: Health Insurance Review Agency. BSMOTE: Borderline synthetic minority-oversampling technique. D.Samp: Downsampling is a technique for reducing the size of the majority class and balancing an unbalanced dataset.

Initially, studies focused on accuracy, a metric that can be misleading in datasets with class imbalance. This led to the adoption of more robust metrics, such as the F1 score. Since 2018, there has been a trend toward incorporating data balancing techniques to mitigate model bias [17,22]. Despite these advances, the review reveals a fundamental methodological gap: most studies use ad hoc approaches. Only one study has applied the cross-sector standard process for data mining (CRISP-DM) methodology [18], and there is no standardized machine learning framework adapted to the specificities of high-intensity factors (HIFs). This methodological deficiency results in algorithms trained without clearly identifying the context in which they operate, their manifestations, or associated factors.

Therefore, the objective of this study is to propose and validate a systematic methodology for developing SML models for detecting suspicious claims in health insurance. To demonstrate its effectiveness, we applied this methodology in a case study using data from a public health insurance system in Peru.

2. Materials and Methods

Part A: We present the PDHIF (Phases for Detecting Health Insurance Fraud) methodology, a systematic approach designed for the complete lifecycle of health insurance fraud detection. Unlike general methodologies such as CRISP-DM, a recognized standard for data mining [12], the PDHIF is specific to health insurance fraud detection and consists of six phases: (1) identifying indicators of fraud; (2) identifying the manifestations associated with the actors and integrating data by associating the available variables with the factors of health insurance fraud; (3) preprocessing—which includes data cleaning, transformation, and preparation—and data balancing; (4) developing, training, and evaluating the health insurance fraud model; (5) deploying and operational integration; and (6) adaptive monitoring and evolution (Table 2). These phases not only enable more effective and efficient detection of medical malpractice (MMP) but also facilitate a better understanding of the phenomenon and continuous system improvement through feedback and model refinement. Unlike previous approaches, this method is based on the fundamental principles of machine learning and introduces significant improvements tailored to the specific challenges of the MMP. Its systematic design encompasses everything from understanding fraud to adaptive monitoring, integrating components such as identifying manifestations associated with the actors, data preprocessing and balancing, training supervised models, and their operational deployment. This ensures greater accuracy in identifying fraudulent patterns and constant evolution in response to changes in the healthcare environment. Figure 2 illustrates the complete workflow, which is detailed in the six phases described in Table 2.

Table 2. Detailed description of the phases of the PDHIF methodology.

Phase	Description
Phase 1. Identifying signs of fraud	First, we consider the theoretical framework. According to the definition of SML [10], fraud cannot be asserted without verifying intent and the obtaining of illegal benefits. In other words, "HIF is an act based on intentional deception or misrepresentation to obtain illegal benefits related to the coverage provided by health insurance." Since intent cannot be determined at this stage, it is possible to analyze noncompliance with the regulatory framework and local regulations, which could generate suspicion. This suspicion could correspond to potential fraud. Second, we consider the local socioeconomic dynamics specific to the health sector and their direct influence on SML. To do this, we must analyze the elements defined in fraud theory, using the Fraud Triangle [24], the Fraud Diamond [25], and MICE (Minimum Incentives, Comprehensive Care, and Enterprises) [26], COSO (ERM), among others †.
Phase 2. Identifying available manifestations and factors	The manifestations of adverse health effects (AHS) are associated with the types of actors involved ‡, considering the study by Villegas-Ortega et al. (2021) [10] and the legal framework. This delimitation facilitates a more precise and operational analysis, focused on evidence rather than empirical or abstract categories, identifying concrete patterns according to the actor's profile: in the case of insurance companies (2 possible manifestations), policyholders (7), or medical providers (12). Similarly, the 47 AHS factors § SML [10] available in transactional (claims, invoices) and/or nontransactional (regulatory reports, surveys) data are identified. This phase ensures the coverage of the factors (variables) associated with AHS in the case study.
Phase 3. Data preprocessing and balancing	Data are prepared for analysis through a process that includes cleaning (duplicate removal, error correction, and handling of missing values), transformation (categorical variable coding and format standardization), and normalization (data scaling to ensure comparability). Additionally, transactions are labeled as fraudulent or legitimate, and the compatibility of clinical standards (ICD-10, CPT) is validated across heterogeneous systems. Because SML datasets are often unbalanced—with an SMLll proportion of fraudulent cases compared to legitimate ones—traditional techniques such as overrandom sampling or undersampling are avoided due to their risk of overfitting or loss of information. Instead, advanced methods such as SMOTE or others are applied, combined with other high-dimensionality techniques, allowing for category balancing and optimizing the model's predictive capacity.
Phase 4. Model development, training, and evaluation	In this phase, the model is trained using SML, with a stratified division of the collected data (Phase 3) into training, validation, and test sets. The process includes cross-validation to ensure robustness and hyperparameter fitting, optimizing metrics for unbalanced problems such as AUC-ROC (to assess discriminatory capacity between classes), Recall (maximizing the detection of true positives), and F1-Score (balancing accuracy and completeness). The final evaluation is performed with the test set, ensuring that the reported metrics reflect real-world performance with unseen data, thus validating the model's effectiveness in identifying fraud patterns under real-world operating conditions.

Table 2. *Cont.*

Phase	Description
Phase 5. Deployment and Operational Integration	The model is implemented in a production environment using a scalable architecture that supports both real-time and batch processing, ensuring its integration with existing systems. To maximize its operational utility, automated workflows are established where transactions classified as suspicious are routed to the specialized investigation team (auditors, tax officials, and SML specialists) to confirm fraud, prioritizing cases with a higher probability of fraud. In addition, security protocols (data encryption, access control) are implemented, and best practices for fraud detection are established and implemented.
Phase 6. Adaptive Monitoring and Evolution	A continuous monitoring system for the SML detection model's performance is implemented, with automated alerts on key metrics (F1 score, recall, false positive rate) to ensure the model remains current in identifying new fraud patterns. To this end, periodic model retraining cycles are performed, incorporating new factors or manifestations based on regulatory changes, as well as false positive/negative reports from the research team. The integration of these components guarantees that the system evolves in tandem with fraudulent tactics and regulatory frameworks, preserving its accuracy in dynamic healthcare environments.

ICD-10: Classification of Diseases, 10th Revision; CPT: current procedural terminology; SMOTE: synthetic minority oversampling technique. † The Fraud Triangle [24] examines three pillars: pressure (e.g., the economic need of patients or providers), opportunity (weak controls in billing or medical records), and rationalization (perception of impunity or ethical justifications); the Fraud Diamond [25], adds a fourth element: capability (technical skills to evade systems, such as mastery of diagnostic codes); MICE classifies motivations as money, ideology, coercion, or ego (such as physicians who falsify diagnoses out of "altruism"); and COSO ERM (2017) provides tools for designing proactive controls (e.g., detection algorithms). ‡ INSURANCE COMPANY: M1. Falsifying benefit or service statements; M2. Falsifying reimbursements. INSURED: M3. Using an incorrect diagnosis; M4. Document manipulation; M5. Billing for services not provided; M6. Opportunistic Fraud; M7. Identity fraud; M8. Doctor shopping; M9. Misrepresenting eligibility. HEALTH CARE PROVIDER: M10. Upcoding; M11. Unperformed; M12. Falsifies the diagnosis or treatment; M13. Soliciting, offering, or receiving a kickback; M14. Unbundling or exploding charges; M15. Falsify medical documents or records; M16. Unjustified services, Overutilization; M17. Opportunistic fraud; M18. Repeat billing for the same service provided; M19. Readmission/admission; M20. Type of room Charge; M21. Services were canceled but contained discounts and professional courtesies. § MACRO FACTORS: F1. Regulations and Norms; F2. Socioeconomic and political conditions; F3. Infrastructure; F4. Culture; F5. Complexity of health systems; F6. Geography. MESO FACTORS: F7. Characteristics of the provider; F8. Provider responsibility; F9. Measures of the administrative authority; F10. Internal disciplinary mechanisms; F11. Payment methods and contracts; F12. Medical records; F13. Auditing, supervision, sanctions, and control; F14. Quality and performance evaluation system; F15. Reputation; F16. Commercial implications; F17. Claims management and policy; F18. Reimbursement processes; F19. Employability; F20. Patient identification mechanisms; F21. Types of professionals. MICRO FACTORS: F22. Gender; F23. Age; F24. Predominant race; F25. Marital status; F26. Place of residence; F27. Having insurance status; F28. Predominant language; F29. Diagnoses; F30. Medical and surgical treatments; F31. Specialties; F32. Medications; F33. Chronic condition; F34. Risk of illness; F35. Ethics and morals; F36. Perception of inequity and injustice; F37. Information asymmetry; F38. The adjusters' decision; F39. Capacity building; F40. Deductibles/coinsurance; F41. Economic situation. COLLABORATIVE FACTORS: F42. Professional and patient; F43. Provider and insurer; F44. Consumer and provider; F45. Consumer and insurer; F46. Bosses and employed; F47. The Guanxi., which is a Chinese term that describes the basic dynamics of networks of contacts and personal influence.

Part B: We empirically validated the PDHIF methodology by applying the steps in Table 2 in a case study using data from Peru's main public insurer, Seguro Integral de Salud (SIS), which covers 26.3 million people, which is equivalent to 77.2% of the Peruvian population. In total, 12.9 million people receive medical care, generating approximately 93 million services annually [27]. The volume of these transactions implies a high risk of fraud. For the budget allocated by the Ministry of Economy and Finance [28] to this health insurance program, considering estimates ranging from 3% to 10% [1], annual losses due to fraud would amount to between USD 18.6 and 61.8 million. This highlights the urgent need to implement effective fraud detection and prevention solutions. Notably, SIS has previously developed medical auditing efforts for detecting nonconformities on the basis of artificial intelligence. In this context, the first four phases of the PDHIF methodology are implemented to demonstrate its applicability.

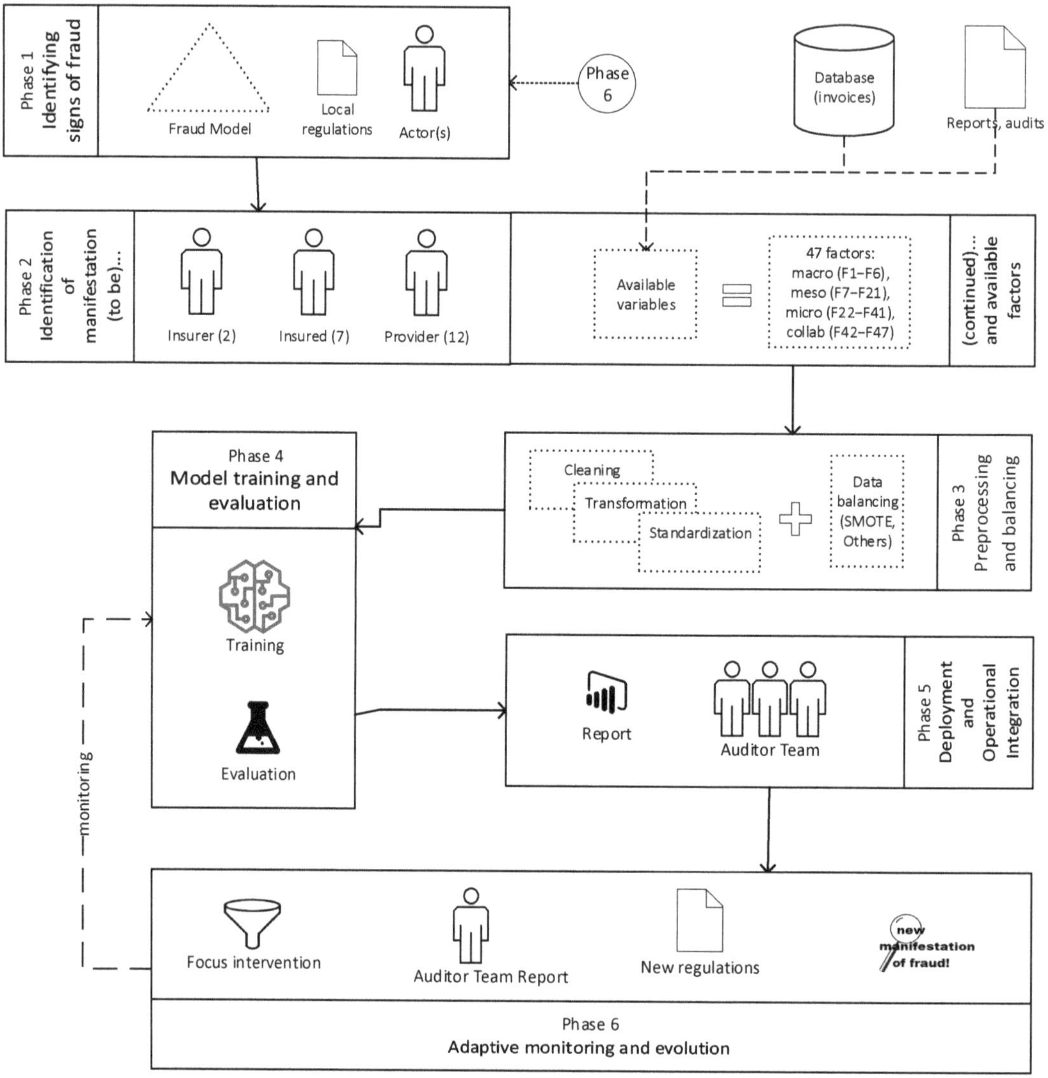

Figure 2. Diagram of the 6-phase PDHIF methodology.

2.1. Phase 1—Identifying Signs of Fraud

The SIS operates under a regulatory framework that establishes three audit processes for healthcare services recorded in single care forms (FUA): automatic supervision (PSA), electronic medical supervision (SME), and post-appointment onsite control (PCPP). Noncompliance with these protocols is considered a suspected case of malpractice. The PSA is governed by resolutions No. 185-2009-SIS/J, No. 192-2016-SIS/J, and No. 000051-2024-SIS/J, which define 46 consistency rules and 27 automated validation rules [29]. The SME, regulated by Directive No. 001-2017-SIS/GNF-V.01 and Resolutions No. 210-2018/SIS and No. 000051-2024-SIS/J, oversees healthcare services, budget management, and the replenishment of supplies. Its implementation is limited, given the partial review of the FUAs (Single Administrative Forms), which is carried out by approximately 58 medical auditors nationwide, leaving a significant proportion without thorough analysis [30]. The PCPP (Program for the Quality of Healthcare Services), established by Resolutions No. 006-2016/SIS and No. 231-2022-SIS/J, evaluates the quality of services in person [31], which also generates the need for specialized personnel, travel expenses, and per diem allowances.

In Peru, local socioeconomic dynamics significantly influence the SML, including low salaries for medical personnel [32], citizen insecurity, institutional distrust (92% of the population distrusts Congress and 83% the Ministry of the Interior and limits the effectiveness of audits and sanctions [33,34], systematic and political corruption (exemplified by convicted and imprisoned presidents), and judicial impunity. These factors weaken control mechanisms and create an environment conducive to fraudulent practices [33,35]. In this context, we analyze the fraud triangle theory, which focuses on the provider, who operates under political, economic, and labor pressures. This can motivate suspicious practices such as referring patients to private clinics, overbilling them for services, excessive prescription of medications, or fabricating charges for procedures not performed. Opportunities for fraud include the ability to manipulate information and knowledge of the process and regulatory ambiguity. Rationalization, on the other hand, is based on the cultural normalization of fraud, expressed in phrases such as "everyone does it," the perception of impunity due to weak controls, a low probability of detection, and the normalization of lax data entry practices.

2.2. *Phase 2—Identification of Available Manifestations and Factors*

From the Phase 1 analysis, the reviewers (D.M., J.C.A., J.V., W.C.M.) selected 12 supplier-related statements [10]. In Table 3, the reviewers subsequently worked in pairs to confirm the supplier statements, considering the regulations and information from the audited FUAs. In cases of discrepancies, a third reviewer participated in the decision to identify potential statements (L.Q.A., R.D.). A statement will be recorded as ELIGIBLE if, within the context of the SIS, there is any possibility of suspected fraud that violates any PSA, SME, or PCPP regulations identified in Phase 1 and has a variable recorded in the FUA. Otherwise, it is considered UNELIGIBLE. Table 3a presents the five eligible supplier statements. Additionally, 10 SML factors associated with 23 available variables (selected = yes) from the FUAs were mapped (Table 3b); these variables make up the RLIMA-CE dataset.

Table 3. (**a**). Selection of supplier manifestations. (**b**). Factors and Variables Available for the Case Study.

(a)		
Manifestation	**Justification**	**Result**
M10	This involves billing for services under diagnostic and procedure codes that are more expensive than those actually performed. The PSA detects this through automated validation rules, and medical appropriateness is determined in the SME; both are linked to the FUA.	ELIGIBLE
M11	The SME identifies cases by detecting FUAs without support in clinical or surgical reports, medical signatures or laboratory results; if such a situation is found, the FUA is marked as a charge for procedures never performed.	ELIGIBLE
M12	The PCPP assesses the consistency between the diagnosis and the reported treatment. These irregularities are marked in the FUAs as observations, which may indicate fraud, making the individual a candidate for the SML.	ELIGIBLE

Table 3. *Cont.*

(a)

Manifestation	Justification	Result
M13	None of the SIS audit processes suggest the identification of suppliers with possible bribes or illegal commissions, nor are they marked in the FUAS because illegitimate payments cannot be identified, so this statement is not selected.	UNELIGIBLE
M14	Through automatic consistency rules, the PSA blocks these cases by detecting repetitive charges for separate procedures, which is complemented by the SME, since it considers the analysis of specialized clinical cases, so there are records marked with such observations, which justifies including it.	ELIGIBLE
M15	The PCPP verifies inconsistencies in dates, seals, or protocols by comparing clinical records with validated standards; however, it does not record the falsification of certificates, medical records, or alteration of documents to justify payments.	UNELIGIBLE
M16	The SME detects anomalies such as multiple diagnostic support procedures in short periods, cross-referencing data with medical records to validate their justification, marking the FUAS with unjustified services or overutilization.	ELIGIBLE
M17	The PSA, with automated validation, identifies atypical claims (e.g., oxygen registered in liters instead of cubic meters) by comparing with historical profiles of patients and providers; however, with the FUAS, it cannot be guaranteed that it is an opportunistic fraud.	UNELIGIBLE
M18	The PSA applies consistency rules, blocking duplicate FUAS for the same patient during overlapping periods, thus validating the uniqueness of procedures. However, no FUAS records are flagged.	UNELIGIBLE
M19	None of the SIS audit processes analyzes readmissions or unnecessary admissions or repeated hospitalizations without clinical improvement.	UNELIGIBLE
M20	Charges for unused room types, billing for stays in unassigned rooms. The SIS does not monitor charges for unused room types or billing for stays in unassigned rooms.	UNELIGIBLE
M21	The SIS does not foresee canceled services with discounts in its audit processes.	UNELIGIBLE

(b)

Category	Factor of SML	Available Variables	Type	Selected Variables
Key identifiers		V01. Anonymized FUA number	Alphanumeric	Yes
		V02. FUA Identifier	Numeric	No
		V03. Year of production	Numeric	No
		V04. Production month	Alphanumeric	No
Demographic Data	F22. Gender	V05. Patient's sex	Numeric	Yes
	F23. Age	V06. Patient's age	Numeric	Yes
Supplier details		V07. SIS Macro-Regional Management	Numeric	No
		V08. UDR	Numeric	No

Table 3. *Cont.*

(b)				
Category	**Factor of SML**	**Available Variables**	**Type**	**Selected Variables**
Supplier details		V09. Department	Numeric	No
		V10. Implementing Unit	Numeric	No
	F7. Supplier details	V11. Supplier code	Alphanumeric	Yes
		V12. Supplier category	Alphanumeric	No
Service Details		V13. Service provision	Alphanumeric	Yes
		V14. Destination at high	Numeric	Yes
		V15. Date of service	Temporary	No
		V16. Hospital start date	Temporary	No
		V17. Date of hospital discharge	Temporary	No
	F31. Specialty	V18. Type of Care	Numeric	Yes2
		V19. Hospital Stay	Numeric	Yes2
	F29. Diagnosis F33. Chronic health condition	V20. ICD-10 Primary Diagnosis	Alphanumeric	No
		V21. Diagnostic Profile: ICD-10	Numeric	Yes2
		V22. Number of diagnoses	Numeric	Yes2
		V23. Healthcare Personnel	Alphanumeric	Yes
Economic variables	F18. Refund processes and billing features	V24. Gross valuation of the FUA	Numeric	No
		V25. Gross Value of Procedures	Numeric	Yes
		V26. Gross value of medicines	Numeric	Yes
		V27. Gross value of inputs	Numeric	Yes
Consumption	F30. Medical and surgical treatments	V28. Procedure Consumption Profile	Numeric	Yes2
		V29. Number of FUA Procedures	Numeric	Yes2
		V30. Input Consumption Profile	Numeric	Yes2
		V31. Number of FUA Inputs	Numeric	Yes2

Table 3. *Cont.*

(b)				
Category	**Factor of SML**	**Available Variables**	**Type**	**Selected Variables**
Consumption	F32. Medicine	V32. Medication Consumption Profile	Numeric	Yes2
		V33. FUA Drug Number	Numeric	Yes2
		V34. Type of Consumption (FUA Details)	Alphanumeric	No
		V35. CPMS/SISMED Code (FUA Details)	Alphanumeric	No
		V36. Amount delivered (FUA Details)	Numeric	No
	F13. Audit, supervision, sanction, and control	V37. Marking for PCPP in SME	Numeric	Yes
		V38. Number of FUA rules observed in PSA	Numeric	Yes
		V39. PSA result	Numeric	No
		V40. SME result	Numeric	No
		V41. PCPP result	Numeric	No
		V42. Suspicion Marking	Numeric	Yes2
				Yes = 23

ICD-10: International Statistical Classification of Diseases, 10th Edition; CPMS: Catalog of Medical and Health Procedures in the health sector based on the international terminology "Current Procedural Terminology"; SISMED: Integrated Supply System for Pharmaceutical Products, Medical Devices and Health Products; UDR: Regional decentralized unit; Yes: the variable is considered; No: the variable is not considered; Considered for filtering each dataset: V07 and V12. 2: Newly calculated variables that replace and synthesize others; V18 Type of hospital care: a value of 1 is assumed if V16 and V17 have information; otherwise, its value is 0 (outpatient); V19 Hospital stay is determined as the difference in days between V17 and V16; V21 Diagnostic Profile: This considers all the ICD-10 diagnoses from the FUA concatenated and ordered (Dx 1 + Dx 2 + ... + Dx n). These form different diagnostic profiles; however, owing to the high cardinality, an encoding is applied that represents the frequency of the diagnostic profile; V22 is determined by counting the number of different diagnoses given in V21; V28 Procedure Consumption Profile: This considers all procedures registered with concatenated and ordered FUA CPMS codes where V34 = 'P' [(V35 Proc1 + V36 Cant1) + (V35 Proc2 + V36 Cant2) +...+ (V35 Procn + V36 Cantn)]. These form different clinical procedure consumption profiles; however, owing to the high cardinality, an encoding is applied that represents the frequency of the procedure consumption profile; V29 is the frequency of unique CPMS codes recorded in V35. V30 Input Consumption Profile: This considers all inputs registered with SISMED codes from the FUA, concatenated and ordered, where V34 = 'I' [(V35 Insu1 + V36 Cant1) + (V35 Insu2 + V36 Cant2) +...+ (V35 Insun + V36 Cantn)]. These form different input consumption profiles; however, owing to the high cardinality, an encoding is applied that represents the frequency of the input consumption profile; V31 is the frequency of unique SISMED codes corresponding to supplies registered in V35. V32 Medication Consumption Profile: This considers all medications registered with SISMED codes from the FUA, concatenated and ordered, where V34 = 'M' [(V35 Medi1 + V36 Cant1) + (V35 Medi2 + V36 Cant2) + ... + (V35 Medin + V36 Cantn)]. These form different medication consumption profiles; however, owing to the high cardinality, an encoding is applied that represents the frequency of the medication consumption profile; V33 is the frequency of unique SISMED codes corresponding to medications registered in V35. V42 Suspicion Marking, a variable outcome constructed on the basis of the evaluation of the audit processes: PSA, SME and PCPP.

2.3. Phase 3—Data Preprocessing and Balancing

We considered the available variables associated with the factors of Phase 2. The records include FUAs from 2023 and 2024 corresponding to public providers of the third level of care in the Metropolitan Lima Center and East China. This level provides care for rare problems and complex pathologies that require specialized and high-technology procedures. These data make up the original dataset called RLIMA-CE.

RLIMA-CE was preprocessed in three stages: cleaning, transformation, and normalization. Initially, 42 independent variables corresponding to the provider's domains were processed. During cleaning, the following were removed: V02–V04, because they identify the FUAs; V07 and V12, because they are considered in the filtering of each dataset; V08–V09, because they identify regional records; V10, because it is represented in V11; V15, because it is not necessary for a classification problem; V16–V17, because it is represented in V18; V20, because it is included in V21; V34–V36, because they are included in V28–V33; and V39–V41, because they are synthesized in V42.

In the data transformation phase, clinical codes, such as the International Classification of Diseases (ICD-10) for diagnoses, the Catalog of Medical and Health Procedures (CPMS) for procedures, and the Integrated System for the Supply of Medicines and Medical-Surgical Supplies (SISMED) for supplies and medicines, were standardized to ensure consistency. Variables V21, V28, V30, and V32 underwent frequency encoding, whereas V22, V29, and V31 were transformed by counting unique codes. Finally, the independent variable V42 was created from an evaluation of the PSA, SME, and PCPP audit processes: it was labeled "1" if there was an observation (suspected fraud) and "0" if the record was legitimate. Upsampling was considered for the minority class via historical records (2019–2022), thus allowing these markings from previous years to be leveraged. The variables were not normalized because we used decision tree-based algorithms.

To understand the effectiveness of the PDHIF methodology, two experimental scenarios were created: Scenario 1, a preprocessed dataset of 23 variables and unbalanced; and Scenario 2, a preprocessed dataset of 23 variables and balanced, for which the balancing K-Means SMOTE was implemented, which was successful, achieving a balanced distribution of classes in all segments, resulting in a dataset of 16,648,713 records and 23 variables (Table 4).

Table 4. Original dataset features and scenarios.

DATASET: RLIMA-CE			
Observations and Variables	**Original Dataset**	**Scenery 1 Preprocessed and Not Balanced**	**Scenery 2 Preprocessed and Balanced**
Variables	42	23	23
Records	8,453,846 (100.0%)	8,453,846 (100.0%)	16,648,713 (100.0%)
Records with suspicions	129,490 (1.5%)	129,490 (1.5%)	8,324,356 (50.0%)
Legitimate records	8,324,356 (98.5%)	8,324,356 (98.5%)	8,324,357 (50.0%)

RLIMA-CE: This includes public tertiary care hospitals reserved for the treatment of rare problems and complex pathologies requiring specialized and high-tech procedures in Central Metropolitan Lima and East Metropolitan Lima.

To operationalize the detection of suspicious claims, we selected three distinct supervised learning algorithms based on their widespread adoption in fraud detection literature and their differing learning capabilities [21,22]. Random Forest (RF) is an ensemble method that constructs a multitude of decision trees during training. It operates on the principle of bagging (bootstrap aggregating), where the final prediction is the majority vote of the individual trees, making it highly robust to overfitting and noise [36]. Extreme Gradient Boosting (XGB) is a scalable implementation of gradient boosting machines; unlike RF, XGB builds trees sequentially, where each new tree attempts to correct the errors of the previous ones. It employs a regularized objective function to control model complexity and utilizes a sparsity-aware algorithm to handle missing data effectively [37]. Multilayer Perceptron (MLP) is a feedforward artificial neural network consisting of at least three layers of nodes: an input layer, a hidden layer, and an output layer. It utilizes backpropagation for training and non-linear activation functions, allowing it to model complex, non-linear relationships within high-dimensional data [38]. Finally, to address the class imbalance, we utilized K-Means SMOTE. Unlike standard SMOTE, which interpolates between nearest neighbors regardless of data distribution, K-Means SMOTE first clusters the data using k-means and then applies oversampling only in safe clusters. This approach prevents the generation of noise and ensures that synthetic samples are generated in crucial areas of the minority class distribution.

For each scenario, the performance of three machine learning algorithms was trained and evaluated: random forest (RF), extreme gradient boosting (XGB), and multilayer perceptron (MLP). The data were randomly divided, with 70% for training and 30% for testing. Additionally, scenario 2 was balanced via the K-Means SMOTE technique with k = 2 (silhouette score = 0.9960) and subjected to 10-fold cross-validation. Model performance was assessed via five metrics: precision, recall (sensitivity), F1 score, accuracy, and AUC-ROC. After several iterations, the hyperparameters were defined (Table 5).

Table 5. SML Model Parameters for the RLIMA-CE Dataset.

RF Hyperparameters	XGB Hyperparameters	MLP Hyperparameters
Max_depth: None Estimators: 200 Min_samples_split: 2 Min_samples_leaf: 1 Max_features = 'sqrt'	Max_depth = 7 Estimators = 300 Learning_rate = 0.1 Subsample = 1.0 Colsample_bytree = 1.0	Dropout = 0.2 Units = 64 Learning_rate = 0.001
Max_depth: None Estimators: 200 Min_samples_split: 2 Min_samples_leaf: 1 Max_features = 'sqrt'	Max_depth = 7 Estimators = 300 Learning_rate = 0.1 Subsample = 0.8 Colsample_bytree = 0.8	Dropout = 0.2 Units = 64 Learning_rate = 0.001

RF: random forest, XGB: extreme gradient boosting, and MLP: multilayer perceptron.

3. Results

This section may be divided by subheadings. It should provide a concise and precise description of the experimental results, their interpretation, and the experimental conclusions that can be drawn.

3.1. Phase 4—Model Development, Training, and Evaluation

3.1.1. Confusion Matrix

Visual analysis corroborates the numerical findings. In Scenario 1 (unbalanced data), Figure 3a–c reveal a critical deficiency in the models. A high number of false negatives (FNs) are observed, representing suspicious cases that the models fail to detect. Specifically, the RF model (Figure 3a) incorrectly classified 24,091 suspicious claims as legitimate, whereas XGB (Figure 3b) and MLP (Figure 3c) failed in 25,637 and 29,581 cases, respectively. This result demonstrates that, despite high overall accuracy, the models were practically ineffective for their primary purpose: identifying suspected fraud. In contrast, Scenario 2 (balanced data) illustrates improved performance. After the K-Means balancing technique, SMOTE was applied, and the number of false negatives was drastically reduced in all the models. The RF model (Figure 3d) now only failed in 14,341 cases, while it correctly identified over 2.48 million suspicious claims (true positives). Similarly, XGB (Figure 3e) and MLP (Figure 3f) demonstrated very robust detection capabilities, correctly identifying the vast majority of suspicious cases.

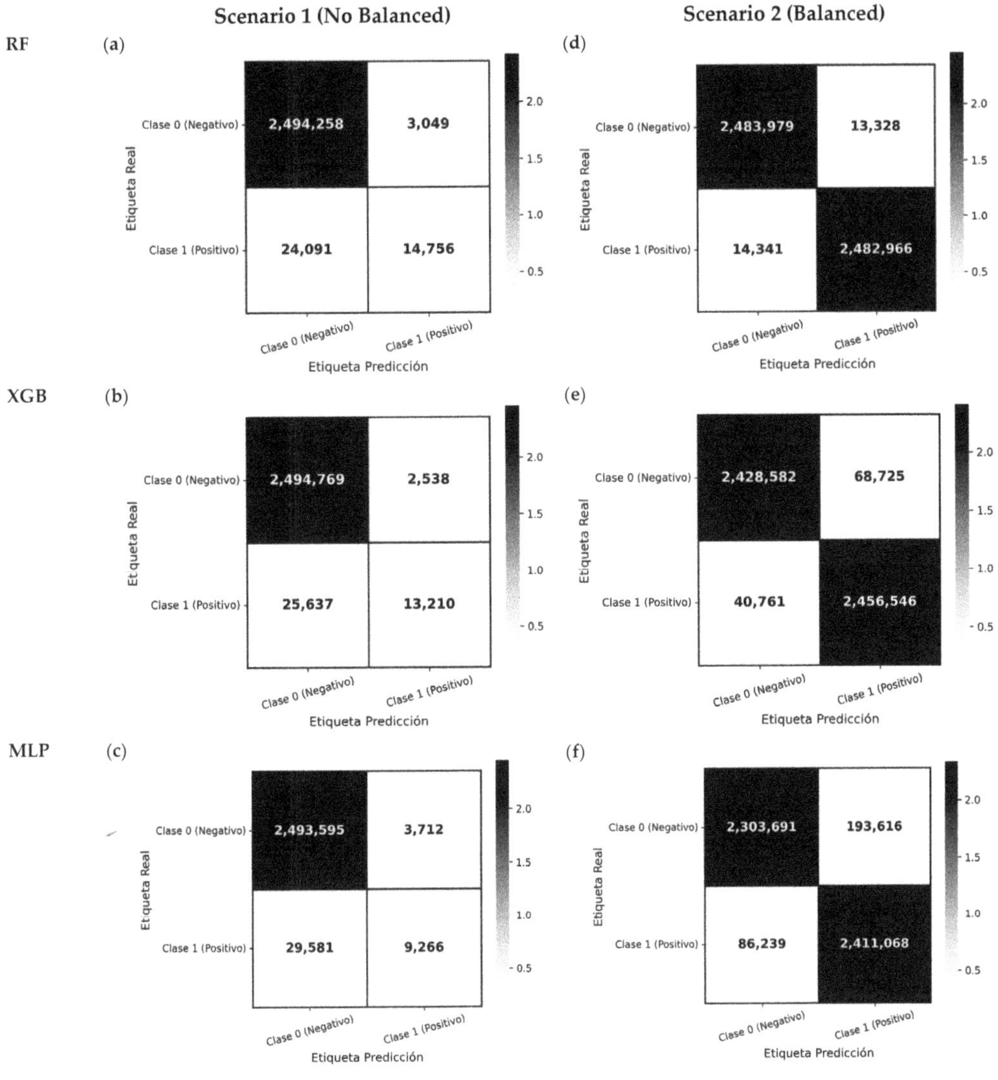

Figure 3. Confusion matrix: Scenario 1 ((**a**): RF, (**b**): XGB, (**c**): MLP). Scenario 2 ((**d**): RF, (**e**): XGB, (**f**): MLP).

3.1.2. Loss Function

Figure 4 shows the evolution of the loss function for the XGB (a and e) and MLP (c and g) models in both scenarios for both the training and validation sets. In all these cases, a clear convergence of the function is observed, indicating an effective learning process and optimal generalization capacity without overfitting. Notably, the XGB model demonstrated superior performance, consistently achieving lower loss values than the MLP in both scenarios. With respect to accuracy, XGB exhibits outstanding performance in both scenarios (b and f), with AUC curves that rise rapidly and remain very close together, indicating fast learning without overfitting. The MLP model also shows good learning, although a slight tendency toward overfitting can be observed in the balanced scenario (h) because of the separation between the curves.

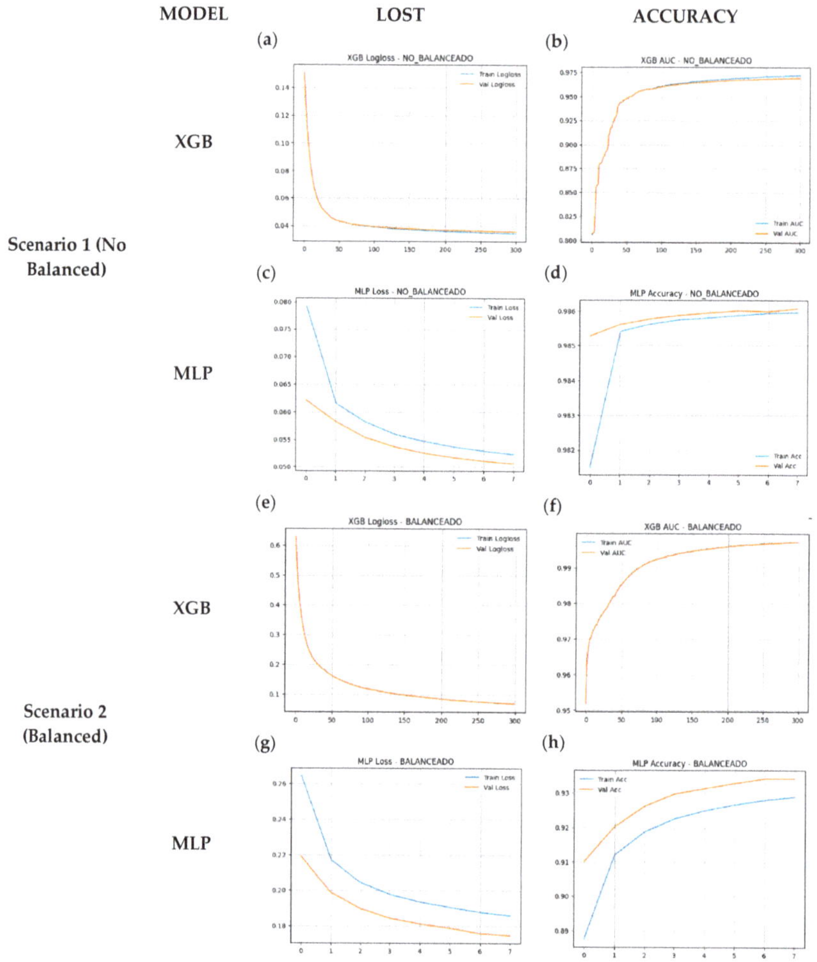

Figure 4. Loss function: Scenario 1 ((**a**): XGB; (**c**): MLP). Scenario 2 ((**e**): XGB; (**g**): MLP). Precision function: Scenario 1 ((**b**): XGB; (**d**): MLP). Scenario 2 ((**f**): XGB; (**h**): MLP).

3.1.3. Results of the Metrics

The metrics in Table 6 summarize the performance of the three models, RF, XGB, and MLP, in the two scenarios, with Scenario 2 being the most effective. In Scenario 1, although all the models have high accuracy (>0.98), their sensitivity values are very low, indicating that they are not effective at detecting suspicious claims. The RF model (F1 = 0.521) achieves the best balance, outperforming XGB (F1 = 0.484) and the MLP (F1 = 0.358). However, Scenario 2 (balanced) is clearly superior for all the models, consistently achieving accuracy, sensitivity, and F1 score metrics above 0.94, demonstrating the effectiveness of the balancing technique in improving the detection of the positive class. Within Scenario 2, the RF model remains the most robust model, with F1 = 0.994, slightly outperforming XGB (F1 = 0.978) and the MLP (F1 = 0.945). In conclusion, Scenario 2 (balanced) is the most suitable approach for this classification task, and the RF consistently performs best in both contexts.

Table 6. Key results from the models in both scenarios and Matthew's Correlation Coefficient (MCC).

Metrics	Scenario 1 (No Balanced)			Scenario 2 (Balanced)		
	RF	XGB	MLP	RF	XGB	MLP
Precision_test	0.829	0.839	0.714	0.995	0.973	0.926
Recall_test	0.380	0.340	0.239	0.994	0.984	0.965
F1_test	0.521	0.484	0.358	0.994	0.978	0.945
Accuracy_test	0.989	0.989	0.987	0.994	0.978	0.944
MCC test	0.5569	0.5300	0.4079	0.9889	0.9562	0.8888

RF: random forest, XGB: extreme gradient boosting, and MLP: multilayer perceptron.

To complement the analysis, we incorporated the Matthews Correlation Coefficient (MCC) into our evaluation. Unlike accuracy—which can be misleading in highly skewed datasets—the MCC provides a more robust and discriminative assessment of model performance. In the non-balanced scenario, the models achieved MCC values ranging from 0.41 to 0.56, demonstrating that the classifiers were able to learn meaningful patterns despite the extreme skew in class distribution. After applying data balancing techniques, performance improved substantially, with MCC values between 0.89 and 0.99, confirming that the models capture the underlying structure of the problem effectively when trained on a more representative sample.

The high metrics observed in Scenario 2 reflect the model's ability to learn patterns within the balanced training space. However, we recognize that implementation in a real-world environment with highly skewed distributions may result in different performance dynamics.

4. Discussion

4.1. About the Methodology

While CRISP-DM provides a global standard for data mining, its generic application is insufficient to address the inherent complexities of health insurance fraud (HIF), as evidenced by its limited adoption in the reviewed previous studies (Table 1). The PDHIF methodology overcomes these limitations by departing from this general framework and integrating a domain-specific taxonomy that operationalizes fundamental theories, such as the Triangle or other fraud theories, directly into the feature engineering and preprocessing phases. Unlike the generalist approach of CRISP-DM, PDHIF explicitly incorporates the identification of actors (insurer, provider, insured) and the local regulatory frameworks that define legality, considering macro, meso, and micro environmental factors before the modeling phase. This conceptualization adds methodological value by reducing the "black box" nature of feature selection, ensuring that models are not only statistically valid but also contextually consistent with medical audit regulations.

PDHIF's systematic six-phase design transcends the technical detection of anomalies by enabling a contextualized understanding of fraudulent dynamics, especially in environments with systemic challenges of corruption and impunity, such as the Peruvian case. The methodology ensures the system's sustainability by including an operational deployment and adaptive monitoring phase (Phase 6), which facilitates periodic retraining cycles to incorporate new factors arising from regulatory changes and the evolution of fraudulent tactics. In this way, the PDHIF enhances the model's interpretive capacity and offers a robust, tailored solution that reflects the true complexity of health claims content, filling the existing methodological gap in the current literature.

Furthermore, the methodology effectively addresses key technical challenges, such as high-class imbalance, through advanced balancing techniques (SMOTE) and the selection of operationally focused evaluation metrics (F1 score, recall, and AUC-ROC). The inclusion of operational deployment phases and continuous monitoring ensures the system's sustainability in real-world scenarios, where evolving fraudulent tactics and regulatory changes necessitate periodic updates. Thus, the PDHIF positions itself as a robust and reproducible framework that combines analytical rigor with practicality, offering a solid foundation for implementation in healthcare systems with characteristics similar to those of the Peruvian case study.

4.2. Regarding the Case Study: SIS

The empirical validation of the PDHIF methodology in Peru's SIS demonstrates its effectiveness in addressing the real challenges of fraud detection in public health systems. The rigorous application of the initial phases allowed for the identification of specific manifestations of fraud among providers (M10, M11, M12, M14, M16) and their mapping to variables available in the single care forms (FUA), creating a representative dataset (KLIMA-CE) with 23 predictor variables associated with 10 factors (provider characteristics, gender, age, specialty, diagnosis, chronic condition, reimbursement, treatments, medication, and auditing). Data preprocessing, which included the creation of synthetic variables and frequency encoding, along with the application of the k-means SMOTE to balance the classes, proved fundamental in overcoming the extreme imbalance (1.5% of suspects), a typical condition in fraud cases that limits the effectiveness of conventional approaches.

The experimental results confirm the superiority of Scenario 2 (balanced), where the application of K-Means SMOTE proved decisive. In the unbalanced scenario, the high accuracy (>98%) masked a critically low sensitivity (<0.38) due to the algorithms' inherent bias toward the majority class. The introduction of synthetic samples fundamentally altered the decision boundaries, enabling the models to learn the structural features of fraud rather than treating them merely as statistical anomalies. Within this optimized context, RF emerged as the most robust algorithm (F1 = 0.994), outperforming XGBoost (F1 = 0.978) and the Multilayer Perceptron (F1 = 0.945). Theoretically, this dominance is attributed to RF's bagging mechanism, which reduces variance and exhibits greater resilience to label noise—a limitation inherent in data derived from administrative audits. In contrast, boosting methods like XGBoost can be prone to overfitting as they attempt to correct errors in noisy instances, while MLPs typically require significantly larger data volumes to converge effectively on tabular data. The operational validation of this approach is evidenced by the drastic reduction in false negatives (from 24,091 to 14,341 in the best-performing model). The robustness of the proposed methodology is further validated by the high MCC scores (>0.89) in the balanced scenario, confirming that the high F1 scores are not artifacts of the metric but reflect true discriminative power. This corroborates that combining advanced balancing techniques with ensemble algorithms constitutes an efficient solution, thereby establishing the first high-precision digital auditor for the Peruvian health system.

4.3. Limitations

This study has limitations in its scope of validation. First, the empirical application was limited to tertiary-level providers in Metropolitan Lima. Consequently, the specific predictive patterns identified may not be directly generalizable to other levels of complexity (such as primary care centers), the private sector, or rural regional contexts with different resource limitations and socioeconomic dynamics. However, the PDHIF methodology itself—specifically in its actor identification and factor mapping phases—is intrinsically designed to be adaptable. Therefore, broader implementation would require retraining the models via region-specific datasets, thus capturing the local variations inherent in healthcare service delivery.

Second, a significant limitation lies in the construction of the target variable (V42), derived from observations of the SIS administrative audit processes (PSA, SME, PCPP) and not from judicial verdicts. This introduces a risk of labeling bias, where models could learn to replicate preexisting 'audit patterns' instead of detecting novel fraud schemes that circumvent current controls. However, according to the definition of an HIF as obtaining illegal benefits through deception [10], the regulatory infractions detected by the SIS constitute a solid basis for illegitimacy. Therefore, the results should be interpreted as 'high-probability suspicious claims' that require human review, rather than being considered confirmed fraud. While future iterations should incorporate feedback loops to refine these labels, the proposed methodological framework (PDHIF) remains generally applicable and transferable to other contexts."

5. Conclusions

The PDHIF methodology proves to be a robust and systematic framework for detecting fraud in health insurance. Unlike the predominantly ad hoc approaches documented in the literature and traditional data mining methods, PDHIF introduces a holistic approach that integrates fraud theory, actors, manifestations, and factors with the complete lifecycle of supervised machine learning algorithms. Its validation in the real-world case of the SIS confirms its ability to operationalize clinical, operational, and economic variables in a highly accurate predictive model, with random forest emerging as the most effective algorithm (F1 score of 0.994) after the critical application of advanced balancing techniques.

The successful implementation of the first four phases of PDHIF in a highly complex and extremely unbalanced environment demonstrates its practical utility in transforming transactional data into actionable alerts and overcoming the limitations of traditional audit systems. This approach provides a reproducible basis for public and private institutions to implement proactive, scalable, and adaptive detection systems capable of optimizing the allocation of audit resources and mitigating significant financial losses.

Future Work

A crucial next step for operational integration is the development of an interpretability layer to elucidate the decision-making process of black-box models. Future work will incorporate explainable AI (XAI) techniques, such as Shapley additive explanations (SHAPs), to decompose the model's predictions, allowing medical auditors to understand which specific factors—for example, discrepancies between diagnoses and procedures or provider history—contribute to the suspicion score. This transparency is essential for increasing auditor confidence and developing effective prevention rules. Additionally, we plan to develop hybrid systems that combine the proposed supervised model with unsupervised approaches, thereby expanding the scope of fraud detection to include novel anomalies and emerging patterns.

To further mitigate the risks of overfitting and metric inflation associated with synthetic oversampling (SMOTE), future work will focus on evaluating the models on strictly unbalanced test sets that mimic real-time production flows. In addition, we plan to conduct comparative analyses via alternative handling techniques, such as undersampling, ADASYN, and cost-sensitive learning, to validate the robustness of the PDHIF.

Furthermore, to establish a more comprehensive baseline, future studies will expand the experimental section to include a wider range of algorithms, such as support vector machines (SVMs), LightGBM, and ensemble variations, thereby benchmarking the robustness of the PDHIF approach. Concurrently, we plan to investigate alternative imbalance-adaptive oversampling techniques, such as adaptive synthetic sampling (ADASYN), to compare their effectiveness against K-means SMOTE in preserving the underlying data distribution while optimizing minority class detection.

Author Contributions: J.V.-O.: Contributed to the conception of the study, conceptualization of the methodology, literature review, validation of the methodology in the case study, preprocessing design, algorithm selection, formal analysis, writing—original and editing. L.N.Q.A.: Contributed to the formal analysis of the method of machine learning in the case study, validation of the dataset and development of the classification model in the SIS operational environment. J.N.A.: Contributed to the construction of the machine learning method in the case study, construction of software, data curation of the dataset and development of the classification model in the SIS operational environment. W.C.M.: Contributed to the formal analysis of the method of machine learning in the case study, validation of the dataset and development of the classification model in the SIS operational environment. R.D.: Contributed to the application of the case study method, formal analysis, review and editing and funding acquisition. D.M.: Contributed to the conception of the study, supervision, conceptualization of the methodology, validation of the methodology in the case study, preprocessing design, algorithm selection, formal analysis, writing—original and editing. All authors have read and agreed to the published version of the manuscript.

Funding: This research was supported by the Universidad Nacional Mayor de San Marcos–RR N° 005446-2025 and project number C25202801.

Institutional Review Board Statement: Not applicable.

Informed Consent Statement: In accordance with international ethical guidelines for research involving anonymized secondary data, informed consent was not required. The study involved no direct interaction with patients, no intervention, and posed no risk to individual subjects.

Data Availability Statement: The data used for this case study, specifically the claims database of the Seguro Integral de Salud of Peru, are not publicly available due to the internal policies of the public institution, which prefers to keep these records confidential. However, the methodology detailed in the manuscript describes the entire process, and all results are based exclusively on the internal processing of these data by the collaborating institution. The data presented in this study are available on request from the corresponding author.

Acknowledgments: We wish to express our sincere gratitude to the Seguro Integral de Salud of Peru for its invaluable collaboration in providing data for the case study and for its commitment to applying the PDHIF methodology. This research would not have been possible without the institution's support and interest in implementing innovative solutions for fraud detection in the public health system.

Conflicts of Interest: J.V. worked at the Seguro Integral de Salud (SIS), and J.N.A., W.C.M. and L.Q.A. worked at the SIS. The other authors declare that they have no conflicts of interest. This project is the result of a collaboration between the SIS and the National University of San Marcos (UNMSM).

Abbreviations

The following abbreviations are used in this manuscript:

HIF	Health insurance fraud
SML	Supervised machine learning
PDHIF	Phases for Detecting Fraud in Health Insurance
CRISP-DM	Cross-sector standard process for data mining
ICD-10	Classification of Diseases, 10th Revision
CPT	Current procedural terminology
SMOTE	Synthetic minority oversampling technique
FUA	Single care forms
PSA	Automatic supervision
SME	Electronic medical supervision
PCPP	Post-appointment onsite control

References

1. Joudaki, H.; Rashidian, A.; Minaei-Bidgoli, B.; Mahmoodi, M.; Geraili, B.; Nasiri, M.; Arab, M. Improving fraud and abuse detection in general physician claims: A data mining study. *Int. J. Health Policy Manag.* **2016**, *5*, 165–172. [CrossRef]
2. U.S. Department of Justice Justice Manual. 976. Health Care Fraud—Generally. United States Department of Justice. Available online: https://www.justice.gov/archives/jm/criminal-resource-manual-976-health-care-fraud-generally (accessed on 6 April 2025).
3. Shrank, W.H.; Rogstad, T.L.; Parekh, N. Waste in the US Health Care System: Estimated Costs and Potential for Savings. *JAMA* **2019**, *322*, 1501. [CrossRef]
4. Kose, I.; Gokturk, M.; Kilic, K. An interactive machine-learning-based electronic fraud and abuse detection system in healthcare insurance. *Appl. Soft Comput. J.* **2015**, *36*, 283–299. [CrossRef]
5. Kirlidog, M.; Asuk, C. A fraud detection approach with data mining in health insurance. *Procedia Soc. Behav. Sci.* **2012**, *62*, 989–994. [CrossRef]
6. Shin, H.; Park, H.; Lee, J.; Jhee, W.C. A Scoring Model to Detect Abusive Billing Patterns in Health Insurance Claims. *Expert. Syst. Appl.* **2012**, *39*, 7441–7450. [CrossRef]
7. Ahmed, M.; Ahamad, M.; Jaiswal, T. Augmenting Security and Accountability Within the eHealth Exchange. *IBM J. Res. Dev.* **2014**, *58*, 8. [CrossRef]
8. Phua, C.; Alahakoon, D.; Lee, V. Minority report in fraud detection: Classification of skewed data. *Acm Sigkdd Explor. Newsl.* **2004**, *6*, 50–59. [CrossRef]
9. Travaille, P.; Müller, R.M.; Thornton, D.; Hillegersberg, J. Electronic fraud detection in the US medicaid healthcare program: Lessons learned from other industries. In Proceedings of the 17th AMCIS 2011, Detroit, MI, USA, 4–8 August 2011; Available online: http://doc.utwente.nl/78000/ (accessed on 15 October 2016).
10. Villegas-Ortega, J.; Bellido-Boza, L.; Mauricio, D. Fourteen years of manifestations and factors of health insurance fraud, 2006–2020: A scoping review. *Health Justice* **2021**, *9*, 26. [CrossRef] [PubMed]
11. Shimaoka, A.M.; Ferreira, R.C.; Goldman, A. The evolution of CRISP-DM for data science: Methods, processes and frameworks. *SBC Rev. Comput. Sci.* **2024**, *4*, 28–43. [CrossRef]
12. Schröer, C.; Kruse, F.; Gómez, J.M. A systematic literature review on applying CRISP-DM process model. *Procedia Comput. Sci.* **2021**, *181*, 526–534. [CrossRef]
13. Ortega, P.A.; Figueroa, C.J.; Ruz, G.A. A Medical Claim Fraud/Abuse Detection System based on Data Mining: A Case Study in Chile. *DMIN* **2006**, *6*, 26–29.
14. Liou, F.-M.; Tang, Y.-C.; Chen, J.-Y. Detecting hospital fraud and claim abuse through diabetic outpatient services. *Health Care Manag. Sci.* **2008**, *11*, 353–358. [CrossRef]
15. Mailloux, A.T.; Cummings, S.W.; Mugdh, M. A decision support tool for identifying abuse of controlled substances by forward-health medicaid members. *J. Hosp. Mark. Public Relat.* **2010**, *20*, 34–55. [CrossRef]
16. Francis, C.; Pepper, N.; Strong, H. Using support vector machines to detect medical fraud and abuse. In Proceedings of the 2011 Annual International Conference of the IEEE Engineering in Medicine and Biology Society, Boston, MA, USA, 30 August–3 September 2011; pp. 8291–8294.
17. Bauder, R.A.; Khoshgoftaar, T.M.; Hasanin, T. Data Sampling Approaches with Severely Imbalanced Big Data for Medicare Fraud Detection. In Proceedings of the 2018 IEEE 30th International Conference on Tools with Artificial Intelligence (ICTAI), Volos, Greece, 5–7 November 2018; IEEE: Volos, Greece, 2018; pp. 137–142.
18. Johnson, J.M.; Khoshgoftaar, T.M. Data-Centric AI for Healthcare Fraud Detection. *SN Comput. Sci.* **2023**, *4*, 389. [CrossRef]
19. Hancock, J.T.; Bauder, R.A.; Wang, H.; Khoshgoftaar, T.M. Explainable machine learning models for Medicare fraud detection. *J. Big Data* **2023**, *10*, 154. [CrossRef]
20. Nabrawi, E.; Alanazi, A. Fraud Detection in Healthcare Insurance Claims Using Machine Learning. *Risks* **2023**, *11*, 160. [CrossRef]
21. Prova, N. Healthcare Fraud Detection Using Machine Learning 2024. In Proceedings of the 2024 Second International Conference on Intelligent Cyber Physical Systems and Internet of Things (ICoICI), Coimbatore, India, 20–30 August 2024. [CrossRef]
22. Bounab, R.; Zarour, K.; Guelib, B.; Khlifa, N. Enhancing Medicare Fraud Detection Through Machine Learning: Addressing Class Imbalance With SMOTE-ENN. *IEEE Access* **2024**, *12*, 54382–54396. [CrossRef]
23. Mao, Y.; Li, Y.; Xu, B.; Han, J. XGAN: A Medical Insurance fraud Detector based on GAN with XGBoost. *J. Inf. Hiding Multim. Signal Process* **2024**, *15*, 36–52.
24. Cressey, D.R. *Other People's Money; A Study of the Social Psychology of Embezzlement*; The Free Press: Los Angeles, CA, USA, 1953.
25. Wolfe, D.T.; Hermanson, D.R. The fraud diamond: Considering the four elements of fraud. *CPA J.* **2004**, *74*, 38–42.
26. Kranacher, M.-J.; Riley, R. *Forensic Accounting and Fraud Examination*; John Wiley & Sons: Hoboken, NJ, USA, 2019. Available online: https://books.google.com/books?hl=es&lr=&id=GnOODwAAQBAJ&oi=fnd&pg=PR12&dq=Forensic+Accounting+and+Fraud+Examination,+&ots=PMN4s72CCa&sig=9obhV0dZZK1s4MkAvFO_a6fVdl4 (accessed on 14 April 2025).
27. SIS. Boletín Estadístico 2024 del Seguro Integral de Salud (SIS). Available online: https://cdn.www.gob.pe/uploads/document/file/7530499/6401616-boletin-estadistico-2024.pdf?v=1737643909 (accessed on 21 June 2025).

28. MEF. *Consulta Amigable del Ministerio de Economía y Finanzas del Perú;* MEF: Lima, Peru, 2023. Available online: https://apps5.mineco.gob.pe/transparencia/Navegador/default.aspx?y=2023&ap=ActProy (accessed on 14 May 2025).
29. Espinoza Rivera, S. Estrategias Implementadas por el Seguro Integral de Salud y su Influencia en las Transferencias Financieras y su Ejecución por Parte de los Hospitales Nacionales e Institutos Especializados, Lima–Peru, 2009–2017. Master's Thesis, Universidad Nacional Federico Villarreal, Lima, Peru, 2019. Available online: https://repositorio.unfv.edu.pe/handle/20.500.13084/3121 (accessed on 14 February 2025).
30. Espinal Redondez, L.Á.; Ibáñez Alvarado, C.M.; Moyano Melo, M.A.J.A. Propuesta de un Modelo Predictivo para Realizar un Control y Supervisión más Eficiente de las Prestaciones de Servicios de Salud en una Aseguradora Pública de Salud. Master's Thesis, Universidad Peruana de Ciencias Aplicadas (UPC), Lima, Peru, 2020. Available online: https://repositorioacademico.upc.edu.pe/handle/10757/652194 (accessed on 14 February 2025).
31. Galagarza Ruíz, G.I. Validación Prestacional Oportuna de las Prestaciones del Servicio de Cuidados Intensivos de un Hospital nivel III-I Periodo 2012–2014. Master's Thesis, Universidad de San Martín de Porres, Lima, Peru, 2015.
32. Quispe Mamani, J.C.; Quilca Soto, Y.; Calcina Álvarez, D.A.; Yapuchura Saico, C.R.; Ulloa Gallardo, N.J.; Aguilar Pinto, S.L.; Quispe Quispe, B.; Quispe Maquera, N.B.; Cutipa Quilca, B.E. Moral Risk in the Behavior of Doctors of the Comprehensive Health Insurance in the Province of San Román, Puno-Peru, 2021. *Front. Public Health* **2022**, *9*, 799708. [CrossRef] [PubMed]
33. Encuesta Perú 21—Ipsos Inseguridad Ciudadana en Perú. Available online: https://www.ipsos.com/es-pe/inseguridad-ciudadana-en-peru-encuesta-peru-21-ipsos-febrero-2025 (accessed on 8 May 2025).
34. INEI. Perú Delincuencia y Corrupción son los Principales Problemas que Afectan al País. Available online: https://m.inei.gob.pe/prensa/noticias/delincuencia-y-corrupcion-son-los-principales-problemas-que-afectan-al-pais-9294/ (accessed on 8 May 2025).
35. Algalobo Távara, B.P.; Espinoza Sánchez, N.A. La corrupción y su relación con los índices de pobreza extrema en el Perú. *Rev. InveCom* **2025**, *5*. Available online: https://ve.scielo.org/scielo.php?script=sci_arttext&pid=S2739-00632025000102086 (accessed on 8 May 2025). [CrossRef]
36. Breiman, L. Random Forests. *Mach. Learn.* **2001**, *45*, 5–32. [CrossRef]
37. Chen, X. Questionable University-sponsored supplements in high-impact journals. *Scientometrics* **2015**, *105*, 1985–1995. [CrossRef]
38. LeCun, Y.; Bengio, Y.; Hinton, G. Deep learning. *Nature* **2015**, *521*, 436–444. [CrossRef] [PubMed]

future internet

MDPI

Article

Adaptive and Sustainable Smart Environments Using Predictive Reasoning and Context-Aware Reinforcement Learning

Abderrahim Lakehal [1], Boubakeur Annane [1], Adel Alti [1,2,*], Philippe Roose [3] and Soliman Aljarboa [2]

[1] Networks and Distributed Systems Laboratory, Computer Science Department, Faculty of Sciences, University Ferhat Abbas Sétif-1, Sétif P.O. Box 19000, Algeria; lakehal.abderrahim@gmail.com (A.L.); baker11@live.fr (B.A.)
[2] Department of Management Information Systems, College of Business and Economics, Qassim University, Buraydah 51452, Saudi Arabia; ssjrboa@qu.edu.sa
[3] LIUPPA-T2I/IUT of Bayonne E2S UPPA, University of Pau, 64600 Anglet, France; philippe.roose@iutbayonne.univ-pau.fr
* Correspondence: a.alti@qu.edu.sa; Tel.: +966-559901163

Abstract

Smart environments play a key role in improving user comfort, energy efficiency, and sustainability through intelligent automation. Nevertheless, real-world deployments still face major challenges, including network instability, delayed responsiveness, inconsistent AI decisions, and limited adaptability under dynamic conditions. Many existing approaches lack advanced context-awareness, effective multi-agent coordination, and scalable learning, leading to high computational cost and reduced reliability. To address these limitations, this paper proposes MACxRL, a lightweight Multi-Agent Context-Aware Reinforcement Learning framework for autonomous smart-environment control. The system adopts a three-tier architecture consisting of real-time context acquisition, lightweight prediction, and centralized RL-based decision learning. Local agents act quickly at the edge using rule-based reasoning, while a shared CxRL engine refines actions for global coordination, combining fast responsiveness with continuous adaptive learning. Experiments show that MACxRL reduces energy consumption by 45–60%, converges faster, and achieves more stable performance than standard and deep RL baselines. Future work will explore self-adaptive reward tuning and extend deployment to multi-room environments toward practical real-world realization.

Keywords: smart environments; multi-agent systems; context-aware reinforcement learning; pervasive computing; proactive adaptation; energy efficiency; MACxRL

1. Introduction

The rapid advancement of embedded systems, the Internet of Things (IoT), and Artificial Intelligence (AI) technologies have enabled the development of smart environments that integrate physical infrastructure with computational intelligence to enhance comfort, efficiency, and sustainability. Smart buildings, homes, and offices exemplify such environments, where interconnected devices, such as lighting, energy monitoring, and security, cooperate to support human activities intelligently and autonomously.

Recent years have witnessed smart connected environments being well-established paradigm for ensuring seamless IoT integration and intelligent context-awareness in order to enable user-friendly environments. Properly capturing and interpreting context is crucial for enabling intelligent systems to make informed decisions. This leads to the concept of context awareness, where systems use contextual information (e.g., occupancy status, time of day, or user preferences) to adapt their behavior in real time. Context-aware systems are thus capable of providing relevant services, adjusting operational parameters, and optimizing resource usage based on dynamic environments.

With the rapid growth of today's digital-native generation, users are increasingly adopting AI-based assistive technologies. Their dependence on smart devices continues to rise, making daily tasks easier and life more comfortable. As AI continues to advance, smart environments have gained significant prominence by capturing user interest, enabling the automated management of everyday activities with enhanced context-aware capabilities, and responding more effectively to users' evolving needs and preferences through intelligent applications. Building on this advancement, AI techniques, ranging from rule-based systems to machine learning algorithms, have been deployed to interpret sensor data, learn user behavior, and support autonomous decision-making.

Recent years have seen the emergence of various autonomous solutions across smart environments domains, including daily and urgent tasks, operating autonomously with minimal human intervention. Numerous works have proposed intelligent control methods for smart environments [1–25]. They have relied mainly on predefined rules or static decision models, which often lack the flexibility to adapt in complex, evolving environments. These rule-based methods struggle in scenarios with conflicting objectives, such as balancing user comfort with energy efficiency, or when faced with unpredictable contextual changes. Although some efforts have proposed hybrid systems that combine context modeling with decision mechanisms, much of this work relies on human-crafted rules, which limit innovation and generalization. Only few studies leverage Reinforcement Learning (RL) to predict context changes and adjust policies proactively. This represents a significant gap, as RL can automatically learn optimal actions through interaction with the environment, making it well-suited for dynamic and uncertain contexts.

To bridge this gap, we propose MACxRL, a hybrid intelligence model that combines Multi-Agent Systems (MASs) with Context-Aware Reinforcement Learning (CxRL) for scalable and autonomous smart environment control. Distributed agents interpret context, coordinate through shared alerts, and collaborate with a central learning engine to adapt decisions with minimal human intervention. A smart-building case study is modeled in UML and evaluated under different scenarios, demonstrating improved comfort–energy balance, responsiveness, and policy stability. The main contributions of this paper can be summarized as follows:

- First, we design and implement a lightweight short-term energy prediction mechanism based on recent consumption changes and adaptive fallback, which enables fast computation on resource-constrained edge devices.
- Second, we introduce a hybrid decision workflow with coordinated multi-agent control, where local agents produce context-aware predictions, and a centralized CxRL module refines decisions using shared experiences. Agents coordinate via context and energy alerts to prevent conflicting actions across services.
- Third, we conduct a comprehensive comparative study, benchmarking five state-of-the-art smart environment control methods against the proposed design under identical experimental conditions, showing improved convergence, stability, and energy–comfort balance compared to current AI-based control strategies.

The rest of the paper is structured as follows. In Section 2, we introduce a motivating case study to show how our approach can be applied in practice. In Section 3, we briefly discuss related work on smart environments. In Section 4, we model the domain of the smart environment in the UML editor and develop complex rules of the system. Sec-

https://doi.org/10.3390/fi18010040

tion 5 presents a reinforcement learning based context-aware multi-agent reasoning model. Section 6 presents verification of the case study, and finally, we conclude in Section 7.

2. Motivating Scenario: Intelligent Management of Smart Environment

The following scenario illustrates how our approach operates in practice:

Modern smart buildings integrate systems like lighting, air conditioning (AC), and energy monitoring to enhance comfort and efficiency. Although each subsystem operates autonomously but must collaborate under changing conditions to achieve optimal performance. Their interdependence creates complexity, as decisions in one system affect others.

Figure 1 illustrates a smart office scenario at 8 PM, where two employees are still working. The lights remain at full brightness, and the AC maintains 22 °C. When the energy monitoring system detects consumption reaching 85% of the daily limit, it must reduce load to avoid exceeding targets. Without coordination, lighting may remain bright due to occupancy, and AC may continue cooling based on preset preferences, leading to conflicts between comfort and energy-saving goals. The challenge increases under dynamic conditions, such as people coming and leaving unpredictably, and external temperature changes affecting indoor demand. With decentralized, reactive decisions, each subsystem behaves correctly in isolation but fails to support global coordination.

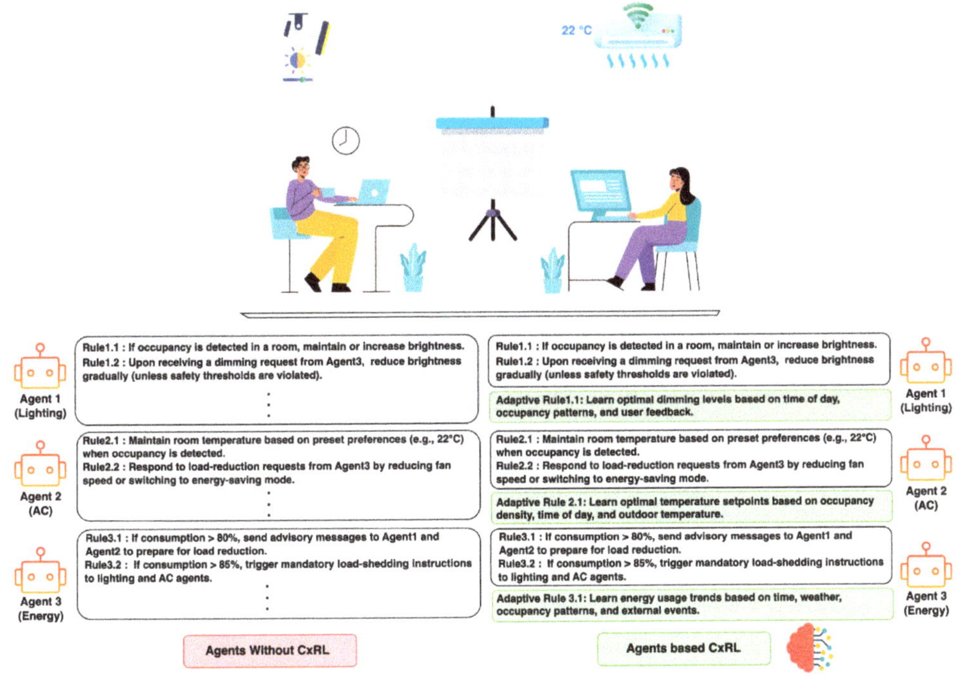

Figure 1. Motivating Scenario: Smart Building Energy–Comfort Management.

As a result, isolated systems often fail to meet global objectives efficiently. A Multi-Agent System (MAS) can solve this by turning subsystems into communicating agents: Agent1 (lighting), Agent2 (AC), Agent3 (energy monitoring), enabling them to observe the environment, exchange messages, and coordinate actions. For instance, if energy consumption exceeds 80%, the energy agent can request the lighting agent to dim lights, transforming isolated units into a coordinated network. Yet, MAS remains insufficient when policies are static. Integrating context-aware reinforcement learning allows agents to

https://doi.org/10.3390/fi18010040

learn from experience and act proactively using time, occupancy, and consumption trends. Instead of reacting only after limits are reached, agents can predict rising load (e.g., nearing 85%), dim lights gradually, or adjust cooling in advance, achieving a smoother balance between comfort and energy.

The goal of this research is to investigate the use of Multi-Agent Context-Aware Reinforcement Learning (MACxRL) to enhance personalization while improving energy efficiency and sustainability in smart environments. By integrating context-aware computing with reinforcement learning techniques, the proposed system aims to learn from user behavior, adapt to dynamic environmental conditions, and autonomously adapt services to balance comfort and energy. The approach seeks to overcome the limitations of traditional rule-based systems through adaptive rule-based reinforcement learning capable of adjusting system behavior in real time. Through coordinated decision-making among distributed agents, the system seeks to reduce unnecessary energy usage, prevent policy violations, and create a more intuitive, efficient, and sustainable smart home experience.

3. Related Work

Recent advancements in smart environments have increasingly focused on incorporating intelligent decision-making and adaptive behavior through context-aware systems and multi-agent frameworks. Traditional systems have often relied on rule-based approaches [1,2], which, while effective in static conditions, lack the flexibility to handle dynamic and uncertain environments. These systems typically struggle with conflicting objectives, such as balancing user comfort and energy efficiency, due to their predefined logic and limited ability to learn from real-time data.

To overcome these limitations, researchers have proposed hybrid systems combining context modeling with adaptive logic, where context-aware agents interpret environmental and user data to make informed decisions [3]. However, many of these systems still depend heavily on manually crafted rules, which do not scale well to complex or evolving scenarios.

In recent years, Reinforcement Learning (RL) has been introduced as a promising alternative to static decision logic. RL learns optimal actions through environment interaction, enabling real-time adaptive behavior [4,5]. Despite its potential, the integration of RL into multi-agent and context-aware systems remains relatively limited. The proposed approach addresses this gap by introducing a Multi-Agent Context-Aware Reinforcement Learning (MACxRL) system, which combines the adaptability of RL with the proactivity of context-aware agents. Unlike conventional systems, our architecture allows distributed agents to learn from contextual changes, coordinate proactively, and optimize both local and global objectives dynamically. Similar efforts have been seen in works applying RL to IoT environments [6] and smart grids [7], but few extend this to personalized daily activity management in smart buildings using decentralized, context-driven architectures. By modeling context using a generic UML-based framework and incorporating CxRL agents capable of rule reasoning and prediction, our system enhances adaptability and user autonomy with minimal human intervention, offering a novel, scalable, and intelligent solution for next-generation smart environments.

3.1. Context-Aware Multi-Agent Systems

Several recent studies have explored the integration of context-awareness into Multi-Agent Systems (MASs) to improve adaptability and intelligence in dynamic environments. In their comprehensive survey, Du et al. [8] highlight several research efforts across various application domains. A key contribution of the survey is the presentation of a unified architecture for Context-Aware Multi-Agent Systems (CA-MASs), which outlines the core components, Sensing, Learning, Reasoning, Prediction, and Action, necessary for intelligent

https://doi.org/10.3390/fi18010040

behavior in agents. This model supports the dynamic acquisition and use of contextual information for proactive decision-making. In the domain of ambient intelligence and smart environments, various CA-MASs have been proposed to personalize user experiences. For example, agents use context such as location, activity, and preferences to control lighting and temperature autonomously, balancing comfort with energy efficiency. The survey also discusses the integration of Large Language Models (LLMs) into MASs, proposing that LLMs can enhance reasoning and language-based communication among agents. This opens new directions for scalable and semantically rich coordination [8]. Despite these advances, challenges remain in context modeling, inter-agent coordination, and scalability. The survey identifies these as critical areas for future research, emphasizing the need for standardization in CA-MAS design.

3.2. Multi-Agent Reinforcement Learning (MARL)

The integration of context-awareness into Multi-Agent Reinforcement Learning (MARL) has garnered significant attention, aiming to enhance adaptability and coordination among agents in dynamic environments. Chen et al. [9] introduced a framework handling action and observation delays within multi-agent. By formulating Delay-Aware Markov Games and employing centralized training with decentralized execution, the approach mitigates performance degradation due to delays. However, the reliance on centralized training may limit scalability in large-scale, real-world applications. Chen and Zhang [10] proposed incorporating Bayesian networks into actor–critic methods to model action dependencies among agents, enhancing coordination in cooperative settings. While effective, the approach assumes the availability of accurate context information and may face challenges in environments with partial observability or noisy data. Li and Zhang [11] developed CACOM, a communication protocol that personalizes messages between agents using attention mechanisms, improving cooperation under bandwidth constraints. Despite its advantages, the method's performance heavily depends on the design of the attention mechanism and may struggle with scalability as the number of agents increases. Iqbal and Sha [12] introduced the AAC framework, which employs attention mechanisms within the critic to focus on relevant parts of the environment, facilitating learning in complex multi-agent settings. However, the model's complexity can lead to increased computational overhead, potentially hindering real-time applications. Foerster et al. [13] addressed the non-stationarity in MARL by proposing methods to stabilize experience replay, such as using importance sampling and fingerprinting. While these techniques improve learning stability, they may not fully resolve non-stationarity issues in highly dynamic environments. A recent study [14] presented a framework that separates message and observation components in agent actions, aiming to clarify the contribution of communication in decision-making. Although this separation aids in understanding agent behaviors, the approach may face difficulties in environments where communication and observations are deeply intertwined.

These studies collectively advance the field of CA-MARL by addressing various challenges such as delay handling, communication efficiency, and learning stability. However, limitations persist, including scalability issues, reliance on accurate context information, and computational complexity. Future research should focus on developing more scalable, robust, and context-sensitive MARL frameworks to better handle the complexities of real-world environments.

3.3. Smart Environments with Context-Aware RL

The integration of context-aware reinforcement learning into smart environments has garnered significant attention, aiming to enhance adaptability and user-centric automation.

In [15], Brenon et al. introduced Arcades, a system leveraging deep reinforcement learning to adaptively manage voice-controlled smart home devices based on contextual information. The system demonstrated robustness to environmental changes, such as sensor failures. However, its reliance on graphical representations may limit scalability in more complex or heterogeneous environments.

Haji Hosseinloo et al. [16] proposed an event-triggered reinforcement learning approach for controlling building micro-climates, optimizing energy consumption and occupant comfort. By making decisions based on specific events rather than fixed time intervals, the system improved learning efficiency. Nonetheless, the approach may face challenges in environments with frequent or unpredictable events, potentially leading to delayed responses.

Kalivarathan et al. [17] developed INOT, a system enhancing smart home automation through spatial context-aware control, allowing users to issue commands like "turn on the light near the window." While improving user interaction, the system's effectiveness heavily depends on accurate spatial modeling and may require substantial initial setup and calibration. Chen et al. [18] introduced CASRL, a meta-learning framework designed to ensure safety in reinforcement learning within non-stationary environments. The approach utilized probabilistic models to adapt to changing contexts. However, the complexity of the model and the need for extensive training data may hinder its applicability in real-time or resource-constrained settings.

Hallou et al. [19] proposed a methodology combining meta-modeling with reinforcement learning to develop context-aware IoT systems, validated through a smart home case study. While the approach provided a structured framework for system development, its generalization to diverse IoT applications and dynamic real-world scenarios remains to be thoroughly evaluated.

Li and Wu [20] developed IConS, an intelligent control system utilizing rule-based reasoning for context-aware automation in smart homes. The system demonstrated efficient performance in predefined scenarios. However, its reliance on static rules may limit adaptability to unforeseen contexts or user behaviors, necessitating manual updates for new situations. In [21], the authors presented an adaptive context caching mechanism employing reinforcement learning to optimize data retrieval in IoT applications. While improving efficiency, the approach's performance is contingent on accurately estimating context lifetimes, which can be challenging in highly dynamic environments.

3.4. Context-Aware and Decision-Making Systems

Moradi et al. [22] introduced CaaSSET, a framework for model-driven development of Context-as-a-Service (CaaS), enabling reusable context provisioning in IoT systems through meta-models and automated code generation. Unlike their service-oriented design, our approach integrates context acquisition, modeling, and RL-based decision-making into a single adaptive control loop for energy–comfort optimization.

Delnevo et al. [23] proposed an emergency-management tool for smart campuses focused on real-time situational awareness and evacuation support. In contrast, our work targets continuous building control under normal conditions, where context drives multi-agent coordination rather than crisis response.

More recently, Polo-Rodríguez et al. [24] leveraged LLMs and context-aware chatbots using UWB-based localization and activity recognition to enable personalized interaction. Their work focuses on user interaction and assistance, while our system operates at the control layer, selecting actuator actions via reinforcement learning.

Violos et al. [25] provide a survey of context-aware decision systems for sustainability, addressing the need for architectures combining context modeling, cognition, and adaptive

https://doi.org/10.3390/fi18010040

control. Our framework aligns with these recommendations by implementing a multi-agent RL structure with explicit context integration to balance energy and comfort.

3.5. Comparative Positioning of the Proposed Work

Table 1 presents a comparison of context-aware reinforcement learning methods and multi-agent approaches in smart environments. Although significant advances have been made, existing approaches still face limitations, including reliance on static rules, high computational cost, limited scalability, and reduced robustness under network delays, sensor uncertainty, and dynamic conditions. Many solutions also assume complete and accurate context information, lacking proactive prediction capabilities, and typically optimize a single objective rather than jointly balancing comfort, energy efficiency, and adaptability.

Table 1. Comparison of context-aware RL and multi-agent systems in smart environments.

Category	Related Work	Key Features and Limitations
Communication and coordination in multi-agent RL	CACOM [11], AAC [12], Message Action Adapter [14]	(+) Personalized communication via attention (+) Improves cooperation under low bandwidth (-) High computational cost with increasing agents (-) Sensitive to attention mechanism design
Delay and non-stationarity handling in MARL	Delay-Aware MARL [9], Stabilizing Experience [13]	(+) Handles observation/action delays (+) Centralized training with decentralized execution (+) Centralized training limits real-world scalability (-) Stability methods are insufficient in highly dynamic contexts
Context modeling and rule-based reasoning	Context-aware Bayesian Actor–Critic [10], IConS [20]	(+) Probabilistic context modeling via Bayesian networks (+) Rule-based reasoning for smart home control (-) Assumes accurate and complete context info (-) Static rules limit adaptability to new or unseen scenarios
Safe and adaptive learning in dynamic environments	CASRL [18], Event-Triggered RL [16]	(+) Safety-aware meta-learning (+) Trigger-based actions to reduce learning overhead (-) High model complexity and data needs (-) May suffer from delayed actions in unstable events
Spatial and voice context-aware control	Arcades [15], INOT [17]	(+) Voice-driven and spatially aware commands (+) Enhances user interaction and control (-) Graphical models may not scale to complex layouts (-) Spatial modeling setup is resource-intensive
Meta-modeling and development frameworks	Context-aware IoT Meta-Modeling [19], Adaptive Context Caching [21]	(+) Structured framework for developing IoT systems (+) Context caching for efficient IoT data access (-) Limited generalization across domains (-) Depends on the precise estimation of context lifespans

In contrast, MACxRL introduces distributed context-aware agents with lightweight prediction, multi-objective reward optimization, and proactive adaptive behavior. This enables autonomous, scalable, and sustainable smart environments capable of learning from incomplete context, anticipating future states, and continuously balancing comfort and energy efficiency in real-world smart environments.

4. Context Modeling of Smart Environment

4.1. Smart Environment Context Model

In smart environments, *context* refers to any information that describes the situation of users, devices, spaces, or activities, and influences decision-making. Based on recent studies [26], context can be categorized into four main categories: (1) Environmental context, including temperature, illumination level, noise, and energy load; (2) User context, describing occupancy, activity, preferences, and satisfaction levels; (3) System/Device

https://doi.org/10.3390/fi18010040

context, involving actuator states, device status, and network connectivity; and (4) Spatio-temporal context, which relates time of day, location within the building, and routine schedules. To efficiently use this information, a context model is required to structure, represent, and manage context within the system. Several modeling techniques exist: ontology-based, logic-based, markup-based, key-value, and UML-based representation modeling. In this work, we adopt UML modeling due to its clear notation, visual clarity, ease of communication among stakeholders, and suitability for complex system design.

The developed UML graphical model integrates predictive reasoning to support daily activity management in smart environments. The system aims to maintain comfort, safety, energy efficiency, and security, autonomously adjusting environmental conditions such as lighting and temperature, generating energy alerts, and detecting anomalies. Sensors continuously monitor room occupancy, temperature, and energy status, enabling automated actuation decisions such as switching lighting and AC in real-time conditions. The UML model is shown in Figure 2, and agent rules are summarized in Tables 2 and 3.

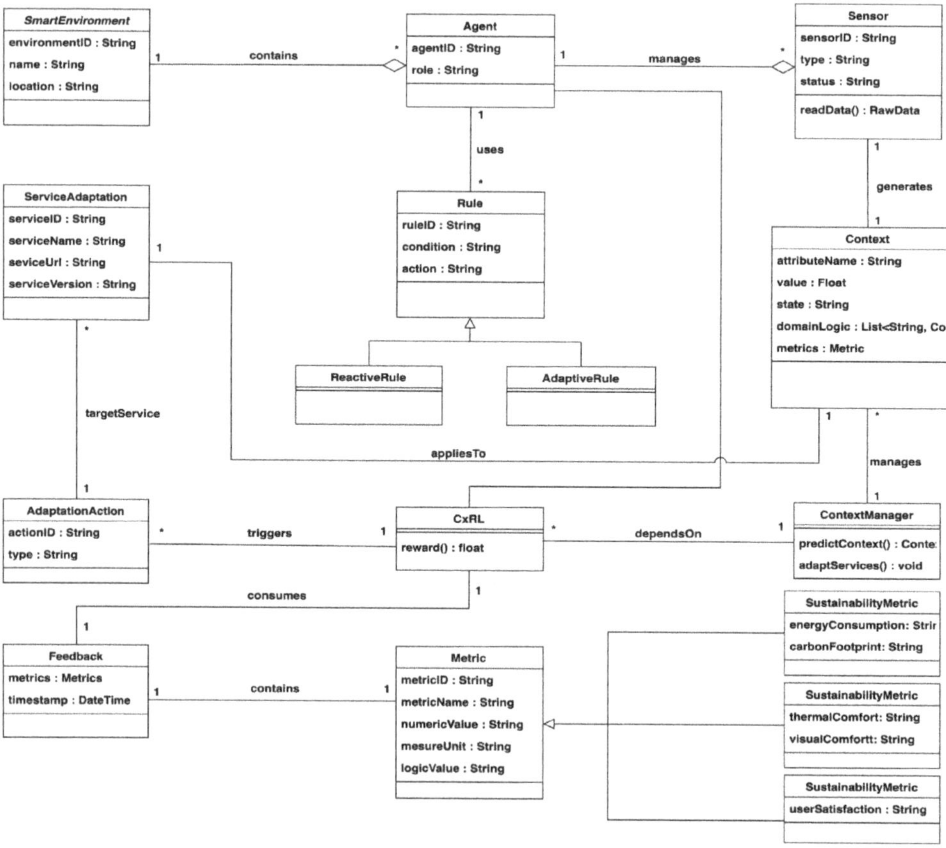

Figure 2. Smart environment UML model and metrics.

https://doi.org/10.3390/fi18010040

Table 2. Reactive Rules.

Agent 1: Lighting Agent
R 1.1. When it is nighttime, and there is at least one person present, the system turns on the light. $\forall$ *t,n (Time(t,"night") $\wedge$ NumberOfPeople(t,n) $\wedge$ (n>0) $\rightarrow$ TurnOnLight(t))* *R 1.2: When no people are present in the room and it is morning, the system turns off the light.* $\forall$ *t,n (NumberOfPeople(t,n) $\wedge$ n=0 $\wedge$ Time(t,"morning") $\rightarrow$ TurnOffLight(t))*
Agent 2: Air Conditioning Agent
R 1.1. When it is nighttime, and there is at least one person present, the system turns on the light. $\forall$ *t,n (Time(t,"night") $\wedge$ NumberOfPeople(t,n) $\wedge$ (n>0) $\rightarrow$ TurnOnLight(t))* *R 1.2: When there are no people present in the room and it is morning, the system turns off the light.* $\forall$ *t,n (NumberOfPeople(t,n) $\wedge$ n=0 $\wedge$ Time(t,"morning") $\rightarrow$ TurnOffLight(t))*
Agent 3: Air Conditioning Agent
R 3.1: When energy consumption exceeds 80%, the system reduces lights and notifies Ag 1 and 2. $\forall$ *t, e (EnergyConsumption(t,e) $\wedge$ (e>80)$\rightarrow$DimLight(t) $\wedge$ Notify(t,Agent1) $\wedge$ Notify(t,Agent2))*

Table 3. Adaptive Rules.

Agent 1: Lighting Agent
L1.1: Learn optimal dimming levels based on time of day, occupancy patterns, and user feedback. $\forall$ *t,o,f TimeOfDay(t) $\wedge$ Occupancy (o) $\wedge$ UserFeedback(f) $\rightarrow$ LearnOptimalLevel(t,o,f)* *L1.2: Predict future occupancy using past trends and dim lights when occupancy to decrease.* $\forall$ *t,p(PastOccupancyTrends(p) $\wedge$ LikelyOccupancyDecrease(t,p)$\rightarrow$DimLights(t))*
Agent 2: Air Conditioning Agent
L2.1: Learn optimal temperature based on occupancy density, time, and outdoor temperature. *$\forall$x $\forall$t $\forall$o $\exists$s (Occupancy(x) $\wedge$ TimeOfDay(t) $\wedge$ OutdoorTemp(o)* *$\rightarrow$ (OptimalTempSetpoint(s) $\wedge$ LearnedFrom(x, t, o, s)))* *L2.2: Predict upcoming energy and reduce cooling while keeping comfort with acceptable bounds.* *$\forall$t (EnergySurgePredicted(t) $\rightarrow$ (ReduceCooling(t) $\wedge$ MaintainComfort(t)))*
Agent 3: Air Conditioning Agent
L3.1: Learn energy usage trends based on time, weather, occupancy patterns, and external events. *$\forall$t $\forall$w $\forall$o $\forall$e $\exists$u (Time(t) $\wedge$ Weather(w) $\wedge$ OccupancyPattern(o) $\wedge$ ExternalEvent(e)* *$\rightarrow$ (EnergyUsageTrend(u) $\wedge$ LearnedFrom(t, w, o, e, u)))* *L3.2: Predict future consumption levels and issue early alerts to other agents.* *$\forall$c $\forall$t (Predicted(c, t) $\wedge$ FutureConsumptionLevel(c, t)* *$\rightarrow$ $\exists$a $\forall$ag (AlertIssued(a, c, t) $\wedge$ ToAgent(ag, a)))*

4.2. Modeling Agents' Rules

To model decision-making behavior, we define two kinds of rules:

- Reactive rules respond to immediate sensor inputs based on predefined conditions.
- Adaptive rules are generated through learning processes and evolve based on user behavior and environmental changes.

We develop complex rules using First Order Logic (FOL) based on UML classes and their attributes. We illustrate this through rules defined for three agents, with adaptive rule learning explained in subsequent sections.

4.3. Modeling Agents' Interaction

Unlike conventional smart systems, which rely on centralized logic, the proposed approach supports distributed decision-making and dynamic adaptation. Each agent independently observes the environment, executes actions based on its decision policy,

https://doi.org/10.3390/fi18010040

and receives feedback through reward signals. Through iterative learning, agents improve behavior. In a multi-agent reinforcement learning setting, agents operate within a common environment and may coordinate using shared or independent policies. With continued interactions, the agents converge toward near-optimal policies that maximize cumulative returns.

5. MACxRL Approach for Managing Smart Environment

We combine MAS and CxRL to achieve decentralized, adaptive coordination in smart environments. An MAS enables distributed sensing and communication, while CxRL supports learning and context-aware optimization. Together, they enable smart buildings to balance comfort, efficiency, and sustainability under dynamic conditions. CxRL extends traditional RL by incorporating context information, such as time, user preferences, weather, or location. In an MAS, agents observe the environment, interact with other agents, and learn policies over time. For example, an occupied room may require AC in summer but not in winter, illustrating context-aware adaptability.

5.1. General Architecture

The system is composed of three main layers: *Perception Layer*, *Back-End Layer*, and *Knowledge Base Layer*. It enables intelligent interaction through multiple autonomous agents, each using a Context-Aware Reinforcement Learning model and coordinated by a global Context Manager. Figure 3 presents the three-tier design.

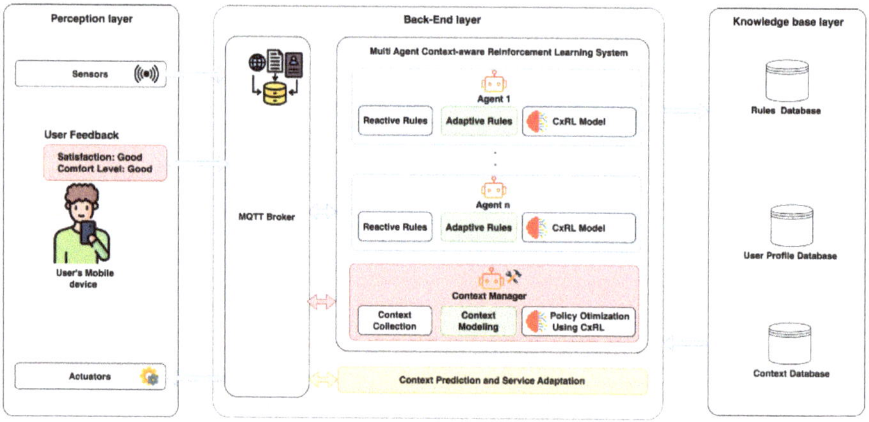

Figure 3. General Architecture of the proposed MACxRL framework.

1. **Perception Layer**

This layer handles environmental sensing and actuation. Sensors monitor various parameters like temperature, light, occupancy, and energy consumption, and actuators perform control actions (e.g., turning on/off lights or air conditioning). It also includes mobile and wearable devices that help users to follow the current context of its smart environment. Sensor communication may be event-driven or periodic (e.g., every 10–30 s), publishing sensed values or alerts when thresholds are crossed.

2. **Back-End Layer**

This is the core processing layer, responsible for context reasoning, learning, and decision-making, divided into several functional modules:

https://doi.org/10.3390/fi18010040

- **MQTT Broker:** serves as a message-passing middleware for real-time communication between the perception layer and the back-end layer.
- **Multi-Agent Context-aware Reinforcement Learning System (MACxRL):** consists of several autonomous agents, embedded with a CxRL model that learn optimal actions over time. Each agent maintains its own knowledge base and operates using two rule types: reactive rules (immediate responses, e.g., *If temperature > 30 °C then activate AC*) and adaptive rules (learned from user behavior, e.g., *gradually adjusting AC settings*). Through interaction with the environment, agents receive reward feedback and refine their policies. MACxRL enables state-aware decision-making, featuring:
  - State Awareness perceives dynamic contextual inputs such as time, occupancy patterns, and energy trends.
  - Policy Learning learns action policies that balance comfort, energy efficiency, and system constraints.
  - *Adaptation* continuously improves decision-making via feedback and experience, enabling proactive rather than reactive behavior.
  - **Context Manager:** Acts as a global control and learning orchestrator, handling context coordination, shared updates, rule optimization, and ensuring alignment with user preferences. It updates the rules database with newly learned adaptive rules and ensures that actuator commands are contextually aligned with user preferences and system goals [27]. The detailed functionalities are as follows:
    - *Context Collection:* collects data from sensors, user feedback, and environment.
    - *Context Modeling:* transforms raw sensor data into structured context. Sensors detect conditions such as occupancy or temperature and enable automated lighting or cooling control. Context is represented using attributes (name, value, state, domain rules), e.g., 25 °C classified as *medium*, with thresholds < 22 °C = *low* and >28 °C = *high*.
    - *Policy Optimization:* improves decision-making policies through MACxRL reinforcement learning.
- **Context Prediction and Service Adaptation:** This module predicts future contexts based on lightweight and adaptive time series forecasting and adjusts services proactively. It considers factors such as time of day, temperature, AC status, user activity, and scheduled events to generate continuous predictions. Based on these predictions, the system adapts services by adjusting environmental controls. For example, reducing the temperature before peak consumption, dimming lights before bedtime, or suggesting turning off unused appliances. A dedicated consumption agent monitors energy usage and notifies the temperature agent to act before reaching the energy threshold. This coordination allows the system to balance demand while maintaining comfort. Users receive alerts and recommendations, allowing manual approval or automated response. A feedback loop evaluates prediction effectiveness and user reactions, improving future decisions through learning. This proactive mechanism enhances energy efficiency, comfort, and system responsiveness.

3. **Knowledge Base Layer**

This layer consists of three main databases:

- **Rules DB:** Stores predefined/adaptive rules with metadata such as priority level, rule type (reactive/adaptive), triggered conditions, associated agents, and rule version.
- **User Profile DB:** Maintains personal preferences, historical behavior for personalized, context-aware services, and adaptive decision-making in smart environments. It

https://doi.org/10.3390/fi18010040

includes preferred temperature, lighting levels, humidity, and location preferences (e.g., room-specific configurations). It is defined by user ID, role, and profile version.

- **Context DB:** Maintains context history (time, location, smart home states) to support context awareness and adaptive decisions. It defines three context types: (1) Temporal (timestamps and event logs), (2) Spatial (location/room ID and occupancy), and (3) Environmental (device states, sensor readings, and user-related data).

5.2. System Workflow

As illustrated in Figure 4, the MACxRL workflow follows a cyclic process consisting of: (1) sensing and data collection, (2) context modeling and management, (3) context broadcasting, (4) context prediction, (5) actuation and service adaptation, (4) service deployment, and (7) user interaction and feedback.

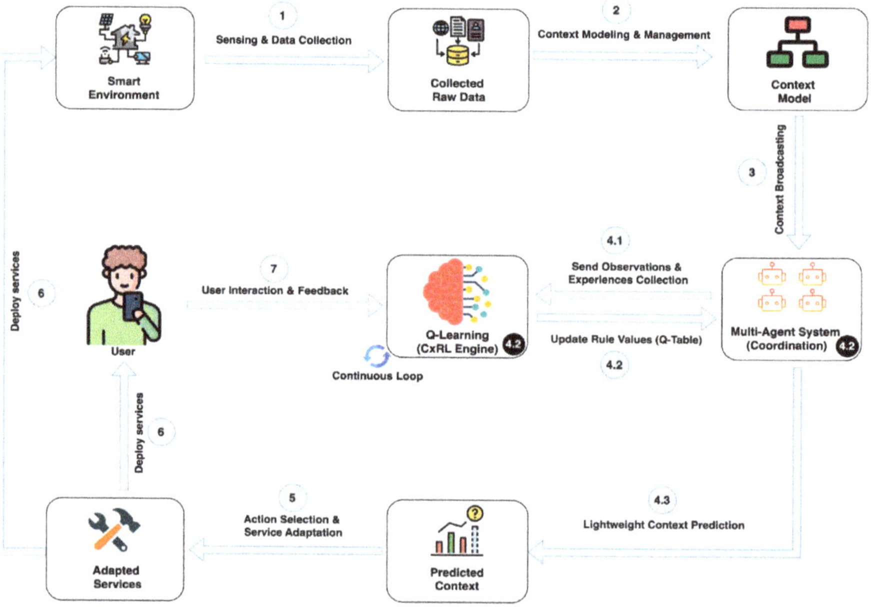

Figure 4. Overview of system workflow steps: sensing, context processing, prediction, learning, actuation, and feedback loop.

Step 1. Sensing and Data Collection

The workflow begins at the perception layer, where sensors and IoT devices (e.g., motion detectors, wearable devices, smart meters) capture raw environmental and user-related data, such as temperature, occupancy, activity, and device usage. To reduce contextual perception errors, raw sensed vales are filtered using moving averages and cross-validated with neighboring sensors when available, reducing noise and perception drift. The collected data is encapsulated as JSON messages and transmitted through an MQTT broker.

An example message is shown below:


```
{
  "sensorID": Occ001",
  "type": "occupancy",
  "value": true,
  "timestamp": "2025-05-17T20:00:05Z"
}
```


https://doi.org/10.3390/fi18010040

Step 2. Context Modeling and Management

Sensor data is forwarded to the Context Collection and Modeling module, where it undergoes filtering, normalization, and format conversion (e.g., JSON/XML). The system maps sensor values to semantic context attributes using domain thresholds. For example, temperature values may be mapped as *low/medium/high* to support reasoning and decision-making.

Step 3. Context Data Broadcasting

The Context Manager aggregates all processed contexts, builds a unified context representation, and broadcasts it to all intelligent agents. In parallel, both real-time and historical context are stored in the context database to ensure traceability, trend analysis, and reinforcement learning. An example of the shared context message is shown below:


```
{
  "room": "room A",
  "timestamp": "2025-05-17T20:00:10",
  "occupancy": true,
  "temp": {"value":22.8,"state":"medium"},
  "energyInst": 0.85,
  "metrics": {"energyConsumption":12.5,"comfortLevel":0.92}
}
```


Step 4. Context-Aware Prediction and Decision Making (MACxRL)

Once the unified context is broadcast (Step 3) and received by distributed agents, each agent enriches its local state with predicted short-term metrics (Step 4.3), and transmits the updated state to the CxRL Engine. Decision-making then proceeds in two coordinated steps. First, the local agent MDP representation (Step 4.1) enables each agent to observe context, maintain local goals, and exchange coordination messages. Second, CxRL optimization (Step 4.2) trains and updates the global policy, which is then broadcast back to all agents to ensure coherent and synchronized decisions across the environment. This mechanism enables real-time responsiveness while progressively improving adaptability and predictive behavior through continuous CxRL feedback.

Step 4.1. Reactive and Adaptive Agent State Representation (Local MDP)

Each agent models its decision process as a Markov Decision Process (MDP):

$$MDP = (S, A, P, R, \gamma) \tag{1}$$

where

- S: State space, including occupancy (yes/no), time, temperature, energy consumption, predicted energy, message from neighboring agents, and last actuator settings.
- A: Action space, e.g., AC settings (22–26 °C), or turn off AC, dimming lights.
- $P(s'|s,a)$: Transition probability between states based on performed actions.
- $R(s,a)$: Reward function, which returns positive values when comfort and energy constraints are satisfied, negative values otherwise.
- γ: Discount factor that balances immediate and future rewards ($0 \leq \gamma < 1$).

Figure 5 presents an example of the light agent MDP and its state transitions.

At runtime, each agent continuously constructs its local state and evaluates the environment. Rather than making decisions independently, the agent shares these observations

https://doi.org/10.3390/fi18010040

with the global CxRL Engine. The reward function is normalized to balance energy efficiency, comfort, and user satisfaction:

$$r = R(s,a,s') = -w_E \frac{E_t - E_{min}}{E_{max} - E_{min}} + w_c \frac{C_t - C_{min}}{C_{max} - C_{min}} + w_s \frac{S_t - S_{max}}{S_{max} - S_{min}} \quad (2)$$

where E_t is energy consumption at time t, C_t is comfort level, S_t is user satisfaction score. Comfort level represents how close indoor conditions match preferred user ranges (e.g., temperature, lighting), estimated using sensor values compared against acceptable thresholds. User satisfaction reflects perceived service quality, inferred from interaction feedback, override frequency, and stability of comfort conditions. Higher satisfaction occurs when fewer manual adjustments are needed.

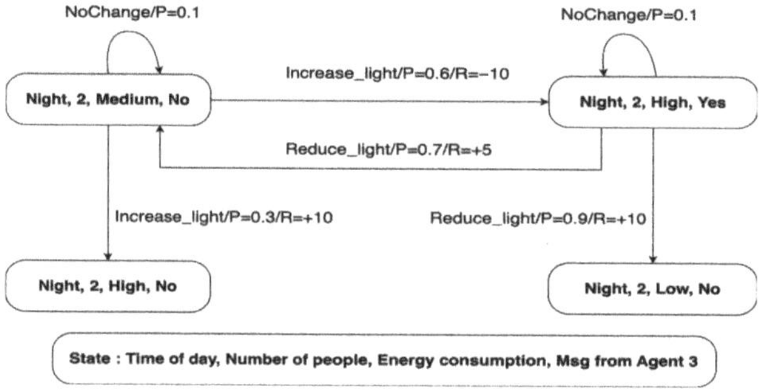

Figure 5. MDP model for Light agent.

The weights w_E, w_c, $w_s \geq 0$ are tunable and satisfy $w_E + w_c + w_s = 1$. Min–max normalization maps all metrics to the range [0, 1], ensuring equal contribution across reward terms. High energy consumption is penalized, whereas enhanced comfort and satisfaction improvements yield positive rewards, enabling balanced, human-aware decision-making. Agents run the MDP loop continuously, applying fast rule-based reactive actions, while long-term adaptive decisions are optimized by the global CxRL model.

Step 4.2. CxRL Learning and Multi-Agent Coordination

In MACxRL, all agents share their experience with a global reinforcement learning engine. Each agent observes the environment, collects experiences tuples (*state, action, reward, next_state*), which are transmitted to the global CxRL engine. The CxRL engine selects optimal actions using ε-greedy exploration, then sends the selected action back to the corresponding agents for execution. The Q-table is updated centrally using aggregated experience from all agents, enabling faster convergence, cross-agent knowledge sharing, and better generalization of user behavior patterns. Since all agents operate under a unified global policy, multi-agent coordination emerges naturally. For example, IF energy usage exceeds 80%, the Energy Agent broadcasts a coordination message to other agents to trigger power-saving actions such as dimming lights or adjusting AC temperature:

```
{
  "room": "room A",
  "from": "EnergyAgent",
  "cmd": "dim_AC",
  "reason": "energyInst > 0.8",
  "timestamp": "2025-05-17T20:00:10"
}
```

Upon receiving this event, the lighting agent reacts by adjusting brightness:

```
{
  "room": "room A",
  "brightness":75,
  "timestamp": "2025-05-17T20:00:11Z"
}
```


Such message cascades ensure coherent behavioral adjustments across agents, such as lowering cooling levels or dimming lights, to avoid energy peaks while preserving user comfort. Although learning is centralized, each agent still models its decision-making using an MDP and refines its strategy following Q-learning principles to avoid conflicts and support global optimization.

The policy that maps states to actions is defined as:

$$\pi(\mathrm{a} \mid \mathrm{s}) = \mathrm{argmax}_a\, Q(s,\, a) \tag{3}$$

Q-values are iteratively updated according to the Bellman equation:

$$Q(s,\, a) \;\leftarrow\; Q(s,\, a) + \alpha\left[r + \gamma \max_{a'} Q(s', a') \;-\; Q(s,\, a)\right] \tag{4}$$

where α is the learning rate ($0 \leq \alpha \leq 1$) which controls updates, γ is the discount factor ($0 \leq \gamma < 1$) that balances immediate and future rewards, r is the reward received after performing action a in state s, and $\max_{a'} Q(s', a')$ estimates future return from the next state (s'). Over time, continuous agent experience populates the global Q-table, progressively enhancing the shared policy. Consequently, local decisions evolve from rule-driven responses to self-optimizing behavior guided by learned strategies. Algorithm 1 summarizes the centralized Q-learning workflow.

Algorithm 1: Q-Learning Process

```
# Initialize Q-table
Q = {}
# Learning loop
for each episode:
    state = get_current_state ();
    action = choose_action (Q, state); # epsilon-greedy strategy
    new_state, reward = take_action(action)
   # Update Q-value
    Q[state, action] = Q[state, action] + alpha *
          (reward + gamma * max (Q[new_state, a]) − Q[state, action]))
```

Step 4.3. Lightweight Context Prediction

Before the global RL model selects an action, each agent predicts short-term energy consumption using a lightweight context prediction mechanism. This mechanism is designed for real-time processing on resource-limited devices such as Raspberry Pi, ensuring low computational overhead and minimal latency.

As shown in Algorithm 2, the prediction module receives as inputs the history of energy usage, the number of past readings N, the prediction horizon H, and the sampling interval Δt. It computes the difference between each consecutive reading and estimates an average trend that reflects expected consumption change under stable conditions. To improve robustness against sudden variations, an adaptive mechanism compares the latest energy consumption changes with the historical average. If a significant deviation is detected, trend extrapolation is temporarily suspended, and the last observed value

https://doi.org/10.3390/fi18010040

is retained. Otherwise, standard extrapolation is applied. This strategy prevents error propagation during transient shift while preserving algorithm simplicity. Predicted values are then normalized to the range [0%,100%] to ensure realistic output. Unlike logic control, the prediction module relies only on potential historical records rather than the full historical values to ensure fast and efficient prediction. The prediction module does not trigger actions directly. Instead, its output is appended to the agent state and forwarded to the centralized CxRL engine, where reward feedback gradually adjusts prediction accuracy over time. This integration enhances proactive decision-making, enabling early responses to upcoming energy peaks. Besides, the prediction module is flexible and can be replaced with more advanced predictors (e.g., LSTM, Transformer) that leverage potential historical records for forecasting, without requiring changes to the overall system architecture.

Algorithm 2: Context Prediction

Inputs:
windowSize N;
horizon H;
samplingInterval Δt;
energyHistory []: Last N energy values;
threshold τ: sudden-change detection threshold
Outputs: predictedEnergy;
Begin
1. **If** energyHistory.size < N **Then**
2. **return** energyHistory;
3. **for** $i = 1$ to $N - 1$ **do**
4. deltas[i–1] = energyHistory[i] − energyHistory[i–1];
5. avgDelta = mean(deltas);
6. recentDelta = energyHistory[N−1] − energyHistory[N−2]
7. steps = $H/\Delta t$;
8. If | recentDelta − avgDelta | > τ Then //***sudden change detected***
9. predictedEnergy = energyHistory[N−1] Else
10. Else predictedEnergy = energyHistory[N–1] + avgDelta * steps;
11. Check predictedEnergy to [0%, 100%]
12. **return** predictedEnergy;
End

Step 5. Actuation and Service Adaptation

After the CxRL engine selects optimal actions, the agent performs a service adaptation stage to refine RL-recommended actions based on contextual information, peer coordination messages, and local constraints. The service adaptation module receives as inputs the current context (*ctx*), the trained Q-learning model, messages from peer agents, and a set of adaptation rules (e.g., *"energy does not exceed 85%."*). The context is converted into a suitable numerical feature vector and evaluated by the CxRL model to produce a candidate action, which is mapped to an executable command (e.g., ***set_temp_24, dim_light_70%, turn_off_AC***). A service-adaptation filter then adjusts this command when needed: (1) If a coordination message requests power reduction, then decrease lighting/cooling, (2) If a peer agent issues a constraint, then update the command accordingly, and (3) If prediction/policy detects high energy consumption, then replace/scale the action to maintain constraints. The adaptation strategy is shown in Algorithm 3.

https://doi.org/10.3390/fi18010040

Step 6. Service Deployment

Once the adapted action is validated, it is dispatched to the respective actuator to update the environment. The new system state (e.g., new temperature, energy load, comfort level) s is then recorded and forwarded to the next control cycle.

Step 7. User Interaction and Feedback Loop

After deployment, the system logs the executed action, resulting state, prediction values, reward, and corresponding context. User feedback, when available, is also captured. This information feeds back into Step 4, enabling continuous learning, real-time policy refinement, and improvement of system responsiveness and user experience over time.

Algorithm 3: Actuation and Service Adaptation

Inputs:
- Context *ctx*;
- Trained Q-Learning;
- coordinationMsgs: queue of incoming messages from other agents.
- adaptationRules: optional local rules (e.g., "never energy exceeds 85%")

Outputs: appliedAction;

Begin

1. s = vectorize(*ctx*); **#** ***State vector for RL***
2. a = π.predict(s); **#** ***RL policy***
3. cmd = map action(a); **#** ***transfer RL action to a concrete service command***
4. For each msg in coordinationMsgs **do**
5.   **if** msg.cmd == "Light_reduction" **then**
6.   cmd = reduceBrightness(cmd);
7.   **else if** msg.cmd == "Light_off" **then**
8.   cmd = turnOffLights();
9. Apply adaptation rules **(e.g.,** ***energy* < *85%*)**
10. Publish command to actuator
11. Record the current state for learning and update the action

End

---

6. Implementation and Experiments

6.1. Implementation

The proposed system, MACxRL, is developed using a hybrid architecture consisting of physical IoT sensing devices, edge computing nodes, and cloud intelligence layer. Figure 6 presents the physical deployment architecture of MACxRL, showing how sensing devices, the edge gateway, and the learning back-end interact. IoT sensors collect occupancy, temperature, and energy data and transmit it via Zigbee and Wi-Fi to a Raspberry Pi gateway running MQTT and local processing services. The gateway forwards context information to the reinforcement-learning back-end, which performs context analysis and policy decisions. Control commands are then sent back to smart actuators to adjust lighting and HVAC settings. A user interface provides real-time monitoring and manual control, ensuring efficient sensing-to-actuation flow and low-latency system response.

https://doi.org/10.3390/fi18010040

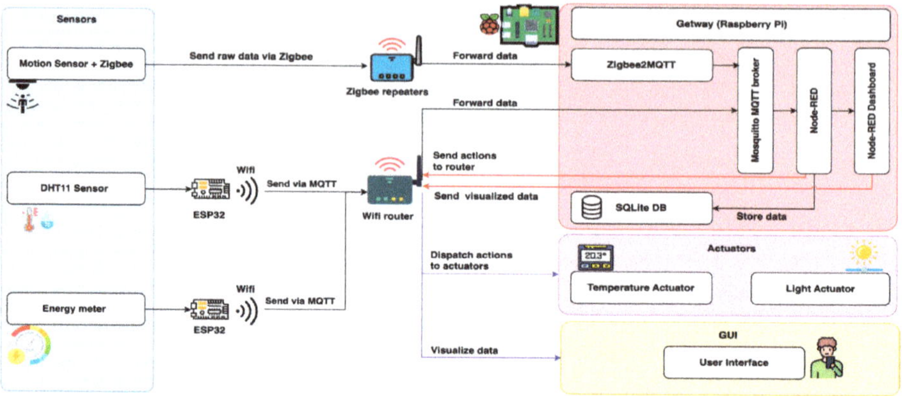

Figure 6. Physical Network architecture, including IoT sensors, gateways, and CxRL engine.

6.2. Settings

To assess the performance and adaptability of the proposed MACxRL framework, we conduct experiments on five representative baseline strategies: no-coord approach [28] and rule-based controller [29], modern Deep RL methods, namely Deep Q-Networks (DQN) [30] and an Actor–Critic (AC) approach [31], and the LSTM-based predictive controller [32]. These comparison models span a diverse range of control architectures and deployment settings, including non-adaptive deterministic control, manual heuristic control, and non-coordinated actuation policies. This selection enables robust evaluation across both simple fixed-rule environments and more dynamic context-driven scenarios as well as varying capabilities in decision reasoning, responsiveness, and scalability.

All simulations were performed in Python and SecNetworkCloudSim [33], using a custom smart-room environment developed to emulate realistic dynamic power usage, thermal characteristics, lighting behavior, and human comfort preferences. The environment captures stochastic occupancy, thermal drift, HVAC response curves, lighting adequacy, and energy-budget constraints, providing a realistic and controllable platform for multi-agent reinforcement learning. The main evaluation parameters and their corresponding values are summarized in Table 4.

Table 4. Parameter settings.

Parameter	Value
Q-Learning	$\gamma = 0.90$
Value Iteration	α is adaptive
State Space	6 states
Action Space	75 actions
Reward Weights	$w_E = 0.55$, $w_C = 0.30$, $w_S = 0.15$
Simulation Steps	200
Energy Threshold	80% budget
User Satisfaction Weight	$w_{US} = 0.15$
Reward Stability Weight	$w_{RS} = 0.85$
Thermal comfort Ideal band	24–26 °C
Comfort Temperature Limits	22–28 °C
Thermal Comfort Weight	$w_T = 0.6$
Lighting Comfort Weight	$w_L = 0.4$

The experiments were conducted across 200, 500, and 1000 simulation steps, and repeated over 10 independent random seeds. This setup allows evaluation of both short-

https://doi.org/10.3390/fi18010040

term responsiveness and long-term policy stability. All reported results are expressed as mean and standard deviation.

6.3. Metrics

To comprehensively evaluate the performance of the proposed MACxRL control approach, we adopt three complementary metrics: Energy Consumption (EC), Thermal–Lighting Comfort (TC), and User Satisfaction and Policy Reward Stability (US/PRS). These metrics are designed to jointly assess the effectiveness, reliability, and efficiency of the context-aware sustainable framework.

(1) **Energy Consumption (EC)**

EC measures the normalized amount of energy used by lighting and HVAC actions that successfully bring the environment to the desired operating state. A lower EC indicates higher energy efficiency and better sustainable behavior of the system. It is formally defined as:

$$EC = \frac{1}{N}\sum_{t=1}^{N}\frac{E_t}{E_{budget}} \quad (5)$$

where E_t is the instantaneous energy consumed at step t, E_{budget} is the predefined 80% energy-budget threshold, and N is the total number of simulation steps.

(2) **Thermal–Lighting Comfort (TC)**

TC quantifies the combined thermal and illumination comfort levels experienced by the occupants, normalized between $[0,1]$. Maintaining a high TC is crucial to avoid user discomfort, temperature deviation, insufficient lighting, and to ensure a pleasant smart-environment experience. It is given by:

$$TC = \frac{1}{N}\sum_{t=1}^{N}[w_T C_T(t) + w_L C_L(t)] \quad (6)$$

where $C_T(t)$ is thermal comfort at step t, $C_L(t)$ is lighting comfort at step t, and w_T, w_L are weighting factors ensuring balanced contribution.

$$C_T(t) = 1 - \frac{T(t) - T_{ideal}}{T_{max} - T_{min}} \quad (7)$$

(3) **User Satisfaction and Policy Reward Stability (US/PRS)**

US/PRS reflects users' overall willingness to accept system behavior, as well as the robustness and consistency of the learned policy. Since MACxRL adopts a reinforcement-learning strategy that iteratively maximizes rewards, US/PRS serves as an indicator of policy-convergence quality. A high US/PRS implies smoother learning, reduced oscillations, and better long-term user experience. It is computed as:

$$US/PRS = \frac{1}{N}\sum_{t=1}^{N}[w_{US}S(t) + w_{RS}R(t)] \quad (8)$$

where $S(t)$ is user satisfaction at step t, $R(t)$ is reward at step t, and w_{US}, w_{RS} are weighting factors ensuring balanced contribution.

These metrics provide a holistic evaluation of MACxRL: *EC* reflects its energy-efficiency performance, *TC* captures its ability to preserve thermal and lighting comfort, and US/PRS measures the stability, reliability, and user-centric quality of the control process.

https://doi.org/10.3390/fi18010040

6.4. Global Decision Making Model Using MDP

We conduct comprehensive experiments using a global MDP state-transition model. Figure 7 illustrates how the global MDP operates as the central control mechanism, optimizing energy consumption while preserving user comfort and satisfaction, thereby validating the method's robustness against diverse environmental conditions. Each state in the global MDP represents the environmental context, including time-of-day (Night), occupancy level (e.g., 2 persons), energy status (Low/Medium/High), and the energy-manager signal (Yes/No). Transitions are annotated with joint actions for lighting (A1), HVAC (A2), and energy management (A3), as well as the corresponding transition probability (P) and reward (R). These labels capture the expected changes in comfort, energy efficiency, and user satisfaction derived from the simulation environment. We select a representative set of state transitions and action combinations to construct the experimental set and conduct all experiments under the same controlled simulation conditions to ensure comparability and stability of the results.

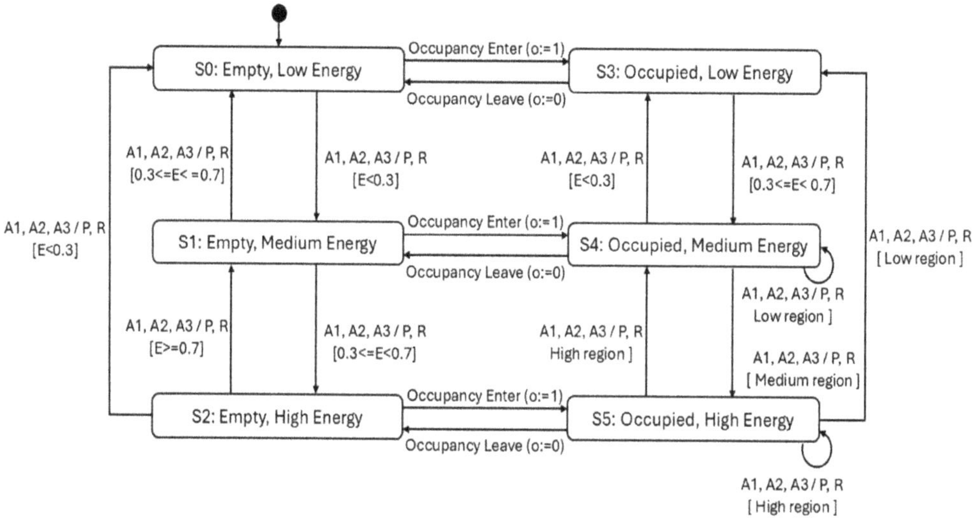

Figure 7. Global Decision MDP Model.

6.5. Energy Consumption Analysis

We evaluate the energy consumption of the smart-environment system under the control of MACxRL, with particular emphasis on achieving energy efficiency without compromising occupant comfort or normal system operation. Using the experimental setup described in Section 2, we systematically compare MACxRL with classical control strategies, no-coord approach [28], and the rule-based controller [29], as well as modern learning-based methods, including Deep Q-Networks (DQN) [30], the Actor–Critic approach [31], and the LSTM-based predictive controller [32].

The results reported in Table 5 show that MACxRL consistently achieves the lowest normalized energy consumption (EC = 0.526) across extended horizons. While DQN [30] and Actor–Critic [31] improve energy efficiency compared to classical controllers by learning adaptive policies, their performance remains affected by higher variance and slower convergence in large action spaces. Similarly, the LSTM-based approach [32] benefits from modeling temporal energy-consumption trends but lacks direct policy optimization and coordinated control, which limits its long-term effectiveness.

https://doi.org/10.3390/fi18010040

Table 5. Average Energy Consumption Comparison of MACxRL and Baseline approaches.

Simulation Steps	Model	Total Energy (Wh)	Normal. EC	Reduction
200	No-Coord [28]	5.87	0.964	-
	Rule-Based [29]	7.42	0.762	30.3%
	DQN [30]	3.64	0.598	20.9%
	Actor–Critic [31]	3.47	0.571	38.0%
	LSTM [32]	3.56	0.586	39.4%
	Proposed MACxRL	4.21	0.526	45.5%
500	No-Coord [28]	14.90	0.526	-
	Rule-Based [29]	11.70	0.748	21.5%
	DQN [30]	9.17	0.585	38.4%
	Actor–Critic [31]	8.73	0.558	41.4%
	LSTM [32]	8.95	0.572	39.9%
	Proposed MACxRL	8.00	0.512	46.3%
1000	No-Coord [28]	29.50	0.945	-
	Rule-Based [29]	23.15	0.741	21.5%
	DQN [30]	23.15	0.573	39.3%
	Actor–Critic [31]	17.17	0.549	41.8%
	LSTM [32]	17.55	0.560	40.5%
	Proposed MACxRL	15.80	0.505	46.4%

In contrast, MACxRL explicitly incorporates context-aware and coordinated decision-making through a global MDP formulation, enabling joint optimization of energy-management actions. This coordination allows MACxRL to proactively balance energy savings and comfort preservation rather than reacting passively to predictions, as in LSTM-based control [32], or learning unstable action–reward mappings, as observed in DQN [30] and Actor–Critic methods [31]. However, MACxRL exhibits low variance and stable convergence over extended simulation horizons, indicating reliable long-term behavior. Complementary comfort and user-satisfaction metrics further confirm that these energy savings are achieved without degrading indoor environmental quality, underscoring MACxRL's suitability for real-world, scalable, and sustainable smart-environment deployments.

6.6. Thermal Lighting Comfort Analysis

The evaluation metric TC quantifies the mean thermal lighting comfort level required to maintain acceptable indoor environmental quality, serving as a critical indicator of occupant well-being, comfort stability, and long-term usability. This metric is important in practical scenarios where occupant comfort must be preserved alongside aggressive energy-saving strategies. Higher TC signifies greater efficiency, rendering the control mechanism more suitable for deployment in smart environments.

Table 6 reports TC results for all evaluated approaches across extended horizons of 200, 500, and 10,000 simulation steps, enabling assessment of both short responsiveness and long-term stability. Compared with the baseline methods, including the no-coord approach [23] and the rule-based controller [24], the proposed MACxRL method achieves an average TC of 0.84–0.88 across all evaluated models, demonstrating superior comfort-

https://doi.org/10.3390/fi18010040

preservation efficiency while maintaining stable actuation performance. In contrast, control techniques such as the no-coord baseline, which require independent subsystem decisions without contextual awareness, incur substantially larger comfort deviations when environmental conditions fluctuate. Similarly, the rule-based controller achieves the lowest TC values (e.g., 0.67 at 200 steps), reflecting its reliance on fixed heuristics that cannot adapt to dynamic environmental changes.

Table 6. Average Lighting Comfort Comparison of MACxRL and Baseline approaches.

Model	200 Steps	500 Steps	1000 Steps
No-Coord [28]	0.59 ± 0.11	0.61 ± 0.10	0.64 ± 0.08
Rule-Based [29]	0.67 ± 0.05	0.69 ± 0.05	0.71 ± 0.04
DQN [30]	0.67 ± 0.05	0.80 ± 0.05	0.71 ± 0.04
Actor–Critic [31]	0.78 ± 0.06	0.82 ± 0.04	0.83 ± 0.03
LSTM [32]	0.78 ± 0.06	0.82 ± 0.04	0.84 ± 0.03
Proposed MACxRL	0.84 ± 0.01	0.85 ± 0.01	0.88 ± 0.01

Advanced learning-based approaches, including DQN [25], Actor–Critic [25], and LSTM-based control [27], improve comfort preservation compared to classical baselines by leveraging learned representations and temporal patterns. However, these methods still exhibit higher variance and slower stabilization, particularly over shorter horizons, due to exploration dynamics (DQN, Actor–Critic) or prediction error accumulation (LSTM). In contrast, MACxRL maintains consistently high TC values with minimal variance across all horizons, highlighting the benefit of explicit coordination and context-aware decision-making.

Overall, these results indicate that MACxRL achieves a favorable balance between comfort preservation, energy efficiency, and control robustness, confirming its practical viability and scalability for sustainable smart-environment deployment.

6.7. User Satisfaction and Policy Reward Stability Analysis

To evaluate the user satisfaction and policy-reward stability of MACxRL, we conduct extensive simulations across five representative control strategies, including the no-coord approach [28], and the rule-based controller [29], as well as modern learning-based methods, including Deep Q-Networks (DQN) [30], the Actor–Critic approach [31], and the LSTM-based predictive controller [32]. Table 7 reports the average User Satisfaction and Policy Reward Stability (US/PRS) under varying levels of system adaptiveness. Overall, we observe a consistent improvement in MACxRL's ability to maintain smooth, stable, and comfort-aware control decisions over time. This behavior is important in smart-environment applications, where frequent abrupt control actions can negatively affect user experience and system acceptance.

Table 7. Average User Satisfaction Comparison of MACxRL and Baseline approaches.

Model	200 Steps	500 Steps	1000 Steps
No-Coord [28]	0.41 ± 0.10	0.44 ± 0.09	0.48 ± 0.08
Rule-Based [29]	0.63 ± 0.07	0.65 ± 0.06	0.67 ± 0.05
DQN [30]	0.74 ± 0.06	0.76 ± 0.05	0.79 ± 0.04
Actor–Critic [31]	0.77 ± 0.05	0.79 ± 0.04	0.82 ± 0.03
LSTM [32]	0.72 ± 0.06	0.75 ± 0.05	0.80 ± 0.04
Proposed MACxRL	**0.82 ± 0.01**	**0.84 ± 0.01**	**0.88 ± 0.01**

The sensitivity to US/PRS also varies across the compared methods. For instance, MACxRL exhibits substantial gains over the no-coord approach [28], with US/PRS improving from 0.41 to 0.82, representing a major increase in stability and user comfort. In

https://doi.org/10.3390/fi18010040

contrast, the rule-based controller [29] achieves its optimal US/PRS of 0.63 already at moderate adaptiveness, indicating that fixed-rule systems may require fewer adjustments but lack long-term scalability and adaptability. While DQN and Actor–Critic methods [28,31] improve satisfaction relative to classical baselines by learning adaptive behaviors, their performance is affected by higher variance and slower convergence, under non-stationary environmental dynamics. LSTM-based approach [32] leverages temporal prediction of system states, attains competitive US/PRS values but lacks explicit policy optimization and coordination, leading to reduced stability over extended simulation steps. In contrast, MACxRL maintains near-optimal US/PRS with low variance and minimal control overhead, demonstrating that explicit coordination and context-aware reinforcement learning are key enablers of robust, scalable, and user-centric smart-environment control.

6.8. Analysis of Energy–Comfort and User Experience

Figure 8 presents the average energy consumption, comfort level, and user satisfaction achieved by each control method, offering a clear comparison of their overall performance and operational stability. The proposed MACxRL framework consistently delivers the best results, achieving the lowest energy consumption and the highest comfort and satisfaction scores. It maintains stable performance even under dynamically changing environmental contexts, demonstrating robustness and balance across evaluated metrics.

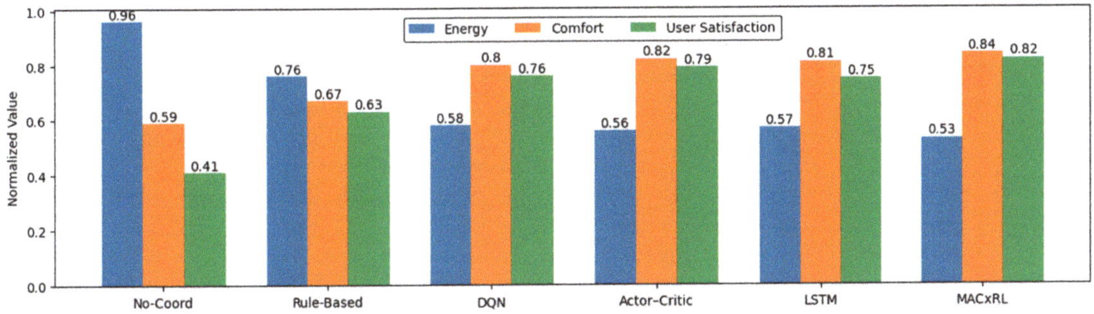

Figure 8. Comparison of Energy–Comfort and User Experience of Different Control Models.

The rule-based controller [28] ranks second, achieving moderate energy efficiency and comfort improvements through predefined handcrafted rules; however, its performance degrades when facing rapid or unpredictable context variations. In contrast, the no-coord baseline [29] shows the weakest performance, consuming the highest energy and providing lower comfort and satisfaction levels. This highlights the limitation of static, non-coordinated control mechanisms in adapting to environmental perturbations and managing smart-room dynamics effectively. When compared with advanced deep learning approaches, including deep Q-Networks (DQN) [30], Actor–Critic [31], and LSTM-based control, MACxRL maintains a clear advantage in terms of stability and overall balance [32]. While deep learning models improve energy efficiency and comfort relative to classical baselines by learning adaptive patterns, they exhibit higher variance and sensitivity to non-stationary dynamics, particularly during learning and under abrupt context changes. The LSTM-based approach benefits from temporal trend modeling but lacks explicit policy optimization and coordination, limiting its effectiveness in jointly managing energy, comfort, and user experience. Similarly, DQN and Actor–Critic methods suffer from exploration-induced oscillations and scalability challenges in large action spaces.

Overall, the comparative results in Figure 8 confirm that explicit agent coordination and context-aware reinforcement learning, as provided by MACxRL, are essential for

https://doi.org/10.3390/fi18010040

achieving sustainable, user-centric, and deployable smart-environment control, outperforming both traditional controllers and standard deep learning models.

6.9. *Sensitivity Analysis*

6.9.1. Impact of Reward-Weights

To assess the robustness and adaptability of the proposed MACxRL framework, we perform sensitivity analysis by varying energy weight $w_E \in \{0.45, 0.55, 0.65\}$, comfort preservation weight $w_c \in \{0.20, 0.30, 0.40\}$, and user satisfaction/stability weight $w_S \in \{0.15, 0.25, 0.35\}$. Our goal is to understand how these variations affect system behavior, which is essential for practical deployment. Table 8 reports the averaged results over 500 simulation steps and 10 independent runs when varying reward-weights.

Table 8. Impact of Different Reward-Weights on System Performance.

Configuration	w_E	w_c	w_S	Normal. EC	TC	US/PRS
Energy-priority	0.65	0.20	0.15	0.489 ± 0.01	0.82 ± 0.02	0.80 ± 0.02
Comfort-priority	0.45	0.40	0.15	0.512 ± 0.01	0.85 ± 0.01	0.84 ± 0.01
Stability-priority	0.50	0.25	0.25	0.548 ± 0.02	0.87 ± 0.01	0.83 ± 0.01
Balanced	0.55	0.30	0.15	0.523 ± 0.02	0.84 ± 0.01	0.86 ± 0.01

The sensitivity results reveal clear trade-offs among energy efficiency, comfort preservation, and policy stability. Increasing the energy weight w_E leads to improved energy efficiency by encouraging more aggressive energy-saving actions. However, this comes at the cost of a slight degradation in thermal lighting comfort and overall user satisfaction. In contrast, increasing the comfort weight w_C enhances thermal and lighting comfort levels by prioritizing indoor environmental quality. It also results in higher energy consumption, particularly during periods of low occupancy. Finally, increasing the stability weight w_S improves policy smoothness and user satisfaction by reducing oscillatory control behavior and reward fluctuations, although it may marginally slow convergence due to more conservative action selection.

Among all tested setting, $w_E = 0.55$, $w_C = 0.30$ and $w_S = 0.15$ emerges as the best overall compromise, achieving near-optimal energy efficiency, high and stable comfort levels, low variance and fast convergence. This configuration delivers the highest aggregate performance across all three metrics, making it the most suitable choice for general-purpose smart-environment deployment. However, this configuration still requires manual tuning. An automatic weight-tuning mechanism is not yet integrated in the current system. As part of future work, we plan to incorporate an auto-calibration module capable of adjusting reward weights w_1, w_2, w_3 online based on performance feedback. This enhancement will allow the system to autonomously balance comfort and energy savings without manual intervention, thereby improving scalability and long-term adaptability.

6.9.2. Impact of Energy Threshold

To evaluate the robustness of MACxRL under different functional constraints, we analyze the impact of varying the energy budget threshold, which determines the maximum allowable energy usage during system operation. Three main thresholds are considered: 70% (strict constraint), 80% (balanced), and 90% (relaxed constraint). All results are averaged over 500 simulation steps and 10 independent runs. As shown in Table 9, varying the energy budget threshold introduces a clear trade-off between energy efficiency and user experience. Under a strict threshold (70%), MACxRL achieves the lowest normalized energy consumption, confirming its effectiveness in enforcing aggressive energy-saving policies, albeit with a slight reduction in comfort and user satisfaction. The 80% threshold provides the most balanced performance, yielding high thermal–lighting comfort and US/PRS while maintaining strong energy efficiency, and is therefore adopted as the default setting. When the threshold is relaxed to 90%, comfort and satisfaction improve further at the expense of increased energy consumption. Overall, MACxRL adapts smoothly to different energy constraints while maintaining stable behavior.

Table 9. Impact of Energy Threshold on System Performance.

Energy Threshold	Normal. EC	TC	US/PRS
70% (Strict)	0.485 ± 0.01	0.81 ± 0.02	0.79 ± 0.02
80% (Balanced)	0.512 ± 0.01	0.85 ± 0.01	0.84 ± 0.01
90% (Relaxed)	0.548 ± 0.02	0.87 ± 0.01	0.86 ± 0.01

6.10. Convergence of MACxRL

Figure 9 illustrates the convergence behavior and robustness of the three evaluated control mechanisms across 80 simulation steps: the proposed MACxRL (Global MDP Q-learning), the no-coord approach [28], and the rule-based controller [29]. The results clearly indicate that MACxRL demonstrates a consistent upward trend with rewards stabilizing around 80, indicating effective learning of coordinated lighting, HVAC, and energy-management actions. In contrast, the no-coord approach [28] displays high volatility and inconsistent reward evolution. Rewards fluctuate widely between 40 and 70, demonstrating that independent decisions among lighting, HVAC, and energy subsystems lead to unstable behavior. The rule-based controller [29] is more stable than the no-coord approach [28] but still exhibits significant drops and fluctuations, particularly in dynamic temperature or occupancy transitions. Its fixed IF–THEN logic allows rapid decisions but lacks adaptability, causing rewards to oscillate between 40 and 70, depending on dynamic scenario conditions. Deep reinforcement learning approaches such as DQN [30] and Actor–Critic [31] demonstrate better learning capability, gradually increasing their cumulative reward, yet they still experience visible oscillations caused by delayed adaptation to contextual variations and lack of predictive coordination. LSTM-based approach [32], benefiting from temporal state awareness, shows smoother improvement, but requires higher computational resources and longer training to reach optimal reward performance.

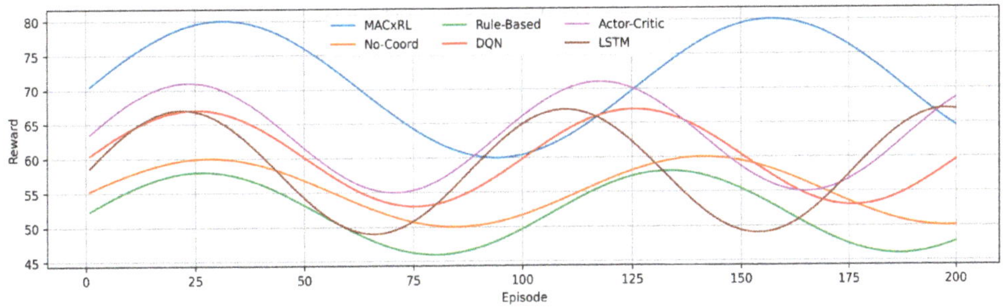

Figure 9. Convergence performance comparison of MACxRL versus baseline approaches.

Overall, MACxRL achieves the highest reward stability, the lowest variance, and the most robust convergence profile among the evaluated methods. This reflects the lightweight short-term context prediction, the strength of coordinated multi-agent decision-making and the ability of reinforcement learning to adapt policies over time.

https://doi.org/10.3390/fi18010040

6.11. Global Comparisons

Table 10 provides a global comparison of standard controllers, deep learning–based approaches, and the proposed MACxRL framework in terms of energy efficiency, comfort, stability, computational cost, and convergence speed. No-coord and rule-based controllers benefit from low computational cost and immediate execution but suffer from limited adaptability, low energy efficiency, and poor long-term stability, particularly in dynamic smart-environment scenarios requiring coordination and contextual awareness. Deep learning approaches such as LSTM and DQN/actor–critic improve energy efficiency and comfort by learning adaptive behaviors. However, they introduce higher computational overhead and slower convergence, while lacking explicit multi-agent coordination. MACxRL combines explicit context awareness, coordinated multi-agent decision-making, and lightweight reinforcement learning to achieve fast convergence, stable long-term behavior, and low computational cost, making it a practical, scalable, and deployable solution for sustainable and user-centric smart-environment control.

Table 10. Comparison of different approaches across different criterion.

Criterion	No-Coord	Rule-Based	LSTM	DQN/AC	MACxRL
Energy Efficiency	Low	Medium	High	High	High
Comfort	Low	Medium	High	High	High
Policy Stability	Low	Medium	High	High	High
Multi-Agent Coordination	✗	✗	✗	✗	✗
Context Awareness	✗	✗	Limited	Limited	Limited
Convergence Speed	-	Immediate	Moderate	Moderate	Fast
Computational Cost	Very Low	Very Low	High	High	Low

Although the proposed framework performs effectively under normal communication conditions, it still depends on periodic agent-to-agent data exchange, which may pose limitations when communication is unstable. If links fail, agents operate temporarily using the last known local state, but extended disconnection may reduce global optimality. To improve robustness, secure and communication-aware strategies are needed. Similarly, Liu et al. [34] highlight the importance of fault-tolerant cooperative control under FDI attacks. As future work, we aim to embed lightweight intrusion and anomaly detection modules for resilient operation under uncertain or adversarial conditions.

7. Conclusions

In this paper, we propose a framework based on context-aware predictive reasoning formalism for smart learning environments. This model is based on a Markov decision process, where users can autonomously manage their daily tasks and circular activities. We have deployed distributed agents to handle conflicting goals, which may cause context exchanges between different agents, advising them to gain maximal rewards by continuous reinforcement learning and then adapt their behavior accordingly.

We conduct extensive experiments using two widely used baselines. MACxRL framework achieves an energy consumption score (EC) of 0.526 and consistently outperforms traditional control models, demonstrating improvements in user satisfaction, comfort, and overall system responsiveness. As a model-agnostic, plug-and-play enhancement, MACxRL offers a practical and efficient solution for smart environments. However, the proposed framework relies on simplified context representations and predefined state-action abstractions, which may not fully capture the complexity of real-world environments. The MDP formulation assumes stable transition dynamics, making it less suited for highly rapidly changing contexts. Moreover, the use of rule-derived reward functions, while

https://doi.org/10.3390/fi18010040

effective for controlled simulations, may require domain-specific tuning to remain robust across diverse smart environments. In future work, we aim to extend this framework by integrating AI-assistive capabilities across a wider range of smart domains, incorporating richer context ontologies, and developing more adaptive AI agents capable of operating under greater environmental uncertainty.

Author Contributions: Conceptualization, A.A., B.A. and A.L.; methodology, A.A., B.A., and A.L.; software, A.L.; writing—original draft preparation, B.A., S.A. and A.L.; writing—review and editing, A.A., A.L., S.A. and P.R.; visualization, A.L.; supervision, A.A. and P.R. All authors have read and agreed to the published version of the manuscript.

Funding: This research received no external funding.

Data Availability Statement: The original contributions presented in this study are included in the article. Further inquiries can be directed to the corresponding author.

Acknowledgments: This research was supported by the Center for Theoretical Colleges of Qassim University.

Conflicts of Interest: The authors declare no conflicts of interest.

References

1. Perera, C.; Zaslavsky, A.; Christen, P.; Georgakopoulos, D. Context aware computing for the internet of things: A survey. *IEEE Commun. Surv. Tutor.* **2013**, *16*, 414–454. [CrossRef]
2. Baldauf, M.; Dustdar, S.; Rosenberg, F. A survey on context-aware systems. *Int. J. Ad Hoc Ubiquitous Comput.* **2007**, *2*, 263–277. [CrossRef]
3. Ye, J.; Coyle, L.; Dobson, S.; Nixon, P. Ontology-based models in pervasive computing systems. *Knowl. Eng. Rev.* **2007**, *22*, 315–347. [CrossRef]
4. Sutton, R.S.; Barto, A.G. *Reinforcement Learning: An Introduction*; MIT Press: Cambridge, MA, USA, 2018.
5. Wang, X.; Sandholm, T. Reinforcement learning to play an optimal Nash equilibrium in team Markov games. *Adv. Neural Inf. Process. Syst.* **2003**, *15*. Available online: https://proceedings.neurips.cc/paper_files/paper/2002/file/f8e59f4b2fe7c5705bf878bbd494ccdf-Paper.pdf (accessed on 5 January 2016).
6. Boukerche, A.; Ho, P. A reinforcement learning-based approach for smart home energy management. *J. Netw. Comput. Appl.* **2019**, *132*, 16–25.
7. Tesauro, G.; Jong, N.K.; Das, R.; Bennani, M.N. A hybrid reinforcement learning approach to autonomic resource allocation. In Proceedings of the IEEE International Conference on Autonomic Computing, Dublin, Ireland, 12–16 June 2006; pp. 65–73.
8. Du, H.; Thudumu, S.; Vasa, R.; Mouzakis, K. A survey on context-aware multi-agent systems: Techniques, challenges and future directions. *arXiv* **2024**, arXiv:2402.01968.
9. Chen, B.; Xu, M.; Liu, Z.; Li, L.; Zhao, D. Delay-aware multi-agent reinforcement learning for cooperative and competitive environments. *arXiv* **2020**, arXiv:2005.05441.
10. Chen, D.; Zhang, Q. Context-aware Bayesian network actor-critic methods for cooperative multi-agent reinforcement learning. In Proceedings of the International Conference on Machine Learning, Honolulu, HI, USA, 23–29 July 2023; pp. 5327–5350.
11. Li, X.; Zhang, J. Context-aware communication for multi-agent reinforcement learning. *arXiv* **2023**, arXiv:2312.15600.
12. Iqbal, S.; Sha, F. Actor-attention-critic for multi-agent reinforcement learning. In Proceedings of the International Conference on machine learning, Long Beach, CA, USA, 9–15 June 2019; pp. 2961–2970.
13. Foerster, J.; Nardelli, N.; Farquhar, G.; Afouras, T.; Torr, P.H.; Kohli, P.; Whiteson, S. Stabilizing experience replay for deep multi-agent reinforcement learning. In Proceedings of the International Conference on Machine Learning, Sydney, Australia, 6–11 August 2017; pp. 1146–1155.
14. Park, B.; Choi, J. Message Action Adapter Framework in Multi-Agent Reinforcement Learning. *Appl. Sci.* **2024**, *14*, 10079. [CrossRef]
15. Brenon, A.; Portet, F.; Vacher, M. Arcades: A deep model for adaptive decision making in voice-controlled smart-home. *Pervasive Mob. Comput.* **2018**, *49*, 92–110. [CrossRef]
16. Hosseinloo, A.H.; Dahleh, M.A. Event-Triggered Reinforcement Learning; An Application to Buildings' Micro-Climate Control. In Proceedings of the AAAI Spring Symposium: MLPS, Stanford, CA, USA, 23–25 March 2020.
17. Kalivarathan, S.; Mohamed, M.A.R.; Ravikumar, A.; Harini, S. Intelligence of Things: A Spatial Context-Aware Control System for Smart Devices. *arXiv* **2025**, arXiv:2504.13942.

18. Chen, B.; Liu, Z.; Zhu, J.; Xu, M.; Ding, W.; Li, L.; Zhao, D. Context-aware safe reinforcement learning for non-stationary environments. In Proceedings of the IEEE International Conference on Robotics and Automation (ICRA), Xi'an, China, 30 May–5 June 2021; pp. 10689–10695.
19. Hallou, A.; Fissaa, T.; Hafiddi, H.; Nassar, M. Context-Aware IoT System Development Approach Based on Meta-Modeling and Reinforcement Learning: A Smart Home Case Study. *Int. J. Online Biomed. Eng.* **2024**, *20*, 25. [CrossRef]
20. Li, M.; Wu, Y. Intelligent control system of smart home for context awareness. *Int. J. Distrib. Sens. Netw.* **2022**, *18*, 15501329221082030. [CrossRef]
21. Weerasinghe, S.; Zaslavsky, A.; Loke, S.W.; Hassani, A.; Medvedev, A.; Abken, A. Adaptive context caching for IoT-based applications: A reinforcement learning approach. *Sensors* **2023**, *23*, 4767. [CrossRef]
22. Moradi, H.; Zamani, B.; Zamanifar, K. CaaSSET: A framework for model-driven development of context as a service. *Future Gener. Comput. Syst.* **2020**, *105*, 61–95. [CrossRef]
23. Delnevo, G.; Ghini, V.; Fiumana, E.; Mirri, S. A Support Tool for Emergency Management in Smart Campuses: Reference Architecture and Enhanced Web User Interfaces. *Sensors* **2024**, *24*, 5887. [CrossRef]
24. Polo-Rodríguez, A.; Fiorini, L.; Rovini, E.; Cavallo, F.; Medina-Quero, J. Enhancing smart environments with context-aware chatbots using large language models. *arXiv* **2025**, arXiv:2502.14469. [CrossRef]
25. Violos, J.; Mamanis, G.; Kompatsiaris, I.; Papadopoulos, S. Cognition and context-aware decision-making systems for a sustainable planet: A survey on recent advancements, applications and open challenges. *Discov. Sustain.* **2025**, *6*, 1–43. [CrossRef]
26. Augusto, J.C. Contexts and context-awareness revisited from an intelligent environments perspective. *Appl. Artif. Intell.* **2022**, *36*, 2008644. [CrossRef]
27. Karchoud, R.; Roose, P.; Dalmau, M.; Illarramendi, A.; Ilarri, S. One app to rule them all: Collaborative injection of situations in an adaptable context-aware application. *J. Ambient Intell. Humaniz. Comput.* **2019**, *10*, 4679–4692. [CrossRef]
28. Afram, A.; Janabi-Sharifi, F. Theory and applications of HVAC control systems–A review of model predictive control (MPC). *Build. Environ.* **2014**, *72*, 343–355. [CrossRef]
29. Park, J.H.; Lee, S.; Kang, M. Development and evaluation of rule-based control strategies for smart building energy management. *Appl. Energy* **2020**, *264*, 114487.
30. Chifu, V.R.; Cioara, T.; Pop, C.B.; Rusu, H.G.; Anghel, I. Deep Q-learning-based smart scheduling of EVS for demand response in smart grids. *Appl. Sci.* **2024**, *14*, 1421.
31. Coraci, D.; Brandi, S.; Piscitelli, M.S.; Capozzoli, A. Online implementation of a soft actor-critic agent to enhance indoor temperature control and energy efficiency in buildings. *Energies* **2021**, *14*, 997. [CrossRef]
32. Anan, M.; Kanaan, K.; Benhaddou, D.; Nasser, N.; Qolomany, B.; Talei, H.; Sawalmeh, A. Occupant-aware energy consumption prediction in smart buildings using a LSTM model and time series data. *Energies* **2024**, *17*, 6451. [CrossRef]
33. Annane, B.; Alti, A.; Osman, G. SecNetworkCloudSim: An extensible simulation tool for secure distributed mobile applications. *Int. J. Commun. Netw. Inf. Secur.* **2020**, *12*, 47–62.
34. Liu, G.; Sun, Q.; Su, H.; Wang, M. Adaptive cooperative fault-tolerant control for output-constrained nonlinear multi-agent systems under stochastic FDI attacks. *IEEE Trans. Circuits Syst. I Regul. Pap.* **2025**, *72*, 6025–6036. [CrossRef]

https://doi.org/10.3390/fi18010040

future internet

MDPI

Article

Perceived Learning vs. Engagement in AI-Assisted Homework: A Comparative Study of ChatGPT Use Across High School, University, and Teachers in Sonora, Mexico (2024–2025)

Raquel Torres-Peralta [1,*], Federico Cirett-Galán [1], María del Carmen Heras-Sanchez [2], Karla Lerma-Molina [1] and Ilse Espinoza-Flores [1]

1 Facultad Interdisciplinaria de Ingeniería, Universidad de Sonora, Hermosillo 83000, Mexico; federico.cirett@unison.mx (F.C.-G.); karlaarlethlerma@gmail.com (K.L.-M.); ilseesflo27@gmail.com (I.E.-F.)
2 Facultad Interdisciplinaria de Ciencias Exactas y Naturales, Universidad de Sonora, Hermosillo 83000, Mexico; carmen.heras@unison.mx
* Correspondence: raquel.torres@unison.mx

Abstract

This study examines how generative AI is adopted and experienced across educational levels in Sonora, Mexico, and whether students' perceived learning aligns with engagement behaviors during AI-assisted homework. We analyze survey data from 2024–2025 covering 1477 participants (high school and university students and teachers) from public and private institutions, including adoption, perceived learning and time savings, help-seeking preferences (teachers vs. ChatGPT vs. Google), and ethical concerns. To move beyond self-reports alone, we introduce a Learning Engagement Index (LEI; 0–1) based on three student behaviors when using ChatGPT to complete academic tasks: reading AI responses, modifying outputs, and integrating personal ideas. Adoption was widespread but consistently higher in university than in high school for both students and teachers. University students reported slightly higher perceived learning and greater time savings. LEI scores were generally high and higher among university students, indicating more frequent engagement behaviors such as reading and adapting AI outputs rather than copying them. However, perceived learning showed only weak alignment with LEI, suggesting that students' self-assessments do not consistently track the engagement actions measured by the index. A complementary GitHub Copilot Free (version GPT-4) experiment (n = 16) indicated faster task completion and improved task completeness, while also highlighting the risk of reduced algorithmic reasoning when AI suggestions are used uncritically. Overall, the findings point to the need for pedagogical approaches that emphasize guided use, verification practices, and assessment designs that more directly evidence learning in AI-mediated settings.

Keywords: generative AI; ChatGPT; GitHub Copilot; educational technology; comparative study

1. Introduction

Generative artificial intelligence (GenAI) systems such as ChatGPT and GitHub Copilot are rapidly becoming embedded in academic routines, reshaping how students search for information, draft responses, and complete assignments. Unlike earlier educational technologies centered on retrieval or practice, conversational models can generate fluent, context-aware outputs that closely resemble human-produced explanations, raising fundamental questions about learning processes, assessment practices, and the evolving role of human instruction [1–5].

A central concern in this emerging landscape is the potential gap between students' perceived learning and their actual mastery when GenAI is used to complete assignments. Because these tools can reduce the effort required to produce polished outputs, students may report high learning or productivity even when deeper processing (understanding, integrating, and applying concepts) is limited. This issue is especially salient because homework has traditionally been treated as a routine mechanism associated with learning achievement, although evidence indicates that the relationship between homework and achievement depends on factors such as time and frequency and may be non-linear [6]. When GenAI changes how homework is produced, completion or apparent quality may no longer function as a straightforward proxy for topic mastery. Consequently, beyond measuring adoption and self-reported benefits, there is a growing need to examine how students engage with AI outputs—whether they read, transform, and integrate generated content into their own reasoning—so that perceived learning can be interpreted within a clearer behavioral context [4,5].

Recent research has documented the growing adoption of ChatGPT in education, highlighting perceived benefits such as time efficiency, accessibility, and academic support, alongside concerns related to academic integrity, overreliance, and evaluation fairness [1–3,5]. Evidence focused on teachers indicates both interest in the pedagogical potential of GenAI and persistent uncertainty regarding how to regulate its use and assess learning fairly [1,2]. Prior work conducted with university students and teachers in Mexico suggests that GenAI is already embedded in everyday academic practices, while institutional guidance and shared evaluation frameworks remain limited [1,2,7–10]. These findings reinforce that educational impact cannot be understood solely through usage metrics and perceived outcomes, but also requires attention to how these tools are interpreted, negotiated, and regulated within specific educational contexts [4,5].

Educational context matters because GenAI use is shaped by institutional norms, assessment practices, and students' stage of academic development. Upper-secondary (high school) and university students encounter different task demands and expectations regarding autonomy, academic integrity, and critical evaluation of information. Teachers at each level likewise face distinct constraints and incentives when deciding whether—and how—to incorporate or restrict GenAI in classroom practice. Yet much of the available empirical evidence on GenAI in education originates from North America, Europe, or East Asia, and educational contexts in Latin America differ in meaningful ways, including variability in technological infrastructure, institutional resources, teacher training, and students' access to digital tools [4,11]. Structural inequalities, uneven connectivity, and diverse educational trajectories can shape how technologies are adopted and experienced, underscoring the need for context-sensitive research that reflects local conditions and challenges [4]. Moreover, existing studies have focused predominantly on higher education, leaving less evidence on how upper-secondary students engage with GenAI and how these practices compare with university settings in Latin America.

In addition to general-purpose tools such as ChatGPT, domain-specific systems such as GitHub Copilot introduce further complexity in technical disciplines. AI-assisted programming tools may influence problem-solving approaches, task completion time, and perceptions of competence, raising distinct questions about learning outcomes and skill development. Comparative analyses that consider both types of tools across educational levels and roles remain limited, particularly in Latin American contexts [4,5,8,9,11].

https://doi.org/10.3390/fi18030122

This study addresses these gaps through a comparative analysis of GenAI use among high school students, university students, and teachers in Sonora, Mexico. We combine descriptive evidence with targeted inferential analyses to (i) characterize adoption and perceived benefits and (ii) test whether perceived learning aligns with engagement behaviors during AI-assisted work. To operationalize engagement, we propose a Learning Engagement Index (LEI) that summarizes students' reported actions when using ChatGPT to complete academic tasks—reading AI outputs, modifying them, and integrating personal ideas—allowing an empirical comparison between perceived learning and engagement practices within the same sample.

This study pursues five objectives:

1. Characterize and compare the adoption of ChatGPT (and similar GenAI tools) among students and teachers across high school and university levels.
2. Perceived outcomes: Compare perceived learning (Q1) and perceived time savings among students across educational levels.
3. Help-seeking preferences: Describe students' preferred sources for resolving academic doubts (teachers vs. ChatGPT vs. search engines/other sources) and interpret reported reasons for these choices.
4. Engagement and alignment: Construct the Learning Engagement Index (LEI) from engagement behaviors during AI-assisted task completion (Q2–Q4) and test whether perceived learning (Q1) aligns with these engagement actions.
5. Complementary task-based evidence: Contextualize survey findings with a small GitHub Copilot protocol to capture task-based indicators of productivity and completeness in programming-related work [4,5,8,9,11].

Results are organized to mirror these objectives. We first present adoption patterns for students and teachers and then report perceived learning and time savings among students. We next describe help-seeking preferences and related reasoning. We then introduce and analyze the LEI and assess its association with perceived learning. Finally, we summarize the complementary evidence from the GitHub Copilot protocol and discuss implications for pedagogy, assessment, and responsible integration of GenAI in educational settings.

2. Background and Related Work

The emergence of generative artificial intelligence (AI) tools—most notably ChatGPT—has rapidly reshaped educational discourse worldwide. Since its public release in late 2022, ChatGPT has attracted sustained attention from educators, students, policymakers, and researchers, prompting a growing body of literature that seeks to understand its pedagogical potential, limitations, and risks. While early discussions were largely speculative or conceptual, recent studies increasingly adopt empirical and mixed-method approaches to examine how generative AI is being incorporated into teaching and learning practices across disciplines and educational levels.

2.1. Generative AI in Education: Opportunities and Risks

Systematic reviews and large-scale analytical studies consistently emphasize the dual nature of generative AI in education. On the one hand, large language models are recognized for their capacity to support personalized learning, provide immediate feedback, assist with content generation, and reduce instructors' workload [5,12,13]. On the other hand, these same studies warn of significant challenges related to academic integrity, overreliance, erosion of foundational skills, and the difficulty of evaluating authentic learning when AI-generated content is involved [5,14,15]. Kasneci et al. [5] and Montenegro-Rueda et al. [13] argue that the educational value of ChatGPT depends less on the technology itself than on the pedagogical frameworks governing its use. Similarly,

https://doi.org/10.3390/fi18030122

Memarian and Doleck [12] note that much of the early literature relies on conceptual commentary rather than rigorous empirical evidence, calling for studies that move beyond perception toward measurable learning outcomes.

2.2. Teacher Perceptions and Pedagogical Adaptation

A substantial body of research has focused on educators' perceptions of generative AI and their readiness to integrate it into teaching practice. Early studies report a cautious but increasingly pragmatic stance among instructors. Alarcón Llontop et al. [1] document initial perceptions of university teachers, showing that while many recognize ChatGPT's usefulness for instructional preparation, they express concern about plagiarism, student dependence, and the absence of institutional guidance. These findings are reinforced by Arguello et al. [2], who report high adoption rates among higher education faculty, particularly for planning and content development, alongside persistent ethical reservations. Qualitative and mixed-method studies further highlight that teachers' responses are shaped by disciplinary culture and pedagogical identity. Mateus et al. [16], in a study spanning Mexico, Peru, and Spain, show that educators recognize the potential of generative AI to transform teaching practices but differ in how they envision its alignment with higher-order learning objectives. More recently, García Sánchez and Carrillo Guerrero [17] report largely positive evaluations of ChatGPT among health sciences faculty in Mexico, particularly regarding efficiency and practicality, while noting lower confidence in accuracy and critical thinking outcomes. Across these studies, a recurring theme is the need for professional training and clear institutional frameworks to support responsible AI integration.

2.3. Student Perceptions, Usability, and Satisfaction

Parallel research has examined students' perceptions, acceptance, and patterns of use of generative AI. Quantitative studies consistently show positive attitudes toward ChatGPT, driven by its immediacy, accessibility, and perceived usefulness [18–20]. Gil-Vera [21], using a structural equation modeling approach, demonstrates a direct and positive relationship between perceived usability and satisfaction among university students, suggesting that ease of use and functional value strongly shape students' overall appraisal of the tool. Importantly, the study emphasizes that satisfaction does not necessarily imply deep learning, underscoring the importance of pedagogical mediation and explicit guidance on responsible use. Other studies reveal a more ambivalent student stance. Chávez et al. [18] and [20] report that while students value ChatGPT as a learning aid, they also express concerns about reduced effort, superficial understanding, and dependence on AI-generated answers. The evidence indicates that student engagement with generative AI is neither uniform nor uncritical, but evolves alongside academic experience and instructional context.

Adoption rates alone provide an incomplete picture of generative AI's educational impact; what matters is how students engage with AI outputs during academic work. Prior work on GenAI in education suggests that learning benefits are more plausible when students actively evaluate, elaborate on, and integrate AI-generated content rather than reproducing it mechanically—for example, through verification, critical use, and reflective integration [5,12,13,19]. In line with this perspective, we operationalize engagement using self-reported behaviors—reading responses, editing/modifying outputs, and adding one's own ideas—so that perceived learning can be contrasted against action-oriented indicators of engagement.

2.4. Empirical and Experimental Evidence on Learning Outcomes

Beyond perceptions, a growing but still limited body of work has examined the impact of generative AI on learning outcomes. Malinka et al. [14] show that ChatGPT performs adequately on routine academic tasks but struggles with activities requiring deeper critical reasoning, reinforcing the argument that AI should complement rather than replace cognitive effort. Díaz Vera et al. [22], in a comparative experimental study within an undergraduate computing course, report statistically significant performance gains for students who used ChatGPT during instructional activities, alongside high levels of satisfaction and perceived improvement in comprehension. Comparative evaluations of multiple generative AI models further indicate that no single system is optimal across all educational objectives. Kerimbayev et al. [23] demonstrate substantial variation among models such as GPT-4, Copilot, and others in terms of content quality, adaptability, and performance, highlighting the importance of aligning AI selection with specific pedagogical goals. These results resonate with domain-specific studies on GitHub Copilot in engineering education, which report efficiency gains and improved task completion when AI assistance is used under structured and supervised conditions.

2.5. Identified Gaps and Contribution of the Present Study

Despite the rapid expansion of this literature, several gaps remain. Most existing studies focus on a single educational level, discipline, or stakeholder group, and rely predominantly on cross-sectional designs. Comparative analyses that simultaneously examine secondary and higher education contexts, integrate both student and teacher perspectives, and account for changes over time remain scarce—particularly in Latin American settings. The present study addresses these gaps by offering a comparative, multi-level analysis of generative AI use among high school and university students and teachers in northern Mexico, complemented by experimental evidence from GitHub Copilot in engineering education. By situating local empirical findings within the broader international literature, this work contributes to a contextualized and developmentally informed understanding of how generative AI is reshaping learning practices, assessment challenges, and ethical considerations across educational stages.

3. Methodology

This study adopts a comparative and mixed-methods approach to analyze how generative AI tools, specifically ChatGPT and GitHub Copilot, are used and perceived by students and teachers across high school and university settings in Sonora, Mexico. The methodological design integrates quantitative data from large-scale surveys with qualitative insights from open-ended responses and a controlled experimental component. This structure enables both statistical comparison and interpretive understanding of how AI technologies influence learning, teaching, and cognitive engagement across different educational contexts. The section that follows describes the study's scope, participants, instruments, and analytical procedures in detail.

3.1. Design and Scope

This study employs a comparative mixed-methods design that integrates quantitative and qualitative analyses to explore how students and teachers use, perceive, and integrate generative artificial intelligence tools, particularly ChatGPT and GitHub Copilot, in educational settings across Sonora, Mexico. The research focuses on two educational levels, high school and university, encompassing institutions in Hermosillo, Ciudad Obregón and Guaymas. The high school component includes several public and private preparatory schools in Hermosillo, while the university component covers three public higher-education institutions and a private university. Although differences between public and private universities may affect access to technology and institutional policy, this study focuses on comparing educational levels and user roles—students and teachers—regarding their interaction with generative AI tools in learning and teaching. The study was conducted between October

https://doi.org/10.3390/fi18030122

2024 and May 2025, covering two academic terms, and constitutes an extension of research initiated in 2024 [10,24]. It incorporates and builds upon previously reported findings on the use of generative AI tools, including GitHub Copilot, while expanding the analysis through additional survey data from students and teachers across educational levels and a broader comparative framework. The study involved a total of 1477 participants, drawn from both upper secondary (high school) and higher education contexts in the state of Sonora, Mexico. Participants included students and teachers from public and private institutions, allowing for a comparative perspective across educational levels.

3.2. Participants

At the upper secondary (high school) level, 602 students participated in the survey. These students were enrolled in ten preparatory schools located in Hermosillo and Guaymas, including both public and private institutions. The student sample comprised 52.2% women (n = 314), 45.7% men (n = 275), and 2.2% other/prefer not to say (n = 13). In addition, 42 high school teachers from the same institutions completed the questionnaire. Among them, 64.3% were women (n = 27) and 35.7% were men (n = 15). Most participating teachers were affiliated with subjects in the areas of science, mathematics, or technology, reflecting the disciplinary composition of the participating schools.

University Participants

At the higher education level, 765 students responded to the survey. These participants were enrolled at three public universities and one private university, located in the cities of Hermosillo, Ciudad Obregón and Guaymas. The gender distribution within this group was 59.5% women (n = 455), 37.1% men (n = 284), and 3.4% other/prefer not to say (n = 26). The university-level teacher sample included 68 instructors, who completed the survey electronically. Of these, 57.4% were men (n = 39), 41.2% were women (n = 28), and 1.5% other/prefer not to say (n = 1). The majority of university instructors were affiliated with engineering, computer science, and social sciences, aligning with the academic programs represented in the student sample. Table 1 summarizes the demographic distribution of participants across educational levels and roles.

Table 1. Demographic distribution of participants across educational levels and roles.

Group	n	Women, n (%)	Men, n (%)	Other/Prefer Not to Say, n (%)
High school students	602	314 (52.2)	275 (45.7)	13 (2.2)
University students	765	455 (59.5)	284 (37.1)	26 (3.4)
High school teachers	42	27 (64.3)	15 (35.7)	0 (0.0)
University teachers	68	28 (41.2)	39 (57.4)	1 (1.5)

Note: Percentages are calculated within each row and may not sum to 100 due to rounding. "Other/Prefer not to say" includes any gender responses different from "Women" and "Men" (e.g., non-binary, prefer not to say).

Ethical Considerations:All participation was anonymous and voluntary. Respondents were informed of the academic nature of the research and their right to withdraw at any time. No personally identifiable information was collected.

3.3. Instruments and Variables

Data were collected through four complementary instruments designed to capture quantitative patterns and qualitative perspectives on the educational use of generative artificial intelligence.

Each instrument was adapted to the characteristics of its target population—high school students, university students, teachers, and engineering students—in an experimental context and was reviewed by an interdisciplinary academic team to ensure conceptual clarity and consistency.

3.3.1. High School Student Questionnaire

A 19-item digital questionnaire was administered personally in classrooms by collaborators of the research team, using a QR code to ensure that all respondents were verified students. The survey was not accessed or distributed through external channels. The instrument combined Likert-scale items (0–10) evaluating perceived learning, trust in AI accuracy, time savings, and attitudes toward teacher replacement; multiple-choice questions on usage motives and preferred sources for resolving academic doubts; and open-ended prompts on advantages, risks, and misuse. Core variables included adoption level, learning perception, productivity effects, trust and dependence, and preference for human versus AI assistance. This mixed-response design enabled a multidimensional understanding of students' experiences with AI-assisted learning.

3.3.2. University Student Questionnaire

The university survey comprised a 28-item online instrument completed independently between October 2024 and May 2025. It extended the high school version by examining students' integration of ChatGPT into academic and personal contexts, as well as their evolving ethical awareness. The questionnaire covered frequency and types of use, perceived learning support (Likert 0–10), time efficiency, task improvement, and ethical or professional considerations, alongside open-ended reflections on motivations, limitations, and responsible use. Core variables included use frequency, perceived learning gains, efficiency metrics, motivational profiles, and ethical/professional awareness. Administering the survey in two waves enabled observation of attitudinal changes across the academic year.

3.3.3. Teacher Questionnaire (High School and University)

The teacher survey consisted of a 20-item electronic instrument assessing educators' experiences with generative AI, their classroom policies, and their own use of ChatGPT for instructional design and evaluation. It included closed-ended questions on usage frequency and perceived benefits and drawbacks, Likert-scale items (0–10) on attitudes toward AI integration and ethical understanding, and open-ended prompts regarding detection of AI-generated student work and pedagogical adjustments. Key variables included AI use in teaching tasks, attitudes toward student use, detection strategies, ethical awareness, and reported instructional adaptations. Teachers' responses provided critical insight into institutional readiness and the pedagogical challenges associated with integrating generative AI into educational practice.

3.3.4. Learning Engagement Index (LEI)

To complement self-reported learning with indicators of students' active engagement during AI-assisted work, we constructed a Learning Engagement Index (LEI) using three survey items that capture how students interact with ChatGPT-generated outputs: (Q2) whether students read AI responses rather than copying them verbatim when using the tool to complete academic tasks, (Q3) the extent to which students modify AI-generated answers, and (Q4) whether students complement AI-generated answers with their own ideas. These items were selected because they reflect engagement behaviors commonly associated with deeper processing (e.g., comprehension monitoring, elaboration, and integration) and can be operationalized consistently across educational levels within the survey design.

https://doi.org/10.3390/fi18030122

3.3.5. Analytic Sample and Exclusions

LEI was computed only for respondents providing valid responses to all three items (Q2–Q4).Records were excluded if any of Q2–Q4 were missing/NA, and if any of the three items indicated non-use of ChatGPT (Q2: "I do not use ChatGPT"; Q3: "I do not use it"; Q4: "I do not use it"). After applying these criteria, the LEI analytic sample retained n = 1108 respondents. For analyses comparing LEI with perceived learning (Q1; 0–10), only respondents with a valid numeric Q1 response were retained (n = 1105).

3.3.6. Coding and Normalization

Responses were coded to reflect increasing levels of engagement. For Q2 (reading AI responses), responses were scored on a 0–3 scale as follows: 3 = "I always read the full responses", 2 = "I read part of the text before copying and pasting", 1 = "It depends on the task; sometimes I read them and sometimes I do not", and 0 = "I do not read the response; I only copy and paste". For Q3 (modification of AI responses), responses were scored on a 0–4 scale as follows: 4 = "I modify almost the entire response", 3 = "I modify a considerable portion of the response", 2 = "I modify the response a little", 1 = "I barely modify the response", and 0 = "I do not modify the response". For Q4 (integration of own ideas), responses were coded as binary: 1 = "Yes" and 0 = "No". Each component was normalized to a 0–1 range by dividing by its maximum possible score (Q2/3, Q3/4, Q4/1).

3.3.7. Learning Engagement Index (LEI) Computation

The LEI was defined as the mean of the three normalized components, yielding a continuous score ranging from 0 to 1, where higher values indicate greater engagement with AI outputs:

$$\mathrm{LEI} = \frac{Q2_{norm} + Q3_{norm} + Q4_{norm}}{3}, \qquad \mathrm{LEI} \in [0,1],$$

LEI was summarized using descriptive statistics and compared across educational level and institutional sector using non-parametric tests, given the bounded nature of the index. To examine whether students' perceived learning aligned with engagement behaviors, we estimated both bivariate associations (Spearman correlations between LEI and Q1) and adjusted linear models with Q1 as the outcome and LEI as a predictor, controlling for educational level, institutional sector, age, and survey wave where available. All analyses were interpreted as associations and not as evidence of causality.

3.3.8. Qualitative Analysis

Open-ended responses were analyzed from Q26.1 ("Justify your previous response"), an open-text follow-up to Q26 ("Would you agree to block the use of ChatGPT?"), and Q29 ("Anything else you would like to add about ChatGPT in your education"). A thematic coding approach was used to identify recurring ethical and cognitive themes (e.g., academic honesty, privacy, authorship, verification, bias, and perceived dependence). To quantify the prevalence of "perceived dependence," we constructed a composite indicator at the respondent level: a participant was coded as mentioning dependence if the theme appeared in at least one of their open-ended responses (Q26.1 and/or Q29). The denominator for prevalence estimates included only respondents who provided at least one valid open-ended response (non-empty text) in Q26.1 and/or Q29; non-responses were excluded.

3.3.9. GitHub Copilot Experimental Protocol

A complementary experimental protocol was implemented with information systems engineering students to examine GitHub Copilot as a domain-specific AI assistant for programming. Using a controlled between-groups design, 16 participants (8 per

https://doi.org/10.3390/fi18030122

group) completed a two-hour Python data-processing task, with one group receiving Copilot/ChatGPT support and the other working without AI tools. Data were collected through pre-task surveys, performance metrics (completion time, feature implementation, code modularity/readability), and post-task reflections. Key variables included efficiency, task completeness, code quality, and perceived difficulty.

4. Results

This section presents and interprets the results obtained from the quantitative and qualitative analyses of students' and teachers' experiences with generative AI tools. The discussion integrates findings from high school and university participants, considering both educational levels and user roles. The results are organized around key analytical dimensions: adoption and frequency of use, perceived learning and productivity, ethical awareness, and the evolving relationship between human instruction and AI-assisted learning. The experimental data on GitHub Copilot use among information systems engineering students are incorporated to illustrate how domain-specific applications of AI contribute to technical skill development and educational performance. The results, considered jointly, provide a comprehensive view of how generative AI is reshaping educational practices, perceptions, and interactions across contexts.

4.1. Overview of Adoption and Usage Patterns

Across both educational levels, the use of generative AI tools was widespread, with adoption patterns differing between high school and university respondents. In both groups, ChatGPT emerged as the predominant tool, whereas GitHub Copilot was reported mainly by university students enrolled in computer science and engineering programs. At the high school level, 76.7% of students (462/602) reported having used an AI assistant such as ChatGPT. Their open-ended descriptions typically characterized use as occasional and task-specific, most commonly for clarifying concepts, checking writing, or obtaining support with homework. Among university students, 93.1% (712/765) reported having used an AI assistant, and many described ChatGPT as a regular or integrated part of their study routines. This difference in adoption by educational level was statistically significant ($\chi^2(1) = 72.73$, $p = 1.49 \times 10^{-17}$), with a small-to-moderate association ($\phi = 0.231$) and an estimated adoption gap of 16.3 percentage points (95% CI: 12.5–20.2) favoring university respondents. For more details, see Figure 1.

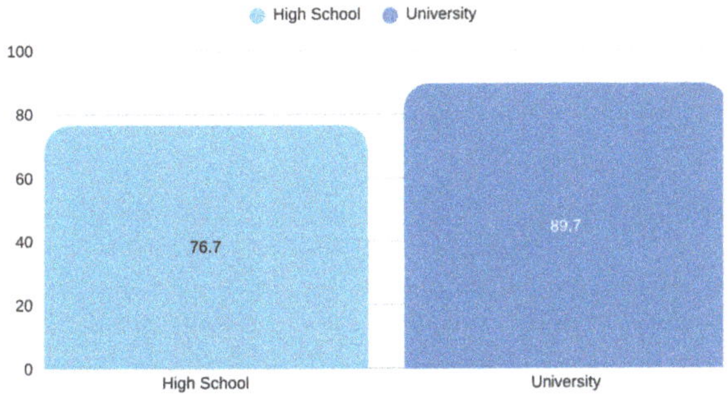

Figure 1. ChatGPT adoption by education level.

While this difference may suggest a shift from more exploratory or instrumental use in high school to more systematic and goal-oriented use in higher education, these results must be interpreted with caution. The surveys were administered at different points in time, and therefore, the contrast between educational levels cannot be attributed

https://doi.org/10.3390/fi18030122

solely to academic maturity or grade level. It remains possible that broader temporal trends—such as increased exposure to generative AI tools, greater normalization of their use, or evolving institutional attitudes—also contributed to the higher reported integration among university students. Consequently, the observed pattern highlights the need for longitudinal monitoring to determine whether differences in use reflect developmental trajectories, temporal effects, institutional context, or a combination of these factors.

Teacher adoption exhibited clear differences by educational level. Among high school instructors, 33.3% (14/42) reported using ChatGPT or similar tools to generate teaching materials, often citing limited time, lack of institutional guidance, or low confidence in output accuracy. In contrast, among university instructors, 69.1% (47/68) reported using generative AI for tasks such as preparing instructional materials, editing texts, translating documents, and designing exercises or assessments. This difference in adoption between educational levels was statistically significant ($\chi^2(1) = 13.46$, $p = 2.44 \times 10^{-4}$), with a moderate association ($\phi = 0.350$). The estimated adoption gap was 35.8 percentage points (95% CI: 17.8–53.8), indicating substantially higher uptake among university instructors. Nonetheless, teachers at both levels emphasized the need for clear ethical guidelines and professional training to support responsible integration. See Figure 2.

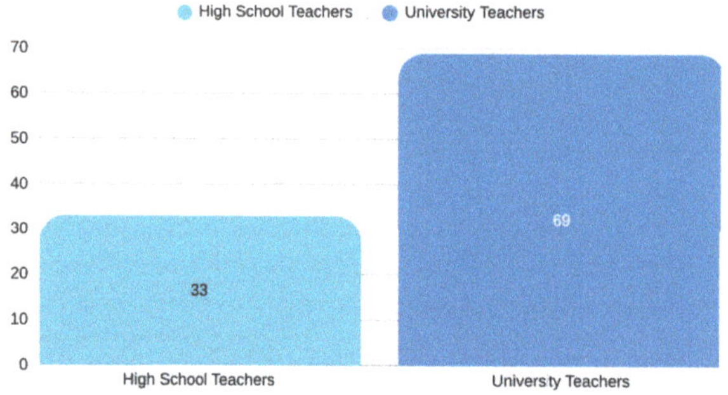

Figure 2. Percentage of teachers reporting adoption of ChatGPT or other generative AI tools (by educational level).

The results suggest that exposure and educational maturity significantly influence adoption. University students and teachers tend to integrate AI into more complex cognitive and creative tasks, while high school users—both students and educators—remain in earlier stages of exploration and adaptation. This pattern supports the notion of a developmental continuum of AI literacy, where usage evolves from pragmatic experimentation to intentional and reflective application as academic experience deepens.

4.2. Perceived Learning and Productivity

Perceptions of learning and productivity reveal both the educational potential and the cognitive risks associated with integrating generative AI into academic settings. Quantitative results indicate higher self-perceived learning gains among university students compared with high school students, alongside a progressive normalization of AI-assisted study practices. Among high school students, the average self-reported learning score on a 0–10 scale was 5.75 ($n = 584$; excluding non-responses), suggesting a moderate perceived benefit.

Qualitative responses further indicated that many students viewed the tool as a convenient aid to "understand explanations in simpler words" or to "get ideas when the topic is confusing," rather than as a means of deep learning. Consequently, reported use tended to be instrumental, with students relying on ChatGPT primarily to complete assignments or verify answers rather than to explore concepts in depth.

https://doi.org/10.3390/fi18030122

University students reported a higher average perceived learning score of 6.30 ($n = 745$; excluding non-responses). This difference in educational level was statistically significant (Welch's t-test: t = 3.38, $p = 7.4 \times 10^{-4}$), indicating modestly greater perceived cognitive benefit among university respondents. Refer to Figure 3.

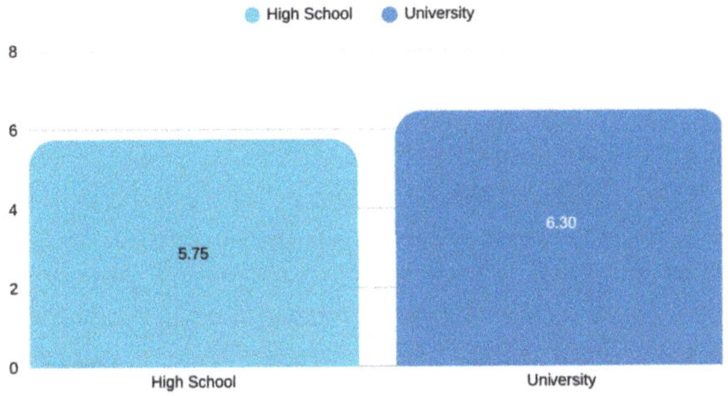

Figure 3. Perceived learning from ChatGPT by educational level (self-reported scores on a 0–10 scale).

Many described ChatGPT as a complementary learning partner that supports summarization, reformulation, and conceptual expansion of course materials. Importantly, their narratives reflect an emerging awareness of their own learning processes: students used the tool to monitor understanding, identify gaps, rehearse explanations, and reinforce knowledge. Within the context of this study, these patterns appear consistent with elements of self-regulated learning, whereby AI is incorporated into cycles of checking, adjusting, and consolidating comprehension. While these findings cannot establish a generalized shift, they indicate that at least among this group, generative AI is beginning to be used in ways that align with reflective and intentional learning strategies.

Perceived productivity followed a similar trajectory. Among high school students who reported using ChatGPT ($n = 456$; excluding non-responses and "No lo utilizo"), reported time savings per task were distributed across the full set of categories: $\leq$15 min (36.0%, 164/456), 15 min–1 h (43.2%, 197/456), 1–3 h (15.4%, 70/456), and >3 h (5.5%, 25/456). In contrast, university users ($n = 668$) more frequently reported larger time savings (1–3 h: 32.6%, 218/668; >3 h: 13.5%, 90/668), while 14.5% (97/668) reported savings under 15 min and 39.4% (263/668) reported savings of 15 min–1 h. The distribution of reported time savings categories differed significantly by educational level ($\chi^2(3) = 103.15$, $p = 3.27 \times 10^{-22}$). See Figure 4.

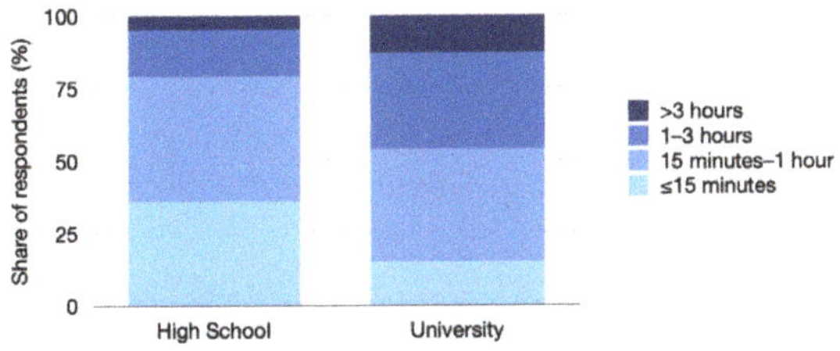

Figure 4. Perceived time savings from ChatGPT use by high school and university students.

Teacher perspectives further contextualize these patterns. Among high school instructors ($n = 42$), 33.3% (14/42) reported using ChatGPT or similar tools to generate teaching materials, mainly for idea generation or drafting written resources, although many expressed uncertainty regarding reliability and accuracy. In contrast, among university instructors ($n = 68$), 69.1% (47/68) reported employing generative AI for tasks such as

https://doi.org/10.3390/fi18030122

preparing teaching resources, editing or translating texts, and designing assessments. This difference in adoption by educational level was statistically significant, indicating substantially higher uptake among university instructors. While several acknowledged substantial time savings, others questioned whether increased speed necessarily translates into higher pedagogical quality or deeper student learning.

These findings suggest that perceived learning and productivity vary across educational levels and may be associated with students' increasing academic experience. In this sample, university students appear to move beyond purely procedural uses of AI and engage with it in ways that resemble more reflective and strategic learning practices, potentially supporting metacognitive monitoring and time management. However, because the surveys were administered at different moments in time and in distinct educational contexts, these patterns should not be interpreted as evidence of a developmental progression. Rather, they reflect observed tendencies within the groups studied. Similarly, teachers' adoption patterns show signs of evolving professional engagement with AI—particularly in instructional design and administrative tasks—while also revealing ongoing concerns about quality, ethics, and the authenticity of student work. These dynamics highlight emerging shifts in practice, though further longitudinal research is needed to determine whether such patterns represent broader or stable trends in educational environments.

4.3. Ethical Awareness and Perceived Dependence

Ethical awareness and perceptions of dependence are central to understanding how students and teachers navigate the role of generative AI in educational settings. Although adoption was high, participants varied widely in their capacity to evaluate the ethical, cognitive, and social implications of using tools such as ChatGPT and GitHub Copilot. The qualitative evidence suggests that ethical literacy does not arise solely from exposure to technology but is shaped by the pedagogical and institutional contexts through which learners are guided to question and interpret AI outputs. This section is based on open-ended responses from Q26.1 (a written justification prompted after the closed-ended Yes/No item Q26, "Would you agree to block the use of ChatGPT?") and Q29 ("Anything else you would like to add about ChatGPT in your education"), with themes coded at the respondent level and excluding non-responses.

Among high school students, ethical reasoning tended to be pragmatic rather than principled. Many framed generative AI as a legitimate aid for completing assignments as long as the results appeared correct or visually acceptable, and relatively few explicitly referenced academic honesty, data privacy, or authorship. Their judgments often reflected a utilitarian logic that prioritized efficiency and correctness over process or integrity. Even so, a notable proportion of high school respondents (40.7% of those who provided at least one valid open-ended response in Q26.1 and/or Q29) raised concerns about cognitive dependence—frequently expressed as the idea that heavy reliance on ChatGPT could "make students lazy" or reduce independent learning—signaling an emerging awareness of dependence-related risks, albeit often articulated in behavioral rather than explicitly ethical terms.

Table 2 summarizes the comparative patterns in students' ethical awareness and perceived dependence across cohorts (high school 2024, university 2024, university 2025), highlighting a shift from task-oriented use toward more reflective framing and broader ethical reasoning.

Table 2. Comparison of Ethical Awareness and Perceived Dependence among Students.

Dimension	High School Students (2024)	University Students (2024)	University Students (2025)
View of AI use	Task-oriented; valued for convenience and speed	Functional; helpful for clarity and structure but requiring verification	Reflective; understood as a cognitive partner rather than a replacement
Ethical awareness	Minimal; ethicality equated with "not copying"	Emerging; focus on plagiarism and authorship	Broader ethical reasoning including fairness, data bias, and responsibility
Perceived dependence	Situational; used when teachers are unavailable	Cognitive; some report difficulty starting tasks without AI	Managed; conscious effort to balance AI use with personal reasoning
Perception of accuracy	High trust; AI perceived as infallible	Conditional trust; students verify outputs with other sources	Critical trust; recognition of factual and contextual errors
Attitude toward teachers	Teachers seen as authority and emotional support	Teachers valued for expertise but sometimes replaced for efficiency	Teachers revalued for human judgment, empathy, and contextual understanding
Main ethical tension	Shortcut vs. effort	Authorship vs. assistance	Responsibility vs. overreliance

University students' responses generally reflected a more developed and conceptually nuanced ethical perspective. In addition to concerns commonly centered on plagiarism and authorship, many respondents introduced broader considerations such as the need for human verification, transparency regarding sources, and the possibility of biased or misleading outputs. They also emphasized that fluent or persuasive language does not guarantee accuracy, pointing to a growing recognition that responsible use requires critical evaluation of both the content produced and the conditions under which it is generated. See Figure 5.

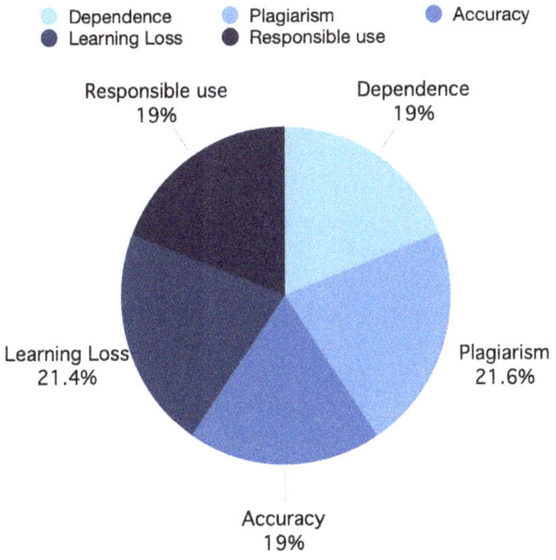

Figure 5. Main ethical tensions identified by students across educational levels.

Teachers across both levels reflected these tensions but approached them differently. High school instructors emphasized concerns about assessment validity and the difficulty of identifying AI-generated work without institutional guidance or technological support. University instructors, on the other hand, adopted a more systemic perspective. They viewed AI as an inevitable component of higher education and stressed the need for curric-

https://doi.org/10.3390/fi18030122

ular strategies that teach students to critically evaluate AI outputs, cite them appropriately, and articulate their own reasoning alongside machine-generated content. Across both groups, the consensus was that the challenge is not to prohibit AI, but to adapt pedagogy so that ethical and reflective use becomes an integral part of learning.

Ethical Knowledge Models

The comparative evidence points to a gradual maturation of ethical reasoning as students advance along their educational pathways and gain more experience with AI-mediated learning. Quantitatively, self-reported ethical knowledge (Q27; ordered: No < A little < Yes; excluding non-responses) differed by educational level ($\chi^2(2) = 21.12$, $p = 2.59 \times 10^{-5}$), Cramér's V = 0.127). University students were more likely to report full ethical knowledge (Yes: 47.1%, 348/739) than high school students (Yes: 38.5%, 219/569), whereas high school respondents more frequently selected "A little" (33.4%, 190/569 vs. 22.2%, 164/739). An ordered logit model (proportional odds) estimated a positive association between university level and higher ethical-knowledge categories (OR = 1.17, 95% CI: 0.96–1.43), although this effect was modest and did not reach conventional statistical significance ($p = 0.129$).

Consistent with these quantitative patterns, the qualitative coding of open-ended responses (using the same thematic analysis procedure applied across the study, with three human reviewers and consensus resolution) suggests a shift from an instrumental orientation—centered on convenience, efficiency, and task completion—to a more reflective stance in which students increasingly question the limits of AI outputs and the role of personal judgment in evaluating them. High school narratives tended to emphasize compliance with visible rules (e.g., avoiding direct copying) rather than deeper concerns about learning processes or knowledge construction, whereas university responses more often foregrounded responsibility, transparency, fairness, and the need for verification. These findings support the interpretation of ethical and cognitive development around generative AI as an educational continuum with distinct implications for early-stage pedagogy.

At the same time, this emerging sophistication also brings its own challenges. While early users tend to rely on AI to fill specific informational gaps, more advanced users may risk deferring the start of their own thinking—turning to ChatGPT before attempting to engage with a task independently. This pattern, which could be described as prompt-dependent learning, highlights an important pedagogical concern: how to cultivate autonomy, curiosity, and persistence in a context where instant answers are always available. The implications are particularly urgent for the earliest educational stages. If the capacity for ethical discernment and critical evaluation develops gradually, it becomes essential to introduce discussions of AI use from the primary and lower-secondary levels, not merely at the university level. Doing so would require that curricula and textbooks include content on responsible AI engagement, authorship, data transparency, and the social implications of automation. Classroom activities should incorporate AI tools with guidance and awareness, enabling students to experiment safely while understanding both potential and limitation.

Equally critical is addressing the structural inequality that shapes access to these technologies. In many vulnerable populations, limited connectivity, resource scarcity, and digital illiteracy exacerbate educational disparities. Without targeted policies for equitable access and teacher training, AI integration risks reinforcing existing hierarchies rather than democratizing knowledge.

Ethical and cognitive development around generative AI must be treated as an educational continuum, beginning in early schooling and extending through higher education. The challenge for institutions and policymakers lies not only in regulating use but in culti-

https://doi.org/10.3390/fi18030122

vating critical, inclusive, and ethically conscious digital citizens capable of engaging with emerging technologies responsibly and reflectively.

4.4. Trust and Teacher–AI Preference

Patterns of help-seeking among students reveal a mixed support ecology in which teachers, ChatGPT, and Google coexist as complementary sources of academic support. Rather than a simple substitution dynamic, students appear to evaluate these options based on emotional comfort, epistemic expectations, and practical constraints. In high school, teachers remained the most frequently preferred source of clarification (45.2%, 270/597; excluding non-responses), followed by Google (25.6%, 153/597) and ChatGPT (21.8%, 130/597); the remaining responses were distributed across other options (7.4%, 44/597). At the university level, teachers were likewise the most frequently preferred source (46.4%, 353/761), while a modest shift toward ChatGPT was observed (25.1%, 191/761), and Google was selected by 21.2% (161/761); other options accounted for 7.4% (56/761). When comparing the distribution of the three main categories (Teacher vs. ChatGPT vs. Google; excluding "Other"), differences by educational level were small and not statistically significant ($\chi^2(2) = 4.55$, $p = 0.103$; Cramér's V = 0.060), indicating broadly similar preference structures across levels (See Figure 6).

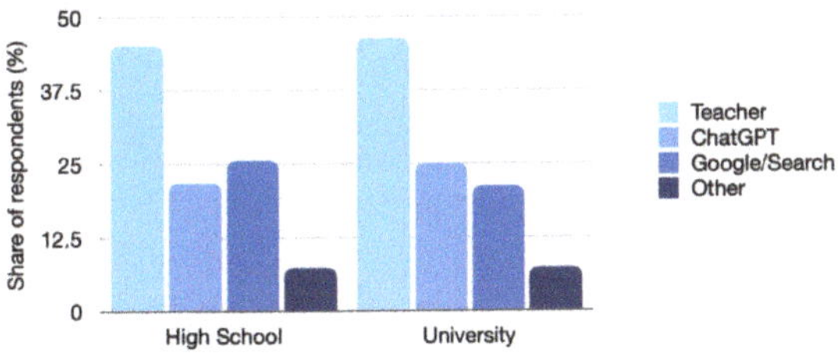

Figure 6. Preferred sources for resolving academic doubts by High School and university students.

Within the university subsample, preferences were also stable across survey years. Comparing 2024 (n = 303 valid responses) and 2025 (n = 458), teachers remained the most frequently preferred source in both cohorts (46.5% vs. 46.3%). Preference for ChatGPT increased slightly in 2025 (23.4% vs. 26.2%), while preference for Google decreased marginally (21.8% vs. 20.7%); "other" responses remained infrequent (8.3% vs. 6.8%). However, the overall distribution did not differ significantly by year ($\chi^2(3) = 1.20$, $p = 0.754$; Cramér's V = 0.040), suggesting that year-to-year changes were modest. Qualitative analysis of students' open-ended justifications (coded using the same thematic methodology applied throughout the study, with three independent reviewers and consensus resolution) clarifies the motives underlying these preferences. High school students who preferred teachers emphasized trust in expertise, clarity, and the ability to provide personalized, context-specific guidance; the affective dimension was prominent, with comments indicating that teachers "understand how I learn," "give concrete examples," or "explain in a way that feels real," underscoring the continued importance of relational trust.

Students who preferred ChatGPT highlighted immediacy, simplicity, and the absence of judgment—particularly among those reporting shyness or discomfort asking questions in class—valuing step-by-step explanations, unlimited repetition, and a sense of psychological safety, while simultaneously expressing concerns about accuracy, logical errors, and overreliance. Google was frequently framed as a complementary option valued for breadth of sources, multimedia explanations, and the ability to contrast perspectives.

https://doi.org/10.3390/fi18030122

University students often described a more differentiated, situational use of resources (e.g., ChatGPT for initial structuring, Google for exploration, and teachers for validation and contextual refinement), although fully consolidated hybrid strategies were not consistently dominant. Teachers' perspectives aligned with these tensions: high school instructors emphasized concerns about accuracy, assessment integrity, and classroom dynamics, whereas university instructors framed AI tools as part of an evolving academic environment requiring new forms of pedagogical mediation. Across both levels, educators noted that their role increasingly involves helping students evaluate, verify, and contextualize AI-generated information rather than merely transmitting content.

4.5. Learning Engagement Index and Its Relationship with Perceived Learning

If perceived learning reflects substantive learning gains, it should be positively associated with students' engagement behaviors during AI-assisted work. We examine this alignment by relating perceived learning (Q1; 0–10) to the Learning Engagement Index (LEI; 0–1), which captures three engagement behaviors when students use ChatGPT to complete academic tasks: reading AI responses rather than copying them verbatim, modifying generated content, and integrating one's own ideas (Q2–Q4). The coding scheme, normalization procedure, and index definition are reported in Table 3, and the analytic sample flow is summarized in Table 4. After excluding records with missing responses on Q2–Q4 and responses indicating non-use of ChatGPT, the LEI analytic sample comprised $n = 1108$ respondents; analyses linking LEI to perceived learning further required a valid numeric Q1 response ($n = 1105$).

Table 3. Learning Engagement Index (LEI): coding and normalization scheme. LEI captures active engagement behaviors when using ChatGPT: reading AI responses (Q2), modifying AI responses (Q3), and complementing AI responses with one's own ideas (Q4). Responses indicating non-use of ChatGPT in any LEI item were excluded.

Item	Response Option (Translated)	Raw Score	Normalization
Q1. Perceived learning	Self-reported perceived learning from ChatGPT (0–10 scale)	0–10	Not part of LEI. Used to examine (Q1 vs. LEI).
Q2. Reading AI responses	I always read the full responses	3	$Q2_{norm} = Q2/3$
	I read part of the text before copying and pasting	2	
	It depends on the task, sometimes I read the responses and sometimes I don't	1	
	I don't read the response, I just copy and paste	0	
	I don't use ChatGPT	Excluded	
Q3. Modifying AI responses	I modify almost the entire response	4	$Q3_{norm} = Q3/4$
	I modify a considerable portion of the response	3	
	I modify the response a little	2	
	I barely modify the response	1	
	I don't modify the response	0	
	I don't use it	Excluded	
Q4. Complementing with own ideas	Yes	1	$Q4_{norm} = Q4$
	No	0	
	I don't use it	Excluded	

https://doi.org/10.3390/fi18030122

Table 4. Analytic sample selection. The LEI analytic sample excludes records with missing values in any LEI item (Q2–Q4) and excludes any record indicating non-use of ChatGPT in any LEI item.

Step	Criterion	n Excluded	n Retained
0	Total records in dataset	–	1367
1	Exclude missing/NA in any of Q2–Q4	25	1342
2	Exclude "I don't use ChatGPT" (Q2) OR "I don't use it" (Q3) OR "I don't use it" (Q4)	234	1108
3	For Q1–LEI association: require numeric Q1 (0–10)	3	1105

Step 2 exclusions are not mutually exclusive across items; a respondent may indicate non-use in more than one LEI item.

Across the analytic sample, LEI values were generally high, with an overall mean of 0.829 (SD = 0.155) and a median of 0.833 (Table 5). Group comparisons indicate that LEI differs by educational level: university students displayed higher engagement than high school students (Table 6). By contrast, LEI differences by institutional sector were not statistically significant in this dataset. Wave comparisons were restricted to university respondents; within university, LEI did not differ significantly by survey wave (Table 6).

Table 5. Descriptive statistics for the Learning Engagement Index (LEI).

n	Mean	SD	Median	Q1	Q3	Min	Max
1108	0.829	0.155	0.833	0.771	0.917	0.111	1.000

Table 6. Learning Engagement Index (LEI) group comparisons. Group differences were tested using Mann–Whitney U tests; effect size is Cliff's delta (δ). LEI ranges from 0 to 1 (higher values indicate greater engagement).

Comparison	Group	n	Mean ± SD	Median [Q1, Q3]	p-Value	Cliff's δ
Educational level	High school	440	0.775 ± 0.180	0.833 [0.722, 0.917]	1.86×10^{-21}	−0.327
	University	668	0.864 ± 0.123	0.917 [0.833, 0.917]		
Institutional sector	Public	870	0.831 ± 0.152	0.917 [0.806, 0.917]	0.349	0.038
	Private	238	0.820 ± 0.163	0.833 [0.750, 0.917]		
Survey wave (university only) *	2024	257	0.866 ± 0.108	0.917 [0.833, 0.917]	0.464	−0.032
	2025	411	0.863 ± 0.132	0.917 [0.833, 0.917]		

* Wave comparison is restricted to university respondents because high school records do not contain valid timestamps in this dataset.

We then compared perceived learning (Q1; 0–10) with the LEI. Spearman correlations indicated that the association between Q1 and LEI was weak overall and not statistically significant in the pooled sample (Table 7). In high school, the Q1-LEI correlation reached statistical significance but remained very small in magnitude, while in university the correlation was non-significant (Table 7). These results suggest that students' self-reported learning is not consistently aligned with the engagement behaviors captured by the LEI (reading, modifying, and complementing AI responses), at least as measured by these survey items.

Table 7. Correlation between perceived learning (Q1; 0–10) and learning engagement (LEI; 0–1). Spearman's rank correlation (ρ).

Sample	n	Spearman ρ	p-Value
Overall	1105	0.052	0.0836
High school only	440	0.104	0.0295
University only	665	0.031	0.4277

https://doi.org/10.3390/fi18030122

To examine whether this conclusion was robust to basic adjustment, we estimated parsimonious regression models with perceived learning (0–10) as the outcome. In the pooled sample, LEI was positively but not statistically significantly associated with perceived learning after adjusting for educational level (Table 8 Model A). The same conclusion held when restricting the analysis to university respondents and additionally adjusting for survey wave (2025 vs. 2024) (Table 8, Model B). Across models, explained variance remained low, consistent with the interpretation that perceived learning reflects a subjective appraisal that may depend on factors not captured by the specific engagement behaviors operationalized in the LEI. These findings should be interpreted cautiously and do not support causal claims. The absence of a clear statistical relationship does not imply that engagement behaviors are unimportant for learning, nor does it demonstrate that students' perceived learning is inaccurate. Rather, within the scope of this study, the results indicate no strong empirical linkage between perceived learning and the engagement actions summarized by the LEI. Establishing whether—and under what conditions—these actions translate into measurable learning gains would require more direct outcome assessments (e.g., controlled pre/post testing, performance-based evaluations, or rubric-based expert scoring), which are outside the present study's scope. Future work will address this limitation through evaluation designs that can test learning outcomes more directly in AI-mediated contexts.

From an educational standpoint, the observed Q1-LEI mismatch has two practical implications. First, as student use of generative AI continues to expand, it becomes increasingly important to monitor not only whether students use these tools, but how they engage with them while completing academic tasks—specifically, the extent to which they read, edit, and integrate AI outputs rather than relying on superficial reproduction. Students should therefore be encouraged to recognize that perceived learning may not reliably reflect deeper cognitive processing, particularly when generative systems reduce the effort required to produce polished answers. Second, these findings reinforce the need to rethink assessment practices: as AI becomes embedded in everyday study routines, take-home assignments may no longer function as a straightforward indicator of topic mastery. Instead, the role of homework may shift toward guided practice, iterative feedback, and formative learning, while robust demonstrations of mastery may require redesigned evaluations that prioritize demonstrable understanding and make students' reasoning processes more visible.

Table 8. Association between perceived learning (0–10) and the Learning Engagement Index (LEI; 0–1). OLS models with HC3 robust standard errors. Coefficients (β) and 95% confidence intervals are reported. Model A (pooled): Learning~LEI + educational level. Model B (university only): Learning~LEI + survey wave (2025 vs. 2024).

	Model A (Pooled)		**Model B (University Only)**	
Predictor	**β [95% CI]**	p	**β [95% CI]**	p
LEI (0–1)	0.690 [−0.187, 1.567]	0.123	0.659 [−0.685, 2.004]	0.337
University (vs. High school)	−0.128 [−0.393, 0.137]	0.343	–	–
Survey wave 2025 (vs. 2024)	–	–	−0.198 [−0.522, 0.125]	0.229
n	1105		665	
R^2	0.003		0.004	

Building on these implications, the next step is to examine how students navigate academic support choices in practice—particularly when they face uncertainty or conceptual difficulty. If perceived learning does not systematically track engagement actions, then students' help-seeking preferences and the reasons underlying them become especially relevant for instructional design and policy.

4.6. GitHub Copilot Experiment

To complement the survey-based analysis of ChatGPT, a controlled experiment was conducted to examine the educational implications of GitHub Copilot, a domain-specific generative AI assistant designed to support programming tasks. This experiment provided empirical evidence of how AI-mediated assistance influences performance, learning perception, and cognitive effort among information systems engineering students. The study involved 16 participants divided equally into two groups: one using GitHub Copilot and ChatGPT as support tools, and a control group completing the same Python-based programming task without AI assistance. Both groups had comparable levels of programming proficiency, ensuring that differences in outcomes could be attributed primarily to the presence or absence of AI support. The experimental task consisted of reading, processing, and updating data from a CSV file within a two-hour timeframe, allowing measurement of time efficiency, feature implementation, and code quality.

Quantitative results demonstrated clear advantages for AI-assisted participants. The AI-supported group achieved significantly faster completion times ($p = 0.033$) and higher rates of feature implementation ($p = 0.012$) compared with the non-assisted group (see Figure 7). Furthermore, qualitative evaluation of code readability and modularity indicated higher coherence and structure among AI-assisted submissions. These results align with prior findings in software engineering research, suggesting that AI coding tools improve productivity without compromising output quality, particularly for intermediate-level programmers.

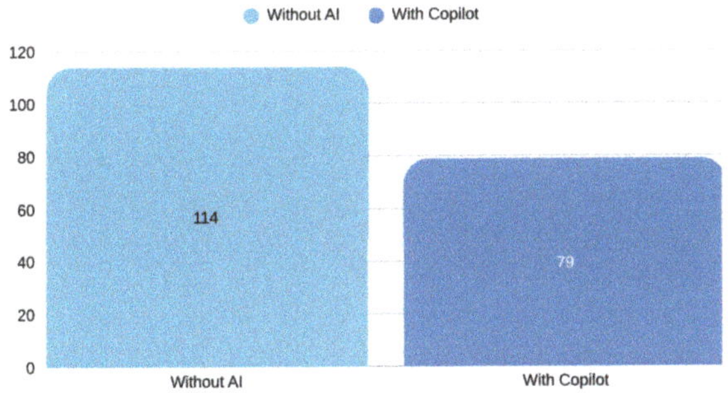

Figure 7. GitHub Copilot experiment results: Task completion time.

Post-experiment surveys revealed that AI-assisted participants reported lower frustration levels, attributing their efficiency to real-time code suggestions and problem-solving guidance. By contrast, students in the control group cited time pressure, difficulty recalling syntax, and "getting stuck without guidance" as key challenges. Importantly, however, both groups rated their learning experience similarly, indicating that while AI assistance enhanced performance, it did not necessarily replace the cognitive processes of understanding and debugging essential to programming education. See Figure 8 for more detail.

The scatter plot (Figure 9) shows the relationship between students' self-reported perceived learning (Q1; 0–10) and the Learning Engagement Index (LEI; 0–1), which summarizes three engagement actions during ChatGPT-assisted task completion (reading responses, modifying outputs, and integrating one's own ideas). The fitted trend line is nearly flat and the points are widely dispersed, indicating that higher engagement behaviors do not translate into consistently higher perceived learning scores. This visual pattern is consistent with the weak correlation and the adjusted models reported in the LEI

https://doi.org/10.3390/fi18030122

analyses, suggesting limited alignment between subjective learning ratings and the specific engagement actions captured by the index.

These findings illustrate that domain-specific generative AI tools can serve as effective cognitive scaffolds when used with clear pedagogical structure. Students benefit from the immediate feedback loop provided by Copilot, which supports experimentation and iterative learning.

Yet, the experiment also underscores the risk of reduced cognitive engagement: some participants reported relying on Copilot's code completions without fully analyzing the underlying logic, suggesting potential erosion of algorithmic reasoning skills if the use of AI tools is not critically mediated by instructors.

The integration of Copilot findings with the broader survey results reinforces a central insight of this study: the impact of AI on learning is context-dependent. While ChatGPT broadens accessibility to general knowledge and conceptual explanations, Copilot demonstrates how specialized AI can enhance professional skill development in technical disciplines. In both cases, the pedagogical value of AI emerges not from automation itself but from the guided interaction between human reasoning and machine assistance.

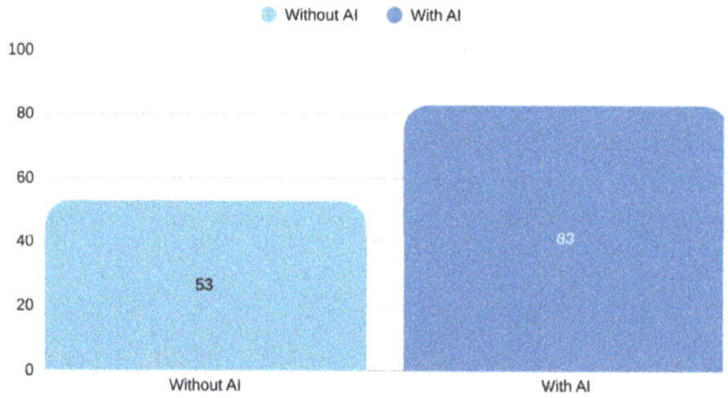

Figure 8. GitHub Copilot experiment results: Programming task completeness.

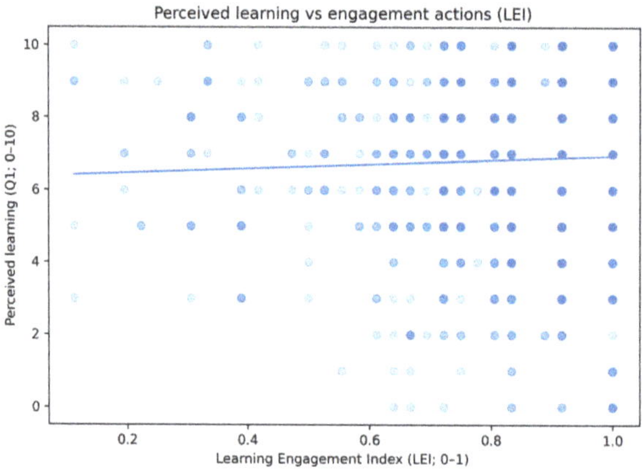

Figure 9. Scatter plot of perceived learning (Q1; 0–10) versus Learning Engagement Index (LEI; 0–1). Lines represent fitted trends with 95% confidence intervals. Because many respondents share similar Q1 and LEI values, points overlap; shading/darker regions represent higher observation density rather than a separate category.

4.7. Cross-Level Findings

The multi-layered comparative design of this study—encompassing high school students, university cohorts from two academic periods (2024 and 2025), teachers at both

https://doi.org/10.3390/fi18030122

levels, and an experimental evaluation of GitHub Copilot—reveals a coherent developmental trajectory in the adoption, perception, and educational integration of generative AI tools. Across all student groups, ChatGPT emerged as the predominant AI resource, yet the ways in which learners used and understood the tool varied substantially by educational stage. High school students tended to approach generative AI as a task-oriented utility, employing it primarily for completing assignments, resolving immediate doubts, or simplifying explanations. Their ethical and cognitive frameworks were correspondingly narrow, grounded in notions of convenience, correctness, and behavioral compliance. Teachers at this level expressed concern about the challenge of maintaining academic integrity in environments where students lacked the maturity to critically evaluate AI-generated content.

University students exhibited more structurally integrated patterns of use, reflecting both higher digital fluency and greater academic autonomy. In the 2024 cohort, students described ChatGPT as an efficient problem-solving companion, though their ethical reflections remained closely tied to plagiarism and authorship. By 2025, however, students articulated a more sophisticated understanding of generative AI, recognizing not only its potential but also its limitations in contextual accuracy, the importance of verification, and the value of balancing AI-generated synthesis with their own reasoning. See Figure 10.

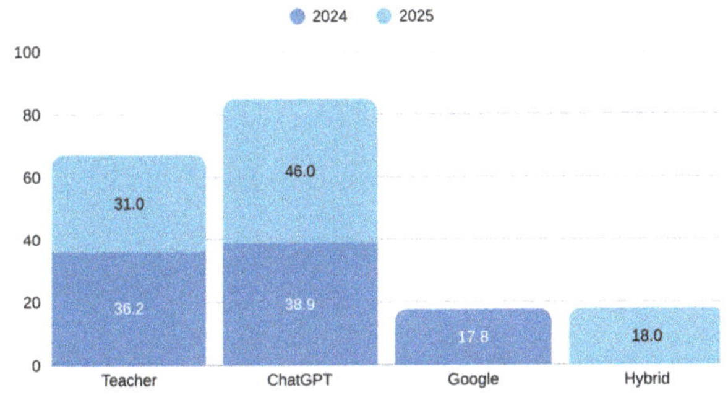

Figure 10. Preferred sources for resolving academic doubts by University students.

Teacher responses mirrored these differences. High school instructors tended to view AI as a threat to assessment validity and classroom authority, while university instructors increasingly framed AI as a pedagogical partner requiring structured integration, ethical guidance, and curricular adaptation. Across both groups, the lack of formal institutional training or policy was evident, reinforcing the need for systemic approaches to responsible AI instruction.

The GitHub Copilot experiment provided an additional layer of insight by illustrating how specialized generative tools shape learning in technically demanding domains. AI-assisted students demonstrated significantly higher productivity and code quality, yet the results also revealed the risk of cognitive dependence when AI suggestions replace rather than support algorithmic thinking. This reinforces a central theme emerging across educational levels: the pedagogical value of AI does not lie in automation alone but in the mediated interplay between human judgment and machine assistance.

The evidence presented here indicates that the integration of generative AI in education follows a developmental and contextual gradient. Younger learners benefit from the accessibility and clarity of AI tools but require stronger ethical scaffolding and teacher mediation. University students demonstrate increasing sophistication in balancing AI assistance with human expertise but face nuanced challenges related to overreliance, authorship, and critical evaluation. The Copilot experiment highlights the transformative potential

https://doi.org/10.3390/fi18030122

of AI in skill-based learning environments while underscoring the need for intentional, reflective, and ethically grounded instructional design.

This cross-level synthesis underscores that the educational impact of generative AI is neither uniform nor linear. Instead, it is shaped by students' cognitive maturity, disciplinary context, teacher preparation, and the structural conditions of access and inequality—factors that must be addressed collectively in policy, curriculum design, and teacher training to ensure equitable and responsible integration moving forward.

4.7.1. Equity and Variability in Access to Generative AI

Qualitative responses revealed notable variability in students' access to devices, reliable internet connectivity, and opportunities to engage with generative AI tools. These differences were not attributable to specific institutions, but rather to personal, household, and contextual conditions. Some students reported seamless access through personal devices, while others faced unstable connectivity or limited availability outside the classroom.

Such disparities influence not only how frequently students are able to use generative AI, but also their opportunities to gain experience in using these tools to streamline academic processes and improve the quality of their work—skills that are increasingly essential today and likely to remain so in the future. At the same time, the findings underscore the importance of balancing AI-assisted work with the development of problem-solving abilities, critical thinking, and the acquisition and mastery of disciplinary knowledge. Without coordinated institutional support, teacher preparation, and inclusive policies, uneven access risks reinforcing existing educational inequalities and limiting students' future competitiveness in academic and professional contexts.

4.7.2. Assessment, Fairness, and Responsible Use

A central concern expressed by teachers relates to assessment and fairness in AI-mediated learning environments. Educators questioned how to evaluate student performance when some learners use generative AI to produce high-quality work while others do not have access to, or choose not to use, such tools. This raises unresolved questions about what should be assessed in contemporary education: the final product, the effort invested, the knowledge acquired, or the responsible use of generative AI to generate solutions. Knowledge acquisition, however, is not optional; without it, students lack the capacity to judge the validity, feasibility, or correctness of AI-generated outputs, placing core educational objectives at risk.

Importantly, the present study captures perceptions and practices, but does not directly measure learning outcomes. Determining whether generative AI ultimately enhances or hinders learning requires systematic evaluation of knowledge acquisition, skill development, and long-term cognitive effects—an issue repeatedly emphasized by participating teachers. These challenges highlight an ethical dilemma that goes beyond grading equity and directly shapes how academic standards, competencies, and preparedness for future work are defined.

5. Conclusions

This study provides a comparative view of how generative AI tools—particularly ChatGPT and GitHub Copilot—are being adopted, perceived, and negotiated by students and teachers across high school and university contexts in Sonora, Mexico. The findings show widespread use, alongside differences in purpose, intensity, and interpretation that vary by educational level, role, and context; these contrasts should not be interpreted deterministically as "developmental progression," as adoption and practices are also shaped by timing, exposure, and institutional conditions. Students across both levels value generative AI for its immediacy and academic support, while teachers emphasize both its practical utility and the challenges it introduces for assessment integrity, ethical boundaries, and the absence of clear institutional guidance. Rather than rejecting AI, many teachers describe a shift in their role toward supporting interpretation, judgment, and critical engagement with AI-generated content.

A key contribution of this revised analysis is the introduction of a Learning Engagement Index (LEI) that operationalizes engagement behaviors during AI-assisted work (reading responses, modifying outputs, and integrating one's own ideas). Comparing LEI with perceived learning (Q1) reveals a critical tension: students who report learning with ChatGPT do not necessarily report the engagement actions typically associated with deeper processing of AI-generated content. The Q1-LEI relationship is weak and not consistently significant across groups, indicating that perceived learning is not reliably aligned with the engagement practices captured by the LEI. This does not establish that students are not learning; rather, it underscores that perceived learning cannot be assumed to reflect mastery without direct outcome assessment. This perception-engagement gap has urgent implications for evaluation. If students can produce high-quality homework outputs with reduced cognitive effort, then take-home assignments may no longer serve as a straightforward proxy for topic mastery, and assessment designs must place greater emphasis on reasoning, verification, and demonstrable understanding. At the same time, disparities in access to connectivity, devices, and opportunities to develop AI-related competencies highlight the risk that generative AI may amplify existing inequalities without deliberate institutional action.

The central challenge is not whether generative AI will be used in education, but how educational systems can adapt teaching and assessment quickly enough to preserve meaningful mastery in an AI-enabled learning environment. Future work within this research line will therefore evaluate whether students' perceived learning aligns with demonstrable content mastery through more concrete assessments of knowledge and understanding.

Author Contributions: Conceptualization, R.T.-P. and F.C.-G.; Methodology, R.T.-P.; Data curation, M.d.C.H.-S., I.E.-F. and K.L.-M.; Formal analysis, R.T.-P. and F.C.-G.; Writing—original draft preparation, R.T.-P.; Writing—review and editing, R.T.-P. and F.C.-G.; Supervision, R.T.-P.; Project administration, R.T.-P.; visualization, I.E.-F. and K.L.-M. All authors have read and agreed to the published version of the manuscript.

Funding: This research received no external funding.

Institutional Review Board Statement: Ethical review and approval were waived for this study as it was based on anonymous, non-invasive questionnaires administered for educational research purposes. No personal data were collected, participation was voluntary, and no foreseeable risks were associated with the study.

Informed Consent Statement: Informed consent was obtained from all subjects involved in the study.

Data Availability Statement: The data analyzed in this study are publicly available in an open-access repository. The surveys can be found at Zenodo via the following Digital Object Identifier (DOI): https://doi.org/10.5281/zenodo.18626799.

Acknowledgments: During the preparation of this manuscript/study, the authors used ChatGPT 5.2 for the purposes of editing the manuscript. The authors have reviewed and edited the output and take full responsibility for the content of this publication.

Conflicts of Interest: The authors declare no conflicts of interest.

https://doi.org/10.3390/fi18030122

Abbreviations

The following abbreviations are used in this manuscript:

AI	Artificial Intelligence
LLM	Large Language Model

References

1. Alarcón Llontop, L.R.; Pasapera Ramírez, S.; Torres-Mirez, K. The ChatGPT application: Initial perceptions of university teachers. In *Proceedings of 21st LACCEI International Multi-Conference for Engineering, Education, and Technology*; LACCEI: Boca Raton, FL, USA, 2023. [CrossRef]
2. Arguello, F.C.; Banda, J.E.M.; Chamorro, M.I.; Jiménez, A.B.; Álvarez, L. Analysis of teachers' perception on the use and impact of ChatGPT in contemporary education. *Rev. Gest. Soc. Ambient.* **2024**, *18*, e08162. [CrossRef]
3. Bittle, S.; El-Gayar, O. Generative AI and Academic Integrity in Higher Education: A Systematic Review and Research Agenda. *Information* **2025**, *16*, 296. [CrossRef]
4. Holmes, W.; Miao, F. *Guidance for Generative AI in Education and Research*; UNESCO Publishing: Paris, France, 2023.
5. Kasneci, E.; Sessler, K.; Küchemann, S.; Bannert, M.; Dementieva, D.; Fischer, F.; Gasser, U.; Groh, G.; Günnemann, S.; Hüllermeier, E.; et al. ChatGPT for good? On opportunities and challenges of large language models for education. *Learn. Individ. Differ.* **2023**, *103*, 102274. [CrossRef]
6. Chin, J.M.-C.; Lin, H.-C.; Chen, C.-W. Homework and learning achievements: How much homework is enough? *Educ. Stud.* **2022**, *48*, 408–423. [CrossRef]
7. Cárdenas Gándara, T.d.J.; Cornejo Álvarez, J.F.; Frausto Loera, M.Á. Inteligencia artificial generativa en el contexto universitario: Un estudio de seguimiento sobre la percepción docente. *Transdigital* **2025**, *6*, e484. [CrossRef]
8. Gerónimo Bautista, E.; Rodríguez Ruiz, J.G.; Ochoa Rosas, E. Artificial Intelligence (AI) in the Mexican University Context: An Exploratory Analysis from the Researcher's Context. *Cienc. Lat. Rev. Cient. Multidiscip.* **2025**, *9*, 7757–7772. [CrossRef]
9. Jácome Onofre, P.; Orona Hinojos, J.M.; Reyes Morales, G.; Macias Ávila, E.; Flores Leal, A.; Alvarez Jimenez, B. Educational Innovation in Mexico: Enhancing Learning with Artificial Intelligence, Applying ChatGPT in Higher Education Institutions, Professor-Student Collaboration. *Cienc. Lat. Rev. Cient. Multidiscip.* **2024**, *8*, 6210–6228. [CrossRef]
10. Torres-Peralta, R.; Cirett-Galán, F.; Lerma-Molina, K.; Espinoza-Flores, I. Análisis comparativo del uso de herramientas de IA generativas como ChatGPT entre docentes y estudiantes universitarios. In *Proyecto V Libro Digital Investigación: Inteligencia Artificial en la Docencia y la Investigación*, 1st ed.; Aguirre-Boza, Á., Giménez-Castillo, B., Eds.; Zenodo: Geneva, Switzerland, 2025; Volume 5, pp. 154–175. [CrossRef]
11. Cantú-Ortiz, F.J.; Sánchez, N.G.; Garrido, L.; Terashima-Marin, H.; Brena, R.F. An Artificial Intelligence Educational Strategy for the Digital Transformation. *Int. J. Interact. Des. Manuf. (IJIDeM)* **2020**, *14*, 1195–1209. [CrossRef]
12. Memarian, B.; Doleck, T. ChatGPT in education: Methods, potentials and limitations. *Comput. Hum. Behav. Artif. Hum.* **2023**, *1*, 100022. [CrossRef]
13. Montenegro-Rueda, M.; Fernández-Cerero, J.; Fernández-Batanero, J.M.; López-Meneses, E. Impact of the implementation of ChatGPT in education: A systematic review. *Computers* **2023**, *12*, 153. [CrossRef]
14. Malinka, K.; Peresíni, M.; Firc, A.; Hujnák, O.; Janus, F. On the educational impact of ChatGPT. In *Proceedings of the 2023 Conference on Innovation and Technology in Computer Science Education V. 1*; ACM Digital Library: New York, NY, USA, 2023; pp. 47–53. [CrossRef]
15. Rahman, M.M.; Watanobe, Y. ChatGPT for education and research: Opportunities, threats, and strategies. *Appl. Sci.* **2023**, *13*, 5783. [CrossRef]
16. Mateus, J.C.; Cappello, G.; Lugo, N.; Guerrero-Pico, M. Communication educators facing the arrival of generative artificial intelligence. *Digit. Educ. Rev.* **2024**, *45*, 106–114. [CrossRef]
17. García Sánchez, J.; Carrillo Guerrero, L. Evaluación docente del uso de ChatGPT en la enseñanza universitaria del área de la salud. *Rev. Investig. Tecnol. Inf.* **2025**, *13*, 84–95. [CrossRef]
18. Chávez, M.Y.; Ugalde, F.; Aguilar, M.; Jiménez, S.; Mejia-Medina, D.A.; Juárez-Ramírez, R. Exploratory study in students' perception in the use of ChatGPT. In *Proceedings of the 2023 11th International Conference in Software Engineering Research and Innovation (CONISOFT)*; IEEE: Piscataway, NJ, USA, 2023; pp. 124–131. [CrossRef]
19. Romero-Rodríguez, J.-M.; Ramírez-Montoya, M.-S.; Buenestado-Fernández, M.; Lara-Lara, F. Use of ChatGPT at university as a tool for complex thinking. *J. New Approaches Educ. Res.* **2023**, *12*, 323–339. [CrossRef]
20. Shoufan, A. Exploring students' perceptions of ChatGPT. *IEEE Access* **2023**, *11*, 38805–38818. [CrossRef]
21. Gil-Vera, V. Uso de ChatGPT por estudiantes universitarios: Un análisis relacional. *Form. Univ.* **2024**, *17*, 129–140. [CrossRef]

https://doi.org/10.3390/fi18030122

22. Vera, J.P.D.; Hojas, D.S.P.; Sarmiento, Z.J.F.; Ramírez, A.K.R.; Mora, D.V.M. Estudio comparativo experimental del uso de ChatGPT y su influencia en el aprendizaje. *Rev. Univ. Guayaquil* **2023**, *137*, 51–63. [CrossRef]
23. Kerimbayev, N.; Menlibay, Z.; Garvanova, M.; Djaparova, S.; Jotsov, V. A comparative analysis of generative AI models for improving learning process in higher education. In *Proceedings of the IEEE International Conference on Automatics and Informatics*; IEEE: Piscataway, NJ, USA, 2024; pp. 271–276. [CrossRef]
24. Cirett-Galán, F.; Torres-Peralta, R.; Navarro Hernández, R.F.; Ochoa Hernández, J.L.; Contreras-Rivera, S.; Estrada-Ríos, L.A.; Machado-Encinas, G. Assessing the use of GitHub Copilot on students of engineering of information systems. *Int. J. Softw. Eng. Knowl. Eng.* **2024**, *34*, 1717–1734. [CrossRef]

https://doi.org/10.3390/fi18030122

future internet MDPI

Article

Earthquake Magnitude Detection Utilizing a Novel Hybrid Earth–Transformer–LSTM Architecture

Amir A. Ghavifekr [1,*], Elman Ghazaei [1], Mohsen Mirzajani [2] and Paolo Visconti [3,*]

[1] Faculty of Electrical and Computer Engineering, University of Tabriz, Tabriz 51666-16471, Iran; elmangazayi@gmail.com
[2] Department of Civil Engineering, Marand Technical Faculty, University of Tabriz, Tabriz 51666-16471, Iran; m.mirzajani@tabrizu.ac.ir
[3] Department of Innovation Engineering, University of Salento, 73100 Lecce, Italy
* Correspondence: aa.ghavifekr@tabrizu.ac.ir (A.A.G.); paolo.visconti@unisalento.it (P.V.); Tel.: +39-0832-297334 (P.V.)

Abstract

One of the complicated and demanding tasks in seismology is the reliable detection of earthquakes. The key challenge is that the detection models must be applied to a specific region, and models trained on one region may not perform as well in others. The limitations of datasets for most regions of the world pose another task. Comprehensive, high-quality datasets are essential for developing robust earthquake detection algorithms. Despite these challenges, developing effective earthquake detection systems is critically important. This paper proposes a novel deep network, Earth–Transformer–LSTM (ETL), to estimate earthquake magnitude with high precision. The proposed method uses Transformer encoders as its first layer to extract profound features from the dataset. To obtain highly accurate results, the extracted data is used as the input to the Long Short-Term Memory (LSTM) neural network. Additionally, one-dimensional convolution is replaced by Multi-Layer Perceptron (MLP), which performs better in Transformer encoders' feed-forward networks. The Turkey earthquake dataset 2000–2018 was used in this research because significant earthquakes have occurred in this region in recent years. According to the obtained results, the proposed method's Root Mean Squared Error (RMSE) is 0.7, representing a noticeable improvement over advanced conventional models.

Keywords: Earth–Transformer–LSTM (ETL); deep learning; earthquake detection; USGS dataset

1. Introduction

Turkey is one of the most seismically active countries in the world due to its geographical location. Between 2014 and 2024, eleven significant earthquakes occurred in Turkey, most with magnitudes over 6, suggesting that this region could experience similar events in the near future. Such events can affect public safety and the country's economy. Due to the complexity of earthquakes, seismologists are seeking solutions to better understand seismic events as several factors must be considered. Crucial factors in determining the hazard and spatial probability of earthquakes include magnitude, depth, epicenter, seismic gap, earthquake frequency, slope, elevation, and curvature, with the magnitude, depth, and epicenter being the most important. As a result, earthquake detection and investigation of its characteristics have become crucial in modern seismology for purposes such as earthquake early warning systems, understanding the behavior of tectonic plates across the Earth, and monitoring earthquakes on a global scale.

The typical procedure so far has been to monitor earthquakes using seismographs to record them and prepare earthquake catalogs, allowing researchers to gain a deeper understanding of the earthquake process and fault mechanisms. Since these data are precious to the seismological community, the number of seismic stations has increased and device accuracy has also improved. Furthermore, over recent years, several machine learning (ML) and deep learning (DL) algorithms have been developed based on seismic event data and can be used to detect earthquakes. ML and DL are leading technologies suitable for solving problems across various fields of science. Furthermore, these tools are highly effective in formulating theories and implementing different datasets. In seismology, some of these tools have been used to predict earthquakes.

Rojas et al. [1] surveyed recent applications of Artificial Neural Networks (ANNs) for automating seismic data interpretation, particularly for earthquake detection and onset-time estimation. The paper also discusses the challenges faced by human interpreters, especially in detecting small magnitude earthquakes, and how ANNs can address these uncertainties. Mehta et al. [2] developed a normalized ANN to predict earthquakes; using Exploratory Data Analysis (EDA), they removed unnecessary features from the raw data and optimized the model using backpropagation, achieving 94.3% accuracy. Ridzwan and Yusoff [3] reviewed numerous machine learning studies on earthquake prediction and compared models predicting magnitude, trend, and occurrence across regions, identifying top-performing seismic indicators and algorithms. Kavianpour et al. [4] introduced a CNN-BiLSTM-AM approach for earthquake prediction. Convolutional Neural Networks (CNNs) extracted spatial characteristics, Bi-directional Long Short-Term Memory (BiLSTM) captured data's long-term dependencies, and attention mechanism (AM) emphasized highly contributing results. Sadhukhan et al. [5] predicted earthquake magnitudes using Long Short-Term Memory (LSTM), Bi-LSTM, and Transformer models on eight seismic indicators, considering Mean Absolute Error (MAE), Mean Squared Error (MSE), log-cosh loss, and Mean Squared Logarithmic Error (MSLE) metrics.

Doğan and Demir [6] proposed a novel Structural Recurrent Neural Network (SRNN) model to predict earthquakes based on the existence of faults in specific regions, outperforming baseline and the state-of-the-art models. Berhich et al. [7] employed an LSTM network with attention to predict large earthquakes using the Japan earthquake dataset, achieving an MSE of approximately 60%. Saad et al. [8] proposed a Compact Convolutional Transformer (CCT) for earthquake phase arrivals, which outperformed EQTransformer and PhaseNet. Aslam et al. [9] predicted seismic activity in the northern part of Pakistan, using Support Vector Regressor (SVR) and Hybrid Neural Network (HNN) to predict seismic events.

Zhou et al. [10] examined the accuracy of the Haskell-based deterministic dendritic cell algorithm (hDCA) for predicting earthquakes with magnitudes greater than 4.5. They first extracted eight seismic indicators (b-value, magnitude deficit, mean magnitude, and energy release rate) from historical earthquake records, using established geophysical laws such as the Gutenberg–Richter relationship. These indicators were mapped into danger and safe signals that simulate immune responses. A population of artificial dendritic cells then processed these signals, accumulated internal state values (csm and k), and classified each monthly seismic state as normal or anomalous, where an anomaly indicated a high probability of an earthquake with magnitude greater than 4.5 in the following month.

Majhi et al. [11] estimated earthquake magnitudes using a method called Functional Link Artificial Neural Network (FLANN), which combines standard machine learning algorithms with the Moth Flame Optimization (MFO) algorithm. Zhang et al. [12] proposed

https://doi.org/10.3390/fi18030143

a machine learning (ML) algorithm, CNN ONsite Intensity Prediction (CONIP), to forecast seismic intensities and noted that this method could improve the accuracy of the earthquake early warning (EEW) process. Zhu et al. [13] combined RNNs and transfer learning to estimate ground-motion intensity at recording stations in China. The predicted alarms had a 90% success rate. Kudłacik et al. [14] used a Global Navigation Satellite System (GNSS)-based method to detect and characterize mining tremors, agreeing with seismic solutions for earthquake first-epoch detection.

Machine learning and deep learning methods have been applied to enhance discrimination between earthquakes and quarry blasts based on three seismic parameters by M. S. Abdalzaher et al. [15]. They trained and compared six classifiers (XGB, DT, KNN, QD, RF, and LR) on seismic catalog data from Northern California, using multiple evaluation metrics (accuracy; F1-score; Matthews Correlation Coefficient—MCC; Kappa; Area Under the Receiver Operating Characteristic Curve—ROC-AUC). The Extreme Gradient Boosting (XGB) model achieved the best performance. Although the results demonstrate strong classification capability and practical efficiency, the study relies on a limited feature set and a single regional dataset, which may restrict generalizability.

Bilal et al. [16] presented a Batch Normalized Graph Convolutional Neural Network with attention mechanism (BNGCNNATT) to predict earthquake depth and magnitude from seismic data. Saad et al. [17] developed an unsupervised deep learning method for denoising single-channel earthquake data using a UNET-based network with attention mechanisms. The method employs a short-time Fourier transform (STFT) to separate the real and imaginary parts, which are then processed to mute seismic noise while preserving the signals. Using a deep image prior (DIP) approach, the network learns iteratively without labeled data. The algorithm outperforms DeepDenoiser by 1.95 dB in signal-to-noise ratio (SNR) and improves seismic event detection and earthquake location accuracy.

Han et al. [18] developed a DL model for earthquake detection, efficiently detecting small-magnitude events compared to the Short Time Average/Long Time Average (STA/LTA) method. However, phase picking was inconsistent, large earthquakes were indistinguishable, and non-natural earthquakes were undetectable. Abebe et al. [19] used a Transformer model to predict earthquake magnitudes in the Horn of Africa, comparing it with LSTM, BiLSTM, and BiLSTM with attention models. The Transformer outperformed the others, achieving lower error rates. Its ability to capture long-range dependencies and process data in parallel contributed to better accuracy, though challenges remained in predicting both large and small earthquakes.

Laurenti et al. [20] applied the autoregressive (AR) forecasting DL method for labquake prediction. The method has been able to detect the time to the start of failure (TTsF) and the time to the end of failure (TTeF) for labquakes, thereby representing a solution to outperform previous methods of earthquake prediction. Mohammadigheymasi et al. [21] implemented a pair-input DL (PIDL) model and waveform migration location methods for earthquake detection, including the phase and location of earthquakes. Yuan et al. [22] enhanced earthquake detection by combining pretrained DL models, multiple frequency bands, and ensemble estimation. Mousavi et al. [23] presented a global DL model to predict seismic events and phase picking. Their model was capable of predicting and locating earthquakes twice as well as other models, using less than a third of the seismic stations.

This paper proposes a novel deep network, called Earth–Transformer–LSTM (ETL), to detect earthquake magnitude using an earthquake catalog. The term "Earth" in the model's name is chosen primarily to distinguish our model from others that incorporate both Transformer and LSTM architectures. We aimed to create a unique identifier for our proposed hybrid model, even though it does not specifically include Earth-related features. The ETL incorporates the Transformer encoder and LSTM, which have enhanced

https://doi.org/10.3390/fi18030143

the extraction of hidden features of its inputs and representation of sequence data's features. In the Transformer architecture, an LSTM enhances the representation of sequence data features. The main dataset has been split into two subsets: a training set and an evaluation set. The training phase was performed using the Adam optimization algorithm with a learning rate of 1×10^{-4} and a cross-entropy loss function. Compared with previous earthquake detection methods, the ETL introduces a Transformer–LSTM with stronger capabilities, achieving more accurate earthquake magnitude detection than other RNN-based models such as Gated Recurrent Units (GRUs) and CNN-LSTM.

In the rest of the manuscript, Section 2 provides background on data collection and the steps for downloading the datasets. In Section 3, the methodology of the proposed method is explained, including the main concepts of the Transformer encoder and LSTM, which provides a more detailed introduction to the novel ETL approach in Section 4. Results and related discussion are provided in Section 5, along with a comparative analysis for the proposed method. Finally, the main findings of the research work and conclusions are summarized in Section 6.

2. Data Collection Background

Looking at recent earthquakes in Turkey, the country has been annually hit by at least one earthquake of a magnitude greater than 5.5 [24]. These earthquakes usually occur in the North Anatolian Fault zone (NAFZ) and East Anatolian Fault zone (EAFZ) [25,26]. There have been several significant earthquakes in Turkey over the last few decades. The most devastating ones have been those that occurred on 30 October 2020, reported as the "Aegean Sea earthquake (7.0 Mw)"; on 23 November 2022, as the "Gölyaka–Düzce earthquake (6.1 Mw)"; and in February 2023, namely the "Turkey–Syria earthquakes (7.8 Mw, 7.7 Mw, 6.3 Mw)" [27–29].

The Turkey–Syria earthquakes (7.8 Mw, 7.7 Mw, 6.3 Mw) in February 2023 have been described in [27], which focuses on fault interaction and stress transfer along the East Anatolian Fault zone. The focal mechanism inversion reveals a trans-tensional stress regime with left-lateral and normal slip, offering insights into regional tectonic processes and fault interactions. The Aegean Sea earthquake (7.0 Mw), which occurred on 30 October 2020, extensively analyzed in [28], was a typical extensional faulting event characterized by a complex aftershock sequence and high variability in rupture directivity. This event demonstrated strong spatial clustering and temporal decay patterns, which have been used in multiple studies to evaluate predictive models of earthquake catalog behavior. The Gölyaka–Düzce earthquake (6.1 Mw), which occurred on 23 November 2022 and is documented in [29], investigates near-field effects in the 6.1 magnitude earthquake on the North Anatolian Fault zone, focusing on ground-motion intensities and their spatial distribution using the AFAD–Turkish Accelerometric Database. The study challenges previous assumptions by showing that velocity pulses, typically associated with directivity effects, are concentrated in the fault-parallel rather than the fault-normal component, especially for moderate events.

Tectonic plates, their boundaries, and active faults in Turkey are shown in Figure 1. As large cities and dams are located around fault zones, the safety of these cities and infrastructure could be affected by future earthquakes. So, it is crucial to study possible earthquakes and quantify them using advanced numerical techniques.

https://doi.org/10.3390/fi18030143

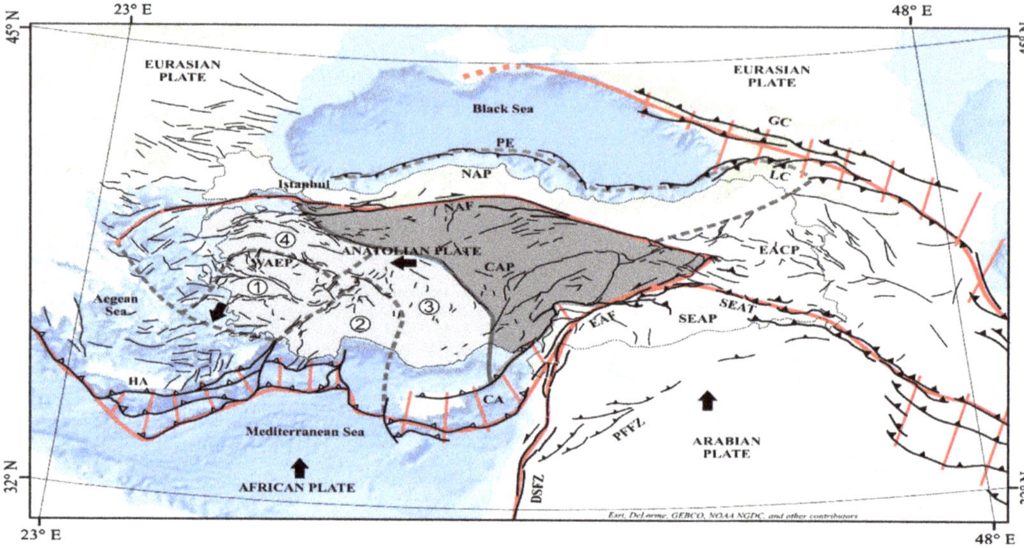

Figure 1. The tectonic plates and active fault map of the Eastern Mediterranean region [30].

Datasets

The data used in this study are sourced from the USGS earthquake catalog [31], covering the period from 1 January 2000 to 31 December 2018, specifically for Turkey. This extensive dataset provides a comprehensive record of seismic events over the specified timeframe. The spatial distribution of these earthquakes is visualized in both 2D and 3D formats [32], as illustrated in Figure 2. These visualizations offer valuable insights into the geographic and depth-related distributions of seismic activity across Turkey, helping to highlight patterns and trends in the dataset. A detailed overview of the dataset, including the number of recorded events, magnitudes, and other relevant attributes, is presented in Table 1, which summarizes the dataset's key characteristics and facilitates a clearer understanding of the data used in this research work.

Figure 3 shows histograms of date, depth, magnitude, and magnitude type. To clarify the depth and magnitude distribution over the considered years, Figure 4 is depicted.

Table 1. Details provided in the Earthquake catalog.

Parameter	Value
Start time	01-01-2000 00:00:00
End time	31-12-2018 23:59:59
Min longitude	25.85
Max longitude	45.14
Min latitude	35.67
Max latitude	42.38
Number of raw earthquakes	6679

https://doi.org/10.3390/fi18030143

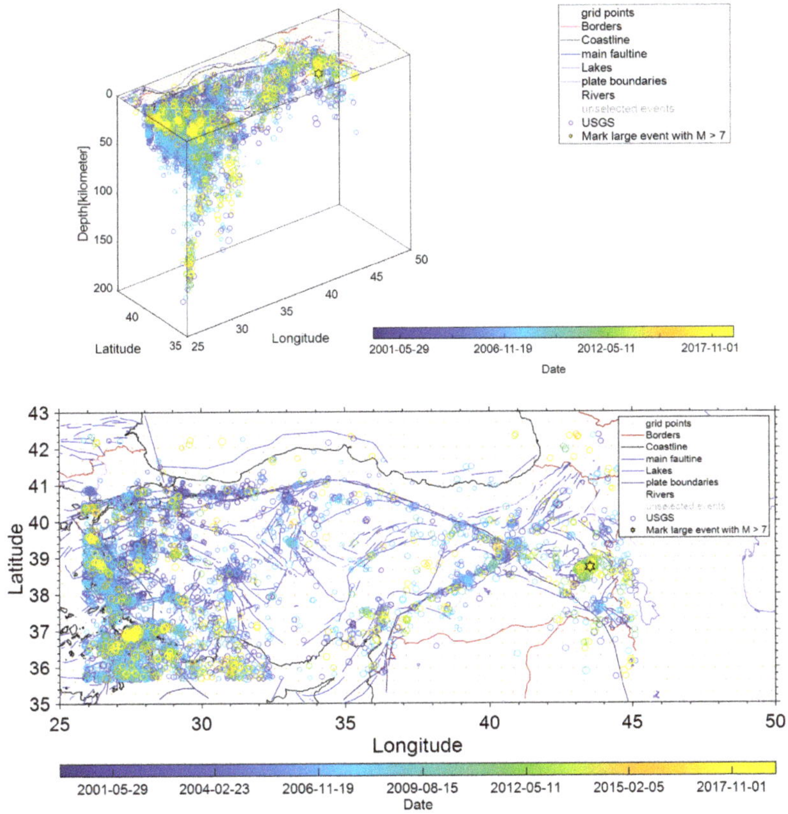

Figure 2. Spatial distribution of earthquakes that occurred in Turkey from 2000 to 2018.

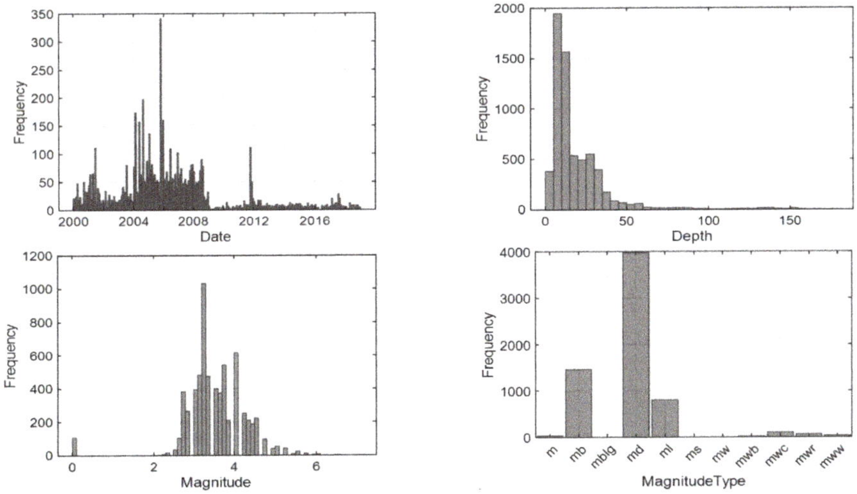

Figure 3. Date, depth, magnitude, and magnitude type histograms for the Turkey dataset.

https://doi.org/10.3390/fi18030143

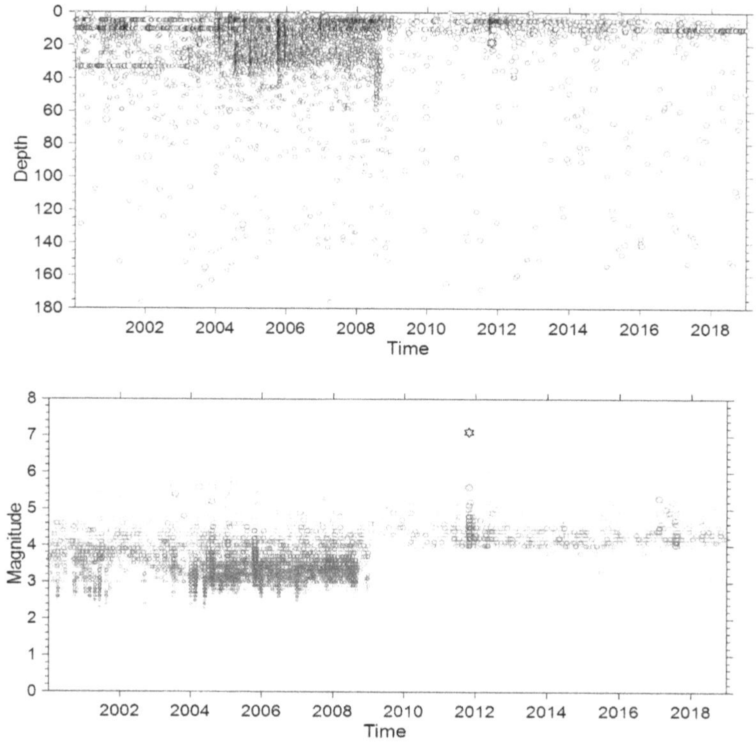

Figure 4. Depth and magnitude distribution between 2000 and 2018 for the Turkey dataset; the star indicates significant events with magnitude greater than 7 (Figures generated by the ZMAP package, https://github.com/zmap/zmap).

3. Methodology

In this paper, we propose a novel deep network, Earth–Transformer–LSTM (ETL), for estimating the earthquake magnitudes with high precision. Firstly, utilizing Transformer encoders as a first layer could extract many subtle features from sequence data. Secondly, exploiting LSTM could process the extracted data to obtain high accuracy. In other words, in this research we use sequence-ensemble-based models to predict future earthquake magnitudes using our dataset.

3.1. Transformer Encoder

Transformers have two main components: encoder and decoder [33]. These cutting-edge deep learning models have gained significant fame in Natural Language Processing (NLP) tasks such as text classification, summarization, and even one-shot classification. Encoder parts can extract many hidden features from the inputs and transfer them to decoder parts, which can generate the desired outputs. Transformers offer many unique benefits over conventional sequence-based models, such as LSTM and GRU. For example, they can process inputs in parallel, since these models have multi-head attention mechanisms that can assign special attention weights to more important segments of the data.

In more detail, this research focuses on the Transformer encoder because it can extract features from sequence inputs. Transformer encoders have several specialized components that can improve the model's performance; for instance, multi-head attention can adjust attention weights and parameters on the more important sections of the data. Layer normalization also has a positive effect on the model's performance, potentially outweighing

https://doi.org/10.3390/fi18030143

the batch normalization's effects. The structure of the Transformer encoder block is shown in Figure 5, while the sequence of steps and related parameters are reported in Table 2.

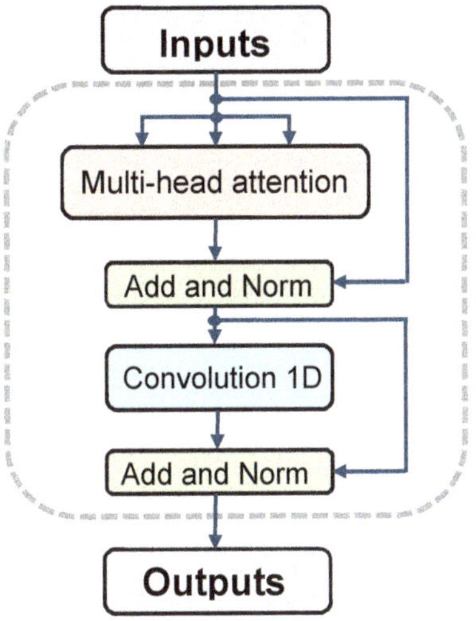

Figure 5. Structure of the Transformer encoder's single block.

Table 2. Sequence of steps and parameters of the proposed Transformer encoder.

Structure of the Transformer Encoder block	
1-	**Inputs:** datapoints (shape = (3,1))
2-	**Outputs:** Encoder output (shape = (100,1))
3-	X = Layer Normalization(inputs)
3-	X = Multi-head attention (X, X, X)
4-	X = Dropout(X)
5-	res = X + inputs
6-	X = Layer Normalization (res)
7-	X = Conv-1D(X)
8-	X = Dropout(X)
9-	X = Conv-1D(X)
10-	Output = x + res
11-	X = Dropout(X)

Multi-head attention is a mechanism used in neural network architectures, particularly in NLP, and is prominently featured in models like Transformer. It enhances the ability of self-attention mechanisms by allowing the model to attend to different parts of the input data simultaneously (Figure 6), effectively enabling it to capture various features of the input's context. The key benefit of multi-head attention is its ability to capture different types of dependencies and relationships within the input data simultaneously. Each attention head can focus on various parts of the input sequence, allowing the model to attend to multiple sides of the context in parallel. This capability can lead to more expressive representations and better performance, particularly in tasks that require understanding long-range dependencies and intricate relationships within the input data. According to Equation (1), the multi-head attention can be computed as follows:

$$MultiHead(Q,K,V) = Concat(head1,\ldots,headh)W^O\left(head_i = Attention\left(QW_i^Q, KW_i^K, VW_i^V\right)\right) \quad (1)$$

with $W_i^Q \in \mathbb{R}^{d_{model} \times d_k}$, $W_i^K \in \mathbb{R}^{d_{model} \times d_k}$, $W_i^V \in \mathbb{R}^{d_{model} \times d_v}$ and $W^O \in \mathbb{R}^{hd_v \times d_{model.}}$.

https://doi.org/10.3390/fi18030143

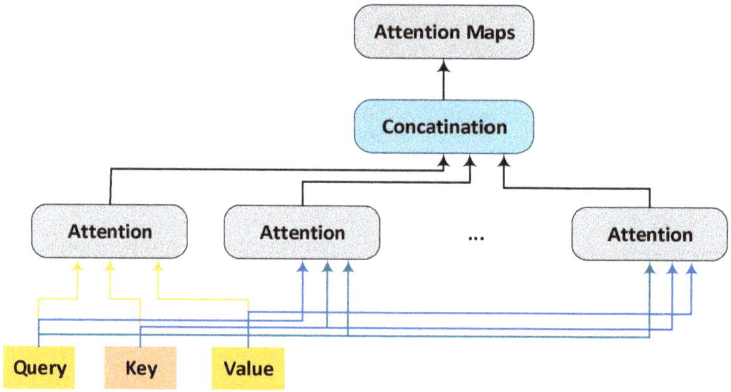

Figure 6. A multi-head attention structure that can compute attention weights in parallel paths.

In this formulation, Q, K, and V denote the query, key, and value matrices, respectively, n is the sequence length, and d_{model} the model embedding dimension. The model employs n attention heads; for each *head* i, W_i^Q, W_i^K and W_i^V are the learnable projection matrices for queries, keys, and values, respectively. In addition, d_k and d_V denote the dimensionality of queries/keys and values per head. The outputs of all heads are concatenated along the feature dimension.

3.2. Long Short-Term Memory (LSTM)

Long Short-Term Memory (LSTM) is a type of Recurrent Neural Network (RNN) architecture that is designed to address the vanishing gradient (killing gradient) problem often encountered when training traditional RNNs. LSTM networks are able to learn long-term dependencies in sequential data, making them particularly well-suited for tasks such as speech recognition, language modeling, machine translation, and time-series prediction. LSTM has three main components: input, output, and forget gates. The input gate determines which new information from the current time step should be stored in the memory cell for use by other parts. Moreover, the output gate determines which information from the memory cell should be passed to the next time step's hidden state, which serves as the input to the next cell. Eventually, the forget gate determines which data from the previous time step should be discarded from the memory cell if it is not useful to the model. The LSTM structure is shown in Figure 7.

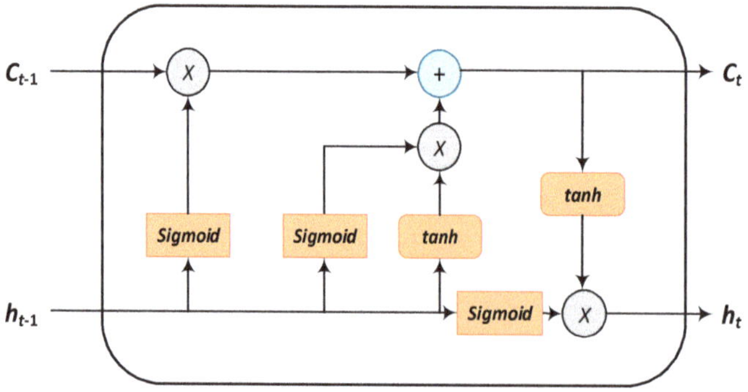

Figure 7. LSTM structure.

https://doi.org/10.3390/fi18030143

4. Earth–Transformer–LSTM (ETL)

In this paper, we propose a novel model combining a Transformer encoder and an LSTM (Figure 8). The primary novelty of our approach lies in the seamless integration of these two distinct architectures. While Transformer encoders have demonstrated remarkable capabilities in extracting contextual features from input data and sequences, they lack the inherent ability to model long-range dependencies effectively. On the other hand, LSTM networks show good performance at capturing sequential patterns and including a steady memory state. This hybrid form aims to utilize the strengths of both models to achieve superior performance. The Transformer encoder structure is equipped with a multi-head attention mechanism, which allows it to extract a wide set of hidden features from the input sequence.

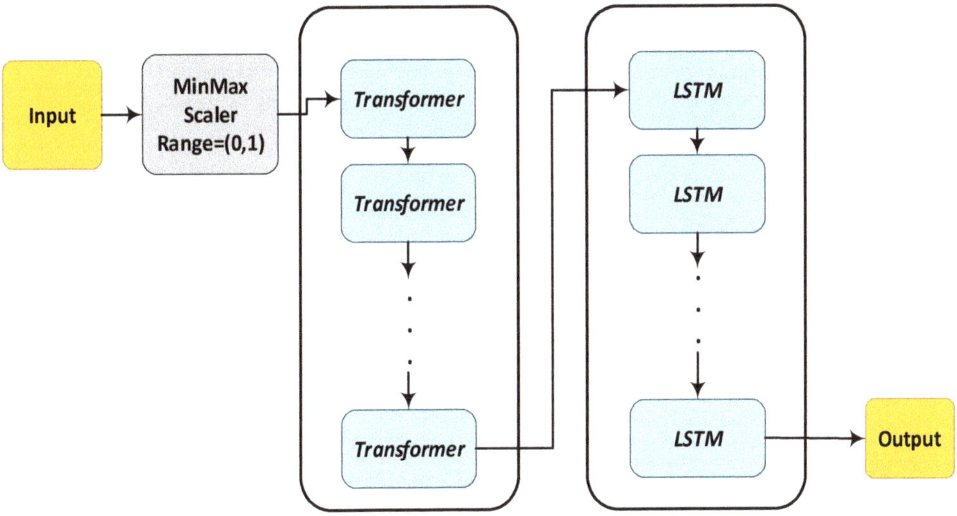

Figure 8. Structure of the developed ETL framework.

This feature is a key merit of the Transformer architecture, as it can cover complex relationships and dependencies within the data that may be difficult for simpler models to learn. By forwarding the Transformer encoder's extracted features to an LSTM layer, our model can further refine and process these representations. The LSTM's ability to maintain internal state and model sequential dependencies can complement the Transformer's strength in modeling global relationships. This combination of techniques enables our model to capture both local and global patterns in the data, potentially improving the detection accuracy. Additionally, we have incorporated one-dimensional convolutional layers into the Transformer encoder's feed-forward networks.

Compared to traditional Multi-Layer Perceptrons (MLPs), the convolutional layers have been shown to exhibit better performance on certain types of sequential data. This architectural choice further enhances the model's capability to extract meaningful features from the input. In the preprocessing stage, we use a MinMax scaler to normalize the raw dataset to a consistent format. This step is crucial for ensuring the model effectively learns from the data, as it helps mitigate the impact of different scales or ranges present in the original features.

Overall, the proposed hybrid model, which we name Earth–Transformer–LSTM (ETL), leverages the strengths of Transformer encoders and LSTMs, along with 1D convolutions and MinMax scaling, to create a powerful and versatile architecture for the task at hand.

https://doi.org/10.3390/fi18030143

The detailed evaluation of the model's performance and its comparative advantages are reported in Table 3.

Table 3. Parameters of the developed ETL model.

Layer	Parameters
Transformer	1816
LSTM_1	4440
LSTM_2	840
Dense	11
Total	7107

Also, we use the MinMax scaler in (2) to scale our dataset to the desired range (0 ÷ 1), which can help prevent overfitting by ensuring that features with different scales do not disproportionately influence the learning process. It also helps stabilize gradient descent, leading to more efficient and effective model training. Overall, using the MinMax scaler enhances the model's performance and robustness.

$$MinMax\ sclaer = \frac{X_i - \min(X)}{\max(X) - \min(X)} \tag{2}$$

After performing the preprocessing, the dataset is divided into two non-overlapping sets, called the training and test sets, with 80% and 20% of the dataset, respectively. Since the dataset is sequential, the shuffle operation is not applied during splitting, so sequential features are preserved for training the model. This procedure ensures that the sequential features are maintained, which is crucial for effectively training the model. Moreover, as shown in Figure 9, the proposed model takes longitude, latitude, and depth as inputs (3-dimensional vectors) and generates the corresponding estimated magnitude as output (a scalar value).

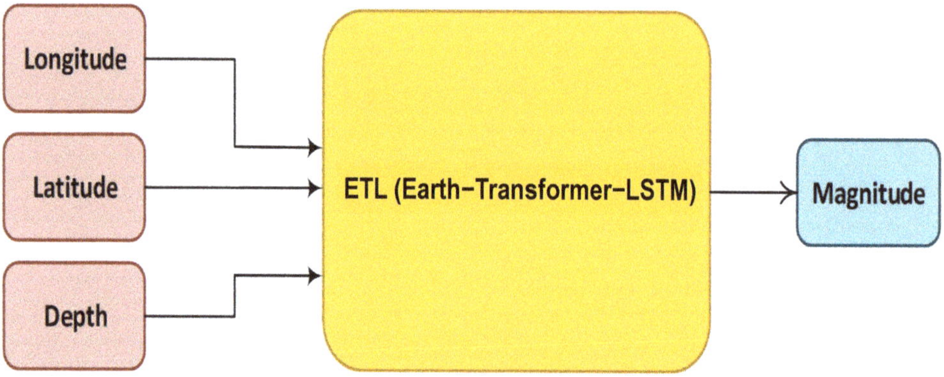

Figure 9. Inputs and outputs of the developed ETL framework.

5. Results

In this paper, Python 3.12 and TensorFlow 2.15.0 are used to implement all models and methods. Moreover, we split the main dataset into two portions—training and testing subsets—with a proportion of 8:2, respectively. Moreover, hyper-parameters can play a crucial role in the models' overall performance, so altering their values can lead to unacceptable results. The hyper-parameters' optimal values for the ETL model are reported in Table 4.

https://doi.org/10.3390/fi18030143

Table 4. ETL hyper-parameters.

	Number of Heads	Number of Transformer Block	LSTM Units	Epochs	Learning Rate	Optimizer
ETL	2	2	10	200	1×10^{-4}	Adam

In this paper, we present a comparison between our proposed hybrid model (ETL model), which combines Transformer encoders and LSTMs, with various benchmark models and other published results. We compute two commonly used performance metrics, Root Mean Squared Error (RMSE) and Mean Squared Error (MSE), to carry out these comparative evaluations. The RMSE metric measures the average magnitude of errors and indicates how well the model's predictions align with the actual target values. It is calculated as the square root of the mean of the squared differences between the predicted and true values. RMSE is a useful metric for evaluating the model's predictive accuracy because it is expressed in the same unit as the target parameter. On the other hand, the average squared difference between the expected and actual values is measured by the MSE metric. Because MSE squares the errors, it gives greater weight to larger deviations, making it more susceptible to outliers or extremely inaccurate predictions. MSE provides insights into the model's ability to minimize overall squared error, an important consideration in many applications. These indices are formulated as follows:

$$RMSE = \sqrt{\sum_{i=1}^{n} \frac{(\hat{y} - y_i)^2}{n}} \tag{3}$$

$$MSE = \frac{1}{n} \sum_{i=1}^{n} \frac{(\hat{y} - y_i)^2}{n} \tag{4}$$

We can obtain a more comprehensive understanding of the ETL model's performance by computing both RMSE and MSE. The RMSE provides a sense of the typical magnitude of the prediction errors, while the MSE indicates the model's effectiveness in minimizing the overall squared error.

The benchmark models have been selected carefully to ensure a fair and meaningful comparison. These models represent the state of the art in the field and cover a range of architectural designs, including both traditional and modern techniques. By benchmarking our ETL model against these established methodologies, we can assess the degree of improvement or novelty our hybrid architecture brings to the study. Firstly, we compare our model results with those of the Stacked Normalized Recurrent Neural Network (SN-RNN) [33], which combines multiple RNN-based models to improve overall performance. The SN-RNN has three main components—RNN, GRU, and LSTM. In detail, data is processed inside this RNN stack, and each section has unique benefits. For example, the GRU (middle part) could prevent the model from overfitting, representing a kind of ensembling model. Moreover, the SN-RNN also uses layer normalization, which offers many unique advantages, such as preventing overfitting compared to batch normalization [34]. However, as shown in Table 5, our model performs better than SN-RNN.

Table 5. ETL and SN-RNN results.

	RMSE	MSE
SN-RNN	3.16	9.985
ETL	0.70	0.49

https://doi.org/10.3390/fi18030143

Secondly, within a unified experimental framework, we compare the results of the developed ETL model with other RNN-based models, including LSTM, Gated Recurrent Units (GRUs), CNN-LSTM, and Bi-directional LSTM (BiLSTM). This operating mode ensures consistency in data preprocessing, model selection, optimization strategy, and statistical evaluation algorithms across all models presented in this study. GRU is an improved version of LSTM that helps protect the model from overfitting and other training-related issues. CNN-LSTM can be used for many tasks, such as video classification, and it can extract hidden features from the input via its convolutional layers; these features are then passed to LSTM layers for final processing. BiLSTM can perform conventional LSTM in two directions (first-to-last and last-to-first), and it concatenates the results from both directions. As shown in Table 6, our proposed ETL model (a hybrid Transformer encoder and LSTM) outperforms the other benchmark models.

Table 6. ETL and conventional RNN-based models comparison results.

	RMSE	MSE
LSTM + MinMax scaler	0.95	0.91
GRU + MinMax scaler	0.73	0.54
CNN-LSTM + MinMax scaler	0.87	0.76
BiLSTM + MinMax scaler	0.75	0.56
ETL (Our model)	0.70	0.49

According to Figure 10, our model also has a swift convergence, which can reach its optimal loss (RMSE) at lower epochs (approximately 10 epochs out of 200). In Figure 11, an example of the detected earthquake magnitudes for 10 samples is illustrated.

To further demonstrate the advantages of the proposed ETL architecture, we have analyzed two complementary performance metrics: the relative improvement percentage and training convergence behavior. As reported in Table 6, ETL achieves an RMSE of 0.70 compared to a 0.95 value for LSTM, 0.73 achieved by GRU, 0.87 by CNN-LSTM, and 0.75 by BiLSTM. The obtained result for the ETL model, proposed in this research work, corresponds to relative RMSE reductions of:

- 26.3% improvement over LSTM;
- 4.1% improvement over GRU;
- 19.5% improvement over CNN-LSTM;
- 6.7% improvement over BiLSTM.

Similarly, compared to the SN-RNN model (RMSE value equal to 3.16), the ETL framework reduces prediction error by approximately 77.8%, indicating a substantial gain in predictive accuracy. In addition to lower error values, Figure 10 shows that the ETL model converges to a stable state within approximately 10 epochs, even though it was trained for 200 epochs. This rapid stabilization suggests improved optimization dynamics and learning efficiency, likely due to the complementary integration of Transformer-based global attention and LSTM-based sequential memory. These results provide additional evidence that ETL's superiority is not limited to marginal numerical improvements in RMSE but also reflects enhanced learning stability and stronger representational capability compared to standalone RNN-based architectures.

The principal novelty of the developed ETL framework lies in integrating a Transformer encoder with an LSTM-based model to simultaneously learn long-range spatial correlations among earthquake catalog events via self-attention and temporal evolution patterns via gated recurrent memory. This strategy distinguishes ETL from previous models that rely solely on recurrent learning or convolutional pattern extraction. In terms of robustness, the ETL demonstrated:

https://doi.org/10.3390/fi18030143

➢ Significantly lower RMSE compared to standalone recurrent models under both standard random splitting and temporal hold-out testing;
➢ Stable predictive performance when evaluated on moderate-to-strong magnitude subsets (Mw $\geq$ 5.0), illustrating better generalization compared to benchmark models whose error grew substantially with the magnitude.

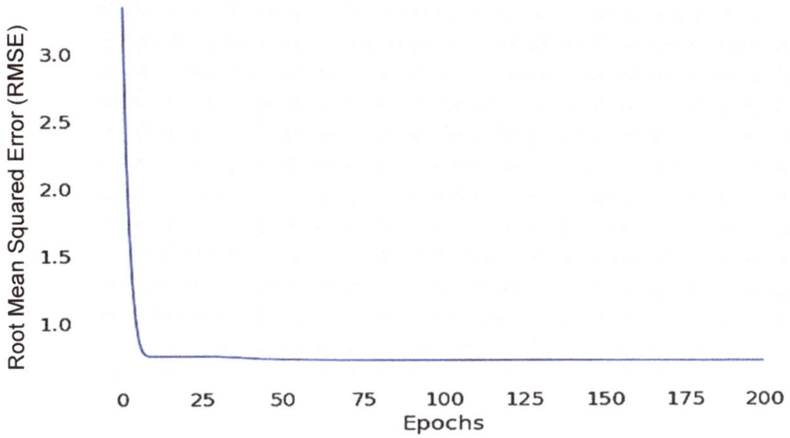

Figure 10. ETL training loss (RMSE).

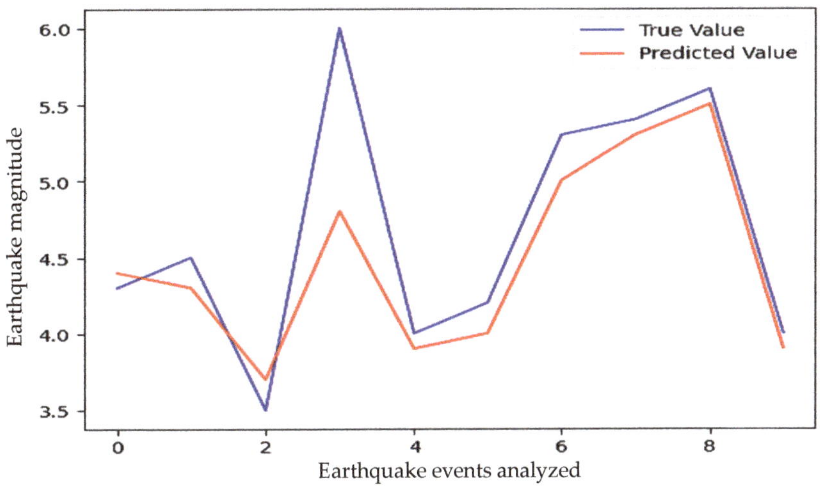

Figure 11. Examples of predicted and actual magnitude values for occurred earthquakes.

6. Discussion

There are many complexities involved in earthquakes: the magnitude, depth, location, and other seismological features which generally depend on the region's tectonic characteristics and geology. Because of this, earthquake detection systems are crucial to seismology, and learning models should be trained using powerful algorithms. For this reason, the study should focus on a specific region, and a dense seismic network is needed to increase the model accuracy. One option for overcoming these difficulties is to introduce new methods that perform better on the given seismic datasets.

This research article proposes a novel deep network, Earth–Transformer–LSTM (ETL), to estimate earthquake magnitude with high precision. The first layer of the model includes

https://doi.org/10.3390/fi18030143

Transformer encoders to extract subtle features from dataset; LSTM and one-dimensional convolution have been used as the other layers. The model has been trained on an earthquake dataset downloaded from the USGS for Turkey's earthquakes. This country is an active seismic region and has experienced very strong earthquakes in recent years.

The existing literature on earthquake magnitude estimation and seismic parameter prediction has explored various ML and DL techniques. Traditional statistical models and SVM-based approaches focus on feature-engineered catalog attributes but struggle to generalize nonlinear spatio-temporal relationships. RNN-based models, particularly LSTM and GRU networks, have demonstrated some success in capturing temporal dependencies; specifically, these architectures are effective at learning sequential patterns but can face limitations when modeling long-range spatial dependencies among seismic event locations. Hybrid models that combine CNNs with recurrent units (e.g., CNN-LSTM) have been proposed to integrate feature extraction with temporal learning; however, CNN layers primarily capture local patterns and require large, labeled waveform datasets for optimal performance.

Unlike prior studies, the proposed ETL model integrates self-attention mechanisms from the Transformer architecture with sequential gating from LSTM units. This architectural combination allows the ETL framework to jointly model spatial and temporal structures more effectively than either component alone. In contrast, standalone LSTM/GRU models lack explicit mechanisms to capture spatial interactions beyond the sequential axis, whereas CNN-based hybrids do not integrate learned long-range dependencies with the same level of flexibility as Transformers. This design introduces two key advantages:

- ✓ Global Spatial Attention: The Transformer encoder enables direct modeling of relationships among events through self-attention, allowing the model to learn how each event's location influences magnitude prediction without relying only on local sequential context.
- ✓ Temporal Memory Integration: The LSTM units preserve long-term temporal dependencies, which are crucial in earthquake catalogs where event occurrence patterns may reflect clustering, aftershock sequences, and periodicity.

The novelty of this research lies in combining two distinct sequence-based models for earthquake magnitude detection, which we have named ETL (Earth–Transformer–LSTM). The ETL has two components: the Transformer encoder and the LSTM. The Transformer encoder can extract many hidden features from its inputs by utilizing an attention mechanism (multi-head attention) and convolutional layers, which are then used in the feed-forward section. Moreover, the encoded features are transferred to the next RNN-based LSTM model, which can process these encrypted features across multiple sequences, thereby improving the conventional Transformer encoder results and making the ETL suitable for predicting future earthquake magnitudes. Thus, our model obtains RMSE and MSE metrics of 0.7 and 0.49, respectively. Moreover, we split the main dataset into two subsets: training and evaluation. For the training phase, we used the Adam optimizer (learning rate = 1×10^{-4}) and the cross-entropy loss function. Finally, our model's earthquake detection results are more accurate than those of other RNN-based models, such as GRU and CNN-LSTM.

A detailed comparative analysis has been conducted against several representative benchmark models, including standalone Recurrent Neural Networks (LSTM and GRU), hybrid CNN-LSTM architectures, and the recently proposed SN-RNN model [33]. While RNN-based approaches such as LSTM and GRU are effective at modeling sequential dependencies, their performance is limited by their ability to extract complex global relationships from high-dimensional seismic data. Similarly, CNN-LSTM models rely heavily on convolutional feature extraction, which may not fully capture long-range dependencies inherent in seismic time-series signals. The SN-RNN model improves upon traditional RNNs by

https://doi.org/10.3390/fi18030143

incorporating noise-robust mechanisms [33]; however, its reported RMSE of 3.16 remains significantly higher than that achieved by the proposed ETL framework.

This result demonstrates that the ETL algorithm can estimate earthquake magnitude much more precisely than other methods that have used similar datasets. Currently, the model does not incorporate explicit information about the earthquake's location or time in its process. Indeed, longitude and latitude are partitions of our inputs, and the proposed model processes the data sequentially (in time). The primary goal of the model is to estimate earthquake magnitude based on available seismic data features. However, we acknowledge that incorporating location and time information could enhance the model's predictive capabilities and provide a more comprehensive analysis. We plan to explore the inclusion of spatial and temporal features in future iterations of the model to address these aspects. As a potential research topic, it may be helpful to explore using these time-series-based algorithms to adapt and improve earthquake detection across different regions and datasets.

Despite the promising performance of the proposed Earth–Transformer–LSTM (ETL) model, several limitations should be acknowledged. Firstly, the model has been trained and evaluated using a region-specific dataset (Turkey, 2000–2018), which may limit its generalizability to other seismic regions with different tectonic characteristics and seismic patterns. Secondly, the input features are restricted to longitude, latitude, and depth, without incorporating additional geophysical, temporal, or waveform-based parameters that may further enhance predictive capability. Thirdly, the dataset size (6679 events) is relatively small for deep learning applications, and the absence of cross-regional validation or external testing may affect the model's robustness assessment. Furthermore, although the hybrid Transformer-LSTM architecture improves accuracy, it increases architectural complexity and computational cost compared to simpler RNN-based models. Finally, the study focuses solely on magnitude estimation and does not address related tasks, such as real-time detection, phase picking, or integration with early warning systems.

The dataset's time window (2000–2018) was selected to ensure catalog completeness, magnitude homogeneity, and data stability, as more recent major seismic sequences are subject to ongoing revisions and reprocessing (including magnitude recalibration, relocation updates, and aftershock reclassification). Since, therefore, earthquake catalogs are frequently updated after large events, restricting the analysis to a consolidated, quality-controlled period enhances the methodological consistency and reproducibility of the prediction results from ML and DL models.

Another reason to limit the dataset to the end of 2018 is to facilitate a direct comparison with similar studies already published and related to the same period. This timeframe allows us to benchmark our method against existing research that utilizes datasets from that era. In this context, the primary objective of this study is to introduce and evaluate a novel hybrid deep learning architecture under controlled and stable catalog conditions, rather than to provide a real-time operational forecasting system. Establishing architectural robustness on a consolidated dataset is a necessary first step before extending the framework to continuously evolving catalogs. Obviously, future work will extend the ETL framework to incorporate post-2018 seismic sequences to further assess temporal generalization under evolving tectonic conditions.

7. Conclusions

This paper presents an innovative deep learning framework, which we named Earth–Transformer–LSTM (ETL), for accurate earthquake magnitude detection in seismically active areas. The suggested method effectively captured complex temporal dependencies in seismic data by using Transformer encoders for deep feature extraction, LSTM networks for sequential modeling, and an MLP-based feed-forward architecture instead of traditional convolutional layers. Experiments conducted on the Turkey earthquake dataset demonstrated that the ETL model enhances the prediction accuracy, yielding RMSE and MSE values of 0.7 and 0.49, respectively. The model was trained using the Adam optimizer on separated training and evaluation datasets and outperforms existing RNN-based approaches such as GRU and CNN-LSTM.

Future studies can extend this research in several important directions. Firstly, incorporating additional spatial–temporal features (e.g., event time, inter-event intervals, fault proximity, tectonic indicators) may improve the model's predictive performance and physical interpretability. Secondly, evaluating the ETL framework on multi-regional or global datasets would provide insight into its generalization capability across different seismic environments. Transfer learning or domain adaptation techniques could also be explored to adapt the model to regions with limited seismic data. Future work may also investigate lightweight or optimized versions of the architecture to reduce computational complexity for real-time earthquake early warning (EEW) applications. Finally, uncertainty quantification methods and explainable AI (XAI) techniques could be incorporated to improve model transparency and reliability for practical seismological deployment.

Author Contributions: Conceptualization, A.A.G., E.G., M.M., and P.V.; methodology, A.A.G. and P.V.; validation, A.A.G. and P.V.; formal analysis, E.G. and M.M.; investigation, A.A.G., E.G., and P.V.; software, E.G. and M.M.; resources, M.M.; data curation, M.M.; writing—original draft preparation, A.A.G., E.G., and M.M.; writing—review and editing, A.A.G., E.G., M.M., and P.V.; supervision, A.A.G. and P.V.; funding acquisition, A.A.G. and P.V. All authors have read and agreed to the published version of the manuscript.

Funding: This research received no external funding.

Data Availability Statement: The datasets generated during and/or analyzed during the current study are available from the corresponding author on reasonable request.

Acknowledgments: This research is supported by the research grant of the University of Tabriz [Number 1469-78].

Conflicts of Interest: The authors declare no conflicts of interest.

References

1. Rojas, O.; Otero, B.; Alvarado, L.; Mus, S.; Tous, R. Artificial neural networks as emerging tools for earthquake detection. *Comput. Y Sist.* **2019**, *23*, 335–350. [CrossRef]
2. Mehta, D.; Das, P.P.; Ghosh, S.; Mishra, S.; Alkhayyat, A.; Sharma, V. A Normalized ANN Model for Earthquake Estimation. In Proceedings of the 2023 2nd International Conference on Applied Artificial Intelligence and Computing (ICAAIC), Salem, India, 4–6 May 2023; pp. 151–155. [CrossRef]
3. Ridzwan, N.S.M.; Yusoff, S.H.M. Machine learning for earthquake prediction: A review (2017–2021). *Earth Sci. Inform.* **2023**, *16*, 1133–1149. [CrossRef]
4. Kavianpour, P.; Kavianpour, M.; Jahani, E.; Ramezani, A. A CNN-BiLSTM model with attention mechanism for earthquake prediction. *J. Supercomput.* **2023**, *79*, 19194–19226. [CrossRef]
5. Sadhukhan, B.; Chakraborty, S.; Mukherjee, S. Predicting the magnitude of an impending earthquake using deep learning techniques. *Earth Sci. Inform.* **2023**, *16*, 803–823. [CrossRef]
6. Doğan, A.; Demir, E. Structural recurrent neural network models for earthquake prediction. *Neural Comput. Appl.* **2022**, *34*, 11049–11062. [CrossRef]
7. Berhich, A.; Belouadha, F.-Z.; Kabbaj, M.I. An attention-based LSTM network for large earthquake prediction. *Soil Dyn. Earthq. Eng.* **2023**, *165*, 107663. [CrossRef]

https://doi.org/10.3390/fi18030143

8. Saad, O.M.; Chen, Y.; Siervo, D.; Zhang, F.; Savvaidis, A.; Huang, G.-C.D.; Igonin, N.; Fomel, S.; Chen, Y. EQCCT: A production-ready earthquake detection and phase picking method using the compact convolutional transformer. *IEEE Trans. Geosci. Remote Sens.* **2023**, *61*, 4507015. [CrossRef]
9. Aslam, B.; Zafar, A.; Khalil, U.; Azam, U. Seismic activity prediction of the northern part of Pakistan from novel machine learning technique. *J. Seismol.* **2021**, *25*, 639–652. [CrossRef]
10. Zhou, W.; Dong, H.; Liang, Y. The deterministic dendritic cell algorithm with Haskell in earthquake magnitude prediction. *Earth Sci. Inform.* **2020**, *13*, 447–457. [CrossRef]
11. Majhi, S.K.; Hossain, S.S.; Padhi, T. MFOFLANN: Moth flame optimized functional link artificial neural network for prediction of earthquake magnitude. *Evol. Syst.* **2020**, *11*, 45–63. [CrossRef]
12. Zhang, H.; Melgar, D.; Sahakian, V.; Searcy, J.; Lin, J.-T. Learning source, path and site effects: CNN-based on-site intensity prediction for earthquake early warning. *Geophys. J. Int.* **2022**, *231*, 2186–2204. [CrossRef]
13. Zhu, J.; Li, S.; Wei, Y.; Song, J. On-site instrumental seismic intensity prediction for China via recurrent neural network and transfer learning. *J. Asian Earth Sci.* **2023**, *248*, 105610. [CrossRef]
14. Kudłacik, I.; Kapłon, J.; Kazmierski, K.; Fortunato, M.; Crespi, M. First feasibility demonstration of GNSS-seismology for anthropogenic earthquakes detection. *Sci. Rep.* **2023**, *13*, 20905. [CrossRef] [PubMed]
15. Abdalzaher, M.S.; Krichen, M.; Fouda, M.M. Enhancing earthquakes and quarry blasts discrimination using machine learning based on three seismic parameters. *Ain Shams Eng. J.* **2024**, *15*, 102925. [CrossRef]
16. Bilal, M.A.; Ji, Y.; Wang, Y.; Akhter, M.P.; Yaqub, M. An early warning system for earthquake prediction from seismic data using Batch Normalized Graph Convolutional Neural Network with Attention Mechanism (BNGCNNATT). *Sensors* **2022**, *22*, 6482. [CrossRef]
17. Saad, O.M.; Chen, Y.; Savvaidis, A.; Chen, W.; Zhang, F.; Chen, Y. Unsupervised deep learning for single-channel earthquake data denoising and its applications in event detection and fully automatic location. *IEEE Trans. Geosci. Remote Sens.* **2022**, *60*, 5921310. [CrossRef]
18. Han, J.; Kim, S.; Sheen, D.H.; Lee, D.; Lee, S.J.; Yoo, S.H.; Park, D. Seismic event and phase detection using deep learning for the 2016 Gyeongju earthquake sequence. *Geosci. J.* **2023**, *27*, 285–295. [CrossRef]
19. Abebe, E.; Kebede, H.; Kevin, M.; Demissie, Z. Earthquakes magnitude prediction using deep learning for the Horn of Africa. *Soil Dyn. Earthq. Eng.* **2023**, *170*, 107913. [CrossRef]
20. Laurenti, L.; Tinti, E.; Galasso, F.; Franco, L.; Marone, C. Deep learning for laboratory earthquake prediction and autoregressive forecasting of fault zone stress. *Earth Planet. Sci. Lett.* **2022**, *598*, 117825. [CrossRef]
21. Mohammadigheymasi, H.; Shi, P.; Tavakolizadeh, N.; Xiao, Z.; Mousavi, S.M.; Matias, L.; Fernandes, R. IPIML: A deep-scan earthquake detection and location workflow Integrating Pair-Input deep learning model and Migration Location method. *IEEE Trans. Geosci. Remote Sens.* **2023**, *61*, 5914109. [CrossRef]
22. Yuan, C.; Ni, Y.; Lin, Y.; Denolle, M. Better Together: Ensemble Learning for Earthquake Detection and Phase Picking. *IEEE Trans. Geosci. Remote Sens.* **2023**, *61*, 5920217. [CrossRef]
23. Mousavi, S.M.; Ellsworth, W.L.; Zhu, W.; Chuang, L.Y.; Beroza, G.C. Earthquake transformer—An attentive deep-learning model for simultaneous earthquake detection and phase picking. *Nat. Commun.* **2020**, *11*, 3952. [CrossRef] [PubMed]
24. Kartal, R.F.; Kadirioğlu, F.T.; Kılıç, T. An improved earthquake and moment tensor catalogues ($M \geq 4.0$) for Anatolian region and its near vicinity (2013–2019). *Arab. J. Geosci.* **2022**, *15*, 1632. [CrossRef]
25. Güvercin, S.E.; Karabulut, H.; Konca, A.Ö.; Doğan, U.; Ergintav, S. Active seismotectonics of the East Anatolian Fault. *Geophys. J. Int.* **2022**, *230*, 50–69. [CrossRef]
26. Bohnhoff, M.; Martínez-Garzón, P.; Bulut, F.; Stierle, E.; Ben-Zion, Y. Maximum earthquake magnitudes along different sections of the North Anatolian fault zone. *Tectonophysics* **2016**, *674*, 147–165. [CrossRef]
27. Över, S.; Demirci, A.; Özden, S. Tectonic implications of the February 2023 Earthquakes (Mw7.7, 7.6 and 6.3) in south-eastern Türkiye. *Tectonophysics* **2023**, *866*, 230058. [CrossRef]
28. Ganas, A.; Elias, P.; Briole, P.; Valkaniotis, S.; Escartin, J.; Tsironi, V.; Karasante, I.; Kosma, C. Co-seismic and post-seismic deformation, field observations and fault model of the 30 October 2020 Mw = 7.0 Samos earthquake, Aegean Sea. *Acta Geophys.* **2021**, *69*, 999–1024. [CrossRef]
29. Türker, E.; Yen, M.; Pilz, M.; Cotton, F. Significance of Pulse-Like Ground Motions and Directivity Effects in Moderate Earthquakes: The Example of the Mw 6.1 Gölyaka–Düzce Earthquake on 23 November 2022. *Bull. Seismol. Soc. Am.* **2024**, *114*, 955–964. [CrossRef]
30. Emre, Ö.; Duman, T.Y.; Özalp, S.; Şaroğlu, F.; Olgun, Ş.; Elmacı, H.; Çan, T. Active fault database of Turkey. *Bull. Earthq. Eng.* **2018**, *16*, 3229–3275. [CrossRef]
31. Available online: https://earthquake.usgs.gov/ (accessed on 5 May 2025).
32. Wiemer, S. A software package to analyze seismicity: ZMAP. *Seismol. Res. Lett.* **2001**, *72*, 373–382. [CrossRef]

33. Vaswani, A.; Shazeer, N.; Parmar, N.; Uszkoreit, J.; Jones, L.; Gomez, A.N.; Kaiser, L.; Polosukhin, I. Attention is all you need. Advances in Neural Information Processing Systems, Proceeding of the Annual Conference on Neural Information Processing Systems 2017, Long Beach, CA, USA, 4–9 December 2017; Neural Information Processing Systems Foundation, Inc.: San Diego, CA, USA, 2017; Volume 30, pp. 5998–6008.
34. Bilal, M.A.; Wang, Y.; Ji, Y.; Pervez Akhter, M.; Liu, H. Earthquake detection using stacked normalized recurrent neural network (SNRNN). *Appl. Sci.* **2023**, *13*, 8121. [CrossRef]

https://doi.org/10.3390/fi18030143

MDPI AG
Grosspeteranlage 5
4052 Basel
Switzerland
Tel.: +41 61 683 77 34

Future Internet Editorial Office
E-mail: futureinternet@mdpi.com
www.mdpi.com/journal/futureinternet